THE CLASSIC DOCTOR WHO DVD COMPENDIUM

THE CLASSIC DOCTOR WHO DVD COMPENDIUM

COMPILED & WRITTEN BY
PAUL SMITH

WONDERFUL
BOOKS

Published in the UK in 2014 by Paul Smith/Wonderful Books

14 St George's Court, Garden Row, London SE1 6HD

www.wonderfulbook.co.uk

The Classic Doctor Who DVD Compendium © Paul Smith, 2014

The moral right of the author has been asserted

Cover photo © James O'Gorman

Printed on demand through CreateSpace

ISBN: 978-0-9576062-1-0

If you enjoy this book or find it useful, please leave a review of it at Amazon, recommend it on your blog or mention it on any other social media you use.

CONTENTS

A HISTORY OF CLASSIC DOCTOR WHO ON DVD

One of the enduring appeals of *Doctor Who*, and a reason why it's still going strong after half a century, is that it's like no other programme on television. Whether you're old enough to have been watching since the first episode in November 1963 or you only became hooked during the series' recent fiftieth anniversary, you can probably list half a dozen ways in which *Doctor Who* stands apart from other shows. Whenever you think you have a handle on what the programme is or can do, it spins off in a new direction, whether as a result of casting a new incarnation of the Doctor himself or by reviving something from its long history that leads you to discover a whole aspect of the series you never realised was there.

That history has never been more accessible than it is now, with all but one surviving episodes — including those rediscovered barely more than a year ago — available to watch in pristine quality on DVD. The current series, of course, has been released in regular series sets since its revival in 2005, just like any modern show. Even if you're just now catching up with the 21st Century adventures of the Doctor, seven series with around a hundred episodes isn't that daunting a prospect in today's scheme of things, when marathoning the whole of a programme like *24* or *Lost* is a popular way to spend one's evenings. However, that's barely a third as long as *Doctor Who*'s initial twenty-six-year run, even accounting for the shorter episodes back then and the fact that many of those from the 1960s are still missing. But that needn't be off-putting for the intrepid viewer interested in dipping into the Doctor's past, and in fact the way the Classic Series has been released on a story-by-story basis, rather than as modern-style season boxsets, makes this easier than it might seem.

A SHOW LIKE NO OTHER

Most drama on television, from the medium's early days right up to the present, fits one of two formats. There's the *serial*, in which a self-contained story is told over a number of episodes, much like a book with chapters (indeed, television serials are often adaptations of books). One needs to watch every episode in order to follow the characters' experiences and enjoy the unfolding of the story. Then there's the *series*, in which each episode generally tells a one-off story (or maybe two as a main plot and a subplot), but there's some continuity of characters, location and situation over the course of the episodes. Thus, once you're familiar with the setup, you can watch random episodes and still get a complete narrative, but there's more depth to be gained from watching them all and following the characters' development.

If a serial is popular it may be brought back to tell further stories with its characters and become a series, although each block of episodes usually tells a self-contained story. An example would be *24*, where each season is yet another day in the life of Jack Bauer and the team at CTU, but over successive seasons there are developments in the characters and their relationships that reward returning viewers. Similarly, a series may run the occasional two- or three-part storyline, especially at the climax of a season, but generally each weekly episode is a largely standalone story. This is the norm for police and medical shows from *Z Cars* to *Juliet Bravo* to *CSI*, and from *Dr Findlay's Casebook* to *Casualty* to *House*, with a case of the week but ongoing characters.

More recent programmes have created slight variations of these standards. Police procedural *Waking the Dead*, for example, was a series that presented each case over two episodes, making it a series of two-part serials, whereas *Lost* had little closure at the end of each season let alone each episode, making it essentially a long serial told over several series. Soap operas are another unique case, being essentially a never-ending serial. And a third, less-common structure is the anthology series, where each episode is a totally new story with fresh characters and situations, but linked by a theme, such as all being murder mysteries or horror stories.

When *Doctor Who* was being devised in 1963, it was always conceived as something different, combining all three formats: an anthology series of serials. There would be continuing characters, as in a typical series — the Doctor and his companions — but they would regularly find themselves in a new location and a new story, as with an anthology. Each adventure would be presented over anything from two to twelve episodes, like a serial. Indeed, with the programme in almost year-round production for its first six years, off the air for only a few weeks during the summer, the idea of annual seasons was somewhat notional. It wasn't until the 1970s when the show was cut back to twenty-six episodes a year that the series aspect became more obvious, but those episodes were still grouped into five or six largely standalone serials.

Doctor Who wasn't unique in this respect. There were programmes before it that had a similar structure — largely adventure series aimed primarily at young boys, appropriately enough — although none had the freedom to regularly place their characters in an entirely new situation anywhere in space and time. For example, Granada Television's 1960 series *Biggles*, based on the books by Captain WE Johns, ran for forty-four half-hour episodes making up eleven stories of between three and six parts. These each ended with a cliff-hanger to tempt the audience back the following week. For a more adult audience there was *The World of Tim Frazer*, created by crime-thriller writer Francis Durbridge, which ran for three six-part stories from November 1960 to March 1961. Durbridge had previously created the popular radio detective series *Paul Temple* (which made the transition to television in 1969 under ex-*Doctor Who* producer Derrick Sherwin), but a closer radio precedent for *Doctor Who*'s style of storytelling was perhaps *Dick Barton – Special Agent*, whose daily serialised adventures were a popular hit from 1946 to 1951 and possibly an influence on the team that created *Doctor Who* a decade later. Other series from later in the 1960s and 70s used the same 'series of serials' format, largely children's and adventure shows such as the BBC's *Quick Before They Catch Us*, Thames Television's *Sexton Blake*, and ATV's *Timeslip* and *Sapphire & Steel*. None but *Doctor Who* persisted for twenty-six years, however, and by the time the original series was suspended in 1989 the format had largely become a relic in the television schedules.

MOVING BEYOND BROADCAST

What this structure did allow for was the series' move into other media. When *Doctor Who* began, television was an ephemeral medium, with programmes broadcast once and then likely never seen again. The idea of selling them in an affordable format that people could watch again at their leisure was inconceivable. Now this is seen as a valuable part of a programme's lifespan and factored into the production process and budget. Shows have even been saved from cancellation or revived thanks to profitable home-video sales, and some are deliberately made to offer deeper understanding through repeated viewing. But back in the 1960s this was unheard of.

There were books, however. Such was the early popular success of *Doctor Who* that a publisher soon approached the BBC about the prospect of novelising the stories. In November 1964 — just as the Daleks were set to make their return appearance on television in *The Dalek Invasion of Earth* — Frederick Muller published *Doctor Who in an Exciting Adventure with the Daleks*, written by David Whitaker (who was the show's story editor for its first year) and based on the seven-part serial *The Daleks* by Terry Nation. It sold so well that it was reprinted the following month, and in September 1965 Frederick Muller published *Doctor Who and the Zarbi* by Bill Strutton, based on his television serial *The Web Planet*. This was followed in February 1966 by *Doctor Who and the Crusaders* by David Whitaker, based on his serial *The Crusade*.

Thanks to the television series' structure as a sequence of standalone stories, each could be presented as a self-contained book without the reader being required to have read others, or even to have seen the programme itself. Indeed, for the first book, Whitaker created an entirely new scenario for Barbara and Ian's meeting with the Doctor and Susan quite unlike that seen on television in *An Unearthly Child*, so that the story's setup could be understood with no prior knowledge of the show. The episodic nature of the stories on television also suited their translation into book form, with Strutton's *Doctor Who and the Zarbi* being split into six chapters that matched the six broadcast episodes, even down to their individual titles.

No more stories were novelised in the 1960s, but in 1973 publisher Universal-Tandem was looking for titles to establish its new Target imprint of children's books. It bought the rights to the three Frederick Muller hardbacks and reissued them in paperback, quickly followed by further adaptations of then-current Third Doctor stories. These were an instant hit and Target went on to publish novelisations of nearly every Classic *Doctor Who* story over the subsequent twenty years.

The other benefit of *Doctor Who*'s structure highlighted by these books was that the stories don't have to be revisited in the order their were originally broadcast. Most television shows, even if they're a series of story-of-the-week episodes, are intended to be watched in sequence because there are often ongoing strands of plot and character that develop across episodes. While you can dip in and watch a particular edition of, say, *Buffy the Vampire Slayer* that features a monster you like, there will be aspects that only make sense if you know the ongoing storyline of the season, if not the entire run. Even the modern series of *Doctor Who* fits this mould. While it has inherited the anthology nature of the Doctor's travels from the original series, such that each episode (or occasional two-part story) is a new self-contained adventure, it also has strands running throughout any one series, like the nature of Bad Wolf or the cause of the crack in Amy's bedroom wall.

Classic *Doctor Who* isn't really like that. Certainly in the early years, when it was an ongoing series with no sense of building up to what we now call a season finale and you only had one chance to see each episode, there was no real overarching narrative. For the first couple of years, when initial companions Barbara and Ian were aboard the TARDIS, there was a nominal question of whether the Doctor would ever get them back to Earth in their own time, but they soon got used to the fact that he couldn't. Subsequent companions frequently had no home to return to and just travelled until the actor or production team felt like a change, while the Doctor himself rarely had a destination in mind. There wasn't even much development of the characters themselves, this being a series focused on adventure and monsters more than emotion. Many a companion actor left the show because they felt that after the initial interest of their introduction their parts went nowhere. Still, thanks to some wonderful casting, the most fondly remembered companions are more often a result of the qualities the actors brought to the roles than the writers' creation of rounded characters.

Occasional attempts were made to give the Doctor's adventures some continuity, such as when he was exiled to Earth in his third incarnation and worked with the military investigation team UNIT, or when he was sent on a mission to find the Key to Time in the 1978/79 season. But for the most part he would spend a few episodes dealing with one problem before moving on to be faced with another in a completely different place in space and time. That was the nature of the show.

Modern television programmes are produced with the expectation of further exploitation after broadcast through some form of consumer release, and the necessary permissions for this are written into the actors' and production crews' contracts. This wasn't the case for archive shows, at least those made before the 1990s. Then, people were paid to make a programme to be aired on television once or perhaps twice, with an allowance for potential sale overseas. No one predicted the BBC would one day want to make further profit from their efforts, and when it became apparent it did, it had to renegotiate its right to do so with every programme contributor. For a typical serial or series with a largely consistent cast this can be straightforward; for *Doctor Who*, with a small regular cast and frequent one-off guest stars, it's a protracted and potentially expensive process, eased by treating each story on its own rather than trying to clear a whole series' worth of serials.

REVISITING THE PAST

So when the home VHS market began to take off in the early 1980s and it was clear that the then-twenty-year back catalogue of *Doctor Who* would be popular releases, there was already familiarity with the ideas that the series' stories could be packaged individually and experienced in any order. The early video cassettes even did away with the original's serialisation by having the episodes edited together into one continuous programme, until fans complained they wanted it split into episodes because the cliff-hanger endings are an integral part of the stories' presentation.

One other unique aspect of *Doctor Who* also came into play: the regular regeneration of the Doctor into a completely new body and personality. This not only allows the programme to keep going indefinitely and attract new generations of followers, but each Doctor is always going to be someone's favourite, whether it's because he's the one they remember watching first or they just prefer the storytelling style of his period of the show's history. To start releasing the series from the very beginning and in original broadcast order would have meant releasing the black-and-white episodes first long after colour television had become the norm. Also, fans of more recent Doctors wouldn't get to see their favourite episodes until much later. And the then-current Doctor, who was most familiar among the general public, wouldn't have his episodes available straight away (at that point the series was still in production so there was not only a large backlist of stories to release but also regular new ones). These were all factors that could have reduced the initial number of potential buyers and made the range unviable before it had even got going.

Jump forward fifteen years and, as the end of the century approached, most of the stories that survived in the BBC's archive (we'll come back to this later) had been released on VHS. But a new format was beginning to make an impact on the home-video market: DVD. This promised greater picture and sound quality through digital reproduction, which meant every copy was exactly the same as the original, rather than slightly degraded as analogue formats like VHS were. It also provided a menu-based structure that allowed for quick navigation of a programme and multiple picture, soundtrack and subtitle options (unlike the linear viewing experience of a tape-based format), as well as having space for additional content.

BBC Video, the division of the BBC's commercial arm BBC Worldwide responsible for issuing programmes on consumer formats, wanted to try out this burgeoning new medium. In 1999 it selected for its initial releases some of its most popular titles, both recent and archive, including *Doctor Who* (see page 354). Although the programme was no longer in production (and showed no signs of coming back), it was still well remembered and a profitable brand thanks to a sizeable fan following. At the time most DVDs were movies or concerts and there was little sign of the full-season boxsets that would eventually become the norm for modern and archive television shows. So given the precedent set by *Doctor Who*'s book and VHS ranges there was no suggestion of changing the release structure for DVD, as all the same reasons still applied. The first release was The Five Doctors Special Edition, as this had been produced for VHS just a few years before using the surviving original video recordings and with new computer-generated effects. It was also a sensible choice because it featured several Doctors so could appeal to a wide range of people (as it was intended to when first broadcast for the show's twentieth anniversary in 1983). It was hoped several extra features would be included to really show off the versatility of the DVD format, although in the end these were pared down to a couple of soundtrack options to keep costs low as it was uncertain how well the release would sell in this nascent market.

Evidently it sold well enough because the following year the *Doctor Who* range was launched in earnest. To make this as enticing as possible in its early days, releases focused on the more well-respected stories while making sure each of the Doctors was represented so none of their fans felt left out (see Appendix 3, page 380). There was also an awareness at BBC Video that many fans of the series had been diligently buying the stories on VHS for the past fifteen years and were still doing so — that range wouldn't be completed until November 2003 — so if they were to be persuaded to collect them again on a new format, the DVDs would have to offer considerable advantages. There were already the inherent benefits of a digital medium, especially reliable quality as VHS tapes were well known to degrade the more you played them, but BBC Video was convinced it needed more. It therefore committed to two factors that made the DVDs a worthwhile upgrade: special features and restoration of the episodes from the best source materials. A catalogue of the extensive range of extras on the *Doctor Who* discs is the primary purpose of this book, but it also summarises what materials were used as the starting point of each serial's restoration, so it's worth considering how the Classic Series was recorded and what survives for us to watch today.

THE ORIGINAL RECORDINGS

The key to selling archive television programmes in any medium is to have an archive of programmes in the first place. It's an unfortunate fact that the BBC (like other television companies) hasn't always kept copies of the shows it makes. The recording of programmes at all was still a relatively new process in the 1960s when *Doctor Who* began. Although BBC Television had then been broadcasting for twenty-five years, most of this was done live, the studio cameras sending signals directly to the transmitters. By the late 1940s, however, there was a growing recognition that programmes should be preserved for future transmission or sale to other broadcasters overseas. Once the BBC resumed its television service in 1946 after the Second World War, tests were made with telerecording, using a film camera to shoot the image on a large, flat television screen.

Before the advent of digital television, video pictures were an analogue signal that was captured by electronic cameras and displayed on a cathode-ray screen as a series of horizontal lines. Unlike a strip of film, which projects a series of still images (frames) fast enough that the human eye perceives the changes between them as movement, an analogue video signal is continuously changing. The electronics of the day were limited in how fast they could capture and display the picture information so, to ensure the viewer didn't see any flickering, the signal was interlaced. This means that the first, third, fifth and so on horizontal lines are scanned first, from top to bottom of the image, then the electron beam jumps back to the top and fills in the second, fourth, sixth and so on lines. If this is done fast enough — in the UK system, fifty times a second — the viewer retains the information of the first set of lines (called a field) as the second set is being scanned, and similarly retains the second field as the first is re-scanned with new picture information, and so on. This is a continuous process so each line presents the view from a fractionally later moment in time (unlike a film frame which shows all the image information from one single moment) and between any two fields there's a differential of a fiftieth of a second (twenty milliseconds).

When it came to telerecording programmes onto film, therefore, the camera was cranked at twenty-five frames per second, initially capturing every alternate field so that it had that 20ms gap in which to wind the film on to the next frame. This was known as suppressed-field recording but was superseded by the stored-field method, which combined pairs of fields on a single film frame by increasing the intensity of the first field so that it persisted on the screen while the next was being displayed and the frame exposed.[1] One of the earliest broadcasts to be telerecorded was the wedding of Princess Elizabeth to Philip Mountbatten in November 1947.

It wasn't until the late 1950s that videotaping became economical, although still expensive. When *Doctor Who* began in 1963, therefore, all studio scenes were captured by electronic cameras recording to two-inch Quadruplex ('Quad') videotape using the then-standard 405-line format. Episodes were recorded weekly a few weeks ahead of transmission, and because video was difficult and expensive to edit they were performed 'as live' — that is, in scene order with as few breaks in recording as possible. Any minor mistakes, therefore, had to go uncorrected.

Episodes also featured filmed inserts, which were telecined at the appropriate points during studio recording. Prime among these was the opening title sequence, which was compiled on 35mm film (although the swirling patterns were generated using video technology). Any scenes that needed to be shot on location were filmed before the episode went into the studio, on 16mm or occasionally 35mm film. The first instance of outside filming was a short scene in episode two of *The Reign of Terror*, followed by more extensive location work for *The Dalek Invasion of Earth* two months later. But some indoor scenes, usually those involving larger sets to accommodate stunt work or particular effects unachievable in a small studio, would also be filmed on sound stages at Ealing. The fight between Kal and Za in *An Unearthly Child* episode four is the first example of this. Model work was also shot on 35mm film, and any stock footage used (such as the thunderstorm in *The Aztecs* episode one) would be on film. One further instance of filmed inserts were the previous-week recaps at the start of an episode. In the very early days of the series these opening scenes were simply re-enacted, sometimes with slightly different dialogue or camera angles. Occasionally, though, the closing scenes of an episode would be telerecorded onto 35mm film (at the same time as

---

1 In principle, it doesn't matter which two video fields are combined onto one film frame, as the content of each is always 20ms apart. It does matter, however, when telerecording video programmes that include portions originally shot on film, as *Doctor Who* often did. The footage would be filmed at twenty-five frames per second and then telecined onto video — the reverse of telerecording — with each frame forming two sequential fields. Ideally, then, when the final programme is telerecorded, each pair of fields from the original film frame is recombined onto a single new frame. In practice, the second field from frame A might be combined with the first field from frame B (which would be a snapshot of the original scene 40ms later), then field two from frame B with field one from frame C and so on. This results in any moving objects being heavily blurred, and if there's a change of shot between say frames B and C, then the telerecorded frame will contain picture content from two totally different images.

the main videotape recording) to be telecined during studio recording the following week.

While most episodes were recorded onto and transmitted from videotape in this way, occasional instalments used film. If an episode required significant editing or a video machine simply wasn't available when the episode was being made, the output of the electronic studio cameras would be sent to a film-recording suite and recorded onto 35mm film — essentially the same process as telerecording. Once any necessary editing was done, this would be the version used for transmission.

Although in the 1960s there was no hint yet of the potential for selling recordings of programmes to the public, that doesn't mean they weren't being marketed at all. BBC Enterprises, as BBC Worldwide was then called, made its own telerecordings onto 16mm film of programmes it thought could be sold to broadcasters overseas. Distributing programmes on film rather than videotape was beneficial for several reasons, not least the expense of video in the 1950s and 60s. Film was also more durable and more easily transported, while the relative newness of video meant many overseas television stations still transmitted from film only. *Doctor Who* was telerecorded from the start and sold to countries from Algeria to Zambia. New Zealand was the first country outside the UK to broadcast the show, followed by Australia and Canada (see Appendix 4, page 385).

Sales began well, with twenty-four countries known to have bought most of the episodes from the first two seasons. This doesn't mean twenty-four prints were struck from BBC Enterprises' telerecording negatives, however. The sales were made over time — for example, Zambia didn't buy even black-and-white episodes until the early 1970s — so new buyers could be sent prints that had been returned by previous buyers after their rights to show the episodes had expired. Similarly, prints were 'bicycled', whereby a television station that held copies it no longer needed was asked to pass them on to another station that had since bought the rights to show the series, rather than return them to BBC Enterprises or destroy them as their contract stipulated. Many of Singapore's film prints came directly from New Zealand, for example.

When BBC2 launched in April 1964 it used the higher-resolution 625-line UHF (ultra high frequency) format for broadcasts, and from July 1967 began some colour transmissions using the PAL system. Because viewers needed a new receiver — that is, a new television set — to watch the new channel, BBC1 stuck with 405-line VHF (very high frequency), not broadcasting on UHF until it too switched to colour in November 1969 (although the BBC continued to simulcast on VHF until 1985). *Doctor Who* began regularly recording in 625 lines from *The Enemy of the World*, the first episode of which was studio recorded on Saturday 2 December 1967, the very day BBC2 became a full-colour service, freeing up the 625-line monochrome cameras for use by BBC1 programmes.

With the introduction of colour on BBC1 at the end of 1969 (although not universally — many programmes were still made in black and white for several more years), in January 1970 the Third Doctor's debut adventure *Spearhead from Space* became the first colour broadcast of *Doctor Who*. It was an atypical beginning, however, as this serial was shot entirely on 16mm colour film owing to industrial action at the BBC closing all the studios. The next story, *Doctor Who and the Silurians*, therefore became the series' first to be recorded on 625-line PAL-colour videotape. Programmes were also much easier to edit by now, being done electronically rather than physically, and incoming producer Barry Letts restructured the shooting of the series so that two episodes were recorded every fortnight rather than one a week. This meant studio work could be structured around which sets were needed, with scenes edited into the appropriate order in post-production.

As colour television began to spread around the world in the early-70s, interest in black-and-white programming diminished. The later Second Doctor stories were bought by far fewer countries than earlier stories had been, predominantly ones in Australasia and Africa where black-and-white broadcasting persisted until the mid-70s. The last *Doctor Who* story to be telerecorded onto 16mm black-and-white film was *Invasion of the Dinosaurs* in July 1974, but neither it nor the preceding season-opener, *The Time Warrior*, is known to have been sold in that format. Australia was the last country to buy 16mm film prints of the show, but only up to the end of the 1972/73 season; national broadcaster ABC transmitted subsequent episodes from PAL copies of the original videotapes.

The Third Doctor episodes were also offered for sale in colour. Although colour telerecording was possible, by this time television stations broadcasting in colour did so from videotape, so episodes were offered as either PAL copies of the originals or, for North American markets, as NTSC conversions made using the BBC-designed MK2B Standards Converter. As this format uses 525-line images interlaced at sixty fields per second, as opposed to PAL's 625 lines at fifty fields per second, the conversion process lost some picture information from the drop in vertical resolution, while duplicating some fields to match the higher field rate.

LOST AND FOUND

Already, though, the Doctor's earliest adventures were being consigned to oblivion. At the time, the BBC saw little value in keeping programmes it could no longer show. Broadcasters saw themselves as producers of new programming, not curators of past shows, and in this they were supported by the unions to which their staff, both technical and creative, belonged. The actors' union Equity in particular limited the number of times a programme could be repeated; it was rightly working to keep its members in employment by encouraging the creation of new material. And in the days long before commercial video and 24-hour multi-channel television, there was no reason to suspect this situation would ever change. Factors like these, plus the expense of videotape, meant storing the original video recordings was of limited value. Once a programme was broadcast, the tape was kept by the BBC Engineering Division's Videotape Section in the basement of Television Centre, with a Retention Authorisation sheet issued for each recording. After telerecordings had been taken and options for repeating the programme had expired, a Wipe/Junk Authorisation would be issued, permitting the Engineering Division to erase the videotape for re-use.

Researchers have unearthed many of the Retention and Wipe/Junk Authorisation sheets for the black-and-white era of *Doctor Who*. The first episodes to be wiped, authorised on 9 March 1967, were all four parts of Second Doctor story *The Highlanders*, followed a few months later by *The Faceless Ones*, *The Moonbase*, *The Underwater Menace* and the bulk of First Doctor episodes. Even while the wiping procedures were in place, there was concern about the policy. In its 23 August 1973 edition, BBC magazine *The Listener* reported on the Corporation's archiving system and criticised it for junking important programmes. "A prime target for quiet indignation over the years has been the BBC's Archive system, and criticism has been growing in recent months. The source of the trouble is a suspicion that the BBC throws away a great many good films and broadcasts which ought to be preserved," it wrote. The following week, Anne Hanford of the BBC Film Library responded, "The policy of the BBC is to spend licence revenue on maintaining what is by now a very full and comprehensive collection of visual material, for its own requirements — either direct re-use in programmes or as a research source." Indeed, as of September 1973, the Engineering Division held more than twenty-thousand hours of programming on tape. Yet the wiping of *Doctor Who*'s original videotape recordings continued until the BBC Film and Videotape Library was formed in 1975 (headed by Hanford) and responsibility for storing tapes was taken out of the hands of the Engineering Division. By then all of the tapes of First and Second Doctor episodes, and most of the Third Doctor's first three seasons, had been erased.

All was not lost, however, because BBC Enterprises still had all of its telerecordings, right? Unfortunately not. Agreements with writers and actors only allowed the BBC five years in which to sell programmes abroad, although this could be extended for a further period if Enterprises felt the expense of further royalties would be covered by sales. By the mid-70s its rights to sell the black-and-white episodes were running out and, although many had been extended once, the demand for these serials was drying up, meaning its store of episodes was losing value and merely taking up space. For each film can, an Accessions card would be filed to show what Enterprises had available for sale. Once the rights to sell a programme had expired it was withdrawn from sale and its card de-accessioned (that is, moved to the 'Junked' file). The relevant film cans — original negatives and any prints that had been returned — were then labelled with the ominous phrase 'Withdrawn, De-Accessioned and Junked' and would eventually be physically destroyed. While records of what telerecordings were junked when are no longer accessible, investigations in 1978 shortly before the policy was officially abandoned indicate the first disposals of *Doctor Who* didn't occur until 1972. Until then Enterprises was offering for sale all stories from the first eight years of the series (except

The Daleks' Master Plan episode seven). Indeed, as late as July 1973 Algeria bought the bulk of the first season. By 1978, however, Enterprises held film copies of just seventeen of the fifty stories from the 1960s, plus black-and-white film copies of the first four Third Doctor seasons.

It was in that year the Film and Videotape Library appointed its first Archive Selector, Sue Malden, to finally establish proper procedures for the retention of current and future programmes, and to see what if anything had survived the junking policies of the past. Malden had been working at the BBC Film Library in Brentford, which was set up in 1948 to store BBC footage on film (as it all was at that time): predominantly news items but over the years it began to take in all sorts of film, from complete programmes to short inserts. As luck would have it, she happened to pick *Doctor Who* to use as a test case for her investigations into how and where wiped programmes might have survived.

The Film Library's own *Doctor Who* holdings were somewhat random. As the programme was predominantly made on videotape, little would be expected to be found at the Film Library, but seven of the eleven episodes recorded onto and broadcast from 35mm film ended up there, along with various filmed inserts, such as shots of the Daleks burning the forest on Kembel from *The Daleks' Master Plan* episode two. But the Library had a junking policy too. Items were graded according to their perceived importance and those of low value — such as inserts that couldn't be re-used and were assumed to exist within an extant programme — would be discarded. Even complete episodes were disposed of, probably on the assumption copies were held by BBC Enterprises. Records show the Library held but junked at various times before 1976 copies of *The Crusade* episode one, *The Ice Warriors* episode three, *The Power of the Daleks* episode six and *The Wheel in Space* episode five, plus film sequences from episode two of *The Celestial Toymaker*. By the time of Sue Malden's audit in 1978, however, it had acquired further episodes, most likely sent to the Library by mistake. These along with the prints she recovered from BBC Enterprises and the surviving colour videotapes formed a solid base from which to start seeking those episodes that were still missing.

With the wiping of transmission tapes coming to an end in 1975, all episodes from the Fourth Doctor's debut onwards survive in their original format. The programme was still recorded largely on videotape with location and model work shot on 16mm or 35mm film, then transferred to video and edited into the episodes. Occasional variations arose, however. The first two Fourth Doctor stories into production in 1974, *Robot* and *The Sontaran Experiment*, were entirely videotaped using the then-new outside broadcast vans for location work, as were the following year's *The Seeds of Doom* and 1978's *The Stones of Blood*. Conversely, the alien jungle settings for *Planet of Evil* and *The Creature from the Pit*, while constructed in a studio, were recorded on film to give them the feel of real locations. This mix of filmed location work and videotaped studio scenes, edited onto and broadcast from tape, continued through the switch to one-inch Type C videotape, which enabled functions that Quad lacked, such as pause, shuttle and variable-speed playback. This was first used for 1984's *Warriors of the Deep* (recorded June/July 1983). Then, when the show returned in 1987 after an eighteen-month break, it was recorded entirely on video. Not only was this cheaper but it gave a more uniform appearance to the picture. Only model work continued to be filmed, the last example being shots of the underwater spaceship in 1989's *Battlefield*.

In 1993 the BBC began transferring all its archived two-inch Quad videotape recordings onto Panasonic D3 digital tapes and the original tapes were donated to the National Film and Television Archive (now the BFI National Archive) in Berkhamstead, Hertfordshire. Material on one-inch Type C tapes was subsequently transferred to Digital Betacam and the originals junked, save for some of the *Doctor Who* recordings which were retained by BBC Video specifically for use when remastering for DVD. The D3 format has now become obsolete itself and those tapes' contents have also been transferred to DigiBeta, although the BBC is now working towards moving all its video material to mass-storage data files as it looks to open up its archive to the public.

So the BBC archive's holdings of Classic *Doctor Who* are a mixed bag of 16mm and 35mm black-and-white film recordings, digital duplicates of one- and two-inch 625-line PAL-colour videotapes, plus episodes converted to 525-line NTSC-colour that were recovered from Canada, off-air Betamax recordings of colour episodes shown in the US (which aren't of broadcast quality but are archived on 525-line U-matic videotape), and various surviving film elements such as location and model footage — all of which is of varying quality depending on its age, where it was originated and how well it has been looked after. There are still many episodes from the 1960s that have not been recovered in any form, however. In some cases complete stories are missing, in others only one or two parts of a serial survive. And for those stories that are complete but for an episode or two, various methods have been tried to fill in the gaps.

When *Doctor Who* was released on VHS, generally whatever source first came to hand was used to produce the tapes, leading to some poor-quality releases, particularly of black-and-white episodes which were often badly transferred from inferior film copies. So deciding what were the best materials to use for the DVDs was a complicated task, one that BBC Video delegated to a group of knowledgeable BBC engineers and video experts known as the Restoration Team.

THE FIRST RESTORATIONS

In 1992, three BBC employees (and *Doctor Who* fans) — Ralph Montagu, Steve Roberts and James Russell — combined their skills in different aspects of video technology and production to trial a technique for restoring the 1971 Third Doctor serial *The Dæmons* to colour. Only one of the story's five episodes survives on its original two-inch colour videotape, the rest wiped probably sometime in 1973 (episode four was spared purely by chance). BBC Enterprises had made telerecordings of all episodes on 16mm black-and-white film and these were subsequently archived by the Film and Videotape Library. While colour video copies converted to the 525-line NTSC format had been sold to US broadcasters in 1972, these too had since been wiped. But on 19 November 1977, KCET in Los Angeles had shown a compilation of *The Dæmons* (that is, the episodes edited together into one long story) which one viewer recorded onto Betamax at the request of British fan and episode collector Ian Levine. He then had the recording transferred to U-matic cassette, a format he could watch back in the UK. This was still in 525 lines and, being a copy of a Betamax recording, wasn't of broadcast quality. The telerecordings were much sharper, however, and Montagu, Roberts and Russell's idea was to combine the two.

An analogue colour television signal is made up of two components: information about the brightness of the image (called luminance) and information about the colour (called chrominance). Because the human eye is more sensitive to changes in brightness than colour, the luminance signal is at full resolution but the chrominance signal is much less detailed — just like the surviving film and video recordings of *The Dæmons*. By combining the luminance of the telerecording with just the chrominance of the off-air video, a full-colour, full-resolution version of the story could be created. It wasn't that straightforward as the telerecording process introduces slight distortions, so the pictures from the two sources don't quite line up. The video also has shots missing where the episodes had been edited together, so they had be coloured by other means. But the attempt was ultimately a success. *The Dæmons* now existed again as a broadcast-quality colour story. Indeed, it was shown on BBC2 in the run-up to Christmas 1992 and released on VHS in March 1993.

So impressive were the results that the Film and Videotape Library and BBC Enterprises provided further funding for the team to recolour three more Third Doctor stories for which the only surviving colour source is off-air recordings from the US: *The Ambassadors of Death*, *Doctor Who and the Silurians* and *Terror of the Autons*. The last two were equally successfully restored and released on VHS in 1993; unfortunately the recording of *The Ambassadors of Death*, transmitted on WNED in Buffalo, New York in 1977, exhibits much interference and the colour for most episodes is uneven. This was eventually released on VHS in May 2002 with as many sections recoloured as could be effectively achieved and the rest left in black and white — it wasn't until new restoration techniques were available for its DVD release in October 2012 that the serial could once again be watched in colour throughout.

Towards the end of 1991 Steve Roberts had been involved in compiling clips from past *Doctor Who* episodes for the BBC2 retrospective *Resistance is Useless*. Then in 1993, with Richard Molesworth and Paul Vanezis (a videotape editor at BBC Pebble Mill in Birmingham), he helped transfer hundreds of clips from their original videotapes for use in Kevin Davies' documentary *30 Years in the TARDIS*. This and further work for BBC Video — including *The Five Doctors Special*

Edition, re-edited from the original studio recordings (later to become the first release on DVD); the release of *The War Machines*, reinstating cut sections newly rediscovered in Australia; and the reconstruction of *The Ice Warriors* episodes two and three from off-screen stills and a recording of the soundtrack, along with a documentary about the missing episodes featuring many surviving clips — gave the Restoration Team a good knowledge of what was in the archive and which were the best copies of episodes, along with close contacts among the staff at the Film and Videotape Library. By the end of the 1990s the team was handling any VHS release that wasn't a straightforward transfer from an original videotape, as they were now sufficiently trusted to be allowed access to the best source materials in the archive and, with new telecine transfers and incoming digital restoration techniques, they were able to present the episodes in the highest possible quality.

When the DVD range began in earnest in 2000, with the desire to make them a worthwhile upgrade from VHS in terms of both picture quality and additional features, the Restoration Team were the obvious people to prepare the discs' contents. Not only did they have the technical skills and contacts, they were also fans of the programme and knew what would constitute an attractive package. Their dedication meant they often went the extra mile to make the releases as good as possible within the limits of time and budget. Now the range is complete, it forms arguably the most comprehensive examination of the series there has ever been, and the episodes themselves look as good as, if not better than they did when originally broadcast, a testament to the talents and devotion of the various members of the Restoration Team over the years.

REMASTERING FOR THE DIGITAL AGE

To maximise the appeal of the new DVD range, the initial releases tended towards the more well-regarded stories, starting with *The Robots of Death*, a popular Fourth Doctor story from 1977. For those episodes for which the original transmission tape survives, the restoration process is usually based on the archive's digital duplicate on D3 tape, which is generally a faithful clone of what was recorded on the Quad tape. (In this first instance it was found some faults had been introduced during the transfer to D3, so the team was given access to the original Quad tape held by the National Film and Television Archive from which a new digital transfer was made.) Even these need some basic restoration work, however, to reduce video noise, correct faults on the original tape (remember, these may have been wiped and reused several times before *Doctor Who* was recorded onto them) and clean up any film inserts. The telecine of the 1970s and 80s wasn't as good as can be achieved today, but sadly most of the location and model film no longer survives. All we have is what was edited into the episodes at the time, which may include dirt and scratches on the original film, now permanently recorded onto the videotape. Fortunately with digital techniques (and time permitting) these can largely be removed and the episodes graded so that all scenes have consistent contrast and colour irrespective of whether they were shot by film cameras on location or electronic cameras in the studio. Where filmed material does still exist and has been newly telecined for the DVDs, this is noted in the relevant entries in this book.

The issue of 'burnt in' defects is worse for the 1960s episodes, which now only exist as tele-recordings. These may incorporate problems from the original film inserts, from the videotape onto which these and the studio scenes were recorded, and from the telerecording process itself. And that's before you consider that many are not the original telerecording negatives, but positive prints copied from those, then sent to overseas broadcasters, maybe bicycled around several television stations, left in a vault for several decades or passed around among film collectors, before finally being recovered and returned to the archive.

When working with such material, the Restoration team has needed to devise some inventive methods to get it looking as close to the original broadcasts as possible. This is not only to make for a more pleasing viewing experience, but also because the better the quality, the more efficiently the data can be compressed when producing the DVDs. One of the earliest and perhaps most revelatory techniques is the Video Field Interpolation Restoration Effect, known as VidFIRE, developed by Peter Finklestone in 2001. As discussed, the 1960s episodes (and some early-70s episodes) survive only as telerecordings — 25-frame-per-second film copies of the 50-interlaced-fields-per-second videotapes — so any motion in the picture is not as smooth as it originally looked. In theory, if the telerecording precisely reproduced the horizontal lines of the video picture, it would be possible to separate out the two video fields in each film frame and re-interlace them to recreate the smoother motion of video. In practice, the telerecording process introduced slight distortions as the film wound through the camera, breaking up the precise horizontal structure of the lines. Also a setting called 'spot wobble' was generally used, whereby the electron beam scanning across the television screen to produce the image was slightly elongated so that the edges of the lines were softened and overlapped to make them less discernible.[2]

Nevertheless, each telerecorded film frame is a blend of two video fields recorded 20ms apart. Copying the film back to interlaced video doesn't make a difference as the original field line structure is lost, so you still get two fields from one static frame, then two more from the next frame 40ms later. What VidFIRE does is compare each pair of frames to assess what parts of the picture have changed and creates a new frame to go between them, then interlaces the first field from an original frame with a second from a new estimated frame. This means the content of each pair of fields (one original, the other computer generated) is again 20ms apart in time, making the motion of the complete video smoother. This only applies to shots originally recorded by video cameras at 50 fields per second, of course, so for the DVDs only those scenes recorded in the studio are treated. The better the film recording (and its clean-up to remove the tell-tale signs of being a film source), the more convincing the appearance of genuine video. The process was later refined so that both fields are computer generated, at 10ms and 30ms after an original frame. This keeps the 20ms gap between fields but gives a more even result as the estimated frames are closer to an original one.

The first release to feature VidFIRE was *Planet of Giants* on VHS in January 2002. Although *The Tomb of the Cybermen* was released on DVD at the same time (the first 1960s story to be issued on disc), its remastering had been completed six months earlier, before the VidFIRE process had been perfected. It was also uncertain the effect would still work after being encoded for DVD, so a short section of episode three was treated and included as an Easter Egg (see Appendix 2, page 367). This demonstrated that the smoother motion was retained and so the next black-and-white release, *The Aztecs* in October 2002, was the first story on DVD to be fully treated with the VidFIRE process. The releases of nearly all subsequent 1960s serials, and those early Third Doctor stories that only survive as telerecordings, have VidFIRE applied to their studio scenes; the only exceptions are episode one of *The Crusade* in the Lost in Time set and *The Time Meddler*, as the surviving copies are too poor for the process to be effective at hiding their film origins.

At the start of the DVD range, just six titles were issued a year. This was partly because the Restoration Team was also still working on the final VHS releases — including recolouring as much of *The Ambassadors of Death* as possible, restoring three First Doctor stories for a boxset release in November 2002, and another set of incomplete serials to finish the range in November 2003 — partly because computing power was lower in those days so the restorations took longer than they would now, and partly because the DVD market was still relatively small, with only an estimated 10% of UK households having a DVD player in 2001. The Restoration Team was also charged with compiling the special features for each disc. Initially these tended towards existing material, such as trailers, behind-the-scenes footage and *Doctor Who*-related clips from other programmes, but there were three newly produced elements that would be maintained for every subsequent release: an audio commentary by people involved in making the serial; information subtitles that provide facts about its production; and a photo gallery of images from the story.

In the second year the team also began to try out ideas for original material, such as newly recorded interviews with cast members and production personnel, optional CGI effects shots, and alternative music-only and surround-sound tracks. All were popular additions and would be offered periodically throughout the range when possible. For example, most of the music recorded for the series survives only on the programme itself, mixed with the dialogue and other sound. Where it

---

2 This is why telerecordings that mix fields from two different frames of a telecined film insert are such a problem, as the fields can no longer be separated and re-synced to match the original film footage.

does exist separately — primarily from the 1980s when much of the music was composed by the BBC Radiophonic Workshop and survives in its archive, maintained and remastered by composer and sound engineer Mark Ayres — it is often presented as an alternative audio track. Similarly a Dolby Digital 5.1 soundtrack can only be created if all the different sound sources — dialogue, background noise, sound effects and music — exist separately. For some serials, again mainly those made during the 1980s, videotapes survive of the original studio sessions with the as-recorded sound, while the music and effects are held in the Radiophonic Workshop archive, enabling Ayres to produce a new surround-sound mix so viewers with a home-cinema setup can experience the story in a fresh way.

New computer-generated visual effects could feasibly be done for any story as they're generally superimposed on top of the existing picture (simply hiding the original effect); in practice there needs to be a sufficient number of effects shots that are worth replacing in order to make the option worthwhile, and a producer keen enough to create them (on budget). A full list of which releases feature CGI effects, music-only or surround-sound tracks is given in Index i starting on page 398. Such alternatives are provided in addition to the original, as-transmitted programme, which is always the default viewing option.

The range received a slight facelift at the start of 2002 when Clayton Hickman, who was then editor of *Doctor Who Magazine*, was commissioned to provide artwork for the covers. He proposed a totally new design, as the existing layout with grey circles taking up half the cover was widely criticised by fans. BBC Video was wary of changing the look so soon in the range, though, especially as previous alterations to the cover design of the VHS releases had also received complaints because fans wanted them to be consistent. So the overall design remained but rather then the single photo or simple montage used on the first year's releases, Hickman supplied more accomplished photo illustrations. He would ultimately produce artwork for 141 covers and slipcases, more than any other artist on the range, accounting for 70% of individual story releases.

Another innovation in restoration came at the end of 2002 with the release of Resurrection of the Daleks. Because the luminance and chrominance components of an analogue television signal were combined (to reduce bandwidth for recording and broadcasting), when this composite signal was decoded by a receiver — that is, the viewer's television — the frequencies of the two components could be confused, leading to fine detail in the picture being interpreted as colour information (known as cross-colour) while areas of colour display a pattern through misinterpretation of the colour information as small variations in brightness (cross-luminance or dot crawl). The mistakes are subtle but visible, producing a noisier picture, which also means more data is needed to encode the image onto DVD. As the Quad videotape recordings of *Doctor Who* (and their archived D3 duplicates) were composite video, these needed to be decoded into their separate components before restoration, but existing decoders were still prone to these misinterpretations of the signal. Jim Easterbrook, working in the BBC's engineering research and development department, therefore devised a new way of retrieving the correct luminance and chrominance signals, using knowledge of how PAL encoding works and complex mathematics to eliminate errors in the decoding process. He then worked with colleague Richard Russell to translate his computer simulations into a physical device, called the Transform PAL Decoder. *The Three Doctors* was actually the first serial to be treated with the Decoder, but its release was pushed back in the schedule leaving Resurrection of the Daleks to be the first DVD showing the much cleaner pictures produced by the Decoder. This was subsequently used in the restoration of all episodes originating on PAL videotape, with those initially released on DVD before its invention having since been re-released as Special Editions.

EXTRA AMBITIONS

In 2003 BBC Video celebrated the series' fortieth anniversary by issuing a story from each Doctor's era (except the Eighth Doctor, whose single outing was already available) and featuring some of the most popular monsters. The seven releases each had a sticker on the box featuring the anniversary logo designed by Hickman, which in Australia was used as the main logo on the covers themselves. The year also saw the first multi-story boxset, a collection of the three Dalek serials released on

DVD to date. This was a limited edition exclusive to UK newsagent chain WHSmith, for which BBC Video had previously provided VHS boxsets of all five Davros stories in 2001 and three Time Lord stories in 2002. The DVD of The Three Doctors, initially scheduled for January, was held back to the anniversary month of November so that as well as being released in a standard case it could be issued as a gift set with a metal model of the Third Doctor's car Bessie, made by Corgi.

The special features were also getting more ambitious, particularly those looking at how the stories were made. While interviews with cast and crew members on the likes of The Aztecs, The Dalek Invasion of Earth and Resurrection of the Daleks had covered many areas of production, the first structured documentary about the making of a story appeared on Earthshock in August 2003. This was much praised and from the following year such documentaries started to become more regular — when there was a worthwhile story to tell about a serial's production.

For some serials footage exists that wasn't used in the final programme, cut to get an episode to the right length, to improve its pacing or because a mistake was made during the recording. Often, however, this material survives in an unbroadcastable form, either as a low-quality VHS copy or with a time-code superimposed over the picture (a counter enabling sections of footage to be found quickly, used as a reference in editing and dubbing). When this is the case and the footage contains some interesting or amusing material, it's included as a selection of deleted scenes or outtakes. In a very few instances full studio recordings survive or an initial, longer edit of an episode before it was cut down to the required length exists clean and in broadcast quality. An extended edit can then be considered, reinstating material that was cut but which adds to or helps the telling of the story, as had been done with The Five Doctors Special Edition.

This mainly applies to stories from the late-80s as, being the most recent, they have the greatest chance of such unused footage surviving. Some of the Seventh Doctor stories were thus re-edited and extended for their VHS releases in the 1990s, partly as an incentive for people who had made their own recording during the original broadcast to purchase the commercial release. As quite a few of these stories were over-length and had to have a lot of material cut out after recording, these longer, more coherent versions became preferred by some fans and it was hoped the DVD range would at least include those that had previously been produced plus any more that were possible. One such was The Curse of Fenric, released on DVD in October 2003 with both the episodes as broadcast and an extended re-edit produced by Mark Ayres, who was the composer for the original serial and so knew how the director wanted to present it before he had to squeeze the material into four 24-minute episodes. This isn't as simple as dropping some scenes back in and maybe re-ordering a few others, as the programme still has to flow and tell the story properly, and new music and effects are likely to be required for the added sections. The opportunity was also taken to update some of the visual effects for the extended version.

In the end, only this and Battlefield had extended versions produced, further attempts succumbing to lack of time and budget. Two other special edits were made of Enlightenment and Planet of Fire, but these actually removed footage in a bid to make them feel more like modern episodes — something that was widely considered to be a pointless exercise. One final special edit was made for Day of the Daleks, which didn't reinstate any deleted material but replaced some shots with newly filmed footage, had new digitally created visual effects and updated some elements of the soundtrack. Confusingly, these alternative edits were labelled 'special editions' before the freshly restored Special Edition re-releases were conceived, so be aware that the latter include only the original as-broadcast serials, not reworked versions.

With the VHS releases coming to an end in 2003, the Restoration Team was free to concentrate on the DVDs, although with the growing sophistication of newly made extras — including features about how the serials were made, people profiles, era overviews and even comedy pieces — from a growing range of producers, they were now beginning work on a title around a year or more ahead of its planned release date, despite the release rate staying at six a year. Thus, when Doctor Who Magazine ran a survey in January 2003 for readers to pick which story they most wanted on DVD, the winner, Pyramids of Mars, didn't hit the shops until March 2004.

That year also saw the next milestone in restoration techniques, this time for those Third Doctor stories that existed only in the NTSC colour format. The problem with these episodes was that their conversion for broadcast in North America not only lost some picture information in the drop from 625 to 525 lines, but the way fields were mixed and retimed to display at 60 instead of 50 times a second made the on-screen movement uneven. When these videotapes were first recovered they were simply run through a standards converter again to return them to 625 lines at 50 fields per second, but that couldn't remove the juddery motion or replace the lost picture resolution. Fortunately the recovered 525-line tapes were retained in the archive and, in 1993, original Restoration Team members Ralph Montagu and Steve Roberts considered a way of undoing the original conversion by mathematically reversing the process applied by the MK2B Standards Converter. Jim Easterbrook worked out the calculations and showed it could work, but at that time there was no money to build the hardware needed to process the analogue videotapes. However, Montagu pursued the idea, dubbed Reverse Standards Conversion (RSC), and as the broadcasting industry moved into the digital age he worked with another BBC research engineer, James Insell, on a PC-based software implementation. With further input from Easterbrook and financing from BBC Worldwide, in 2004 the process was realised, unpicking the original fields from the conversion and digitally interpolating the missing 100 lines.[3] The result is smoother motion and restored resolution, although there is some image flickering especially along near-horizontal edges owing to the repeated changes in vertical resolution. The processing also introduces a lot of picture noise that has to subsequently be reduced with standard restoration techniques.

RSC was first applied to *The Claws of Axos*, which required only two of its four episodes to be reverse converted, and this story was released on DVD in April 2005. All episodes recovered on NTSC videotape were then treated for their initial DVD issue — *Colony in Space*, *The Curse of Peladon*, *Inferno*, *The Mutants* episodes one and two, *The Sea Devils* episodes one to three, and *The Time Monster* — but when *The Claws of Axos* and *Inferno* were revisited for their later Special Edition releases a new technique was applied. Because of the imperfections still evident in the reverse-converted material, this time just its chrominance component was used, combined with the luminance from restored and VidFIRE-processed 16mm black-and-white telerecordings of the episodes. It might seem odd to resort to using film copies when a version exists that has always existed in the video domain (and therefore was never prone to the dirt and distortion of film), but the team now has so much experience of restoring the telerecordings that their images are sharper than even the reverse-converted video copies, and using just the latter's colour information minimises the noise and flicker they exhibit.

GETTING REANIMATED

During this period, two events occurred that would impact the DVD range. The first was the announcement in late-September 2003 that *Doctor Who* would be returning to television with a new series under the creative direction of Russell T Davies. The second was the merger in September 2004 of BBC Video with Woolworths Group's Video Collection International to form a new DVD publishing company, 2 entertain. Although the joint venture was 60% owned by BBC Worldwide, it operated as its own business, licensing from its parent the rights to issue BBC programmes, including *Doctor Who*. It was happy to retain the Restoration Team's services as they were clearly providing what the audience wanted, but as the new business became established (the first release with 2 entertain branding wasn't until Revelation of the Daleks in July 2005) it did make one notable change to the process. In the autumn of 2005 it appointed Dan Hall as commissioning editor of the range. He would now handle the editorial side of the releases — managing budgets and schedules, and choosing and commissioning the special features — while the Restoration Team would focus on remastering the episodes.

One of the aims of spreading the workload in this way was to enable the release rate to be increased. Those doing the actual restoration work were now a core team of three: Jonathan Wood

---

3 Strictly speaking, the UK PAL system uses only 576 of its 625 lines for actual picture information, while the US NTSC system uses 480 of its 525 lines for the image, so the resolution of the latter is only 96 lines less.

at BBC Studios & Post Production performing the initial transfer of the source materials to Digital Betacam and the final colour-grading of the restored episodes; Peter Crocker at SVS Resources carrying out the picture repair and clean-up; and Mark Ayres handling the remastering of the soundtrack and any other audio elements commissioned, such as isolated music scores and surround-sound mixes. Their work was co-ordinated by Steve Roberts, who was now responsible for ensuring all content met the technical specifications and was delivered to 2 entertain ready for the discs to be pressed, with notes about how the content should be presented in the DVD menus. He reported to Hall, who decided what special features to produce, apportioned them budget and contracted producers to make them. Hall brought in several new contributors alongside those who had already been working on the extras, and sought to expand the features beyond the esoteric world of *Doctor Who* and show how the series connected with real history, literature and science.

Given the lead times the Restoration Team was working to, the schedule for 2006 was already in place and Dan Hall's influence wouldn't be felt until the following year, his first credit as executive producer of the extras appearing on *Robot* in June 2007. In the meantime there were a couple of milestones already in the pipeline. January 2006 saw the first boxset of newly released stories. The Beginning contained the first three *Doctor Who* serials from 1963/64 plus all the material from the initial recording of the debut episode. Some digital restoration of these episodes had been done for a VHS boxset in 1999 that ultimately never happened (the three stories were re-released separately instead) and the idea of redoing the work more meticulously for DVD had been around since before the New Series was announced. The set was initially planned for release in November 2005 alongside the Series One boxset, but was later pushed back to January (with The Web Planet pulled forward to maintain six releases in 2005). This established a trend for boxsets at the start of the year (when buyers had Christmas gift money to spend), with the New Beginnings, Beneath the Surface, E-Space Trilogy and Peladon Tales sets following suit over subsequent years. Further sets of two or three stories were released at other times of the year as the range progressed (see Appendix 3), along with occasional re-packagings of previous releases into themed sets, such as The Complete Davros Collection and Bred for War: The Sontaran Collection.

In November 2006 came the first example of animation being used to recreate episodes of which no film copy is known to exist, with the release of *The Invasion*. This eight-part serial is missing episodes one and four, which were animated by Cosgrove Hall as a follow-up to its 2003 webcast *Scream of the Shalka* after that project was dropped owing to the revival of the television series (see page 361). Because the animation had already been done and paid for by BBC Interactive, 2 entertain was able to license it for DVD release at a manageable cost and so issue *The Invasion* as a now-complete story. It was well received and raised hopes that further stories with only one or two missing episodes could be similarly treated. For a long time, however, it merely meant other methods of filling these gaps — such as reconstructions using off-screen stills and soundtrack, as done for the VHS releases of *The Ice Warriors* and *The Tenth Planet* — were seen as less acceptable even though the now-preferred animation route was too expensive for 2 entertain to commission from scratch. Eventually, as technology developed and a new generation of animators arrived who were willing to work for lower rates in order to establish their credentials on a prestigious project like *Doctor Who*, a way was found to finance animations for the missing episodes of *The Ice Warriors*, *The Moonbase*, *The Tenth Planet* and *The Reign of Terror*, and these all had standalone releases as complete serials.[4]

4 It's possible a further Second Doctor story, *The Underwater Menace*, will be released with animated episodes. Initially only one episode of this four-part serial was held in the archive, and this was restored and released on DVD with other solo episodes in the Lost in Time set in November 2004. Then in September 2011 episode two was recovered from film collector Terry Burnett. This meant only two episodes were now missing, making the serial a viable candidate for completion through animation. Such a release was planned, previewed on the DVD of *The Moonbase* in January 2014, with special features known to have been produced and indications that Planet 55 Studios was handling the animated episodes. Since then there have been suggestions the release is delayed while Planet 55 completes other work, and at the time of writing no announcement has been made by BBC Worldwide about when *The Underwater Menace* will be released or whether it will still be completed with animation, or instead match off-screen images to the soundtrack, as was done for the missing episode three of *The Web of Fear* released in February 2014.

With the New Series proving an immediate popular hit and raising the profile of the Classic Series alongside, 2 entertain was keen to capitalise on the brand's renewed prominence and 2007 saw a bumper crop of DVD releases. As well as six first-time single-story releases there were three boxsets containing a further eleven unreleased serials (including all six stories of the Key to Time season), a fourth grouping together five previously issued stories with several related CD audio adventures produced by Big Finish, plus re-releases of eight discs from early in the range at a discounted price. Much of this new momentum was sustained in subsequent years with a mix of single and boxset releases allowing the number of stories issued each year to triple without impacting the quality of the product. Each still received full restoration plus audio commentary, information subtitles and a photo gallery as the bare minimum, with most also getting further extras of both archive material and newly made interviews and documentaries.

In fact, such was the quality of the additional features by now that the very early releases, innovative at the time, looked rather plain in comparison. With the release of The Complete Davros Collection in 2007, the opportunity was taken to revisit the restoration of *Remembrance of the Daleks* with the new techniques and experience that had been gained since it was first issued in February 2001 (and to correct a couple of small errors that had slipped through on that previous disc). Some newly recorded extras for the story were also added to bring it up to the standard of more recent releases. Inevitably there was an outcry from fans, who complained the only way to get this improved release was by buying an expensive boxset, most of the content of which they already owned. Eventually 2 entertain released the Special Edition of *Remembrance of the Daleks* on its own, having also re-released the content of the very first DVD release, The Five Doctors Special Edition, alongside the original, as-transmitted version of the story for the first time — plus lots of new extras — as The Five Doctors 25th Anniversary Edition.

This showed there was a demand for early discs to be revisited, especially if there were now improvements that could be made to the quality of the restoration, but also if there was scope for the addition of major special features such as making-of documentaries and any contemporary footage that hadn't been included first time around. Thus ten of the earliest DVD releases were selected as viable candidates for smartening up, scheduled for release in various boxsets. Such was the improvement that these sold as well as the regular releases and further standalone Special Editions were added to the schedule. In all eighteen serials got the Special Edition treatment (not including *The Five Doctors*), mostly for stories initially released in the first two years of the range (the table of stories on page 26 shows which these are).

The range was now on a roll with monthly one-, two- or three-story releases. For the first time people began to anticipate when it might reach the end. The fiftieth anniversary in 2013 began to be seen by both the disc producers and fans as a handy target: if hit, it would have taken just thirteen years to issue all stories on DVD, versus the twenty years it took for the VHS range to be completed. Even the worsening economy didn't cause the releases to slow down. As Woolworths Group went into administration in early 2009, BBC Worldwide began negotiations to acquire the remaining 40% stake in 2 entertain, which it completed in March 2010, eventually folding the DVD publishing operation into its Consumer Products division. Dan Hall remained as commissioning editor, although on a freelance basis, eventually setting up his own company Pup Ltd to produce content for the *Doctor Who* discs under licence to BBC Worldwide. And of course he kept the members of the Restoration Team on contract to perform the remastering work.

There was one final hurdle to overcome in terms of restoration technology before the range could be satisfactorily completed. As we've seen, while some Third Doctor episodes survive on their original PAL colour videotapes, others are reconverted from NTSC copies and some required a combination of telerecordings with off-air recordings to return them to colour. This still left several of which only black-and-white film copies were known to exist: most of *The Ambassadors of Death*, all of *The Mind of Evil* and one episode each of *Invasion of the Dinosaurs* and *Planet of the Daleks*. How could these be restored to their original colour when no colour copies survived?

Step forward James Insell (who had worked on developing Reverse Standards Conversion).

When watching a broadcast of one of these episodes on satellite channel UK Gold in 1994, he noticed patches of colour appearing in the black-and-white image. As we saw when discussing the development of the Transform PAL Decoder, the luminance and chrominance components of a composite video signal can interfere and be misinterpreted by a receiver. Although when the Third Doctor episodes were telerecorded the process used a black-and-white monitor (as it was being recorded onto black-and-white film anyway), that was being fed by a colour video signal, either directly from videotape or, more usually, the same broadcast signal being watched by viewers at home. If not filtered out, the chrominance signal would cause cross-luminance artefacts on the screen — a fine pattern of moving dots caused by the signal being interpreted as brightness information — which were recorded onto the film. Insell wondered if this pattern could be decoded back into the original colour information.

Unable to get backing from his bosses at BBC Research & Development, he set up an online forum for people to suggest ways in which this decoding could be achieved. One contributor was Richard Russell, who had built the Transform PAL Decoder and now devised a successful way to decode the cross-luminance pattern, or 'chroma dots' (the very effect the Decoder had been designed to remove). With a high-resolution scan of the original telerecording negative, the chrominance information can be separated and, by understanding how it was originally modulated onto the luminance signal, decoded to restore the original colours of the image. This Colour Recovery process is not perfect, depending on the quality of the telerecording and requiring much manual adjustment to ensure the signal is translated into the correct colours. But the fact alone that usable colour information can be extracted from a black-and-white film recording is simply staggering.[5] The first commercial application of the technique was to an episode of *Dad's Army* that was subsequently transmitted on BBC2 in December 2002, seen for the first time in colour since its original broadcast in 1969.

While Insell and Russell were developing Colour Recovery during 2008, the DVD of *Planet of the Daleks* was in preparation. With only one of its six episodes not existing in colour, 2|entertain agreed to having it coloured by Legend Films in California, a company with much experience at digitally colouring old black-and-white movies. This is an expensive and time-consuming process whereby selected frames are manually coloured and then a computer extrapolates that colour information across subsequent frames until it loses synchronisation as objects move around or come into the picture. Legend was sent the restored telerecording as a sequence of frames, which it coloured with reference to the other episodes (guessing at appropriate colours for items that didn't appear elsewhere). The result was treated with the VidFIRE process to restore the smoother motion of video and this version was intended for the DVD release. It was at this point that Insell showed the Restoration Team the results of the Colour Recovery process. While the computer colouring was crisp and stable, it was rather flat, relying on the luminance of the telerecording for tonal variation. Colour Recovery, on the other hand, produced rather noisy, unstable colour but it had the subtle variations that made it more convincing, and was closer to the true colour as originally seen. The team realised that by combining the two colour sources they could get the best of both. The result is all but indistinguishable from a genuine colour videotape.

Only the Colour Recovery process was subsequently applied to the other black-and-white-only Third Doctor episodes that had the necessary chroma dots. Legend raised its prices for further computer-colouring work which, with a less favourable exchange rate, made it uneconomical, whereas with effort the recovered colour could be improved sufficiently to produce acceptable results at a much lower cost. Indeed, when watching the DVD of *The Ambassadors of Death* — of

---

5 One aspect of the Colour Recovery process uses the chroma dot patterning to calculate how to straighten out the slight distortions in the image introduced by the telerecording process. This is necessary to correctly decode the chrominance signal, but is also useful when combining a telerecording with a colour video recording, as the two images match up much more precisely. Previously the colour recording was digitally warped to match the telerecording, but for later recolourisations such as *The Dæmons*, *Terror of the Autons* and the Special Editions of *The Claws of Axos* and *Inferno*, the film frames were run through the Colour Recovery software to undistort them (even though any recovered colour was not to be used) so that the colour source was easier to align.

which parts are colour recovered and parts coloured from an off-air NTSC video recording — the former arguably look more like the original PAL colour video of the surviving episode one. Only two episodes couldn't have suitable colour recovered. It was found the telerecording of *The Mind of Evil* episode one does have the chrominance signal filtered out (as strictly speaking all telerecordings of colour material were supposed to have — how lucky we are the technicians making them didn't always do so), therefore no colour information is contained on the film. Instead this was computer-coloured by Peter Crocker and Stuart Humphreys, a *Doctor Who* fan who for years has been colouring clips and off-screen stills from 1960s episodes, using essentially the same technique as Legend but at a fraction of the cost (although with a huge degree of dedication). And while episode one of *Invasion of the Dinosaurs* does have chroma dots evident, the quality of the telerecording means they aren't clear enough to decode fully, generally missing any blue hues. This was corrected to a degree through digital colour grading, but the result was deemed unsuitable to be the version of the episode that plays by default on the disc, although it can still be viewed.

SURPRISE ENDING

With the completion of the DVD range in sight, Dan Hall and 2 entertain were keen for it to go out on a high; in the event, it was to see an unexpected climax. They felt that the VHS range, by releasing the most highly regarded stories earlier on, had been left with less popular serials at the end, so the DVDs were scheduled much more evenly. A few well-respected stories were deliberately held back to close the range, notably *Terror of the Zygons*, a much-wanted Fourth Doctor story and a particular favourite of Hall's. The Third Doctor episodes that only existed in black-and-white were delayed in the hope of finding an affordable way to recolour them, a decision that proved correct thanks to the timely development of Colour Recovery. Similarly, the 1960s serials with one or two missing episodes were eventually able to be completed with animation. Both groups contained some highly regarded stories, such as *The Mind of Evil* and *The Tenth Planet*, that kept anticipation high through to the end.

These were partly given more time to get the treatment they deserved by the scheduling of further Special Editions which, while re-releases, were much improved on the original discs and broadly welcomed by collectors. There was even scope to put out unexpected bonuses like *Shada*, *Scream of the Shalka* and the *More Than 30 Years in the TARDIS* documentary (see Appendix 1) before the tentative November 2013 deadline was reached. *Terror of the Zygons* and *The Tenth Planet* were duly issued in the months leading up to the fiftieth anniversary, and although an animated release of *The Moonbase* was known to be due in early 2014, this was very much a late addition (the two surviving episodes having already been released in the Lost in Time set with no expectation that the missing episodes would ever be animated), as was the eventual standalone release of *The Underwater Menace* after another of its episodes was recovered in 2011. To all intents and purposes, by the anniversary the range was finally complete and fans could watch every existing episode of *Doctor Who* in pristine quality. Then nine more were discovered.

The announcement in October 2013 that *The Enemy of the World* and all but one episode of *The Web of Fear* had been recovered from a television station in Nigeria left *Doctor Who* fans around the world astonished and overjoyed. What better anniversary present could they have asked for? Unsurprisingly the two stories became the fastest selling DVDs in the range, even though they had already been made available as downloads from Apple iTunes. Although the episodes were fully restored by the experts of the Restoration Team, the DVDs have no additional features as their preparation might have made the discovery known before the big reveal. With *The Enemy of the World* released the Monday after the anniversary itself and *The Web of Fear* three months later, the *Doctor Who* DVD range culminated in the best way possible: with episodes that when the releases began fourteen years previously no one knew existed or could have hoped would ever be found. Then again, can the range ever be considered truly complete while there are still episodes missing? One can only hope that more will one day be found and join their fellows on DVD.

But the legacy of the range goes beyond the episodes themselves, however much the work done to restore them to the highest quality is appreciated, particularly being able to watch the Third

Doctor era in full colour at last. The exhaustive array of special features shows how Classic *Doctor Who* is the most analysed, debated and loved television programme there has ever been. If there's anything you want to know about the series, it'll be on these meticulously produced discs. They form the perfect celebration of a show that has brought fifty years of pleasure to viewers everywhere.

USING THE DVD COMPENDIUM

This book has been designed as a buying guide for those new to or still picking up the Classic *Doctor Who* DVDs, to help you make your selections and giving pointers to other stories you might like (although of course we recommend getting them all eventually). Once your collection is underway, or if you've already completed it, the book acts as a handy digest of the discs' contents so you can easily find any feature you want to watch.

The main section lists every DVD in alphabetical order for easy reference. A table of the stories in the order they were broadcast precedes the listings (overleaf) and they are listed in release order in Appendix 3. Related titles that were released as part of the range but aren't broadcast *Doctor Who* stories are covered in Appendix 1.

Each entry begins with a tally of the episodes and extras, for use as a point of comparison when deciding which disc to buy next if you're still building your collection. The main characters, enemies and locations of each story are listed to help new viewers find elements they know they like without giving away too much ahead of watching the story, plus some basic details about the DVD release to guide buyers searching for them online or in shops.

A **Story Teaser** gives a brief summary of the premise of the story to remind long-time fans without spoiling it for first-time viewers (at least, nothing that isn't revealed by the packaging). **Connections** lists other titles that feature some of the same themes, events, locations, characters and key contributors. **Worth Watching** suggests some of the highlights of each serial that make it worthy of adding to your collection.

The contents of each disc are given in the sequence they are presented on the DVD menus. As all releases offer Play All, Episode Selection or Scene Selection options for viewing the episodes, **The Episodes** gives a brief summation of what sources were used in their restoration and any key techniques that were applied, as discussed in the introduction. **Special Features** are described with timings and key contributors.

Finally, if a disc contains hidden **Easter Eggs**, the number is noted under the entry so you know how many to look for if you desire, or if you'd rather just be told where they are (or can't find any) you can look them up in Appendix 2. **Related Extras** lists other titles that also contain significant coverage of the story's elements or production.

Note that throughout the book, story titles in *serif italics* refer to the programme while those in sans serif type refer to the DVD release of that story.

ACKNOWLEDGEMENTS

First and foremost I'd like to thank everyone who has contributed in any way to the Classic *Doctor Who* DVDs over the years — this Compendium is a salute to all their hard work and you'll find many of them listed in Index vi at the back of the book. While I have catalogued the contents by watching the discs themselves, much of my knowledge of the range has been gained from years of reading interviews in Panini's *Doctor Who Magazine*, the in-depth articles on the Restoration Team website at restoration-team.co.uk and online forums to which the content producers have kindly contributed information, and I thank them all for their engagement with viewers, helping us appreciate the dedication involved in working on the DVDs. While I've made every effort to ensure the details in this book are accurate, any errors are entirely my own. For help with clarifying specific facts about particular items, I'd like to thank Mark Ayres, Richard Bignell, David Brunt, Chris Chapman, Sue Cowley, Derek Handley, Vanessa Jackson, Allison Jones, Moray Laing, Dennis Lensveld, Pete McTighe, Steve Manfred, Linda Ming, Richard Molesworth, Jon Preddle, Steve Roberts, Gavin Rymill, Paul Scoones, Paul Shields, Stephen James Walker and Martin Wiggins.

CLASSIC DOCTOR WHO TV STORIES

● Yes ◐ Some episodes ○ No ● Animated

Story No.	Season No.		On DVD	SE
1963				
		FIRST DOCTOR: William Hartnell		
1	1:1	An Unearthly Child	●	
2	1:2	The Daleks	●	
1964				
3	1:3	The Edge of Destruction	●	
4	1:4	Marco Polo	○	
5	1:5	The Keys of Marinus	●	
6	1:6	The Aztecs	●	*
7	1:7	The Sensorites	●	
8	1:8	The Reign of Terror	◐ (animated)	
9	2:1	Planet of Giants	●	
10	2:2	The Dalek Invasion of Earth	●	
1965				
11	2:3	The Rescue	●	
12	2:4	The Romans	●	
13	2:5	The Web Planet	●	
14	2:6	The Crusade	◐	
15	2:7	The Space Museum	●	
16	2:8	The Chase	●	
17	2:9	The Time Meddler	●	
18	3:1	Galaxy 4	◐	
19	3:2	Mission to the Unknown	○	
20	3:3	The Myth Makers	○	
21	3:4	The Daleks' Master Plan	◐	
1966				
22	3:5	The Massacre	○	
23	3:6	The Ark	●	
24	3:7	The Celestial Toymaker	◐	
25	3:8	The Gunfighters	●	
26	3:9	The Savages	○	
27	3:10	The War Machines	●	
28	4:1	The Smugglers	○	
29	4:2	The Tenth Planet	● (animated)	
		SECOND DOCTOR: Patrick Troughton		
30	4:3	The Power of the Daleks	○	
31	4:4	The Highlanders	○	
1967				
32	4:5	The Underwater Menace	◐	
33	4:6	The Moonbase	◐	
34	4:7	The Macra Terror	○	
35	4:8	The Faceless Ones	◐	
36	4:9	The Evil of the Daleks	◐	
37	5:1	The Tomb of the Cybermen	●	*
38	5:2	The Abominable Snowmen	◐	
39	5:3	The Ice Warriors	◐ (animated)	
40	5:4	The Enemy of the World	●	
1968				
41	5:5	The Web of Fear	●	
42	5:6	Fury from the Deep	○	
43	5:7	The Wheel in Space	◐	
44	6:1	The Dominators	●	
45	6:2	The Mind Robber	●	
46	6:3	The Invasion	● (animated)	
47	6:4	The Krotons	●	
1969				
48	6:5	The Seeds of Death	●	*
49	6:6	The Space Pirates	◐	
50	6:7	The War Games	●	
1970				
		THIRD DOCTOR: Jon Pertwee		
51	7:1	Spearhead from Space	●	*
52	7:2	Doctor Who and the Silurians	●	
53	7:3	The Ambassadors of Death	●	
54	7:4	Inferno	●	*
1971				
55	8:1	Terror of the Autons	●	
56	8:2	The Mind of Evil	●	
57	8:3	The Claws of Axos	●	*
58	8:4	Colony in Space	●	
59	8:5	The Dæmons	●	
1972				
60	9:1	Day of the Daleks	●	
61	9:2	The Curse of Peladon	●	
62	9:3	The Sea Devils	●	
63	9:4	The Mutants	●	
64	9:5	The Time Monster	●	
65	10:1	The Three Doctors	●	*
1973				
66	10:2	Carnival of Monsters	●	*
67	10:3	Frontier in Space	●	
68	10:4	Planet of the Daleks	●	
69	10:5	The Green Death	●	*
70	11:1	The Time Warrior	●	
1974				
71	11:2	Invasion of the Dinosaurs	●	
72	11:3	Death to the Daleks	●	
73	11:4	The Monster of Peladon	●	
74	11:5	Planet of the Spiders	●	
		FOURTH DOCTOR: Tom Baker		
75	12:1	Robot	●	
1975				
76	12:2	The Ark in Space	●	*
77	12:3	The Sontaran Experiment	●	

Story No.	Season No.		ON DVD	SE
78	12:4	Genesis of the Daleks	●	
79	12:5	Revenge of the Cybermen	●	
80	13:1	Terror of the Zygons	●	
81	13:2	Planet of Evil	●	
82	13:3	Pyramids of Mars	●	
83	13:4	The Android Invasion	●	
1976				
84	13:5	The Brain of Morbius	●	
85	13:6	The Seeds of Doom	●	
86	14:1	The Masque of Mandragora	●	
87	14:2	The Hand of Fear	●	
88	14:3	The Deadly Assassin	●	
1977				
89	14:4	The Face of Evil	●	
90	14:5	The Robots of Death	●	*
91	14:6	The Talons of Weng-Chiang	●	*
92	15:1	Horror of Fang Rock	●	
93	15:2	The Invisible Enemy	●	
94	15:3	Image of the Fendahl	●	
95	15:4	The Sun Makers	●	
1978				
96	15:5	Underworld	●	
97	15:6	The Invasion of Time	●	
98	16:1	The Ribos Operation	●	
99	16:2	The Pirate Planet	●	
100	16:3	The Stones of Blood	●	
101	16:4	The Androids of Tara	●	
102	16:5	The Power of Kroll	●	
1979				
103	16:6	The Armageddon Factor	●	
104	17:1	Destiny of the Daleks	●	
105	17:2	City of Death	●	
106	17:3	The Creature from the Pit	●	
107	17:4	Nightmare of Eden	●	
108	17:5	The Horns of Nimon	●	
1980				
109	18:1	The Leisure Hive	●	
110	18:2	Meglos	●	
111	18:3	Full Circle	●	
112	18:4	State of Decay	●	
1981				
113	18:5	Warriors' Gate	●	
114	18:6	The Keeper of Traken	●	
115	18:7	Logopolis	●	
FIFTH DOCTOR: Peter Davison				
1982				
116	19:1	Castrovalva	●	
117	19:2	Four to Doomsday	●	
118	19:3	Kinda	●	

Story No.	Season No.		ON DVD	SE
119	19:4	The Visitation	●	
120	19:5	Black Orchid	●	*
121	19:6	Earthshock	●	
122	19:7	Time-Flight	●	
1983				
123	20:1	Arc of Infinity	●	
124	20:2	Snakedance	●	
125	20:3	Mawdryn Undead	●	
126	20:4	Terminus	●	
127	20:5	Enlightenment	●	
128	20:6	The King's Demons	●	
129		The Five Doctors	●	*
1984				
130	21:1	Warriors of the Deep	●	
131	21:2	The Awakening	●	
132	21:3	Frontios	●	
133	21:4	Resurrection of the Daleks	●	*
134	21:5	Planet of Fire	●	
135	21:6	The Caves of Androzani	●	*
SIXTH DOCTOR: Colin Baker				
136	21:7	The Twin Dilemma	●	
1985				
137	22:1	Attack of the Cybermen	●	
138	22:2	Vengeance on Varos	●	*
139	22:3	The Mark of the Rani	●	
140	22:4	The Two Doctors	●	
141	22:5	Timelash	●	
142	22:6	Revelation of the Daleks	●	
1986				
143	23:1	The Trial of a Time Lord	●	
1987				
SEVENTH DOCTOR: Sylvester McCoy				
144	24:1	Time and the Rani	●	
145	24:2	Paradise Towers	●	
146	24:3	Delta and the Bannermen	●	
147	24:4	Dragonfire	●	
1988				
148	25:1	Remembrance of the Daleks	●	*
149	25:2	The Happiness Patrol	●	
150	25:3	Silver Nemesis	●	
151	25:4	The Greatest Show in the Galaxy	●	
1989				
152	26:1	Battlefield	●	
153	26:2	Ghost Light	●	
154	26:3	The Curse of Fenric	●	
155	26:4	Survival	●	
1996				
EIGHTH DOCTOR: Paul McGann				
156		The Movie	●	*

THE **ABOMINABLE SNOWMEN**
STORY No.38 SEASON No.5:2

One surviving episode (part 2 of 6) released in the **LOST IN TIME** *set*

TARDIS TEAM Second Doctor, Jamie, Victoria
TIME AND PLACE Himalayan Buddhist monastery, 1930s
ADVERSARIES Great Intelligence and its Yeti robots (1st appearance)
FIRST ON TV 7 October 1967
DVD RELEASE BBCDVD1353, 1 November 2004, PG

● *See* Lost in Time *for full details*

RELATED EXTRAS
Original trailer — The Tomb of the Cybermen (and Special Edition)
Sylvia James - In Conversation — The War Games

ACE ADVENTURES
Boxset of **DRAGONFIRE** and **THE HAPPINESS PATROL**

DVD RELEASE BBCDVD3387, 7 May 2012, PG
SLIPCASE Photo illustration by Clayton Hickman, silvered logo and titles, blue background
ORIGINAL RRP £30.63

WHAT'S IN THE BOX
Two stories featuring popular late-80s companion Ace — the street-wise teenager who likes to mix up her own explosives, played by Sophie Aldred — alongside the Seventh Doctor. *Dragonfire* (1987) sees the introduction of Ace as the Doctor and Mel arrive on Iceworld only to find their old acquaintance the dodgy dealer Glitz in trouble with the authorities there. To help extricate him, the Doctor joins him on a hunt for some very special treasure. *The Happiness Patrol* (1988) features a pastiche of Thatcherite Britain as colony world Terra Alpha is ruled with an iron first and a smile by Helen A and her executioner the Kandyman. Can the Doctor and Ace bring down their corrupt government in just one night?

● *See individual stories for full contents*

THE **AMBASSADORS OF DEATH**
STORY No.53 SEASON No.7:3

Two discs with seven episodes (172 mins) and 46 minutes of extras, plus commentary track, production subtitles and PDF items
Audio navigation of each disc's contents available by pressing Enter after the BBC ident

TARDIS TEAM Third Doctor, Liz, Brigadier and UNIT
TIME AND PLACE Contemporary England
ADVERSARIES Radioactive astronauts and their human kidnappers
FIRST ON TV 21 March–2 May 1970
DVD RELEASE BBCDVD3484, 1 October 2012, PG (episodes and extras bar DVD trailer U)
COVER Photo illustration by Lee Binding, light orange strip; version with older BBC logo on reverse
ORIGINAL RRP £20.42

STORY TEASER
Contact has been lost with the astronauts on Britain's first manned mission to Mars and, when a rescue rocket is sent to investigate, it stops responding too. The recovery pod returns to Earth but its three occupants are kidnapped by mercenaries and, being highly radioactive, are used to steal and kill. While UNIT tracks down who is controlling the astronauts, the Doctor takes a rocket into space to learn what they are and where they're really from.

CONNECTIONS

Although the Doctor doesn't land on Mars in this story, he does make it there in *Pyramids of Mars* (1975) and *The Waters of Mars* (2009). Dangerous characters in helmeted spacesuits feature in *Silence in the Library/Forest of the Dead* (2008) and in *The Impossible Astronaut* (2011), while the technician androids in *The Android Invasion* (1975) have a similar look. UNIT has further trouble liaising with the regular army in *The Claws of Axos* (1971) and *Invasion of the Dinosaurs* (1974). This is the last story credited to David Whitaker, who was the first story editor on *Doctor Who*, although the bulk of it was written by Malcolm Hulke, who had just finished the preceding story *Doctor Who and the Silurians* and wrote for each of the four subsequent seasons. Michael Ferguson previously directed *The War Machines* (1966) and *The Seeds of Death* (1969), and later *The Claws of Axos*. Ronald Allen, playing Professor Cornish, is Rago in *The Dominators* (1968), while John Abineri appears as Van Lutyens in *Fury from the Deep* (1968), Railton in *Death to the Daleks* (1974) and Ranquin in *The Power of Kroll* (1978/79). *The Ambassadors of Death* sees the first appearance in *Doctor Who* of Michael Wisher, who returns the next year as Rex Farrel in *Terror of the Autons* (1971) and, most significantly, was the first actor to play Davros, in *Genesis of the Daleks* (1975). Cyril Shaps is another familiar face, playing John Viner in *The Tomb of the Cybermen* (1967), Professor Clegg in *Planet of the Spiders* (1974) and the Archimandrite in *The Androids of Tara* (1978).

WORTH WATCHING

Made just six months after the first manned Moon landing, this story ties into the optimism and excitement around space travel that existed at the time, with its suggestion that Britain has sent a manned mission to Mars, and model shots of space capsules docking reminiscent of those in *2001: A Space Odyssey*. It doesn't skimp on action, either, with impressive stunt and fight sequences by the HAVOC team who appeared often in *Doctor Who* over the next few years.

DISC ONE

THE EPISODES

This is the first release of the serial in complete colour since its original broadcast. Episode one is restored from a digital duplicate of the original two-inch colour videotape recording used for broadcast (the series' earliest surviving video recording) and its mono soundtrack remastered. The other six episodes are restored from 16mm black-and-white film copies of the original colour videotape recordings. Episodes five and six have been recoloured using copies of lower-resolution home-video recordings made when the serial was broadcast in America in 1977. For episodes two, three, four and seven, the quality of these colour copies is inconsistent owing to interference in the transmission being recorded, so they could only be used to recolour parts of these episodes; colour for the remaining sections has been restored from information in the mono images on the film that relates to the original colour of the video picture being filmed, using the Colour Recovery process. Episodes two to seven have the VidFIRE process applied to studio-recorded shots to recapture the smoother motion of video, and their mono soundtracks are remastered. The title sequences on all seven episodes are replaced by a modern transfer of the original 35mm film with credits remade to match the originals.

SPECIAL FEATURES

AUDIO OPTIONS Select **Commentary** to play the audio commentary in place of the main sound-track when watching the episodes. This is moderated by actor and comedian Toby Hadoke, talking with stuntman Derek Ware [eps 1,2,3,5], script editor Terrance Dicks [1,4,5], director Michael Ferguson [1,4,5,6,7], Nicholas Courtney (the Brigadier) [1,4,6,7], stuntmen Roy Scammell and Derek Martin [2,3], Caroline John (Liz Shaw) [3,5,7], Peter Halliday (alien voices) [6] and Geoffrey Beevers (Private Johnson) [7].

— Select **Feature Audio** to reinstate the main soundtrack when watching the episodes.

INFO TEXT Select **On** to view subtitles when watching the episodes that provide information and anecdotes about the development, production, broadcast and history of *The Ambassadors of Death*. Written by Martin Wiggins.

SUBTITLES

Select **On** to view subtitles for all episodes (none for commentary).

SPECIAL FEATURES

MARS PROBE 7: MAKING THE AMBASSADORS OF DEATH (25m51s) A look at the production of the serial, covering the problems with getting the script into shape; the formation of *Doctor Who*'s regular stunt team HAVOC and the action sequences they arranged for this story; and creating the sense of space travel in the studio. With contributions from script editor Terrance Dicks, director Michael Ferguson, assistant floor manager Margot Hayhoe, and stunt performers Roy Scammell and Derek Ware. Produced by Chris Chapman.

TRAILER (1m28s) Preview shown after the previous story, *Doctor Who and the Silurians*, combining clips with specially shot footage of Jon Pertwee as the Doctor. Reconstructed by matching an audio recording made at the time of broadcast to the restored footage from the episodes and a manually recoloured black-and-white film copy of the Doctor sections. *Also on* Doctor Who and the Silurians

TOMORROW'S TIMES – THE THIRD DOCTOR (13m7s) Coverage of *Doctor Who* in the national newspapers during the Third Doctor's era from 1970 to 1974. Presented by Peter Purves, written and directed by Marcus Hearn. *See Index iii for further editions*

PHOTO GALLERY (4m26s) Slideshow of colour and black-and-white photos taken during production of *The Ambassadors of Death*, including design department photos of the sets, behind-the-scenes shots and photos taken by *Radio Times*. Set to sound effects and music from the story. Compiled by Paul Shields.

PDF MATERIALS Accessible via a computer are the seven episode listings from *Radio Times* for the original BBC1 broadcast of *The Ambassadors of Death*.

SUBTITLES Select **On** to view subtitles for all Special Features on disc two.

COMING SOON (1m4s) Trailer for the Special Edition DVD release of *The Claws of Axos*.

RELATED EXTRAS

Coming Soon trailer — Vengeance on Varos Special Edition

AN UNEARTHLY CHILD

STORY No.1   SEASON No.1:1

Released with **THE DALEKS** and **THE EDGE OF DESTRUCTION** in **THE BEGINNING** boxset
One disc with four broadcast episodes (96 mins), the unbroadcast recording of the first episode (25 mins) and 65 minutes of extras, plus commentary track for two episodes and production subtitles

TARDIS TEAM First Doctor, Susan, and introducing Barbara Wright and Ian Chesterton
TIME AND PLACE The Stone Age
ADVERSARIES Cavemen
FIRST ON TV 23 November–14 December 1963
DVD RELEASE BBCDVD1882(A), 30 January 2006, U (boxset 12)
COVER Photo illustration by Clayton Hickman, dark pink strip
ORIGINAL RRP £29.99 (boxset)

STORY TEASER

Teachers Barbara Wright and Ian Chesterton are puzzled by the erratic knowledge of their pupil Susan Foreman so they decide to visit her home to talk to her grandfather. But what they discover is something they could never have imagined. Against their will, they are transported back in time to the Stone Age, where all four must work together to avoid being sacrificed by a tribe of cavemen.

CONNECTIONS

Being the wellspring of the subsequent fifty years (and counting) of adventures, referencing the first episode of *Doctor Who* is used in later stories to add significance. When the Doctor tries to repair the TARDIS's chameleon circuit in *Attack of the Cybermen* (1985) (and publicity at the time suggested the show might indeed replace the police box) the ship returns to the junkyard in Totter's Lane. To mark the show's twenty-fifth year, *Remembrance of the Daleks* (1988) sees the Doctor revisit both the yard and Coal Hill School, this time with added Daleks. And by the time of the fiftieth anniversary, companion Clara is teaching at the school in *The Day of the Doctor* (2013). In *City of Death* (1979) Scaroth claims to have taught Man how to make fire, so presumably this tribe was away that day. Waris Hussein directed only this and *Marco Polo* a couple of months later but went on to a successful career in television and films. Derek Newark (Za) plays drilling engineer Greg Sutton in *Inferno* (1970), while Alethea Charlton (Hur) moves forward to Saxon times in *The Time Meddler* (1965). Jeremy Young (Kal) is in *Mission to the Unknown* (1965), and Eileen Way (Old Mother) seems little older when she returns to play Karela in 1979's *The Creature from the Pit*.

WORTH WATCHING

This is where it all started and, despite the creakiness of its production by today's standard, it still stands out as something unique. Now everyone knows about the TARDIS being bigger on the inside, but watching this you can still sense the astonishment the original audience must have felt when the secret of the police box is revealed. While the adventure in the Stone Age is often dismissed, it subtly relates the Doctor's treatment of the teachers to their attitude towards the cavemen, and gives a solid introduction to the four main characters.

THE EPISODES

All four episodes and the pilot are restored from 16mm film copies of the original black-and-white video recordings that survived in the archives. Their mono soundtracks are remastered and the VidFIRE process is applied to studio-recorded shots to recapture the smoother motion of video. The title sequences are replaced by a modern transfer of the best surviving copy of the original 35mm film with end credits remade to match the originals.

● Selecting **Play All** *plays the pilot followed by the four broadcast episodes (therefore playing both versions of episode one).*

SPECIAL FEATURES

PILOT EPISODE STUDIO RECORDING (35m38s) The full studio recording made on Friday 27 September 1963 of the initial attempt at episode one, including mistakes and retakes, restored from a 16mm film copy of the original black-and-white video recording. The production was deemed unsuitable for broadcast and restaged a few weeks later. The version played under **Episode Selection** is a new edit from this material of how the episode might have been presented had it been shown. When the audio commentary for the episodes is selected, producer Verity Lambert and director Waris Hussein can be heard talking about this footage also.

THEME MUSIC VIDEO (2m37s) The full-length version of the original *Doctor Who* theme music, composed by Ron Grainer and produced by Delia Derbyshire and Dicks Mills of the BBC Radiophonic Workshop in 1963. Set to graphics footage shot for the first title sequence created by Bernard Lodge, including elements not used in the final titles. Select to listen in original mono, or new Dolby Digital stereo or Dolby Digital 5.1 Surround mixes created for this release from the original tape recordings.

COMEDY SKETCHES (17m6s) Four short comedy sketches. 'The Pitch of Fear' (3m44s), 'The Web of Caves' (3m51s) and 'The Kidnappers' (3m38s) were written by and star David Walliams and Mark Gatiss (with a cameo in the last by Peter Davison) for *Doctor Who Night* on BBC2 on Saturday 13 November 1999. 'The Corridor Sketch' (5m53s), featuring Nicholas Briggs and a cameo by Nicholas Courtney, was made by fans in 1991.

GALLERY (6m3s) Slideshow of black-and-white photos taken during production of *An Unearthly Child*, plus contemporary photos of the cast and shots of the commentary participants. Set to sound effects from the story. Compiled by Ralph Montagu.

AUDIO OPTIONS Select **Commentary On** to play audio commentaries in place of the main sound-track when watching episodes one and four, and the pilot episode studio recording. These are moderated by author and journalist Gary Russell, talking with producer Verity Lambert [ep 1], William Russell (Ian) [1,4], Carole Ann Ford (Susan) [1,4] and director Waris Hussein [4].

INFORMATION TEXT Select **On** to view subtitles when watching the episodes that provide information and anecdotes about the development, production, broadcast and history of *An Unearthly Child*. Written by Martin Wiggins.

SUBTITLES
Select **On** to view subtitles for all episodes and Special Features (except commentaries).
RELATED EXTRAS
Five Faces of Doctor Who trailer — Carnival of Monsters (and Special Edition),
The Three Doctors (and Special Edition)
PDF Documents — The Edge of Destruction

THE **ANDROID INVASION**

STORY No.83   SEASON No.13:4

Released with **INVASION OF THE DINOSAURS** in the **U.N.I.T FILES** boxset
One disc with four episodes (97 mins) and 75 minutes of extras, plus commentary track,
production subtitles and PDF items
Audio navigation of disc contents available by pressing Enter after the BBC ident

TARDIS TEAM Fourth Doctor, Sarah Jane
TIME AND PLACE English village of Devesham, planet Oseidon
ADVERSARIES Rhino-like Kraals; human-duplicate androids; astronaut Guy Crayford
FIRST ON TV 22 November–13 December 1975
DVD RELEASE BBCDVD3376B, 9 January 2012, PG
COVER Photo illustration by Clayton Hickman, light orange strip;
version with older BBC logo on reverse
ORIGINAL RRP £30.63 (boxset)

STORY TEASER
The Doctor tries to get Sarah back home but the village they arrive in is familiar yet strange. Sarah realises she has visited before when she reported on the launch of a rocket from the nearby Space Research Station, but the villagers behave as if hypnotised, a dead man comes back to life, and faceless androids patrol the streets. Even at the research base their UNIT friends are unwelcoming and the Doctor realises no one is really who they seem, not even Sarah.

CONNECTIONS
This is a rare instance of the TARDIS arriving somewhere that isn't where it appears to be, as only otherwise happens in *Carnival of Monsters* (1973), *Enlightenment* (1983) and *The God Complex* (2011). An android doppelgänger first appears in *The Chase* (1965) when the Daleks duplicate the Doctor in order to infiltrate and kill the TARDIS crew, and further robot replicas of the Doctor's companions appear in *The Androids of Tara* (1978) and *The Caves of Androzani* (1984). The Sontarans prefer cloning techniques to create a double of Martha in *The Sontaran Stratagem/The Poison Sky* (2007), Harry is doubled by a Zygon in *Terror of the Zygons* (1975), Amy is swapped for a Flesh avatar during Series Six, while both Mickey and Rory are replicated by Autons in *Rose* (2005) and *The Pandorica Opens/The Big Bang* (2010) respectively. The Urbankans in *Four to Doomsday* (1982) can build androids that look like real people (with similarly detachable faces), and the Daleks have improved their skills by the time of *Victory of the Daleks* (2010). Irradiated planets the Doctor stumbles upon include Skaro in *The Daleks* (1963) and *Destiny of the Daleks* (1979), Uxaerius in *Colony in Space* (1971) and Argolis in *The Leisure Hive* (1980). The Kraals have a nose like a rhino horn, which a rhino-headed Judoon would probably snort at. This is one of only two Terry Nation scripts that don't feature the Daleks, the other being 1964's *The Keys of Marinus*, and is the last serial directed by Barry Letts, producer of the Third Doctor era (*see Index v*). John Levene and Ian Marter — Sergeant Major Benton and Lieutenant Harry Sullivan — are the only two returning UNIT characters, previously seen in *Terror of the Zygons* at the start of this season and here making their final appearances in the show. Milton Johns, playing Guy Crayford, is also Benik in *The Enemy of the World* (1967/68) and Castellan Kelner in *The Invasion of Time* (1978), in the latter of which Max Faulkner (Corporal Adams) plays Nesbin. Peter Welch (pub landlord Morgan) is redcoat sergeant Klegg in *The Highlanders* (1966/67), while Roy Skelton (Chedaki) is best known for providing Dalek

voices but also plays Norton in *Colony in Space*, Wester in *Planet of the Daleks* (1973), Mr James in *The Green Death* (1973) and King Rokon in *The Hand of Fear* (1976).

WORTH WATCHING

There may not be Daleks, but plenty of other Terry Nation ideas are stirred into the mix, although as often they combine in new ways. It's unfortunate that *Terror of the Zygons* was held back to kick off the 1975/76 season and so aired just two months before this, as it too features doubles, including one of a companion. But watched on its own now, *The Android Invasion* has a good sense of strangeness in its early episodes and a memorably realised monster in the Kraals.

THE EPISODES

All four episodes are restored from digital duplicates of the original two-inch colour videotape recordings used for broadcast and their mono soundtracks remastered. The title sequences are replaced by a modern transfer of the original 35mm film with credits remade to match the originals.

SPECIAL FEATURES

THE VILLAGE THAT CAME TO LIFE (30m57s) Actor and writer Nicholas Briggs visits East Hagbourne in Oxfordshire, where much of *The Android Invasion* was filmed, to present a look at the making of the serial. He discusses how Terry Nation came to write the story; the last appearances of Harry Sullivan and Benton; the role of the director; how Tom Baker was mobbed on location by local children; rehearsals and studio recording; creating the Kraals; and the successful partnership of Baker's Doctor and Elisabeth Sladen's Sarah Jane Smith. With contributions from producer Philip Hinchcliffe, director Barry Letts (interviewed in 2008), and actors Martin Friend and Milton Johns, plus memories from villagers who watched the location filming. Produced by Ed Stradling.

LIFE AFTER WHO PHILIP HINCHCLIFFE (29m37s) The producer of Tom Baker's first three years as the Doctor looks back at his long television career after *Doctor Who*, in discussion with his daughter, television sports presenter Celina Hinchcliffe.

PHOTO GALLERY (4m52s) Slideshow of colour and black-and-white photos taken during production of *The Android Invasion*, including design department photos of the sets and behind the scenes at the location filming. Set to sound effects and music from the story. Compiled by Paul Shields.

WEETABIX ADVERT (33s) Television commercial from 1977 in which a Dalek promotes the breakfast cereal's *Doctor Who* promotion.

NEXT

AUDIO OPTIONS Select **Commentary** to play the audio commentary in place of the main soundtrack when watching the episodes. This is moderated by actor and comedian Toby Hadoke, talking with producer Philip Hinchcliffe [eps 1,2,3,4], Milton Johns (Guy Crayford) [1,2,3,4], production assistant Marion McDougall [1,3,4] and Martin Friend (Styggron) [2,3,4].
— Select **Feature Audio** to reinstate the main soundtrack when watching the episodes.

INFO TEXT Select **On** to view subtitles when watching the episodes that provide information and anecdotes about the development, production, broadcast and history of *The Android Invasion*. Written by Nicholas Pegg.

PDF MATERIALS Accessible via a computer are the four episode listings from *Radio Times* for the original BBC1 broadcast of *The Android Invasion*.
— Packaging with six cut-out background scenes and TARDIS model, twenty-four character cards and promotional materials from the 1975 *Doctor Who* promotion by Weetabix breakfast cereal.
— Packaging with four game boards and rules, eighteen character cards and promotional materials from the 1977 *Doctor Who* promotion by Weetabix breakfast cereal.

COMING SOON (59S) Trailer for the DVD release of *The Sensorites*.

SUBTITLES

Select **On** to view subtitles for all episodes and Special Features (except commentary).

EASTER EGG

There is one hidden feature on this disc to find. *See Appendix 2 for details*

RELATED EXTRAS

Coming Soon trailer — Colony in Space

The UNIT Family — Terror of the Zygons

THE **ANDROIDS OF TARA**

Released with **THE ARMAGEDDON FACTOR, THE PIRATE PLANET, THE POWER OF KROLL, THE RIBOS OPERATION** and **THE STONES OF BLOOD** in **THE KEY TO TIME** boxset

One disc with four episodes (98 mins) and 51½ minutes of extras, plus commentary track, production subtitles and PDF items

TARDIS TEAM Fourth Doctor, First Romana, K9
TIME AND PLACE Planet Tara
ADVERSARIES Count Grendel of Gracht
FIRST ON TV 25 November–16 December 1978
DVD RELEASE BBCDVD2335(D), 24 September 2007, PG
COVER Photo illustration by Clayton Hickman, red strip
ORIGINAL RRP £69.99 (boxset)

STORY TEASER

Romana takes charge of finding the fourth segment of the Key to Time while the Doctor goes fishing, but both soon find themselves caught up in political rivalry over the succession to the throne of Tara. Count Grendel of Gracht is seeking to depose the rightful ruler, Prince Reynart, and when he discovers Romana is the spitting image of the prince's bride-to-be, she become very important to his plans. The matter is confused by the Tarans' expertise in making realistic androids, meaning no one can ever be sure who is really who.

CONNECTIONS

The Tarans' skill at building androids that are indistinguishable from real people rivals that of the Kraals (*The Android Invasion*, 1975) and the Urbankans (*Four to Doomsday*, 1982), and surpasses that of the Daleks based on the evidence of their duplicate of the Doctor in *The Chase* (1965) — although their techniques have improved by the time of *Victory of the Daleks* (2010) as Bracewell doesn't even realise he is an android. Whoever originally constructed the Movellans (*Destiny of the Daleks*, 1979) only made the mistake of placing their power supplies on the outside (and giving them easily detachable arms), while the Karfelons for some reason gave their otherwise convincing androids blue faces (*Timelash*, 1985). The Fourth Doctor had already demonstrated his sword-fighting skill in *The Masque of Mandragora* (1976), inherited perhaps from the Third Doctor who duelled the Master in *The Sea Devils* (1972) and Irongron in *The Time Warrior* (1973/74). It was a talent he retained, his fifth incarnation battling the Master in *The King's Demons* (1983) and his tenth fighting the Sycorax leader in *The Christmas Invasion* (2005), even though he temporarily lost a hand. David Fisher also wrote the preceding story, *The Stones of Blood*, as well as *The Creature from the Pit* (1979) and *The Leisure Hive* (1980), while director Michael Hayes returned for this season's finale, *The Armageddon Factor*, and 1979's *City of Death*. Peter Jeffrey (Count Grendel) also plays the Pilot in *The Macra Terror* (1967), Simon Lack (Zadek) is Professor Kettering in *The Mind of Evil* (1971), while Cyril Shaps takes his last role in the series, having been John Viner in *The Tomb of the Cybermen* (1967), Dr Lennox in *The Ambassadors of Death* (1970) and Professor Clegg in *Planet of the Spiders* (1974). Mary Tamm actually plays four parts here: Romana and Princess Strella, and android doubles of them both.

WORTH WATCHING

This continues the Doctor's quest for the Key to Time, which formed the whole of the 1978/79 season. The story is based broadly on Anthony Hope's novel *The Prisoner of Zenda* — although with lots more doppelgängers than the book's single pairing — and provides a splendid villain in Peter Jeffrey's Count Grendel. It also gives Mary Tamm's Romana a more central role and shows how much she has already learned since joining the Doctor.

THE EPISODES

All four episodes are restored from digital duplicates of the original two-inch colour videotape recordings used for broadcast and their mono soundtracks remastered. The title sequences are replaced by a modern transfer of the original 35mm film with credits remade to match the originals.

SPECIAL FEATURES

THE HUMANS OF TARA (21m12s) The making of *The Androids of Tara*, including the writing of the story as an homage to *The Prisoner of Zenda*; working with the director; location filming at Leeds Castle; the cast and getting to play two versions of their characters; and shooting the climactic sword fight. With contributions from script editor Anthony Read, writer David Fisher, director Michael Hayes, and actors Neville Jason, Paul Lavers and Mary Tamm. Produced by Steve Broster and Ed Stradling.

NOW & THEN – THE ANDROIDS OF TARA (10m19s) Comparing the filming locations in and around Leeds Castle in Kent as they look today with how they appeared in late-July 1978 when used for *The Androids of Tara*. Narrated by Paul Lavers, produced by Richard Bignell. *See Index iii for further editions*

DOUBLE TROUBLE (11m4s) The use of doubles and doppelgängers throughout the history of Classic *Doctor Who*, discussed by fan journalists Moray Laing, Paul Lang and Tom Spilsbury. Directed by Marcus Hearn.

PHOTO GALLERY (7m46s) Slideshow of colour and black-and-white photos taken during production of *The Androids of Tara*, including design department photos of the dungeon sets. Set to sound effects from the story. Compiled by Derek Handley.

NEXT

AUDIO OPTIONS Select **Commentary** to play the audio commentary, recorded for an earlier US-only release, in place of the main soundtrack when watching the episodes. With Tom Baker, Mary Tamm (Romana) and director Michael Hayes on all four episodes.
— Select **Feature Audio** to reinstate the main soundtrack when watching the episodes.

INFO TEXT Select **On** to view subtitles when watching the episodes that provide information and anecdotes about the development, production, broadcast and history of *The Androids of Tara*. Written by Richard Molesworth.

COMING SOON (1m) Trailer for the DVD release of *Planet of Evil*.

RADIO TIMES LISTINGS Accessible via a computer is a PDF file of the four episode listings for the original BBC1 broadcast of *The Androids of Tara*, and a cartoon by Marc Boxer of the Doctor and K9 published the week of episode one.

SUBTITLES

Select **On** to view subtitles for all episodes and Special Features (except commentary).

RELATED EXTRAS

Directing Who — The Armageddon Factor
Coming Soon trailer — The Time Warrior

ARC OF INFINITY

STORY No.123   SEASON No.20:1

Released in a boxset with **TIME-FLIGHT**
One disc with four episodes (98½ mins) and 76½ minutes of extras, plus optional CGI effects, commentary and music-only tracks, production subtitles and PDF items

TARDIS TEAM Fifth Doctor, Nyssa, and re-meeting Tegan
TIME AND PLACE Contemporary Amsterdam and Time Lord homeworld Gallifrey
ADVERSARIES Omega (2nd appearance); renegade Time Lord
FIRST ON TV 3–12 January 1983
DVD RELEASE BBCDVD2327B, 6 August 2007, PG
COVER Photo illustration by Dan Budden, dark purple strip
ORIGINAL RRP £29.99 (boxset)

STORY TEASER

A creature composed of anti-matter, shielded by the properties of the Arc of Infinity, attacks the Doctor in the TARDIS in a bid to bond with him and become normal matter. Fearing another attempt and the universal obliteration it could cause, the Time Lords recall the Doctor to Gallifrey and sentence him to death. But the creature has help among the Time Lord High Council — as well as an unexpected hostage from Earth — and is determined to live again.

CONNECTIONS

The Doctor has been ordered back to Gallifrey several times during his travels, always in a different way. In *The War Games* (1969), when we first learn of and meet the Time Lords, they give him a chance to return voluntarily and only when he tries to hide do they take control of the TARDIS. In *The Deadly Assassin* (1976) the Doctor receives a psychic call about the resignation of the president that he feels compelled to attend. In *Meglos* (1980) the Doctor simply receives a message to return Romana home and seems happy to comply, prevented only by getting trapped in E-Space. In *Arc of Infinity* the console flashes to alert the Doctor that the TARDIS has again been forcibly returned to Gallifrey, while in *The Trial of a Time Lord* (1986) it's beamed out of time and space entirely. Omega was introduced in *The Three Doctors* (1972/73), the first story of the tenth season, so he was brought back for the first story of the twentieth, a sign of the growing influence fans had over the production of the series. However, that serial had been repeated on BBC2 just over a year earlier (seen by some 5m people, just 2m less than watched *Arc of Infinity*) so his return wasn't completely out of the blue, and his backstory is restated for new viewers anyway. President Borusa is on his third incarnation in as many stories, having been a cardinal in *The Deadly Assassin* and chancellor by the time of *The Invasion of Time* (1978), and has regenerated again by his next and final appearance in *The Five Doctors* (1983). This trip to Amsterdam is the first time the Doctor is seen on the streets of a city outside the UK since his holiday in Paris in *City of Death* (1979), followed shortly by a visit to Seville in *The Two Doctors* (1985) and then not again until he's in New York in *Daleks in Manhattan* (2007). Johnny Byrne also wrote *The Keeper of Traken* (1981), which introduced Nyssa, and *Warriors of the Deep* (1984), which brought back another old enemy. Ron Jones had started his directing career on *Doctor Who* the season before and would handle three more serials (*see Index v*). Michael Gough (Hedin) is remembered among *Doctor Who* fans for playing the Toymaker in *The Celestial Toymaker* (1966), and Ian Collier (Omega) is seen as Stuart Hyde in *The Time Monster* (1972). Paul Jerricho (Castellan) returns in the same role in *The Five Doctors*, while Colin Baker (Maxil) is the only Doctor to have been in the series previously, although several companion actors have been promoted from earlier roles, including Peter Purves (Steven), Ian Marter (Harry), Lalla Ward (Romana), Freema Agyeman (Martha) and Karen Gillan (Amy).

WORTH WATCHING

The return of Omega may have been inspired by fan feeling but, as mentioned above, it's not as if the general viewers were being expected to remember plot points from ten years earlier. Indeed, writer Johnny Byrne builds nicely on the Doctor's previously stated admiration for Omega and even makes him sympathetic by the end of the story. As with *City of Death*, it's nice to see the Doctor running around some different streets for a change, although they are just streets as the location is less well integrated into the plot than Paris had been. The return of Tegan was always planned but it's nice to see Nyssa getting more to do as sole companion, even if only briefly.

THE EPISODES

All four episodes are restored from digital duplicates of the original two-inch colour videotape recordings used for broadcast and their mono soundtracks remastered. The title sequences are replaced by a modern transfer of the original 35mm film with credits remade to match the originals.

SPECIAL FEATURES

ANTI-MATTER FROM AMSTERDAM (34m56s) Sophie Aldred is joined by writer Johnny Byrne in Amsterdam, where much of *Arc of Infinity* was filmed, to present a look at the making of the serial. She discusses the writing of the story; the logistics of filming on location outside the UK; reactions to the look of the Ergon and Ian Collier's problems with his costume; the characterisation of the Time Lords and the casting of Colin Baker (plus who Ermintrude the Chicken was); the bigger role for Nyssa in this story; and opinions of the finished serial. With contributions from script editor Eric Saward, and actors Colin Baker, Ian Collier, Alistair Cumming, Peter Davison, Paul Jerricho and Sarah Sutton. Produced by Keith Barnfather.

THE OMEGA FACTOR (14m56s) The people who wrote and portrayed renegade Time Lord Omega discuss his character and motivations. With contributions from writers Bob Baker, Johnny Byrne and Nev Fountain, and actors Ian Collier and Stephen Thorne. Narrated by Ian Collier, produced by Keith Barnfather.

DELETED SCENES (2m54s) A selection of scenes from episode four not used in the final programme, taken from a VHS copy of an earlier edit of the episode with on-screen time-code.

UNDER ARC LIGHTS (11m32s) Footage from the full studio recording sessions in early-June 1982 of scenes in Omega's TARDIS and on Gallifrey, including retakes and shots unused in the final programme, taken from a copy with on-screen time-code.

CGI EFFECTS Select **CGI Effects On** to view updated computer-generated effects in place of some of the original visual effects when watching the episodes.

CONTINUITIES (3m13s) Trailer for episode one and continuity announcements from the original BBC1 broadcasts of all four episodes of *Arc of Infinity*, with an announcement of the celebratory event held at Longleat in April 1983.

NEXT

AUDIO OPTIONS Select **Commentary** to play the audio commentary in place of the main soundtrack when watching the episodes. With Peter Davison, Sarah Sutton (Nyssa) and Colin Baker (Maxil) on all four episodes, joined from episode two by Janet Fielding (Tegan).
— Select **Isolated Music** to hear only Roger Limb's music when watching the episodes.
— Select **Feature Audio** to reinstate the main soundtrack when watching the episodes.

INFO TEXT Select **On** to view subtitles when watching the episodes that provide information and anecdotes about the development, production, broadcast and history of *Arc of Infinity*. Written by Richard Molesworth.

PHOTO GALLERY (7m47s) Slideshow of colour and black-and-white photos taken during production of *Arc of Infinity*, including design department photos of the sets. Set to music and sound effects from the story. Compiled by Ralph Montagu.

DOCTOR WHO ANNUAL Accessible via a computer is a PDF file of the 1983 *Doctor Who Annual*, published by World Distributors the autumn before *Arc of Infinity* was broadcast. With stories featuring the Doctor, Adric, Nyssa and Tegan, plus behind-the-scenes and science features.

RADIO TIMES LISTINGS Accessible via a computer is a PDF file of the four episode listings for the original BBC1 broadcast of *Arc of Infinity*.

COMING SOON TRAILER (1m) Trailer for the DVD release of *The Time Warrior*.

SUBTITLES
Select **On** to view subtitles for all episodes and Special Features (except commentary).

EASTER EGG
There is one hidden feature on this disc to find. *See Appendix 2 for details*

RELATED EXTRAS
The Rise and Fall of Gallifrey — The Invasion of Time
Coming Soon trailer — Timelash

THE **ARK**

STORY No.23   SEASON No.3:6

One disc with four episodes (98 mins) and 43 minutes of extras, plus commentary track, production subtitles and PDF items
Audio navigation of disc contents available by pressing Enter after the BBC ident

TARDIS TEAM First Doctor, Dodo, Steven
TIME AND PLACE Human colony spaceship and planet Refusis II, distant future
ADVERSARIES One-eyed Monoids
FIRST ON TV 5–26 March 1966
DVD RELEASE BBCDVD2957, 14 February 2011, PG (episodes U)

COVER Photo illustration by Lee Binding (Ark by Gavin Rymill), green strip; version with older BBC logo on reverse

ORIGINAL RRP £19.99

STORY TEASER

Far in the future, as the Earth faces destruction by the expanding Sun, the human race evacuates in a giant ark ship, taking with them all of the planet's forms of life, plus the subservient alien Monoids. But the arrival of the TARDIS threatens them with a long-forgotten danger. Dodo has a cold and the virus is deadly to these people, who have long since outgrown their immunity. The Doctor fights to save them, unaware that the disease will have an unexpected long-term effect that it will become his responsibility to put right sooner than he imagines.

CONNECTIONS

While here the suggestion is the Ark houses the entire human population escaping the doomed Earth, *Frontios* (1984) indicates there are other people who evacuated at the same time (and have better dress sense), while in *The End of the World* (2005) we learn Mankind long ago propagated among the stars, as well as seeing our world's demise close-up. Assuming *The Ark* is also set around the year five billion, it has probably long been forgotten that sometime around the 60th Century humans similarly miniaturised Earth's flora and fauna and loaded it and themselves aboard a space station to wait out the planet's desolation by solar flares (*The Ark in Space*, 1975). The Monoids are treated much as the Ood are in *The Impossible Planet/The Satan Pit* (2006) and are talked of as being willing servants in the same way. Other one-eyed species include the Daleks, in both machine and mutant forms, the latter at least post-Time War according to *Dalek* (2005) and most notably *The Evolution of the Daleks* (2007); the Alpha Centaurians (*The Curse of Peladon*, 1972);, the Jagaroth (*City of Death*, 1979); and seemingly the Eknodine (*Amy's Choice*, 2010). The Atraxi appear to be nothing but one giant eyeball (*The Eleventh Hour*, 2010). The ageing Doctor tells the children of Christmas town on Trenzalore of adventures with the Monoids (*The Time of the Doctor*, 2013), suggesting further encounters perhaps. Terence Bayler (Yendom) also plays Major Barrington in *The War Games* (1969); Roy Spencer (Manyak) is Frank Harris in *Fury from the Deep* (1968); Michael Sheard (Rhos) returns as Dr Summers in *The Mind of Evil* (1971), Laurence Scarman in *Pyramids of Mars* (1975), Lowe in *The Invisible Enemy* (1977), Mergrave in *Castrovalva* (1982) and the headmaster of Coal Hill School in *Remembrance of the Daleks* (1988); and Terence Woodfield is alien delegate Celation in *The Daleks' Master Plan* (1965/66). Richard Beale (Refusian voice) provides further voices in *The Macra Terror* (1967) and appears in person as Bat Masterson in *The Gunfighters* (1966) and the Ecology Minister in *The Green Death* (1973).

WORTH WATCHING

One of the few surviving stories from the largely missing 1965/66 season, this is a rare chance to see William Hartnell completely settled into the role of the Doctor, along with a pre-*Blue Peter* Peter Purves as Steven. It also plays with the format of the series at the time, when each episode had an individual title rather than an overall story title. As viewers wouldn't know when the serial was due to end, it uses the cliffhanger of episode two to unique effect, something that's partly lost now we label and watch the whole thing as a four-part serial.

THE EPISODES

All four episodes are restored from 16mm film copies of the original black-and-white video recordings, recovered from BBC Enterprises in 1978. Their mono soundtracks are remastered and the VidFIRE process is applied to studio-recorded shots to recapture the smoother motion of video. The title sequences are replaced by a modern transfer of the best surviving copy of the original 35mm film with end credits remade to match the originals.

SPECIAL FEATURES

ALL'S WELLS THAT ENDS WELLS (13m15s) The influence of the novels and ideas of HG Wells on *Doctor Who*, particularly in stories like *The Ark* and *Timelash* (1985). With contributions from academic Dr Tony Keen, novelist and critic Kim Newman, historian and writer Dominic Sandbrook, literary editor Graham Sleight, and writer and broadcaster Matthew Sweet. Produced by Thomas Guerrier.

A

ONE HIT WONDER (4m35s) Why the Monoids were relegated to the ranks of monsters that appeared in *Doctor Who* only once. With contributions from authors Kim Newman, Jacqueline Rayner, Dominic Sandbrook and Matthew Sweet. Produced by Thomas Guerrier.

RIVERSIDE STORY (20m19s) Matthew Sweet presents a tribute to the BBC's Riverside Studios, where many early *Doctor Who* episodes were recorded. He discusses how sets and camera movements were coordinated, and how serials like *The Ark* were rehearsed and recorded, with director Michael Imison and actor Peter Purves. Produced by Thomas Guerrier.

PHOTO GALLERY (3m30s) Slideshow of black-and-white photos taken during production of *The Ark*, including design department photos of the sets and publicity shots of Jackie Lane on Wimbledon Common. Set to music from the story (composed for *The Daleks*). Compiled by Paul Shields.

NEXT

AUDIO OPTIONS Select **Commentary** to play the audio commentary in place of the main soundtrack when watching the episodes. This is moderated by actor and comedian Toby Hadoke, talking with Peter Purves (Steven) and director Michael Imison on all four episodes.

— Select **Feature Audio** to reinstate the main soundtrack when watching the episodes.

INFO TEXT Select **On** to view subtitles when watching the episodes that provide information and anecdotes about the development, production, broadcast and history of *The Ark*. Written by Jim Smith.

PDF MATERIALS Accessible via a computer are the four episode listings from *Radio Times* for the original BBC1 broadcast of *The Ark* and a short article that introduced the story.

COMING SOON (1m14s) Trailer for the DVD releases of *Kinda* and *Snakedance* in the Mara Tales boxset.

SUBTITLES

Select **On** to view subtitles for all episodes and Special Features (except commentary).

RELATED EXTRAS

Coming Soon trailer — The Mutants

THE **ARK IN SPACE**

STORY No.76   SEASON No.12:2

One disc with four episodes (99 mins) and 30 minutes of extras, plus optional CGI effects, commentary track, production subtitles and image content

TARDIS TEAM Fourth Doctor, Harry, Sarah Jane

TIME AND PLACE Human space station Nerva in the far future

ADVERSARIES Wirrn, man-sized insects

FIRST ON TV 25 January–15 February 1975

DVD RELEASE BBCDVD1097, 8 April 2002, U

COVER Photo illustration by Clayton Hickman, green strip

ORIGINAL RRP £19.99

STORY TEASER

When Harry meddles with the controls, the TARDIS is thrown into the far future, landing on a space station where humans are in suspended animation, waiting for the Earth to recover from solar flare damage. But something else has broken in and delayed their awakening so it can use their sleeping bodies. The Doctor fights to resuscitate the station's crew, but some have already been infected.

CONNECTIONS

The idea of humans packing themselves along with examples of flora and fauna onto a space vessel to escape a dying Earth also forms the basis of 1966's *The Ark*. The following story, *The Sontaran Experiment*, indicates the Nerva ark disappeared and became a myth, which is odd given it's seen in orbit around the Earth. The Doctor returns to Nerva at an earlier point in its history in *Revenge of the Cybermen* later in this season when it comes under attack by, well, you can guess. The Cybermen also encounter the Doctor on a space station in *The Wheel in Space* (1968), while he again visits an orbiting platform at different times in its history in the New Series' *The Long Game* and *Bad Wolf/ The Parting of the Ways* (both 2005). Insects clearly make for creepy monsters, as seen in *The Web Planet* (1965) with its numerous species of insectoid life, *Frontios* (1984) with its woodlice-like Tractators, *The Unicorn and the Wasp* (2008) in which again a man turns into a giant wasp, and *Turn Left* (2008) when a Time Beetle hitches a lift on Donna's back. More grisly is the idea of people being mutated into monsters, never better presented than in *The Ark in Space*, but also the modus operandi of the Varga plants in *Mission to the Unknown* (1965), the Krynoids in *The Seeds of Doom* (1976), the Haemovores in *The Curse of Fenric* (1989) and the Flood in *The Waters of Mars* (2009). Robert Holmes had barely begun as script editor on the series before he had to write a replacement for a failed script by Louis Marks, but by now was an old hand at *Doctor Who* (*see Index v*), while director Rodney Bennett worked on this and *The Sontaran Experiment* together before returning to direct *The Masque of Mandragora* in 1976. Kenton Moore (Noah) briefly appears as a Roboman in the opening scene of *The Dalek Invasion of Earth* (1964), while Richardson Morgan (Rogin) lasts at least a few episodes as Corporal Blake in *The Web of Fear* (1968).

WORTH WATCHING

This is the second Fourth Doctor story to be broadcast, although third made, and yet already Tom Baker seems totally at home in the part and is making the character clearly different to Jon Pertwee's portrayal. It's also the first example of the kind of creepiness verging on horror that came to typify the next three years of the show under producer Philip Hinchcliffe and script editor Robert Holmes. The Wirrn are a memorable monster, and while the realisation of Noah's transformation is crude by today's standards it's still a disturbing idea made believable by the strength of the performance.

THE EPISODES

All four episodes are restored from digital duplicates of the original two-inch colour videotape recordings used for broadcast and their mono soundtracks remastered.

SPECIAL FEATURES *ALSO ON SPECIAL EDITION

*NEW CGI MODEL SEQUENCES (1m32s) Watch all the new computer-generated model shots in sequence, or select **CGI Effects On** to view them in place of the original model footage when watching the episodes.

*UNUSED TITLE SEQUENCE (42s) The initial version of Bernard Lodge's opening title sequence for the Fourth Doctor.

*ORIGINAL MODEL EFFECTS (7m10s) Silent 16mm colour film footage of the original model work, including used and unused shots of the Ark, its rocket and the Wirrn outside the space station. Set to sound effects from the story.

*TRAILER FOR EPISODE 1 (51s) Preview of the first episode shown on BBC1 the day before on Friday 24 January 1975.

TOM BAKER INTERVIEW (5m55s) Report from the Friday 22 November 1974 edition of BBC local news programme *Points West*, shot on location at Wookey Hole, Somerset the day before and broadcast a few weeks ahead of the showing of Tom Baker's first story. Includes the first television interview with Baker since becoming the Doctor and behind-the-scenes footage of the location filming for *Revenge of the Cybermen*. *Also on* **Revenge of the Cybermen**

PHOTO GALLERY Scroll through 31 colour and black-and-white photos taken during production of *The Ark in Space*. Compiled by Ralph Montagu.

▶

*SPACE STATION SCHEMATICS (1m9s) Technical schematic of the Ark and its rocket, created by the team that produced the CGI model effects.

INFORMATION TEXT Select **On** to view subtitles when watching the episodes that provide information and anecdotes about the development, production, broadcast and history of *The Ark in Space*. Written by Richard Molesworth.

*ROGER MURRAY-LEACH INTERVIEW (10m28s) The set designer of *The Ark in Space*, Roger Murray-Leach, talks about his work on this story and other *Doctor Who* serials he designed: *The Sontaran Experiment* (1975), *Planet of Evil* (1975), *The Deadly Assassin* (1976) and *The Talons of Weng-Chiang* (1977).

*AUDIO OPTIONS Select **Commentary On** to play the audio commentary in place of the main soundtrack when watching the episodes. With Tom Baker, Elisabeth Sladen (Sarah) and producer Philip Hinchcliffe on all four episodes.

*TARDIS–CAM (1m23s) A short scene featuring the TARDIS, originally made for the BBCi *Doctor Who* website in 2001. The TARDIS stands on a barren planet near a crashed Cybermen spaceship (model).

SUBTITLES
Select **On** to view subtitles for all episodes and Special Features, or for the commentary.

EASTER EGGS
There are three hidden features on this disc to find. *See Appendix 2 for details*

THE **ARK IN SPACE** SPECIAL EDITION

STORY No.76   SEASON No.12:2

Two discs with four episodes (99 mins) and 168½ minutes of extras, plus optional CGI effects, commentary track, production subtitles and PDF items
Audio navigation of each disc's contents available by pressing Enter after the BBC ident

TARDIS TEAM Fourth Doctor, Harry, Sarah Jane
TIME AND PLACE Human space station Nerva in the far future
ADVERSARIES Wirrn, man-sized insects
FIRST ON TV 25 January–15 February 1975
DVD RELEASE BBCDVD3672, 25 February 2013, PG (episodes and extras bar DVD trailer U)
COVER Photo illustration by Lee Binding, dark green strip; version with older BBC logo on reverse
ORIGINAL RRP £20.42

STORY TEASER
When Harry meddles with the controls, the TARDIS is thrown into the far future, landing on a space station where humans are in suspended animation, waiting for the Earth to recover from solar flare damage. But something else has broken in and delayed their awakening so it can use their sleeping bodies. The Doctor fights to resuscitate the station's crew, but some have already been infected.

CONNECTIONS
The idea of humans packing themselves along with examples of flora and fauna onto a space vessel to escape a dying Earth also forms the basis of 1966's *The Ark*. The following story, *The Sontaran Experiment*, indicates the Nerva ark disappeared and became a myth, which is odd given it's seen in orbit around the Earth. The Doctor returns to Nerva at an earlier point in its history in *Revenge of the Cybermen* later in this season when it comes under attack by, well, you can guess. The Cybermen also encounter the Doctor on a space station in *The Wheel in Space* (1968), while he again visits an orbiting platform at different times in its history in the New Series' *The Long Game* and *Bad Wolf/ The Parting of the Ways* (both 2005). Insects clearly make for creepy monsters, as seen in *The Web Planet* (1965) with its numerous species of insectoid life, *Frontios* (1984) with its woodlice-like Tractators, *The Unicorn and the Wasp* (2008) in which again a man turns into a giant wasp, and *Turn Left* (2008) when a Time Beetle hitches a lift on Donna's back. More grisly is the idea of people being mutated into monsters, never better presented than in *The Ark in Space*, but also the modus operandi of the Varga plants in *Mission to the Unknown* (1965), the Krynoids in *The Seeds of Doom* (1976), the Haemovores in *The Curse of Fenric* (1989) and the Flood in *The Waters of Mars* (2009). Robert Holmes had barely begun as script editor on the series before he had to write a replacement for a failed script by Louis Marks, but by now was an old hand at *Doctor Who* (see Index v), while director Rodney Bennett worked on this and *The Sontaran Experiment* together before returning to direct *The Masque of Mandragora* in 1976. Kenton Moore (Noah) briefly appears as a Roboman in the opening scene of *The Dalek Invasion of Earth* (1964), while Richardson Morgan (Rogin) lasts at least a few episodes as Corporal Blake in *The Web of Fear* (1968).

WORTH WATCHING

This Special Edition features more advanced clean-up of the episodes compared to the previous release and additional Special Features. *The Ark in Space* is the second Fourth Doctor story to be broadcast, although third made, and yet already Tom Baker seems totally at home in the part and is making the character clearly different to Jon Pertwee's portrayal. It's also the first example of the kind of creepiness verging on horror that came to typify the next three years of the show under producer Philip Hinchcliffe and script editor Robert Holmes. The Wirrn are a memorable monster, and while the realisation of Noah's transformation is crude by today's standards it's still a disturbing idea made believable by the strength of the performance.

DISC ONE

THE EPISODES

All four episodes are newly restored from digital duplicates of the original two-inch colour videotape recordings used for broadcast and their mono soundtracks remastered using more advanced techniques than the previous release. The title sequences are replaced by a modern transfer of the original 35mm film (episode one's graded to match the original's faulty film transfer) with credits remade to match the originals.

SPECIAL FEATURES *REPEATED FROM PREVIOUS RELEASE

A NEW FRONTIER (29m53s) The making of *The Ark in Space*, including the new producer's ambitions for *Doctor Who* and the impact these had on the script for this story; how the cast approached their roles and their thoughts about Tom Baker as the Doctor; designing and lighting the sets to be as convincing as possible; realising the Wirrn and Noah's transformation; how one scene came to be cut; and the success of the finished programme. With contributions from producer Philip Hinchcliffe, director Rodney Bennett, designer Roger Murray-Leach, actors Kenton Moore and Wendy Williams, and fan Nicholas Briggs. Produced by Chris Chapman.

*ROGER MURRAY–LEACH INTERVIEW (10m28s) The set designer of *The Ark in Space*, Roger Murray-Leach, talks about his work on this story and other *Doctor Who* serials he designed: *The Sontaran Experiment* (1975), *Planet of Evil* (1975), *The Deadly Assassin* (1976) and *The Talons of Weng-Chiang* (1977).

*MODEL EFFECTS ROLL (7m10s) Silent 16mm colour film footage of the original model work, including used and unused shots of the Ark, its rocket and the Wirrn outside the space station. Set to sound effects from the story.

*CGI EFFECTS ROLL (1m32s) Watch all the new computer-generated model shots in sequence.

*3D TECHNICAL SCHEMATICS (1m9s) Technical schematic of the Ark and its rocket, created by the team that produced the CGI model effects.

*TRAIL (51s) Preview of the first episode shown on BBC1 on Friday 24 January 1975.
NEXT

*ALTERNATIVE TITLES (42s) The initial version of Bernard Lodge's opening title sequence for the Fourth Doctor.

*ALTERNATIVE CGI SEQUENCES Select **On** to view the computer-generated model shots produced for the previous release in place of the original model footage when watching the episodes.

*TARDIS-CAM NO.1 (1m23s) A short scene featuring the TARDIS, originally made for the BBCi *Doctor Who* website in 2001. The TARDIS stands on a barren planet near a crashed Cybermen spaceship (model).

PHOTO GALLERY (7m5s) Slideshow of colour and black-and-white photos taken during production of *The Ark in Space*, including design department photos of the sets. Set to sound effects from the story. Compiled by Paul Shields.

INFO TEXT Select **On** to view subtitles when watching the episodes that provide information and anecdotes about the development, production, broadcast and history of *The Ark in Space*, updated and expanded from the previous release. Written by Martin Wiggins.

*AUDIO OPTIONS Select **Commentary** to play the audio commentary recorded for the previous release in place of the main soundtrack when watching the episodes. With Tom Baker, Elisabeth Sladen (Sarah) and producer Philip Hinchcliffe on all four episodes.

— Select **Feature Audio** to reinstate the main soundtrack when watching the episodes.

SUBTITLES

Select **On** to view subtitles for all episodes and Special Features on disc one (except commentary).

DISC TWO

SPECIAL FEATURES

THE ARK IN SPACE – MOVIE VERSION (69m50s) Version of the story edited down into a single episode, as broadcast on BBC1 on Wednesday 20 August 1975, the week before the next season began. Presented unrestored from the original two-inch colour videotape used for broadcast.

DOCTOR FOREVER! LOVE & WAR (27m36s) Examining how *Doctor Who* has spread beyond the television screen, this edition looks at the books from the 1990s and early 2000s that continued the Doctor's story when he was no longer on television. With contributions from Virgin Publishing editor Peter Darvill-Evans, BBC Books editors Steve Cole and Justin Richards, actor Lisa Bowerman, journalist David Richardson, and authors Paul Cornell, Russell T Davies, Mark Gatiss, Joseph Lidster, Gary Russell and Robert Shearman. Presented by Ayesha Antoine, produced by James Goss. *See Index iii for further editions*

SCENE AROUND SIX (7m35s) Film footage from the BBC Belfast news programme of Tom Baker's visit to Derry to turn on the Christmas lights outside the Guildhall on Saturday 9 December 1978; and of an earlier visit to Belfast between production of *The Pirate Planet* and *The Stones of Blood*, in which he meets children of Mersey Street Primary School, is interviewed for BBC Radio Ulster and in the street by Patrick Burns, and visits a hospital, broadcast on Thursday 8 June 1978.

ROBOT 8MM LOCATION FILM (1m10s) Silent colour film footage shot in late-April 1974 during location recording for Tom Baker's debut story *Robot*.

PDF MATERIALS Accessible via a computer are the four episode listings from *Radio Times* for the original BBC1 broadcast of *The Ark in Space*.

— Packaging and the six chocolate bar wrappers from the 1975 Nestlé *Doctor Who* promotion.

— Baked bean packaging, promotional material and colouring-in booklet from the 1977 Crosse & Blackwell *Doctor Who* offer.

— *The Doctor Who Technical Manual* by Mark Harris, published by Severn House in March 1983, featuring blueprint-style drawings of various props, mechanical creatures and spaceships, including the TARDIS, Daleks and Cybermen.

SUBTITLES Select **On** to view subtitles for all Special Features on disc two.

COMING SOON (1m12s) Trailer for the Special Edition DVD release of *The Aztecs*.

EASTER EGGS

There are three hidden features on these discs to find. *See Appendix 2 for details*

RELATED EXTRAS

Coming Soon trailer — The Reign of Terror

THE **ARMAGEDDON FACTOR**

STORY No.103 SEASON No.16:6

Released with **THE ANDROIDS OF TARA, THE PIRATE PLANET, THE POWER OF KROLL, THE RIBOS OPERATION** and **THE STONES OF BLOOD** in **THE KEY TO TIME** boxset
Two discs with six episodes (148½ mins) and 136 minutes of extras, plus two commentary tracks, production subtitles and PDF items

TARDIS TEAM Fourth Doctor, First Romana, K9

TIME AND PLACE Warring planets Atrios and Zeos

ADVERSARIES Atrian warmonger the Marshal; the Shadow; the Black Guardian (1st appearance)

FIRST ON TV 20 January–24 February 1979

DVD RELEASE BBCDVD2335(F), 24 September 2007, PG (disc one U; cover wrongly labelled U)

COVER Photo illustration by Clayton Hickman, orange strip

ORIGINAL RRP £69.99 (boxset)

STORY TEASER

The planet Atrios has long been at war with its neighbour in space Zeos, but neither side seems to be making much progress towards victory. The Atrian military leader the Marshal is getting help from a mysterious third party, but it seems more interested in the planet's princess, Astra. The Doctor finds he's not the only one seeking to assemble the Key to Time.

CONNECTIONS

The Atrios-Zeos war is the first time two inhabited planets within the same solar system are featured, a situation that often leads to conflict it seems. While Tigella and Zolfa-Thura seem to have avoided contact by virtue of the latter's population dying out (virtually) a long time ago (*Meglos*, 1980), the humanoid Thoros Alphans were somehow completely subdued by their amphibious neighbours from Thoros Beta (*The Trial of a Time Lord: Mindwarp*, 1986). The inhabitants of Bandril were generally at peace with those of nearby Karfel, although war was almost provoked in *Timelash* (1985), while Androzani Minor seemed to be inhabited only by refugees from industrialised Androzani Major (*The Caves of Androzani*, 1984). Only the Traken planetary system seems to find a way for everyone to just be terribly nice to each other (*The Keeper of Traken*, 1981). Of course, Earth itself had a twin planet, Mondas, that was on an orbit that took it to the edge of the system and back (by nature or accident is unclear), which proved catastrophic for the latter when it returned (*The Tenth Planet*, 1966), and at some point Mars was also home to an advanced civilisation, the Ice Warriors. Time loops are also deployed in *The Claws of Axos* (1971), *Image of the Fendahl* (1977), *The Invasion of Time* (1978), *Meglos* and *The Big Bang* (2010). Drax is another of those Time Lords who have quit the society of Gallifrey yet managed to evade attention from their peers, such as K'anpo (*Planet of the Spiders*, 1974), Professor Chronotis (*Shada*, 1980) and Azmael (*The Twin Dilemma*, 1984). This was the last story written by Bob Baker and Dave Martin, who had been contributing stories almost yearly throughout the 1970s (*see Index v*), although Baker wrote one more solo: *Nightmare of Eden* (1979). Director Michael Hayes came to *The Armageddon Factor* fresh from directing *The Androids of Tara*, and followed it with *City of Death* (1979). Barry Jackson (Drax), an ex-stuntman, plays Ascaris in *The Romans* (1965) and Jeff Garvey in *Mission to the Unknown* (1965), Valentine Dyall returns as the Black Guardian for a trilogy of stories in 1983 — *Mawdryn Undead*, *Enlightenment* and *Terminus* — and Lalla Ward (Princess Astra) was cast as the second incarnation of Romana before *The Armageddon Factor* had finished being broadcast.

WORTH WATCHING

This concludes the Doctor's quest for the Key to Time, which formed the whole of the 1978/79 season. Bringing the season's arc story to a climactic close was always going to be a tall order on *Doctor Who*'s meagre resources, yet series stalwarts Bob Baker and Dave Martin incorporate some epic ideas, and there are strong performances from the regulars plus renowned actors John Woodvine and William Squire.

DISC ONE

THE EPISODES

All six episodes are restored from digital duplicates of the original two-inch colour videotape recordings used for broadcast and their mono soundtracks remastered. The title sequences are replaced by a modern transfer of the original 35mm film with credits remade to match the originals.

SPECIAL FEATURES

COMING SOON (1m) Trailer for the DVD release of *Planet of Evil*.

AUDIO OPTIONS Select **Commentary 1** to play the audio commentary recorded for an earlier US-only release of the story in place of the main soundtrack when watching the episodes. With Mary Tamm (Romana), John Woodvine (Marshal) and director Michael Hayes on all six episodes.

— Select **Commentary 2** to play the audio commentary recorded for this release when watching the episodes, with Tom Baker, Mary Tamm and John Leeson (K9 voice) on all six episodes.

— Select **Feature Audio** to reinstate the main soundtrack when watching the episodes.

INFO TEXT Select **On** to view subtitles when watching the episodes that provide information and anecdotes about the development, production, broadcast and history of *The Armageddon Factor*. Written by Richard Molesworth.

DOCTOR WHO ANNUAL Accessible via a computer is a PDF file of the 1979 *Doctor Who Annual*, published by World Distributors the autumn before *The Armageddon Factor* was broadcast. With stories featuring the Doctor and Leela, plus science features, puzzles and games.

RADIO TIMES LISTINGS Accessible via a computer is a PDF file of the six episode listings for the original BBC1 broadcast of *The Armageddon Factor*, and a two-page article published at the start of the season in the 31 August 1978 edition looking at the Doctor's past female companions.

SUBTITLES

Select **On** to view subtitles for all episodes and the Coming Soon trailer (none for commentary).

DISC TWO

PLAY ALL

Plays each of the Special Features in sequence.

SPECIAL FEATURES

DEFINING SHADOWS (15m39s) The making of *The Armageddon Factor*, including the ideas involved in developing the story; working with the director; designing the sets; the characters and cast; the process of studio recording; and last-minute changes to the script. With contributions from writers Bob Baker and Dave Martin, director Michael Hayes, designer Richard McManan-Smith, and actors Davyd Harries, Barry Jackson and Lalla Ward. Produced by Ed Stradling.

ALTERNATIVE | EXTENDED SCENE (2m52s) Longer version of a scene from episode three, taken from a low-quality black-and-white copy of the studio recording with as-recorded sound and on-screen time-code.

DIRECTING WHO (8m26s) Michael Hayes talks about directing *The Androids of Tara* (1978), *The Armageddon Factor* and *City of Death* (1979), including his initial reluctance to work on the programme and going on location to Paris.

ROGUE TIME LORDS (13m11s) A rundown of those members of the Doctor's own people who got up to no good, including the Monk, the War Chief, the Master, Omega, Borusa, Hedin, the Rani, the Valeyard and, of course, the Doctor himself. With contributions from writers Pip and Jane Baker and Terrance Dicks, actor Nicholas Courtney, and fan journalists Moray Laing, Paul Lang and Tom Spilsbury. Produced by Anthony Caulfield and Richard Adamson.

PEBBLE MILL AT ONE (8m30s) Extract from the Tuesday 16 January 1979 edition of the BBC1 lunchtime magazine show, in which Donny MacLeod interviews Tom Baker about the continued popularity of *Doctor Who* after five hundred episodes.

RADIOPHONIC FEATURE (4m28s) Extract from the Wednesday 11 April 1979 (not March as stated at the end) edition of BBC1 lunchtime magazine programme *Pebble Mill at One*, in which reporter Tony Francis visits the BBC's Radiophonic Workshop in Maida Vale, London and talks to Dick Mills and Brian Hodgson about creating the sound effects for *Doctor Who*, demonstrated using a clip from *The Armageddon Factor*.

NEXT

THE NEW SOUND OF MUSIC (1m) Extract from this BBC1 documentary in which Michael Rodd investigated the development of electronic music, broadcast on Tuesday 5 June 1979. Dick Mills shows how he creates sound effects for *Doctor Who* using an example from *The Armageddon Factor*.

MERRY CHRISTMAS, DOCTOR WHO (1m13s) Comedy sketch featuring Tom Baker, Mary Tamm and John Leeson voicing K9, recorded on the set of *The Armageddon Factor* for the 1978 BBC staff Christmas tape.

CONTINUITIES (2m56s) Continuity announcements from the original BBC1 broadcasts of all six episodes of *The Armageddon Factor*, reconstructed by matching audio recordings made at the time of broadcast to clips from the episodes.

PHOTO GALLERY (4m48s) Slideshow of colour and black-and-white photos taken during production of *The Armageddon Factor*, including design department photos of the sets. Set to sound effects from the story. Compiled by Derek Handley.

LATE NIGHT STORY (70m30s) This BBC2 series from Christmas 1978 featured Tom Baker reading spooky stories relating to childhood just before the channel's closedown at the end of the evening. Select from 'The Photograph' by Nigel Kneale (shown Saturday 23 December 1978, 14m32s);

'The Emissary' by Ray Bradbury (Monday 25 December, 13m44s); 'Nursery Tea' by Mary Danby (Tuesday 26 December, 14m19s); 'The End of the Party' by Graham Greene (Thursday 28 December, 15m2s); and 'Sredni Vashtar' by Hector Hugh Munro (12m53s), which was planned to launch the run on Friday 22 December 1978 but wasn't broadcast owing to strike disruption.

SUBTITLES
Select **On** to view subtitles for all Special Features on disc two.

EASTER EGG
There is one hidden feature on these discs to find. *See Appendix 2 for details*

RELATED EXTRAS
Coming Soon trailer — The Time Warrior

ATTACK OF THE CYBERMEN
STORY No.137   SEASON No.22:1

One disc with two episodes (89 mins) and 80 minutes of extras, plus commentary and music-only tracks, production subtitles and PDF items
Audio navigation of disc contents available by pressing Enter after the BBC ident

TARDIS TEAM Sixth Doctor, Peri
TIME AND PLACE Contemporary London and future Telos
ADVERSARIES Cybermen (9th appearance); mercenary Lytton (2nd appearance)
FIRST ON TV 5–12 January 1985
DVD RELEASE BBCDVD2436, 16 March 2009, U
COVER Photo illustration by Clayton Hickman, pale blue strip
ORIGINAL RRP £19.56

STORY TEASER
Tracking an alien distress signal to Earth, the Doctor discovers a squad of Cybermen hiding in London's sewers. They have travelled back in time to 1985 to use Halley's Comet as a missile to destroy the world and thus prevent the impending death of their own home planet Mondas. Helped by the mercenary Lytton, the Cybermen take charge of the TARDIS and return to their adopted home of Telos, where their Controller has murderous plans for its indigenous people.

CONNECTIONS
Attack of the Cybermen is renowned for being so overloaded with links and references to past stories that it's assumed to be impenetrable to new viewers. Firstly it's a sequel to the Cybermen's original appearance in *The Tenth Planet* (1966), in which their planet Mondas returned from the depths of space to absorb energy from the Earth but ended up disintegrating. *The Tomb of the Cybermen* (1967) introduced the titular catacombs on Telos, a world they are said to have occupied following the loss of their own. Then in *The Invasion* (1968) the Cybermen launch an attack on Earth beginning in London, where they emerge from the sewers. Although not explicitly linked, they tried to destroy the Earth in the future by crashing a missile into it but were successfully shifted back in time so that it killed only the dinosaurs as history records (*Earthshock*, 1982). That story also introduced this design of Cybermen, which lasted until the end of the Classic Series. As the Doctor finally (if temporarily) repairs the chameleon circuit that enables the TARDIS to blend in with its surroundings, the ship materialises back at the junkyard in Totter's Lane where the circuit broke down, as related in the very first story *An Unearthly Child* (1963). He previously tried to mend it with the help of Logopolitan mathematics in *Logopolis* (1981). Finally, the character of Lytton debuted in *Resurrection of the Daleks* (1984), escaping the defeat of his eponymous employers by disguising himself as a policeman in contemporary London, along with two of his henchman, also returning in *Attack of the Cybermen*. While the authorship of the script is debated, Eric Saward would have had a major input as script editor, as he had done uncredited for *The Twin Dilemma* (1984) as well as those stories that did go out under his name (*see Index v*), such as *Resurrection of the Daleks*, which was also directed by Matthew Robinson. As well as Maurice Colbourne as Lytton,

along with Mike Braben and Michael Jeffries as his silent aides, Terry Molloy (Russell) returns from *Resurrection of the Daleks*, in which he plays Davros for the first time, a role he revisits in *Revelation of the Daleks* (1985) and *Remembrance of the Daleks* (1988). David Banks once again plays the Cyberleader, as in *Earthshock*, *The Five Doctors* (1983) and *Silver Nemesis* (1988), while Michael Kilgarriff reprises his role of the Cyber Controller from *The Tomb of the Cybermen*.

WORTH WATCHING

It's arguably true that there's rather too much reference to past adventures in *Attack of the Cybermen*, but less supportable is the suggestion this makes it too convoluted for newcomers. All the relevant points are explained, and they're just the backstory to the action, as valid as any newly created explanation. The story is directed with panache by Matthew Robinson but perhaps fails to give the still-new Sixth Doctor a strong enough role for the start of his first full season.

THE EPISODES

Both episodes are restored from digital duplicates of the original one-inch colour videotape recordings used for broadcast and their mono soundtracks remastered. The title sequences are replaced by a modern transfer of the original 35mm film with credits remade to match the originals.

SPECIAL FEATURES

AUDIO OPTIONS Select **Commentary** to play the audio commentary in place of the main soundtrack when watching the episodes. With Colin Baker and Nicola Bryant (Peri) on both episodes, joined by Terry Molloy (Russell) on episode one and Sarah Berger (Rost) on episode two.

— Select **Isolated Score** to hear only Malcolm Clarke's music when watching the episodes.

— Select **Feature Audio** to reinstate the main soundtrack when watching the episodes.

INFO TEXT Select **On** to view subtitles when watching the episodes that provide information and anecdotes about the development, production, broadcast and history of *Attack of the Cybermen*.

THE COLD WAR (27m28s) The making of *Attack of the Cybermen*, covering the effects of moving to 45-minute episodes for the 1985 season; disagreement over who really wrote the story; the references to past stories; Matthew Robinson's direction; bringing back Lytton; the guest cast; location filming in London and a Buckinghamshire quarry; the portrayal of the Cryons; creating the right atmosphere in the studio; and criticisms of overt violence. With contributions from script editor Eric Saward, continuity advisor Ian Levine, director Matthew Robinson, film cameraman Godfrey Johnson, and actors Colin Baker, Sarah Berger, Nicola Bryant and Terry Molloy. Narrated by Stephen Greif, produced by John Kelly.

THE CYBER STORY (22m51s) A history of the Cybermen's appearances in the original series of *Doctor Who*, running through each of their stories, plus how their look changed over the years and how plausible they are in reality. With contributions from writer Eric Saward, director Morris Barry (interviewed in 1992), costume designers Dinah Collin and Sandra Reid, actors Mark Hardy and Roy Skelton, and cybernetics professor Kevin Warwick. Narrated by James Coombes, produced by Brendan Sheppard.

HUMAN CYBORG (8m10s) Kevin Warwick, professor of cybernetics at Reading University, talks about the existing possibilities for augmenting our senses with technology.

NEXT

PHOTO GALLERY (8m12s) Slideshow of colour photos taken during production of *Attack of the Cybermen*, set to music from the story. Compiled by Ralph Montagu.

THE CYBER-GENERATIONS (7m50s) Slideshow of colour and black-and-white photos of Cybermen from all their Classic *Doctor Who* appearances, set to music from the relevant serials. Compiled by Ralph Montagu.

TRAILS AND CONTINUITY (3m12s) Trailers and continuity announcements from the original BBC1 broadcasts of both episodes of *Attack of the Cybermen*.

RADIO TIMES LISTINGS Accessible via a computer is a PDF file of the two episode listings for the original BBC1 broadcast of *Attack of the Cybermen*, and a two-page article that introduced the 1985 season (with *Doctor Who*-themed puzzles).

— The eight episode listings from *Radio Times* for the original BBC1 broadcast of *The Invasion* (1968), and an article about Cybermen creator Dr Kit Pedler published the week of episode four.

— Also on the disc but not listed in the menus is a PDF file of a three-page article from the 10 July 1969 edition of the BBC's *The Listener* magazine written by Kit Pedler, about technologies mimicking biological processes.

COMING SOON (1m5s) Trailer for the DVD release of *Image of the Fendahl*.

SUBTITLES
Select **On** to view subtitles for all episodes and Special Features (except commentary).

EASTER EGG
There is one hidden feature on this disc to find. *See Appendix 2 for details*

RELATED EXTRAS
Coming Soon trailer — The Rescue, The Romans

THE **AWAKENING**
STORY No.131   SEASON No.21:2

Released with **THE GUNFIGHTERS** in the **EARTH STORY** boxset
One disc with two episodes (50 mins) and 54½ minutes of extras, plus commentary and music-only tracks, production subtitles and PDF items
Audio navigation of disc contents available by pressing Enter after the BBC ident

TARDIS TEAM Fifth Doctor, Tegan, Turlough
TIME AND PLACE Village of Little Hodcombe
ADVERSARIES The Malus; local squire Sir George Hutchinson
FIRST ON TV 19–20 January 1984
DVD RELEASE BBCDVD3380B, 20 June 2011, PG
COVER Photo illustration by Clayton Hickman, blue strip; version with older BBC logo on reverse
ORIGINAL RRP £30.63 (boxset)

STORY TEASER
The Doctor takes Tegan to the village of Little Hodcombe to visit her grandfather, but they find he has disappeared and the villagers are vigorously re-enacting a local battle from the English Civil War. Meanwhile, in the nearby dilapidated church, something dangerous is stirring that could make the war games very real indeed.

CONNECTIONS
The idea of a sleepy English village hiding peculiar goings-on is less common in *Doctor Who* than you might think, with only *The Dæmons* (1971), *The Android Invasion* (1975), *The Awakening* and, most recently, *The Eleventh Hour* (2010) really using such a setting (and *Terror of the Zygons* (1975) if we include Scottish villages as well). The other, often mentioned connection between *The Awakening* and *The Dæmons* is their focus on a church and its eventual destruction. Although here we only see and hear echoes of the English Civil War, Will Chandler is transported forward in time from the real period, as are a troop of Roundheads in *The Time Monster* (1972). (Lady Peinforte and her servant Richard Maynarde left Stuart England shortly before the onset of the war, although the latter must have survived the conflict as the Doctor returns him to 1638 and his gravestone says he died in 1657.) While various species have practised forms of mind control, hypnosis and telepathy, the only ones with manifest psychic powers like the Malus are the giant spiders of Metebelis 3 (*Planet of the Spiders*, 1974), the Sisterhood of Karn (*The Brain of Morbius*, 1976), the Mentiads of Zanak (*The Pirate Planet*, 1978), and possibly the Time Lords. Andrew Verney, Tegan's grandfather, is the second member of her family seen, after her aunt Vanessa in *Logopolis* (1981). As Tegan's surname is Jovanka, presumably Verney's daughter emigrated to Australia and married Vanessa's brother. While writer Eric Pringle and director Michael Owen Morris made only this single contribution to *Doctor Who*, *The Awakening* is the last story designed by Barry Newbery, whose contribution goes back to the very first serial, *An Unearthly Child* (1963). Glyn Houston (Ben Wolsey) plays Professor Watson in *The Hand of Fear* (1976), while Dennis Lill (Sir George Hutchinson) is Dr Fendleman in *Image of the Fendahl* (1977).

WORTH WATCHING

This short story from Peter Davison's final season is a tight, exciting adventure that takes an inventively different approach to the series' usual ways of presenting historical events, by showing the later consequences of an alien incursion into the past. This means it can enjoy the feel and detail of a period drama without getting bogged down in debates about changing history. The huge Malus face is a memorable creation and is effectively creepy when leering out from behind a wall.

THE EPISODES

Both episodes are restored from digital duplicates of the original one-inch colour videotape recordings used for broadcast, with location sequences newly transferred from the original 16mm colour film. Their mono soundtracks are remastered and the title sequences replaced by a modern transfer of the original 35mm film with credits remade to match the originals.

SPECIAL FEATURES

RETURN TO LITTLE HODCOMBE (19m35s) Director Michael Owen Morris, script editor Eric Saward, and actors Janet Fielding and Keith Jayne return to the villages in Dorset where they filmed much of *The Awakening*, recalling their involvement in making the story. With memories from villagers Jane Butler, John Chappell and Maureen Crumpler who watched the location filming. Produced by Chris Chapman.

MAKING THE MALUS (7m15s) Visual effects designer Tony Harding and model maker Richard Gregory discuss designing and building the Malus as they examine the original prop again, with its current owner Paul Burrows.

NOW & THEN (7m26s) Comparing the filming locations in Shapwick and Tarrant Monkton in Dorset and Martin in Hampshire as they look today with how they appeared in mid-July 1983 when used for *The Awakening*. Narrated and produced by Richard Bignell. *See Index iii for further editions*

FROM THE CUTTING ROOM FLOOR (9m30s) Deleted and extended scenes from both episodes — including one with Kamelion — taken from a VHS copy of earlier edits with as-recorded sound and on-screen time-code, and from the full location film footage. The sections in black and white appear in the final episodes while those in colour are the unused scenes, to show where they would have fitted into the story. Plus unused silent 16mm colour film footage from the location shoot, with explanatory captions, set to music from the story. Includes the countdown clock for the studio recording of episode one.

THE GOLDEN EGG AWARDS (2m22s) Extract from the Saturday 10 December 1983 edition of BBC1 entertainment programme *The Noel Edmonds Late Late Breakfast Show* in which Peter Davison receives an award for a blooper from *The Awakening* involving a wilful horse.

PHOTO GALLERY (7m9s) Slideshow of colour photos taken during production of *The Awakening*, including design department photos of the sets, behind the scenes at rehearsals and on location, and shots of the model filming. Set to music from the story. Compiled by Paul Shields.

NEXT

AUDIO OPTIONS Select **Commentary** to play the audio commentary in place of the main soundtrack when watching the episodes. This is moderated by actor and comedian Toby Hadoke, talking with script editor Eric Saward and director Michael Owen Morris on both episodes.

— Select **Isolated Score** to hear only Peter Howell's music when watching the episodes.

— Select **Feature Audio** to reinstate the main soundtrack when watching the episodes.

INFO TEXT Select **On** to view subtitles when watching the episodes that provide information and anecdotes about the development, production, broadcast and history of *The Awakening*. Written by Paul Scoones.

PDF MATERIALS Accessible via a computer are the two episode listings from *Radio Times* for the original BBC1 broadcast of *The Awakening*.

COMING SOON (1m20s) Trailer for the DVD release of *Paradise Towers*.

SUBTITLES

Select **On** to view subtitles for all episodes and Special Features (except commentary).

RELATED EXTRAS

Coming Soon trailer — Frontios

THE **AZTECS**

STORY No.6   SEASON No.1:6

One disc with four episodes (99 mins) and 74½ minutes of extras, plus commentary and foreign-dub tracks, and production subtitles

TARDIS TEAM First Doctor, Barbara, Ian, Susan
TIME AND PLACE Aztec city, 15th Century
ADVERSARIES Priest of sacrifice Tlotoxl
FIRST ON TV 23 May–13 June 1964
DVD RELEASE BBCDVD1099, 21 October 2002, U
COVER Photo illustration by Clayton Hickman, red strip
ORIGINAL RRP £19.99

STORY TEASER

The TARDIS arrives in the tomb of the high priest Yetaxa during the reign of the Aztecs. When Barbara emerges she is mistaken for a reincarnation of the priest and venerated. However, she is soon seduced by the power this gives her to try to end the Aztec practice of human sacrifice, despite the Doctor's warnings that history is not so easily changed. And she reckons without the devious scheming of Tlotoxl, high priest of sacrifice.

CONNECTIONS

Although the Doctor doesn't visit Central America on screen again, he's back in the 15th Century, this time in what will be Italy, in *The Masque of Mandragora* (1976). He does encounter other societies that perform ritual sacrifice, although is usually too busy being on the end of it to try to change their ways, such as the Atlanteans in *The Underwater Menace* (1967), the Sisterhood of Karn in *The Brain of Morbius* (1976), the Seers in *Underworld* (1978), the Swampies in *The Power of Kroll* (1978/79), and the Tigellans in *Meglos* (1980). Although the Doctor insists to Barbara that she can't change history, given later stories such as *The Time Meddler* (1965), *The Time Warrior* (1974), *Pyramids of Mars* (1975) and *The King's Demons* (1983), this would seem to be a moral rather than a practical issue. John Lucarotti wrote this and *Marco Polo* for the series' first year, but soon his style of straightforward historical tale was being usurped by incoming story editor Dennis Spooner's more relaxed approach, and only *The Crusade* (1965) by David Whitaker and *The Massacre* (1966) — initially by Lucarotti but heavily reworked by Spooner's replacement Donald Tosh — follow in the style of *The Aztecs*. John Ringham (Tlotoxl) also plays Josiah Blake in the penultimate First Doctor story *The Smugglers* (1966) and is Robert Ashe in *Colony in Space* (1971); Margot van der Burgh (Cameca) returns as another wise old lady, Katura, in *The Keeper of Traken* (1981); while David Anderson (Guard Captain) has larger roles as Sir Raynier de Marun in *The Crusade* and Viking raider Sven in *The Time Meddler*. Walter Randall (Tonila) became one of director David Camfield's repertoire of actors, appearing in *The Crusade*, *The Daleks' Master Plan* (1965/66), *The Invasion* (1968) and *Inferno* (1970).

WORTH WATCHING

Doctor Who originally alternated between science fiction and historical adventures, and this is the earliest of the latter that's known to survive. It shows that human drama can be just as compelling as alien societies, with thought-provoking ideas and strong performances, especially from Jacqueline Hill, who relishes Barbara's central role in the story.

THE EPISODES

All four episodes are restored from 16mm film copies of the original black-and-white video recordings, recovered from BBC Enterprises in 1978. Their mono soundtracks are remastered, the VidFIRE process is applied to studio-recorded shots to recapture the smoother motion of video, and end credits are remade to match the originals. When selecting **Play All**, one of six messages recorded by cast members in character will play before the first episode.

SPECIAL FEATURES *ALSO ON SPECIAL EDITION

*REMEMBERING THE AZTECS (28m19s) Three actors from *The Aztecs* — Ian Cullen, Walter Randall and John Ringham — recall the process of rehearsing and recording this serial, including working with the rest of the cast, memories of director John Crockett, and the authenticity of the costumes.

***CORTEZ & MONTEZUMA** (5m55s) Extract from the Monday 21 September 1970 edition of BBC1 children's magazine programme *Blue Peter* (just its third edition transmitted in colour) in which Valerie Singleton, in Mexico City, relates the history of the Aztec civilisation and its demise at the hands of the Spanish Conquistadors.

***RESTORING THE AZTECS** (8m8s) Comparisons of picture and sound quality before and after restoration, demonstrating the techniques used on this and other black-and-white episodes, including the VidFIRE motion-smoothing process. With explanatory captions.

***TARDIS- CAM NO. 3** (1m5s) Short scene featuring the TARDIS, originally made for the BBCi *Doctor Who* website in 2001. The TARDIS stands on a barren, windswept planet (model).

***INTRO SEQUENCES** Caption explaining the messages played when selecting **Play All**.

▶

INFORMATION TEXT Select **On** to view subtitles when watching the episodes that provide information and anecdotes about the development, production, broadcast and history of *The Aztecs*. Written by Richard Molesworth.

***DESIGNING THE AZTECS** (24m33s) Set designer Barry Newbery talks about his work on *The Aztecs*, including the research required; designing the sets; selecting props; the trickiness of using backcloths in a small studio and putting up the sets; budgeting; coping with missing scenery; the designer's role during studio rehearsals; the requirements when shooting in black and white; and his success with creating the tipping tomb doorway. Featuring many of Barry's set photos.

***MAKING COCOA** (2m29s) Animation of Tlotoxl and Tonila, voiced by John Ringham and Walter Randall, describing how the Aztecs prepared cocoa.

***AUDIO OPTIONS** Select **Commentary On** to play the audio commentary in place of the main soundtrack when watching the episodes. With Carole Ann Ford (Susan), William Russell (Ian) and producer Verity Lambert on all four episodes.
— Select **Arabic Audio for Episode 4** to hear the soundtrack with dialogue dubbed into Arabic when watching episode four, made for sales of the programme to Middle Eastern broadcasters. This also features different incidental music to that used in the UK broadcast.

***PHOTO GALLERY** (3m51s) Slideshow of colour and black-and-white photos taken during production of *The Aztecs*, including design department photos of the sets. Set to sound effects. Compiled by Ralph Montagu.

SUBTITLES
Select **On** to view subtitles for all episodes and Special Features (except Arabic soundtrack), or for the commentary.

EASTER EGG
There is one hidden feature on this disc to find. *See Appendix 2 for details*

THE **AZTECS** SPECIAL EDITION

STORY No.6   SEASON No.1:6

Two discs with four episodes (99 mins), reconstruction of Galaxy 4 *including the one surviving episode (65 mins) and 224½ minutes of extras, plus commentary and foreign dub tracks, production subtitles and PDF items*
Audio navigation of each disc's contents available by pressing Enter after the BBC ident

TARDIS TEAM First Doctor, Barbara, Ian, Susan
TIME AND PLACE Aztec city, 15th Century
ADVERSARIES Priest of sacrifice Tlotoxl
FIRST ON TV 23 May–13 June 1964
DVD RELEASE BBCDVD3689, 11 March 2013, PG (episodes U)
COVER Photo illustration by Lee Binding, dark red strip; version with older BBC logo on reverse
ORIGINAL RRP £20.42

STORY TEASER

The TARDIS arrives in the tomb of the high priest Yetaxa during the reign of the Aztecs. When Barbara emerges she is mistaken for a reincarnation of the priest and venerated. However, she is soon seduced by the power this gives her to try to end the Aztec practice of human sacrifice, despite the Doctor's warnings that history is not so easily changed. And she reckons without the devious scheming of Tlotoxl, high priest of sacrifice.

CONNECTIONS

Although the Doctor doesn't visit Central America on screen again, he's back in the 15th Century, this time in what will be Italy, in *The Masque of Mandragora* (1976). He does encounter other societies that perform ritual sacrifice, although is usually too busy being on the end of it to try to change their ways, such as the Atlanteans in *The Underwater Menace* (1967), the Sisterhood of Karn in *The Brain of Morbius* (1976), the Seers in *Underworld* (1978), the Swampies in *The Power of Kroll* (1978/79), and the Tigellans in *Meglos* (1980). Although the Doctor insists to Barbara that she can't change history, given later stories such as *The Time Meddler* (1965), *The Time Warrior* (1974), *Pyramids of Mars* (1975) and *The King's Demons* (1983), this would seem to be a moral rather than a practical issue. John Lucarotti wrote this and *Marco Polo* for the series' first year, but soon his style of straightforward historical tale was being usurped by incoming story editor Dennis Spooner's more relaxed approach, and only *The Crusade* (1965) by David Whitaker and *The Massacre* (1966) — initially by Lucarotti but heavily reworked by Spooner's replacement Donald Tosh — follow in the style of *The Aztecs*. John Ringham (Tlotoxl) also plays Josiah Blake in the penultimate First Doctor story *The Smugglers* (1966) and is Robert Ashe in *Colony in Space* (1971); Margot van der Burgh (Cameca) returns as another wise old lady, Katura, in *The Keeper of Traken* (1981); while David Anderson (Guard Captain) has larger roles as Sir Raynier de Marun in *The Crusade* and Viking raider Sven in *The Time Meddler*. Walter Randall (Tonila) became one of director David Camfield's repertoire of actors, appearing in *The Crusade*, *The Daleks' Master Plan* (1965/66), *The Invasion* (1968) and *Inferno* (1970).

WORTH WATCHING

This Special Edition features more advanced clean-up of the episodes compared to the previous release and additional Special Features. *Doctor Who* originally alternated between science fiction and historical adventures, and this is the earliest of the latter that's known to survive. It shows that human drama can be just as compelling as alien societies, with thought-provoking ideas and strong performances, especially from Jacqueline Hill, who relishes Barbara's central role in the story.

DISC ONE

THE EPISODES

All four episodes are newly restored from 16mm film copies of the original black-and-white videotape recordings, recovered from BBC Enterprises in 1978, using more advanced techniques than the previous release. Their mono soundtracks are remastered and a refined version of the VidFIRE process is applied to studio-recorded shots to recapture the smoother motion of video. The title sequences are replaced by a modern transfer of the best surviving copy of the original 35mm film with credits remade to match the originals. When selecting **Play All**, one of six messages recorded by cast members in character will play before the first episode.

SPECIAL FEATURES *REPEATED FROM PREVIOUS RELEASE

*REMEMBERING THE AZTECS (28m19s) Three actors from *The Aztecs* — Ian Cullen, Walter Randall and John Ringham — recall the process of rehearsing and recording this serial, including working with the rest of the cast, memories of director John Crockett, and the authenticity of the costumes.

*DESIGNING THE AZTECS (24m33s) Set designer Barry Newbery talks about his work on *The Aztecs*, including the research required; designing the sets; selecting props; the trickiness of using backcloths in a small studio and putting up the sets; budgeting; coping with missing scenery; the designer's role during studio rehearsals; the requirements when shooting in black and white; and his success with creating the tipping tomb doorway. Featuring many of Barry's set photos.

*CORTEZ AND MONTEZUMA (5m55s) Extract from the Monday 21 September 1970 edition of BBC1 children's magazine programme *Blue Peter* (just its third edition transmitted in colour) in which

Valerie Singleton, in Mexico City, relates the history of the Aztec civilisation and its demise at the hands of the Spanish Conquistadors.

*RESTORING THE AZTECS (8m8s) Comparisons of picture and sound quality before and after restoration, demonstrating the techniques used on this and other black-and-white episodes, including the VidFIRE motion-smoothing process. Turn on **Info Text** to view with explanatory captions.

*AUDIO OPTIONS Select **Commentary** to play the audio commentary recorded for the previous release in place of the main soundtrack when watching the episodes. With Carole Ann Ford (Susan), William Russell (Ian) and producer Verity Lambert on all four episodes.

— Select **Episode 4 Arabic Audio** to hear the soundtrack with dialogue dubbed into Arabic when watching episode four, made for sales of the programme to Middle Eastern broadcasters. This also features different incidental music to that used in the UK broadcast.

— Select **Feature Audio** to reinstate the main soundtrack when watching the episodes.

INFO TEXT Select **On** to view subtitles when watching the episodes that provide information and anecdotes about the development, production, broadcast and history of *The Aztecs*, updated and expanded from the previous release. Written by Matthew Kilburn.

NEXT

*MAKING COCOA (2m29s) Animation of Tlotoxl and Tonila, voiced by John Ringham and Walter Randall, describing how the Aztecs prepared cocoa.

*TARDIS-CAM NO. 3 (1m5s) Short scene featuring the TARDIS, originally made for the BBCi *Doctor Who* website in 2001. The TARDIS stands on a barren, windswept planet (model).

*PHOTO GALLERY (3m51s) Slideshow of colour and black-and-white photos taken during production of *The Aztecs*, including design department photos of the sets. Set to sound effects. Compiled by Ralph Montagu.

*INTRO SEQUENCES Caption explaining the messages played when selecting **Play All**.

SUBTITLES

Select **On** to view subtitles for all episodes and Special Features on disc one (except commentary and Arabic soundtrack).

DISC TWO

SPECIAL FEATURES

GALAXY 4 (64m44s) Reconstruction of the mostly-missing serial that opened *Doctor Who*'s third season in September 1965. Episodes one, two and four are represented by extracts from an audio recording of the original soundtrack matched to surviving clips — including a six-minute clip from episode one that survived because part of it was used in the 1977 *Whose Doctor Who* documentary — photos and computer-generated animation. Episode three is presented in full (chapters 7 to 12), restored from a 16mm film copy of the original black-and-white videotape recording, returned by Terry Burnett in July 2011. Its mono soundtrack is remastered and the VidFIRE process is applied to studio-recorded shots to recapture the smoother motion of video. The title sequence is replaced by a modern transfer of the best surviving copy of the original 35mm film with end credits remade to match the originals. Reconstruction produced by Derek Handley.

CHRONICLE – THE REALMS OF GOLD (49m51s) Edition of the BBC2 history series broadcast on Saturday 8 February 1969, in which John Julius Norwich visits the remains of the Aztec civilisation of Mexico and relates its conquest by the Spanish under Hernan Cortes in 1519. With music by Delia Derbyshire of the BBC Radiophonic Workshop.

DOCTOR FOREVER! – CELESTIAL TOYROOM (22m35s) Examining how *Doctor Who* has spread beyond the television screen, this edition looks at the range of toys and games, from the early boom in Dalek merchandise in the 1960s to a growing diversity of toys in the 1970s, targeting the fan market in the 1980s, going retro in the 1990s after the series had ended, and a new explosion of products with the New Series. With Classic Series producer Verity Lambert (interviewed in 2003), New Series showrunner Russell T Davies, BBC Worldwide's product licensing executive Richard Hollis, product approval executive Dave Turbitt and range editor Steve Cole, AudioGo commissioning editor Michael Stevens, Character Options product development director Alasdair Dewar, toy reviewer Jim Sangster, writers Paul Cornell, Mark Gatiss, Joseph Lidster and

Robert Shearman, and actor Ian McNiece discussing the Winston Churchill figure based on him. Presented by Ayesha Antoine, produced by James Goss. *See Index iii for further editions*

IT'S A SQUARE WORLD (7m22s) Sketch from the Tuesday 31 December 1963 edition of the BBC comedy show starring Michael Bentine, in which Clive Dunn as Doctor Fotheringown (dressed as the Doctor) demonstrates his new space rocket and accidentally launches Television Centre into space. This is the first known *Doctor Who* parody on television, shown between episodes two and three of *The Daleks*.

A WHOLE SCENE GOING (4m32s) Extract from the Wednesday 16 March 1966 edition of the BBC1 arts programme, featuring an interview with Gordon Flemyng, director of the two 1960s Dalek movies, and behind-the-scenes footage of the filming of *Daleks Invasion Earth: 2150AD*, still in production at the time. Introduced by Barry Fantoni.

PDF MATERIAL Accessible via a computer are the four episode listings from *Radio Times* for the original BBC1 broadcast of *The Aztecs* and an article that introduced the story.

SUBTITLES Select **On** to view subtitles for all Special Features on disc two.

COMING SOON (54s) Trailer for the DVD release of *The Ice Warriors*.

EASTER EGG

There is one hidden feature on these discs to find. *See Appendix 2 for details*

RELATED EXTRAS

Coming Soon trailer — The Ark in Space Special Edition

BATTLEFIELD

STORY No.152   SEASON No.26:1

Two discs with four episodes (97 mins), a new 95-minute Special Edition and 83 minutes of extras, plus commentary and music-only tracks, production subtitles and PDF items
Audio navigation of each disc's contents available by pressing Enter after the BBC ident

TARDIS TEAM Seventh Doctor, Ace

TIME AND PLACE Village of Carbury, near-future

ADVERSARIES Sorceress Morgaine; her son Mordred

FIRST ON TV 6–27 September 1989

DVD RELEASE BBCDVD2440, 29 December 2008, PG

COVER Photo illustration by Clayton Hickman, light green strip

ORIGINAL RRP £19.99

STORY TEASER

Advanced knights from another dimension arrive on Earth in search of King Arthur and Excalibur. When the Doctor turns up just as a conflict between rival knights threatens a UNIT convoy transporting a nuclear missile, Brigadier Lethbridge-Stewart is brought out of retirement to sort out the situation. But the sorceress Morgaine is interested only in the lost king and threatens to unleash the Destroyer on the world if he is not brought before her.

CONNECTIONS

It's somewhat surprising that it took *Doctor Who* so long to engage with the Arthurian legends, given they're exactly the sort of boys' adventure fiction the programme pays homage to throughout its history. The Doctor visits medieval times on occasion, such as in *The Crusade* (1965), *The Time Warrior* (1973/74) and *The King's Demons* (1983), stories which feature knights and sword fights, but they don't reference the myths of Arthur, Merlin and the Round Table (although these have turned up in other stories in annuals and comic strips). The suggestion here that Merlin is really a future incarnation of the Doctor is such an obvious conceit that perhaps it was simply dismissed before now. *Battlefield* appropriately casts the series' own legendary noble leader of men in the King Arthur role: Brigadier Alistair Gordon Lethbridge-Stewart, who led the British wing of UNIT in the fight against invading forces from *The Invasion* (1968) to *Terror of the Zygons* (1975), before retiring to teach in a public school (*Mawdryn Undead*, 1983). This is his last appearance in the

B

Classic Series, although he is referred to in the New Series and helps old friend Sarah Jane Smith in *The Sarah Jane Adventures: Enemy of the Bane* (2008). Following actor Nicholas Courtney's death in February 2011, his character was similarly reported to have passed away in *The Wedding of River Song* (2011), although his daughter Kate has since featured (*The Power of Three*, 2012; *The Day of the Doctor*, 2013). UNIT themselves appear without the Brigadier in *The Android Invasion* (1975) and *The Seeds of Doom* (1976), as well as the New Series, briefly in *Aliens of London* (2005) and more notably in *The Christmas Invasion* (2005), *The Sontaran Stratagem/The Poison Sky* (2008) and *Planet of the Dead* (2009). Ben Aaronovitch also wrote the previous season's opening story *Remembrance of the Daleks* (1988) and was a possible candidate to take over from Andrew Cartmel as script editor had the series not been suspended. As well as playing Lethbridge-Stewart, Courtney is Bret Vyon in *The Daleks' Master Plan* (1965/66), in which Jean Marsh plays his sister Sara Kingdom, who briefly travels with the Doctor. She is also Princess Joanna in *The Crusade*. June Bland (Elizabeth Rowlinson) appears as Lieutenant Berger in *Earthshock* (1982), and Marek Anton (the Destroyer) can be seen in the flesh as Vershinin in *The Curse of Fenric* (1989).

WORTH WATCHING

When *Doctor Who* finally connects with the King Arthur legend, it does so tangentially. Rather than telling one of the familiar stories but revealing how the Doctor was really involved, whether as Merlin or not, it allows those tales to stand and instead uses alternative-dimension versions of the characters at a time after Arthur's death, lending an added poignancy to their situation. Nicholas Courtney is as distinguished as ever and the Brigadier gets to meet yet another incarnation of the Doctor (the fifth of seven at the time), while Jean Marsh was renowned for playing witch-queen roles in the 1980s. The Destroyer is also an impressive creation, showing how sophisticated the show's effects were becoming.

DISC ONE

THE EPISODES

On this disc are the four original broadcast episodes, recompiled and restored from digital duplicates of the earliest edits of the original one-inch colour videotape recordings. Their stereo soundtracks are remastered and the computer-generated title sequences replaced by a digital duplicate of the original one-inch colour videotape recording with credits remade to match the originals.

SPECIAL FEATURES

STORM OVER AVALLION (22m31s) The making of *Battlefield*, including the location recording, casting and costume design; choreographing the stunts and battles; creating the Destroyer; and the message of the story. With contributions from script editor Andrew Cartmel, writer Ben Aaronovitch, director Michael Kerrigan and actors Sophie Aldred, Angela Bruce, Nicholas Courtney, Marcus Gilbert, Jean Marsh and Sylvester McCoy. Produced by Steve Broster.

PAST AND FUTURE KING (12m2s) Ben Aaronovitch and Andrew Cartmel take a detailed look at the writing of *Battlefield*. With additional comments from Sophie Aldred, Angela Bruce, Nicholas Courtney, Michael Kerrigan and Sylvester McCoy.

WATERTANK (6m37s) Sophie Aldred, Andrew Cartmel, Michael Kerrigan and Sylvester McCoy recount a near-fatal accident with a watertank in the studio. With footage from the original videotape recording on Thursday 1 June 1989, which was retained by the BBC for use in safety training. Produced by Steve Broster.

STUDIO RECORDING (18m57s) Footage from the full studio recording on Thursday 1 June 1989 of scenes in the underwater spaceship and the brewery outhouse, including retakes and shots unused in the final programme.

FROM KINGDOM TO QUEEN (8m8s) Actor Jean Marsh talks about her three roles in *Doctor Who*, as Princess Joanna in *The Crusade* (1965), Sara Kingdom in *The Daleks' Master Plan* (1965/66) and Morgaine in *Battlefield*.

NEXT

TRAILS AND CONTINUITY (5m10s) Previews and continuity announcements from the original BBC1 broadcasts of all four episodes of *Battlefield*, with a plug for *Doctor Who* on video and an ad for the BBC's *Fast Forward* magazine; and from the repeat showings of episodes one and two on BBC2 in April 1993. Includes the BBC1 evening schedule for Wednesday 6 September 1989.

PHOTO GALLERY (7m1s) Slideshow of colour and black-and-white photos taken during production of *Battlefield*, set to music from the story. Compiled by Derek Handley.

AUDIO OPTIONS Select **Commentary** to play the audio commentary in place of the main sound-track when watching the episodes. With Sophie Aldred (Ace), Angela Bruce (Bambera), Nicholas Courtney (the Brigadier), script editor Andrew Cartmel and writer Ben Aaronovitch on all four episodes.

— Select **Isolated Music** to hear only Keff McCulloch's music when watching the episodes.

— Select **Feature Audio** to reinstate the main soundtrack when watching the episodes.

INFO TEXT Select **On** to view subtitles when watching the episodes that provide information and anecdotes about the development, production, broadcast and history of *Battlefield*. Written by Richard Molesworth.

PDF MATERIALS Accessible via a computer are the four episode listings from *Radio Times* for the original BBC1 broadcast of *Battlefield*, a half-page article that introduced the 1989 season's monsters, and a letter complaining about the lack of coverage for *Doctor Who* in the magazine.

SUBTITLES
Select **On** to view subtitles for all episodes and Special Features on disc one (except commentary).

DISC TWO

SPECIAL EDITION
On this disc is a new edit of the story as a single 95-minute episode, compiled and restored from digital duplicates of the earliest edits of the original one-inch colour videotape recordings, reinstating scenes originally cut for time. With updated computer-generated visual effects and optional Dolby Digital 5.1 surround sound.

SPECIAL FEATURES
SEASON 26 TRAILER (1m33s) Preview made for the press launch of the BBC Autumn Season on Wednesday 16 August 1989, featuring clips from all four stories in the 1989 season and with specially composed music by Keff McCulloch.

COMING SOON (1m12s) Trailer for the DVD releases of *Full Circle*, *State of Decay* and *Warriors' Gate* in The E-Space Trilogy boxset.

AUDIO OPTIONS
Select to play the Special Edition with either stereo or Dolby Digital 5.1 soundtrack.

SUBTITLES
Select **On** to view subtitles for the Special Edition and Special Features on disc two.

RELATED EXTRAS
The UNIT Family — Terror of the Zygons
Coming Soon trailer — The War Machines

THE **BEGINNING**

Boxset of **AN UNEARTHLY CHILD**, **THE DALEKS** and **THE EDGE OF DESTRUCTION**

DVD RELEASE BBCDVD1882, 30 January 2006, 12

SLIPCASE Photo illustration by Clayton Hickman, silvered logo and title, purple/black background

ORIGINAL RRP £29.99

WHAT'S IN THE BOX
As the name indicates, these are the first three serials of *Doctor Who*, broadcast from November 1963 to February 1964, along with the original unbroadcast recording of the very first episode and a shortened retelling of the fourth serial, *Marco Polo* — the only story from *Doctor Who*'s first year that is completely missing from the archives. These stories offer a fascinating look at the very early days of the programme, when no one was really quite sure what it would be or how it would be received, yet which contain many of the foundations for the show as we know it today.

● *See individual stories for full contents*

BENEATH THE SURFACE

Boxset of **DOCTOR WHO AND THE SILURIANS, THE SEA DEVILS** and
WARRIORS OF THE DEEP

DVD RELEASE BBCDVD2438, 14 January 2008, PG
SLIPCASE Photo illustration by Clayton Hickman, silvered logo and title,
turquoise/black background
ORIGINAL RRP £39.99

WHAT'S IN THE BOX

These are the three Classic Series stories featuring the Silurians and their aquatic cousins the Sea
Devils — intelligent reptile creatures that ruled the Earth long before mankind evolved, went into
hibernation to avoid a catastrophe but were never revived and continued to sleep while humans
developed into the dominant species on the planet. *Doctor Who and the Silurians* (1970) and *The
Sea Devils* (1972) feature the Third Doctor during his exile on Earth, while *Warriors of the Deep*
(1984) is set in the near future and features the Fifth Doctor. A new species of Silurian appears in
the New Series opposite the Eleventh Doctor.

● *See individual stories for full contents*

THE **BLACK GUARDIAN TRILOGY**

Boxset of **ENLIGHTENMENT, MAWDRYN UNDEAD** and **TERMINUS**

DVD RELEASE BBCDVD2596, 10 August 2009, PG
SLIPCASE Photo illustration by Clayton Hickman, silvered logo and title, green/black background
ORIGINAL RRP £39.14

WHAT'S IN THE BOX

Three consecutive stories from the twentieth season (1983) in which the Black Guardian — whom
the Fourth Doctor foiled at the end of the Key to Time saga (1978/79) — seeks revenge by tricking
an alien schoolboy, Turlough, into assassinating the Fifth Doctor. The plots of the three stories are
unconnected but chart Turlough's increasing anxiety until, at the end of *Enlightenment*, he is forced
to choose who he will follow.

● *See individual stories for full contents*

BLACK ORCHID

STORY No.120   SEASON No.19:5

*One disc with two episodes (49½ mins) and 53 minutes of extras, plus commentary track,
production subtitles and PDF items*

TARDIS TEAM Fifth Doctor, Adric, Nyssa, Tegan
TIME AND PLACE Cranleigh Hall, 1920s England
ADVERSARIES Disfigured man
FIRST ON TV 1–2 March 1982
DVD RELEASE BBCDVD2432, 14 April 2008, PG
COVER Photo illustration by Clayton Hickman, purple strip
ORIGINAL RRP £12.99

STORY TEASER

The TARDIS arrives at a country train station in 1925 where, through mistaken identity, the Doctor
finds himself indulging in a pleasant afternoon's cricket and a fancy dress ball at Cranleigh Hall.
Mischief is on hand when it's discovered Nyssa is the spitting image of Lord Cranleigh's fiancée Ann,
but the family harbours a dark secret that threatens both girls when a mysterious prisoner being
held in the attic breaks free.

CONNECTIONS

Apart from his outfit and some improbable ball skills in *Four to Doomsday* (1982), this features the only evidence of the Fifth Doctor's predilection for cricket. Still, it's the first time the TARDIS crew are seen relaxing and having fun since the Fourth Doctor and Romana's trip to Paris in *City of Death* (1979). *Black Orchid* is also notably the first story since the mid-60s set in the past with no alien activity other than the Doctor and company's presence. It's more like the latter historicals such as *The Smugglers* (1966) or *The Highlanders* (1966/67) in evoking a feel for the period rather than portraying known events as in *The Reign of Terror* (1964) or *The Romans* (1965), and strays into the territory of *The Time Meddler* (1965) when it uses the TARDIS as a way to prove the Doctor's honesty (somehow) and even gives some of the locals a short trip in it. Terence Dudley also wrote *Four to Doomsday* earlier in the season and *The King's Demons* (1983), as well as the spin-off *K9 and Company* (1981), while this was Ron Jones first job as a director and the first of six *Doctor Who* serials he directed (*see Index v*). Ivor Salter (Sergeant Markham) plays the Morok commander in *The Space Museum* (1965) and Odysseus in *The Myth Makers* (1965), while Michael Cochrane (Lord Cranleigh) returns as explorer Redvers Fenn-Cooper in *Ghost Light* (1989).

WORTH WATCHING

Black Orchid's claim as the only pure historical story since the 1960s is of little merit when it has less of a period feel than the preceding story, *The Visitation*, and treats a disfigured and piteous man as its *de facto* monster. While the narrative is slight, the serial does offer a delightful cast and a nice double role for the often under-used Sarah Sutton. And while Peter Davison isn't fond of it, the Fifth Doctor does fit surprisingly well into this story's milieu.

THE EPISODES

Both episodes are restored from digital duplicates of the original two-inch colour videotape recordings used for broadcast, with location sequences newly transferred from the original 16mm colour film negatives. Their mono soundtracks are remastered and the title sequences replaced by a modern transfer of the original 35mm film with credits remade to match the originals.

SPECIAL FEATURES

NOW AND THEN (9m3s) Comparing the filming locations at Quainton station in Buckinghamshire and the Buckhurst Estate in Withyam, East Sussex as they look today with how they appeared in early-October 1981 when used for *Black Orchid*. Narrated by IT Williams, produced by Richard Bignell. *See Index iii for further editions*

DELETED SCENES (7m4s) A selection of scenes not used in the final programme, taken from the full location film footage and a VHS copy of the studio recording with on-screen time-code. The sections in monochrome appear in the final episodes while those in colour are the unused scenes, to show where they would have fitted into the story.

FILM RESTORATION (2m41s) Demonstration of how the original location film negatives were newly scanned and restored for this release, with explanatory captions.

BLUE PETER (8m38s) Extract from the Thursday 10 December 1981 edition of the BBC1 children's magazine programme in which presenters Simon Groom and Sarah Greene visit theatrical costumier Bermans & Nathans. Includes a preview clip from *Black Orchid* for which the company had recently provided period outfits.

STRIPPED FOR ACTION – THE FIFTH DOCTOR (16m9s) *Doctor Who* comic strips have run in various publications since the early days of the television series. This examines the Fifth Doctor's comic strip adventures in Marvel Comics UK's *Doctor Who Monthly/Magazine*. With contributions from magazine editors Alan Barnes and Gary Russell, comics editor Alan McKenzie, and artist Dave Gibbons. Directed by Marcus Hearn. *See Index iii for further editions*

NEXT

AUDIO OPTIONS Select **Commentary** to play the audio commentary in place of the main soundtrack when watching the episodes. With Peter Davison, Janet Fielding (Tegan), Sarah Sutton (Nyssa) and Matthew Waterhouse (Adric) on both episodes.

— Select **Feature Audio** to reinstate the main soundtrack when watching the episodes.

INFO TEXT Select **On** to view subtitles when watching the episodes that provide information and anecdotes about the development, production, broadcast and history of *Black Orchid*. Written by Karen Davies.

POINTS OF VIEW (2m26s) Extract from the Friday 29 January 1982 edition of the BBC1 viewer feedback show hosted by Barry Took, featuring letters regarding *Doctor Who*'s switch from Saturdays to weekday evenings.

PHOTO GALLERY (4m40s) Slideshow of colour and black-and-white photos taken during production of *Black Orchid*, including design department photos of the sets. Set to 1920s music heard in the story and Roger Limb's incidental music. Compiled by Derek Handley.

COMING SOON (1m16s) Trailer for the DVD release of *The Trial of a Time Lord*.

RADIO TIMES LISTINGS Accessible via a computer is a PDF file of the two episode listings for the original BBC1 broadcast of *Black Orchid*.

SUBTITLES

Select **On** to view subtitles for all episodes and Special Features (except commentary).

EASTER EGG

There is one hidden feature on this disc to find. *See Appendix 2 for details*

THE **BRAIN OF MORBIUS**

STORY No.84   SEASON No.13:5

One disc with four episodes (100 mins) and 51½ minutes of extras, plus commentary track, production subtitles and PDF items

TARDIS TEAM Fourth Doctor, Sarah Jane

TIME AND PLACE Planet Karn

ADVERSARIES Surgeon Mehendri Solon; Time Lord criminal Morbius

FIRST ON TV 3–24 January 1976

DVD RELEASE BBCDVD1816, 21 July 2008, PG

COVER Photo illustration by Clayton Hickman, dark red strip

ORIGINAL RRP £19.99

STORY TEASER

On the storm-ravaged planet of Karn, the Doctor and Sarah discover the Time Lord criminal Morbius, believed to have been executed long ago, is not entirely dead. One of his followers, the crazed surgeon Mehendri Solon, was able to rescue his brain and has kept it alive while he creates a new body for his master. All he needs is a suitable head to house the megalomaniac's brain, and a passing Time Lord would be perfect.

CONNECTIONS

Doctor Who under producer Philip Hinchcliffe and script editor Robert Holmes is renowned for taking inspiration from classic horror literature and film, notably *Planet of Evil*, *Pyramids of Mars* (both 1975), *The Hand of Fear* and *The Deadly Assassin* (both 1976). But *The Brain of Morbius* is perhaps the most blatant example, being quite clearly a reworking of the Frankenstein story. To be fair to original writer Terrance Dicks, he at least tried to flip things by having the creature (a robot) build a perfect body, but Holmes reversed it to the standard mad surgeon stitching together parts of corpses, leading to Dicks taking his name off the serial. The Morpho creatures exist as disembodied brains in jars in *The Keys of Marinus* (1964) and Lady Cassandra's bottled brain is linked to a sheet of skin with a face in *The End of the World* (2005) and *New Earth* (2006), whereas the giant brain the Rani cultivates in *Time and the Rani* (1987) and the even bigger hive brain of the Ood (*Planet of the Ood*, 2008) seem to survive happily *au naturel*. The Sisterhood of Karn are seen again in *The Night of the Doctor*, the online prequel to the fiftieth anniversary special *The Day of the Doctor* (2013). *The Brain of Morbius* is the penultimate serial directed by Christopher Barry, whose association with the show goes back to the first Dalek story in 1963 (*see Index v*). Philip Madoc (Solon) also plays Eelek in *The Krotons* (1969), the War Lord in *The War Games* (1969) and Fenner in *The Power of Kroll* (1979), while Michael Spice (Morbius) is the titular villain in *The Talons of Weng-Chiang* (1977).

WORTH WATCHING

This is one of the most popular Fourth Doctor stories, a dark and in places violent tale based on the story of Frankenstein (more the Universal horror movie than the original novel). It features an impressive performance by Philip Madoc, providing a strong foil for Tom Baker, and Michael Spice's voice work for Morbius is chilling.

THE EPISODES

All four episodes are restored from digital duplicates of the original two-inch colour videotape recordings used for broadcast and their mono soundtracks remastered. The title sequences are replaced by a modern transfer of the original 35mm film with credits remade to match the originals.

SPECIAL FEATURES

GETTING A HEAD (32m6s) The making of *The Brain of Morbius*, including the origins of the story and how the script editor's rewrites upset the original author; selecting the cast; choreography for the Sisterhood; the make-up and set design; scoring the incidental music; interpretations of the mind-bending contest; and criticism of the growing horror in *Doctor Who* at the time. With contributions from producer Philip Hinchcliffe, writer Terrance Dicks, director Christopher Barry, designer Barry Newbery, composer Dudley Simpson, and actors Gillian Brown, Colin Fay, Cynthia Grenville and Philip Madoc. Narrated by Paul McGann, illustrations by Russell Owen, produced by Brendan Sheppard.

DESIGNS ON KARN (6m11s) Barry Newbery talks about his set designs for Solon's castle, the landscape of Karn and the Sisterhood's shrine, illustrated with his original design sketches.

SET TOUR (2m12s) Computer-generated recreation of the arrangement of sets in the studio based on the original design plans. Graphics by Rob Semenoff.

PHOTO GALLERY (4m36s) Slideshow of colour and black-and-white photos taken during production of *The Brain of Morbius*, including design department photos of the sets. Set to sound effects from the story. Compiled by Derek Handley.

SKETCH GALLERY (2m23s) Slideshow of Barry Newbery's design sketches, set to sound effects from the story, plus concept artwork of the original storyline produced for the making-of feature.

NEXT

AUDIO OPTIONS Select **Commentary** to play the audio commentary in place of the main soundtrack when watching the episodes. With Tom Baker, Elisabeth Sladen (Sarah), Philip Madoc (Solon), producer Philip Hinchcliffe and director Christopher Barry on all four episodes.

— Select **Feature Audio** to reinstate the main soundtrack when watching the episodes.

INFO TEXT Select **On** to view subtitles when watching the episodes that provide information and anecdotes about the development, production, broadcast and history of *The Brain of Morbius*. Written by Richard Molesworth.

RADIO TIMES LISTINGS Accessible via a computer is a PDF file of the four episode listings for the original BBC1 broadcast of *The Brain of Morbius*, and a letter about the characters' eating habits.

COMING SOON TRAILER (1m16s) For the DVD release of *The Trial of a Time Lord*.

SUBTITLES

Select **On** to view subtitles for all episodes and Special Features (except commentary).

EASTER EGGS

There are two hidden features on this disc to find. *See Appendix 2 for details*

RELATED EXTRAS

Coming Soon trailer — The Invisible Enemy, K9 and Company

BRED FOR WAR THE SONTARAN COLLECTION

Boxset of **THE INVASION OF TIME, THE SONTARAN EXPERIMENT, THE TIME WARRIOR** and **THE TWO DOCTORS**

DVD RELEASE BBCDVD2617, 5 May 2008, PG

SLIPCASE Photo illustration by Clayton Hickman, silvered logo and title, orange/black background

ORIGINAL RRP £39.99

WHAT'S IN THE BOX

This set collects all the Classic Series stories featuring the Sontarans, the potato-headed clone warriors that return in the New Series. Each story has the same contents and packaging as the individual releases held in a cardboard slipcase.

● See individual stories for full contents

CARNIVAL OF MONSTERS

STORY No.66 SEASON No.10:2

One disc with four episodes (98 mins) and 24 minutes of extras, plus commentary track and production subtitles

TARDIS TEAM Third Doctor, Jo

TIME AND PLACE Planet Inter Minor

ADVERSARIES Alien bureaucrats; Drashig swamp monsters

FIRST ON TV 27 January–17 February 1973

DVD RELEASE BBCDVD1098, 15 July 2002, U

COVER Photo illustration by Clayton Hickman, yellow strip

ORIGINAL RRP £19.99

— Also released in The Third Doctor Collection; BBCDVD2263, £49.99, 6 November 2006

STORY TEASER

The Doctor promises to take Jo to Metebelis 3, the famous blue planet, but the TARDIS brings them to a steamer, the SS Bernice, crossing the Indian Ocean in 1926. The Doctor recalls that the ship never reached its destination; could its disappearance be something to do with the repeated attacks by a prehistoric creature? Meanwhile two entertainers arrive on a bureaucratic alien world with their Miniscope, a peepshow of miniaturised creatures like the ferocious Drashigs — and a boatload of humans from 1920s Earth…

CONNECTIONS

This is the first time a story has used the idea of the Doctor not being where he thinks he is, perhaps because it's the first time he's actually aiming for somewhere specific following the return of his knowledge of flying the TARDIS, which seems to give back greater control than he ever had before his exile. The following season's Invasion of the Dinosaurs plays a similar trick on Sarah Jane, but only The Android Invasion (1975), Enlightenment (1983) and The God Complex (2011) stick with the same idea for any length of time. In Enlightenment the TARDIS again lands on a ship that's not on Earth, whereas at least in The Curse of the Black Spot (2011) the boat it arrives on is at sea. The Miniscope itself resembles the CET machine in Nightmare of Eden (1979), to which the Doctor also takes a dislike, and to the swamp monsters caught within it. This was Robert Holmes' fifth script for Doctor Who (see Index v) and so impressed producer Barry Letts that he chose to direct it himself, as he had done with Holmes' Terror of the Autons (1971). Letts recasts Michael Wisher (Kalik) and Andrew Staines (SS Bernice captain) from that story, the former going on to be the first actor to play Davros while the latter was a regular collaborator with Letts. Terence Lodge (Orum) also plays Medok in The Macra Terror (1967), while Peter Halliday (Pletrac) plays villain's henchman Packer in The Invasion (1968) and smaller roles in City of Death (1979) and Remembrance of the Daleks (1988). Ian Marter (Andrews) narrowly missed playing UNIT regular Captain Yates but was soon cast by Letts as Fourth Doctor companion Harry Sullivan, appearing throughout the 1975 season.

WORTH WATCHING

This is the Doctor's first flight in the TARDIS after the Time Lords restore his control in the previous story, The Three Doctors. Robert Holmes is by now beginning to flex his satirical muscles, seemingly poking a little fun at the programme itself, but showing his usual skill at creating engaging characters. Despite the writer's initial doubts about how they'd be realised, the Drashigs are an impressively scary creation, memorable as much for their terrifying scream as their appearance.

THE EPISODES

All four episodes are restored from digital duplicates of the original two-inch colour videotape recordings used for broadcast and their mono soundtracks remastered. The opening title sequences are replaced by a modern transfer of the original 35mm film with title captions overlaid from the episode recordings.

SPECIAL FEATURES *ALSO ON SPECIAL EDITION

*EXTENDED AND DELETED SCENES (3m53s) Three scenes from episode two cut or shortened in the final programme, taken from an earlier edit of the episode.

*DIRECTOR'S AMENDED ENDING (1m18s) For a repeat of this serial in November 1981, director Barry Letts requested the final scene be edited to remove a shot he was unhappy with.

*FIVE FACES OF DOCTOR WHO (4m10s) Trailer for the series of repeats on BBC2 in November 1981 that included *Carnival of Monsters*, along with *An Unearthly Child* (1963), *The Krotons* (1968/69), *The Three Doctors* (1972/73) and *Logopolis* (1981). Also on **The Three Doctors** (and Special Edition)

*DELAWARE OPENING TITLES (1m23s) The opening and closing title sequences from *Carnival of Monsters* with a new arrangement of the theme music produced by Delia Derbyshire and Paddy Kingsland of the BBC Radiophonic Workshop on the EMS Synthi 100 'Delaware' synthesiser. This was intended to be used from 1973 onwards but ultimately the existing theme was kept. Taken from an earlier edit of episode two onto which the new theme was dubbed before being dropped.

*VISUAL EFFECTS TEST FILM (4m22s) Silent 16mm colour film footage of the model work for *Carnival of Monsters*, including unused shots of the Drashig puppets and spaceship landing, set to matching sound effects from the story.

*PHOTO GALLERY (1m52s) Slideshow of colour and black-and-white photos from *Carnival of Monsters*, plus shots of the commentary participants and Frank Bellamy's illustrations for the *Radio Times* billings of this story. Set to sound effects from the story. Compiled by Ralph Montagu.

▶

INFORMATION TEXT Select **On** to view subtitles when watching the episodes that provide information and anecdotes about the development, production, broadcast and history of *Carnival of Monsters*. Written by Richard Molesworth.

*BEHIND THE SCENES (1m44s) Film footage shot during the studio recording of *Carnival of Monsters* episode four on Monday 3 and Tuesday 4 July 1972 for the documentary programme *Looking In* about the BBC's thirty years of broadcasting, shown on Tuesday 7 November 1972.

*TARDIS–CAM NO. 2 (46s) Short scene featuring the TARDIS, originally made for the BBCi *Doctor Who* website in 2001. The TARDIS flies through the space-time vortex (CGI).

*AUDIO OPTIONS Select **Commentary On** to play the audio commentary in place of the main soundtrack when watching the episodes. With Katy Manning (Jo) and producer/director Barry Letts on all four episodes.

*CSO DEMO (3m8s) Demonstration of the possibilities of using CSO (colour separation overlay, the precursor to green screen), from a BBC training film presented by Barry Letts in the early-70s.

SUBTITLES

Select **On** to view subtitles for all episodes and Special Features, or for the commentary.

EASTER EGGS

There are two hidden features on this disc to find. *See Appendix 2 for details*

RELATED EXTRAS

Dressing Doctor Who — The Mutants

CARNIVAL OF MONSTERS SPECIAL EDITION

STORY No.66   SEASON No.10:2

Released with **RESURRECTION OF THE DALEKS SPECIAL EDITION** and **THE SEEDS OF DEATH SPECIAL EDITION** in the **REVISITATIONS 2** boxset
Two discs with four episodes (98 mins) and 123½ minutes of extras, plus two commentary

tracks, production subtitles and PDF items
Audio navigation of each disc's contents available by pressing Enter after the BBC ident

TARDIS TEAM Third Doctor, Jo
TIME AND PLACE Planet Inter Minor
ADVERSARIES Alien bureaucrats; Drashig swamp monsters
FIRST ON TV 27 January–17 February 1973
DVD RELEASE BBCDVD2956B, 28 March 2011, PG (episodes and extras bar DVD trailer U)
COVER Photo illustration by Clayton Hickman, orange strip;
version with older BBC logo on reverse
ORIGINAL RRP £39.99 (boxset)

STORY TEASER

The Doctor promises to take Jo to Metebelis 3, the famous blue planet, but the TARDIS brings them to a steamer, the SS Bernice, crossing the Indian Ocean in 1926. The Doctor recalls that the ship never reached its destination; could its disappearance be something to do with the repeated attacks by a prehistoric creature? Meanwhile two entertainers arrive on a bureaucratic alien world with their Miniscope, a peepshow of miniaturised creatures like the ferocious Drashigs — and a boatload of humans from 1920s Earth…

CONNECTIONS

This is the first time a story has used the idea of the Doctor not being where he thinks he is, perhaps because it's the first time he's actually aiming for somewhere specific following the return of his knowledge of flying the TARDIS, which seems to give back greater control than he ever had before his exile. The following season's *Invasion of the Dinosaurs* plays a similar trick on Sarah Jane, but only *The Android Invasion* (1975), *Enlightenment* (1983) and *The God Complex* (2011) stick with the same idea for any length of time. In *Enlightenment* the TARDIS again lands on a ship that's not on Earth, whereas at least in *The Curse of the Black Spot* (2011) the boat it arrives on is at sea. The Miniscope itself resembles the CET machine in *Nightmare of Eden* (1979), to which the Doctor also takes a dislike, and to the swamp monsters caught within it. This was Robert Holmes' fifth script for *Doctor Who* (*see Index v*) and so impressed producer Barry Letts that he chose to direct it himself, as he had done with Holmes' *Terror of the Autons* (1971). Letts recasts Michael Wisher (Kalik) and Andrew Staines (SS Bernice captain) from that story, the former going on to be the first actor to play Davros while the latter was a regular collaborator with Letts. Terence Lodge (Orum) also plays Medok in *The Macra Terror* (1967), while Peter Halliday (Pletrac) plays villain's henchman Packer in *The Invasion* (1968) and smaller roles in *City of Death* (1979) and *Remembrance of the Daleks* (1988). Ian Marter (Andrews) narrowly missed playing UNIT regular Captain Yates but was soon cast by Letts as Fourth Doctor companion Harry Sullivan, appearing throughout the 1975 season.

WORTH WATCHING

This Special Edition features more advanced clean-up of the episodes compared to the previous release and additional Special Features. This is the Doctor's first flight in the TARDIS after the Time Lords restore his control in the previous story, *The Three Doctors*. Robert Holmes is by now beginning to flex his satirical muscles, seemingly poking a little fun at the programme itself, but showing his usual skill at creating engaging characters. Despite the writer's initial doubts about how they'd be realised, the Drashigs are an impressively scary creation, memorable as much for their terrifying scream as their appearance.

DISC ONE

THE EPISODES

All four episodes are newly restored from digital duplicates of the original two-inch colour videotape recordings used for broadcast and their mono soundtracks remastered using more advanced techniques than the previous release. The title sequences are replaced by a modern transfer of the original 35mm film with credits remade to match the originals.

SPECIAL FEATURES *REPEATED FROM PREVIOUS RELEASE

EPISODE TWO – EARLY EDIT (29m44s) The full-length initial edit of episode two featuring scenes cut from the final broadcast episode. Includes the countdown clock for the studio recording and the ultimately unused 'Delaware' version of the theme music (these were presented separately on the previous release).

*BEHIND THE SCENES (1m44s) Film footage shot during the studio recording of *Carnival of Monsters* episode four on Monday 3 and Tuesday 4 July 1972 for the documentary programme *Looking In* about the BBC's thirty years of broadcasting, shown on Tuesday 7 November 1972.

VISUAL EFFECTS MODELS (8m42s) Silent 16mm colour film footage of the model work for *Carnival of Monsters*, including unused shots of the Drashig puppets and spaceship landing, set to matching sound effects from the story. Extended from the previous release.

*'FIVE FACES OF DOCTOR WHO' TRAILER (4m10s) Trailer for the series of repeats on BBC2 in November 1981 that included *Carnival of Monsters*, along with *An Unearthly Child* (1963), *The Krotons* (1968/69), *The Three Doctors* (1972/73) and *Logopolis* (1981). *Also on* The Three Doctors *(and* Special Edition*)*

*DIRECTOR'S AMENDED ENDING (1m19s) For a repeat of this serial in November 1981, director Barry Letts requested the final scene be edited to remove a shot he was unhappy with.

NEXT

*CSO DEMO (3m8s) Demonstration of the possibilities of using CSO (colour separation overlay, the precursor to green screen), from a BBC training film presented by Barry Letts in the early-70s.

*TARDIS CAM NO.2 (46s) Short scene featuring the TARDIS, originally made for the BBCi *Doctor Who* website in 2001. The TARDIS flies through the space-time vortex (CGI).

AUDIO OPTIONS Select ***Commentary 1** to play the audio commentary recorded for the previous release in place of the main soundtrack when watching the episodes. With Katy Manning (Jo) and producer/director Barry Letts on all four episodes.

— Select **Commentary 2** to play the audio commentary recorded for this release when watching the episodes. This is moderated by actor and comedian Toby Hadoke, talking with Peter Halliday (Pletrac) [eps 1,2], Cheryl Hall (Shirna) [1,2,4], Jenny McCracken (Claire Daly) [1,3,4], special sounds creator Brian Hodgson [2,3] and script editor Terrance Dicks [3,4].

— Select **Feature Audio** to reinstate the main soundtrack when watching the episodes.

INFO TEXT Select **On** to view subtitles when watching the episodes that provide information and anecdotes about the development, production, broadcast and history of *Carnival of Monsters*, updated and expanded from the previous release. Written Richard Bignell.

PDF MATERIALS Accessible via a computer are the four episode listings from *Radio Times* for the original BBC1 broadcast of *Carnival of Monsters*, with illustrations by Frank Bellamy.

COMING SOON (1m35s) Trailer for the DVD release of *Planet of the Spiders*.

SUBTITLES

Select **On** to view subtitles for all episodes and Special Features on disc one (except commentaries).

DISC TWO

SPECIAL FEATURES

DESTROY ALL MONSTERS! (23m12s) The making of *Carnival of Monsters*, including the development of the script; location shooting on a ship (with one light-fingered member of the cast) and in an Essex marsh; the creation of the Drashigs; casting and clothing Vorg and Shirna; the look of the Inter Minorians; and the decision to change the theme music. With contributions from producer and director Barry Letts (interviewed in 2008), script editor Terrance Dicks, assistant floor manager Karilyn Collier, visual effects assistant Colin Mapson, and actors Cheryl Hall, Peter Halliday and Katy Manning. Narrated by Marc Silk, produced by Chris Chapman.

ON TARGET WITH IAN MARTER (16m9s) The Target range of *Doctor Who* novelisations was for years the only way to experience past stories, and its regular authors were very influential on their child readers. This examines the books and career of Ian Marter, who also played Fourth Doctor companion Harry Sullivan on television. With contributions from fellow author Terrance Dicks, writer Gary Russell, and actors Tom Baker, Nicholas Courtney and Elisabeth Sladen. Narrated by Jonathan Rigby, readings by Nigel Plaskitt, directed by Marcus Hearn.

THE A–Z OF GADGETS AND GIZMOS (11m22s) A light-hearted rundown of the most notable technical devices seen in Classic *Doctor Who*, including K9, the chameleon circuit, the randomiser and, of course, the sonic screwdriver. Narrated by Paul Jones, produced by Brendan Sheppard.

MARY CELESTE (18m2s) Discussion of real-life shipping mysteries by academic Roger Lockhurst and maritime historians Ian Murphy and John McAleer. They consider the disappearances of the SS Poet in 1980, the SS Marine Sulphur Queen in 1963, the USS Cyclops in 1918 and, most famously, the mystery of the Mary Celeste in 1872 — as 'explained' in *The Chase* (1965). Produced by Stella Broster.

PHOTO GALLERY (2m55s) Slideshow of colour and black-and-white photos taken during production of *Carnival of Monsters*, plus shots of the commentary participants and Frank Bellamy's illustrations for the *Radio Times* billings. Set to music and sound effects from the story. Re-edited and expanded from the previous release by Paul Shields.

SUBTITLES Select **On** to view subtitles for all Special Features on disc two.

EASTER EGG
There is one hidden feature on these discs to find. *See Appendix 2 for details*

RELATED EXTRAS
Coming Soon trailer — Kinda, Snakedance
Dressing Doctor Who — The Mutants

CASTROVALVA
STORY No.116   SEASON No.19:1

Released with **THE KEEPER OF TRAKEN** and **LOGOPOLIS** in the **NEW BEGINNINGS** boxset
One disc with four episodes (96½ mins) and 82½ minutes of extras, plus commentary and music-only tracks, production subtitles and PDF items

TARDIS TEAM Fifth Doctor, Adric, Nyssa, Tegan
TIME AND PLACE Inside the TARDIS, city of Castrovalva on unknown planet
ADVERSARIES Third Master (2nd appearance)
FIRST ON TV 4–12 January 1982
DVD RELEASE BBCDVD1331(C), 29 January 2007, U (boxset 12)
COVER Photo illustration by Clayton Hickman, light pink strip
ORIGINAL RRP £29.99 (boxset)

STORY TEASER
The newly regenerated Doctor is very weak but the Master is still hounding him. The evil Time Lord kidnaps Adric and sets the Doctor's TARDIS on a course to destruction. But there is one place in the universe where the Doctor can recover, if he can get there.

CONNECTIONS
This follows directly on from the previous season's finale *Logopolis* (1981), and was the first ever episode of *Doctor Who* to begin with a pre-titles sequence — standard practice in modern *Doctor Who*. We see more of the inside of the TARDIS, mainly corridors but also a changing room and, notably, the zero room (look out for the same set, painted black, being used as the Master's TARDIS). The idea of deleting rooms was introduced in *Logopolis*, when the Doctor deletes Romana's bedroom to escape a gravity bubble. It's not clear here if Event One is the creation of our galaxy or the universe itself, although it's suggested to be the latter in *Terminus* (1983), in which the cause of the Big Bang is revealed. The TARDIS finds itself on a similarly dangerous reverse-time trip in *The Edge of Destruction* (1964). The recursive occlusion that engulfs Castrovalva is not dissimilar to the way people seem to end up going in circles in the TARDIS's own corridors, notably in *Journey to the Centre of the TARDIS* (2013). Christopher Bidmead stepped in late in the day to write *Castrovalva* as the Fifth Doctor's debut, having scripted the Fourth Doctor's swan song *Logopolis*; his last contribution to the series was *Frontios* in 1984. This was director Fiona Cumming's first of four Fifth Doctor serials, followed by *Snakedance* (1983), *Enlightenment* (1983) and *Planet of Fire* (1984). Michael Sheard (Shardovan) plays several roles throughout Classic *Doctor Who*, from Rhos in *The Ark* (1966) to the headmaster of Coal Hill School in *Remembrance of the Daleks* (1988) but is most

fêted for his part as Laurence Scarman in *Pyramids of Mars* (1975). Dallas Cavell (Pharos security chief) had an even longer history with the series, appearing as the roadworks overseer whom the Doctor clobbers in the first season's *The Reign of Terror* (1964), as well as Bors in *The Daleks' Master Plan* (1965/66), Sir James Quinlan in *The Ambassadors of Death* (1970) and, most significantly, the villainous slave-trader Captain Trask in *The Highlanders* (1966/67).

WORTH WATCHING

The title is taken from a drawing by MC Escher, the Dutch artist best known for his optical illusion pictures, which themselves were inspiration for the concept of recursive occlusion in the way a space seems to circle round on itself. The video effects technology of the early-80s can't quite pull off such a visual (just squint and imagine a convoluted CGI landscape) but it's one moment in a story with lots of charm. This is also the only story of the season to really take note of *Doctor Who*'s new transmission schedule of two episodes per week, with the first half set mainly in the TARDIS and the second half in Castrovalva itself.

THE EPISODES

All four episodes are restored from digital duplicates of the original two-inch colour videotape recordings used for broadcast, with location sequences newly transferred from the original 16mm colour film negatives. This has required shots that mix film and video elements to be recomposited and some video effects recreated. The episodes' mono soundtracks are remastered and the title sequences replaced by a modern transfer of the original 35mm film with credits remade to match the originals.

SPECIAL FEATURES

SWAP SHOP – PETER DAVISON (20m42s) Extract from the 9 January 1982 edition of the BBC1 Saturday morning children's show in which Noel Edmonds interviews Peter Davison about taking on the role of the Doctor and they take viewers' questions on the phone.

BLUE PETER – PETER DAVISON (9m16s) Extract from the Monday 10 November 1980 edition of the BBC1 children's magazine programme in which Simon Groom and Sarah Greene look at past highlights of *Doctor Who* (using largely the same script written for its marking of the series' tenth anniversary, included on The Tenth Planet and The Three Doctors) and Greene interviews Peter Davison shortly after the announcement of his casting as the new Doctor. With Peter Duncan.

DIRECTING CASTROVALVA (11m19s) Director Fiona Cumming talks about her experiences of her first *Doctor Who* story, including working with the regular cast, filming on location, keeping the limited TARDIS set looking like new areas, and presenting the distorted Castrovalva.

BEING DOCTOR WHO (13m31s) Peter Davison recalls his thoughts at taking on the part of the Doctor, including his performance and costume (and his ironic distaste for celery), as well as his reasons for leaving after three years.

THE CROWDED TARDIS (11m26s) The end of the 1980/81 season introduced three new companions for the Doctor, rather than the one or two he usually travelled with. Discussing the pros and cons are script editor Christopher H Bidmead, director John Black, and actors Tom Baker, Peter Davison and Sarah Sutton. Narrated by George Williams, produced by Steve Broster and Paul Vanezis.

DELETED SCENES (1m36s) Two scenes not used in the final programme, taken from the location film.

NEXT

CONTINUITIES AND TRAILERS (5m29s) Previews and continuity announcements from the original BBC1 broadcasts of all four episodes of *Castrovalva*, with a plug for the *Doctor Who* display at Madame Tussauds. Includes the BBC1 evening schedules for Monday 4, Tuesday 5, Monday 11 and Tuesday 12 January 1982.

THEME MUSIC VIDEO (3m34s) The full version of Peter Howell's rearrangement of the *Doctor Who* theme remastered in stereo from the original recording, set to footage from the title sequences designed by Sid Sutton for the Fourth and Fifth Doctors. *Also included on* Four to Doomsday *with an option to listen in Dolby Digital 5.1*

PHOTO GALLERY (5m19s) Slideshow of colour and black-and-white photos taken during production of *Castrovalva*, including design department photos of the sets. Set to music from the story. Compiled by Ralph Montagu.

RADIO TIMES LISTINGS Accessible via a computer is a PDF file of the four episode listings for the original BBC1 broadcast of *Castrovalva*, an article that introduced the 1982 season, and readers' letters about the new Doctor and the move from a Saturday timeslot (published the week of episodes one and two of *Kinda*).

DOCTOR WHO ANNUAL Accessible via a computer is a PDF file of the 1982 *Doctor Who Annual*, published by World Distributors the autumn before *Castrovalva* was broadcast. With stories featuring the Doctor, Adric and K9, plus science features and puzzles.

— Also on the disc but not listed in the menus is a PDF file of BBC Enterprises' sales document for the 1982 season, describing its seven stories for potential overseas broadcasters.

INFO TEXT Select **On** to view subtitles when watching the episodes that provide information and anecdotes about the development, production, broadcast and history of *Castrovalva*. Written by Martin Wiggins.

AUDIO OPTIONS

Select **Commentary** to play the audio commentary in place of the main soundtrack when watching the episodes. With Peter Davison, Janet Fielding (Tegan), writer Christopher H Bidmead and director Fiona Cumming on all four episodes.

— Select **Isolated Music** to hear only Paddy Kingsland's music when watching the episodes.

— Select **Feature Audio** to reinstate the main soundtrack when watching the episodes.

SUBTITLES

Select **On** to view subtitles for all episodes and Special Features (except commentary).

EASTER EGG

There is one hidden feature on this disc to find. *See Appendix 2 for details*

THE **CAVES OF ANDROZANI**

STORY No.135   SEASON No.21:6

One disc with four episodes (100 mins) and 21 minutes of extras, plus commentary and music-only tracks, production subtitles and image content

TARDIS TEAM Fifth Doctor, Peri
TIME AND PLACE Twin planets Androzani Major and Androzani Minor
ADVERSARIES Businessman Morgus; fugitive Sharaz Jek; gunrunner Stotz
FIRST ON TV 8–16 March 1984
DVD RELEASE BBCDVD1042, 18 June 2001, PG
COVER Photo montage, red strip
ORIGINAL RRP £19.99

STORY TEASER

The TARDIS arrives on Androzani Minor but it's not a healthy place to be. In a network of caves the army is seeking the hideout of Sharaz Jek, who controls the only source of spectrox, a powerful drug that the rulers of sister planet Androzani Major are desperate to regain access to. Accidentally infected by raw spectrox, all the Doctor is interested in is finding a cure for himself and Peri, but the various fighting forces won't believe the pair don't have more cunning motives and are prepared to kill them to find out.

CONNECTIONS

This was Robert Holmes' first *Doctor Who* script in five years, having written regularly for the series throughout the 1970s (*see Index v*), so perhaps not surprisingly it reworks a few ideas from his past stories. The ruthless company man paying a gunrunner to supply his enemies in order to justify military action against them is taken from *The Power of Kroll* (1979); a deformed scientist hiding in tunnels also features in *The Talons of Weng-Chiang* (1977); and a president is murdered so that his killer might gain greater power, as in *The Deadly Assassin* (1976). But these are just concepts that Holmes blends skilfully into a new and wonderfully self-contained situation that is only disrupted (fatally for all) by the chance arrival of the Doctor. Morgus fits into a line of corrupt businessmen, including Salamander and Giles Kent in *The Enemy of the World* (1967/68), Tobias Vaughan in *The Invasion* (1968), Jocelyn Stevens in *The Green Death* (1973), Henry Van Statten in *Dalek* (2005), John Lumic in *Rise of the Cybermen/The Age of Steel* (2006) and Klineman Halpen in *Planet of the Ood* (2008). Graeme Harper makes his directorial debut on *Doctor Who* here, having worked as a production assistant on earlier serials, and clearly stands apart from those around him. He returned the following year to direct *Revelation of the Daleks* with equal panache and is the only Classic Series director to work on the New Series too, reintroducing the Cybermen and helming several more Dalek stories. Of the main cast, only John Normington returns, in the rather less juicy role of Trevor Sigma in *The Happiness Patrol* (1988).

WORTH WATCHING

This is the final Fifth Doctor story and the feeling throughout of danger and impending disaster is palpable. Even Peri almost dies and it's only her second adventure! *The Caves of Androzani* is considered by many to be the finest of Peter Davison's adventures — even the best of all Classic *Doctor Who* — with a strong script and powerful direction.

THE EPISODES

All four episodes are restored from digital duplicates of the original one-inch colour videotape recordings used for broadcast, with most location sequences newly transferred from the original 16mm colour film and matte shots stabilised.

SPECIAL FEATURES *ALSO ON SPECIAL EDITION

*BEHIND THE SCENES: THE REGENERATION (7m38s) Unbroadcast footage from the end of episode four featuring the shooting of the regeneration and Colin Baker's first performance as the Doctor, recorded on Thursday 12 January 1984. When the audio commentary for the episodes is selected, the three participants can be heard discussing this footage also.

*ORIGINAL OPENING SCENE For this DVD release, director Graeme Harper requested that a section in episode one where a painted landscape had been added to a location shot be corrected so that the two elements didn't wobble as they had done originally. Press ▶ on the first caption page, then select **Play Episode** to view episode one with the original unstable effect as broadcast.

*EXTENDED SCENE (2m29s) Longer version of a scene from episode two, taken from the original 16mm colour film location footage. When the audio commentary for the episodes is selected, Peter Davison and Graeme Harper can be heard discussing this footage also.

*CREATING SHARAZ JEK (5m5s) An audio interview with Christopher Gable about his performance as Sharaz Jek, illustrated with clips from the story and behind-the-scenes footage.

*BBC1 TRAILER (33s) Preview of episode one broadcast on BBC1 on Wednesday 7 March 1984.

*AUDIO OPTIONS Select **Commentary On** to play the audio commentary in place of the main sound-track when watching the episodes and some Special Features (see above). With Peter Davison, Nicola Bryant (Peri) and director Graeme Harper on all four episodes.

— Select **Isolated Music On** to hear only Roger Limb's music when watching the episodes.

▶

*BBC ONE O'CLOCK NEWS 28/07/1983 (24s) Report from the BBC1 lunchtime news bulletin announcing Peter Davison's decision to quit the role of the Doctor.

*BBC NINE O'CLOCK NEWS 28/07/1983 (1m23s) Report from the main BBC1 evening news covering Peter Davison's resignation as the Doctor, with Michael Buerke introducing a report by Kate Adie in which she talks to Davison.

*SOUTH EAST AT SIX 29/07/1983 (3m37s) Extract from the BBC1 regional news programme in which Fran Morrison and Sue Cook interview Peter Davison and producer John Nathan-Turner.

INFORMATION TEXT Select **On** to view subtitles when watching the episodes that provide infor-mation and anecdotes about the development, production, broadcast and history of *The Caves of Androzani*. Written by Richard Molesworth.

PHOTO GALLERY Scroll through 56 colour photos taken during production of *The Caves of Androzani*. Compiled by Ralph Montagu.

SUBTITLES

Select **On** to view subtitles for all episodes and Special Features, or for the commentary.

THE **CAVES OF ANDROZANI** SPECIAL EDITION

STORY No.135   SEASON No.21:6

Released with **THE MOVIE SPECIAL EDITION** and **THE TALONS OF WENG-CHIANG SPECIAL EDITION** in the **REVISITATIONS 1** boxset
Two discs with four episodes (100 mins) and 89½ minutes of extras, plus commentary and music-only tracks, production subtitles and PDF items
Audio navigation of each disc's contents available by pressing Enter after the BBC ident

TARDIS TEAM Fifth Doctor, Peri
TIME AND PLACE Twin planets Androzani Major and Androzani Minor
ADVERSARIES Businessman Morgus; fugitive Sharaz Jek; gunrunner Stotz
FIRST ON TV 8–16 March 1984
DVD RELEASE BBCDVD2806(B), 4 October 2010, PG (boxset 12)
COVER Photo illustration by Clayton Hickman, purple strip; version with older BBC logo on reverse
ORIGINAL RRP £39.99 (boxset)
— Episodes released in the **Regeneration** box; BBCDVD3801, £61.27, 24 June 2013

STORY TEASER

The TARDIS arrives on Androzani Minor but it's not a healthy place to be. In a network of caves the army is seeking the hideout of Sharaz Jek, who controls the only source of spectrox, a powerful drug that the rulers of sister planet Androzani Major are desperate to regain access to. Accidentally infected by raw spectrox, all the Doctor is interested in is finding a cure for himself and Peri, but the various fighting forces won't believe the pair don't have more cunning motives and are prepared to kill them to find out.

CONNECTIONS

This was Robert Holmes' first *Doctor Who* script in five years, having written regularly for the series throughout the 1970s (*see Index v*), so perhaps not surprisingly it reworks a few ideas from his past stories. The ruthless company man paying a gunrunner to supply his enemies in order to justify military action against them is taken from *The Power of Kroll* (1979); a deformed scientist hiding in tunnels also features in *The Talons of Weng-Chiang* (1977); and a president is murdered so that his killer might gain greater power, as in *The Deadly Assassin* (1976). But these are just concepts that Holmes blends skilfully into a new and wonderfully self-contained situation that is only disrupted (fatally for all) by the chance arrival of the Doctor. Morgus fits into a line of corrupt businessmen, including Salamander and Giles Kent in *The Enemy of the World* (1967/68), Tobias Vaughan in *The Invasion* (1968), Jocelyn Stevens in *The Green Death* (1973), Henry Van Statten in *Dalek* (2005), John Lumic in *Rise of the Cybermen/The Age of Steel* (2006) and Klineman Halpen in *Planet of the Ood* (2008). Graeme Harper makes his directorial debut on *Doctor Who* here, having worked as a production assistant on earlier serials, and clearly stands apart from those around him. He returned the following year to direct *Revelation of the Daleks* with equal panache and is the only Classic Series director to work on the New Series too, reintroducing the Cybermen and helming several more Dalek stories. Of the main cast, only John Normington returns, in the rather less juicy role of Trevor Sigma in *The Happiness Patrol* (1988).

WORTH WATCHING

This Special Edition features more advanced clean-up of the episodes compared to the previous release and additional Special Features. This is the final Fifth Doctor story and the feeling throughout of danger and impending disaster is palpable. Even Peri almost dies and it's only her second adventure! *The Caves of Androzani* is considered by many to be the finest of Peter Davison's adventures — even the best of all Classic *Doctor Who* — with a strong script and powerful direction.

DISC ONE

THE EPISODES

All four episodes are newly restored from digital duplicates of the original one-inch colour videotape recordings used for broadcast, with location sequences transferred from the original 16mm colour film and matte shots stabilised. Their mono soundtracks are remastered using more advanced techniques than the previous release, and title sequences replaced by a modern transfer of the original 35mm film with credits remade to match the originals.

SPECIAL FEATURES *REPEATED FROM PREVIOUS RELEASE

*BEHIND THE SCENES THE REGENERATION (7m54s) Unbroadcast footage from the end of episode four featuring the shooting of the regeneration and Colin Baker's first performance as the Doctor, recorded on Thursday 12 January 1984. Select either **Studio Sound** to view with the original as-recorded sound or **Commentary** to hear an audio commentary by Graeme Harper, Peter Davison and Nicola Bryant.

*BEHIND THE SCENES CREATING SHARAZ JEK (5m5s) An audio interview with Christopher Gable about his performance as Sharaz Jek, illustrated with clips from the story and behind-the-scenes footage.

EXTENDED SCENES (4m12s) Three longer versions of scenes from episode two, taken from the full location film footage and a copy of the studio recording with on-screen time-code. Select either **Studio Sound** to view with the original as-recorded sound or **Commentary** to hear an audio commentary by Graeme Harper and Peter Davison on the first scene.

*TRAILER (33s) Preview of episode one broadcast on BBC1 on Wednesday 7 March 1984.
NEXT

*NEWS (5m23s) Three BBC1 news reports on Peter Davison's decision to quit the role of the Doctor. From the *One O'Clock News* on Thursday 28 July 1983; the *Nine O'Clock News* the same day, with Michael Buerke introducing a report by Kate Adie in which she talks to Davison; and regional programme *South East at Six* the following evening, in which Fran Morrison and Sue Cook interview Peter Davison and producer John Nathan-Turner.

*AUDIO OPTIONS Select **Commentary** to play the audio commentary recorded for the previous release in place of the main soundtrack when watching the episodes. With Peter Davison, Nicola Bryant (Peri) and director Graeme Harper on all four episodes.
— Select **Isolated Score** to hear only Roger Limb's music when watching the episodes.
— Select **Feature Audio** to reinstate the main soundtrack when watching the episodes.

INFO TEXT Select **On** to view subtitles when watching the episodes that provide information and anecdotes about the development, production, broadcast and history of *The Caves of Androzani*, updated and expanded from the previous release. Written by Paul Scoones.

PDF MATERIALS Accessible via a computer are the four episode listings from *Radio Times* for the original BBC1 broadcast of *The Caves of Androzani*.

COMING SOON (51s) Trailer for the DVD release of *The Seeds of Doom*.

SUBTITLES
Select **On** to view subtitles for all episodes and Special Features on disc one, including the **Extended Scenes** and **Regeneration** commentaries, but not the episodes commentary.

DISC TWO

SPECIAL FEATURES

CHAIN REACTION (36m5s) Writer and broadcaster Matthew Sweet looks at the making of *The Caves of Androzani* to gauge whether it really is the best *Doctor Who* story ever, as many claim. He examines the return of popular writer Robert Holmes to the show after five years; the challenges facing a novice director; the characters and cast; filming on location; and recording and scoring the regeneration. With contributions from script editor Eric Saward, director Graeme Harper, designer John Hurst, composer Roger Limb, and actors Nicola Bryant, Martin Cochrane, Peter Davison, Robert Glenister and Maurice Roëves. Produced by Paul Vanezis.

DIRECTING WHO: THEN & NOW (11m46s) Graeme Harper talks about the differences in the styles and techniques of directing television between the 1980s and the 2000s, illustrated with behind-the-scenes footage from *The Caves of Androzani*, *Revelation of the Daleks* (1985), *Doomsday* (2006) and *Journey's End* (2008).

RUSSELL HARTY (8m38s) Extract from the Tuesday 20 March 1984 edition of the BBC1 early-evening chat show *Harty* in which the titular host interviews Peter Davison and Colin Baker, and talks to some costumed fans in the audience.

PHOTO GALLERY (4m58s) Slideshow of colour photos taken during production of *The Caves of Androzani*, including design department photos of the sets, plus black-and-white shots of Anthony Ainley as the Master. Set to music from the story. Compiled by Paul Shields.

SUBTITLES Select **On** to view subtitles for all Special Features on disc two.

EASTER EGG

There is one hidden feature on these discs to find. *See Appendix 2 for details*

RELATED EXTRAS

Coming Soon trailer — Time and the Rani

THE **CELESTIAL TOYMAKER**

STORY No.24   SEASON No.3:7

*One surviving episode (part 4 of 4) released in the **LOST IN TIME** set*

TARDIS TEAM First Doctor, Dodo, Steven

TIME AND PLACE Toymaker's domain

ADVERSARIES The Toymaker

FIRST ON TV 23 April 1966

DVD RELEASE BBCDVD1353, 1 November 2004, PG

● *See* Lost in Time *for full details*

THE **CHASE**

STORY No.16   SEASON No.2:8

Released in a boxset with **THE SPACE MUSEUM**
Two discs with six episodes (148½ mins) and 132 minutes of extras, plus commentary track, production subtitles and PDF items
Audio navigation of each disc's contents available by pressing Enter after the BBC ident

TARDIS TEAM First Doctor, Barbara, Ian, Vicki, and introducing Steven Taylor

TIME AND PLACE Planet Aridius, then pursued through various Earth locations to planet Mechanus

ADVERSARIES Daleks (3rd appearance); octopoid Mire Beasts; Mechonoid robots

FIRST ON TV 22 May–26 June 1965

DVD RELEASE BBCDVD2809(B), 1 March 2010, PG (disc two U)

COVER Photo illustration by Clayton Hickman, light purple strip;
         version with older BBC logo on reverse

ORIGINAL RRP £29.99 (boxset)

STORY TEASER

The Daleks have built their own time machine and set out to exterminate the Doctor once and for all, tracking him to the desert planet Aridius, where the oceans have dried up leaving the bottom-dwelling Mire Beasts to feed on the few surviving Aridians. Narrowly escaping in the TARDIS, the crew go on the run but find that with each subsequent landing the Daleks are getting closer and a confrontation in inevitable.

CONNECTIONS

The Daleks are a hit, you've brought them back as the conquerors of our own world (*The Dalek Invasion of Earth*, 1964), what next? For their third appearance creator Terry Nation decided the next step up was to give the Daleks the same capabilities as the Doctor and have them chase him through time. This is the first time a story has been focused on the Doctor himself, rather than the places he visits, something that happened rarely before the New Series. Although Nation more or less repeats the strategy in his next serial, *The Daleks' Master Plan* (1965/66), as a way to extend it to the desired twelve episodes. The Daleks arrive at the top of the Empire State Building presumably unaware that they actually helped to build it (*Daleks in Manhattan/Evolution of the Daleks*, 2007).

Peter Purves becomes the first companion cast because he impressed in an earlier role, and uniquely in the same serial, here playing Morton Dill in episode three then returning as Steven Taylor three weeks later (hey, the kids won't remember, and besides, he has a beard now). Subsequently Ian Marter was cast as Harry Sullivan in the 1975 season having played Andrews in *Carnival of Monsters* (1973); Lalla Ward was cast as the second incarnation of Romana having played Astra in *The Armageddon Factor* (1979); Freema Agyeman was cast as Martha Jones in the 2007 series having played, it was later revealed, her cousin in *Army of Ghosts* (2006); and Karen Gillan was cast as Amy Pond having played one of the Sibylline Sisterhood in *The Fires of Pompeii* (2008). Director Richard Martin had become the go-to man for Dalek serials, having directed them in episodes of their debut *The Daleks* (1963/64) and *The Dalek Invasion of Earth*, as well as handling *The Web Planet* (1965), although this was his last work on *Doctor Who*. Ian Thompson, playing Aridian Malsan, is Hetra in *The Web Planet*, while Arne Gordon (Empire State guide) and Roslyn de Winter (Grey Lady) are fellow Menoptra Hrostar and Vrestin respectively. The officers of the Mary Celeste don't disappear after all, David Blake Kelly (Captain Briggs) returning as innkeeper Kewper in *The Smugglers* (1966) and Dennis Chinnery (First Mate Richardson) playing Gharman in *Genesis of the Daleks* (1975) and Professor Sylvest in *The Twin Dilemma* (1984). Edmund Warwick, not entirely convincing as the robot Doctor duplicate, is also Darrius in *The Keys of Marinus*, while glimpsed on the Time and Space Visualiser are Hugh Walters as William Shakespeare and Roger Hammond as Roger Bacon: the former plays Runcible in *The Deadly Assassin* (1976) and Vogel in *Revelation of the Daleks* (1985), while the latter is Dr Runciman in *Mawdryn Undead* (1983).

WORTH WATCHING

This was the second time the Daleks returned to *Doctor Who*, by now at the height of their popularity, although there are hints in this story that writer Terry Nation was getting a little tired of only being associated with his creations as he sends them up at times. However, this is an ambitious production and a suitably epic story for original companions Barbara and Ian to leave in.

DISC ONE

THE EPISODES

All six episodes are restored from 16mm film copies of the original black-and-white video recordings, recovered from BBC Enterprises in 1978. Their mono soundtracks are remastered and the VidFIRE process is applied to studio-recorded shots to recapture the smoother motion of video. The title sequences are replaced by a modern transfer of the best surviving copy of the original 35mm film with end credits remade to match the originals.

SPECIAL FEATURES

CUSICK IN CARDIFF (12m45s) Raymond Cusick, one of the first set designers on *Doctor Who* and the man who created the look of the Daleks, is given a tour of the New Series prop store and art department by production designer Edward Thomas and concept designer Peter McKinstry, and visits the Ninth/Tenth Doctor TARDIS set. Cusick discusses his original ideas for the Daleks and how television production design has changed since the 1960s. Directed by Paul Giddings.

AUDIO OPTIONS Select **Commentary** to play the audio commentary in place of the main soundtrack when watching the episodes. This is moderated by Peter Purves — who appears in episodes three and six — talking with Maureen O'Brien (Vicki) [eps 1,2,4,5,6], William Russell (Ian) [1,2,5,6] and director Richard Martin [1,3,4,5,6].
— Select **Feature Audio** to reinstate the main soundtrack when watching the episodes.

INFO TEXT Select **On** to view subtitles when watching the episodes that provide information and anecdotes about the development, production, broadcast and history of *The Chase*. Written by Richard Bignell.

PDF MATERIALS Accessible via a computer are the six episode listings from *Radio Times* for the original BBC1 broadcast of *The Chase* and a one-page article that introduced the story.

COMING SOON (1m34s) Trailer for the DVD release of the Myths and Legends boxset containing *The Horns of Nimon*, *The Time Monster* and *Underworld*.

SUBTITLES

Select **On** to view subtitles for all episodes and Special Features on disc one (except commentary).

DISC TWO

SPECIAL FEATURES

THE THRILL OF THE CHASE (10m26s) Director Richard Martin talks about the production of *The Chase*, including how he and story editor Dennis Spooner refined the scripts, working with the cast, the limits of studio recording at the time, and filming the climactic battle at Ealing Studios.

LAST STOP WHITE CITY (13m15s) A look at the characters of original companions Barbara Wright and Ian Chesterton, and their portrayal by Jacqueline Hill and William Russell. With contributions from director Richard Martin, vision mixer Clive Doig, author Simon Guerrier and William Russell himself. Produced by James Goss.

DALEKS CONQUER AND DESTROY (22m38s) The Daleks were an instant hit and put *Doctor Who* on the cultural map. Some of the people who were there at the Daleks' creation in 1963, and those who helped to put them back on television in 2005, discuss their enduring appeal. With contributions from original series producer Verity Lambert (interviewed in 2003), Dalek designer Raymond Cusick, director Richard Martin, actor Carole Ann Ford, New Series writer Robert Shearman and designer Matthew Savage, prop maker Mike Tucker and Dalek voice actor Nicholas Briggs. Produced by James Goss.

DALEKS BEYOND THE SCREEN (21m55s) A look at some of the enormous range of Dalek-inspired merchandise from both the 1960s and 2000s, plus the creatures' appearances outside the television series in comic strips, on the stage, in audio dramas and even as a target of humour. With contributions from original series producer Verity Lambert (interviewed in 2003), Dalek designer Raymond Cusick, director Richard Martin, New Series writer Robert Shearman and designer Matthew Savage, prop maker Mike Tucker, Dalek voice actor Nicholas Briggs, BBC Worldwide's Dave Turbitt and Kate Walsh, *Private Eye* journalist Adam MacQueen, and Dalek collector Mick Hall. Produced by James Goss.

SHAWCRAFT – THE ORIGINAL MONSTER MAKERS (17m) A history of Shawcraft Models, which produced many of the props, models, effects and monsters for early *Doctor Who*, including the Daleks and Mechonoids. With contributions from BBC designers Spencer Chapman, Raymond Cusick, Barry Newbery and John Wood, and Shawcraft owner Bill Roberts' daughter Annette Basford. Narrated by Philip Kelly, produced by John Kelly.

NEXT

FOLLOW THAT DALEK (12m) Silent 8mm colour film footage of Shawcraft Models' workshop, shot in early 1967 by home-movie maker Gerry Irwin. It shows many props used in *Doctor Who* and construction of the model Chitty Chitty Bang Bang car used in the 1968 film. Set to sound effects from 1960s *Doctor Who* stories.

— Select **Info Text On** to view explanatory subtitles while watching the footage.

GIVE–A–SHOW SLIDES (12m15s) Slideshow presentation of the cartoon slides — sixteen stories of seven slides each, five featuring the Daleks — from the 1965 *Doctor Who* Give-A-Show Projector toy made by Chad Valley. *The last two stories featuring the Zarbi are also on* The Web Planet

PHOTO GALLERY (5m9s) Slideshow of colour and black-and-white photos taken during production of *The Chase*, including design department photos of the sets. Set to sound effects from the story. Compiled by Derek Handley.

SUBTITLES Select **On** to view subtitles for all Special Features on disc two.

EASTER EGG

There is one hidden feature on these discs to find. *See Appendix 2 for details*

RELATED EXTRAS

Terror Nation — Destiny of the Daleks

The Dalek Tapes — Genesis of the Daleks

Coming Soon trailer — The Masque of Mandragora

The Doctor's Composer — The War Games

CITY OF DEATH

STORY No.105   SEASON No.17:2

Two discs with four episodes (100 mins) and 102 minutes of extras, plus commentary track, production subtitles and PDF items

C

TARDIS TEAM Fourth Doctor, Second Romana

TIME AND PLACE Contemporary Paris, 16th Century Florence, primeval Earth

ADVERSARIES Art thief Count Scarlioni; Scaroth, last of the Jagaroth

FIRST ON TV 29 September–20 October 1979

DVD RELEASE BBCDVD1664, 7 November 2005, PG (episodes U)

COVER Photo illustration by Clayton Hickman, yellow strip

ORIGINAL RRP £19.99

STORY TEASER

Taking a holiday in modern-day Paris, the Doctor and Romana begin experiencing ripples in the flow of time. While visiting the Louvre to view the Mona Lisa, they become embroiled in a rich Count's plans to steal the painting and sell it to raise funds for the time experiments he's performing in his cellar. But his scheme is grander than even the Doctor realises, and threatens not just the population of Paris but the very existence of all life on Earth.

CONNECTIONS

More often than not, when the Doctor visits France he ends up in to Paris: to break his friends out of prison in *The Reign of Terror* (1964), to visit an apothecary in *The Massacre* (1966), getting a snog from Reinette Poisson in *The Girl in the Fireplace* (2006), and once more to visit an art gallery in *Vincent and the Doctor* (2010). The birth of life was the earliest point in Earth's history he had visited until he went to see the planet itself begin forming in *The Runaway Bride* (2006), before landing on its still-cooling surface in *Hide* (2013). A scientist benevolently running time experiments funded by someone more affluent but less altruistic features in *The Evil of the Daleks* (1967), and as here he ends up serving a one-eyed horror. Kerensky's apparatus is not dissimilar to that in *The Lazarus Experiment* (2007), which appears more successful at reversing time but ends as tragically for the professor involved. While based on ideas from a story by David Fisher, the final script was written by Douglas Adams, which accounts for the sophistication of its humour, ably handled by Michael Hayes, who also directed the previous season's *The Androids of Tara* and *The Armageddon Factor*. Julian Glover is wonderfully dry as Count Scarlioni, a change from his fiery King Richard in *The Crusade* (1965), while Tom Chadbon (Duggan) takes a less memorable part in *The Trial of a Time Lord: The Mysterious Planet* (1986). Peter Halliday (Guard) also has stronger roles as Packer in *The Invasion* (1968) and Pletrac in *Carnival of Monsters* (1973), returning once more for *Remembrance of the Daleks* (1988). David Graham (Kerensky) provided Dalek voices for their early stories, but can be seen as Charlie the barman in *The Gunfighters* (1966), while Eleanor Bron has a fuller role as Kara in *Revelation of the Daleks* (1985); John Cleese has yet to return to the series.

WORTH WATCHING

This highly regarded story was largely written by Douglas Adams and demonstrates much of his stylish wit and wordplay, combining humour with genuine threat. The deft dialogue amuses while leaving you in no doubt about the seriousness of the plot, aided by commanding performances throughout, although Tom Baker and Julian Glover play against each other especially well. There is some excellent effects work, and famously this is the story which convinced New Series executive producer Julie Gardner that *Doctor Who* could do great things.

DISC ONE

THE EPISODES

All four episodes are restored from digital duplicates of the original two-inch colour videotape recordings used for broadcast and their mono soundtracks remastered. The title sequences are replaced by a modern transfer of the original 35mm film with credits overlaid from the episode recordings.

SPECIAL FEATURES

INFORMATION TEXT Select **On** to view subtitles when watching the episodes that provide information and anecdotes about the development, production, broadcast and history of *City of Death*. Written by Martin Wiggins.

AUDIO OPTIONS Select **Commentary On** to play the audio commentary in place of the main soundtrack when watching the episodes. With Tom Chadbon (Duggan), Julian Glover (Scarlioni) and director Michael Hayes on all four episodes.

SUBTITLES

Select **On** to view subtitles for all episodes (none for commentary).

DISC TWO

SPECIAL FEATURES

PARIS IN THE SPRINGTIME (44m4s) The making of *City of Death* and the contribution to *Doctor Who* of writer Douglas Adams. Including the origins of the story — with an illustrated summary of David Fisher's original storyline 'The Gamble with Time' — and how extensive reworking led to it going out under a pseudonym; how Adams began writing for *Doctor Who* and went on to become script editor, just as *The Hitchhiker's Guide to the Galaxy* took off; filming in Paris; the characters and cast; and the popular legacy of the story among fans. With contributions from script editors Douglas Adams (interviewed in 1985 and 1992) and Anthony Read, writer David Fisher, directors Michael Hayes and Pennant Roberts, actors Tom Chadbon, Julian Glover and Catherine Schell, and New Series writers Steven Moffat and Robert Shearman. Written by Jonathan Morris, narrated by Toby Longworth, illustrations by Jason Lythgoe-Hay, produced by Ed Stradling.

PARIS, W12 (20m5s) Footage from the full studio recording in May/June 1979 of scenes in the chateau, Louvre, Da Vinci's studio and of Kerensky's death, including retakes and shots unused in the final programme. Taken from a low-quality black-and-white video copy with on-screen timecode. Select **Optional subtitles On** before pressing ▶ to view explanatory captions about the scenes being recorded when watching.

PREHISTORIC LANDSCAPES (2m27s) Silent 35mm colour film footage of the model prehistoric landscape and Jagaroth spaceship, including shots not used in the final programme. Set to matching sound effects from the story.

CHICKEN WRANGLER (2m46s) Silent 35mm colour film footage of visual effects designer Ian Scoones shooting the 'ageing chicken' sequence. Set to 'Chicken Man' by Alan Hawkshaw (better known as the original *Grange Hill* theme).

PHOTO GALLERY (8m40s) Slideshow of colour and black-and-white photos taken during production of *City of Death*, including design department photos of the sets, studio plans and prop blueprints, plus publicity photos of Lalla Ward in the costume she wore for *City of Death*. Set to sound effects from the story. Compiled by Ralph Montagu.

EYE ON...BLATCHFORD (13m) Spoof regional news report following Sardoth, second-to-last of the Jagaroth, as he tries to mix village life with saving his species. Written by Robert Hammond, produced by Matt West.

DOCTOR WHO ANNUAL Accessible via a computer is a PDF file of the 1980 *Doctor Who Annual*, published by World Distributors the autumn that *City of Death* was broadcast. With stories featuring the Doctor, Romana and K9, plus science features, puzzles and games.

SUBTITLES Select **On** to view subtitles for all Special Features on disc two.

EASTER EGGS

There are five hidden features on these discs to find. *See Appendix 2 for details*

RELATED EXTRAS

Directing Who — The Armageddon Factor
The Doctor's Composer — The Sun Makers

THE **CLAWS OF AXOS**

STORY No.57   SEASON No.8:3

One disc with four episodes (97½ mins) and 69½ minutes of extras, plus commentary track and production subtitles

TARDIS TEAM Third Doctor, Jo, Brigadier and UNIT
TIME AND PLACE Contemporary England
ADVERSARIES First Master (3rd appearance); shape-shifting Axons
FIRST ON TV 13 March–3 April 1971
DVD RELEASE BBCDVD1354, 25 April 2005, U
COVER Photo illustration by Clayton Hickman, orange strip
ORIGINAL RRP £19.99

— Also released in The Third Doctor Collection; BBCDVD2263, £49.99, 6 November 2006

STORY TEASER

A strange alien craft lands in Southern England near a nuclear power station and UNIT is sent to investigate. The golden-skinned humanoid Axons claim to be refugees seeking assistance in return for Axonite, a substance that can fulfil all energy needs. The authorities begin negotiations but the Doctor is suspicious about the craft's proximity to the nuclear reactor. His concern increases when he discovers the Master is in league with the Axons.

CONNECTIONS

Axos's scheme of seeking refuge but really coming here to consume is similar to that of the Nimon in *The Horns of Nimon* (1979/80) and the Gelth in *The Unquiet Dead* (2005). The boot is arguably on the other foot, however, when humans gain space travel themselves, as in both *The Sensorites* (1964) and *The Trial of a Time Lord: Terror of the Vervoids* (1986) they're seen as leeches of other planets' natural resources. The Axons are the first aliens in *Doctor Who* with shape-shifting abilities (if you don't count the Doctor's regenerating), ahead of the Zygons in *Terror of the Zygons* (1975) and *The Day of the Doctor* (2013), the Rutan in *Horror of Fang Rock* (1977), the Carrionites in *The Shakespeare Code* (2007), the Vespiform in *The Unicorn and the Wasp* (2008) and Prisoner Zero in *The Eleventh Hour* (2010). Another first comes in the writing partnership of Bob Baker and Dave Martin, who went on to script serials throughout the 1970s (*see Index v*), including *The Three Doctors* (1973), the first multi-Doctor story; *The Hand of Fear* (1976), which wrote out Sarah Jane; and *The Invisible Enemy* (1977), which introduced K9. However, it was the last for Michael Ferguson, who previously directed *The War Machines* (1966), *The Seeds of Death* (1969) and *The Ambassadors of Death* (1970). Peter Bathurst (Chinn) plays a similarly overbearing politician, Hensell, in *The Power of the Daleks* (1966), while David Savile (Winser) is the reliable Lieutenant Carstairs in *The War Games* (1969) and Colonel Crichton in *The Five Doctors* (1983). Tim Pigott-Smith (Captain Harker) in on the Doctor's side as Marco in *The Masque of Mandragora* (1976), and Bernard Holley (Axon man) is more recognisable but short-lived as Peter Haydon in *The Tomb of the Cybermen* (1967).

WORTH WATCHING

This is early-70s *Doctor Who* at its most psychedelic, making full use of the opportunities provided by the recent introduction of colour television to present an environment that is truly alien. Although they only appeared in the series once, the Axons are a memorable monster, in both their humanoid and especially their tentacled forms. And of course there's another stylish performance from Roger Delgado as the original Master.

THE EPISODES

Episodes one and four are restored from digital duplicates of the original two-inch colour videotape recordings used for broadcast. Episodes two and three are reverse-converted and restored from digital duplicates of conversions of the original two-inch colour videotape recordings in a lower-resolution format, recovered from a Canadian broadcaster in 1981. Some studio scenes in episodes one and two are restored from a higher quality two-inch colour videotape of the original studio recording. All episodes' mono soundtracks are remastered and title sequences replaced by a modern transfer of the original 35mm film with credits remade to match the originals.

SPECIAL FEATURES *ALSO ON SPECIAL EDITION

*DELETED AND EXTENDED SCENES (26m59s) A selection of scenes and retakes not used in the final programme, taken from the full studio recording of scenes for episodes one and two on Friday 22 January 1971. Includes the opening graphics showing the original story title 'The Vampire from Space' and the full disintegration effect for Pigbin Josh. Explanatory subtitles can be turned on under **Information Text**.

*NOW AND THEN FEATURETTE (6m35s) Comparing the filming locations in and around Dungeness in Kent as they look today with how they appeared in early January 1971 when used for *The Claws of Axos*. Narrated by Katy Manning, produced by Richard Bignell. *See Index iii for further editions*

*REVERSE STANDARDS CONVERSION (10m10s) An explanation of how television programmes in the 1970s were converted from the UK PAL system to the North American NTSC standard, and what was involved in developing a means to reverse this process and recover some of the lost picture quality, as used in the restoration of episodes two and three of *The Claws of Axos*. Presented by Jack Pizzey, produced by John Kelly.

*INFORMATION TEXT Select **On** to view subtitles when watching the episodes that provide information and anecdotes about the development, production, broadcast and history of *The Claws of Axos* (written by Martin Wiggins), or for explanatory captions when watching **Deleted and Extended Scenes** (written by Richard Bignell).

*DIRECTING WHO (14m44s) Director Michael Ferguson talks about the filming and recording of *The Claws of Axos*, and the creativity *Doctor Who* allowed directors compared to other programmes.

*PHOTO GALLERY (10m56s) Slideshow of colour and black-and-white photos taken during production of *The Claws of Axos*, plus shots of the commentary participants. Set to sound effects from the story. Compiled by Ralph Montagu.

AUDIO OPTIONS
Select ***Commentary On** to play the audio commentary in place of the main soundtrack when watching the episodes. With Katy Manning (Jo), Richard Franklin (Captain Yates) and producer Barry Letts on all four episodes.

SUBTITLES
Select **On** to view subtitles for all episodes and Special Features, or for the commentary.

EASTER EGG
There is one hidden feature on this disc to find. *See Appendix 2 for details*

RELATED EXTRAS
The UNIT Family — Day of the Daleks

THE **CLAWS OF AXOS** SPECIAL EDITION

STORY No.57   SEASON No.8:3

Two discs with four episodes (97½ mins) and 206 minutes of extras, plus commentary track, production subtitles and PDF items
Audio navigation of each disc's contents available by pressing Enter after the BBC ident

TARDIS TEAM Third Doctor, Jo, Brigadier and UNIT

TIME AND PLACE Contemporary England

ADVERSARIES First Master (3rd appearance); shape-shifting Axons

FIRST ON TV 13 March–3 April 1971

DVD RELEASE BBCDVD3670, 22 October 2012, PG (episodes U)

COVER Photo illustration by Lee Binding, orange strip; version with older BBC logo on reverse

ORIGINAL RRP £20.42

STORY TEASER
A strange alien craft lands in Southern England near a nuclear power station and UNIT is sent to investigate. The golden-skinned humanoid Axons claim to be refugees seeking assistance in return for Axonite, a substance that can fulfil all energy needs. The authorities begin negotiations but the

Doctor is suspicious about the craft's proximity to the nuclear reactor. His concern increases when he discovers the Master is in league with the Axons.

CONNECTIONS

Axos's scheme of seeking refuge but really coming here to consume is similar to that of the Nimon in *The Horns of Nimon* (1979/80) and the Gelth in *The Unquiet Dead* (2005). The boot is arguably on the other foot, however, when humans gain space travel themselves, as in both *The Sensorites* (1964) and *The Trial of a Time Lord: Terror of the Vervoids* (1986) they're seen as leeches of other planets' natural resources. The Axons are the first aliens in *Doctor Who* with shape-shifting abilities (if you don't count the Doctor's regenerating), ahead of the Zygons in *Terror of the Zygons* (1975) and *The Day of the Doctor* (2013), the Rutan in *Horror of Fang Rock* (1977), the Carrionites in *The Shakespeare Code* (2007), the Vespiform in *The Unicorn and the Wasp* (2008) and Prisoner Zero in *The Eleventh Hour* (2010). Another first comes in the writing partnership of Bob Baker and Dave Martin, who went on to script serials throughout the 1970s (*see Index v*), including *The Three Doctors* (1973), the first multi-Doctor story; *The Hand of Fear* (1976), which wrote out Sarah Jane; and *The Invisible Enemy* (1977), which introduced K9. However, it was the last for Michael Ferguson, who previously directed *The War Machines* (1966), *The Seeds of Death* (1969) and *The Ambassadors of Death* (1970). Peter Bathurst (Chinn) plays a similarly overbearing politician, Hensell, in *The Power of the Daleks* (1966), while David Savile (Winser) is the reliable Lieutenant Carstairs in *The War Games* (1969) and Colonel Crichton in *The Five Doctors* (1983). Tim Pigott-Smith (Captain Harker) in on the Doctor's side as Marco in *The Masque of Mandragora* (1976), and Bernard Holley (Axon man) is more recognisable but short-lived as Peter Haydon in *The Tomb of the Cybermen* (1967).

WORTH WATCHING

This Special Edition features more advanced clean-up of the episodes compared to the previous release and additional Special Features. This is early-70s *Doctor Who* at its most psychedelic, making full use of the opportunities provided by the recent introduction of colour television to present an environment that is truly alien. Although they only appeared in the series once, the Axons are a memorable monster, in both their humanoid and especially their tentacled forms. And of course there's another stylish performance from Roger Delgado as the original Master.

DISC ONE

THE EPISODES

Episodes one and four are restored from digital duplicates of the original two-inch colour videotape recordings used for broadcast. Episodes two and three are restored from 16mm black-and-white film copies of the original two-inch colour videotape recordings that survived in the archives; the VidFIRE process is applied to studio-recorded shots to recapture the smoother motion of video and they are recoloured using reverse-converted digital duplicates of conversions of the original two-inch colour videotape recordings in a lower-resolution format (recovered from a Canadian broadcaster in 1981). Some studio scenes in episodes one and two are restored from a higher quality two-inch colour videotape of the original studio recording. All episodes' mono soundtracks are remastered and the title sequences replaced by a modern transfer of the original 35mm film with credits remade to match the originals.

SPECIAL FEATURES *REPEATED FROM PREVIOUS RELEASE

*DELETED AND EXTENDED SCENES (26m59s) A selection of scenes and retakes not used in the final programme, taken from the full studio recording of scenes for episodes one and two on Friday 22 January 1971. Includes the opening graphics showing the original story title 'The Vampire from Space' and the full disintegration effect for Pigbin Josh. Explanatory subtitles can be turned on under **Info Text**.

*AUDIO OPTIONS Select **Commentary** to play the audio commentary recorded for the previous release in place of the main soundtrack when watching the episodes. With Katy Manning (Jo), Richard Franklin (Captain Yates) and producer Barry Letts on all four episodes.
— Select **Feature Audio** to reinstate the main soundtrack when watching the episodes.

INFO TEXT Select **On** to view subtitles when watching the episodes that provide information and anecdotes about the development, production, broadcast and history of *The Claws of Axos*, updated from the previous release (written by Martin Wiggins), and for explanatory captions when watching **Deleted and Extended Scenes** (written by Richard Bignell).

SUBTITLES
Select **On** to view subtitles for all episodes and Special Features on disc one (except commentary).

DISC TWO

SPECIAL FEATURES *REPEATED FROM PREVIOUS RELEASE

AXON STATIONS! (26m40s) The making of *The Claws of Axos*, including how 'the Bristol Boys' started writing for *Doctor Who* and their initial ideas for this story; weather problems during the location filming at Dungeness; making the costumes for both forms of Axon; designing the set for Axos; and getting psychedelic with the visual effects. With contributions from script editor Terrance Dicks, writer Bob Baker, director Michael Ferguson, stuntman Derek Ware, and actors Paul Grist, Bernard Holley and Katy Manning. Produced by Chris Chapman.

*****NOW & THEN** (6m35s) Comparing the filming locations in and around Dungeness in Kent as they look today with how they appeared in early January 1971 when used for *The Claws of Axos*. Narrated by Katy Manning, produced by Richard Bignell. *See Index iii for further editions*

*****DIRECTING WHO** (14m44s) Director Michael Ferguson talks about the filming and recording of *The Claws of Axos*, and the creativity *Doctor Who* allowed directors compared to other programmes.

STUDIO RECORDING (72m47s) The full, unedited studio recording of episodes one and two made on the evening of Friday 22 January 1971, from which the deleted and extended scenes were taken.

SUBTITLES Select **On** to view subtitles for all Special Features on disc two.

NEXT

LIVING WITH LEVENE (35m10s) Actor and comedian Toby Hadoke spends a weekend with the eccentric John Levene, who played UNIT Sergeant Benton during the Third Doctor era, to get to know the man behind the stripes. Produced by Chris Chapman.

*****PHOTO GALLERY** (10m56s) Slideshow of colour and black-and-white photos taken during production of *The Claws of Axos*, plus shots of the commentary participants. Set to sound effects from the story. Compiled by Ralph Montagu.

PDF MATERIALS Accessible via a computer are the four episode listings from *Radio Times* for the original BBC1 broadcast of *The Claws of Axos*, and an article about Bernard Holley published the week of episode one.

COMING SOON (2m14s) Trailer for the DVD releases of *More Than 30 Years in the TARDIS* and *Shada* in The Legacy Collection boxset.

EASTER EGG
There is one hidden feature on these discs to find. *See Appendix 2 for details*

RELATED EXTRAS
Coming Soon trailer — The Ambassadors of Death
The UNIT Family — Day of the Daleks

COLONY IN SPACE

STORY No.58   SEASON No.8:4

One disc with six episodes (146 mins) and 45 minutes of extras, plus commentary track, production subtitles and PDF items
Audio navigation of disc contents available by pressing Enter after the BBC ident

TARDIS TEAM Third Doctor, Jo
TIME AND PLACE Planet Uxaerius
ADVERSARIES First Master (4th appearance); Interplanetary Mining Corporation
FIRST ON TV 10 April–15 May 1971
DVD RELEASE BBCDVD3381, 3 October 2011, PG (episodes and extras bar commentary U)
COVER Photo illustration by Lee Binding, light green strip; version with older BBC logo on reverse
ORIGINAL RRP £20.42

STORY TEASER

The Time Lords send the Doctor to the planet Uxaerius to prevent the Master from retrieving an ancient weapon of devastating power. He is hindered not only by the primitive aliens who guard the weapon, but also a territorial dispute between a settlement of human colonists and a mining company that wants to strip the planet of its resources. And things only get worse when a familiar arbitrator from Earth arrives.

CONNECTIONS

This is the first journey in the TARDIS to another world since the Doctor was exiled to Earth in *The War Games* (1969), although apparently under the direction of the Time Lords. They will again take control of the Ship in *The Curse of Peladon* (1972), *The Mutants* (1972), *Planet of the Daleks* (1973), *The Brain of Morbius* (1976), *Arc of Infinity* (1983) and *The Trial of a Time Lord* (1986). Planets made barren by the radiation from powerful weapons include Skaro (*The Daleks*, 1963; *Destiny of the Daleks*, 1979), Oseidon (*The Android Invasion*, 1975), Argolis (*The Leisure Hive*, 1980), and parts of Dulkis (*The Dominators*, 1968) and Atrios (*The Armageddon Factor*, 1979), although Uxaerius is at least recovering and now habitable. *Frontios* (1984) features a colony struggling to survive on an uninviting world, although there people were banned from digging into the ground. Mining companies like IMC are generally seen as corporate monsters in *Doctor Who*, such as the copper-mining company run by Morgus in *The Caves of Androzani* (1984) and the Galatron Mining Company represented by Sil in *Vengeance on Varos* (1985). Although not in charge, Captain Dent is just the sort yes-man who personifies his company's amorality as is Gatherer Hade in *The Sun Makers* (1977), Thawn in *The Power of Kroll* (1978/79), Sil in *The Trial of a Time Lord: Mindwarp* (1986) and the Editor in *The Long Game* (2005). This is the only time in the Third Doctor era the Master's plan isn't focused on dominating the Earth but has a more universal outlook, an ambition he'll have more often in his post-thirteenth incarnation. Malcolm Hulke wrote scripts for each year of the Third Doctor era, including two more Master stories, while this was the first of six serials directed by Michael E Briant (*see Index v*). John Ringham (Robert Ashe) plays high priest of sacrifice Tlotoxl in *The Aztecs* (1964) and Josiah Blake in *The Smugglers* (1966); Bernard Kay (Caldwell) is Tyler in *The Dalek Invasion of Earth* (1964), Saladin in *The Crusade* (1965) and Inspector Crossland in *The Faceless Ones* (1967); Tony Caunter (Morgan) is Thatcher in *The Crusade* and Jackson in *Enlightenment* (1983); John Herrington (Jim Holden) is Rhynmal in *The Daleks' Master Plan* (1965/66); and Norman Atkyns (Guardian) can be seen as the Rear Admiral in *The Sea Devils* (1972). Roy Skelton (Norton) provides numerous voices throughout the Classic series, most notably for the Daleks, but also plays individual roles in *Planet of the Daleks* (1973), *The Green Death* (1973), *The Android Invasion* and *The Hand of Fear* (1976).

WORTH WATCHING

In just the second year of the Third Doctor's exile to Earth, the limitations of the format were becoming clear, so means were devised to get him back into space occasionally. This sees his first trip to another planet, although he still runs up against the Master, as in all the stories of the 1971 season. The storyline has echoes of movie Westerns but writer Malcolm Hulke enhances it with contemporary issues of sustainable living and corrupt corporations.

THE EPISODES

All six episodes are reverse-converted and restored from digital duplicates of conversions of the original two-inch colour videotape recordings in a lower-resolution format, recovered from a Canadian broadcaster in 1983. Their mono soundtracks are remastered and the title sequences replaced by a modern transfer of the original 35mm film with credits remade to match the originals.

SPECIAL FEATURES

IMC NEEDS YOU! (25m2s) The making of *Colony in Space*, including the political ideas in the script; the direction and controversial casting ideas; finding the futuristic buggies; the trials of filming in a clay quarry in Cornwall in February; devising the look of the Uxaerians; and problems with the servo robot prop. With contributions from producer Barry Letts (interviewed in 2008), script editor Terrance Dicks, director Michael E Briant, assistant floor manager Graeme Harper, and actors Bernard Kay and Katy Manning. Narrated by Marc Silk, produced by Chris Chapman.

FROM THE CUTTING ROOM FLOOR (12m52s) Silent 16mm colour film footage from the location filming at Old Baal Clay Pit, Cornwall in mid-February 1971, and of the model filming, including retakes and shots unused in the final programme. With explanatory captions.

PHOTO GALLERY (5m52s) Slideshow of colour and black-and-white photos taken during production of *Colony in Space*, set to sound effects from the story. Compiled by Paul Shields.

AUDIO OPTIONS Select **Commentary** to play the audio commentary in place of the main soundtrack when watching the episodes. This is moderated by actor and comedian Toby Hadoke, talking with script editor Terrance Dicks [eps 1,2], director Michael E Briant [1,2,3,4,5,6], Katy Manning (Jo) [1,2,3,5], assistant floor manager Graeme Harper [1,3,4,6], Bernard Kay (Caldwell) [2,4,5,6] and Morris Perry (Captain Dent) [3,4,5,6].

— Select **Feature Audio** to reinstate the main soundtrack when watching the episodes.

INFO TEXT Select **On** to view subtitles when watching the episodes that provide information and anecdotes about the development, production, broadcast and history of *Colony in Space*. Written by David Brunt.

PDF MATERIALS Accessible via a computer are the six episode listings from *Radio Times* for the original BBC1 broadcast of *Colony in Space*, the three-page comic strip by Frank Bellamy and article that introduced the story, and artwork by Bellamy that accompanied the episode one billing.

COMING SOON (1m27s) Trailer for the DVD releases of *The Android Invasion* and *Invasion of the Dinosaurs* in the U.N.I.T Files boxset.

SUBTITLES

Select **On** to view subtitles for all episodes and Special Features (except commentary).

RELATED EXTRAS

Coming Soon trailer — Day of the Daleks

THE **COMPLETE DAVROS COLLECTION**

Boxset of **DESTINY OF THE DALEKS, GENESIS OF THE DALEKS, REMEMBRANCE OF THE DALEKS SPECIAL EDITION, RESURRECTION OF THE DALEKS** and **REVELATION OF THE DALEKS**, plus eight audio dramas featuring Davros

DVD RELEASE BBCDVD2508, 26 November 2007, PG

SLIPCASE Photo illustration by Clayton Hickman, silvered logo and title, purple/black background
— With cover sticker reading 'INCLUDES: New Remembrance of the Daleks Special Edition /
   New Documentary: Davros Connections / New Audio Drama: The Davros Mission /
   Extensive DVD Special Features / 12 Page Collector's Booklet'

ORIGINAL RRP £99.99

WHAT'S IN THE BOX

This set collects all the Classic Series stories featuring Davros, creator of the Daleks, together with several audio dramas produced by Big Finish that examine the character further. It was released in a limited edition of 10,000 numbered copies. Each television story has the same contents as the individual releases but the discs are in a folded digipack within a cardboard slipcase, rather than separate cases. They are printed with different artwork to the regular releases, featuring the title 'Davros' beneath the *Doctor Who* logo and a picture of Davros or a Dalek appropriate to the story on the disc. This was the first release of Remembrance of the Daleks Special Edition, featuring more advanced restoration and additional extras than its previous release, but which was subsequently reissued separately in July 2009. Resurrection of the Daleks has also since been re-released as a Special Edition version.

— The final disc contains eight full-cast audio dramas starring Terry Molloy as Davros, the first seven previously released on CD by Big Finish. These are *Davros* (2003), featuring Colin Baker as the Doctor and set shortly before *Revelation of the Daleks*; *The Juggernauts* (2005), featuring Colin Baker as the Doctor and Bonnie Langford as Mel, set between *Revelation* and *Remembrance of the Daleks*; *Terror Firma* (2005), featuring Paul McGann as the Doctor and set after *Remembrance*; and the four-part *I, Davros* (2006), which tells the story of Davros's life before *Genesis of the Daleks*. Lastly, *The Davros Mission* was exclusive to this set (but released separately by Big Finish in January 2012) and follows Davros after his capture by the Daleks in *Revelation*. Also included is an audio documentary about the making of the *I, Davros* series.

● *See individual television stories for full contents*

THE **CREATURE FROM THE PIT**

STORY No.106   SEASON No.17:3

One disc with four episodes (97 mins) and 43 minutes of extras, plus commentary track, production subtitles and PDF items
Audio navigation of disc contents available by pressing Enter after the BBC ident

TARDIS TEAM Fourth Doctor, Second Romana, K9

TIME AND PLACE Planet Chloris

ADVERSARIES Lady Adrasta

FIRST ON TV 27 October–17 November 1979

DVD RELEASE BBCDVD2849, 3 May 2010, PG

COVER Photo illustration by Clayton Hickman, pale green strip;
  version with older BBC logo on reverse

ORIGINAL RRP £19.99

STORY TEASER

Following a distress call brings the Doctor and Romana to the forest world of Chloris, where Lady Adrasta rules with an iron fist. Anyone who tries to usurp her monopoly over the low metal reserves on the planet is thrown into the Pit and killed by a shapeless creature that dwells there. When the Doctor is condemned to the same fate, he learns the true extent of Adrasta's villainy.

CONNECTIONS

Having tried to present the largest monster ever for the previous season's *The Power of Kroll* (1978/79), with limited success using models, it's perhaps odd that the production team went for the idea again and then tried to achieve it with a practical costume. The result is…ambitious, let down as much by Tom Baker's interactions with the creature as the realisation itself. When the New Series wanted a giant amorphous monster it was fortunately able to use CGI for the Jagrafess (*The Long Game*, 2005). Lady Adrasta is a rare example in the Classic Series not only of a female lead villain but one who's in charge of a community; other examples include Catherine de Medici in *The Massacre* (1966), Hilda Winters in *Robot* (1974), Captain Wrack in *Enlightenment* (1983), Kara in *Revelation of the Daleks* (1985) and Helen A in *The Happiness Patrol* (1988). Fortunately Organon is a more reputable astrologer than the last one the Doctor met: Hieronymous in *The Masque of Mandragora* (1976). David Fisher wrote two stories for the previous season, *The Stones of Blood* and *The Androids of Tara*, provided the initial storyline that Douglas Adams rewrote as *City of Death* (1979) and lastly wrote *The Leisure Hive* the following year. This was director Christopher Barry's last work on *Doctor Who*, having most recently directed *The Brain of Morbius* (1976) but whose contribution went right back to the first Dalek story in 1963 (*see Index v*). The involvement of Eileen Way (Karela) goes back even further, as she plays Old Mother in the very first story *An Unearthly Child* (1963), while Edward Kelsey (Edu) is the slave buyer in *The Romans* (1965) and Resno in *The Power of the Daleks* (1966), and Tim Munro (Ainu) returns as Sigurd in *Terminus* (1983). Morris Barry, playing Tollund in episode one, had previously been a director and for *Doctor Who* directed *The Moonbase* (1967), *The Tomb of the Cybermen* (1967) and *The Dominators* (1968).

WORTH WATCHING

This was the first story to be script edited by Douglas Adams and the influence of his humour is noticeable in many aspects, particularly in the actions of the Doctor himself. Myra Frances as Adrasta makes a great villain, and while the attempt to feature the largest monster ever in *Doctor Who* was a valiant ambition, you'll have to judge the results for yourself.

THE EPISODES

All four episodes are restored from digital duplicates of the original two-inch colour videotape recordings used for broadcast and their mono soundtracks remastered. The title sequences are replaced by a modern transfer of the original 35mm film with credits remade to match the originals.

SPECIAL FEATURES

CHRISTOPHER BARRY: DIRECTOR (19m3s) Director Christopher Barry returns to the village of Aldbourne in Wiltshire, where he filmed *The Dæmons* (1971), to look back over his life and career in film and television, and the *Doctor Who* stories he directed.

TEAM ERATO (14m48s) The visual effects team that worked on *The Creature from the Pit* discuss the challenges they faced in building and operating a giant amorphous monster. With contributions from effects designer Mat Irvine and his assistants Steve Bowman, Steve Lucas and Morag McLean, plus director Christopher Barry. Produced by Chris Chapman.

ANIMAL MAGIC (2m37s) Extract from the Tuesday 1 May 1979 edition of the BBC1 children's wildlife show in which Tom Baker, in character, talks about some of the deadly creatures he has encountered as the Doctor: the Shrivenzale, the Krynoid, the Wirrn and the Fendahl. Shot on the jungle set for *The Creature from the Pit* at Ealing Studios on Monday 26 March 1979.

PHOTO GALLERY (4m51s) Slideshow of colour photos taken during production of *The Creature from the Pit*, set to sound effects from the story. Compiled by Derek Handley.

EXTENDED SCENE (24s) Longer version of a scene in episode three taken from an earlier edit.

NEXT

AUDIO OPTIONS Select **Commentary** to play the audio commentary in place of the main soundtrack when watching the episodes. With Lalla Ward (Romana), Myra Frances (Adrasta), visual effects designer Mat Irvine and director Christopher Barry on all four episodes.

— Select **Feature Audio** to reinstate the main soundtrack when watching the episodes.

INFO TEXT Select **On** to view subtitles when watching the episodes that provide information and anecdotes about the development, production, broadcast and history of *The Creature from the Pit*. Written by Nicholas Pegg.

PDF MATERIALS Accessible via a computer are the four episode listings from *Radio Times* for the original BBC1 broadcast of *The Creature from the Pit*.

COMING SOON (1m18s) Trailer for the DVD releases of *The King's Demons* and *Planet of Fire* in the Kamelion Tales boxset.

SUBTITLES

Select **On** to view subtitles for all episodes and Special Features (except commentary).

RELATED EXTRAS

Coming Soon trailer — The Horns of Nimon, The Time Monster, Underworld

THE **CRUSADE**

STORY No.14 SEASON No.2:6

Two surviving episodes (parts 1 and 3 of 4) released in the **LOST IN TIME** *boxset*

TARDIS TEAM First Doctor, Barbara, Ian, Vicki

TIME AND PLACE Jaffa, 12th Century Palestine

ADVERSARIES Saracen emir El Akir

FIRST ON TV 27 March and 10 April 1965

DVD RELEASE BBCDVD1353, 1 November 2004, PG

● *See* Lost in Time *for full details*

RELATED EXTRAS

The Doctor's Composer — The War Games
From Kingdom to Queen — Battlefield

THE **CURSE OF FENRIC**

STORY No.154   SEASON No.26:3

Two discs with four episodes (97 mins), a new 104-minute Special Edition and 124 minutes of extras, plus commentary and music-only tracks, and production subtitles

TARDIS TEAM Seventh Doctor, Ace

TIME AND PLACE 1940s naval base in the North of England

ADVERSARIES Vampiric Haemovores; ancient evil force Fenric

FIRST ON TV 25 October–15 November 1989

DVD RELEASE BBCDVD1154, 6 October 2003, PG

COVER Photo illustration by Clayton Hickman, dark purple strip

— Original release with cover sticker reading 'Doctor Who 40th Anniversary 1963–2003'

ORIGINAL RRP £19.99

STORY TEASER

Dark forces are gathering at a naval base in northern England during World War Two. A Russian attack squad has come ashore to steal the British deciphering apparatus, and the base's commander is only too happy to let them. But when the machine is set to translate an ancient Viking inscription, hideous blood-sucking creatures rise from the sea and attack local villagers, soldiers and infiltrators alike. For they have all been gathered for a more sinister purpose that only the Doctor suspects, one that involves his companion Ace.

CONNECTIONS

This is the Doctor's first on-screen involvement in the Second World War, despite the fact that by *Victory of the Daleks* (2010) he's positively pally with Winston Churchill and helping out in the heart of the Cabinet War Rooms. Perhaps he didn't get to know the prime minister until after helping save blitzed East London from confused nanogenes in *The Empty Child/The Doctor Dances* (2005). The Doctor describes the Haemovores as having an insatiable taste for blood, rather like the Ogri in *The Stones of Blood* (1978), the servants of the Great One in *State of Decay* (1980), the Tetraps in *Time and the Rani* (1987) and the Plasmavore the Judoon are tracking in *Smith and Jones* (2007). There are a few formless intelligences like Fenric roaming the universe with nebulous evil intent, such as the Great Intelligence in *The Abominable Snowmen* (1967), *The Web of Fear* (1968), *The Snowmen* (2012), *The Bells of Saint John* (2013) and *The Name of the Doctor* (2013); the Mandragora Helix in *The Masque of Mandragora* (1976); the Mara in *Kinda* (1982) and *Snakedance* (1983); the Wire in *The Idiot's Lantern* (2006); and the entity in *Midnight* (2008). Ian Briggs also scripted Ace's introduction in *Dragonfire* (1987) so was best placed to fill in more of her backstory, while Nicholas Mallett directed *The Trial of a Time Lord: The Mysterious Planet* in 1986 and *Paradise Towers* the year after. Marek Anton (Vershinin) hides his good looks behind the Destroyer's grimacing blue visage in *Battlefield* (1989), while Anne Reid (Nurse Crane) appears in the New Series as not-so-nice granny Florence Finnegan in *Smith and Jones*.

WORTH WATCHING

It's perhaps surprising that *Doctor Who* took so long to use the Second World War as a backdrop to a story (although even as early as *The Dalek Invasion of Earth* it was evoking blitzed London). As *The Curse of Fenric* was produced fifty years after the outbreak of hostilities, one can perhaps look on it as the show's way of marking the anniversary by celebrating the war-winning work of Alan Turing and the Enigma code-breaking machine, mirrored here in Dr Judson's Ultima machine. With mythology, war and memorable monsters all combining to make a chilling tale, *The Curse of Fenric* is one of the best stories from the last few years of *Doctor Who*'s original run. This incarnation of the Doctor is at his most devious, manipulating all around him, even Ace, whose story arc over the last two years reaches a climax here.

DISC ONE

THE EPISODES

All four episodes are restored from digital duplicates of the original one-inch colour videotape recordings used for broadcast and their stereo soundtracks remastered.

SPECIAL FEATURES

INFORMATION TEXT Select **On** to view subtitles when watching the episodes that provide information and anecdotes about the development, production, broadcast and history of *The Curse of Fenric*. Written by Martin Wiggins.

MODELLING THE DEAD (5m11s) Demonstration by model makers Stephen Mansfield and Sue Moore of how the Haemovore masks were created, broadcast on Sunday 23 September 1990 as part of BSB's '31 Who' *Doctor Who* Weekend. Presented by Debbie Flint.

CLAWS AND EFFECT (17m39s) Footage shot during the location recce for *The Curse of Fenric* as the director and his crew plan out their shoot, visiting a military training camp in Crowborough, East Sussex, locations in Hawkhurst, Kent, and the ultimately unused Covehurst Bay near Hastings, East Sussex. Includes test footage of various visual effects for the story. With explanatory subtitles.

TITLE SEQUENCES (2m13s) Full opening and closing title sequences with Keff McCulloch's theme arrangement used for Seventh Doctor episodes from 1987 to 1989. Select to view in either original stereo or newly mixed Dolby Digital 5.1 surround sound.

PHOTO GALLERY (5m45s) Slideshow of colour and black-and-white photos taken during production of *The Curse of Fenric*, including behind-the-scenes shots of the location recording. Set to sound effects from the story. Compiled by Ralph Montagu.

AUDIO OPTIONS Select **Commentary On** to play the audio commentary in place of the main soundtrack when watching the episodes. With Sylvester McCoy, Sophie Aldred (Ace) and Nicholas Parsons (Wainwright) on all four episodes.
— Select **Isolated Score** to hear only Mark Ayres' music when watching the episodes. Note, on episode two the titles play with just the theme music, no sound effects, while on episode three you can hear just the titles' sound effects.

NEBULA 90 (20m47s) Highlights from an interview panel featuring cast and crew who worked on *The Curse of Fenric* held at the *Doctor Who* convention in Liverpool on Sunday 7 October 1990. With writer Ian Briggs, model makers Stephen Mansfield and Sue Moore, composer Mark Ayres, and actors Sophie Aldred, Tomek Bork and Joann Kenny, being interviewed by Gary Russell.

TAKE TWO (4m31s) Extract from the Wednesday 19 April 1989 edition of the BBC1 children's viewer feedback programme in which Philip Schofield introduces a behind-the-scenes report on creating the effect of the dying vampire girls, including comments from Sylvester McCoy and Sophie Aldred on location.

SUBTITLES

Select **On** to view subtitles for all episodes and Special Features on disc one, or for the commentary.

DISC TWO

SPECIAL FEATURES

SHATTERING THE CHAINS (24m52s) Writer Ian Briggs talks about the ideas and themes he wanted to include when scripting *The Curse of Fenric*, and his thoughts on the final programme.

RECUTTING THE RUNES (15m6s) Composer Mark Ayres discusses the reasons for producing the Special Edition for this release, the techniques involved in mixing the 5.1 surround soundtrack, and changes to the editing, music, video effects and grading.

40TH ANNIVERSARY CELEBRATION (3m) Compilation of clips from all eras of Classic *Doctor Who*, set to Orbital's version of the theme music, included on all releases in 2003.

COSTUME DESIGN (17m5s) Costume designer Ken Trew talks about creating the various period costumes for *The Curse of Fenric*, as well as the Haemovores, illustrated with many of his original design sketches.

SPECIAL EDITION (103m44s) A new edit of the story as a single episode, compiled and restored from digital duplicates of the earliest edit of the original one-inch colour videotape recordings, reinstating scenes originally cut for time. With updated computer-generated visual effects and Dolby Digital 5.1 surround sound.

SUBTITLES Select **On** to view subtitles for all Special Features on disc two.

EASTER EGGS

There are three hidden features on these discs to find. *See Appendix 2 for details*

THE **CURSE OF PELADON**

STORY No.61   SEASON No.9:2

Released with **THE MONSTER OF PELADON** in the **PELADON TALES** boxset
*One disc with four episodes (98 mins) and 56½ minutes of extras, plus commentary track,
production subtitles and PDF items*
Audio navigation of disc contents available by pressing Enter after the BBC ident

C

TARDIS TEAM Third Doctor, Jo

TIME AND PLACE Planet Peladon

ADVERSARIES Ice Warriors (3rd appearance); high priest Hepesh

FIRST ON TV 29 January–19 February 1972

DVD RELEASE BBCDVD2744(A), 18 January 2010, PG

COVER Photo illustration by Clayton Hickman, purple strip; version with older BBC logo on reverse

ORIGINAL RRP £29.99 (boxset)

STORY TEASER

When the Doctor appears to get the TARDIS working, he and Jo find themselves on the stormy planet Peladon, the rulers of which are negotiating for its acceptance into the Galactic Federation. Mistaken for the delegate from Earth, the Doctor seeks a favourable decision from the attending alien ambassadors. But as these include the Ice Warriors, he has doubts, especially as someone is willing to kill to keep Peladon independent.

CONNECTIONS

The Ice Warriors return for the first time in colour, having previously faced the Second Doctor in *The Ice Warriors* (1967) and *The Seeds of Death* (1969). They are back, along with some of the other species seen here, in this story's sequel *The Monster of Peladon* (1974) and then don't appear on television again until 2013's *Cold War*. Such a conglomeration of creatures isn't seen again until *The End of the World* (2005) and *The Pandorica Opens* (2010). The Doctor visits Earth's Middle Ages in *Marco Polo* (1964), *The Crusade* (1965), *The Time Warrior* (1973/74) and *The King's Demons* (1983), but he encounters medieval societies like Peladon's on Ribos in *The Ribos Operation* (1978), Chloris in *The Creature from the Pit* (1979), a planet in E-Space in *State of Decay* (1980), and the titular city in *Castrovalva* (1982). As well as the four Ice Warrior stories from the Classic Series, Brian Hayles wrote *The Smugglers* (1966) and first drafts of *The Celestial Toymaker* (1966), although the final scripts were rewritten by Donald Tosh. Lennie Mayne directed both Peladon stories plus *The Three Doctors* (1972/73) and *The Hand of Fear* (1976). David Troughton (King Peladon) has a small role as Private Moor in *The War Games* (1969) and appears in the New Series as Professor Hobbes in *Midnight* (2008). Alan Bennion (Izlyr) plays Ice Lords Slaar in *The Seeds of Death* and Azaxyr in *The Monster of Peladon*, and Sonny Caldinez is inside Ice Warrior costumes for all of their Classic Series appearances and is seen as Kemel in *The Evil of the Daleks* (1967). Similarly Stuart Fell and Ysanne Churchman repeat their double-act as the body and voice respectively of Alpha Centauri in *The Monster of Peladon*, while Churchman also provides spider voices in *Planet of the Spiders* (1974).

WORTH WATCHING

In just the Third Doctor's second trip away from Earth, the production team grasps the opportunity to present a wealth of diverse and bizarre aliens, making *The Curse of Peladon* one of the most exotic stories of the era. It was also topical for its time, debating whether individual nations should join with others for mutual benefit, a question that still concerns countries around the world today.

THE EPISODES

All four episodes are reverse-converted and restored from digital duplicates of conversions of the original two-inch colour videotape recordings in a lower-resolution format, recovered from a Canadian broadcaster in 1981. Some filmed scenes are newly transferred from the original 16mm colour film. The title sequences are replaced by a modern transfer of the original 35mm film with credits remade to match the originals.

SPECIAL FEATURES

THE PELADON SAGA – PART ONE (23m25s) The making of *The Curse of Peladon* and *The Monster*

of Peladon, including Brian Hayles' scripts; *Curse*'s reflections of Britain's joining the European Common Market; *Monster*'s similarities to the contemporary coal miners' strikes; memories of director Lennie Mayne; studio filming at Ealing; shooting the model effects; the set design; creating the visual effects for *Monster*; the unique Peladon hairstyles; and the incidental music and sound effects. With contributions from producer Barry Letts, script editor Terrance Dicks, production assistant Chris D'Oyly-John, make-up supervisors Sylvia James and Elizabeth Moss, visual effects designer Peter Day, special sounds creator Brian Hodgson, and actors Donald Gee, Katy Manning, Nina Thomas and Ralph Watson. Narrated by David Hamilton, produced by John Kelly. *Part two is on* The Monster of Peladon

WARRIORS OF MARS (14m55s) A rundown of the Ice Warriors' four appearance in the Classic Series, examining the creation of their costumes and characters, the development of the Ice Lords, realising the Warriors' sonic weapons, and their changing motivations. With contributions from producer Barry Letts, script editor Terrance Dicks, director Michael Ferguson, make-up supervisor Sylvia James, visual effects designer Peter Day, special sounds creator Brian Hodgson, and Ice Warrior performers Alan Bennion, Bernard Bresslaw (from an archive audio interview) and Sonny Caldinez. Narrated by Donald Gee, produced by John Kelly.

JON AND KATY (7m8s) Katy Manning talks about playing Jo Grant and her close friendship with Jon Pertwee. With contributions from producer Barry Letts and script editor Terrance Dicks. Narrated by David Hamilton.

STORYBOARD COMPARISON (2m18s) Design sketches of the model filming for *The Curse of Peladon* intercut with the final shots from the programme.

AUDIO OPTIONS Select **Commentary** to play the audio commentary in place of the main soundtrack when watching the episodes. This is moderated by actor and comedian Toby Hadoke, talking with Katy Manning (Jo), producer Barry Letts, script editor Terrance Dicks and production assistant Chris D'Oyly-John on all four episodes.

— Select **Feature Audio** to reinstate the main soundtrack when watching the episodes.

NEXT

INFO TEXT Select **On** to view subtitles when watching the episodes that provide information and anecdotes about the development, production, broadcast and history of *The Curse of Peladon*. Written by Martin Wiggins.

PHOTO GALLERY (7m31s) Slideshow of colour and black-and-white photos taken during production of *The Curse of Peladon*, including design department photos of the sets and monster costumes. Set to sound effects from the story. Compiled by Derek Handley.

PDF MATERIALS Accessible via a computer are the four episode listings from *Radio Times* for the original BBC1 broadcast of *The Curse of Peladon*, with illustrations by Frank Bellamy.

— BBC Enterprises' sales document for *The Curse of Peladon*, describing the serial for potential overseas broadcasters.

COMING SOON (59s) Trailer for the DVD release of *The Masque of Mandragora*.

SUBTITLES
Select **On** to view subtitles for all episodes and Special Features (except commentary).

THE **CYBERMEN COLLECTION**

Boxset of **EARTHSHOCK**, **THE INVASION** and **THE TOMB OF THE CYBERMEN**

DVD RELEASE BBCDVD2262, 6 November 2006, PG

SLIPCASE Photo illustration by Clayton Hickman, silvered logo and title, blue background

ORIGINAL RRP £39.99

WHAT'S IN THE BOX

This set was released exclusively by Amazon.co.uk in a limited edition. Each story has the same contents and packaging as the individual releases — at the time all the Cybermen stories that were out on DVD — held in a cardboard slipcase. *The Tomb of the Cybermen* has since been re-released

as a Special Edition version with more advanced restoration and additional features.
- *A selection of New Series episodes was also released in a set titled 'The Cybermen Collection' in April 2009.*
- *See individual stories for full contents*

THE **DÆMONS**

STORY No.59   SEASON No.8:5

D

Two discs with five episodes (122½ mins) and 107 minutes of extras, plus commentary track, production subtitles and PDF items
Audio navigation of each disc's contents available by pressing Enter after the BBC ident

TARDIS TEAM Third Doctor, Jo, Brigadier and UNIT
TIME AND PLACE English village of Devil's End
ADVERSARIES First Master (5th appearance); living statue Bok; demonic alien Azal
FIRST ON TV 22 May–19 June 1971
DVD RELEASE BBCDVD3383, 19 March 2012, PG
COVER Photo illustration by Lee Binding, orange strip; version with older BBC logo on reverse
ORIGINAL RRP £20.42
— 'Limited Edition Convention Special' sold by Forbidden Planet in a sleeve with alternative illustration by Binding, content identical to regular release

STORY TEASER

The opening of a prehistoric burial mound near the village of Devil's End has unexpected consequences when an ancient force is released. The Doctor and UNIT race to the scene to find the Master posing as the local vicar and the village cut off by an impenetrable barrier. With seemingly magical powers at work, the Doctor must face the wrath of the Devil himself.

CONNECTIONS

For all the time he spends stuck on Earth in his third incarnation, the Doctor is mostly seen in scientific establishments rather than country villages (although he does find time to visit the circus in *Terror of the Autons* at the start of this season). Devil's End is the only one he visits before his exile is lifted, and after that he only goes to four more: Tulloch in *Terror of the Zygons* (1975), Devesham in *The Android Invasion* (1975), Little Hodcombe in *The Awakening* (1984) and Leadworth in *The Eleventh Hour* (2010). Perhaps the mystical traditions followed by the villagers here put him off rural life. Certainly similar demonic powers are on display in *The Awakening*, which also climaxes with an exploding church. The debate over science versus magic is considered again in *The Masque of Mandragora* (1976) and sort of in *The Shakespeare Code* (2007), although despite championing science, the Doctor's technobabble relies as ever on Arthur C Clarke's magic/advanced technology equivalence. While the Dæmon species is said to be at the root of our conception of the Devil, the Doctor apparently meets the origin of all such myths throughout the universe in *The Satan Pit* (2006). Bok, the sculpted grotesque brought to life (he's not actually a gargoyle), prefigures the Weeping Angels introduced in *Blink* (2007). After appearing in every story of this season, the Master will make less frequent comebacks, next seen in *The Sea Devils* (1972) and then just two more stories in this incarnation owing to the untimely death of Roger Delgado. This is the first story written by Robert Sloman and producer Barry Letts, here under a pseudonym, then under Sloman's name alone for the next three season finales *The Time Monster* (1972), *The Green Death* (1973) and *Planet of the Spiders* (1974). Christopher Barry returned to direct having not worked on *Doctor Who* since 1966's *The Power of the Daleks* (*see Index v*). Stephen Thorne (Azal) is cast again for his booming voice as Omega in *The Three Doctors* (1972/73) and Eldrad in *The Hand of Fear* (1976), Stanley Mason (Bok) is the Uxaerian priest in the previous story *Colony in Space*, Alec Linstead (Sergeant Osgood) plays Arnold Jellicoe in *Robot* (1974/75) and Arthur Stengos in *Revelation of the Daleks* (1985), David Simeon (reporter Alastair Fergus) is UNIT Private Latimer in *Inferno* (1970), and Christopher Wray (PC Groom) is seaman Lovell in *The Sea Devils*.

WORTH WATCHING

This is the favourite story of many of the people who worked on it thanks to the extensive location filming and familiarity of the regular cast by the end of the 1971 season. It's clear to see why as they all have significant roles in the story, as well as accommodating a notable guest spot for Damaris Hayman as the redoubtable Miss Hawthorne, arguing for the existence of the supernatural against the Doctor's scientific rationale.

D

DISC ONE

THE EPISODES

Episodes one, two, three and five are restored from 16mm black-and-white film copies of the original two-inch colour videotape recordings, recoloured using copies of lower-resolution home-video recordings made when the serial was broadcast in America in 1978, and with the VidFIRE process applied to studio-recorded shots to recapture the smoother motion of video. Episode four is restored from a digital duplicate of the original two-inch colour videotape recording used for broadcast. All have their mono soundtracks remastered and title sequences replaced by a modern transfer of the original 35mm film with credits remade to match the originals.

SPECIAL FEATURES

AUDIO OPTIONS Select **Commentary** to play the audio commentary in place of the main soundtrack when watching the episodes. With Katy Manning (Jo), Richard Franklin (Captain Yates), Damaris Hayman (Miss Hawthorne) and director Christopher Barry on all five episodes.

— Select **Feature Audio** to reinstate the main soundtrack when watching the episodes.

INFO TEXT Select **On** to view subtitles when watching the episodes that provide information and anecdotes about the development, production, broadcast and history of *The Dæmons*. Written by Martin Wiggins.

SUBTITLES

Select **On** to view subtitles for all episodes (none for commentary).

DISC TWO

SPECIAL FEATURES

THE DEVIL RIDES OUT (28m39s) The making of *The Dæmons*, including the origins of the story as an audition piece; the truth behind the pseudonym Guy Leopold; the director's return to *Doctor Who* after five years; Damaris Hayman's role as white witch Miss Hawthorne; filming on location in Aldbourne; creating Bok; problems with Jon Pertwee; and the casting of Azal. With contributions from producer/writer Barry Letts (interviewed in 2008), script editor Terrance Dicks, director Christopher Barry, assistant floor manager Sue Hedden, and actors Richard Franklin, Damaris Hayman and Katy Manning. Narrated by Hannah Lucas, produced by Chris Chapman.

REMEMBERING BARRY LETTS (33m35s) Profile of actor, writer, director and producer Barry Letts, who died in 2009. His sons Crispin and Dominic recount his early life and career, with input from Barry himself taken from past interviews, while colleagues Terrance Dicks, Ronald Marsh and Derrick Sherwin reminisce about his *Doctor Who* years. Illustrated with photos and clips from productions Barry appeared in and worked on. Narrated by Glen Allen, produced by Ed Stradling.

LOCATION FILM (6m42s) Silent 8mm colour film footage shot by a villager in Aldbourne on Friday 30 April 1971 during location filming for *The Dæmons*, showing the cast and crew at work.

COLOURISATION TEST (25m) In 1992 a group of BBC engineers investigated the feasibility of combining colour off-air video recordings with black-and-white film recordings in order to restore to colour the many Third Doctor stories that no longer exist on their original colour videotape (as demonstrated in the *Tomorrow's World* extract below). They went on to refine their techniques and are responsible for the restoration of all Classic *Doctor Who* for the DVD range, but this is their very first attempt on the first episode of *The Dæmons*.

SUBTITLES Select **On** to view subtitles for all Special Features on disc two.

NEXT

TOMORROW'S WORLD (5m13s) Extract from the Thursday 19 November 1992 edition of the BBC1 science and technology programme in which Howard Stableford reports on the techniques used in the first colour-restoration of *The Dæmons*. Introduced by Judith Hann.

PHOTO GALLERY (6m11s) Slideshow of colour and black-and-white photos taken during production of *The Dæmons*, including design department photos of the sets. Set to the Master's theme and sound effects from the story. Compiled by Paul Shields.

PDF MATERIALS Accessible via a computer are the five episode listings from *Radio Times* for the original BBC1 broadcast of *The Dæmons*, with artwork by Frank Bellamy that accompanied episode one's billing, an article about Katy Manning published the week of episode two, and one about Jon Pertwee published later the same year.

COMING SOON (1m55s) Trailer for the DVD release of *Nightmare of Eden*.

RELATED EXTRAS

Christopher Barry: Director — The Creature from the Pit

The UNIT Family — Day of the Daleks

Coming Soon trailer — The Face of Evil

The Doctor's Composer — The Sun Makers

THE **DALEK COLLECTION**

Boxset of **THE DALEK INVASION OF EARTH, GENESIS OF THE DALEKS, REMEMBRANCE OF THE DALEKS, RESURRECTION OF THE DALEKS** and **REVELATION OF THE DALEKS**

DVD RELEASE BBCDVD2261, 27 January 2007, PG

SLIPCASE Photo illustration by Clayton Hickman on purple spine with silvered logo and title, black gloss circles on front/back

ORIGINAL RRP £79.99

WHAT'S IN THE BOX

This set was released exclusively by Amazon.co.uk in a limited edition. Each story has the same contents and packaging as the individual releases — at the time, all the Dalek stories that were out on DVD except *The Daleks* — held in a cardboard slipcase. Resurrection of the Daleks and Remembrance of the Daleks have since been re-released as Special Edition versions with more advanced restoration and additional features.

● *The two 1960s Dalek movies were also released in a set titled 'The Dalek Collection' by Optimum Home Entertainment in September 2006, as were a selection of New Series episodes in October 2009.*

● *See individual stories for full contents*

DALEK COLLECTOR'S EDITION

Boxset of **THE DALEK INVASION OF EARTH, REMEMBRANCE OF THE DALEKS** and **RESURRECTION OF THE DALEKS**

DVD RELEASE BBCDVD1384, 6 October 2003, PG

SLIPCASE Artwork incorporating Dalek painting by Andrew Skilleter, silvered fortieth anniversary logo, pink/black background

ORIGINAL RRP £39.99

WHAT'S IN THE BOX

This set was released exclusively by WHSmith to celebrate the fortieth anniversary of *Doctor Who*. Each story has the same contents as the individual releases — at the time, all the Dalek stories that were available on DVD — but the discs are in a folded digipack within a cardboard slipcase, rather than individual cases. They are printed with the fortieth anniversary logo and a picture of the relevant Doctor from each story. The set had a limited release of 5,000 numbered copies. Resurrection of the Daleks and Remembrance of the Daleks have since been re-released as Special Edition versions with more advanced restoration and additional features.

— Also known as '40th Anniversary 1963–2003 (Limited Edition)'

● *See individual stories for full contents*

THE **DALEK INVASION OF EARTH**

STORY No.10   SEASON No.2:2

Two discs with six episodes (148½ mins) and 128 minutes of extras, plus optional CGI effects, commentary track and production subtitles

TARDIS TEAM First Doctor, Barbara, Ian, Susan
TIME AND PLACE 22nd Century ruined London and Bedfordshire
ADVERSARIES Daleks (2nd appearance); humans converted into Robomen
FIRST ON TV 21 November–26 December 1964
DVD RELEASE BBCDVD1156, 16 June 2003, PG
COVER Photo illustration by Clayton Hickman, purple strip
— Original release with cover sticker reading 'Doctor Who 40th Anniversary 1963–2003'
ORIGINAL RRP £19.99
— Also released in **Dalek Collector's Edition**; BBCDVD1384, £39.99, 6 October 2003
— Also released in **The Dalek Collection**; BBCDVD2261, £79.99, 27 January 2007

STORY TEASER

The Doctor gets Ian and Barbara back to London but two hundred years in their future. The city is in ruins and deserted except for patrolling Robomen, and the reason soon becomes apparent: the Earth has been invaded by Daleks. Not all humans have been subjugated, however, and the travellers team up with local rebels to outwit the Daleks. But the Doctor finds he faces a difficult choice.

CONNECTIONS

This appears to be an entirely different 22nd Century Dalek invasion from the one seen then erased in *Day of the Daleks* (1972) as these Daleks weakened humanity with meteorite bombardments rather than waiting for them to start their own war. Despite both defeats, the metal meanies try again in *The Parting of the Ways* (2005) and finally succeed in moving the whole planet in *The Stolen Earth* (2008), in which the Doctor directly references their scheme here. They also enslave humans and force them into mining duties in *Day of the Daleks*, *Death to the Daleks* (1974) and *Destiny of the Daleks* (1979), while the Dalek agents in *Asylum of the Daleks* (2012) and *The Time of the Doctor* (2013) are basically more gruesome Robomen. Notable, of course, is the departure of Susan, the first TARDIS traveller to stay behind. Other companions who leave the Doctor to be with a loved one include Vicki (*The Myth Makers*, 1965), Jo (*The Green Death*, 1973), Leela (*The Invasion of Time*, 1978) and Amy (*The Angels Take Manhattan*, 2012), as well, perhaps, as Mel (*Dragonfire*, 1987). Faced with popular demand to bring back the Daleks after killing them off in their debut, Terry Nation simply disregards their previous history with a single line of dialogue and re-establishes them as planetary conquerors. After this the series will take it as read that there are Dalek forces out there in the universe up to no good for the Doctor to encounter and temporarily defeat whenever it needs him to. This was the first full story directed by relative novice Richard Martin and he seems to have won a reputation for handling the technicalities of the show well as he was subsequently given *The Web Planet* and *The Chase* (both 1965) to direct, although the latter apparently defeated him as he never worked on the series afterwards. Bernard Kay (Tyler) is back a few months later playing Saladin in *The Crusade* (1965), then returns as Detective Inspector Crossland in *The Faceless Ones* (1967) and Caldwell in *Colony in Space* (1971), while Michael Goldie (Craddock) having succumbed to Daleks also falls to the Cybermen in *The Wheel in Space* (1968).

WORTH WATCHING

Viewers were asking for the Daleks to return almost as soon as their first story had been shown, such was the immediacy of their appeal. And so rather than occupying a mysterious city on a distant planet, they were brought right down to Earth and shown to be in charge of our world. The scenes of a ruined London would have been familiar to many just twenty years after World War Two. To modern viewers it's more of an exciting romp but still carries an eye-watering sting in its tail.

DISC ONE

THE EPISODES

Episodes one, two, three, four and six are restored from 16mm film copies of the original black-and-white video recordings, recovered from BBC Enterprises in 1978, while episode five is restored from the 35mm black-and-white film onto which it was originally recorded in the studio. Their mono soundtracks are remastered, the VidFIRE process is applied to studio-recorded shots to recapture the smoother motion of video, and end credits are remade to match the originals.

SPECIAL FEATURES

CGI EFFECTS SEQUENCES (1m12s) Watch all the new computer-generated model shots in sequence, with explanatory captions and set to music from the story, or select **CGI Effects On** to view them in place of the original model footage when watching the episodes.

BBC1 TRAILERS (1m43s) Two previews broadcast on BBC1 in the week leading up to episode one, restored from the original 16mm black-and-white film negatives.

COMMENTARY Select **On** to play the audio commentary in place of the main soundtrack when watching the episodes. This is moderated by author and journalist Gary Russell, talking with director Richard Martin [eps 1,2,3,4,5,6], producer Verity Lambert [1,2,3,4,6], William Russell (Ian) [2,4,5,6] and Carole Ann Ford (Susan) [3,4,5,6].

INFORMATION TEXT Select **On** to view subtitles when watching the episodes that provide information and anecdotes about the development, production, broadcast and history of *The Dalek Invasion of Earth*. Written by Martin Wiggins.

SUBTITLES

Select **On** to view subtitles for all episodes, or for the commentary.

DISC TWO

SPECIAL FEATURES

FUTURE VISIONS (17m48s) Set designer Spencer Chapman talks about how he came to work on *Doctor Who*, how the sets for *The Dalek Invasion of Earth* benefited from the serial being recorded in the larger studios at Riverside, the filming at Ealing and on location, and the adaptations he made to the Dalek props.

FUTURE MEMORIES (45m22s) Cast members of *The Dalek Invasion of Earth* recall the characters they played; how they came to be cast; working with director Richard Martin and the regular cast; shooting on location; working with the Daleks and the Slyther; the pressures of studio recording; the legacy of their appearance; and the appeal of the Daleks and *Doctor Who*. With contributions from Ann Davies (Jenny), Peter Fraser (David), Bernard Kay (Tyler), Nicholas Smith (Wells), Dalek operators Nick Evans and Robert Jewell (interviewed in 1983), and Dalek voice actors David Graham and Peter Hawkins (interviewed in 1985). Produced by Peter Finklestone.

TALKING DALEKS (10m30s) Voice actors David Graham and Peter Hawkins (interviewed at a convention in 1985), and Brian Hodgson of the Radiophonic Workshop talk about how they devised the distinctive voices for the Daleks. With additional comments from actor Nicholas Smith.

NOW AND THEN (6m58s) Comparing the filming locations in West and Central London, and at John's Hole quarry in Kent as they look today with how they appeared in August 1964 when used for *The Dalek Invasion of Earth*. Narrated by Gary Russell, produced by Richard Bignell. *See Index iii for further editions*

SCRIPT TO SCREEN (6m2s) Using the studio plan, camera script and clips from episode six of *The Dalek Invasion of Earth*, this shows how an episode of *Doctor Who* was recorded in the studio during the 1960s. Produced by John Kelly.

BLUE PETER (7m3s) Extract from the Thursday 3 February 1966 edition of the BBC1 children's magazine programme in which Valerie Singleton shows how to make three different edible Daleks. With Christopher Trace and real Dalek props.

▶

WHATEVER HAPPENED TO SUSAN? (27m49s) A light-hearted play broadcast on BBC Radio 4 on Saturday 9 July 1994, suggesting that Susan imagined her adventures aboard the TARDIS. Starring Jane Asher as Susan Foreman and James Grout as Ian Chesterton. Written by Adrian Mourby, produced by Brian King.

REHEARSAL FILM (1m42s) Silent 8mm colour film footage shot by Carole Ann Ford during studio rehearsals for episode six of *The Dalek Invasion of Earth* on Friday 23 October 1964. Ford accidentally used the film again so the resulting footage is double-exposed.

PHOTO GALLERY (3m46s) Slideshow of black-and-white photos taken during production of *The Dalek Invasion of Earth*, plus shots of the commentary participants and the cover of the 19 November 1964 edition of *Radio Times* (issue 2141). Set to sound effects from the story. Compiled by Ralph Montagu.

SUBTITLES Select **On** to view subtitles for all Special Features on disc two.

EASTER EGGS

There are two hidden features on these discs to find. *See Appendix 2 for details*

RELATED EXTRAS

Terror Nation — Destiny of the Daleks

The Dalek Tapes — Genesis of the Daleks

DALEK WAR

Boxset of **FRONTIER IN SPACE** and **PLANET OF THE DALEKS**

DVD RELEASE BBCDVD2614, 5 October 2009, PG

SLIPCASE Photo illustration by Clayton Hickman, silvered logo and title, green/black background

ORIGINAL RRP £34.26

WHAT'S IN THE BOX

Two consecutive stories from the tenth season (1973) in which the Daleks make a bid to conquer the Earth empire, using the Master to foment war between humans and Draconians, while they prepare a massive army of Daleks on the planet Spiridon.

● *See individual stories for full contents*

THE **DALEKS**

STORY No.2   **SEASON No.1:2**

Released with **AN UNEARTHLY CHILD** and **THE EDGE OF DESTRUCTION** in **THE BEGINNING** boxset

One disc with seven episodes (171½ mins) and 22½ minutes of extras, plus commentary track for three episodes and production subtitles

TARDIS TEAM First Doctor, Barbara, Ian, Susan

TIME AND PLACE Planet Skaro

ADVERSARIES Daleks (1st appearance)

FIRST ON TV 21 December 1963–1 February 1964

DVD RELEASE BBCDVD1882(B), 30 January 2006, 12 (episodes PG)

COVER Photo illustration by Clayton Hickman, dark purple strip

ORIGINAL RRP £29.99 (boxset)

— Episodes released in The Monster Collection: The Daleks; BBCDVD3813, £9.99, 30 September 2013

STORY TEASER

Horrified to learn that the Doctor can't control the TARDIS and return them home, Ian and Barbara are further shocked when they find themselves on their first alien world: the barren, radiation-ravaged Skaro. When the Doctor tricks his companions into exploring a strange metal city they become prisoners of the Daleks — creatures like nothing they could have imagined. They are forced to help the Daleks gain anti-radiation drugs from their enemies, the Thals, only to find themselves in the final battle of a long-running war between the two races.

CONNECTIONS

The Daleks were an immediate success and became the first adversary to make a return appearance, less than a year later in *The Dalek Invasion of Earth* (1964), and were the only monsters to do so until the Cybermen got a second chance in *The Moonbase* (1967). Here, they're not yet the xenophobes we now think of them as, however, merely seeking to survive even though everyone else will die as a result. This is subtly addressed in *Genesis of the Daleks* (1975), where Davros's goal in creating the Daleks is indeed simply the survival of his people at all costs, but the Daleks themselves see this as possible only by wiping out all potential threats from other species. Skaro itself is only returned to for significant moments in Dalek history: their creation in *Genesis of the Daleks*, their supposed destruction in *The Evil of the Daleks* (1967) and Davros's resurrection in *Destiny of the Daleks* (1979). It was apparently destroyed by the Doctor in *Remembrance of the Daleks* (1988), but was intact again after the Time War in *Asylum of the Daleks* (2012). The Thals themselves are seen even less, returning only in *Planet of the Daleks* (1973) and *Genesis of the Daleks*. Both directors of this story handled further Dalek encounters (*see Index v*), while of the guest cast only the Dalek operators and voice actors returned for the creatures' rematches.

WORTH WATCHING
This is the first ever Dalek story and arguably the one that sealed *Doctor Who*'s success. But that was all unknown when this was being made, of course, so the Daleks are subtly different here from the legendary monsters they were to become, with their motivation being their own survival rather than everyone else's extermination. For the series' first foray to another planet, it lays on the creepiness most effectively, but becomes perhaps a little simple once the Thals are introduced.

THE EPISODES
All seven episodes are restored from 16mm film copies of the original black-and-white video recordings, recovered from BBC Enterprises in 1978. A short section from episode five is restored from a 35mm film copy of the original video recording made for use in the Monday 9 March 1964 edition of *Blue Peter*, while the film of the last five minutes of episode seven is damaged so this section is restored from a one-inch black-and-white video copy made in 1993 before the damage occurred. The episodes' mono soundtracks are remastered and the VidFIRE process is applied to studio-recorded shots to recapture the smoother motion of video. The title sequences are replaced by a modern transfer of the best surviving copy of the original 35mm film and end credits remade to match the originals.

SPECIAL FEATURES
CREATION OF THE DALEKS (17m10s) Examining how the Daleks were originated for their first story, including the development of writer Terry Nation's script with story editor David Whitaker, the look and sound of the creatures themselves, and how they were operated. With contributions from head of drama Sydney Newman (interviewed in 1984), producer Verity Lambert, director Richard Martin, designer Raymond Cusick, special sounds creator Brian Hodgson, Dalek operator Michael Summerton and Dalek voice actor David Graham. Produced by John Kelly.

GALLERY (5m33s) Slideshow of colour and black-and-white photos taken during production of *The Daleks*, including behind-the-scenes and publicity images, plus shots of the commentary participants. Set to sound effects from the story. Compiled by Ralph Montagu.

AUDIO OPTIONS Select **Commentary On** to play the audio commentary in place of the main soundtrack when watching episodes two, four and seven. This is moderated by author and journalist Gary Russell, talking with producer Verity Lambert [ep 2], director Christopher Barry [2,4], William Russell (Ian) [4,7], Carole Ann Ford (Susan) [4,7] and director Richard Martin [7].

INFORMATION TEXT Select **On** to view subtitles when watching the episodes that provide information and anecdotes about the development, production, broadcast and history of *The Daleks*. Written by Martin Wiggins.

SUBTITLES
Select **On** to view subtitles for all episodes and Special Features (except commentary).

RELATED EXTRAS
Daleks Conquer and Destroy — The Chase
Christopher Barry: Director — The Creature from the Pit
Talking Daleks — The Dalek Invasion of Earth
Terror Nation — Destiny of the Daleks
The Dalek Tapes — Genesis of the Daleks

THE **DALEKS' MASTER PLAN**

STORY No.21   SEASON No.3:4

Three surviving episodes (parts 2, 5 and 10 of 12) released in the **LOST IN TIME** *boxset*

TARDIS TEAM First Doctor, Steven, Katarina, Sara

TIME AND PLACE Jungle planet Kembel, 51st Century Earth, swamp planet Mira, Ancient Egypt

ADVERSARIES Daleks (5th appearance); ruler of Earth Mavic Chen; renegade Time Lord the Monk (2nd appearance)

FIRST ON TV 20 November and 11 December 1965 and 15 January 1966

DVD RELEASE BBCDVD1353, 1 November 2004, PG

● See Lost in Time *for full details*

RELATED EXTRAS

From Kingdom to Queen — Battlefield

Terror Nation — Destiny of the Daleks

PDF Documents — The Edge of Destruction

The Dalek Tapes — Genesis of the Daleks

DAY OF THE DALEKS

STORY No.60   SEASON No.9:1

Two discs with four episodes (96½ mins), a new four-part Special Edition (96½ mins) and 134 minutes of extras, plus commentary track, production subtitles and PDF items

Audio navigation of each disc's contents available by pressing Enter after the BBC ident

TARDIS TEAM Third Doctor, Jo, Brigadier and UNIT

TIME AND PLACE Contemporary and 22nd Century England

ADVERSARIES Daleks (8th appearance); ape-like Ogrons (1st appearance)

FIRST ON TV 1–22 January 1972

DVD RELEASE BBCDVD3043, 12 September 2011, PG (episodes U)

COVER Photo illustration by Lee Binding (Daleks by Gavin Rymill), dark orange strip; version with older BBC logo on reverse

ORIGINAL RRP £20.42

STORY TEASER

Rebels from the future travel back to the present day in order to kill a diplomat who they believe will cause a worldwide war that will eventually enable the Daleks to conquer the Earth. When the Doctor and Jo investigate they find themselves transported into that future, where life under Dalek rule is hard. But the cause is not what it seems.

CONNECTIONS

Is this Dalek occupation of Earth in the 22nd Century the same as that seen in *The Dalek Invasion of Earth* (1964)? Ignoring differences in Dalek design, both stories feature humans used as slave labour and a struggling resistance group. But these Daleks use Ogrons rather than Robomen as goons, there's no suggestion of them mining out the core of the planet, and the way the invasion is described is different in each story. The Daleks here also declare, "We have invaded Earth again. We have changed the pattern of history." So the implication is these are Daleks from even further in the future, who saw the failure of the original invasion and travelled back to try again. Their time technology here is similar to that used in *Resurrection of the Daleks* (1984) and *Remembrance of the Daleks* (1988), but we know they have full-on time machines from *The Chase* (1965) and *The Daleks' Master Plan* (1965/66). Perhaps it's their rewriting of the original course of history that makes this timeline sufficiently fragile for the Doctor to successfully erase it. The Ogrons return in *Frontier in Space* (1973), apparently working for the Master although their true loyalty becomes apparent. Louis Marks wrote for *Doctor Who* in its early days with *Planet of Giants* (1964), and later under Robert Holmes' script-editorship he contributed *Planet of Evil* (1975) and *The Masque of Mandragora* (1976). This was the first of three serials directed by Paul Bernard, followed by *The Time Monster* (1972) and *Frontier in Space*. Scott Frederick (Boaz) returns to play Max Stael in *Image of the Fendahl* (1977).

WORTH WATCHING

This was the Daleks' first appearance in *Doctor Who* for more than four years, and the first time they were seen in colour (on television at least). Despite the gap, they were well remembered as the Doctor's prime enemy and dominated the publicity for the start of the 1972 season. More surprisingly, it's one of the few times the Classic Series really played with the possibilities and effects of time travel and the paradoxes that can result, inspiring many later Steven Moffat storylines.

DISC ONE

THE EPISODES

All four episodes are restored from digital duplicates of the original two-inch colour videotape recordings used for broadcast and their mono soundtracks remastered. The title sequences are replaced by a modern transfer of the original 35mm film with credits remade to match the originals.

SPECIAL FEATURES

BLASTING THE PAST (30m33s) The making of *Day of the Daleks*, including the original Dalek-less script by Louis Marks; the paradoxes of time-travel stories; the common roots with James Cameron's *The Terminator*; the motives of the guerilla characters; memories of director Paul Bernard; designing the Ogrons; working with the Daleks; the similarities between the Third Doctor and Jon Pertwee; filming on location; questions of pacing; and staging the climactic battle. With contributions from producer Barry Letts (interviewed in 2009), script editor Terrance Dicks, monster maker John Friedlander, Dalek operator Ricky Newby, actors Anna Barry, Katy Manning and Jimmy Winston, Dalek voice actor Nicholas Briggs, and writers Ben Aaronovitch, Paul Cornell and Dave Owen. Produced by Steve Broster.

A VIEW FROM THE GALLERY (20m) Producer Barry Letts and vision mixer Mike Catherwood revisit the production gallery for Studio 2 in Television Centre to discuss the techniques of directing and editing television in the 1970s.

NATIONWIDE (3m24s) Extract from the Tuesday 22 February 1972 edition of the BBC1 news magazine programme in which the pupils of Balgowan Primary School in Beckenham, Kent receive their prize — a mini-Dalek — for winning the competition in the New Year edition of *Radio Times* that promoted *Day of the Daleks*.

BLUE PETER (4m48s) Extract from the Monday 25 October 1971 edition of the BBC1 children's programme in which Peter Purves recalls his time on *Doctor Who* as Steven (with a clip from the now-missing episode 4 of *The Daleks' Master Plan*) and Daleks invade the studio ahead of their return to *Doctor Who* in *Day of the Daleks*. With Valerie Singleton and John Noakes.

NEXT

PHOTO GALLERY (5m31s) Slideshow of colour and black-and-white photos taken during production of *Day of the Daleks*, including design department photos of the sets. Set to sound effects from the story. Compiled by Paul Shields.

AUDIO OPTIONS Select **Commentary** to play the audio commentary in place of the main soundtrack when watching the episodes. With Jimmy Winston (Shura) [eps 1,2*], vision mixer Mike Catherwood [1,2,3], script editor Terrance Dicks [1,2,4], producer Barry Letts [1,3,4] and Anna Barry (Anat) [2,4]. (* Jimmy Winston also comments on the last three minutes of episode four.)
— Select **Feature Audio** to reinstate the main soundtrack when watching the episodes.

INFO TEXT Select **On** to view subtitles when watching the episodes that provide information and anecdotes about the development, production, broadcast and history of *Day of the Daleks*. Written by Martin Wiggins.

PDF MATERIALS Accessible via a computer are the four episode listings from *Radio Times* for the original BBC1 broadcast of *Day of the Daleks*, the cover of the 30 December 1971 edition (issue 2512) with artwork by Frank Bellamy and competition page promoting episode one, and a one-page article about Katy Manning published the week of episode two.

COMING SOON (1m36s) Trailer for the DVD release of *Colony in Space*.

SUBTITLES
Select **On** to view subtitles for all episodes and Special Features on disc one (except commentary).

DISC TWO
SPECIAL EDITION
On this disc are the four restored episodes augmented with newly shot footage, computer-generated visual effects and updated Dalek voices by New Series voice actor Nicholas Briggs.

SPECIAL FEATURES

D

THE MAKING OF DAY OF THE DALEKS – SPECIAL EDITION (13m34s) Steve Broster, producer of the Special Edition, discusses how and why the story was updated with new visuals and audio. With Mark Ayres, Nicholas Briggs, Toby Chamberlain, John Kelly, Kevan Looseley and Nick Nicholson.

NOW AND THEN (5m22s) Comparing the filming locations at Dropmore Park, Buckinghamshire, Harvey House in Brentford, and Bull's Bridge near Hayes in Middlesex as they look today with how they appeared in mid-September 1971 when used for *Day of the Daleks*. Narrated by Toby Hadoke, produced by Steve Broster. *See Index iii for further editions*

THE UNIT FAMILY PART TWO (31m22s) Examination of the UNIT era story by story, by the people involved in creating it. This edition covers *Terror of the Autons* to *The Green Death* (1971–73), including the casting of Jo Grant, the introduction of the Master, the addition of Captain Yates, the return of the Daleks, the death of Roger Delgado, and the departure of Katy Manning. With contributions from producer Barry Letts (interviewed in 2005), script editor Terrance Dicks, stuntman Derek Ware, and actors Nicholas Courtney (the Brigadier), Richard Franklin (Yates), John Levene (Sergeant Benton), Katy Manning (Jo) and Fernanda Marlowe (Corporal Bell). Produced by Steve Broster. *Part one is on* Inferno *(and* Special Edition*); part three is on* Terror of the Zygons

THE UNIT DATING CONUNDRUM (9m3s) It has always been unclear when the Classic era UNIT stories were supposed to be set: the present day or some years in the future? This takes a light-hearted look at the conflicting evidence presented in the show, with contributions from script editor Terrance Dicks, writer Ben Aaronovitch, and fans Nicholas Briggs and Dave Owen. Narrated by Toby Hadoke, produced by Steve Broster.

THE CHEATING MEMORY (8m26s) Psychology lecturer Dr Sarita Robinson discusses how memory is currently believed to work and why the *Doctor Who* we remember watching as children can be dramatically different from the actual version made. With Ben Aaronovitch and Nicholas Briggs. Narrated by Steve Broster.

TEASER (18s) A trail for this Special Edition that appeared online ahead of the DVD release.

SUBTITLES
Select **On** to view subtitles for the Special Edition and Special Features on disc two.

RELATED EXTRAS
The Dalek Tapes — Genesis of the Daleks
Coming Soon trailer — The Sun Makers

THE **DEADLY ASSASSIN**
STORY No.88   SEASON No.14:3

One disc with four episodes (95 mins) and 63½ minutes of extras, plus commentary track, production subtitles and PDF items
Audio navigation of disc contents available by pressing Enter after the BBC ident

TARDIS TEAM Fourth Doctor
TIME AND PLACE Time Lord homeworld Gallifrey
ADVERSARIES Second Master (1st appearance)
FIRST ON TV 30 October–20 November 1976
DVD RELEASE BBCDVD2430, 11 May 2009, PG
COVER Photo illustration by Clayton Hickman, dark green strip
ORIGINAL RRP £19.56

STORY TEASER

Returning to Gallifrey for the inauguration of a new Time Lord president, the Doctor has a premonition of himself shooting the outgoing president. While avoiding the zealous security around the Capitol, he tries to warn the authorities, only to find himself unable to avert the assassination and arrested as prime suspect. Before he's tried and executed, he must uncover the real assassin. But an old enemy is waiting in the shadows determined to restore himself to life.

CONNECTIONS

While viewers see glimpses of Gallifrey in *Colony in Space* (1971) and *The Three Doctors* (1972/73), this is the first time the Doctor goes back there since his capture in *The War Games* (1969), in which he also ends up on trial. He'll be back in *The Invasion of Time* (1978), *Arc of Infinity* (1983), *The Five Doctors* (1983) and finally (to date) *The Day of the Doctor* (2013). But it's in *The Deadly Assassin* that much of Time Lord lore is established: the various ranks and chapters, the Capitol and Panopticon, the Matrix, artron energy, Rassilon and his many artefacts, and the limit on the number of regenerations a Time Lord can undergo. The last is introduced mainly as motivation for the Master, making him desperate to find a way to extend his life; in contrast, when the Doctor's time is up he's happy to settle down and spend his dotage on Trenzalore (*The Time of the Doctor*, 2013). This is the Master's first appearance since the death of Roger Delgado, who played the character during the Third Doctor era, debuting in *Terror of the Autons* (1971). He's back in this decrepit form in *The Keeper of Traken* (1981) after which he succeeds in acquiring a new lease of life and is played by Anthony Ainley through to the end of the original run (*Survival*, 1989), and by Eric Roberts in *The Movie* (1996) — the only other time the Doctor starts and ends an adventure without a regular companion, until the New Series. Writer Robert Holmes was also script editor of the series at the time but had permission to write one or two stories each season, while David Maloney had been directing for the show since 1969, although this was his penultimate serial (*see Index v*). Bernard Horsfall (Chancellor Goth) was cast by the director several times, as Gulliver in *The Mind Robber* (1968), a Time Lord in *The War Games* and Taron in *Planet of the Daleks* (1973). Angus Mackay (Cardinal Borusa) plays Turlough's headmaster in *Mawdryn Undead* (1983), George Pravda (Castellan Spandrell) is Alexander Denes in *The Enemy of the World* (1967/68) and Professor Jaeger in *The Mutants* (1972), Eric Chitty (Coordinator Engin) is Charles Preslin in *The Massacre* (1966), and Hugh Walters (Commentator Runcible) is Shakespeare in *The Chase* (1965) and Vogel in *Revelation of the Daleks* (1985). Peter Mayock (Solis) plays Ibrahim Namin in *Pyramids of Mars* (1975), while Helen Blatch (Computer voice) appears as Commander Fabian in *The Twin Dilemma* (1984).

WORTH WATCHING

Previous glimpses of the Doctor's home planet had suggested the Time Lords were a powerful, mysterious elite, but for this, the first story set entirely on Gallifrey, Robert Holmes based the society more on a dusty, archaic university, and the Time Lords became a bunch of fuddy-duddies. This provides a stark contrast to the Fourth Doctor's ebullience, while the political plotting makes for a thrilling adventure — and the unexpected appearance of an old villain.

THE EPISODES

All four episodes are restored from digital duplicates of the original two-inch colour videotape recordings used for broadcast and their mono soundtracks remastered. The cliffhanger to part three was trimmed by some six seconds after broadcast owing to complaints, but has been reconstructed from lower-resolution video recordings. The title sequences are replaced by a modern transfer of the original 35mm film with credits remade to match the originals.

SPECIAL FEATURES

THE MATRIX REVISITED (29m17s) The making of *The Deadly Assassin*, including *Doctor Who*'s place in the BBC's popular Saturday-night schedule; the opportunity to have no companion for the Doctor; the roots of the story; co-ordinating the design elements; the decision to resurrect the Master, choosing his look and casting; the location filming; fan backlash against the portrayal of the Time Lords; and complaints from a viewers' watchdog. With contributions from producer Philip Hinchcliffe, director David Maloney (interviewed in 1999 and 2003), designer Roger Murray-Leach, actors Tom Baker and Bernard Horsfall, campaigner Mary Whitehouse (interviewed in

1993), and fan Jan Vincent-Rudzki. Narrated by Sara Griffiths, produced by Paul Vanezis.

THE GALLIFREYAN CANDIDATE (10m31s) Discussion by Newcastle University literature lecturer Dr Stacy Gillis and Oxford University's Andrew Shail of the extent to which *The Deadly Assassin* draws on ideas from *The Manchurian Candidate*, with readings from the 1959 novel written by Richard Condon and clips from the 1962 film directed by John Frankenheimer. Narrated by Carl Kennedy, produced by Chris Chapman.

THE FRIGHTEN FACTOR (16m38s) Do viewers, particularly children, experience genuine fear when watching television shows like *Doctor Who*, and how scary does and should the programme get? Including some of the scariest moments from the Classic and New Series. With contributions from producer Barry Letts, script editor Terrance Dicks, education psychologist Lucy Lewis, church minister Peter Cavanna, writer John Dorney, television archivist Jim Sangster, fan journalists Annabel Gibson, Moray Laing, Tom Spilsbury and Peter Ware, and fan Alex Lydiate. Narrated by Simon Ockenden, produced by Brendan Sheppard.

PHOTO GALLERY (5m37s) Slideshow of colour and black-and-white photos taken during production of *The Deadly Assassin*, including design department photos of the sets. Set to sound effects from the story. Compiled by Derek Handley.

NEXT

AUDIO OPTIONS Select **Commentary** to play the audio commentary in place of the main soundtrack when watching the episodes. With Tom Baker, Bernard Horsfall (Goth) and producer Philip Hinchcliffe on all four episodes.

— Select **Feature Audio** to reinstate the main soundtrack when watching the episodes.

INFO TEXT Select **On** to view subtitles when watching the episodes that provide information and anecdotes about the development, production, broadcast and history of *The Deadly Assassin*. Written by Niall Boyce.

PDF MATERIALS Accessible via a computer are the four episode listings from *Radio Times* for the original BBC1 broadcast of *The Deadly Assassin*.

COMING SOON (1m1s) Trailer for the DVD release of *Delta and the Bannermen*.

SUBTITLES

Select **On** to view subtitles for all episodes and Special Features (except commentary).

EASTER EGG

There is one hidden feature on this disc to find. *See Appendix 2 for details*

RELATED EXTRAS

Roger Murray-Leach Interview — The Ark in Space (and Special Edition)
Coming Soon trailer — Image of the Fendahl
The Rise and Fall of Gallifrey — The Invasion of Time
Dressing Doctor Who — The Mutants

DEATH TO THE DALEKS

STORY No.72   SEASON No.11:3

One disc with four episodes (98 mins) and 79½ minutes of extras, plus commentary and music-only tracks, production subtitles and PDF items
Audio navigation of disc contents available by pressing Enter after the BBC ident

TARDIS TEAM Third Doctor, Sarah Jane

TIME AND PLACE Planet Exxilon

ADVERSARIES Daleks (10th appearance); primitive Exxilons

FIRST ON TV 23 February–16 March 1974

DVD RELEASE BBCDVD3483, 18 June 2012, PG (episodes and extras bar DVD trailer U)

COVER Photo illustration by Lee Binding (Dalek by Gavin Rymill), blue strip; version with older BBC logo on reverse

ORIGINAL RRP £20.42

STORY TEASER

The TARDIS is stranded on the planet Exxilon when all its power is inexplicably drained. The Doctor and Sarah find a human expedition similarly marooned when they came to find a cure for a plague that's ravaging the galaxy. An ancient city built by the Exxilons' ancestors is the cause of the power drain, but before the Doctor can investigate, another spaceship arrives, one full of Daleks.

CONNECTIONS

It's a 1970s Terry Nation story so of course plague is involved: the Daleks planned to release one on Spiridon in *Planet of the Daleks* (1973); here a disease is killing millions and the Daleks plan to drop a plague bomb on Exxilon; in *Genesis of the Daleks* (1975) the Doctor tempts Davros with a hypothetical virus; and in *The Android Invasion* (1975) the Kraals intend to kill off mankind with a plague. Between writing the two latter serials, Nation had created the series *Survivors*, which sees the world's population decimated by a virus. The Daleks also act more deviously than usual, more a trait of David Whitaker's 1960s Dalek stories than Nation's. There's a military group, the Marine Space Corp here being reminiscent of the Space Security Service in *Mission to the Unknown* (1965) and *The Daleks' Master Plan* (1965/66) and the Thal force in *Planet of the Daleks*. The TARDIS loses all power again when it runs out of Zeiton-7 in *Vengeance on Varos* (1985). The Exxilons' regression from a more advanced species is similar to the Uxaerians' in *Colony in Space* (1971), the Sevateem's in *The Face of Evil* (1977) and the Trogs' in *Underworld* (1978). Michael E Briant was a regular director and handled the return of the Cybermen in *Revenge of the Cybermen* the following season (*see Index v*). John Abineri (Railton) also plays Van Lutyens in *Fury from the Deep* (1968), General Carrington in *The Ambassadors of Death* (1970) and Ranquin in *The Power of Kroll* (1978/79).

WORTH WATCHING

The hook of this story is how scary are the Daleks without the power to exterminate, and there is some early intrigue while they are forced to work with the humans for mutual benefit. Unfortunately the Daleks overcome this disability pretty quickly, but there is still interest in the nature of the 'living' city and the character of Bellal, who makes a unique temporary assistant for the Doctor.

THE EPISODES

Episode one is restored from a digital duplicate of a two-inch colour videotape copy of the episode made for broadcast in Dubai and returned from there in 1991, while episodes, two three and four are restored from digital duplicates of the original two-inch colour videotape recordings used for broadcast in the UK. The episodes' mono soundtracks are remastered and the title sequences replaced by a modern transfer of the original 35mm film with credits remade to match the originals.

SPECIAL FEATURES

BENEATH THE CITY OF THE EXXILONS (26m46s) The making of *Death to the Daleks*, including Terry Nation's script; filming on location in a Dorset quarry and getting the Daleks to glide over sand; some unusual Dalek behaviour; creating the Exxilons; problems with the studio recording; the character of Bellal; the life and death of the Exxilon city; and Carey Blyton's incidental music. With contributions from director Michael E Briant, assistant floor manager Richard Leyland, costume designer L Rowland Warne, actors Julian Fox and Arnold Yarrow, and Dalek voice actor Nicholas Briggs. Narrated by a Dalek (Briggs), produced by Chris Chapman.

STUDIO RECORDING (23m35s) Footage from the studio recording on Tuesday 4 December 1973 of scenes around the Dalek spaceship, including retakes and shots unused in the final programme. With explanatory captions.

ON THE SET OF DR WHO AND THE DALEKS (7m49s) Silent 16mm black-and-white film footage shot for the ITV programme *Movie Magazine* showing behind the scenes of the 1965 movie *Dr Who and the Daleks*, directed by Gordon Flemyng and starring Peter Cushing. With comment from film historian Marcus Hearn, the director's son actor Jason Flemyng, assistant first director on the movie Anthony Waye and Dalek operator Bryan Hands. Produced by John Kelly.

DOCTOR WHO STORIES – DALEK MEN (12m59s) Recorded in 2003 for BBC2's *The Story of Doctor Who*, actors Nick Evans and John Scott Martin recall their experiences of operating the Daleks and other monster costumes.

PHOTO GALLERY (5m50s) Slideshow of colour and black-and-white photos taken during production of *Death to the Daleks*, including design department photos of the sets. Set to music from the story. Compiled by Paul Shields.

NEXT

AUDIO OPTIONS Select **Commentary** to play the audio commentary in place of the main soundtrack when watching the episodes. This is moderated by actor and comedian Toby Hadoke, talking with special sounds creator Dick Mills [eps 1,2,3], Julian Fox (Peter Hamilton) [1,2,3,4], director Michael E Briant [1,2,3,4], assistant floor manager Richard Leyland [1,2,4], costume designer L Rowland Warne [1,3,4] and Dalek operator Cy Town [2,3,4]. Hadoke also relays written comments from Joy Harrison (Jill Tarrant).

— Select **Isolated Score** to hear only Carey Blyton's music when watching the episodes.

— Select **Feature Audio** to reinstate the main soundtrack when watching the episodes.

INFO TEXT Select **On** to view subtitles when watching the episodes that provide information and anecdotes about the development, production, broadcast and history of *Death to the Daleks*. Written by Martin Wiggins.

PDF MATERIALS Accessible via a computer are the four episode listings from *Radio Times* for the original BBC1 broadcast of *Death to the Daleks*, with illustrations by Peter Brookes.

COMING SOON (1m19s) Trailer for the DVD release of *The Krotons*.

SUBTITLES

Select **On** to view subtitles for all episodes and Special Features (except commentary).

EASTER EGG

There is one hidden feature on this disc to find. *See Appendix 2 for details*

RELATED EXTRAS

Terror Nation — Destiny of the Daleks
Coming Soon trailer — Dragonfire, The Happiness Patrol
The Dalek Tapes — Genesis of the Daleks

DELTA AND THE BANNERMEN

STORY No.146   SEASON No.24:3

One disc with three episodes (73½ mins) and 103 minutes of extras, plus commentary track, production subtitles and PDF items
Audio navigation of disc contents available by pressing Enter after the BBC ident

TARDIS TEAM Seventh Doctor, Mel

TIME AND PLACE 1950s holiday camp in Wales

ADVERSARIES Assassins the Bannermen and their vicious leader Gavrok

FIRST ON TV 2–16 November 1987

DVD RELEASE BBCDVD2599, 22 June 2009, PG

COVER Photo illustration by Clayton Hickman, turquoise strip

ORIGINAL RRP £19.56

STORY TEASER

The Doctor and Mel win a trip on a Navarino Nostalgia Tour to 1950s Disneyland, but a collision with an American satellite causes their ship (disguised as a coach) to crash-land instead by the less salubrious Shangri-La holiday camp in South Wales. Also aboard is Delta, last survivor of the Chimeron species, who are being hunted to extinction by Gavrok and his Bannermen — and they are already in hot pursuit.

CONNECTIONS

This is the Doctor's second trip to Wales, having visited in *The Green Death* (1973); he returns in *The Unquiet Dead* (2005), *Boom Town* (2005), *Utopia* (2007), *Last of the Time Lords* (2007) and *The Hungry Earth* (2010). The motivation of the Bannermen is unclear (for all we know the Chimeron were once their oppressors), but the only other instance of a group of aggressors hunting down the last of a species in order to wipe them out is the Cybermen's attack on Voga in *Revenge of the*

Cybermen (1975), and arguably the Silents' attempts to kill the Doctor before he reaches Trenzalore. Chris Clough directed *Delta and the Bannermen* along with the following story, *Dragonfire*, as one production of six episodes, as with his handling of *The Trial of a Time Lord* episodes nine to fourteen (1986), and *The Happiness Patrol* and *Silver Nemesis* (1988). Of the main guest cast, only Tim Scott (male Chimeron) has another speaking role, as Earnest P in *The Happiness Patrol*.

WORTH WATCHING

This is *Doctor Who* at perhaps its most fun and light-hearted, perfectly capturing the atmosphere of its holiday camp setting and wallowing in the rock'n'roll music of the era. And yet the plotline of a militaristic group attempting genocide is treated as straightforward malevolence, with no attempt to fit it into the context of the setting, making for an awkward mix. Starting to emerge, however, in Sylvester McCoy's early portrayal of the Doctor are signs of the darker characterisation to come.

THE EPISODES

All three episodes are restored from digital duplicates of the original one-inch colour videotape recordings used for broadcast and their mono soundtracks remastered. The computer-generated title sequences are replaced by a digital duplicate of the original one-inch colour videotape recording with credits remade to match the originals (although one caption slide from episode two is mislabelled).

SPECIAL FEATURES

BUT FIRST THIS (6m2s) Extract from the Monday 31 August 1987 edition of the BBC1 children's summer-holiday morning programme in which Andy Crane introduces a report from the location recording of *Delta and the Bannermen* in early-July 1987, including interviews with Sylvester McCoy, Bonnie Langford and Ken Dodd.

WALES TODAY (2m16s) Report from the BBC local news programme on Friday 3 July 1987 about the recording that day of *Delta and the Bannermen* at Butlins in Barry Island, South Wales, including Sylvester McCoy and producer John Nathan-Turner interviewed by reporter Elfyn Thomas.

EPISODE ONE – FIRST EDIT (30m29s) The initial, longer edit of episode one, with as-recorded sound before the addition of music or sound effects, featuring a different arrangement of some scenes and material cut from the final programme.

INTERVIEW RUSHES (16m32s) The full interviews with Sylvester McCoy, Bonnie Langford and Ken Dodd filmed for *But First This*.

HUGH AND US (7m4s) Actor Hugh Lloyd, who plays Goronwy in *Delta and the Bannermen*, talks about his long career in entertainment, from variety to *Hancock's Half Hour*, *Hugh and I* and his appearance in *Doctor Who*.

CLOWN COURT (5m41s) Extract from the 8 October 1988 edition of *The Noel Edmonds Saturday Roadshow* featuring outtakes from the recording of *Delta and the Bannermen*, plus one from *The Awakening* (1984), and fluffed lines from the recording of the sketch itself. With Sylvester McCoy (in costume as the Doctor) and Noel Edmonds.

NEXT

STRIPPED FOR ACTION (21m33s) *Doctor Who* comic strips have run in various publications since the early days of the television series. This examines the Seventh Doctor's comic strip adventures in Marvel Comics UK's *Doctor Who Magazine* and *The Incredible Hulk Presents*, plus the return of earlier Doctors to the strip when it looked like the programme really wasn't coming back. With contributions from magazine editors Alan Barnes, John Freeman and Gary Russell, comics writers Paul Cornell, Simon Furman and Scott Gray, artist Lee Sullivan, and *Doctor Who* script editor Andrew Cartmel. Directed by Marcus Hearn. *See Index iii for further editions*

TRAILS AND CONTINUITY (3m18s) Previews and continuity announcements from the original BBC1 broadcasts of episode four of the preceding story, *Paradise Towers*, and all three episodes of *Delta and the Bannermen*, with previous-episode summaries and a plug for the 1986 theme single.

PHOTO GALLERY (8m21s) Slideshow of colour and black-and-white photos taken during production of *Delta and the Bannermen*. Set to music from the story. Compiled by Derek Handley.

AUDIO OPTIONS Select **Commentary** to play the audio commentary in place of the main soundtrack when watching the episodes. With Sylvester McCoy, script editor Andrew Cartmel and director

Chris Clough on all three episodes, joined halfway through episode one by Sara Griffiths (Ray).
— Select **Feature Audio** to reinstate the main soundtrack when watching the episodes.

INFO TEXT Select **On** to view subtitles when watching the episodes that provide information and anecdotes about the development, production, broadcast and history of *Delta and the Bannermen*. Written by Andrew Pixley.

PDF MATERIALS Accessible via a computer are the three episode listings from *Radio Times* for the original BBC1 broadcast of *Delta and the Bannermen*.

COMING SOON (1m36s) Trailer for the DVD release of *The War Games*.

SUBTITLES
Select **On** to view subtitles for all episodes and Special Features (except commentary).

RELATED EXTRAS
Coming Soon trailer — The Deadly Assassin

DESTINY OF THE DALEKS

STORY No.104 SEASON No.17:1

One disc with four episodes (100 mins) and 54 minutes of extras, plus optional CGI effects, commentary track, production subtitles and PDF items

TARDIS TEAM Fourth Doctor, and introducing Second Romana
TIME AND PLACE Dalek homeworld Skaro
ADVERSARIES Daleks (12th appearance); Davros (2nd appearance); Movellans
FIRST ON TV 1–22 September 1979
DVD RELEASE BBCDVD2434, 26 November 2007, PG
COVER Photo illustration by Lee Binding, dark pink strip
ORIGINAL RRP £19.99
— Also released in The Complete Davros Collection; BBCDVD2508, £99.99, 26 November 2007

STORY TEASER
The TARDIS arrives on a barren world that gives the Doctor a foreboding sense of *déjà vu*. He and Romana encounter the Movellans, a group of stylish soldiers who reveal this is Skaro, home of their enemies the Daleks. Together they investigate the signs of underground drilling and discover the Daleks are searching for their long-dead creator. The Doctor agrees to help the Movellans get to Davros first to discover if the evil scientist can possibly still be alive, but he soon learns that his enemy's enemies aren't necessarily his friends.

CONNECTIONS
Pleased with the portrayal and impact of Davros in his debut *Genesis of the Daleks* (1975), writer Terry Nation was keen to use him again when he was invited to write a new Dalek story (and had deliberately written the conclusion to the former serial so that Davros wasn't seen to be killed). Unfortunately Michael Wisher, who originally played the character, was unavailable when *Destiny of the Daleks* was being recorded and the part had to be recast, although the same mask and costume as before were used. This story also introduced the Movellans, a species of robot that was deadlocked in battle with the Daleks — an odd outcome given the Daleks were never previously presented as slaves to logic, with viewers frequently reminded that there were thinking creatures inside the metal shells. While the Movellans themselves don't appear in the series again, in the next Dalek serial, *Resurrection of the Daleks* (1984), it's revealed they have gained the upper hand by developing a virus that kills only Daleks. They seek out Davros again to save them, and it isn't until the New Series that we see Dalek stories without him, although he eventually pops up in *The Stolen Earth/Journey's End* (2008). Skaro is seen for the last time in the Classic Series, having previously been visited in *The Daleks* (1963/64), *The Evil of the Daleks* (1967) and *Genesis of the Daleks*, although it's seemingly destroyed in *Remembrance of the Daleks* (1988) yet seen from space in *The Movie* (1996) and revisited in *Asylum of the Daleks* (2012). This was Terry Nation's final work on *Doctor Who* (*see Index v*), having helped ensure its early success by creating the Daleks, and was the sole

serial directed by Ken Grieve. Of the guest cast, only Tony Osoba (Lan) appears again, as Kracauer in *Dragonfire* (1987).

WORTH WATCHING

Although it was four years since the Daleks had appeared in *Doctor Who* on television, they were a continuing presence in the public eye, name-checked whenever an item about the show featured in another programme and even having their own series of annual storybooks from 1975 to 1978. But following *Destiny of the Daleks* this attention seemed to decline. Was this serial to blame? Certainly the Dalek props are at their most dilapidated on screen, and losing to a bunch of disco robots does little for their scariness. Post-*Star Wars*, they just looked far too cheap. But more significantly the show itself was heading towards a change. Nation's simple adventure plots were no longer what audiences wanted and when the Daleks did return, as inevitably they always do, it was in more complex, continuity-heavy stories.

THE EPISODES

All four episodes are restored from digital duplicates of the original two-inch colour videotape recordings used for broadcast and their mono soundtracks remastered. The title sequences are replaced by a modern transfer of the original 35mm film with credits remade to match the originals.

SPECIAL FEATURES

TERROR NATION (27m49s) Profile of writer Terry Nation, who died in 1997, looking at how he came to work on *Doctor Who*, the creation of the Daleks and his presentation of them in his own scripts, and his non-Dalek stories. Includes comments from Nation himself taken from past radio interviews and clips from the edition of BBC2 documentary series *Whicker's World* broadcast on Saturday 27 January 1968. With contributions from producers Philip Hinchcliffe and Barry Letts, script editor Terrance Dicks, director Richard Martin, and Dalek voice actor Nicholas Briggs. Produced by Richard Molesworth.

DIRECTING WHO (9m28s) Director Ken Grieve talks about his approach to the filming and recording of *Destiny of the Daleks*, including working with Douglas Adams and Tom Baker, and using a Steadicam in its early days.

CGI EFFECTS Select **CGI Effects On** to view updated computer-generated effects in place of some of the original visual effects when watching the episodes.

TRAILS AND CONTINUITY (3m45s) The specially recorded teaser for the new season and the return of the Daleks, broadcast on Saturday 25 August 1979; a preview and continuity announcements from the original BBC1 broadcast of episode one of *Destiny of the Daleks*, with a plug for the *Genesis of the Daleks* LP; plus a trailer for the repeat showing of the story in August 1980.

PHOTO GALLERY (8m14s) Slideshow of colour and black-and-white photos taken during production of *Destiny of the Daleks*, set to sound effects from the story. Compiled by Derek Handley.

NEXT

AUDIO OPTIONS Select **Commentary** to play the audio commentary in place of the main soundtrack when watching the episodes. With Lalla Ward (Romana) and director Ken Grieve on all four episodes, joined from episode two by David Gooderson (Davros).

— Select **Feature Audio** to reinstate the main soundtrack when watching the episodes.

INFO TEXT Select **On** to view subtitles when watching the episodes that provide information and anecdotes about the development, production, broadcast and history of *Destiny of the Daleks*. Written by Richard Molesworth.

PRIME COMPUTER ADVERTS (3m7s) Four television commercials with Tom Baker and Lalla Ward, as the Doctor and Romana, made for Prime Computer in Australia in 1980 and 1981.

COMING SOON (1m6s) Trailer for the DVD releases of *Doctor Who and the Silurians*, *The Sea Devils* and *Warriors of the Deep* in the Beneath the Surface boxset.

RADIO TIMES LISTINGS Accessible via a computer is a PDF file of the four episode listings for the original BBC1 broadcast of *Destiny of the Daleks*, a one-page article introducing the 1979/80 season, and a poem by Roger Woddis published the week of episode four.

 ● *The initial release of this disc (and that in the* Complete Davros Collection *boxset) accidentally omitted the PDF. A corrected disc was subsequently reissued.*

SUBTITLES
Select **On** to view subtitles for all episodes and Special Features (except commentary).

EASTER EGG
There is one hidden feature on this disc to find. *See Appendix 2 for details*

RELATED EXTRAS
The Dalek Tapes — Genesis of the Daleks
Coming Soon trailer — Planet of Evil

DOCTOR WHO AND THE SILURIANS

STORY No.52   SEASON No.7:2

Released with **THE SEA DEVILS** and **WARRIORS OF THE DEEP** in the
BENEATH THE SURFACE boxset

Two discs with seven episodes (167 mins) and 91½ minutes of extras, plus commentary and music-only tracks, production subtitles and PDF items

TARDIS TEAM Third Doctor, Liz, Brigadier and UNIT

TIME AND PLACE Contemporary research centre in Derbyshire

ADVERSARIES Silurians (1st appearance)

FIRST ON TV 31 January–14 March 1970

DVD RELEASE BBCDVD2438(A), 14 January 2008, PG

COVER Photo illustration by Clayton Hickman, dark green strip

ORIGINAL RRP £39.99 (boxset)

— Episodes released in The Monster Collection: The Silurians; BBCDVD3811, £9.99,
30 September 2013

STORY TEASER
Now stuck on Earth and working as scientific advisor to UNIT, the Doctor joins the Brigadier and Liz in an investigation of mysterious power losses at a nuclear research station situated underground in Derbyshire. They discover a species of ancient reptiles are waking from their long hibernation and consider Earth their world, and mankind a mere pest to be eradicated.

CONNECTIONS
The species name of the intelligent reptile-like creatures that once had a civilisation on Earth is sometimes doubted. Here the name 'Silurian' is first used by the Doctor, although he has seen Dr Quinn's notes on the Silurian period which, as Miss Dawson also uses the name unprompted, presumably suggest this. In *The Sea Devils*, the Doctor makes a point of rejecting the name (as life had barely crawled out of the oceans at that time — "The chap who discovered them must have got the period wrong," he says) and suggests 'Eocene' is more accurate. This is sometimes refuted as it comes after the extinction of the dinosaurs at the end of the Cretaceous, which is mistakenly assumed to be the event the Silurians were sheltering from. However, while mammals multiplied in the absence of large predatory dinosaurs, for all we know a surviving reptilian species evolved intelligence, and would have coexisted with early hominids if they were around into the Oligocene period — the Silurians here talks of 'apes' raiding their crops. The Doctor ascribes their hibernation to the arrival of the Moon, which is ludicrous (maybe the Time Lords accidentally messed with that bit of his memory when taking away his TARDIS knowledge), so perhaps an approaching dwarf planet really did threaten to strip away the atmosphere, which was cooling anyway following the Azolla event. In *Warriors of the Deep*, they refer to themselves as Silurians, but then they also call their aquatic cousins Sea Devils, a term originated by a frightened workman in the story of that name and again propagated by the Doctor. After flirting with the oxymoronic 'Homo Reptilia' (again coined by the Doctor — he's not having much luck with this) in *The Hungry Earth/Cold Blood* (2010), the New Series has settled on Silurian, but does seem to treat them as contemporaneous with Cretaceous dinosaurs (*Dinosaurs on a Spaceship*, 2012). So it's most likely they do call themselves Silurians, which coincidentally sounds to us like one of our geological periods, and Dr Quinn heard

it from them in the first place. Of course, writer Malcolm Hulke was just choosing a name he thought sounded good, as he did with the Draconians, his other species of reptilian bipeds featured in *Frontier in Space* (1973). Director Timothy Combe was a production assistant on some early *Doctor Who* serials but directed only this and the following year's *The Mind of Evil*. Peter Miles (Dr Lawrence) makes his first appearance in the programme, returning as Professor Whitaker in *Invasion of the Dinosaurs* (1974) and, most notably, as Davros's deputy Nyder in *Genesis of the Daleks* (1975). Norman Jones (Major Baker) plays Krisong in *The Abominable Snowmen* (1967) and Hieronymous in *The Masque of Mandragora* (1976), Paul Darrow (Captain Hawkins) is Tekker in *Timelash* (1985), Richard Steele (Sergeant Hart) is Commandant Gorton in *The War Games* (1969), and Derek Pollitt (Private Wright) is the cowardly Driver Evans in *The Web of Fear* (1968). Geoffrey Palmer (Edward Masters) plays the Administrator in *The Mutants* (1972) and appears in the New Series as the Titanic's Captain Hardaker in *Voyage of the Damned* (2007).

WORTH WATCHING

This is the story that introduces the idea that once the Earth was inhabited by bipedal reptiles who went into hibernation to avoid a worldwide catastrophe and never woke up — famously as a way to have a story on Earth without it involving either invading aliens or mad scientists. It's a great premise and the Silurian masks are an effective design, sadly realised less well in later appearances. The scenes of plague victims in London are not as commonly lauded as the Auton attack in the preceding *Spearhead from Space*, but are just as chilling. This story also sees the Doctor settling into his work with UNIT and getting a new car, the yellow roadster Bessie.

DISC ONE

THE EPISODES

To maximise their quality on the DVDs, episodes one to four are on disc one and episodes five to seven are on disc two. All four episodes on this disc are restored from 16mm black-and-white film copies of the original two-inch colour videotape recordings and recoloured using copies of lower-resolution home-video recordings made when the serial was broadcast in America in 1977. A short section at the start of episode three missing from the colour copy is recoloured manually, digitally painting in colour for key frames which is then extrapolated across further frames. The episodes' mono soundtracks are remastered and the VidFIRE process is applied to studio-recorded shots to recapture the smoother motion of video. The title sequences are replaced by a modern transfer of the original 35mm film with credits remade to match the originals.

SPECIAL FEATURES

AUDIO OPTIONS Select **Commentary** to play the audio commentary in place of the main soundtrack when watching the episodes. With Caroline John (Liz) [eps 1,2,3], producer Barry Letts [1,2,3,4], director Timothy Combe [1,2,3,4], Peter Miles (Dr Lawrence) [1,2,4] and script editor Terrance Dicks [1,3,4].
— Select **Isolated Music** to hear only Carey Blyton's music when watching the episodes.
— Select **Feature Audio** to reinstate the main soundtrack when watching the episodes.

WHAT LIES BENEATH (35m12s) The cultural and political factors of the late-60s and early-70s that influenced the writing of *Doctor Who and the Silurians* and how audiences at the time viewed the show. Including the BBC's earlier ventures into science fiction as a reflection of society; the expansion of *Doctor Who*'s audience to include adults as well as children; the political views of writer Malcolm Hulke; the scientific plausibility of the ideas in *The Silurians*; a contemporary audience's views of scientists, politicians and the military; reflections of the Cold War; the influence of the BBC's own structures; and contemporary race relations. With contributions from producer Barry Letts, script editor Terrance Dicks, director Timothy Combe, actors Nicholas Courtney, Caroline John and Peter Miles, New Series writer Paul Cornell, and former MP Roy Hattersley. Written by David Harley, narrated by Geoffrey Palmer, produced by Steve Broster.

INFO TEXT Select **On** to view subtitles when watching the episodes that provide information and anecdotes about the development, production, broadcast and history of *Doctor Who and the Silurians*. Written by Martin Wiggins.

SUBTITLES

Select **On** to view subtitles for all episodes and Special Features on disc one (except commentary).

DISC TWO

THE EPISODES

Episodes five, six and seven on this disc are restored from 16mm black-and-white film copies of the original two-inch colour videotape recordings and recoloured using copies of lower-resolution home-video recordings made when the serial was broadcast in America in 1977. A section at the end of episode five missing from the colour copy reuses the computer colourisation produced for the serial's VHS release in July 1992. The episodes' mono soundtracks are remastered and the VidFIRE process is applied to studio-recorded shots to recapture the smoother motion of video. The title sequences are replaced by a modern transfer of the original 35mm film with credits remade to match the originals.

D

SPECIAL FEATURES

AUDIO OPTIONS Select **Commentary** to play the audio commentary in place of the main soundtrack when watching the episodes. With Peter Miles (Dr Lawrence) [eps 5,6], Geoffrey Palmer (Masters) [5,6], Nicholas Courtney (the Brigadier) [5,6,7], Caroline John (Liz) [5,7], producer Barry Letts [6,7] and script editor Terrance Dicks [6,7].

— Select **Isolated Music** to hear only Carey Blyton's music when watching the episodes.
— Select **Feature Audio** to reinstate the main soundtrack when watching the episodes.

INFO TEXT Select **On** to view subtitles when watching the episodes that provide information and anecdotes about the development, production, broadcast and history of *Doctor Who and the Silurians*. Written by Martin Wiggins.

GOING UNDERGROUND (19m9s) The making of *Doctor Who and the Silurians*, including the challenges of creating a realistic cave system in the television studio; devising the Silurians' point-of-view shots; the Silurian costumes; the location filming; the guest cast; and how the Doctor's car Bessie wasn't strictly road legal. With contributions from producer Barry Letts, script editor Terrance Dicks, director Timothy Combe, designer Barry Newbery, and actors Nicholas Courtney, Caroline John and Peter Miles. Produced by Steve Broster.

NEXT

NOW & THEN (9m41s) Comparing the filming locations in Shepherd's Bush and Marylebone Station, London, and around Tilford and Godalming in Surrey as they look today with how they appeared in November 1969 when used for *Doctor Who and the Silurians*. Narrated by Geoffrey Palmer, produced by Richard Bignell. *See Index iii for further editions*

MUSICAL SCALES (13m55s) Discussion of Carey Blyton's exotic incidental music for *Doctor Who and the Silurians*, and the equally experimental scores by Malcolm Clarke for its sequel *The Sea Devils* (1972) and Tristram Cary for *The Mutants* (1972). With contributions from producer Barry Letts, directors Christopher Barry, Michael E Briant and Timothy Combe, and composers Mark Ayres and Malcolm Clarke (at a convention in 1998). Produced by John Kelly.

COLOUR SILURIAN OVERLAY (4m44s) How this story was restored to colour by combining a black-and-white film copy with a low-quality off-air video copy, as the original colour videotapes no longer exist. Narrated by IT Williams, produced by Steven Bagley.

NEXT

PHOTO GALLERY (6m3s) Slideshow of colour and black-and-white photos taken during production of *Doctor Who and the Silurians*, plus publicity shots of Jon Pertwee, Caroline John and Nicholas Courtney, and photos of the season's monsters taken for *Radio Times*. Set to music from the story. Compiled by Ralph Montagu.

COMING SOON: THE TIME MEDDLER (1m4s) Trailer for the DVD release of *The Time Meddler*.

RADIO TIMES LISTINGS Accessible via a computer is a PDF file of the seven episode listings for the original BBC1 broadcast of *Doctor Who and the Silurians*, and a one-page article about Jon Pertwee and Bessie published the week of episode one.

SUBTITLES

Select **On** to view subtitles for all episodes and Special Features on disc two (except commentary).

EASTER EGG

There is one hidden feature on these discs to find. *See Appendix 2 for details*

THE **DOMINATORS**

STORY No.44   SEASON No.6:1

One disc with five episodes (121½ mins) and 46 minutes of extras, plus commentary track, production subtitles and PDF items
Audio navigation of disc contents available by pressing Enter after the BBC ident

TARDIS TEAM Second Doctor, Jamie, Zoe
TIME AND PLACE Planet Dulcis
ADVERSARIES Warmongering Dominators; robot Quarks
FIRST ON TV 10 August–7 September 1968
DVD RELEASE BBCDVD2807, 12 July 2010, PG (episodes and extras bar DVD trailer U)
COVER Photo illustration by Clayton Hickman, light purple strip;
version with older BBC logo on reverse
ORIGINAL RRP £19.99

STORY TEASER

The peaceful Dulcians have renounced violence and the radiation-soaked Island of Death stands as monument to the follies of their past. But when a group of students journey to the island they find no contamination. Unknown to them, a pair of vicious Dominators have landed and are preparing to incinerate the planet. It falls to the Doctor to convince the Dulcians to fight or be annihilated.

CONNECTIONS

This story is written by Mervyn Haisman and Henry Lincoln, who scripted the two stories from the previous season featuring the Great Intelligence and its robot Yeti: *The Abominable Snowmen* (1967) and *The Web of Fear* (1968). However, they fell out with the production team over changes made to their script for *The Dominators* and took their names off it, as well as abandoning a planned third Yeti story that would have written out Jamie. It was hoped the Quarks would prove as successful as the Daleks or Cybermen but they make only a brief cameo at the end of *The War Games* (1969) and are never seen again on screen. The Dulcians are reminiscent of the Thals in *The Daleks* (1963/64) in their refusal to use violence, as is the situation they face as a ruthless species plans to wipe them out in the process of generating the radiation it needs. This was the last of three serials directed by Morris Barry, the others featuring Cybermen: *The Moonbase* (1967) and *The Tomb of the Cybermen* (1967). Ronald Allen (Rago) plays Professor Cornish in *The Ambassadors of Death* (1970), Brian Cant (Tensa) is Kert Gantry in *The Daleks' Master Plan* (1965/66), Malcolm Terris (Etnin) is the Skonnon pilot in *The Horns of Nimon* (1979), and Philip Voss (Wahed) is Acomat in *Marco Polo* (1964). Arthur Cox (Cully) appears in the New Series as Mr Henderson in *The Eleventh Hour* (2010).

WORTH WATCHING

Perhaps because of the extensive reworking of the script that so upset its writers, *The Dominators* doesn't quite hit home with its ideas. It has been suggested the intention was to criticise contemporary anti-war feeling among the younger generation by showing the danger of pacifism in the face of a greater aggressive force, yet it's the old leaders here who refuse to fight and the young bucks who argue for its necessity. And the Dominators are hardly invincible, despite their robot Quarks (too endearing to be fearsome), as their underestimation of the Doctor and friends proves their undoing.

THE EPISODES

Episodes one, two, four and five are restored from 16mm film copies of the original black-and-white video recordings, held by the BFI, while episode three is restored from the 35mm black-and-white film onto which it was originally recorded in the studio. Their mono soundtracks are remastered and the VidFIRE process is applied to studio-recorded shots to recapture the smoother motion of video. The title sequences are replaced by a modern transfer of the original 35mm film with end credits remade to match the originals.

SPECIAL FEATURES

RECHARGE AND EQUALISE (22m58s) The making of *The Dominators*, including inspirations for the story; problems with the scripting; cast opinions of the story; unrealised merchandising hopes for the Quarks leading to an abandoned third Yeti story; the style of director Morris Barry; the casting and look of the Dominators and Dulcians; the location filming; working with the Quarks and developing their sound; recreating the filming location in the studio and other sets; and designing the soundscape in place of music. With contributions from script editor Derrick Sherwin, co-writer Mervyn Haisman, designer Barry Newbery, make-up supervisor Sylvia James, special sounds creator Brian Hodgson, and actors Giles Block, Arthur Cox, Felicity Gibson and Frazer Hines. Narrated by Stephen Greif, produced by John Kelly.

TOMORROW'S TIMES – THE SECOND DOCTOR (13m15s) Coverage of *Doctor Who* in the national newspapers during the Second Doctor's era from 1966 to 1969. Presented by Caroline John, written and directed by Marcus Hearn. *See Index iii for further editions*

PHOTO GALLERY (5m47s) Slideshow of black-and-white photos taken during production of *The Dominators*, including design department photos of the sets. Set to sound effects from the story. Compiled by Derek Handley.

AUDIO OPTIONS Select **Commentary** to play the audio commentary in place of the main soundtrack when watching the episodes. This is moderated by actor and comedian Toby Hadoke, talking with Giles Block (Teel) [eps 1,2,3], Arthur Cox (Cully) [1,2,4,5], Frazer Hines (Jamie) [1,2,4,5], make-up supervisor Sylvia James [1,3] and Wendy Padbury (Zoe) [2,3,4,5].
— Select **Feature Audio** to reinstate the main soundtrack when watching the episodes.

INFO TEXT Select **On** to view subtitles when watching the episodes that provide information and anecdotes about the development, production, broadcast and history of *The Dominators*. Written by Martin Wiggins.

PDF MATERIALS Accessible via a computer are the five episode listings from *Radio Times* for the original BBC1 broadcast of *The Dominators*, a short article introducing the story, and one about Wendy Padbury published the week of episode four.

COMING SOON (1m24s) Trailer for the DVD releases of *Revenge of the Cybermen* and *Silver Nemesis*.

SUBTITLES

Select **On** to view subtitles for all episodes and Special Features (except commentary).

EASTER EGG

There is one hidden feature on this disc to find. *See Appendix 2 for details*

RELATED EXTRAS

Coming Soon trailer — The King's Demons, Planet of Fire
Sylvia James - In Conversation — The War Games

DRAGONFIRE

STORY No.147   SEASON No.24:4

Released with **THE HAPPINESS PATROL** in the **ACE ADVENTURES** boxset
One disc with three episodes (73½ mins) and 79½ minutes of extras, plus commentary and music-only tracks, production subtitles and PDF items
Audio navigation of disc contents available by pressing Enter after the BBC ident

TARDIS TEAM Seventh Doctor, Mel, and introducing Ace

TIME AND PLACE Future Iceworld trading outpost on planet Svartos

ADVERSARIES Exiled criminal Kane

FIRST ON TV 23 November–7 December 1987

DVD RELEASE BBCDVD3387A, 7 May 2012, PG

COVER Photo illustration by Clayton Hickman, dark blue strip; version with older BBC logo on reverse

ORIGINAL RRP £30.63 (boxset)

STORY TEASER

Iceworld appears to be a simple trading outpost but behind the scenes proprietor Kane is recruiting an army of mercenaries in deep freeze and there are tales of a fire-breathing dragon roaming the lower levels. When the Doctor crosses paths again with dodgy dealer Glitz, he's lured into helping him with a treasure hunt, but Kane is tracking them and has his own reasons for finding the dragon that guards a valuable prize.

CONNECTIONS

The Doctor first finds himself in a freezing environment in *Marco Polo* (1964), when the TARDIS lands on the plain of Pamir in the Himalayas. His friends venture into ice caves in episode four of *The Keys of Marinus*, 'The Snows of Terror' (1964) but the Doctor himself is keeping cosy in the city of Millennius. A visit to the South Pole in *The Tenth Planet* (1966) leads to his first encounter with the Cybermen, while a later meeting is in their frozen hibernation complex in *The Tomb of the Cybermen* (1967). He's back in the Himalayas in *The Abominable Snowmen* (1967), although on the milder foothills, but with his very next trip ends up during a future ice age in *The Ice Warriors*. He travels by plane to Antarctica again in *The Seeds of Doom* (1976), seeks the Key to Time on Ribos during its ice time in *The Ribos Operation* (1978), revisits the frozen city of the Cybermen on Telos in *Attack of the Cybermen* (1985) and, after Iceworld, arrives on the snowy Ood-Sphere in *Planet of the Ood* (2008) and again in *The End of Time* (2009/10). The TARDIS itself freezes up as it appears to approach a cold star in *Amy's Choice* (2010), and the Doctor is deposited on the icy planet that forms the *Asylum of the Daleks* (2012). Glitz, played by Tony Selby, first appears in *The Trial of a Time Lord: The Mysterious Planet* (1986) and at its conclusion when he first meets Mel. Ian Briggs also wrote *The Curse of Fenric* (1989), which explains how Ace ended up on Iceworld, while *Dragonfire* was part of Chris Clough's second stint as director on *Doctor Who* (see *Index v*). Tony Osoba (Kracauer) plays one of the glam Movellans, Lan, in *Destiny of the Daleks* (1979), while Shirin Taylor (Stellar's mother) comes to a grisly end in *The Stones of Blood* (1978).

WORTH WATCHING

By the end of the 1987 season new script editor Andrew Cartmel was finally getting his vision for *Doctor Who* into the scripts (if not quite onto the screen yet) and *Dragonfire* moves some way towards the more serious tone of the next two years, helped by the departure of Bonnie Langford's Mel and the introduction of bellicose teenager Ace, played by Sophie Aldred. There's also a fun return by Tony Selby as Glitz from the previous season, and a particularly impressive visual effect at the climax that echoes *Raiders of the Lost Ark*.

THE EPISODES

All three episodes are restored from digital duplicates of the original one-inch colour videotape recordings used for broadcast and their mono soundtracks remastered.

SPECIAL FEATURES

FIRE AND ICE (35m6s) The making of *Dragonfire*, including the development of the script; the decision to write out companion Mel; casting Sophie Aldred as Ace and the character's background; writing Mel's leaving scene; Sylvester McCoy's developing interpretation of the Doctor; the guest cast; creating Iceworld in the studio; designing the dragon; working with the director; how the cliffhanger to episode one differed from script to screen; and controversy over the villain's gruesome demise. With contributions from script editor Andrew Cartmel, writer Ian Briggs, director Chris Clough, and actors Sophie Aldred, Sylvester McCoy and Edward Peel. Produced by Ed Stradling.

DELETED & EXTENDED SCENES (9m57s) A selection of scenes from all three episodes not used in the final programme and alternative takes, taken from earlier edits with as-recorded sound, some from a VHS copy with on-screen time-code. The sections in black and white appear in the final episodes while those in colour are the unused scenes, to show where they would have fitted into the story.

THE DOCTOR'S STRANGE LOVE (15m42s) Writers Simon Guerrier and Joseph Lidster and comedian Josie Long discuss the highs and lows of *Dragonfire* from a fan's point of view. *See Index iii for further editions*

THE BIG BANG THEORY (12m33s) New series special effects supervisor Danny Hargreaves examines some of the more explosive effects from the Classic Series and how the techniques used then compare to modern effects work, illustrated with clips from both the Classic and New Series.

PHOTO GALLERY (4m48s) Slideshow of colour photos taken during production of *Dragonfire*, set to music and sound effects from the story. Compiled by Paul Shields.

NEXT

AUDIO OPTIONS Select **Commentary** to play the audio commentary in place of the main soundtrack when watching the episodes. This is moderated by composer and sound engineer Mark Ayres, talking with script editor Andrew Cartmel [eps 1,2], Sophie Aldred (Ace) [1,2,3], Edward Peel (Kane) [1,2,3], writer Ian Briggs [1,3], composer Dominic Glynn [2] and director Chris Clough [2,3].

— Select **Isolated Score** to hear only Dominic Glynn's music when watching the episodes.

— Select **Feature Audio** to reinstate the main soundtrack when watching the episodes.

INFO TEXT Select **On** to view subtitles when watching the episodes that provide information and anecdotes about the development, production, broadcast and history of *Dragonfire*. Written by Paul Scoones.

PDF MATERIALS Accessible via a computer are the three episode listings from *Radio Times* for the original BBC1 broadcast of *Dragonfire*, a one-page article about all the Doctors promoting this as the one hundred and fiftieth story (by counting *The Trial of a Time Lord* as four stories), and letters about the season so far.

COMING SOON (1m36s) Trailer for the DVD release of *Death to the Daleks*.

SUBTITLES

Select **On** to view subtitles for all episodes and Special Features (except commentary).

RELATED EXTRAS

Coming Soon trailer — Nightmare of Eden

THE **E-SPACE TRILOGY**

Boxset of **FULL CIRCLE**, **STATE OF DECAY** and **WARRIORS' GATE**

DVD RELEASE BBCDVD1835, 26 January 2009, PG

SLIPCASE Photo illustration by Clayton Hickman, silvered logo and title, green/black background

ORIGINAL RRP £34.99

WHAT'S IN THE BOX

Three consecutive stories from the eighteenth season (1980/81) in which the TARDIS is sucked into an alternative universe, known as E-Space. After picking up a stowaway on the planet Alzarius, and solving a mystery from the legends of Gallifreyan history, the Doctor finds a way back into the normal universe but not all aboard will make it out of E-Space.

● *See individual stories for full contents*

EARTH STORY

Boxset of **THE AWAKENING** and **THE GUNFIGHTERS**

DVD RELEASE BBCDVD3380, 20 June 2011, PG

SLIPCASE Photo illustration by Clayton Hickman, silvered logo and titles, green background

ORIGINAL RRP £30.63

WHAT'S IN THE BOX

Two stories with little connection other than they take place on Earth and feature historical aspects. *The Gunfighters* (1966) brings the Doctor to Tombstone in 1881 just in time to get embroiled in the gunfight at the OK Corral. *The Awakening* (1984) sees the Fifth Doctor caught up in a re-enactment of the English Civil War that's getting out of hand thanks to a long-hidden alien presence.

● *See individual stories for full contents*

EARTHSHOCK

STORY No.121   SEASON No.19:6

One disc with four episodes (97½ mins) and 62 minutes of extras, plus optional CGI effects, commentary and music-only tracks, and production subtitles

TARDIS TEAM Fifth Doctor, Adric, Nyssa, Tegan

TIME AND PLACE Future Earth and approaching space freighter

ADVERSARIES Cybermen (7th appearance); androids

FIRST ON TV 8–16 March 1982

DVD RELEASE BBCDVD1153, 18 August 2003, PG

COVER Photo illustration by Clayton Hickman, dark purple strip

— Original release with cover sticker reading 'Doctor Who 40th Anniversary 1963–2003'

ORIGINAL RRP £19.99

— Also released in The Cybermen Collection; BBCDVD2262, £39.99, 6 November 2006

— Reissued in sleeve with orange logo and cover illustration in a circle against dark purple background; BBCDVD2471, £9.99, 2 July 2007

STORY TEASER

Within a cave system full of dinosaur fossils, a scientific expedition has been massacred. Sole survivor Professor Clifford calls in military help and Captain Scott soon has his prime suspects: the Doctor and his friends, who have recently materialised in the caves. But when they uncover a hidden hatch the real murderers reveal themselves: a pair of androids programmed to protect the hatch at all costs. But it's their controllers the Doctor needs to worry about, as they're intent on destroying all life of Earth, and for once not even he can prevent them.

CONNECTIONS

The Cybermen return after a seven-year absence from the show, last seen in *Revenge of the Cybermen* (1975), and before then not since *The Invasion* (1968). In fact their plan here is surprisingly similar to that of their last outing: destroy a planet with a bomb or, failing that, by crashing a spacecraft into it. At least this time it actually makes an impact. For their revival they get a new look, which lasts mostly unchanged through *The Five Doctors* (1983) and *Attack of the Cybermen* (1985) to their last Classic Series appearance in *Silver Nemesis* (1988). Eric Saward had written the same season's *The Visitation*, which won him the script editor's role just as another serial fell through. He also wrote *Resurrection of the Daleks* (1984) and *Revelation of the Daleks* (1985), as well as much of *The Twin Dilemma* (1984) and *Attack of the Cybermen* (1985). This was Peter Grimwade's last *Doctor Who* serial as director, having directed *Full Circle* (1980), *Logopolis* (1981) and *Kinda* (1982), although he had been scheduled to helm the return of the Daleks for the next season before strike action delayed the serial. June Bland (Berger) is also in *Battlefield* (1989), while David Banks and Mark Hardy re-don the Cyber-armour for later stories.

WORTH WATCHING

It's impossible now to avoid the spoiler that this story saw the return of the Cybermen after seven years, but at the time it was a genuine shock for the audience, the production team even turning down a *Radio Times* cover to preserve the surprise. If it weren't for this story and the impact it had, the Cybermen might have been relegated to a little-remembered 1960s monster, but *Earthshock* brought them to life again for a generation of viewers and fans who only knew them from books, in turn making them a must-have for the New Series. Compared to that, the bombshell at the end feels rather inconsequential in hindsight.

THE EPISODES

All four episodes are restored from digital duplicates of the original two-inch colour videotape recordings used for broadcast, with location sequences newly transferred from the original 16mm colour film negatives. Their mono soundtracks are remastered and the title sequences replaced by a modern transfer of the original 35mm film with end credits remade to match the originals (except episode four).

SPECIAL FEATURES

PUTTING THE SHOCK INTO EARTHSHOCK (32m27s) The making of *Earthshock* and its impact on the audience, including the changes introduced in the 1982 season; efforts made to keep the Cybermen's return a secret and their shock appearance at the end of episode one; updating the Cybermen costumes; the anachronistic emotion of these Cybermen; using clips from old episodes; star casting; working with the director; heightening the sense of realism; writing out a companion; and ending in silence. With contributions from writer/script editor Eric Saward, director Peter Grimwade (interviewed in 1987), actors David Banks, Peter Davison, Sarah Sutton and Matthew Waterhouse, and fans Tim Collins MP, Mark Gatiss, Gary Gillatt, Ian Levine, Steven Moffat, Steve O'Brien and Gary Russell. Produced by Ed Stradling.

40TH ANNIVERSARY CELEBRATION (3m) A compilation of clips from all eras of Classic *Doctor Who*, set to Orbital's version of the theme music, included on all releases in 2003.

FILM SEQUENCES (8m47s) The full, restored location film footage, including dialogue only heard on communicators in the final episodes, shot at Springwell Lock Quarry in Hertfordshire on Thursday 29 October 1981.

DID YOU SEE? (10m16s) Extract from the Saturday 13 March 1982 edition of the BBC2 television review programme in which presenter Gavin Scott considers the history of monsters in *Doctor Who*, including the Daleks, Menoptra (*The Web Planet*, 1965), Cybermen, Yeti, Sea Devils, Sontarans, Mandrels (*Nightmare of Eden*, 1979) and Marshmen (*Full Circle*, 1980).

CGI EFFECTS Select **CGI Effects On** to view updated computer-generated effects in place of some of the original visual effects when watching the episodes.

▶

INFORMATION TEXT Select **On** to view subtitles when watching the episodes that provide information and anecdotes about the development, production, broadcast and history of *Earthshock*. Written by Richard Molesworth.

PHOTO GALLERY (4m40s) Slideshow of colour photos taken during production of *Earthshock*, and of the commentary participants. Set to sound effects from the story. Compiled by Ralph Montagu.

AUDIO OPTIONS Select **Commentary On** to play the audio commentary in place of the main soundtrack when watching the episodes. With actors Peter Davison, Sarah Sutton (Nyssa), Janet Fielding (Tegan) and Matthew Waterhouse (Adric) on all four episodes.

— Select **Isolated Music** On to hear only Malcolm Clarke's music when watching the episodes.

EPISODE 5 (1m39s) Comedy animated short suggesting what happened to Adric after the end of *Earthshock*. Produced by Simon Berman.

SUBTITLES

Select **On** to view subtitles for all episodes and Special Features, or for the commentary.

EASTER EGG

There is one hidden feature on this disc to find. *See Appendix 2 for details*

RELATED EXTRAS

The Cyber-Generations — Attack of the Cybermen
The Cyber Story — Attack of the Cybermen
Peter Grimwade - Directing with Attitude — Kinda

THE **EDGE OF DESTRUCTION**

STORY No.3   SEASON No.1:3

Released with **AN UNEARTHLY CHILD** and **THE DALEKS** in **THE BEGINNING** boxset
One disc with two episodes (47 mins) and 142½ minutes of extras, plus foreign-dub track, production subtitles and PDF items

TARDIS TEAM First Doctor, Barbara, Ian, Susan
TIME AND PLACE Inside the TARDIS
ADVERSARIES none

FIRST ON TV 8–15 February 1964
DVD RELEASE BBCDVD1882(C), 30 January 2006, PG (boxset 12)
COVER Photo illustration by Clayton Hickman, light blue strip
ORIGINAL RRP £29.99 (boxset)

STORY TEASER

Trying to return to Earth from Skaro in the far future, the TARDIS suffers a systems breakdown that leaves its occupants bewildered and increasingly suspicious of each other. The outside doors open and close on their own, and everyone is behaving oddly. Nothing seems to be broken and yet the ship is out of control. When the Doctor accuses Ian and Barbara of sabotage, tensions mount, blinding the travellers to the real danger.

CONNECTIONS

This is the only regular episode set entirely within the TARDIS, although various New Series mini-episodes use only the control room set, starting with the Children In Need special in 2005 that shows the Tenth Doctor's first post-regeneration moments. We don't see much more of the inside of the ship until *The Masque of Mandragora* (1976), when we learn of a boot cupboard and a second control room, while in *The Invasion of Time* (1978) much more is shown (looking suspiciously like an old hospital building). We mainly see only corridors, but also a cloister and bedrooms, in *Logopolis* (1981), *Castrovalva* (1982) and *Terminus* (1983), and that's all until we get almost a grand tour in *Journey to the Centre of the TARDIS* (2013). Despite the Doctor's accusation here, the only companions to willingly try to kill him (before they really knew him) are Sara and Turlough.

WORTH WATCHING

Written as a filler when it wasn't sure *Doctor Who* would last beyond its first few stories, this two-parter by story editor David Whitaker takes the opportunity to work through the character dynamics of the regular cast, wisely getting them to a point where they can trust each other enough to work as a team in future adventures. The story, such as it is, is decidedly odd but again helps to establish early that this is a series that can try anything and won't be pigeonholed.

THE EPISODES

Both episodes are restored from 16mm film copies of the original black-and-white video recordings, recovered from BBC Enterprises in 1978. Their mono soundtracks are remastered and the VidFIRE process is applied to studio-recorded shots to recapture the smoother motion of video. The title sequences are replaced by a modern transfer of the best surviving copy of the original 35mm film and end credits remade to match the originals.

SPECIAL FEATURES

DOCTOR WHO: ORIGINS (53m51s) A thorough examination of the creation of *Doctor Who* in 1963, from developing the initial ideas to the transmission of the first episode. Including changes in attitudes at the BBC since the launch of ITV; the appointment of Sydney Newman to revamp the drama department; the need for a family show to hold onto the Saturday evening audience; ideas for a science fiction serial; the initial production team; development of the main characters; early script changes; bringing in Verity Lambert as producer and story editor David Whitaker; finding the main cast; creation of the theme music, TARDIS sound and title sequence; the first recording session and changes made for the remake; and last-minute doubts about the series among BBC management. With contributions from head of drama Sydney Newman (interviewed in 1984), producer Verity Lambert, directors Waris Hussein and Richard Martin, special sounds creator Brian Hodgson, graphic designer Bernard Lodge, actors Carole Ann Ford and William Russell, and film historian Marcus Hearn. Narrated by Terry Molloy, produced by Richard Molesworth.

OVER THE EDGE (29m22s) The making of and concepts in *The Edge of Destruction*, including the script; exploration of the four characters; the styles of the serial's two directors; the use of stock music; working with the TARDIS console; the Doctor's past travels; William Hartnell's performance; and the nature of the TARDIS. With contributions from producer Verity Lambert, directors Frank Cox, Waris Hussein and Richard Martin, designer Raymond Cusick, special sounds creator Brian Hodgson, actors Carole Ann Ford and William Russell, documentary producer Keith Barnfather, and writers Peter Anghelides, Jeremy Bentham and Richard Landen. Produced by Ian Levine.

INSIDE THE SPACESHIP (10m14s) Recollections of working on the TARDIS set. With contributions from producer Verity Lambert, directors Frank Cox, Waris Hussein and Richard Martin, designer Raymond Cusick, special sounds designer Brian Hodgson, and actors Carole Ann Ford and William Russell. Produced by Ian Levine.

MASTERS OF SOUND (12m23s) Examining how the theme music and special sounds for *Doctor Who* were realised, using previously unseen footage shot in 1993 for the documentary *30 Years in the TARDIS*, featuring comments from producer Verity Lambert and Radiophonic Workshop members Delia Derbyshire, Brian Hodgson and Dick Mills, who created the theme from Ron Grainer's score. Directed by Kevin Davies, produced by Steve Roberts.

MARCO POLO (31m25s) A cut-down reconstruction of the missing fourth *Doctor Who* story, *Marco Polo,* using surviving images from the serial matched to remastered recordings of the soundtrack made on audio tape when the serial was originally broadcast. Edited by Derek Handley.

▶

GALLERY (5m9s) Slideshow of black-and-white photos taken during production of *The Edge of Destruction* and colour photos from *Marco Polo*. Set to sound effects from the series. Compiled by Ralph Montagu.

AUDIO OPTIONS Select **Arabic for Episode 2 On** to hear the soundtrack with dialogue dubbed into Arabic when watching episode two, made for sales of the programme to Middle Eastern broadcasters. This also features different incidental music to that used in the UK broadcast.

PDF DOCUMENTS Accessible via a computer are the episode listings from *Radio Times* for the original BBC1 broadcasts of *An Unearthly Child*, *The Daleks*, *The Edge of Destruction* and *Marco Polo*, plus the articles that introduced each story and the covers for the 21 November 1963 (issue 2089) and 20 February 1964 (issue 2102) editions, the latter the first to headline *Doctor Who*.

— The camera script for the very first episode of *Doctor Who*, 'An Unearthly Child'.

INFORMATION TEXT Select **On** to view subtitles when watching the episodes that provide information and anecdotes about the development, production, broadcast and history of *The Edge of Destruction*. Written by Martin Wiggins.

SUBTITLES
Select **On** to view subtitles for all episodes and Special Features (except Arabic soundtrack).

THE **ENEMY OF THE WORLD**

STORY No.40   SEASON No.5:4

One disc with six episodes (140½ mins) and 1 minute of extras
Audio navigation of disc contents available by pressing Enter after the BBC ident

TARDIS TEAM Second Doctor, Jamie, Victoria

TIME AND PLACE Future Earth

ADVERSARIES Ruthless magnate (and the Doctor's double) Salamander

FIRST ON TV 23 December 1967–27 January 1968

DVD RELEASE BBCDVD3866, 25 November 2013, PG

COVER Full-cover photo illustration by Lee Binding; version with standard cover style, dark orange strip, on reverse

ORIGINAL RRP £20.42

— Limited Edition sold by BBCShop.com in a sleeve with alternative illustration by Binding

— Episode three originally released in the Lost in Time set; BBCDVD1353, £29.99, 1 November 2004

STORY TEASER
On Earth in the mid-21st Century one man has gained great power and influence through his development of the Suncatcher device, which has boosted food production and ended starvation. Salamander is thus a hero to most, but those closest to him know he is ruthless in his desire for world domination. When the Doctor arrives and is found to be the exact double of Salamander, he struggles not to get embroiled in plans to assassinate the would-be despot.

CONNECTIONS

With no monster, a charismatic main villain and political intrigue, this is more like one of the history-based stories from the First Doctor era, such as *The Aztecs* (1964) or *The Massacre* (1966), despite being set in the future. (Now we can see it, we know it to be set in 2018, so fifty years ahead at the time it was written but now disturbingly close.) The twist, of course, is that Salamander looks like the Doctor (or vice versa), another similarity with *The Massacre* and also used in *Meglos* (1980), where the titular villain takes on the Doctor's appearance. Omega briefly does the same in *Arc of Infinity* (1983), which also sees guard commander Maxil prefiguring the Sixth Doctor's appearance. Further robotic doubles of the Doctor are constructed in *The Chase* (1965), *The Android Invasion* (1975) and *The Caves of Androzani* (1984), while a Flesh duplicate is seen in *The Rebel Flesh/The Almost People* (2011). Writer David Whitaker started out on *Doctor Who* as its first story editor then wrote for the series regularly throughout the 1960s (*see Index v*). This was the first serial directed by Barry Letts, who became the show's producer from 1970 to 1975 but also directed during that time and afterwards (*see Index v*). Colin Douglas (Donald Bruce) returns as Reuben in *Horror of Fang Rock* (1977), Milton Johns (Benik) is astronaut Guy Crayford in *The Android Invasion* and Castellan Kelner in *The Invasion of Time* (1978), and George Pravda (Alexander Denes) plays Professor Jaeger in *The Mutants* (1972) and Castellan Spandrell in *The Deadly Assassin* (1976). Christopher Burgess (Swann) became a regular actor for Letts, appearing in *Terror of the Autons* (1971) and *Planet of the Spiders* (1974), as does Andrew Staines (Sergeant).

WORTH WATCHING

In a season best known for its monsters, *The Enemy of the World* stands out as an atypical foray into more political machinations, likened by some to a James Bond storyline. The key hook is that the Doctor and Salamander look identical, and this offers a showcase for Patrick Troughton's acting skills, convincing us not only that each is a different character but also cleverly portraying the Doctor pretending to be Salamander as subtly different to the man himself. And, of course, this is one of the most recently rediscovered stories, returned to the archives just months before its release fully cleaned up and restored.

THE EPISODES

Episodes one, two, four, five and six are restored from 16mm film copies of the original black-and-white video recordings, recovered from a Nigerian broadcaster by Philip Morris and returned in May 2013; episode three is restored from a higher quality 16mm film copy of the original black-and-white video recording that survived in the archive. Their mono soundtracks are remastered and the VidFIRE process is applied to studio-recorded shots to recapture the smoother motion of video. The title sequences are replaced by a modern transfer of the original 35mm film with credits remade to match the originals.

SUBTITLES

Select **On** to view subtitles for all episodes and the Coming Soon trailer.

COMING SOON

Trailer for the DVD release of *The Web of Fear* (51s).

RELATED EXTRAS

Sylvia James - In Conversation — The War Games
Available Now trailer — The Web of Fear

ENLIGHTENMENT

STORY No.127   SEASON No.20:5

Released with **MAWDRYN UNDEAD** and **TERMINUS** in **THE BLACK GUARDIAN TRILOGY** boxset

Two discs with four episodes (98 mins), a new 74-minute Special Edition and 116 minutes of extras, plus commentary and music-only tracks, production subtitles and PDF items
Audio navigation of each disc's contents available by pressing Enter after the BBC ident

TARDIS TEAM Fifth Doctor, Tegan, Turlough
TIME AND PLACE Edwardian sailing yacht The Shadow
ADVERSARIES Bored superbeings the Eternals; the Black Guardian (4th appearance)
FIRST ON TV 1–9 March 1983
DVD RELEASE BBCDVD2596C [discs 2596C-1 and 2596C-2], 10 August 2009, PG
COVER Photo illustration by Clayton Hickman, light blue strip
ORIGINAL RRP £39.14 (boxset)

STORY TEASER

The Black Guardian gives Turlough his last chance to kill the Doctor when the TARDIS arrives in the hold of an Edwardian sailing ship. But the Doctor has been warned by the White Guardian that all is not as it seems in the ship's race for the ultimate prize. They find its officers behave strangely and the crew are almost scared to go up on deck. When the true nature of the race becomes apparent, Turlough faces one final choice.

CONNECTIONS

Whenever the TARDIS lands on a ship things are never as they seem. Shortly after it arrives aboard one in *The Chase* (1965), Daleks follow and resolve a long-standing maritime mystery; it materialises in the hold of the SS Bernice in *Carnival of Monsters* (1973) only to be plucked out by a giant hand; in *Enlightenment* the Shadow is not sailing where one would expect it to be; and in *The Curse of the Black Spot* (2011) the Fancy is haunted by a phantom with a strange approach to triage. The Eternals, immortal beings with a desire to be entertained, are reminiscent of the Toymaker (*The Celestial Toymaker*, 1966) and the Gods of Ragnarok (*The Greatest Show in the Galaxy*, 1988/89). Tegan's aunt Vanessa is seen (well, a little of her) in *Logopolis* (1981) and provides another touchstone for Tegan when she leaves the Doctor in *Resurrection of the Daleks* (1984). This is the only *Doctor Who* story both written and directed by women, Fiona Cumming also directing *Castrovalva* (1982), *Snakedance* (1983) and *Planet of Fire* (1984). Valentine Dyall makes his last appearance as the Black Guardian while Cyril Luckham reprises his role as the White Guardian from *The Ribos Operation* (1978). Lynda Baron (Captain Wrack) sings 'The Ballad of the Last Chance Saloon' in *The Gunfighters* (1966) and appears in the New Series as Val in *Closing Time* (2011), while Tony Caunter (Jackson) plays Thatcher in *The Crusade* (1965) and Morgan in *Colony in Space* (1971).

WORTH WATCHING

This is the final story in the trilogy about the Black Guardian's attempt to use Turlough to eliminate the Doctor, and while the Time Lord's survival is never in question, it's the actions of the schoolboy that provide the character drama. This is also a strong story for Tegan as she fends off the advances of a being who can't understand his fascination for her. It's a sumptuous production overall, with especially good model work of the ships in the race.

DISC ONE

THE EPISODES

All four episodes are restored from digital duplicates of the original two-inch colour videotape recordings used for broadcast and their mono soundtracks remastered. The title sequences are replaced by a modern transfer of the original 35mm film with credits remade to match the originals (although one caption slide is accidentally omitted from episode one).

SPECIAL FEATURES

AUDIO OPTIONS Select **Commentary** to play the audio commentary in place of the main soundtrack when watching the episodes. With Peter Davison, Mark Strickson (Turlough), writer Barbara Clegg and director Fiona Cumming on all four episodes.
— Select **Isolated Music** to hear only Malcolm Clarke's music when watching the episodes.
— Select **Feature Audio** to reinstate the main soundtrack when watching the episodes.
INFO TEXT Select **On** to view subtitles when watching the episodes that provide information and anecdotes about the development, production, broadcast and history of *Enlightenment*. Written by Richard Molesworth.
WINNER TAKES ALL (23m48s) The making of *Enlightenment*, including writing the script; working with the director; the set design and lighting; delays in production owing to strikes at the BBC

and their impact on the casting; the period costumes; injury during filming of Turlough's fall overboard; and the climax of his storyline. With contributions from writer Barbara Clegg, director Fiona Cumming, costume designer Dinah Collin, camera supervisor Alec Wheal, and actors Keith Barron, Christopher Brown, Peter Davison, Janet Fielding, Leee John and Mark Strickson. Narrated by Floella Benjamin, produced by Brendan Sheppard.

CASTING OFF! (10m35s) The cast of *Enlightenment* talk about their characters and approaches to acting. With contributions from Keith Barron, Christopher Brown, Peter Davison, Janet Fielding, Leee John and Mark Strickson, and director Fiona Cumming.

SINGLE WRITE FEMALE (5m14s) Barbara Clegg talks about her life and career, starting out as an actor before becoming a writer for radio and television, including *Mrs Dale's Diary*, *Coronation Street*, *Crossroads* and *The Chrysalids*.

THE STORY OF THE GUARDIANS (11m55s) Profile of the two actors who played the White and Black Guardians in 1978 and their return in 1983 — Cyril Luckham, who died in 1989, and Valentine Dyall, who died in 1985 — and what we learn about the Guardians' natures. With contributions from Cyril's son Robert Luckham, Valentine's daughter Sarah Leppard, and fan journalists Moray Laing and Tom Spilsbury. Produced by Brendan Sheppard.

NEXT

STORYBOARDS (5m58s) View the design sketches for the model filming alongside the finished shots, including footage not seen in the final episodes, with a commentary by visual effects designer Mike Kelt. Select **Original Storyboards** to see the storyboards and film footage side by side, or **Full Frame Model Sequences** to view just the final shots. Use the Angle button on your remote to switch between the two views as you watch.

PHOTO GALLERY (6m52s) Slideshow of colour and black-and-white photos taken during production of *Enlightenment*, including design department photos of the sets and behind-the-scenes shots of the model filming. Set to music from the story. Compiled by Derek Handley.

PDF MATERIALS Accessible via a computer are the four episode listings from *Radio Times* for the original BBC1 broadcast of *Enlightenment*.

— Storyboard sketches by Russell Owen for the new CGI effects shots for the Special Edition.

COMING SOON (1m2s) Trailer for the DVD release of *The Twin Dilemma*.

SUBTITLES

Select **On** to view subtitles for all episodes and Special Features on disc one (except commentary).

DISC TWO

SPECIAL EDITION

On this disc is a new edit of the story as a single 74-minute episode in widescreen, with updated computer-generated visual effects and model shots, new music cues, and stereo or Dolby 5.1 surround soundtrack. With an introduction by director Fiona Cumming about her aims for the Special Edition (1m30s).

SPECIAL FEATURES

AUDIO OPTIONS Select **Dolby Digital 5.1** or **Dolby Digital 2.0** for the Special Edition soundtrack.

RE-ENLIGHTENMENT (14m21s) Special Edition producer Brendan Sheppard, original director Fiona Cumming, storyboard artist Russell Owen and 3D animator Rob Semenoff plan what changes and additions they want to make to *Enlightenment*.

ORIGINAL EDIT COMPARISON (2m36s) Scenes from the initial edit of episode three, taken from a copy with as-recorded sound and on-screen time-code, alongside the final transmitted version. With captions explaining the differences.

FILM TRIMS (5m33s) 16mm colour film footage from the Ealing Studio filming in early-November 1982 of scenes on the Shadow deck, showing setups and takes not used in the final episodes.

FINDING MARK STRICKSON (8m30s) Mark Strickson, who played Turlough in 1983/84, talks about his life and career, from musician to actor to nature documentary producer, and his return to *Doctor Who* on audio.

FINDING SARAH SUTTON (7m47s) Sarah Sutton, who played Nyssa from 1981 to 1983, talks about her life and career, from child dancer and actor to her return to *Doctor Who* on audio.

NEXT

RUSSELL HARTY CHRISTMAS PARTY (3m32s) Extract from the Tuesday 21 December 1982 Christmas edition on BBC2 of the *Russell Harty* chat show, in which Peter Davison and Sandra Dickinson perform a routine from the pantomime *Cinderella* in which they were appearing at Tunbridge Wells from 23 December.

CONTINUITY (2m11s) Continuity announcements from the original BBC1 broadcasts of all four episodes of *Enlightenment*, with plugs for the *Doctor Who The Music* album and the Longleat celebratory weekend in April 1983.

PDF MATERIALS Accessible via a computer is the *Doctor Who* production team's handbook of internal memos and documents pertaining to the production of the show and working practices at the BBC in 1983.

— The *Radio Times 20th Anniversary Special* magazine, published by the BBC in November 1983. It profiles the first five Doctors, their companions and the Master; interviews production people; reports on fan gatherings in the UK and America; features a short story about why the Doctor first left Gallifrey, written by script editor Eric Saward; and has a guide to all stories up *The King's Demons*, with previews of *The Five Doctors* and the 1984 season (yet to be broadcast at the time), and an interview with newly announced Sixth Doctor Colin Baker.

SUBTITLES

Select **On** to view subtitles for the Special Edition and Special Features on disc two.

EASTER EGGS

There are three hidden features on these discs to find. *See Appendix 2 for details*

RELATED EXTRAS

Coming Soon trailer — The War Games

THE **EVIL OF THE DALEKS**

STORY No.36   SEASON No.4:9

One surviving episode (part 2 of 7) released in the **LOST IN TIME** *set*

TARDIS TEAM Second Doctor, Jamie, and introducing Victoria Waterfield

TIME AND PLACE Contemporary London and 19th Century mansion

ADVERSARIES Daleks (7th appearance); Victorian businessman Theodore Maxtible

FIRST ON TV 27 May 1967

DVD RELEASE BBCDVD1353, 1 November 2004, PG

● *See* Lost in Time *for full details*

RELATED EXTRAS

The Dalek Tapes — Genesis of the Daleks

The Last Dalek — Lost in Time, Resurrection of the Daleks Special Edition, The Seeds of Death

The Final End — The Tomb of the Cybermen (and Special Edition)

The Doctor's Composer — The War Games

THE **FACE OF EVIL**

STORY No.89   SEASON No.14:4

One disc with four episodes (99½ mins) and 78 minutes of extras, plus commentary track, production subtitles and PDF items
Audio navigation of disc contents available by pressing Enter after the BBC ident

TARDIS TEAM Fourth Doctor, and introducing Leela

TIME AND PLACE Unknown planet in the future

ADVERSARIES Artificial intelligence Xoanon

FIRST ON TV 1–22 January 1977

DVD RELEASE BBCDVD3379, 5 March 2012, PG
COVER Photo illustration by Lee Binding, turquoise strip; version with older BBC logo on reverse
ORIGINAL RRP £20.42

STORY TEASER

The Doctor, travelling alone, encounters the Sevateem, an apparently primitive jungle tribe and yet their holy relics are, unbeknown to them, clearly technological artefacts from a spaceship. They also fear the Doctor as 'the Evil One' who has imprisoned their god Xoanon and whose invisible monsters attack the tribe. And when he discovers a giant carving of his face in a cliff he begins to wonder if they might be right.

CONNECTIONS

The Doctor encounters tribes at a basic level of society in *An Unearthly Child* (1963), *The Savages* (1966), *Colony in Space* (1971), *The Mutants* (1972), *Death to the Daleks* (1974), *The Power of Kroll* (1979) and *The Trial of a Time Lord: The Mysterious Planet* (1986). Like the Sevateem, the Tribe of the Free in the last have regressed and lost their knowledge of advanced technology, as have the Primitives on Uxaerius in *Colony in Space*, the Exxilons in *Death to the Daleks* and to a degree the occupants of *Paradise Towers* (1987). Invisible creatures are encountered in *The Daleks' Master Plan* (1965/66), *The Ark* (1966), *Planet of the Daleks* (1973), *Planet of Evil* (1975) and *Vincent and the Doctor* (2010). The Doctor deals with other crazed computers such as WOTAN in *The War Machines* (1966), BOSS in *The Green Death* (1973), the Oracle in *Underworld* (1978) and Mentalis in *The Armageddon Factor* (1979). His sixth incarnation also has his features carved in stone, but on a much smaller scale (*Revelation of the Daleks*, 1985), and he finds himself having to tie up loose ends from earlier visits in *The Ark* (1966), *Timelash* (1985) and *Bad Wolf* (2005). This was the first script by Chris Boucher, who also wrote *The Robots of Death* (1977) and *Image of the Fendahl* (1977), and the first serial directed by Pennant Roberts who worked on the show into the 1980s (*see Index v*). David Garfield (Neeva) and Leslie Schofield (Calib) are both in *The War Games* (1969) as Von Weich and Leroy respectively.

WORTH WATCHING

This is the first story featuring Leela, played by Louise Jameson, the aggressive yet intelligent member of the Sevateem who joins the Doctor on his travels. It's also a rare instance of the Doctor arriving somewhere he has been before (although in this case not on screen) and having to deal with the consequences of his earlier actions.

THE EPISODES

All four episodes are restored from digital duplicates of the original two-inch colour videotape recordings used for broadcast and their mono soundtracks remastered. The title sequences are replaced by a modern transfer of the original 35mm film with credits remade to match the originals.

SPECIAL FEATURES

INTO THE WILD (25m11s) The making of *The Face of Evil*, including initial story ideas; devising a companion to replace Sarah Jane Smith and the casting of Louise Jameson; creating the stone face carving; designing the sets; working with Tom Baker; making the visual effects; how a ten-year-old fan got a part in *Doctor Who*; public reaction to Leela; and memories of the late director. With contributions from producer Philip Hinchcliffe, director Pennant Roberts (interviewed in 2005), designer Austin Ruddy, visual effects designer Mat Irvine, actor Louise Jameson, and Anthony Frieze. Produced by Chris Chapman.

FROM THE CUTTING ROOM FLOOR (9m4s) Silent 16mm colour film footage from the Ealing Studio filming in late-September 1976 unused in the final programme, with sound and shots from the final programme for comparison and explanatory captions.

TOMORROW'S TIMES THE FOURTH DOCTOR (14m6s) Coverage of *Doctor Who* in the national newspapers during the Fourth Doctor's era from 1974 to 1981. Presented by Wendy Padbury, written and directed by Marcus Hearn. *See Index iii for further editions*

DOCTOR WHO STORIES: LOUISE JAMESON (17m21s) Recorded in 2003 for BBC2's *The Story of Doctor Who*, actor Louise Jameson recalls her experiences of playing companion Leela from 1977 to 1978.

SWAP SHOP (4m28s) Extract from the 12 February 1977 edition of the BBC1 Saturday morning children's show in which Noel Edmonds interviews Louise Jameson about playing Leela.

DENYS FISHER TOYS ADVERT (32s) Television commercial for the Denys Fisher range of *Doctor Who* dolls, including Leela, released in autumn 1977.

PHOTO GALLERY (5m42s) Slideshow of colour photos taken during production of *The Face of Evil*, including design department photos of the sets and publicity shots of Louise Jameson as Leela. Set to sound effects from the story. Compiled by Paul Shields.

NEXT

AUDIO OPTIONS Select **Commentary** to play the audio commentary in place of the main sound-track when watching the episodes. This is moderated by actor and comedian Toby Hadoke, talking with Harry H Fielder (Tribesman) [ep 1], film cameraman John McGlashan [1,2], Louise Jameson (Leela) [1,2,3,4], Leslie Schofield (Calib) [1,2,3,4], David Garfield (Neeva) [1,2,3,4], Mike Elles (Gentek) [3,4] and producer Philip Hinchcliffe [3,4]. Hadoke also relays written comments from writer Chris Boucher throughout.

— Select **Feature Audio** to reinstate the main soundtrack when watching the episodes.

INFO TEXT Select **On** to view subtitles when watching the episodes that provide information and anecdotes about the development, production, broadcast and history of *The Face of Evil*. Written by Martin Wiggins.

PDF MATERIALS Accessible via a computer are the four episode listings from *Radio Times* for the original BBC1 broadcast of *The Face of Evil*, including artwork by Roy Ellsworth that accompanied the billing for episode one.

— Packaging, promotional material, poster, twelve stickers and the complete *The Amazing World of Doctor Who* storybook, which reprinted stories from the World Distributors annuals, from the 1976 *Doctor Who* promotion by Ty-Phoo Tea.

COMING SOON (1m26s) Trailer for the DVD release of *The Dæmons*.

SUBTITLES

Select **On** to view subtitles for all episodes and Special Features (except commentary).

RELATED EXTRAS

Coming Soon trailer — The Robots of Death Special Edition, The Three Doctors Special Edition, The Tomb of the Cybermen Special Edition

THE **FACELESS ONES**

STORY No.35   SEASON No.4:8

Two surviving episodes (parts 1 and 3 of 6) released in the **LOST IN TIME** *set*

TARDIS TEAM Second Doctor, Ben, Jamie, Polly

TIME AND PLACE Contemporary Gatwick airport

ADVERSARIES Body-snatching Chameleons

FIRST ON TV 8 and 22 April 1967

DVD RELEASE BBCDVD1353, 1 November 2004, PG

● *See* Lost in Time *for full details*

THE **FIVE DOCTORS** 25TH ANNIVERSARY EDITION

STORY No.129

Two discs with one episode (90½ mins), a 100½-minute Special Edition and 162 minutes of extras, plus three commentary and two music-only tracks, production subtitles for each version and PDF items

TARDIS TEAM Fifth Doctor, Tegan, Turlough; First Doctor, Susan; Second Doctor, the Brigadier; Third Doctor, Sarah Jane; Fourth Doctor, Second Romana

TIME AND PLACE Time Lord homeworld Gallifrey

ADVERSARIES Third Master (5th appearance); Cybermen (8th appearance)

FIRST ON TV 23 November 1983 (US); 25 November 1983 (UK)

DVD RELEASE BBCDVD2450, 3 March 2008, PG (episode U)

COVER Photo illustration by Clayton Hickman, yellow strip

SLEEVE Full version of cover illustration, orange logo, dark red background

ORIGINAL RRP £19.99

STORY TEASER

One by one the first five incarnations of the Doctor are plucked out of time and deposited in a barren wasteland that he soon learns is the Death Zone on Gallifrey, an arena where the ancient Time Lords placed lesser species to fight. With several formidable adversaries also roaming the Zone, the Doctors must work together to discover who has revived the deadly Game of Rassilon.

CONNECTIONS

From the moment plans started being made to mark *Doctor Who*'s twenty-fifth anniversary (as early as August 1981) it was conceived as featuring past Doctors, even though one of the actors was dead and another had recently quit the role and would be unlikely to return so soon. That this should be the default approach to an anniversary special is telling of the impact 1973's *The Three Doctors* had. Although that had launched the show's tenth season, broadcast shortly after its ninth anniversary, uniting all the Doctor's incarnations quickly became accepted by viewers and the production team as an obvious way to honour the contributions the lead actors had made to the programme's longevity. When it was clear the twentieth anniversary would be reached, a combination of producer John Nathan-Turner's knowledge of the show's past, the input of fan advisors and the rerun in November 1981 of *The Three Doctors* meant repeating the idea was inescapable. No one thought twice about recasting the First Doctor — a suggestion that was often treated as offensive by fans anticipating the fiftieth anniversary, when two further lead actors had passed away — and early storylines even included a reason why he didn't quite look the same. *The Five Doctors* went further, however, by including several past companions and popular enemies as well, becoming largely an exercise in nostalgia, whereas *The Three Doctors* had been about moving the show forward. That feeling extended to the production, with old-school writers and directors initially approached to work on it. After Robert Holmes' story ideas didn't work out Terrance Dicks was brought in, whose connection to the show went back even further (*see Index v*). Similarly the series' original director Waris Hussein was sounded out, as was Douglas Camfield, who hadn't worked on *Doctor Who* since 1976. Once they proved unavailable the task fell to Peter Moffatt who worked on several 1980s serials (*see Index v*). With so many returning actors, as Doctors, companions and monsters, the guest cast was largely new. Paul Jerricho had played the Castellan earlier in the year in *Arc of Infinity*, Stuart Blake (Guard Commander) was short-lived guard Zoldaz in *State of Decay* (1980) and returns as Silurian Scibus in *Warriors of the Deep* (1984), while David Savile (Colonel Crichton) was Lieutenant Carstairs in *The War Games* (1969) and Dr Winser in *The Claws of Axos* (1971). For further links between *The Five Doctors* and other stories, see **The Ties That Bind Us** on disc two.

WORTH WATCHING

A one-off story to celebrate *Doctor Who*'s twentieth anniversary, *The Five Doctors* brought together three of the four surviving actors to play the Doctor (sadly Tom Baker declined to take part but was present via clips from the unbroadcast story *Shada*), with Richard Hurndall cast to stand in for the late William Hartnell (who died in 1975). The result is more of a nostalgic romp than an intricate thriller, but then it's meant as a celebration and experienced *Doctor Who* writer Terrance Dicks keeps the many elements well balanced.

DISC ONE

THE EPISODE

On this disc is the original broadcast episode, recompiled and restored from digital duplicates of the original two-inch colour videotape recordings, with location sequences newly transferred from the original 16mm colour film. This has required shots that mix film and video elements to be recomposited and some video effects recreated. The episode's mono soundtrack is remastered and the title sequences are replaced by a modern transfer of the original 35mm film with credits remade to match the originals.

SPECIAL FEATURES

AUDIO OPTIONS Select **Companions Commentary** to play the audio commentary recorded for this release in place of the main soundtrack when watching the episode. With Nicholas Courtney (the Brigadier), Carole Ann Ford (Susan), Elisabeth Sladen (Sarah Jane) and Mark Strickson (Turlough).

— Select **Isolated Music** to hear only Peter Howell's music when watching the episodes.

— Select **Feature Audio** to reinstate the main soundtrack when watching the episodes.

INFO TEXT Select **On** to view subtitles when watching the episodes that provide information and anecdotes about the development, production, broadcast and history of *The Five Doctors*. Written by Richard Molesworth.

CELEBRATION (52m16s) Twenty years on air is a significant milestone for any television series and in 1983 numerous events celebrated *Doctor Who*'s anniversary, building up to the transmission of *The Five Doctors*. Sixth Doctor Colin Baker presents a look back at the year, from the twentieth season to the increasing publicity around the show under producer John Nathan-Turner, with appearances by present and past cast members on news and children's programmes; early plans for the anniversary special and the struggle to find a workable story, Tom Baker's declining to take part and the returns of Patrick Troughton and Jon Pertwee; working with the director, recasting the First Doctor, filming for *The Five Doctors* in North Wales, redesigning the TARDIS console, casting the Time Lords and the studio recording; BBC Enterprise's unprecedented celebration at Longleat which drew far bigger crowds than anyone expected; the announcements of Peter Davison's decision to leave *Doctor Who* and his replacement Colin Baker, and further publicity nearer the anniversary itself and the broadcast of *The Five Doctors*. With contributions from writer Terrance Dicks, director Peter Moffatt, visual effects designer Mike Kelt, actors Nicholas Courtney, Peter Davison, Janet Fielding, Carole Ann Ford, Richard Franklin, Caroline John, John Leeson, Elisabeth Sladen and Mark Strickson, New Series writers Paul Cornell and Gareth Roberts, and fans Andrew Beech, James Goss, Ian Levine and Richard Molesworth. Produced by Steve Broster.

TRAILS & CONTINUITY (19m13s) Previews and continuity announcements from the original BBC1 broadcast of *The Five Doctors* as part of the BBC's Children In Need appeal, with a plug for the *Radio Times Doctor Who 20th Anniversary Special* magazine; and from the story's repeat showing in four parts on BBC1 in August 1984 (including unscripted cliffhangers). Includes the BBC1 evening schedule for Thursday 16 August 1984.

PHOTO GALLERY (8m14s) Slideshow of colour photos taken during production of *The Five Doctors*. Set to music from the story remixed in stereo and including new cues written for the extended Special Edition. Compiled by Derek Handley.

RADIO TIMES LISTINGS Accessible via a computer is a PDF file of the episode listing for the original broadcast of *The Five Doctors*, the cover for the 17 November 1983 edition (issue 3132) and the clean artwork by Andrew Skilleter, a three-page article about the companions who appear in the special, and subsequent letters about the story.

SUBTITLES

Select **On** to view subtitles for the episode and all Special Features on disc one (except commentary).

DISC TWO

THE EPISODE

On this disc is the Special Edition first produced for home video release in November 1995 and previously released on DVD in November 1999 (*see Appendix 1*). It features extra scenes originally cut from the broadcast version, with updated visual effects, new music cues, and Dolby Surround or Dolby Digital 5.1 sound. The Special Edition was recompiled from digital duplicates of the original two-inch colour videotape recordings and further clean-up work has been done for this release, with location sequences newly transferred from the original 16mm colour film. This has required shots that mix film and video elements to be recomposited and some video effects recreated. Credits are remade with Special Edition producers added.

SPECIAL FEATURES

AUDIO OPTIONS Select **Production Commentary** to play the audio commentary recorded for an earlier US-only release of the story in place of the main soundtrack when watching the episode. With Peter Davison and writer Terrance Dicks.

— Select **Isolated Music** to hear only Peter Howell's music when watching the Special Edition, with the new cues recorded for added scenes.

— Select **Feature Audio 5.1** to hear the soundtrack in Dolby Digital 5.1 when watching the Special Edition, remixed for the previous DVD release.

— Select **Feature Audio Dolby Surround** to hear the soundtrack mixed for the original VHS release (which plays in stereo on systems without surround-sound capability) when watching the Special Edition.

THE TIES THAT BIND US (15m57s) Links between *The Five Doctors* and previous *Doctor Who* adventures, and elements that were reused in later stories. Narrated by Paul McGann, produced by Brendan Sheppard.

FIVE DOCTORS, ONE STUDIO (18m47s) Footage from the full studio recording on Thursday 31 March 1983 of scenes on the Tomb of Rassilon set, including retakes and shots unused in the final programme.

OUT-TAKES (6m36s) Bloopers and fluffed lines taken from the original studio recordings, including a Dalek getting rather carried away.

(NOT SO) SPECIAL EFFECTS (9m) Footage from the studio recordings of scenes involving visual effects, including unused shots and retakes with as-recorded sound.

NEXT

SATURDAY SUPERSTORE (10m31s) Extract from the 26 March 1983 edition of the BBC1 Saturday morning children's show in which Mike Read interviews Peter Davison, Janet Fielding and Mark Strickson, and they take viewers' questions on the phone.

BLUE PETER (8m4s) Extract from the Monday 21 November 1983 edition of the BBC1 children's magazine programme in which Peter Duncan, Janet Ellis and Simon Groom mark *Doctor Who*'s twentieth anniversary with a look at some of his best known enemies, meeting Daleks, Cybermen, Yeti, Axons, Sea Devils and Kraals in the studio. Peter Davison and Richard Hurndall appear in costume with a Variety Club Sunshine Coach paid for from donations by visitors to the Longleat celebration weekend.

NATIONWIDE (9m10s) Extract from the Friday 18 March 1983 edition of the BBC1 news magazine programme in which Richard Kershaw looks at the twenty-year history of *Doctor Who* and interviews original producer Verity Lambert about the series' inception, while Sue Lawley talks to Patrick Troughton, Jon Pertwee and Peter Davison.

BREAKFAST TIME (2m46s) Extract from the Tuesday 1 March 1983 edition of the BBC1 morning news magazine programme in which Frank Bough and Selina Scott interview Patrick Troughton and Peter Davison to promote the Longleat celebration weekend.

COMING SOON (1m4s) Trailer for the DVD release of *The Invasion of Time*.

INFO TEXT Select **On** to view subtitles when watching the episode that provide information about the production of *The Five Doctors* Special Edition and its differences from the broadcast version. Written by Richard Molesworth.

SUBTITLES

Select **On** to view subtitles for the Special Edition and all Special Features on disc two (except commentary).

EASTER EGGS

There are two hidden features on these discs to find. *See Appendix 2 for details*

RELATED EXTRAS

The Cyber-Generations — Attack of the Cybermen

The UNIT Family — Terror of the Zygons

Coming Soon trailer — The Time Meddler

Directing Who — The Visitation (and Special Edition)

THE **FIVE DOCTORS** SPECIAL EDITION

Original DVD release of the extended version produced for home video. While this was the first *Doctor Who* DVD to be issued, in November 1999, it only included a re-edited version of *The Five Doctors*, not the broadcast original, which wasn't made available until March 2008 in the 25th Anniversary Edition release. The packaging and menu design of this Special Edition are also different from the rest of the releases once the range was established.

● *See Appendix 1 for full details*

FOUR TO DOOMSDAY

STORY No.117   SEASON No.19:2

F

One disc with four episodes (97 mins) and 53 minutes of extras, plus commentary track, production subtitles and PDF items

TARDIS TEAM Fifth Doctor, Adric, Nyssa, Tegan

TIME AND PLACE Giant spaceship approaching Earth

ADVERSARIES Urbankans and their androids

FIRST ON TV 18–26 January 1982

DVD RELEASE BBCDVD2431, 15 September 2008, PG

COVER Photo illustration by Clayton Hickman, light green strip

ORIGINAL RRP £19.99

STORY TEASER

The TARDIS arrives on an enormous spaceship that is just four days away from reaching the Earth. After exploring its empty corridors, the Doctor and friends are eventually brought before Monarch, ruler of the Urbankans, and learn that the ship has made the long journey between Earth and Urbanka several times, collecting representatives of human societies from different periods in history. This time, however, Monarch plans to stay and replace the human race with his own people — or something very like them.

CONNECTIONS

Stories that unfold entirely in space are perhaps surprisingly rare in *Doctor Who*. *The Wheel in Space* (1968) is the first, set aboard a space station and a couple of ships, as is *Terminus* (1983), while *The Ark in Space* (1975) takes place solely within a space station. Like *Four to Doomsday*, *Nightmare of Eden* (1978), *Enlightenment* (1983) and *The Trial of a Time Lord: Terror of the Vervoids* (1986) are the only stories set wholly on spaceships. Strictly *The Trial of a Time Lord: The Ultimate Foe* all takes place on the Time Lord's spaceship court, but the scenes in the Matrix include the illusion of a world. In the New Series, only *42* (2007), *The Beast Below* (2010) and *Journey to the Centre of the TARDIS* (2013) feature no characters making planet fall. (The same qualification applies to *Amy's Choice* (2010) as *The Ultimate Foe*.) The Daleks create the first realistic android in the show, duplicating the Doctor in *The Chase* (1965), a skill shared by the Kraals in *The Android Invasion* (1975), the Tarans in *The Androids of Tara* (1978) and the Movellans in *Destiny of the Daleks* (1979). The Daleks have got better at it by the time they construct Bracewell in *Victory of the Daleks* (2010). Terence Dudley also wrote *Black Orchid* (1982) and *The King's Demons* (1983), although his first script for the series was actually its spin-off *K9 and Company* (1981), directed by John Black before he moved on to *Four to Doomsday*, having previously handled *The Keeper of Traken* (1981). Stratford Johns (Monarch) is the first ex-*Z Cars* star to appear in *Doctor Who*, followed in relatively short order by Frank Windsor in *The King's Demons* (and again in *Ghost Light*, 1989), Brian Blessed in *The Trial of a Time Lord: Mindwarp* (1986) and James Ellis in *Battlefield* (1989).

WORTH WATCHING

Although broadcast as the second story of the 1982 season, *Four to Doomsday* was recorded before the season opener and thus was Peter Davison's first time playing the Doctor. As such it's interesting to note which aspects of his interpretation of the character were kept or discarded as the actor settled into the role. The relationship between the Doctor and his three companions is still fragile too as they come to terms with his new personality.

THE EPISODES

All four episodes are restored from digital duplicates of the original two-inch colour videotape recordings used for broadcast and their mono soundtracks remastered. The title sequences are replaced by a modern transfer of the original 35mm film with credits remade to match the originals.

SPECIAL FEATURES

STUDIO RECORDING (27m13s) Footage from the full studio recording on Monday 13 April 1981, Peter Davison's first day playing the Doctor on camera (also his thirtieth birthday), of scenes in the spaceship laboratory, including retakes and shots unused in the final programme.

SATURDAY NIGHT AT THE MILL (14m26s) Extract from the BBC1 evening magazine programme recorded at Pebble Mill studios in Birmingham, actually a Boxing Day edition broadcast on Friday 26 December 1980, in which Bob Langley interviews Peter Davison about his time in *All Creatures Great and Small* and his recent casting as the Doctor, and Davison makes a chocolate milkshake for his wife Sandra Dickinson.

THEME MUSIC VIDEO (3m35s) The full version of Peter Howell's rearrangement of the *Doctor Who* theme remastered from the original recording, set to footage from the title sequences designed by Sid Sutton for the Fourth and Fifth Doctors. Select to listen in either stereo or Dolby Digital 5.1. *Also included on* **Castrovalva** *with stereo option only*

PHOTO GALLERY (6m40s) Slideshow of colour and black-and-white photos taken during production of *Four to Doomsday*, including shots of Stratford Johns having his mask applied and design department photos of the sets. Set to the ethnic music used in the story and Roger Limb's incidental music. Compiled by Derek Handley.

AUDIO OPTIONS Select **Commentary** to play the audio commentary in place of the main soundtrack when watching the episodes. With Peter Davison, Janet Fielding (Tegan), Sarah Sutton (Nyssa), Matthew Waterhouse (Adric) and director John Black on all four episodes.

— Select **Feature Audio** to reinstate the main soundtrack when watching the episodes.

NEXT

INFO TEXT Select **On** to view subtitles when watching the episodes that provide information and anecdotes about the development, production, broadcast and history of *Four to Doomsday*. Written by Richard Molesworth.

RADIO TIMES LISTINGS Accessible via a computer is a PDF file of the four episode listings for the original BBC1 broadcast of *Four to Doomsday*.

COMING SOON (1m5s) Trailer for the DVD release of *The War Machines*.

SUBTITLES

Select **On** to view subtitles for all episodes and Special Features (except commentary).

RELATED EXTRAS

Coming Soon trailer — The Trial of a Time Lord: The Ultimate Foe

FRONTIER IN SPACE

STORY No.67   SEASON No.10:3

Released with **PLANET OF THE DALEKS** in the **DALEK WAR** boxset
Two discs with six episodes (144 mins) and 105 minutes of extras, plus commentary track, production subtitles and PDF items
Audio navigation of each disc's contents available by pressing Enter after the Doctor Who *DVDs promo on disc one or after the BBC ident on disc two*

TARDIS TEAM Third Doctor, Jo

TIME AND PLACE Future Earth and planet Draconia

ADVERSARIES First Master (8th appearance); ape-like Ogrons (2nd appearance); lizard-like Draconians

FIRST ON TV 24 February–31 March 1973
DVD RELEASE BBCDVD2614(A) [discs 2614(1) and 2614(2)], 5 October 2009, PG
(episodes and disc two U)
COVER Photo illustration by Clayton Hickman, light purple strip;
version with older BBC logo on reverse
ORIGINAL RRP £34.26 (boxset)

STORY TEASER

Avoiding a collision with a ship in hyperspace, the Doctor materialises the TARDIS within its hold, only to find himself and Jo then accused of being stowaways. When the ship is attacked and the TARDIS stolen along with its cargo, the pair find themselves arrested for piracy and taken to Earth for sentencing. They learn Earth is on the brink of war with the empire of Draconia, but no one will believe their claims that the Draconians weren't behind the attack as suspected, and that the real enemy is far more dangerous.

CONNECTIONS

Although written as a standalone story, this sets up and leads directly into the events of *Planet of the Daleks*, together forming a twelve-part epic to rival that of *The Daleks' Master Plan* (1965/66). In writer Malcolm Hulke's penultimate script for the series, he picks up on several ideas from his earlier stories, including a rivalry between humans and a reptilian species, as in *Doctor Who and the Silurians* (1970) and *The Sea Devils* (1972); a misguided general who feels compelled to start a war, whereas the supposed aggressors are innocent, as in *The Ambassadors of Death* (1970); and a third party duping two others into conflict for its own ends, as the IMC mission does with the human colonists and Uxaerian locals in *Colony in Space* (1971). The Draconians are reminiscent of the Silurians although in appearance are closer to the kind seen in the New Series in *The Hungry Earth* (2010) *et seq*, while the Ogrons first appear in *Day of the Daleks* (1972). Although unwillingly incarcerated on the Moon here, the Doctor also spends time there in *The Moonbase* (1967), *The Seeds of Death* (1969) and *Smith and Jones* (2007). Hulke's last script for *Doctor Who* is the following season's *Invasion of the Dinosaurs* (*see Index v*), while Paul Bernard also directed *Day of the Daleks* and *The Time Monster* in the previous season. Sadly this is the last time Roger Delgado plays the Master owing to his tragic death just months after *Frontier in Space* was broadcast (*see Index iv for his other appearances*). John Woodnutt, playing the Draconian Emperor, can be seen as George Hibbert in *Spearhead from Space* (1970) and as the Duke or Forgill in *Terror of the Zygons* (1975), in which he is also Zygon leader Broton. Barry Ashton (Lieutenant Kemp) plays Franz in *The Moonbase* and Proctor in *The Time Monster*, Richard Shaw (Cross) is Lobos in *The Space Museum* (1965) and Lakh in *Underworld* (1978), Caroline Hunt (Technician) is Danielle Renan in *The Reign of Terror* (1964), while Louis Mahoney (Newscaster) is Ponti in *Planet of Evil* (1975) and appears in the New Series as the older Billy Shipton in *Blink* (2007).

WORTH WATCHING

This story by Malcolm Hulke, perhaps *Doctor Who*'s most political writer during the 1970s, uses the grand scale of two neighbouring space empires — with extensive spaceship model filming — to examine some of the more down-to-earth reasons why nations go to war and how good intentions can be cynically manipulated by others. Such thoughts are wrapped up in something of a runaround, however, with the Doctor and Jo escaping from one prison after another. And while long scenes of people space-walking might have been exciting in the age of NASA's Apollo missions, to modern eyes they offer little engagement.

DISC ONE

THE EPISODES

Episodes one, two and three are restored from digital duplicates of two-inch colour videotape copies of the episodes made for broadcast in Australia and returned from there in 1983, while episodes four, five and six are restored from digital duplicates of the original two-inch colour videotape recordings used for broadcast in the UK. The episodes' mono soundtracks are remastered and the title sequences replaced by a modern transfer of the original 35mm film with credits remade to match the originals.

AUDIO OPTIONS

Select **Commentary** to play the audio commentary in place of the main soundtrack when watching the episodes. This is moderated by writer and journalist Clayton Hickman, talking with Katy Manning (Jo), producer Barry Letts and script editor Terrance Dicks on all six episodes.

— Select **Feature Audio** to reinstate the main soundtrack when watching the episodes.

SUBTITLES

Select **Subtitles On** to view subtitles for all episodes (none for commentary).

— Select **Info Text On** to view subtitles when watching the episodes that provide information and anecdotes about the development, production, broadcast and history of *Frontier in Space*. Written by Martin Wiggins.

DISC TWO

SPECIAL FEATURES

THE PERFECT SCENARIO: LOST FRONTIERS (30m4s) Part one of a dramatised scenario in which hibernating humans of the 26th Century are kept entertained by stories projected into their sleeping minds. One of the official storytellers, Zed, is starting to run out of original plots and so accesses historical data about *Doctor Who*, specifically *Frontier in Space*, in order to get fresh ideas. His research covers influences of and connections to contemporary life in the writing and production of the story. With input from producer Barry Letts, script editor Terrance Dicks, visual effects designers John Friedlander and Mat Irvine, and actors Janet Fielding, Vera Fusek, Michael Hawkins and Katy Manning. Written by David Harley and featuring Rich Batsford, Mick Broster, Tony Broster, Henry Dunn, Paul Ewing and Gemma Layton; produced by Steve Broster. *Part two is on* Planet of the Daleks

THE SPACE WAR (17m57s) The making of *Frontier in Space*, including working with director Paul Bernard; the model and effects work; creating the Draconian masks; the costumes; filming the space-walk scenes at Ealing Studios; the character of General Williams; and the surprise return of…well, you'll have to watch and see. With contributions from actors Vera Fusek, Michael Hawkins and Katy Manning, and visual effects designers John Friedlander and Mat Irvine. Produced by Steve Broster.

ROGER DELGADO: THE MASTER (31m46s) Profile of the life and career of actor Roger Delgado, who died in 1973, best remembered for playing the Master during the Third Doctor era. With memories from Roger's wife Kismet Marlowe, actor/director/producer Barry Letts (interviewed in 2003), script editor Terrance Dicks, director Christopher Barry, stuntman Derek Ware, and actors William Gaunt, Damaris Hayman, Frazer Hines, Katy Manning, Linda Thorson and Harry Towb. Illustrated with photos and clips from Roger's stage, radio and television work. Narrated by Stephen Greif, produced by John Kelly.

STRIPPED FOR ACTION: THE THIRD DOCTOR (16m6s) *Doctor Who* comic strips have run in various publications since the early days of the television series. This examines the Third Doctor's adventures in Polystyle Publications' *TV Comic*, *Countdown* and *TV Action*. With contributions from magazine editors Alan Barnes and Gary Russell, and comics historians John Ainsworth, Jeremy Bentham and Paul Scoones. Directed by Marcus Hearn. *See Index iii for further editions*

PHOTO GALLERY (6m9s) Slideshow of colour and black-and-white photos taken during production of *Frontier in Space*, including design department photos of the sets and behind-the-scenes shots of the location filming at Beachfields Quarry, Surrey. Set to sound effects from the story. Compiled by Ralph Montagu.

PDF MATERIALS Accessible via a computer are the six episode listings from *Radio Times* for the original BBC1 broadcast of *Frontier in Space*, with illustrations by Frank Bellamy.

— Designer Cynthia Kljuco's blueprints for the cargo ship, the Master's spaceship and the lunar prison sets.

— BBC Enterprises' sales document for *Frontier in Space*, describing the serial for potential overseas broadcasters.

COMING SOON (1m17s) Trailer for the DVD releases of *The King's Demons* and *Planet of Fire*.

SUBTITLES Select **On** to view subtitles for all Special Features on disc two.

EASTER EGG
There is one hidden feature on these discs to find. *See Appendix 2 for details*

RELATED EXTRAS
Coming Soon trailer — The Keys of Marinus

FRONTIOS

STORY No.132   SEASON No.21:3

One disc with four episodes (98½ mins) and 55½ minutes of extras, plus commentary and music-only tracks, production subtitles and PDF items
Audio navigation of disc contents available by pressing Enter after the BBC ident

TARDIS TEAM Fifth Doctor, Tegan, Turlough
TIME AND PLACE Planet Frontios, distant future
ADVERSARIES Giant insect-like Tractators
FIRST ON TV 26 January–3 February 1984
DVD RELEASE BBCDVD3004, 30 May 2011, PG
COVER Photo illustration by Lee Binding, light turquoise strip;
  version with older BBC logo on reverse
ORIGINAL RRP £20.42

STORY TEASER
Drifting into the far future when mankind has abandoned the dying Earth, the TARDIS is mysteriously pulled down to the planet Frontios where one of the last colonies of humans is struggling to survive, having also crashed there. With their society crumbling, rumours of the planet itself burying the dead and the TARDIS apparently destroyed, the Doctor realises the source of everyone's problems must lie underground, but even he doesn't appreciate the full gravity of the situation.

CONNECTIONS
The indication is that the humans in *Frontios* left Earth to escape its destruction by the expanding sun, as did those seen in *The Ark* (1966), although *The End of the World* (2005), which depicts that event, suggests humans had long since spread out into the universe. A group of humans attempting to survive on a world barely able to sustain life features in *Colony in Space* (1971). The Tractators were inspired by woodlice, joining the ranks of insectoid aliens such as the Zarbi, Menoptra and Optera in *The Web Planet* (1965), the Mutts in *The Mutants* (1972), the Wirrn in *The Ark in Space* (1975), the Vespiform in *The Unicorn and the Wasp* (2008) and the Time Beetle in *Turn Left* (2008). The TARDIS exterior is supposed to be indestructible, surviving plunges off cliffs in *The Romans* (1965) and *The Curse of Peladon* (1972) and down a mine shaft in *The Mark of the Rani* (1985), although it is seen to break apart in *The Mind Robber* (1968) and the spaceship Titanic crashes through into the internal dimension in *Last of the Time Lords* (2007). Christopher H Bidmead was script editor for the 1980/81 season and wrote the last Fourth Doctor story, *Logopolis* (1981), as well as its sequel introducing the Fifth Doctor, *Castrovalva* (1982). This was director Ron Jones' fourth serial, his first directing job having been on 1982's *Black Orchid* (see Index v). Of the main guest cast, only Leslie Dunlop (Norna Range) appears again, as Susan Q in *The Happiness Patrol* (1988).

WORTH WATCHING
Having played a major part in developing the character of the Fifth Doctor, writer Christopher H Bidmead returned to contribute to Peter Davison's final season with a story that highlights this incarnation's wit and authority, which had previously been underplayed. The Tractators are also an inventive addition to the *Doctor Who* pantheon, even if Bidmead had to tone down some of his ideas considered too gruesome for a family show.

THE EPISODES
All four episodes are restored from digital duplicates of the original one-inch colour videotape recordings used for broadcast and their mono soundtracks remastered. The title sequences are replaced by a modern transfer of the original 35mm film with credits remade to match the originals.

DRIVEN TO DISTRACTION (32m52s) The making of *Frontios*, including the origins of the story; designing the above- and below-ground sets; exploring the nature of the TARDIS; the impact of the murder of actor Peter Arne who had been cast as Mr Range; the quality of the guest cast; developing the characters of the Doctor and Turlough; working with director Ron Jones; realising the tunnelling machine and the Tractators; and the pressures of recording in the studio. With contributions from script editor Eric Saward, writer Christopher H Bidmead, designer David Buckingham, and actors Peter Davison, John Gillett, Jeff Rawle and Mark Strickson. Narrated by Paul Jones, produced by Ed Stradling.

DELETED AND EXTENDED SCENES (15m37s) A selection of scenes from all four episodes not used in the final programme, taken from copies of earlier edits with on-screen time-code.

PHOTO GALLERY (5m23s) Slideshow of colour and black-and-white photos taken during production of *Frontios*, including design department photos of the sets. Set to music and sound effects from the story. Compiled by Paul Shields.

NEXT

AUDIO OPTIONS Select **Commentary** to play the audio commentary in place of the main soundtrack when watching the episodes. With special sounds creator Dick Mills [eps 1,2], Peter Davison [1,2,3,4], Jeff Rawle (Plantagenet) [1,2,3,4], script editor Eric Saward [1,2,3,4] and John Gillett (the Gravis) [3,4].
— Select **Isolated Score** to hear only Paddy Kingsland's music when watching the episodes.
— Select **Feature Audio** to reinstate the main soundtrack when watching the episodes.

INFO TEXT Select **On** to view subtitles when watching the episodes that provide information and anecdotes about the development, production, broadcast and history of *Frontios*. Written by Paul Scoones.

PDF MATERIALS Accessible via a computer are the four episode listings from *Radio Times* for the original BBC1 broadcast of *Frontios*.

COMING SOON (1m45s) Trailer for the DVD releases of *The Awakening* and *The Gunfighters* in the Earth Story boxset.

SUBTITLES

Select **On** to view subtitles for all episodes and Special Features (except commentary).

RELATED EXTRAS

Coming Soon trailer — Spearhead from Space Special Edition, Terror of the Autons

FULL CIRCLE

STORY No.111   SEASON No.18:3

Released with **STATE OF DECAY** and **WARRIORS' GATE** in **THE E-SPACE TRILOGY** boxset
One disc with four episodes (93 mins) and 61½ minutes of extras, plus commentary and music-only tracks, production subtitles and PDF items
Audio navigation of disc contents available by pressing Enter after the BBC ident

TARDIS TEAM Fourth Doctor, Second Romana, K9, and introducing Adric

TIME AND PLACE Planet Alzarius

ADVERSARIES Marshmen swamp creatures

FIRST ON TV 25 October–15 November 1980

DVD RELEASE BBCDVD1835(A), 26 January 2009, U (boxset PG)

COVER Photo illustration by Clayton Hickman, dark green strip

ORIGINAL RRP £34.99 (boxset)

STORY TEASER

Heading home to Gallifrey, the Doctor and Romana unexpectedly find themselves on a different planet and realise the TARDIS has been pulled into the pocket universe of Exo Space. Here on Alzarius they encounter the occupants of a crashed spaceship, the Starliner, who seem to be taking an unusually long time to make the necessary repairs. Then when Mistfall comes and the land is shrouded in fog, horrifying creatures rise from the swamp and giant spiders hatch from fruit. Somehow all these events are connected.

CONNECTIONS

This begins a trilogy of stories in which the TARDIS is trapped in E-Space and the Doctor and Romana seek a way back into the normal universe. The causes of this are explained at the end of the season in *Logopolis* (1981). E-Space is different to parallel universes or dimensions, as visited in *Inferno* (1970) and *Rise of the Cybermen/The Age of Steel* (2006) or mentioned in *Battlefield* (1989), but may or may not be related to the bubble universe where House dwelled in *The Doctor's Wife* (2011). Evolution on Alzarius appears to happen unusually quickly, as it does on Solos in *The Mutants* (1972) and for the Survey agent who becomes Josiah in *Ghost Light* (1989). The scene of Marshmen rising from the water is reminiscent of the Sea Devils emerging from the sea in *The Sea Devils* (1973) and the Haemovores in *The Curse of Fenric* (1989). This was the first serial directed by Peter Grimwade, who had previously been a production assistant on the programme; he also directed *Logopolis*, *Kinda* (1982) and *Earthshock* (1982). Two of the Deciders had previous experience of *Doctor Who*: James Bree (Nefred) plays the Security Chief in *The War Games* (1969) and the Keeper of the Matrix in *The Trial of a Time Lord: The Ultimate Foe* (1986), while Alan Rowe (Garif) is Dr Evans in *The Moonbase* (1967), Edward of Wessex in *The Time Warrior* (1973/74) and Colonel Skinsale in *Horror of Fang Rock* (1977).

WORTH WATCHING

A key ambition for script editor Christopher H Bidmead was to bring more genuine science into the Doctor's adventures and he worked closely with *Full Circle*'s eighteen-year-old writer Andrew Smith to develop the story's ideas about evolution. With news breaking that Romana and K9 would soon be leaving the series, this story also began a run of plots that left viewers unsure if they would survive to the end. One character Smith was instructed to include in his script was a cheeky young mischief-maker called Adric, who was in line to become the Doctor's latest companion.

THE EPISODES

All four episodes are restored from digital duplicates of the original two-inch colour videotape recordings used for broadcast and their mono soundtracks remastered. The title sequences are replaced by a modern transfer of the original 35mm film with credits remade to match the originals.

SPECIAL FEATURES

AUDIO OPTIONS Select **Commentary** to play the audio commentary in place of the main soundtrack when watching the episodes. With Matthew Waterhouse (Adric), script editor Christopher H Bidmead and writer Andrew Smith on all four episodes.

— Select **Isolated Score** to hear only Paddy Kingsland's music when watching the episodes.

— Select **Feature Audio** to reinstate the main soundtrack when watching the episodes.

INFO TEXT Select **On** to view subtitles when watching the episodes that provide information and anecdotes about the development, production, broadcast and history of *Full Circle*. Written by Richard Bignell.

ALL ABOARD THE STARLINER (24m20s) The making of *Full Circle*, including development of the script; the introduction of Adric; the young cast playing the Outlers and more experienced actors as the Deciders; working with the director and Tom Baker; and the location filming at Black Park in Buckinghamshire. With contributions from script editor Christopher H Bidmead, writer Andrew Smith, director Peter Grimwade (interviewed in 1987), film cameraman Max Samett, and actors George Baker, John Leeson, Bernard Padden and Lalla Ward. Produced by Steve Broster.

K9 IN E-SPACE (4m38s) The reasons behind the decision to write out K9 during the E-Space trilogy. With contributions from script editor Christopher H Bidmead, writers Andrew Smith and Terrance Dicks, and actors John Leeson and Lalla Ward. Produced by Steve Broster.

SWAP SHOP (8m8s) Extract from the 1 November 1980 edition (its one-hundredth) of the BBC1 Saturday morning children's show, in which Noel Edmonds interviews Matthew Waterhouse about his recent introduction as Adric and they take viewers' questions on the phone.

NEXT

E-SPACE – FACT OR FICTION? (14m35s) To what extent is there genuine science behind the idea of E-Space? Experts discuss our current knowledge of cosmology and the possibility of other universes. With contributions from script editor Christopher H Bidmead, visual effects designer (and Fellow of the British Interplanetary Society) Mat Irvine, astronomer Sir Patrick Moore, planetary scientist Dr Andrew Ball, and authors Stephen Baxter and Paul Parsons. Narrated by Sophie Aldred, produced by Keith Barnfather.

CONTINUITY (2m56s) Continuity announcements from the original BBC1 broadcasts of all four episodes of *Full Circle*, with plugs for the theme music single, the *Doctor Who* display at Madame Tussauds, and the following story, *State of Decay*.

PHOTO GALLERY (5m49s) Slideshow of colour and black-and-white photos taken during production of *Full Circle*, including design department photos of the sets, shots taken for the View-Master release of this story (not stereoscopic), and the photo call for Matthew Waterhouse and Andrew Smith on the Starliner laboratory set. Set to music from the story. Compiled by Derek Handley.
— Select **Info Text On** before selecting **Play Gallery** to view descriptive captions while watching the slideshow.

RADIO TIMES LISTINGS Accessible via a computer is a PDF file of the four episode listings for the original BBC1 broadcast of *Full Circle*, plus an article about Matthew Waterhouse and Andrew Smith published the week of episode one, a letter about the departure of K9 published the week of episode two, and one about casting a female Doctor published the week of episode four.

COMING SOON (1m14s) Trailer for the DVD releases of *The Rescue* and *The Romans*.

SUBTITLES
Select **On** to view subtitles for all episodes and Special Features (except commentary).

RELATED EXTRAS
Coming Soon trailer — Battlefield
Peter Grimwade - Directing with Attitude — Kinda

GALAXY 4

STORY No.18   SEASON No.3:1

Reconstruction incorporating one surviving episode (part 3 of 4) and a six-minute clip from episode one released on The Aztecs Special Edition

TARDIS TEAM First Doctor, Steven, Vicki
TIME AND PLACE Unknown planet
ADVERSARIES Drahvin soldiers
FIRST ON TV 11 September–2 October 1965
DVD RELEASE BBCDVD3689, 11 March 2013, PG
● *See* The Aztecs Special Edition *for full details*

GENESIS OF THE DALEKS

STORY No.78   SEASON No.12:4

Two discs with six episodes (143 mins) and 137 minutes of extras, plus commentary track, production subtitles and PDF items

TARDIS TEAM Fourth Doctor, Harry, Sarah Jane
TIME AND PLACE Dalek homeworld Skaro
ADVERSARIES Daleks (11th appearance); Davros (1st appearance); his henchman Nyder
FIRST ON TV 8 March–12 April 1975
DVD RELEASE BBCDVD1813, 10 April 2006, PG
COVER Photo illustration by Clayton Hickman, green strip
— Original release with cover sticker reading 'Doctor Who No. 1 story EVER'
ORIGINAL RRP £19.99

- Also released in The Dalek Collection; BBCDVD2261, £79.99, 27 January 2007
- Reissued in sleeve with orange logo and cover illustration in a circle against dark purple background; BBCDVD2469, £9.99, 2 July 2007
- Also released in The Complete Davros Collection; BBCDVD2508, £99.99, 26 November 2007
- Episodes released in The Monster Collection: Davros; BBCDVD3810, £9.99, 30 September 2013

STORY TEASER

The Time Lords send the Doctor to Skaro, in the last days of the war between the Thals and the Kaleds, his mission to find a way to avoid or limit the creation of the Daleks and alter their destiny of universal domination. Caught between the two factions, the Doctor, Sarah and Harry experience the true horrors of atomic warfare and discover the lengths to which mutated scientist Davros will go in order to ensure his people's survival.

CONNECTIONS

A slightly different but not incompatible account of the war on Skaro is given in the Daleks' debut story, The Daleks (1963/64), in which it's said they were originally called Dals. During the Doctor's exile on Earth the Time Lords use him as a deniable agent for missions in Colony in Space (1971), The Curse of Peladon (1972) and The Mutants (1972), but since lifting his sentence this is their first approach, although they do help him track down the Daleks in Planet of the Daleks (1973). Even though he arguably fails by their criteria, they call on him again in The Brain of Morbius (1976) to counter another threat to themselves (you can see why he left Gallifrey). So effective is the character of Davros that Terry Nation brought him back in Destiny of the Daleks (1979) — the writer's last Doctor Who story — and stipulated that he be included in subsequent Dalek stories written by others. He eventually returned in the New Series too in The Stolen Earth/Journey's End (2008). The Thals are less of a staple, this being their last appearance after The Daleks and Planet of the Daleks. David Maloney is most responsible for the grim atmosphere of this story, encouraged by the production team's desire to make the series more gritty — compare this to his previous handling of the Daleks in Planet of the Daleks. It was a tone he maintained for his remaining Doctor Who assignments (see Index v). Michael Wisher was chosen to play Davros, having provided Dalek voices for the previous two Dalek stories but appearing in person in The Ambassadors of Death (1970), Terror of the Autons (1971), Carnival of Monsters (1973) and Planet of Evil (1975), as well as behind another mask in Revenge of the Cybermen (1975). Peter Miles (Nyder) plays equally uptight villains in Doctor Who and the Silurians (1970) and Invasion of the Dinosaurs (1974), while Dennis Chinnery (Gharman) and Tom Georgeson (Kavell) have smaller roles in The Twin Dilemma (1984) and Logopolis (1981) respectively. Stephen Yardley (Sevrin) is Arak in Vengeance on Varos (1985).

WORTH WATCHING

This is a landmark story for Doctor Who, often voted among the top three of all time. Although it was over eleven years since the Daleks' debut on television, this was the first time their creation had been addressed in detail. And writer Terry Nation created a second cultural icon to almost match the Daleks themselves — their creator Davros — helped in no small part by his astounding portrayal here by Michael Wisher. The story and direction make this one of the most serious and grimmest Doctor Who stories, fitting to its subject matter. With the New Series' depiction of the Great Time War between Daleks and Time Lords, this adventure is now seen by many as one of the first strikes in that war, as the Doctor's people use him to try to wipe out the Daleks before they can become such a terrifying threat.

DISC ONE

THE EPISODES

All six episodes are restored from digital duplicates of the original two-inch colour videotape recordings used for broadcast and their mono soundtracks remastered. The title sequences are replaced by a modern transfer of the original 35mm film with credits remade to match the originals.

SPECIAL FEATURES

INFORMATION TEXT Select **On** to view subtitles when watching the episodes that provide information and anecdotes about the development, production, broadcast and history of Genesis of the Daleks. Written by Richard Molesworth.

AUDIO OPTIONS Select **Commentary On** to play the audio commentary in place of the main soundtrack when watching the episodes. With Elisabeth Sladen (Sarah) [eps 1,2,3,4,5,6], Tom Baker [1,2,4,5,6], director David Maloney [1,3,5,6] and Peter Miles (Nyder) [2,3,4,6].

SUBTITLES
Select **On** to view subtitles for the episodes (none for commentary).

DISC TWO
SPECIAL FEATURES

GENESIS OF A CLASSIC (62m8s) The making of *Genesis of the Daleks*, including development of the script during a change of production team and leading man; the input of the director and script editor; echoes of the Nazi regime in the script; the moral discussions in the story; the degree of violence; the importance of dramatic studio lighting; working with Tom Baker and his approach to the role of the Doctor; creating Davros and Michael Wisher's performance; operating and voicing the Daleks; and the legacy of *Genesis of the Daleks*. Interspersed with lessons in how to talk like a Dalek. With contributions from outgoing production team Barry Letts and Terrance Dicks, producer Philip Hinchcliffe, director David Maloney, lighting director Duncan Brown, make-up supervisor Sylvia James, visual effects designer Peter Day, special sounds creator Dick Mills, Dalek voice actor Roy Skelton, Dalek operators John Scott Martin and Cy Town, and actors Tom Baker, Dennis Chinnery, James Garbutt, Peter Miles, Guy Siner, Elisabeth Sladen and Michael Wisher (interviewed in 1984). Produced by Ian Levine.

THE DALEK TAPES (53m20s) A history of the Daleks' appearances in the original series of *Doctor Who*, running through each of their stories, plus how they were conceived, what it's like playing a Dalek, facts about the Dalek machines and hierarchy, and their appearances outside the television series. With contributions from producer Philip Hinchcliffe, directors Timothy Combe, Ken Grieve, Graeme Harper, David Maloney and Richard Martin, writers/script editors Terrance Dicks and Eric Saward, designer Derek Dodd, visual effects designer Peter Day, Dalek voice actors Nicholas Briggs, Royce Mills and Roy Skelton, Dalek operator Cy Town, actors Terry Molloy and Anneke Wills, film critic Kim Newman, and fans Andrew Beech and Ian McLachlan. Narrated by Terry Molloy, produced by John Kelly.

CONTINUITY COMPILATION (6m15s) Continuity announcements from the original BBC1 broadcasts of episode two of the preceding story, *The Sontaran Experiment*; episodes three and six of *Genesis of the Daleks*; episode four of *The Android Invasion* announcing the omnibus repeat of *Genesis of the Daleks* on Saturday 27 December 1975; plus repeats on BBC1 under the 'Doctor Who and the Monsters' banner in July/August 1982, and on BBC2 in January/February 1993 and February 2000 (including trail and BBC2 Dalek ident).

BLUE PETER (7m12s) Extract from the Thursday 20 March 1975 edition of the BBC1 children's magazine programme shown between episodes two and three of *Genesis of the Daleks*, in which John Noakes and Peter Purves showcase teenager Jonathan Sellers' impressive models of *Doctor Who* sets and monsters. With Lesley Judd.

PHOTO GALLERY (7m56s) Slideshow of colour and black-and-white photos taken during production of *Genesis of the Daleks*, including publicity shots of Tom Baker with the Daleks. Set to sound effects from the story. Compiled by Ralph Montagu.

DOCTOR WHO ANNUAL Accessible via a computer is a PDF file of the 1976 *Doctor Who Annual*, published by World Distributors the autumn after *Genesis of the Daleks* was broadcast. With stories featuring the Doctor, Sarah, Harry and the Brigadier, plus science features, puzzles and games.

RADIO TIMES BILLINGS Accessible via a computer is a PDF file of the six episode listings for the original BBC1 broadcast of *Genesis of the Daleks*, articles about Terry Nation published the weeks of episodes one and six, and the listing for the 27 December 1975 omnibus repeat, with illustration by Frank Bellamy.

SUBTITLES Select **On** to view subtitles for all Special Features on disc two.

RELATED EXTRAS
Terror Nation — Destiny of the Daleks
The Doctor's Composer — The Sun Makers

GHOST LIGHT

STORY No.153   SEASON No.26:2

One disc with three episodes (73 mins) and 98½ minutes of extras, plus commentary, music-only and surround-sound tracks, and production subtitles

TARDIS TEAM Seventh Doctor, Ace

TIME AND PLACE Gabriel Chase house, late-19th Century

ADVERSARIES Josiah Samuel Smith; alien entity known as Light

FIRST ON TV 4–18 October 1989

DVD RELEASE BBCDVD1352, 20 September 2004, PG

COVER Photo illustration by Clayton Hickman, light purple strip

ORIGINAL RRP £19.99

STORY TEASER

The Doctor brings Ace to a Victorian household with some very strange inhabitants. There's owner Josiah Smith, who has some blasphemous theories about evolution, and his creepy ward Gwendoline; a stern housekeeper and her maids who only come out at night; a big-game hunter who is stalking a peculiar form of prey; and locked in the cellar is something very dangerous to all life on Earth. When Ace recognises the house, light begins to dawn on the Doctor's scheming.

CONNECTIONS

Doctor Who has used the setting of a haunted house surprisingly rarely, perhaps deterred by its comical first outing in *The Chase* (1965). *Image of the Fendahl* (1977) features an old mansion and talks about ghosts but doesn't pursue the connection, while *Pyramids of Mars* (1975) and *Black Orchid* (1982) don't make their stately homes especially spooky. Not until 2013's *Hide* do we get a story of a house haunted by a chilling spectre. Dangerous things dwelling in cellars feature in *The Brain of Morbius* (1976), *The Talons of Weng-Chiang* (1977) and, less gothically, *Paradise Towers* (1987). This was the last Classic *Doctor Who* serial made, in the same block as *Survival*, both directed by Alan Wareing who first worked on the series the previous season directing *The Greatest Show in the Galaxy* (1988/89). Carl Forgione (Nimrod) appears as Land in *Planet of the Spiders* (1974), while Michael Cochrane (Redvers) plays Lord Cranleigh in *Black Orchid*, and Frank Windsor (Inspector Mackenzie) is Sir Ranulf Fitzwilliam in *The King's Demons* (1983).

WORTH WATCHING

More than most previous companions — and prefiguring the New Series — Sophie Aldred's Ace became as central a character to the series as the Doctor himself, an aspect of her past forming the core around which the stories were constructed. This reached its height with *Ghost Light*, in which the Doctor returns Ace to a place that terrified her as a girl and forces her to confront her fears. The story, heavily compressed to fit three episodes, is subsequently dense with meaning and metaphor that repays repeated viewing.

THE EPISODES

All three episodes are restored from digital duplicates of the original one-inch colour videotape recordings used for broadcast and their stereo soundtracks remastered. The computer-generated title sequences are replaced by a digital duplicate of the original one-inch colour videotape recording, with credits remade to match the originals (and correcting an actor's misspelled name on broadcast).

SPECIAL FEATURES

DELETED AND EXTENDED SCENES (18m3s) A selection of scenes not used in the final programme, taken from VHS copies of the studio recordings, some with on-screen time code. With captions explaining where they originally fitted into the episodes.

INFORMATION TEXT Select **On** to view subtitles when watching the episodes that provide information and anecdotes about the development, production, broadcast and history of *Ghost Light*. Written by Martin Wiggins.

WRITER'S QUESTION TIME (12m10s) Writer Marc Platt on stage at the PanoptiCon *Doctor Who* convention in Coventry on Saturday 20 October 1990 talking about how he came to write for *Doctor*

G

Who, working with script editor Andrew Cartmel, the original ideas for his story, the character of Ace, the complexity of *Ghost Light*, and influences on his work.

LIGHT IN DARK PLACES (38m51s) The making of *Ghost Light*, including the unusual intricacy of the script; the quality of the guest cast; having fun in rehearsals; the design of the sets; recording in the studio; adding to the Doctor's mystery and Ace's background; making cuts to fit the running time; problems with the sound mix; and what it all means. With contributions from script editor Andrew Cartmel, composer Mark Ayres, and actors Sophie Aldred, Michael Cochrane, Sharon Duce, Ian Hogg, Sylvester McCoy and Katharine Schlesinger. Produced by Richard Molesworth.

SHOOTING GHOSTS (19m8s) Footage from the full studio recording on Tuesday 1 August 1989, including retakes and shots unused in the final programme.

PHOTO GALLERY (5m29s) Slideshow of colour photos taken during production of *Ghost Light*, set to sound effects from the story. Compiled by Ralph Montagu.

AUDIO OPTIONS

Select **Commentary** to play the audio commentary in place of the main soundtrack when watching the episodes. With Sophie Aldred (Ace), script editor Andrew Cartmel, writer Marc Platt and composer Mark Ayres on all three episodes.

— Select **Isolated Music** to hear only Mark Ayres' music when watching the episodes.

— Select **Dolby Digital 5.1 Surround Mix** to hear the surround soundtrack when watching the episodes, newly remixed for this release.

— Select **Stereo** to reinstate the main soundtrack when watching the episodes.

SUBTITLES

Select **On** to view subtitles for all episodes and Special Features, or for the commentary.

EASTER EGGS

There are two hidden features on this disc to find. *See Appendix 2 for details*

THE **GREATEST SHOW IN THE GALAXY**

STORY No.151   **SEASON No.25:4**

One disc with four episodes (98 mins) and 76 minutes of extras, plus commentary, music-only and surround-sound tracks, production subtitles and PDF items
Audio navigation of disc contents available by pressing Enter after the BBC ident

TARDIS TEAM Seventh Doctor, Ace

TIME AND PLACE Planet Segonax

ADVERSARIES Android clowns and their Chief Clown; ancient Gods of Ragnarok

FIRST ON TV 14 December 1988–4 January 1989

DVD RELEASE BBCDVD3481, 30 July 2012, PG

COVER Photo illustration by Lee Binding, purple strip; version with older BBC logo on reverse

ORIGINAL RRP £20.42

STORY TEASER

The Doctor and Ace take a trip to the Psychic Circus on the planet Segonax, a once great show that's now struggling to get an audience for its tired acts. The Ringmaster and Chief Clown are in charge of finding new talent from among the few visitors, but as it's hard to please the mysterious audience, people don't last long in the ring. Can the Doctor keep everyone entertained long enough for the power behind the curtain to be exposed?

CONNECTIONS

The last circus the Doctor investigated was in *Terror of the Autons* (1971). Bellboy's skill at making robots matches that of the Karfelons in *Timelash* (1985), Sharaz Jek in *The Caves of Androzani* (1984), the Urbankans in *Four to Doomsday* (1982), Madame Lamia in *The Androids of Tara* (1978), the Kraals in *The Android Invasion* (1975), and even the Daleks' slightly dodgy efforts in *The Chase* (1965), although they have got better at it by the time of *Victory of the Daleks* (2010). The Gods of Ragnarok's desire to be entertained by lesser beings is reminiscent of the Toymaker in *The Celestial*

Toymaker (1966) and the Eternals in *Enlightenment* (1983). Steven Wyatt also wrote the previous season's *Paradise Towers* (1987), while director Alan Wareing so impressed he was given two stories to handle the following year, *Ghost Light* and *Survival*. Dean Hollingsworth playing the Bus Conductor robot had previously been an android in *Timelash*, while Christopher Guard's (Bellboy) brother Dominic is Olvir in *Terminus* (1983).

WORTH WATCHING

There are subtle and not-so-subtle parallels between this story and *Doctor Who* itself as it was in 1988 — a once-popular show brought down my dark powers but still loved by geeky fans — and for those who were watching the programme at the time these are fun to spot. For newcomers there's still much to enjoy, including creepy clowns, an impressive performance by Ian Reddington as the Chief Clown, and strong direction.

THE EPISODES

Episodes one, two and three are recompiled and restored from digital duplicates of the earliest surviving edits of the original one-inch colour videotape recordings, while episode four is restored from a digital duplicate of the original one-inch colour videotape recording used for broadcast. All episodes' stereo soundtracks are remastered.

SPECIAL FEATURES

THE SHOW MUST GO ON (30m16s) The making of *The Greatest Show in the Galaxy*, including developing the script; the character and performance of the Chief Clown; the location recording; the destruction of the Bus Conductor; modelling the big top; a hot moment for Sylvester McCoy; how the serial was nearly cancelled owing to studio problems and the serendipity of the story's setting in a tent; a painful moment for Ian Reddington; Sylvester doing his own stunts and magic tricks; and shooting the explosive climax. With contributions from producer John Nathan-Turner (interviewed in 1999), script editor Andrew Cartmel, director Alan Wareing, designer David Laskey, visual effects assistant Mike Tucker, and actors Sophie Aldred and Ian Reddington. Produced by Chris Chapman.

DELETED AND EXTENDED SCENES (11m9s) A selection of scenes from the first three episodes not used in the final programme, taken from earlier edits. The sections in black and white appear in the final episodes while those in colour are the unused scenes, to show where they would have fitted into the story.

LOST IN THE DARKNESS (2m7s) Visual effects assistant Mike Tucker discusses why scripted scenes of the advertising robot approaching the TARDIS in space were filmed with models but ultimately not used in the final programme, illustrated with the unused footage.

THE PSYCHIC CIRCUS (3m52s) Music video for the song written and recorded by members of the cast and composer Mark Ayres during production of *The Greatest Show in the Galaxy*. Select to play with stereo or Dolby Digital 5.1 audio.

REMEMBRANCE 'DEMO' (3m23s) Two music cues composed by Mark Ayres in 1988 when he was pitching for work on *Doctor Who*, for scenes from *Remembrance of the Daleks*. Select to play with stereo or Dolby Digital 5.1 audio.

TOMORROW'S TIMES – THE SEVENTH DOCTOR (14m30s) Coverage of *Doctor Who* in the national newspapers during the Seventh Doctor's era from 1987 to 1990. Presented by Anneke Wills, written and directed by Marcus Hearn. *See Index iii for further editions* NEXT

VICTORIA WOOD SKETCH (1m14s) Skit from the Friday 18 December 1987 edition of BBC2 comedy show *Victoria Wood As Seen on TV*, featuring Jim Broadbent as the Doctor and Georgia Allen as Fiona facing the evil Crayola, voiced by Duncan Preston.

PHOTO GALLERY (7m19s) Slideshow of colour and black-and-white photos taken during production of *The Greatest Show in the Galaxy*, including design sketches, studio plans and behind-the-scenes shots of the restaged studio recording. Set to music from the story. Compiled by Paul Shields.

AUDIO OPTIONS Select **Commentary** to play the audio commentary in place of the main soundtrack when watching the episodes. This is moderated by actor and comedian Toby Hadoke, talking with writer Stephen Wyatt [eps 1,2,3], Christopher Guard (Bellboy) [1,2,3], Sophie Aldred (Ace) [1,2,3,4], composer Mark Ayres [1,2,4], Jessica Martin (Mags) [2,3,4] and script editor Andrew Cartmel [3,4]. They also answer questions from fans submitted via Twitter.

— Select **Isolated Score** to hear only Mark Ayres' music when watching the episodes.

— Select **5.1 Audio** to hear the soundtrack in Dolby Digital surround when watching the episodes, newly remixed for this release.

— Select **Stereo Audio** to reinstate the main soundtrack when watching the episodes.

INFO TEXT Select **On** to view subtitles when watching the episodes that provide information and anecdotes about the development, production, broadcast and history of *The Greatest Show in the Galaxy*. Written by Richard Bignell.

PDF MATERIALS Accessible via a computer are the four episode listings from *Radio Times* for the original BBC1 broadcast of *The Greatest Show in the Galaxy*.

— Storyboard and design sketches for the model filming of the advertising robot.

COMING SOON (1m3s) Trailer for the DVD release of *Planet of Giants*.

SUBTITLES
Select **On** to view subtitles for all episodes and Special Features (except commentary).

EASTER EGG
There is one hidden feature on this disc to find. *See Appendix 2 for details*

RELATED EXTRAS
Coming Soon trailer — The Krotons

THE **GREEN DEATH**
STORY No.69   SEASON No.10:5

One disc with six episodes (154½ mins) and 49½ minutes of extras, plus commentary track and production subtitles

TARDIS TEAM Third Doctor, Jo, Brigadier and UNIT

TIME AND PLACE South Welsh village Llanfairfach

ADVERSARIES Oil company Global Chemicals; giant maggots

FIRST ON TV 19 May–23 June 1973

DVD RELEASE BBCDVD1142, 10 May 2004, U

COVER Photo illustration by Clayton Hickman, red strip

ORIGINAL RRP £19.99

— Also released in The Third Doctor Collection; BBCDVD2263, £49.99, 6 November 2006

STORY TEASER
Reports of a dead miner glowing bright green bring UNIT to the Welsh village of Llanfairfach, while Jo tags along to support environmental campaigner Clifford Jones, who is protesting against the nearby oil refinery of Global Chemicals. Investigation of the disused coal mine reveals giant maggots mutated by the luminous green sludge the chemical company is pumping down there. But worse, these are just a side effect of the bid for world domination by the firm's true boss.

CONNECTIONS
The Doctor reaches Metebelis 3, having failed to in *Carnival of Monsters* (1973), although it's not a nice place and the consequences of his visit are seen in *Planet of the Spiders* (1974). He's back in South Wales in *Delta and the Bannermen* (1987) and surprisingly rarely in the New Series, most notably visiting Cardiff in *The Unquiet Dead* (2005) and *Boom Town* (2005), and the village of Cwmtaff in *The Hungry Earth/Cold Blood* (2010). Large corporations are usually up to no good in *Doctor Who*, often involving mining, such as the Issigri Mining Company under Caven's control in *The Space Pirates* (1969), the identically initialled Interplanetary Mining Corporation in *Colony in Space* (1971), Morgus's copper-mining company in *The Caves of Androzani* (1984) and Klineman Halpen's slave-trading Ood Operations in *Planet of the Ood* (2008). If creepy crawlies like maggots are icky, then obviously giant versions will be worse, such as the giant fly (relatively) in *Planet of Giants* (1964), the Metebelis spiders in *Planet of the Spiders*, Greel's mutated rats in *The Talons of*

Weng-Chiang (1977), the waspish Vespiform in *The Unicorn and the Wasp* (2008) and the literal Time Beetle in *Turn Left* (2008). Robert Sloman co-wrote *The Green Death* with producer Barry Letts, as he did *The Dæmons* (1971), *The Time Monster* (1972) and *Planet of the Spiders*, while Michael E Briant went on to direct Daleks and Cybermen in his next two serials (*see Index v*). John Rolfe (Ralph Fell) plays an army captain in *The War Machines* (1966) and crewman Sam Becket in *The Moonbase* (1967), while Talfryn Thomas (Dave) is sneaky porter Mullins in *Spearhead from Space* (1970). Roy Evans (Bert) plays another miner, Rima, in *The Monster of Peladon* (1974) having been Trantis in *The Daleks' Master Plan* (1965/66); Richard Beale (Ecology Minister) also provides voices in *The Ark* (1966) and *The Macra Terror* (1967), and appears as Bat Masterson in *The Gunfighters* (1966); and John Dearth (BOSS) can be seen as Lupton in *Planet of the Spiders*.

WORTH WATCHING

Doctor Who under early-70s producer Barry Letts was more political than at any other point in its history, and this story is a direct result of his views on the state of the environment and the rising power of corporations at the time, raising many points that are still being debated today. It certainly struck a chord with viewers, being remembered as "the one with the maggots". It also marks the last hurrah of the UNIT 'family' that had helped the show become massively popular over the previous three years, as companion Jo Grant leaves in one of the Classic Series' most touching scenes.

THE EPISODES

Episodes one, two, three, four and six are restored from digital duplicates of the original two-inch colour videotape recordings used for broadcast, while episode five is restored from a digital duplicate of an earlier edit on two-inch colour videotape and re-cut to match the broadcast episode. Their mono soundtracks are remastered and title sequences replaced by a modern transfer of the original 35mm film with credits remade to match the originals.

SPECIAL FEATURES *ALSO ON SPECIAL EDITION

*INTERVIEW WITH ROBERT SLOMAN (6m52s) Writer Robert Sloman talks about the ideas and principles behind his scripting of *The Green Death* and how the issues persist to this day.

*INTERVIEW WITH STEWART BEVAN (7m42s) Actor Stewart Bevan, who played Professor Clifford Jones, talks about the character, the foresight of the story, and his memories of the recording.

INFORMATION TEXT Select **On** to view subtitles when watching the episodes that provide information and anecdotes about the development, production, broadcast and history of *The Green Death*. Written by Richard Molesworth.

*GLOBAL CONSPIRACY? (10m52s) Spoof news investigation recounting the events in Llanfairfach in 1973 and their ongoing legacy. Written by and starring Mark Gatiss as journalist Terry Scanlon, with original cast members of *The Green Death*. Produced by Gatiss and Paul Vanezis.

*VISUAL EFFECTS (11m40s) Effects designer Colin Mapson talks about the various techniques used in creating the giant maggots and other creatures, plus the model filming for *The Green Death*, and demonstrates how he originally made the maggots.

*PICTURE GALLERY (8m11s) Slideshow of colour and black-and-white photos taken during production of The *Green Death*, including design department photos of the sets, plus Frank Bellamy's illustrations for the *Radio Times* billings and shots of Katy Manning and Stewart Bevan taken for the *Radio Times Doctor Who 10th Anniversary Special* magazine. Set to sound effects from the story. Compiled by Ralph Montagu.

AUDIO OPTIONS

Select ***Commentary On** to play the audio commentary in place of the main soundtrack when watching the episodes. With Katy Manning (Jo), producer Barry Letts and script editor Terrance Dicks on all six episodes.

SUBTITLES

Select **On** to view subtitles for all episodes and Special Features, or for the commentary.

EASTER EGG

There is one hidden feature on this disc to find. *See Appendix 2 for details*

RELATED EXTRAS

The UNIT Family — Day of the Daleks

THE **GREEN DEATH** SPECIAL EDITION

STORY No.69   SEASON No.10:5

Two discs with six episodes (154½ mins) and 110½ minutes of extras (including two-part The Sarah Jane Adventures *story* The Death of the Doctor *(52½ mins) with commentary track), plus two commentary tracks, production subtitles and PDF items*
Audio navigation of each disc's contents available by pressing Enter after the BBC ident

TARDIS TEAM Third Doctor, Jo, Brigadier and UNIT
TIME AND PLACE South Welsh village Llanfairfach
ADVERSARIES Oil company Global Chemicals; giant maggots
FIRST ON TV 19 May–23 June 1973
DVD RELEASE BBCDVD3778, 5 August 2013, PG (disc one U)
COVER Photo illustration by Lee Binding, green strip; version with older BBC logo on reverse
ORIGINAL RRP £20.42

STORY TEASER

Reports of a dead miner glowing bright green bring UNIT to the Welsh village of Llanfairfach, while Jo tags along to support environmental campaigner Clifford Jones, who is protesting against the nearby oil refinery of Global Chemicals. Investigation of the disused coal mine reveals giant maggots mutated by the luminous green sludge the chemical company is pumping down there. But worse, these are just a side effect of the bid for world domination by the firm's true boss.

CONNECTIONS

The Doctor reaches Metebelis 3, having failed to in *Carnival of Monsters* (1973), although it's not a nice place and the consequences of his visit are seen in *Planet of the Spiders* (1974). He's back in South Wales in *Delta and the Bannermen* (1987) and surprisingly rarely in the New Series, most notably visiting Cardiff in *The Unquiet Dead* (2005) and *Boom Town* (2005), and the village of Cwmtaff in *The Hungry Earth/Cold Blood* (2010). Large corporations are usually up to no good in *Doctor Who*, often involving mining, such as the Issigri Mining Company under Caven's control in *The Space Pirates* (1969), the identically initialled Interplanetary Mining Corporation in *Colony in Space* (1971), Morgus's copper-mining company in *The Caves of Androzani* (1984) and Klineman Halpen's slave-trading Ood Operations in *Planet of the Ood* (2008). If creepy crawlies like maggots are icky, then obviously giant versions will be worse, such as the giant fly (relatively) in *Planet of Giants* (1964), the Metebelis spiders in *Planet of the Spiders*, Greel's mutated rats in *The Talons of Weng-Chiang* (1977), the waspish Vespiform in *The Unicorn and the Wasp* (2008) and the literal Time Beetle in *Turn Left* (2008). Robert Sloman co-wrote *The Green Death* with producer Barry Letts, as he did *The Dæmons* (1971), *The Time Monster* (1972) and *Planet of the Spiders*, while Michael E Briant went on to direct Daleks and Cybermen in his next two serials (*see Index v*). John Rolfe (Ralph Fell) plays an army captain in *The War Machines* (1966) and crewman Sam Becket in *The Moonbase* (1967), while Talfryn Thomas (Dave) is sneaky porter Mullins in *Spearhead from Space* (1970). Roy Evans (Bert) plays another miner, Rima, in *The Monster of Peladon* (1974) having been Trantis in *The Daleks' Master Plan* (1965/66); Richard Beale (Ecology Minister) also provides voices in *The Ark* (1966) and *The Macra Terror* (1967), and appears as Bat Masterson in *The Gunfighters* (1966); and John Dearth (BOSS) can be seen as Lupton in *Planet of the Spiders*.

WORTH WATCHING

This Special Edition features more advanced clean-up of the episodes compared to the previous release and additional Special Features. *Doctor Who* under early-70s producer Barry Letts was more political than at any other point in its history, and this story is a direct result of his views on the state of the environment and the rising power of corporations at the time, raising many points that are still being debated today. It certainly struck a chord with viewers, being remembered as "the one with the maggots". It also marks the last hurrah of the UNIT 'family' that had helped the show become massively popular over the previous three years, as companion Jo Grant leaves in one of the Classic Series' most touching scenes.

DISC ONE

THE EPISODES

All six episodes are newly restored from digital duplicates of the original two-inch colour videotape recordings used for broadcast and their mono soundtracks remastered using more advanced techniques than the previous release. The title sequences are replaced by a modern transfer of the original 35mm film with credits remade to match the originals.

SPECIAL FEATURES *REPEATED FROM PREVIOUS RELEASE

AUDIO OPTIONS Select *Commentary to play the audio commentary recorded for the previous release in place of the main soundtrack when watching the episodes. With Katy Manning (Jo), producer Barry Letts and script editor Terrance Dicks on all six episodes.

— Select **Bonus Commentary** to play the audio commentary recorded for this release when watching episodes three to six. On episodes three to five, actor and comedian Toby Hadoke talks with visual effects designer Colin Mapson and Mitzi McKenzie (Nancy), joined from episode four by Richard Franklin (Yates). Commenting on episode six are Katy Manning and New Series showrunner Russell T Davies.

— Select **Feature Audio** to reinstate the main soundtrack when watching the episodes.

INFO TEXT Select **On** to view subtitles when watching the episodes that provide information and anecdotes about the development, production, broadcast and history of *The Green Death*, updated and expanded from the previous release. Written by Richard Bignell.

SUBTITLES

Select **On** to view subtitles for all episodes (none for commentary).

DISC TWO

SPECIAL FEATURES *REPEATED FROM PREVIOUS RELEASE

THE ONE WITH THE MAGGOTS (26m23s) The making of *The Green Death*, including the origins of the script in the producer's environmental concerns; casting Katy Manning's boyfriend as Jo's love interest; working with live maggots and making the giant maggot puppets; filming on location at a working colliery in South Wales, getting the final shot, filming the Metebelis 3 scenes, and realising the giant fly; recording the mine scenes in the studio; creating a luminous infection; coping with cast illness; and recording Jo's tearful departure. With contributions from producer Barry Letts (interviewed in 2008), script editor Terrance Dicks, director Michael E Briant, assistant floor manager Karilyn Collier, visual effects designer Colin Mapson, and actors Stewart Bevan and Katy Manning. Produced by Chris Chapman.

*****GLOBAL CONSPIRACY?** (10m52s) Spoof news investigation recounting the events in Llanfairfach in 1973 and their ongoing legacy. Written by and starring Mark Gatiss as journalist Terry Scanlon, with original cast members of *The Green Death*. Produced by Gatiss and Paul Vanezis.

*****VISUAL EFFECTS** (11m40s) Effects designer Colin Mapson talks about the various techniques used in creating the giant maggots and other creatures, plus the model filming for *The Green Death*, and demonstrates how he originally made the maggots.

*****ROBERT SLOMAN INTERVIEW** (6m52s) Writer Robert Sloman talks about the ideas and principles behind his scripting of *The Green Death* and how the issues persist to this day.

*****STEWART BEVAN INTERVIEW** (7m42s) Actor Stewart Bevan, who played Professor Clifford Jones, talks about the character, the foresight of the story, and his memories of the recording.

WALES TODAY (2m29s) Silent 16mm colour film footage shot on Thursday 15 March 1973 at Ogilvie Colliery during location filming of *The Green Death* for the BBC1 local news programme; and a report by Tony O'Shaughnessy from Friday 8 April 1994 of Jon Pertwee opening the visitor centre for Parc Cwm Darran country park, built on the site of the colliery.

DOCTOR FOREVER – THE UNQUIET DEAD (23m8s) Examining how *Doctor Who* has spread beyond the television screen, this edition looks at the events that led to the show's return in 2005 after a long struggle to convince many people it could be a success. With New Series showrunner Russell T Davies and BBC controller of drama Jane Tranter. Narrated by Zeb Soanes, produced by James Goss. *See Index iii for further editions*

NEXT

WHAT KATY DID NEXT (5m39s) Clips from the BBC1 arts and craft series *Serendipity*, which ran for ten weeks from Sunday 30 September 1973 and was presented by Katy Manning, her first job after leaving *Doctor Who*. Introduced with an extract from BBC1 news magazine programme *Nationwide* in which Frank Bough previews Manning's departure, shown on Friday 22 June 1973, the day before the final episode of *The Green Death*.

THE SARAH JANE ADVENTURES – DEATH OF THE DOCTOR (52m37s) A two-part story from the CBBC drama series starring Elisabeth Sladen, broadcast on Monday 25/Tuesday 26 October 2010. Written by Russell T Davies, it features Katy Manning reprising the role of Jo Jones (née Grant) for the first time on television since 1973, as well as Matt Smith as the Eleventh Doctor. Select to watch each part individually, and to play with optional commentary by Davies and Manning.

PHOTO GALLERY (9m51s) Slideshow of colour and black-and-white photos taken during production of *The Green Death*, including design department photos of the sets, plus Frank Bellamy's illustrations for the *Radio Times* billings and shots of Katy Manning and Stewart Bevan taken for the *Radio Times Doctor Who 10th Anniversary Special* magazine. Expanded from the previous release and set to sound effects from the story. Compiled by Ralph Montagu.

PDF MATERIALS Accessible via a computer are the six episode listings from *Radio Times* for the original BBC1 broadcast of *The Green Death*, with illustrations by Frank Bellamy; letters about star appearances outside the show and Katy Manning's departure, with replies from producer Barry Letts; and the billing for the omnibus repeat of *The Green Death* on Thursday 27 December 1973.

SUBTITLES Select **On** to view subtitles for all Special Features on disc two.

COMING SOON (54s) Trailer for the DVD release of *The Ice Warriors*.

EASTER EGGS
There are two hidden features on these discs to find. *See Appendix 2 for details*

RELATED EXTRAS
The UNIT Family — Day of the Daleks
Coming Soon trailer — Spearhead from Space Blu-ray

THE **GUNFIGHTERS**
STORY No.25   SEASON No.3:8

Released with **THE AWAKENING** in the **EARTH STORY** boxset
One disc with four episodes (96 mins) and 63½ minutes of extras, plus commentary track, production subtitles and PDF items
Audio navigation of disc contents available by pressing Enter after the BBC ident

TARDIS TEAM First Doctor, Dodo, Steven
TIME AND PLACE 19th Century Tombstone, Arizona
ADVERSARIES Cowboys the Clanton brothers
FIRST ON TV 30 April–21 May 1966
DVD RELEASE BBCDVD3380A, 20 June 2011, PG
COVER Photo illustration by Clayton Hickman, orange strip; version with older BBC logo on reverse
ORIGINAL RRP £30.63 (boxset)

STORY TEASER
The Doctor needs a cure for toothache but the TARDIS lands in Tombstone, Arizona in 1881, where the only dentist is the notorious Doc Holliday. Also in town are the rowdy Clanton brothers, who have less professional reasons for seeking out Holliday, while lawmen Wyatt Earp and Bat Masterson try to keep the peace. But when the Clantons call in killer Johnny Ringo, the Doctor and his friends are drawn into events leading inexorably to the infamous showdown.

CONNECTIONS
This is the Doctor's third on-screen landing in America, having been to the Empire State Building in New York in *The Chase* (1965) and a Hollywood movie studio in *The Daleks' Master Plan* (1965/66). He doesn't return until his seventh incarnation regenerates in San Francisco in *The Movie*, then the

Ninth Doctor lands in Henry Van Statten's bunker under Utah in *Dalek* (2005), the Tenth Doctor is back at the Empire State Building during its construction in *Daleks in Manhattan/Evolution of the Daleks* (2007), while the Eleventh Doctor and friends tour the country in *The Impossible Astronaut/Day of the Moon* (2011), revisit the Wild West in *A Town Called Mercy* (2012), and New York in *The Angels Take Manhattan* (2012). Donald Cotton also wrote *The Myth Makers* (1965), while director Rex Tucker had been involved in the creation of *Doctor Who*. Richard Beale (Bat Masterson) is the voice of the Refusians in *The Ark* (1966) and plays the Ecology Minister in *The Green Death* (1973); David Graham (Charlie the barman) voiced Daleks during the First Doctor era and is Professor Kerensky in *City of Death* (1979); Martyn Huntley (Warren Earp) is one of the unhinged humans in *The Sensorites* (1964) and a Roboman in *The Dalek Invasion of Earth* (1964); and Laurence Payne (Johnny Ringo) plays Argolin leader Morix in *The Leisure Hive* (1980) and genetic scientist Dastari in *The Two Doctors* (1985). The song throughout the story is sung by Lynda Baron, who plays Captain Wrack in *Enlightenment* (1983) and Val in *Closing Time* (2011), while Anthony Jacobs (Doc Holliday) was the grandfather of Matthew Jacobs, who wrote *The Movie*.

WORTH WATCHING

Given the popularity of Westerns on television in the 1950s and 60s, it's surprising it took *Doctor Who* three years to venture into the Wild West. But once it did, what more famous historical event to visit than the gunfight at the OK Corral? The story itself is a strange mixture, as was writer Donald Cotton's previous serial *The Myth Makers*, starting out as rather broad comedy but finishing with a vicious shoot-out more in keeping with the historical reality. *The Gunfighters* also features the first song written specifically for *Doctor Who*, cropping up throughout the story with lyrics that essentially narrate the on-screen events.

THE EPISODES

All four episodes are restored from 16mm film copies of the original black-and-white video recordings, recovered from BBC Enterprises in 1978. Their mono soundtracks are remastered and the VidFIRE process is applied to studio-recorded shots to recapture the smoother motion of video. The title sequences are replaced by a modern transfer of the best surviving copy of the original 35mm film with end credits remade to match the originals.

SPECIAL FEATURES

THE END OF THE LINE (43m27s) After two years of great success, particularly with the Daleks, *Doctor Who*'s third year started to see that initial popularity settle down. This examination of the busy year that proved to be William Hartnell's last as the Doctor includes the first change in producer from Verity Lambert to John Wiles, and his unhappiness with the stories already lined up for production; the sudden writing out of companion Vicki, but second thoughts over her replacement character Katarina; dealing with the scripting problems for the twelve-part *The Daleks' Master Plan* (including a Christmas episode stuck in the middle of the story); the increasing irascibility and forgetfulness of Hartnell and his deteriorating relationship with Wiles, leading to the producer's decision to leave; the true writer of John Lucarotti's *The Massacre*; the appointment of reluctant new producer Innes Lloyd; further rewriting controversy with story editor Gerry Davis's take-over from Donald Tosh; falling audience popularity reaching a nadir with *The Gunfighters*; the switch of companions from Steven and Dodo to Ben and Polly; boosting the science content of the show; Hartnell's worsening illness and the inevitable decision to replace him; the introduction of the Cybermen; and the landmark first changeover of Doctors. With contributions from story editor Donald Tosh, actors Maureen O'Brien, Peter Purves and Anneke Wills, and fans Ian Levine and Gareth Roberts. Written by Jonathan Morris, narrated by Jenny Farish, produced by Ed Stradling.

TOMORROW'S TIMES THE FIRST DOCTOR (14m16s) Coverage of *Doctor Who* in the national newspapers during the First Doctor's era from 1963 to 1966. Presented by Mary Tamm, written and directed by Marcus Hearn. *See Index iii for further editions*

PHOTO GALLERY (4m19s) Slideshow of black-and-white photos taken during production of *The Gunfighters*, including design department photos of the sets. Set to 'The Ballad of the Last Chance Saloon'. Compiled by Paul Shields.

AUDIO OPTIONS Select **Commentary** to play the audio commentary in place of the main soundtrack when watching the episodes. This is moderated by actor and comedian Toby Hadoke, talking with Shane Rimmer (Seth Harper) [eps 1,2], David Graham (Charlie) [1,2,3], Peter Purves (Steven) [1,2,3,4], production assistant Tristan de Vere Cole [1,2,3,4] and Richard Beale (Bat Masterson) [2,3,4].
— Select **Feature Audio** to reinstate the main soundtrack when watching the episodes.

INFO TEXT Select **On** to view subtitles when watching the episodes that provide information and anecdotes about the development, production, broadcast and history of *The Gunfighters*. Written by David Brunt.

PDF MATERIALS Accessible via a computer are the four episode listings from *Radio Times* for the original BBC1 broadcast of *The Gunfighters* and an article introducing the story.

COMING SOON (1m20s) Trailer for the DVD release of *Paradise Towers*.

SUBTITLES
Select **On** to view subtitles for all episodes and Special Features (except commentary).

RELATED EXTRAS
Coming Soon trailer — Frontios

THE **HAND OF FEAR**

STORY No.87   SEASON No.14:2

H

One disc with four episodes (99 mins) and 69½ minutes of extras, plus commentary track, production subtitles and PDF items

TARDIS TEAM Fourth Doctor, Sarah Jane

TIME AND PLACE Contemporary England and planet Kastria

ADVERSARIES Alien criminal Eldrad (and his disembodied hand)

FIRST ON TV 2–23 October 1976

DVD RELEASE BBCDVD1833, 24 July 2006, PG

COVER Photo illustration by Lee Binding, light purple strip
— Original release with cover sticker reading 'Sarah Jane Smith's Final Classic Story'

ORIGINAL RRP £19.99
— Reissued in sleeve with orange logo and cover illustration in a circle against dark purple background; BBCDVD2474, £9.99, 2 July 2007

STORY TEASER
Returning to present-day Earth, the Doctor and Sarah are caught in a quarrying explosion. Sarah is rushed to hospital clutching a fossilised hand wearing a glowing ring. When she recovers she takes the hand and uses the ring to force her way into the nearby nuclear power station. There the hand comes alive and begins to regenerate the rest of its body, feeding off the radiation from a reactor now running dangerously out of control, with Sarah right by the core.

CONNECTIONS
Bob Baker and Dave Martin's first script for *Doctor Who*, *The Claws of Axos* in 1971, also features a nuclear power station's output being drained by an alien creature, almost sending it into meltdown. Indeed, the complex in *The Hand of Fear* was meant to be the same one but the name was changed when a different filming location was chosen. The discovery of an inert object buried long ago but which comes to life when unearthed is reminiscent of the seeds pods found in the Antarctic ice in the previous season's finale *The Seeds of Doom*, while the return of an ancient criminal seeking revenge on his accusers is similar to *Pyramids of Mars* (1975); its last episode also features a trap-laden trip through the villain's domain ending in his defeat via an endless tunnel. The departure of Sarah Jane was added by script editor Robert Holmes but rewritten in rehearsals by Tom Baker and Elisabeth Sladen. While Sarah is right to deduce that the Doctor has failed to return her to South Croydon, it's not until her return in *School Reunion* (2006) that we learn he leaves her in Aberdeen. This was director Lennie Mayne's last *Doctor Who* serial, having directed three Third Doctor stories: *The Curse of Peladon* (1972), *The Three Doctors* (1972/73) and *The Monster of Peladon* (1974). Rex

Robinson's (Dr Carter) previous roles in the series had been in the last two of those, as Dr Tyler and Gebek respectively. Glyn Houston (Professor Watson) plays Ben Wolsey in *The Awakening* (1984), while Stephen Thorne makes his last *Doctor Who* appearance having first played Azal in *The Dæmons* (1971) and Omega in *The Three Doctors*, plus an Ogron in *Frontier in Space* (1973).

WORTH WATCHING

This story is most notable for being the last to feature companion Sarah Jane Smith, played by Elisabeth Sladen. During her three years on *Doctor Who* she became one of the most popular assistants in the show's history, so it feels right and proper that her final story puts her at the centre of the action. It's a shame, though, that her actual departure only arises in the (admittedly sweet) coda rather than progressing from the story itself. Still, this left it open for her to return and indeed when children of the time were grown up and working in television themselves, such was their fondness for Sarah (and Lis) that they were instrumental in bringing the character back to our screens to charm a whole new generation.

THE EPISODES

All four episodes are restored from digital duplicates of the original two-inch colour videotape recordings used for broadcast and their mono soundtracks remastered. The title sequences are replaced by a modern transfer of the original 35mm film with credits remade to match the originals.

SPECIAL FEATURES

CHANGING TIME (50m27s) The making of *The Hand of Fear* and a look at the close bond between the Doctor and Sarah Jane Smith. Including how the cast and crew began their careers; the casting of Elisabeth Sladen; the changeover from Jon Pertwee to Tom Baker; devising the character of the Fourth Doctor and the strong working relationship between Tom and Lis; developing the script for *The Hand of Fear* as Sarah's swan song; filming on location in a genuine power station and quarry; memories of director Lennie Mayne; the techniques used for the moving disembodied hand; having a female adversary; and collaborating on Sarah's leaving scene. With contributions from producers Barry Letts and Philip Hinchcliffe, script editor Terrance Dicks, writer Bob Baker, visual effects designer Colin Mapson, and actors Tom Baker, Glyn Houston, Rex Robinson, Elisabeth Sladen and Stephen Thorne. Produced by Steve Broster.

CONTINUITIES (1m24s) Continuity announcements from the original BBC1 broadcasts of episode four of the preceding story, *The Masque of Mandragora*, with a plug for the Blackpool and Longleat exhibitions; and episode four of *The Hand of Fear*, with a plug for the following story, *The Deadly Assassin* (also on **The Deadly Assassin**).

SWAP SHOP (10m55s) Extract from the very first edition on 2 October 1976 of the BBC1 Saturday morning children's show *Multi-Coloured Swap Shop*, in which Noel Edmonds interviews Tom Baker and Elisabeth Sladen to promote the first episode of *The Hand of Fear* and they take viewers' questions on the phone.

PHOTO GALLERY (5m6s) Slideshow of colour and black-and-white photos taken during production of *The Hand of Fear*, including design department photos of the sets and contemporary shots of the filming locations. Set to sound effects from the story. Compiled by Derek Handley.

NEXT

COMMENTARY Select **On** to play the audio commentary in place of the main soundtrack when watching the episodes. With Tom Baker [eps 1,2,3,4], writer Bob Baker [1,2,3,4], Elisabeth Sladen (Sarah) [1,2,4] and Judith Paris (Eldrad) [3,4], plus additional comments throughout from producer Philip Hinchcliffe.

INFO TEXT Select **On** to view subtitles when watching the episodes that provide information and anecdotes about the development, production, broadcast and history of *The Hand of Fear*. Written by Martin Wiggins.

DOCTOR WHO ANNUAL Accessible via a computer is a PDF file of the 1977 *Doctor Who Annual*, published by World Distributors the autumn that *The Hand of Fear* was broadcast. With stories featuring the Doctor, Sarah, Harry and the Brigadier, plus science features, puzzles and games.

RADIO TIMES BILLINGS Accessible via a computer is a PDF file of the four episode listings for the original BBC1 broadcast of *The Hand of Fear*, plus an item about the launch of *Swap Shop*.

SUBTITLES
Select **On** to view subtitles for all episodes and Special Features (except commentary).

EASTER EGG
There is one hidden feature on this disc to find. *See Appendix 2 for details*

THE **HAPPINESS PATROL**

STORY No.149   SEASON No.25:2

Released with **DRAGONFIRE** in the **ACE ADVENTURES** boxset
One disc with three episodes (74 mins) and 100½ minutes of extras, plus commentary and music-only tracks, production subtitles and PDF items
Audio navigation of disc contents available by pressing Enter after the BBC ident

TARDIS TEAM Seventh Doctor, Ace
TIME AND PLACE Planet Terra Alpha
ADVERSARIES Tyrant Helen A; police squad the Happiness Patrol; executioner the Kandyman
FIRST ON TV 2–16 November 1988
DVD RELEASE BBCDVD3387B, 7 May 2012, PG
COVER Photo illustration by Clayton Hickman, pink strip; version with older BBC logo on reverse
ORIGINAL RRP £30.63 (boxset)

H

STORY TEASER
The law of Terra Alpha demands its citizens be happy at all times. Policing the streets are the trigger-happy Happiness Patrol, and those found showing the slightest signs of sorrow are treated to the dubious delights cooked up by the cruel Kandyman. The Doctor makes it his mission to show despotic ruler Helen A the upside of feeling down.

CONNECTIONS
Helping oppressed societies to free themselves from tyrannical rule is, of course, something the Doctor does often, including in *The Keys of Marinus* (1964), *The Space Museum* (1965), *The Ark* (1966), *The Savages* (1966), *The Macra Terror* (1967), *The Krotons* (1969), *The Face of Evil* (1977), *The Sun Makers* (1977), *The Pirate Planet* (1978), *The Horns of Nimon* (1979/80), *State of Decay* (1980), *Vengeance on Varos* (1985), *Timelash* (1985), *Paradise Towers* (1987), *The Long Game* (2005) and *Planet of the Ood* (2008). The Drahvins in *Galaxy 4* (1965) are a similarly female-dominated society, and Helen A is one of a string of ruthless ruling women along with Maaga in *Galaxy 4*, Queen Xanxia in *The Pirate Planet*, Lady Adrasta in *The Creature from the Pit* (1979), Lexa in *Meglos* (1980), Captain Wrack in *Enlightenment* (1983), Kara in *Revelation of the Daleks* (1985), Rosanna Calvierri in *The Vampires of Venice* (2010) and Madame Kovarian in *A Good Man Goes to War* (2011). This was director Chris Clough's last *Doctor Who* serial, having already recorded *Silver Nemesis* on location even though it was broadcast after *The Happiness Patrol*. Lesley Dunlop (Susan Q) plays Norma Range in *Frontios* (1984), and John Normington (Trevor Sigma) is more fêted as Morgus in *The Caves of Androzani* (1984).

WORTH WATCHING
While on the surface a typical story of the Doctor helping the oppressed to freedom, *The Happiness Patrol* takes a much more socio-political stance than most stories, with some subtle and not-so-subtle swipes at familiar personalities. Helen A is an obvious mirror of then-Prime Minister Margaret Thatcher, both in the scripting and especially Sheila Hancock's performance, but there are also echoes of contemporary government social policies.

THE EPISODES
All three episodes are restored from digital duplicates of the original one-inch colour videotape recordings used for broadcast and their stereo soundtracks remastered.

SPECIAL FEATURES
HAPPINESS WILL PREVAIL (23m46s) The making of *The Happiness Patrol*, including the development and themes of the script; the influence of Margaret Thatcher on the character of Helen A;

devising and realising the Kandyman; Sylvester McCoy's performance as the Doctor; the guest cast; trying to create an outside feel inside the studio; and the importance of the right music score. With contributions from script editor Andrew Cartmel, writer Graeme Curry, director Chris Clough, and actors Sophie Aldred and David John Pope. Produced by Ed Stradling.

DELETED & EXTENDED SCENES (23m19s) A selection of scenes from all three episodes not used in the final programme, including the original cliffhanger to episode two, taken from earlier edits with as-recorded sound. The sections in black and white appear in the final episodes while those in colour are the unused scenes, to show where they would have fitted into the story.

WHEN WORLDS COLLIDE (46m4s) Examining the degree to which *Doctor Who* has reflected the ideologies of the times it was made and how science fiction allows writers to express their political and moral views in a metaphorical way, with examples from throughout the Classic and New Series. With contributions from 1970s producer Barry Letts (interviewed in 2008), script editors Andrew Cartmel and Terrance Dicks, writers Bob Baker, Graeme Curry and Gareth Roberts, and fan journalist Steve O'Brien. Written by Nicholas Pegg, presented by BBC political reporter Shaun Ley, produced by Ed Stradling.

PHOTO GALLERY (5m47s) Slideshow of colour and black-and-white photos taken during production of *The Happiness Patrol*, including design department photos of the sets. Set to music and sound effects from the story. Compiled by Paul Shields.

AUDIO OPTIONS Select **Commentary** to play the audio commentary in place of the main soundtrack when watching the episodes. This is moderated by actor and comedian Toby Hadoke, talking with composer Dominic Glynn [ep 1], writer Graeme Curry [1,2], Sophie Aldred (Ace) [1,2,3], script editor Andrew Cartmel [1,3] and director Chris Clough [2,3].

— Select **Isolated Score** to hear only Dominic Glynn's music when watching the episodes.

— Select **Feature Audio** to reinstate the main soundtrack when watching the episodes.

INFO TEXT Select **On** to view subtitles when watching the episodes that provide information and anecdotes about the development, production, broadcast and history of *The Happiness Patrol*. Written by Charles Norton.

PDF MATERIALS Accessible via a computer are the three episode listings from *Radio Times* for the original BBC1 broadcast of *The Happiness Patrol*.

COMING SOON (1m36s) Trailer for the DVD release of *Death to the Daleks*.

SUBTITLES
Select **On** to view subtitles for all episodes and Special Features (except commentary).

RELATED EXTRAS
Coming Soon trailer — Nightmare of Eden

THE **HORNS OF NIMON**
STORY No.108   SEASON No.17:5

Released with **THE TIME MONSTER** and **UNDERWORLD** in the **MYTHS AND LEGENDS** boxset
One disc with four episodes (101 mins) and 49½ minutes of extras, plus commentary track, production subtitles and PDF items
Audio navigation of disc contents available by pressing Enter after the BBC ident

TARDIS TEAM Fourth Doctor, Second Romana, K9

TIME AND PLACE Planets Skonnos and Crinoth

ADVERSARIES Minotaur-like Nimon; its humanoid lackey Soldeed

FIRST ON TV 22 December 1979–12 January 1980

DVD RELEASE BBCDVD2851(C), 29 March 2010, PG (episodes and extras bar DVD trailer U; boxset 12)

COVER Photo illustration by Clayton Hickman, red strip; version with older BBC logo on reverse

ORIGINAL RRP £49.99 (boxset)

STORY TEASER

The TARDIS is caught in a gravity whirlpool along with a spaceship that is transporting both human and mineral offerings back to Skonnos to present to the mighty Nimon. The Doctor frees the stricken ship, only to be abandoned in the vortex while Romana is taken to join the tribute. She finds Skonnos a decaying world, its past empire crumbled. The Nimon has promised its people greatness again in return for the sacrifices. But safe at the centre of its power complex, the creature has very different plans for the planet.

CONNECTIONS

The Doctor meets an alien Minotaur, said to be a distant relative of the Nimon, in *The God Complex* (2011) and seemingly the real thing in *The Time Monster* (1972), having previously dismissed it as mythical in *The Mind Robber* (1968). The Skonnons' dwindling empire is reminiscent of that of the Moroks in *The Space Museum* (1965). Writer Anthony Read had been the programme's script editor during 1977/78 and wrote *The Invasion of Time* (1978) with producer Graham Williams under a pseudonym. John Bailey (Sezom) also plays the commander in *The Sensorites* (1964) and more notably Edward Waterfield in *The Evil of the Daleks* (1967), while Janet Ellis (Teka) is one of three well-known *Blue Peter* presenters with roles in *Doctor Who*, alongside Peter Purves, who played companion Steven Taylor in 1965/66 (before he was on *Blue Peter*), and Sarah Greene as Varne, one of the Cryons in *Attack of the Cybermen* (1985).

WORTH WATCHING

The most obvious source for *The Horns of Nimon* is the Greek myth of the Minotaur, with a bull-headed creature at the centre of a labyrinth being presented with sacrificial offerings from a defeated peoples, but here given a typical *Doctor Who* twist. More interesting is the strong role it affords Romana, who for much of the story is leading the plot while the Doctor is stranded. There is also a memorable performance by Graham Crowden — who had been considered for the role of the Fourth Doctor in 1974 — as Soldeed, although whether this is for its entertainment or excess you'll have to decide for yourself.

THE EPISODES

All four episodes are restored from digital duplicates of the original two-inch colour videotape recordings used for broadcast and their mono soundtracks remastered. The title sequences are replaced by a modern transfer of the original 35mm film with credits remade to match the originals.

SPECIAL FEATURES

WHO PETER – PARTNERS IN TIME (29m57s) BBC1 children's magazine programme *Blue Peter* has been a frequent promoter of *Doctor Who* throughout both series' histories. Gethin Jones presents a rundown of *Blue Peter*'s items about *Doctor Who* during the Classic Series, and examines what makes the two shows such close bedfellows. With contributions from *Blue Peter* editors Biddy Baxter and Richard Marson, presenters Janet Ellis and Peter Purves, New Series showrunner Russell T Davies, writers Clayton Hickman and Robert Shearman, and Steve Thompson, winner of *Blue Peter*'s first ever Design a *Doctor Who* Monster competition in 1967. Produced by Chris Chapman. *Part two looking at the New Series years is on* The Movie Special Edition

READ THE WRITER (6m29s) Writer Anthony Read talks about handing over the script editor role to Douglas Adams and his subsequent commission to write *The Horns of Nimon*, his sources for the story, giving Romana a stronger role, and his view of the final production.

PETER HOWELL MUSIC DEMOS (2m58s) The opening section of *The Horns of Nimon* episode two re-scored by composer Peter Howell in 1980 to demonstrate how the BBC Radiophonic Workshop could do the incidental music for *Doctor Who*.

PHOTO GALLERY (7m53s) Slideshow of colour and black-and-white photos taken during production of *The Horns of Nimon*, including design department photos of the sets. Set to sound effects from the story. Compiled by Derek Handley.

NEXT

AUDIO OPTIONS Select **Commentary** to play the audio commentary in place of the main soundtrack when watching the episodes. With Lalla Ward (Romana), Janet Ellis (Teka) and writer Anthony Read on all four episodes, joined part-way through episode one by Graham Crowden (Soldeed).

— Select **Feature Audio** to reinstate the main soundtrack when watching the episodes.

INFO TEXT Select **On** to view subtitles when watching the episodes that provide information and anecdotes about the development, production, broadcast and history of *The Horns of Nimon*. Written by Niall Boyce.

PDF MATERIALS Accessible via a computer are the four episode listings from *Radio Times* for the original BBC1 broadcast of *The Horns of Nimon*.

— Designer Graeme Story's blueprints for the spaceship, labyrinth, Power Complex entrance and council chamber sets (not studio floorplans as indicated in the menu).

COMING SOON (41s) Trailer for the DVD release of *The Creature from the Pit*.

SUBTITLES

Select **On** to view subtitles for all episodes and Special Features (except commentary).

EASTER EGG

There is one hidden feature on this disc to find. *See Appendix 2 for details*

RELATED EXTRAS

Coming Soon trailer — The Chase, The Space Museum

HORROR OF FANG ROCK

STORY No.92   SEASON No.15:1

One disc with four episodes (95½ mins) and 58½ minutes of extras, plus commentary track and production subtitles

TARDIS TEAM Fourth Doctor, Leela

TIME AND PLACE Early-20th Century lighthouse

ADVERSARIES Shape-shifting Rutan

FIRST ON TV 3–24 September 1977

DVD RELEASE BBCDVD1356, 17 January 2005, U

COVER Photo illustration by Clayton Hickman, dark blue strip

ORIGINAL RRP £19.99

STORY TEASER

A fireball falls into the sea near the lonely island of Fang Rock and a mysterious mist sweeps in as the three lighthouse keepers struggle to maintain the new electric lamp. The first vessel to lose its way in the fog is the TARDIS, followed by a yacht that crashes onto the rocks. The survivors take refuge in the lighthouse, only to find they have locked themselves inside with a creature that can take human form and whose touch kills instantly.

CONNECTIONS

The Doctor is used to finding himself confined in one location along with a source of danger, such as the Cybermen-infiltrated bases in *The Tenth Planet* (1966) and *The Moonbase* (1967), their hibernation caverns in *The Tomb of the Cybermen* (1967), the Yeti-occupied Tube tunnels in *The Web of Fear* (1968), the Wirrn-infested Nerva station in *The Ark in Space* (1975), Scarman's walled-in estate in *Pyramids of Mars* (1975), the robot-run sandmine in *The Robots of Death* (1977), the titular *Paradise Towers* (1987), the sabotaged Platform One in *The End of the World* (2005), the devilish Sanctuary Base Six in *The Impossible Planet/The Satan Pit* (2006), the stranded Crusader 50 bus in *Midnight* (2008), the inundated Bowie Base One in *The Waters of Mars* (2009), the Siren-haunted Fancy in *The Curse of the Black Spot* (2011), the Minotaur's prison in *The God Complex* (2011) and a Russian submarine with on-board Ice Warrior in *Cold War* (2013). He combats other shape-shifters such as Axons in *The Claws of Axos* (1971), Zygons in *Terror of the Zygons* (1975) and *The Day of the Doctor* (2013), a Vespiform in *The Unicorn and the Wasp* (2008), and Prisoner Zero in *The Eleventh Hour* (2010). Terrance Dicks had written a vampire story to launch the 1977/78 season but this was vetoed by the BBC in case it undermined the adaptation of *Dracula* that was in production, even though this wasn't broadcast until three months after Dicks' replacement, *Horror of Fang Rock*. His original script sat on the shelf until it was eventually reworked and produced as

State of Decay in 1980. This was director Paddy Russell's last *Doctor Who* serial, having directed *The Massacre* (1966), *Invasion of the Dinosaurs* (1974) and *Pyramids of Mars*. Colin Douglas (Reuben and Rutan voice) plays Donald Bruce in *The Enemy of the World* (1967/68), Ralph Watson (Ben) lasts longer but is equally doomed as Captain Knight in *The Web of Fear* (1968) and Ettis in *The Monster of Peladon* (1974), and Alan Rowe (Skinsale) is controlled by Cybermen as Dr Evans in *The Moonbase* (1967), besieged by a Sontaran as Edward of Wessex in *The Time Warrior* (1974) and stalked by Marshmen as Decider Garif in *Full Circle* (1980).

WORTH WATCHING

This is a tight, atmospheric tale adopting the classic horror story technique of trapping a small group of people in a restricted location with an unknown enemy killing them off one by one. The excellent lighthouse sets perfectly convey the sense of claustrophobia, and the characters are pitched just right so that you both dread and relish their demises. Leela has a particularly good role, being in her element and refusing to fit any female stereotypes.

THE EPISODES

All four episodes are restored from digital duplicates of the original two-inch colour videotape recordings used for broadcast and their mono soundtracks remastered. The title sequences are replaced by a modern transfer of the original 35mm film with credits overlaid from the episode recordings.

SPECIAL FEATURES

TERRANCE DICKS: FACT & FICTION (36m6s) Terrance Dicks talks about his career as a writer, script editor and novelist, frequently for *Doctor Who*. From script editing during the Third Doctor era to becoming producer of the BBC's classic serials in the 1980s, while also writing children's books and many of the Target range of books based on past *Doctor Who* serials, as well as further original novels. With contributions from colleagues Christopher Barry, Paul Cornell, Peter Darvill-Evans, Brenda Gardner, Barry Letts, Louis Marks and Eric Saward. Produced by Keith Barnfather.

PADDY RUSSELL – A LIFE IN TELEVISION (14m3s) Director Paddy Russell talks about her career, from working with respected director Rudolph Cartier in the early days of television, such as on the *Quatermass* serials (and with footage of them working on the BBC's production of *Mother Courage and Her Children*, broadcast on Tuesday 30 June 1959), to becoming one of the few female directors at the BBC, including on the *Doctor Who* stories *The Massacre* (1966), *Invasion of the Dinosaurs* (1974), *Pyramids of Mars* (1975) and *Horror of Fang Rock*.

THE ANTIQUE DOCTOR WHO SHOW (4m48s) Antiques expert Justin Pressland examines items of *Doctor Who* memorabilia — including talking K9 toys, Nestlé chocolate wrappers (*as included on* The Ark in Space Special Edition) and an original script from the 1960s — brought along to an antiques fair at Kensington Town Hall on Saturday 6 November 1993. Broadcast on BBC1 on Friday 12 November 1993 under the banner 'Doctor Who and the Daleks' preceding the repeat of *Planet of the Daleks* episode two.

INFORMATION TEXT Select **On** to view subtitles when watching the episodes that provide information and anecdotes about the development, production, broadcast and history of *Horror of Fang Rock*. Written by Richard Molesworth.

PHOTO GALLERY (3m27s) Slideshow of colour and black-and-white photos taken during production of *Horror of Fang Rock*, including storyboard sketches for the model filming. Set to sound effects from the story. Compiled by Ralph Montagu.

AUDIO OPTIONS Select **Commentary On** to play the audio commentary in place of the main soundtrack when watching the episodes. With Louise Jameson (Leela), John Abbot (Vince) and writer Terrance Dicks on all four episodes.

SUBTITLES

Select **On** to view subtitles for all episodes and Special Features, or for the commentary.

EASTER EGG

There is one hidden feature on this disc to find. *See Appendix 2 for details*

RELATED EXTRAS

Built for War — The Sontaran Experiment

THE **ICE WARRIORS**

STORY No.39   SEASON No.5:3

Two discs with four original and two animated episodes (147 mins) and 85 minutes of extras, plus commentary track, production subtitles and PDF items
Audio navigation of each disc's contents available by pressing Enter after the BBC ident

TARDIS TEAM Second Doctor, Jamie, Victoria
TIME AND PLACE Scientific base by glacier, future Earth
ADVERSARIES Ice Warriors (1st appearance)
FIRST ON TV 11 November–16 December 1967
DVD RELEASE BBCDVD3558, 26 August 2013, PG
COVER Photo illustration by Lee Binding, dark purple strip; version with older BBC logo on reverse
ORIGINAL RRP £20.42

STORY TEASER

A thousand years in the future, human activity has induced a new ice age and glaciers are threatening to overwhelm much of the northern hemisphere, held back only by computer-controlled ionisers. When a humanoid figure is discovered inside the ice, it's brought to Brittanicus Base to be thawed, only for an alien warrior to be unleashed. It escapes to release more warriors, and threatens to destroy the base and its ioniser to protect its still-frozen spaceship. With the scientists' computer refusing to let them use the ioniser to fire on the ship in case the explosion also destroys the base, a risky move is needed to break the stalemate.

CONNECTIONS

As mentioned by Jamie, the TARDIS has just come from the chilly foothills of the Himalayas (*The Abominable Snowmen*) and before that the travellers were trapped in the frozen city of the Cybermen (*The Tomb of the Cybermen*), which the Doctor returns to in *Attack of the Cybermen* (1985). He also visits Antarctica in *The Tenth Planet* (1966) and *The Seeds of Doom* (1976), lands on Ribos during its ice time in *The Ribos Operation* (1978), goes on a treasure hunt beneath Iceworld in *Dragonfire* (1987), visits the snowy Ood-Sphere in *Planet of the Ood* (2008) and *The End of Time* (2009/10), and is deposited on the Daleks' frozen stronghold in *Asylum of the Daleks* (2012). The giant armoured Martians are here nicknamed 'Ice Warriors' by the humans, a term others pick up from Jamie in their next appearance in *The Seeds of Death* (1969) and one they themselves respond to in *The Curse of Peladon* (1972), although they don't use it themselves except once in *The Monster of Peladon* (1974). Whatever they call themselves, another is discovered frozen in ice and is equally belligerent when defrosted in *Cold War* (2013). Brian Hayles also wrote *The Smugglers* (1966) and the first draft of *The Celestial Toymaker* (1966) as well as creating the Ice Warriors, while Derek Martinus had directed serials each year until this, his penultimate work on *Doctor Who* (*see Index v*). Angus Lennie (Storr) returns as pub landlord Angus McRanald in *Terror of the Zygons* (1975), while Peter Sallis (Penley) was cast as Captain Striker in *Enlightenment* (1983) before altered recording dates meant he was unavailable.

WORTH WATCHING

Of the many monsters that first appeared during the 1967/68 season, the Ice Warriors became one of the most enduring, making an immediate impact with their size and appearance. With six-foot-plus actors cast as the Warriors — including star of the *Carry On* films Bernard Bresslaw as their leader — they towered over the deliberately short guest cast (and the regulars), making them most intimidating. The tension of the stand-off between humans and Warriors is well presented, and while we might no longer sympathise with the script's suspicious attitude towards computers, the questions it raises are still relevant.

DISC ONE

THE EPISODES

Episodes one, four, five and six are restored from 16mm film copies of the original black-and-white video recordings, discovered at BBC Enterprises in August 1988. Their mono soundtracks are remastered and the VidFIRE process is applied to studio-recorded shots to recapture the smoother motion of video. The title sequences are replaced by a modern transfer of the original 35mm film with end credits remade to match the originals. Episodes two and three, of which no film copies are known to exist, are recreated with black-and-white animation by Qurios Entertainment with reference to surviving images from the serial and matched to a remastered recording of the soundtrack made on audio tape when the episodes were originally broadcast.

SPECIAL FEATURES

AUDIO OPTIONS Select **Commentary** to play the audio commentary in place of the main soundtrack when watching the episodes. On episodes one, four, five and six this is moderated by actor and comedian Toby Hadoke, talking with Sonny Caldinez (Turoc) [eps 1,4], grams operator Pat Heigham [1,4], Frazer Hines (Jamie) [1,4,5,6], Deborah Watling (Victoria) [1,4,5,6] and designer Jeremy Davies [5,6]. On episode two Hadoke presents extracts from archive audio interviews with Peter Barkworth (Clent), Bernard Bresslaw (Varga) and writer Brian Hayles, new interviews with Wendy Gifford (Miss Garrett) and make-up supervisor Sylvia James, readings of written interviews with director Derek Martinus and costume designer Martin Baugh, and reads memories from further late cast and crew members. On episode three Hadoke talks with Patrick Troughton's son Michael.
— Select **Feature Audio** to reinstate the main soundtrack when watching the episodes.

INFO TEXT Select **On** to view subtitles when watching episodes one, four, five and six that provide information and anecdotes about the development, production, broadcast and history of *The Ice Warriors*. Written by Martin Wiggins.

SUBTITLES

Select **On** to view subtitles for the episodes (none for commentary).

DISC TWO

SPECIAL FEATURES

COLD FUSION (24m33s) The making of *The Ice Warriors*, including casting the giant Ice Warriors; filming the icy exteriors at Ealing Studios, including the use of a live bear; the need to redesign the Ice Warrior helmets before studio recording; the guest cast; designing the sets and costumes; and the success of the Ice Warriors. With contributions from designer Jeremy Davies, Bernard Bresslaw's son James, and actors Sonny Caldinez, Frazer Hines and Deborah Watling. Produced by Chris Chapman.

BENEATH THE ICE (10m35s) How the animation team at Qurios approached the task of recreating the two missing episodes as faithfully as possible to the originals, from drawing the characters and sets, to working out the action from the few surviving photos and soundtrack. With producers Chris Chapman and Niel Bushnell, animation director Chris Chatterton and animator Nick Patrick. Produced by Chris Chapman.

VHS LINKS (19m21s) When *The Ice Warriors* was released on home video in November 1998 the two missing episodes were filled in by this shortened reconstruction using off-screen photos and audio recordings of the soundtrack, with an introduction by Frazer Hines and Deborah Watling. Includes the contemporary BBC Video ident.

BLUE PETER – DESIGN–A–MONSTER (10m6s) Extract from the Monday 27 November 1967 edition of the BBC1 children's magazine programme in which John Noakes, Peter Purves and Valerie Singleton invite viewers to design their own monster to challenge the Doctor; and from the Thursday 14 December edition in which they reveal the three winners and the costumes produced from their designs by the BBC Visual Effects department.

ORIGINAL TRAILER (1m23s) Specially recorded introduction to *The Ice Warriors* broadcast after the preceding serial, *The Abominable Snowmen*, featuring Peter Barkworth as Clent and Peter Sallis as Penley explaining the setting for the story. Recreated with animation by Qurios matched to an audio recording made at the time of broadcast.

NEXT

DOCTOR WHO STORIES – FRAZER HINES PART TWO (13m51s) Recorded in 2003 for BBC2's *The Story of Doctor Who*, actor Frazer Hines recalls his experiences of playing companion Jamie McCrimmon from 1966 to 1969. *Part one is on* **The Krotons**

PHOTO GALLERY (3m55s) Slideshow of colour and black-and-white photos taken during production of *The Ice Warriors*, including Bernard Bresslaw's costume fitting and make-up application. Set to music and sound effects from the story. Compiled by Paul Shields.

PDF MATERIALS Accessible via a computer are the six episode listings from *Radio Times* for the original BBC1 broadcast of *The Ice Warriors*, an article introducing the story and an item promoting the *Blue Peter* Design-a-Monster competition published the week of episode three.

SUBTITLES Select **On** to view subtitles for all Special Features on disc two.

COMING SOON (1m19s) Trailer for the DVD release of *Scream of the Shalka*.

RELATED EXTRAS

Coming Soon trailer — The Aztecs Special Edition, The Green Death Special Edition
Warriors of Mars — The Curse of Peladon
Sylvia James - In Conversation — The War Games

IMAGE OF THE FENDAHL

STORY No.94   SEASON No.15:3

One disc with four episodes (94½ mins) and 45 minutes of extras, plus commentary track, production subtitles and PDF items
Audio navigation of disc contents available by pressing Enter after the BBC ident

TARDIS TEAM Fourth Doctor, Leela
TIME AND PLACE Priory near English village of Fetchborough
ADVERSARIES Giant leech-like Fendahleen
FIRST ON TV 29 October–19 November 1977
DVD RELEASE BBCDVD1820, 20 April 2009, PG
COVER Photo illustration by Clayton Hickman, dark orange strip
ORIGINAL RRP £19.56

STORY TEASER

An unstable time fissure draws the TARDIS to Earth, where a group of scientists are investigating the discovery of a human skull older than mankind itself. Their leader, Dr Fendleman, has invented a Time Scanner to see into the past and learn who the skull belonged to. But by tapping the fissure he's unwittingly feeding the skull the energy it needs to recreate its original, deadly form.

CONNECTIONS

Creepy goings-on at an old priory are the focus of *Pyramids of Mars* (1975), and the two were actually filmed at the same location, although *Image of the Fendahl* benefits from some generous night shooting to aid the spooky atmosphere. Here the focus is on occult happenings, rather than the Egyptology of the former story. The buildings in both stories also burn down, which seems to be the answer to haunted houses as Ace does the same to Gabriel Chase (*Ghost Light*, 1989). Frankly, Caliburn House is fortunate to remain intact after the cause of its haunting is resolved in *Hide* (2013). This was the last story commissioned by Robert Holmes before he stepped down as the series' script editor, with scripts by Chris Boucher, who also wrote *The Face of Evil* and *The Robots of Death* (both 1977), while George Spenton-Foster also directed *The Ribos Operation* (1978). Wanda Ventham (Thea Ransome) plays Jean Rock in *The Faceless Ones* (1967) and Faroon in *Time and the Rani* (1987), Dennis Lill (Dr Fendleman) is Sir George Hutchinson in *The Awakening* (1984), Scott Fredericks (Max Stael) appears as Boaz in *Day of the Daleks* (1972), and Geoffrey Hinsliff (Jack Tyler) is Waterguard Fisk in *Nightmare of Eden* (1979).

WORTH WATCHING

Like earlier stories during the Fourth Doctor's first few seasons, *Image of the Fendahl* draws on various conventions from horror literature and film, although without being tied to a particular source. It instead using more general ideas of haunted houses, ancient evils being resurrected and creatures that kill by inducing sheer terror. Of course, this can only be taken so far within a family adventure series, and everything is given a rational explanation, but there are some dark ideas at play in this eerie tale.

All four episodes are restored from digital duplicates of the original two-inch colour videotape recordings used for broadcast and their mono soundtracks remastered. The title sequences are replaced by a modern transfer of the original 35mm film with credits remade to match the originals.

SPECIAL FEATURES

AFTER IMAGE (26m20s) The making of *Image of the Fendahl*, including the changeover of script editors; assembling the cast; the rehearsal process and working with Tom Baker; creating a foggy night on location; making the glowing skull prop; Leela's new costume; the transformation of Thea; realising the Fendahleen creatures; and keeping a lid on the level of horror. With contributions from script editor Anthony Read, visual effects designer Colin Mapson, and actors Edward Arthur, Louise Jameson and Wanda Ventham. Produced by Richard Molesworth.

DELETED AND EXTENDED SCENES (11m27s) A selection of scenes not used in the final programme, taken from a low-quality black-and-white video copy of the full location film with on-screen time-code. Sections in colour are those used in the final episodes.

TRAILER (20s) Preview of the story that was shown on BBC1 the week before episode one. *Also on* The Invisible Enemy

PHOTO GALLERY (5m35s) Slideshow of colour and black-and-white photos taken during production of *Image of the Fendahl*, including design department photos of the sets. Set to sound effects from the story. Compiled by Derek Handley.

NEXT

AUDIO OPTIONS Select **Commentary** to play the audio commentary in place of the main soundtrack when watching the episodes. With Tom Baker, Louise Jameson (Leela), Edward Arthur (Adam Colby) and Wanda Ventham (Thea Ransome) on all four episodes.

— Select **Feature Audio** to reinstate the main soundtrack when watching the episodes.

INFO TEXT Select **On** to view subtitles when watching the episodes that provide information and anecdotes about the development, production, broadcast and history of *Image of the Fendahl*. Written by Richard Molesworth.

PDF MATERIALS Accessible via a computer are the four episode listings from *Radio Times* for the original BBC1 broadcast of *Image of the Fendahl*.

COMING SOON (56s) Trailer for the DVD release of *The Deadly Assassin*.

SUBTITLES

Select **On** to view subtitles for all episodes and Special Features (except commentary).

EASTER EGG

There is one hidden feature on this disc to find. *See Appendix 2 for details*

RELATED EXTRAS

Coming Soon trailer — Attack of the Cybermen
The Doctor's Composer — The Sun Makers

INFERNO

STORY No.54   SEASON No.7:4

Two discs with seven episodes (166½ mins) and 89 minutes of extras, plus commentary track, production subtitles and PDF items

TARDIS TEAM Third Doctor, Liz, Brigadier and UNIT

TIME AND PLACE Contemporary England and a parallel universe equivalent

ADVERSARIES Professor Stahlman; fascist version of UNIT; primeval humanoid Primords

FIRST ON TV 9 May–20 June 1970

DVD RELEASE BBCDVD1802, 19 June 2006, PG

COVER Photo illustration by Clayton Hickman, red strip

ORIGINAL RRP £19.99

— Also released in The Third Doctor Collection; BBCDVD2263, £49.99, 6 November 2006

STORY TEASER

Professor Stahlman is heading a project to drill through the Earth's crust and tap a layer of gas he believes will provide the world with unlimited energy. But so determined is he to prove his theories that he ignores all safety advice, even as a boiling green slime begins to leak from the drill shaft and has horrifying effects on those who come into contact with it. Meanwhile, using the project's nuclear reactor to try to repair the TARDIS console, the Doctor is accidentally thrown into a parallel dimension where England is under fascist rule. Here Stahlman's project is more advanced — and closer to destroying the planet.

CONNECTIONS

The early Third Doctor/UNIT stories have a predilection for scientific establishments — a nuclear research centre in *Doctor Who and the Silurians*, Britain's space mission control in *The Ambassadors of Death*, and a drilling project here — a hangover from the Second Doctor's propensity to encounter the same, such as the weather-controlling moonbase in *The Moonbase* (1967), the ioniser-controlling establishment in *The Ice Warriors* (1967), the gas refinery in *Fury from the Deep* (1968) and the transmat-controlling moonbase in *The Seeds of Death* (1969). Scientists are again attempting a deep bore in *The Hungry Earth* (2010) but don't reach the same depths before they encounter monsters, while somehow Torchwood manages to excavate a hole to the very centre of the Earth right under London without anyone noticing prior to *The Runaway Bride* (2006). If only the Daleks had that technology, then installing their engine to drive the planet would have been much easier (*The Dalek Invasion of Earth*, 1964). The Doctor visits another parallel Earth in *Rise of the Cybermen/ The Age of Steel* (2006), a version in which presumably Stahlman never existed, or perhaps was a builder of airships. Douglas Camfield had been a regular director on *Doctor Who* since its start (*see Index v*) but was taken ill while working on *Inferno* (producer Barry Letts took over directing duties working to Camfield's shooting plans), so moved away from the complex series until wooed back to direct Robert Banks Stewart stories *Terror of the Zygons* (1975) and *The Seeds of Doom* (1976). Don Houghton also wrote the following season's *The Mind of Evil* (1971). Derek Newark, playing Greg Sutton, is in the very first *Doctor Who* story, as caveman Za (*An Unearthly Child*, 1963), while Christopher Benjamin (Sir Keith Gold) is more often fêted for his role as Henry Gordon Jago in *The Talons of Weng-Chiang* (1977) and appears in the New Series as Colonel Hugh Curbishley in *The Unicorn and the Wasp* (2008). Ian Fairbairn (Bromley), Walter Randall (Slocum) and Sheila Dunn (Petra Williams) were all regular actors in Camfield-directed productions, in *Doctor Who* and elsewhere (the last being his wife), while David Simeon (Private Latimer) plays fawning reporter Alastair Fergus in *The Dæmons* (1971).

WORTH WATCHING

Coming at the end of the seventh season of *Doctor Who*, the first in colour and in which the Doctor was exiled on Earth, *Inferno* is the climax of that year's attempts to make the show more scientific and serious, a stance that was relaxed the following season as new producer Barry Letts moved the series in the direction he preferred. The result is an incredibly tense story that really puts its characters through the wringer. The use of a parallel universe where everyone is the same only 'evil' may seem a bit of a sci-fi cliché but here it's used well to really highlight the Doctor's plight and show what could happen without his help.

DISC ONE

THE EPISODES

All seven episodes are reverse-converted and restored from digital duplicates of conversions of the original two-inch colour videotape recordings in a lower-resolution format, recovered from a Canadian broadcaster in 1983. A two-second section of damage in episode six is replaced by a black-and-white film copy with the VidFIRE process applied and recoloured using a nearby section from the video recording. The episodes' mono soundtracks are remastered and the sequence of lava at the start of each episode is newly transferred from the original 16mm colour film footage. The title sequences are replaced by a modern transfer of the original 35mm film with credits remade to match the originals.

*INFORMATION TEXT Select **On** to view subtitles when watching the episodes that provide information and anecdotes about the development, production, broadcast and history of *Inferno*. Written by Martin Wiggins.

*AUDIO OPTIONS Select **Commentary On** to play the audio commentary in place of the main soundtrack when watching the episodes. With Nicholas Courtney (the Brigadier) [eps 1,2,3,4,6,7], producer Barry Letts [1,2,4,6,7] and script editor Terrance Dicks [1,2,4,6,7], plus separate comments from John Levene (Benton) [1,3,4,5,6,7].

SUBTITLES

Select **On** to view subtitles for all episodes (none for commentary).

DISC TWO

*CAN YOU HEAR THE EARTH SCREAM? (34m48s) The making of *Inferno*, including developing the script; memories of director Douglas Camfield; the guest cast; the hardships of filming on location at an oil refinery; arranging the stunts, including an especially high fall and an unfortunate accident; having fun in rehearsals; the director's being taken ill; playing alternative versions of familiar characters; making a last-minute cut; and the morals of the story. With contributions from producer Barry Letts, script editor Terrance Dicks, stuntman Derek Ware, and actors Nicholas Courtney, Ian Fairbairn, Caroline John and John Levene. Narrated by David Harley, produced by Steve Broster.

*THE UNIT FAMILY – PART ONE (35m36s) Examination of the UNIT era story by story, by the people involved in creating it. This edition covers *The Web of Fear* to *Inferno* (1968–70), including the reasons for exiling the Doctor to Earth; the casting of Brigadier Lethbridge-Stewart; the establishment of UNIT; the impromptu rise of Sergeant Benton; working with Jon Pertwee; the casting of Liz Shaw; the use of the HAVOC stunt team; and the decision to drop Liz. With contributions from producers Barry Letts and Derrick Sherwin, script editor Terrance Dicks, stuntman Derek Ware, and actors Nicholas Courtney (the Brigadier), Caroline John (Liz) and John Levene (Benton). Produced by Steve Broster. *Part two is on* **Day of the Daleks***; part three is on* Terror of the Zygons

*VISUAL EFFECTS PROMO FILM (6m1s) Short film made in 1970 showcasing the work of the BBC Visual Effects department, including model work from *The Ambassadors of Death* and *Inferno*, as well as other television programmes including *Doomwatch* and Marty Feldman's *Marty Amok*.

*DELETED SCENE (1m57s) A scene cut from UK broadcast of episode five featuring a voiceover by Jon Pertwee that was considered too recognisable, taken from the video recording recovered from Canada where the scene was broadcast in situ.

NEXT

*PERTWEE YEARS INTRO (2m44s) Jon Pertwee's introduction to the final episode of *Inferno*, recorded for the March 1992 VHS release *The Pertwee Years*, discussing his casting and working with Nicholas Courtney. With clips from *Spearhead from Space*.

*PHOTO GALLERY (6m11s) Slideshow of colour and black-and-white photos taken during production of *Inferno*, including behind-the-scenes shots of the location filming and contemporary photos of the production team. Set to music used in the story. Compiled by Ralph Montagu.

*DOCTOR WHO ANNUAL Accessible via a computer is a PDF file of the 1971 *Doctor Who Annual*, published by World Distributors the autumn after *Inferno* was broadcast. With stories featuring the Doctor, Liz and the Brigadier, plus science features, puzzles and games.

*RADIO TIMES BILLINGS Accessible via a computer is a PDF file of the seven episode listings for the original BBC1 broadcast of *Inferno*, a four-page article about the series' production published the week of episode one, and a pin-up of Jon Pertwee published the week of episode six.

SUBTITLES Select **On** to view subtitles for all Special Features on disc two.

EASTER EGGS

There are two hidden features on these discs to find. *See Appendix 2 for details*

INFERNO SPECIAL EDITION

STORY No.54   SEASON No.7:4

Two discs with seven episodes (166½ mins) and 150½ minutes of extras, plus commentary track, production subtitles and PDF items
Audio navigation of each disc's contents available by pressing Enter after the BBC ident

TARDIS TEAM Third Doctor, Liz, Brigadier and UNIT

TIME AND PLACE Contemporary England and a parallel universe equivalent

ADVERSARIES Professor Stahlman; fascist version of UNIT; primeval humanoid Primords

FIRST ON TV 9 May–20 June 1970

DVD RELEASE BBCDVD3671, 27 May 2013, PG

COVER Photo illustration by Lee Binding, dark pink strip; version with older BBC logo on reverse

ORIGINAL RRP £20.42

STORY TEASER

Professor Stahlman is heading a project to drill through the Earth's crust and tap a layer of gas he believes will provide the world with unlimited energy. But so determined is he to prove his theories that he ignores all safety advice, even as a boiling green slime begins to leak from the drill shaft and has horrifying effects on those who come into contact with it. Meanwhile, using the project's nuclear reactor to try to repair the TARDIS console, the Doctor is accidentally thrown into a parallel dimension where England is under fascist rule. Here Stahlman's project is more advanced — and closer to destroying the planet.

CONNECTIONS

The early Third Doctor/UNIT stories have a predilection for scientific establishments — a nuclear research centre in *Doctor Who and the Silurians*, Britain's space mission control in *The Ambassadors of Death*, and a drilling project here — a hangover from the Second Doctor's propensity to encounter the same, such as the weather-controlling moonbase in *The Moonbase* (1967), the ioniser-controlling establishment in *The Ice Warriors* (1967), the gas refinery in *Fury from the Deep* (1968) and the transmat-controlling moonbase in *The Seeds of Death* (1969). Scientists are again attempting a deep bore in *The Hungry Earth* (2010) but don't reach the same depths before they encounter monsters, while somehow Torchwood manages to excavate a hole to the very centre of the Earth right under London without anyone noticing prior to *The Runaway Bride* (2006). If only the Daleks had that technology, then installing their engine to drive the planet would have been much easier (*The Dalek Invasion of Earth*, 1964). The Doctor visits another parallel Earth in *Rise of the Cybermen/The Age of Steel* (2006), a version in which presumably Stahlman never existed, or perhaps was a builder of airships. Douglas Camfield had been a regular director on *Doctor Who* since its start (*see Index v*) but was taken ill while working on *Inferno* (producer Barry Letts took over directing duties working to Camfield's shooting plans), so moved away from the complex series until wooed back to direct Robert Banks Stewart stories *Terror of the Zygons* (1975) and *The Seeds of Doom* (1976). Don Houghton also wrote the following season's *The Mind of Evil* (1971). Derek Newark, playing Greg Sutton, is in the very first *Doctor Who* story, as caveman Za (*An Unearthly Child*, 1963), while Christopher Benjamin (Sir Keith Gold) is more often fêted for his role as Henry Gordon Jago in *The Talons of Weng-Chiang* (1977) and appears in the New Series as Colonel Hugh Curbishley in *The Unicorn and the Wasp* (2008). Ian Fairbairn (Bromley), Walter Randall (Slocum) and Sheila Dunn (Petra Williams) were all regular actors in Camfield-directed productions, in *Doctor Who* and elsewhere (the last being his wife), while David Simeon (Private Latimer) plays fawning reporter Alastair Fergus in *The Dæmons* (1971).

WORTH WATCHING

This Special Edition features more advanced clean-up of the episodes compared to the previous release and additional Special Features. Coming at the end of the seventh season of *Doctor Who*, the first in colour and in which the Doctor was exiled on Earth, *Inferno* is the climax of that year's attempts to make the show more scientific and serious, a stance that was relaxed the following season as new producer Barry Letts moved the series in the direction he preferred. The result is an incredibly tense story that really puts its characters through the wringer. The use of a parallel universe where everyone is the same only 'evil' may seem a bit of a sci-fi cliché but here it's used well to really highlight the Doctor's plight and show what could happen without his help.

DISC ONE

THE EPISODES

All seven episodes are restored from 16mm black-and-white film copies of the original two-inch colour videotape recordings, recovered from BBC Enterprises in 1978; the VidFIRE process is applied to studio-recorded shots to recapture the smoother motion of video and they are recoloured using reverse-converted digital duplicates of conversions of the original two-inch colour videotape recordings in a lower-resolution format (recovered from a Canadian broadcaster in 1983). The episodes' mono soundtracks are remastered and the sequence of lava at the start of each episode is newly transferred from the original 16mm colour film footage. The title sequences are replaced by a modern transfer of the original 35mm film with credits remade to match the originals.

SPECIAL FEATURES *REPEATED FROM PREVIOUS RELEASE

*AUDIO OPTIONS Select **Commentary** to play the audio commentary recorded for the previous release in place of the main soundtrack when watching the episodes. With Nicholas Courtney (the Brigadier) [eps 1,2,3,4,6,7], producer Barry Letts [1,2,4,6,7] and script editor Terrance Dicks [1,2,4,6,7], plus separate comments from John Levene (Benton) [1,3,4,5,6,7].
— Select **Feature Audio** to reinstate the main soundtrack when watching the episodes.

*INFO TEXT Select **On** to view subtitles when watching the episodes that provide information and anecdotes about the development, production, broadcast and history of *Inferno*. Written by Martin Wiggins.

SUBTITLES

Select **On** to view subtitles for all episodes (none for commentary).

DISC TWO

SPECIAL FEATURES *REPEATED FROM PREVIOUS RELEASE

*CAN YOU HEAR THE EARTH SCREAM? (34m48s) The making of *Inferno*, including developing the script; memories of director Douglas Camfield; the guest cast; the hardships of filming on location at an oil refinery; arranging the stunts, including an especially high fall and an unfortunate accident; having fun in rehearsals; the director's being taken ill; playing alternative versions of familiar characters; making a last-minute cut; and the morals of the story. With contributions from producer Barry Letts, script editor Terrance Dicks, stuntman Derek Ware, and actors Nicholas Courtney, Ian Fairbairn, Caroline John and John Levene. Narrated by David Harley, produced by Steve Broster.

HADOKE VERSUS HAVOC (27m34s) Actor and comedian Toby Hadoke meets members of the 1970s stunt team HAVOC — Stuart Fell, Derek Martin, Roy Scammell and Derek Ware — to discuss their careers and work on *Doctor Who*, and reunites them to teach him how to be a stuntman. Produced by Chris Chapman.

DOCTOR FOREVER! – LOST IN THE DARK DIMENSION (27m26s) Examining how *Doctor Who* has spread beyond the television screen, this edition looks at the attempts to bring back the series during the 1990s, some of which got closer to making it onto the screen than others. With New Series showrunner Russell T Davies, BBC Worldwide range editor Steve Cole, *Doctor Who Magazine* editors John Freeman, Gary Russell and Tom Spilsbury, writer Adrian Rigelsford, director Graeme Harper and actor David Burton. Narrated by Zeb Soanes, produced by James Goss. *See Index iii for further editions*

*THE UNIT FAMILY – PART ONE (35m36s) Examination of the UNIT era story by story, by the people involved in creating it. This edition covers *The Web of Fear* to *Inferno* (1968–70), including the reasons for exiling the Doctor to Earth; the casting of Brigadier Lethbridge-Stewart; the establishment of UNIT; the impromptu rise of Sergeant Benton; working with Jon Pertwee; the casting of Liz Shaw; the use of the HAVOC stunt team; and the decision to drop Liz. With contributions from producers Barry Letts and Derrick Sherwin, script editor Terrance Dicks, stuntman Derek Ware, and actors Nicholas Courtney (the Brigadier), Caroline John (Liz) and

John Levene (Benton). Produced by Steve Broster. *Part two is on* **Day of the Daleks**; *part three is on* **Terror of the Zygons**

⁎VISUAL EFFECTS PROMO FILM (6m1s) Short film made in 1970 showcasing the work of the BBC Visual Effects department, including model work from *The Ambassadors of Death* and *Inferno*, as well as other television programmes including *Doomwatch* and Marty Feldman's *Marty Amok*.
NEXT

⁎DELETED SCENE (1m57s) A scene cut from UK broadcast of episode five featuring a voiceover by Jon Pertwee that was considered too recognisable, taken from the video recording recovered from Canada where the scene was broadcast in situ.

⁎PERTWEE YEARS INTRO (2m44s) Jon Pertwee's introduction to the final episode of *Inferno*, recorded for the March 1992 VHS release *The Pertwee Years*, discussing his casting and working with Nicholas Courtney. With clips from *Spearhead from Space*.

⁎PHOTO GALLERY (6m11s) Slideshow of colour and black-and-white photos taken during production of *Inferno*, including behind-the-scenes shots of the location filming and contemporary photos of the production team. Set to music used in the story. Compiled by Ralph Montagu.

⁎PDF MATERIALS Accessible via a computer are the seven episode listings from *Radio Times* for the original BBC1 broadcast of *Inferno*, a four-page article about the series' production published the week of episode one, and a pin-up of Jon Pertwee published the week of episode six.

— The 1971 *Doctor Who Annual*, published by World Distributors the autumn after *Inferno* was broadcast. With stories featuring the Doctor, Liz and the Brigadier, plus science features, puzzles and games.

SUBTITLES Select **On** to view subtitles for all Special Features on disc two.

COMING SOON (1m13s) Trailer for the DVD release of *The Mind of Evil*.

EASTER EGGS
There are three hidden features on these discs to find. *See Appendix 2 for details*

RELATED EXTRAS
Coming Soon trailer — The Visitation Special Edition

THE **INVASION**

STORY No.46   SEASON No.6:3

Two discs with six original and two animated episodes (190½ mins) and 91½ minutes of extras, plus commentary track and production subtitles

TARDIS TEAM Second Doctor, Jamie, Zoe
TIME AND PLACE Contemporary England
ADVERSARIES Cybermen (5th appearance); businessman Tobias Vaughn
FIRST ON TV 2 November–21 December 1968
DVD RELEASE BBCDVD1829, 6 November 2006, PG
COVER Photo illustration by Clayton Hickman, blue strip
— Original release with cover sticker reading 'Special Edition DVD! The missing episodes 1 & 4 now recreated with brand-new animation and the original TV soundtracks', with drawing of the Second Doctor
ORIGINAL RRP £19.99
— Also released in **The Cybermen Collection**; BBCDVD2262, £39.99, 6 November 2006

STORY TEASER
Tobias Vaughan has revolutionised the electronics industry with his invention of the micro-monolithic circuit, but the Doctor recognises the technology as alien. After a narrow escape from Vaughan's security forces, he discovers Brigadier Lethbridge-Stewart and the newly formed United Nations Intelligence Taskforce — UNIT — also have their eye on the industrialist's activities. But Vaughan has allies of his own and when they launch an attack on London the Doctor realises he has badly underestimated the situation.

CONNECTIONS

After several convoluted plans to attack the Earth, this is the first time we see the Cybermen actually set foot on the planet since their debut in *The Tenth Planet* (1966), and even then they were shown only indoors. Their appearance outside a well-known London venue — St Paul's cathedral — follows that of the Daleks patrolling Trafalgar Square in *The Dalek Invasion of Earth* (1964), WOTAN's battle computers by the Post Office Tower in *The War Machines* (1966) and the Yeti stalking Covent Garden market in *The Web of Fear* (1968). Cybermen are still roaming the sewers in *Attack of the Cybermen* (1985), possibly upgraded remnants of this invasion force. Several elements are also reworked for the New Series alternative-universe Cybermen in *Rise of the Cybermen/The Age of Steel* (2006), such as International Electromatics, stored dormant Cybermen and their defeat by giving them back their emotions. This story sees the debut of UNIT, the military group tasked with combating alien incursions, formed in the wake of the Great Intelligence's attack in *The Web of Fear*. Deliberately created to provide a format for the Doctor to spend more time on Earth, UNIT features primarily in the Third Doctor era, with returns for a few early Fourth Doctor stories, *Battlefield* in 1989, and in the New Series briefly in *Aliens of London* (2005) and more significantly in *The Sontaran Stratagem* (2008). When he was writing *The Invasion*, Derrick Sherwin was handing over script editing duties to Terrance Dicks as he prepared to co-produce the series with Peter Bryant. Frequent *Doctor Who* director Douglas Camfield was assigned after his success with *The Web of Fear* (*see Index v*), which featured the debut of Nicholas Courtney as Lethbridge-Stewart, here promoted from colonel to brigadier. Robert Sidaway (Captain Turner) is also Avon in *The Savages* (1966), Clifford Earl (Major Branwell) is a police sergeant in *The Daleks' Master Plan* (1965/66), Norman Hartley (Sergeant Peters) is Ulf in *The Time Meddler* (1965), and Stacy Davies (Private Perkins) is Veros in *State of Decay* (1980). Kevin Stoney, playing Tobias Vaughan, is lead villain Mavic Chen in *The Daleks' Master Plan* (1965/66), also directed by Camfield, and faces the Cybermen again as Councillor Tyrum in *Revenge of the Cybermen* (1975). Vaughan's henchman Packer is played by Peter Halliday, who is also Pletrac in *Carnival of Monsters* (1973), along with small roles in *City of Death* (1979) and *Remembrance of the Daleks* (1988), while Edward Burnham (Professor Watkins) appears as the similarly compromised Professor Kettlewell in *Robot* (1974/75). Geoffrey Cheshire (Tracy), Sheila Dunn (Telephone operator), Ian Fairbairn (Gregory) and Walter Randall (IE guard) were all regular actors for Camfield, appearing in several of his *Doctor Who* serials.

WORTH WATCHING

With the introduction of UNIT, this serial was a dry run for the money-saving idea of having the Doctor stranded on Earth and helping out the military, which indeed became the case the following year. As such the production had the help of the British Army to swell the ranks of UNIT soldiers and make the climactic battle go with a bang. Although the Cybermen themselves are reduced to generic drones, their strategic presence represented by the Cyberplanner, the inclusion of human collaborator Tobias Vaughan gives a stronger (and certainly clearer) voice to their goals and is a gripping portrayal by Kevin Stoney.

DISC ONE

THE EPISODES

To maximise their quality on the DVD, episodes one to four are on disc one and episodes five to eight are on disc two. Episodes one and four, of which no film copies are known to exist, are recreated with black-and-white animation by Cosgrove Hall Films with reference to surviving photos from the serial and matched to a remastered recording of the soundtrack (with some small edits) made on audio tape when the episodes were originally broadcast. Episodes two and three are restored from 16mm film copies of the original black-and-white video recordings that survived in the archives. Their mono soundtracks are remastered and the VidFIRE process is applied to studio-recorded shots to recapture the smoother motion of video. The title sequences are replaced by a modern transfer of the original 35mm film with credits remade to match the originals.

SPECIAL FEATURES

FLASH FRAMES (11m30s) The team at Cosgrove Hall discuss how they came to animate the two missing episodes of *The Invasion*, having produced *Scream of the Shalka* for BBCi in 2003, and the techniques and challenges involved. With executive producer Jon Doyle, animation director Steve Maher, lead animator Claire Grey and BBC producer James Goss, plus actor Frazer Hines. Produced by James Goss.

LOVE OFF-AIR (15m16s) *Doctor Who* fans David Holman, Justin Richards, Gary Russell and Michael Stevens discuss how when they were children, in the days before home video recording was possible, they made audio recordings of their favourite programme as it was being broadcast so they could listen to the stories over and over again. With some of these recordings now being the only surviving copies of the original episodes, Mark Ayres talks about how they were used to recreate the soundtrack to which the two missing episodes of *The Invasion* were animated. Produced by Rob Francis and James Goss.

ANIMATION TRAILERS (1m8s) Two previews of the animation for *The Invasion*, including shots not used in the final animated episodes.

CHARACTER DESIGN (2m51s) Concept designs for the main characters in *The Invasion*, including an animated version of the opening title sequence. Set to music from the story.

SET UP

COMMENTARY Select **On** to play the audio commentary in place of the main soundtrack when watching the episodes. On episode one are animation director Steve Maher, producer James Goss and sound restorer Mark Ayres discussing the process for the animated episodes. On the next three episodes are Nicholas Courtney (the Brigadier) [eps 2,3,4], Frazer Hines (Jamie) [2,3,4], Wendy Padbury (Zoe) [2,4] and production assistant Chris D'Oyly-John [3].

INFORMATION TEXT Select **On** to view subtitles when watching the episodes that provide information and anecdotes about the development, production, broadcast and history of *The Invasion*. Written by Martin Wiggins.

SUBTITLES Select **On** to view subtitles for all episodes and Special Features on disc one (except commentary).

DISC TWO

THE EPISODES

Episodes five, six, seven and eight on this disc are restored from 16mm film copies of the original black-and-white video recordings that survived in the archives. Their mono soundtracks are remastered and the VidFIRE process is applied to studio-recorded shots to recapture the smoother motion of video. The title sequences are replaced by a modern transfer of the original 35mm film with credits remade to match the originals.

SPECIAL FEATURES

EVOLUTION OF THE INVASION (50m25s) The making of *The Invasion*, including Patrick Troughton's increasing tiredness with the relentless production schedule leading to his decision shortly before *The Invasion* went into production to leave *Doctor Who*; the struggle to find suitable scripts for the 1968/69 season; memories of director Douglas Camfield; the origination of UNIT and the return of Lethbridge-Stewart; the characters and cast; redesigning the Cybermen; filming on location with a helicopter, early morning in the City of London and at the Guinness Factory in Acton; bringing in the British Army for the final battle; rehearsing for the studio recordings; description of a cut location scene that was rewritten for the studio; Don Harper's incidental music; and the legacy of *The Invasion*. With contributions from script editor Terrance Dicks, production assistant Chris D'Oyly-John, and actors Edward Burnham, Nicholas Courtney, Ian Fairbairn, Sally Faulkner, Peter Halliday, Frazer Hines, Wendy Padbury and Kevin Stoney. Narrated by Frazer Hines, illustrations by Robert Hammond, produced by John Kelly.

1993 VHS LINKS (2m59s) Nicholas Courtney's introduction to *The Invasion* and summaries of its two missing episodes, recorded for the serial's release on home video in June 1993. Includes the thirtieth-anniversary ident that featured at the start of all *Doctor Who* videos released that year.

PHOTO GALLERY (7m22s) Slideshow of colour and black-and-white photos taken during production of *The Invasion*, including behind-the-scenes photos of the location filming, plus shots of the commentary participants. Set to music from the story, including cues not used in the final programme. Compiled by Ralph Montagu.

COMMENTARY Select **On** to play the audio commentary in place of the main soundtrack when watching the episodes. With production assistant Chris D'Oyly-John [eps 5,6,7,8], Wendy Padbury (Zoe) [5,6,7,8], Frazer Hines (Jamie) [5,6,8] and Nicholas Courtney (the Brigadier) [5,7,8].

INFORMATION TEXT Select **On** to view subtitles when watching the episodes that provide information and anecdotes about the development, production, broadcast and history of *The Invasion*. Written by Martin Wiggins.

SUBTITLES Select **On** to view subtitles for all episodes and Special Features on disc two (except commentary).

RELATED EXTRAS
The Cyber-Generations — Attack of the Cybermen
Radio Times Listings — Attack of the Cybermen

INVASION OF THE DINOSAURS

STORY No.71   SEASON No.11:2

Released with **THE ANDROID INVASION** in the **U.N.I.T FILES** boxset
Two discs with six episodes (147½ mins), option to view episode one in partial colour, and 85 minutes of extras, plus commentary track, production subtitles and PDF items
Audio navigation of each disc's contents available by pressing Enter after the BBC ident

TARDIS TEAM Third Doctor, Sarah Jane, Brigadier and UNIT
TIME AND PLACE Contemporary London
ADVERSARIES Dinosaurs; environmental conspirators
FIRST ON TV 12 January–16 February 1974
DVD RELEASE BBCDVD3376A, 9 January 2012, PG (disc two U)
COVER Photo illustration by Clayton Hickman, orange strip; version with older BBC logo on reverse
ORIGINAL RRP £30.63 (boxset)

STORY TEASER
The Doctor returns Sarah Jane to 20th Century London only to find it all but deserted. The reason becomes clear when they encounter living prehistoric creatures roaming the streets. UNIT have organised the evacuation of the city and hope the Doctor can discover how and why the dinosaurs are appearing. But how much can they learn when those responsible have connections at the highest levels and are planning a more permanent end to modern life?

CONNECTIONS
Spurred by the success of the Drashigs in *Carnival of Monsters* (1973), the production team were assured dinosaurs could be effectively shown on a *Doctor Who* budget. The results are not entirely convincing, but not all as laughable as some would claim, and better than the previous dinosaur seen in the show, in *Doctor Who and the Silurians* (1970). Nor did it stop a new production team going ahead with a similar attempt for the Skarasen in *Terror of the Zygons* (1975), although again with debatable efficacy. Suffice to say dinosaurs don't appear in the programme again until CGI was suitably advanced (*Dinosaurs on a Spaceship*, 2012). Perhaps more surprising given the preceding four years is that the Doctor hasn't faced monsters in a recognisable London since *The Invasion* (1968); other instances include *The War Machines* (1966), *The Web of Fear* (1968), *Resurrection of the Daleks* (1984), *Attack of the Cybermen* (1985), *Remembrance of the Daleks* (1988) and numerous New Series episodes. Professor Whitaker's work is well ahead of its time, seeming to combine the later Time Scanner Dr Fendleman invents to view the past (*Image of the Fendahl*, 1977) with the time manipulation of Professor Kerensky's machine in *City of Death* (1979). And like Scaroth in the latter, Whitaker's goal is to rewind time to an earlier age, an effect the Doctor is seen to be able to withstand in both stories. Captain Yates' uncertainty of purpose is initiated by events in *The Green Death* (1973) and he is working to resolve them in *Planet of the Spiders* (1974). *Invasion of the Dinosaurs* is Malcolm Hulke's last work for the series having written for it throughout the Third

Doctor era (*see Index v*), while Paddy Russell also directed *The Massacre* (1966), *Pyramids of Mars* (1975) and *Horror of Fang Rock* (1977). John Bennett (General Finch) is more fêted for his role as Li H'sen Chang in *The Talons of Weng-Chiang* (1977), Martin Jarvis (Butler) is Menoptra Hilio in *The Web Planet* (1965) and the Governor in *Vengeance on Varos* (1985), Noel Johnson (Charles Grover) is King Thous in *The Underwater Menace* (1967), Peter Miles is most renowned for playing Nyder in *Genesis of the Daleks* (1975) but is also Dr Lawrence in *Doctor Who and the Silurians* (1970), and Carmen Silvera (Ruth) plays numerous roles in *The Celestial Toymaker* (1966).

WORTH WATCHING

As long as you don't come to this expecting it to be like *Jurassic Park*, there's a lot to enjoy. Perhaps it was over-ambitious of the producers to put dinosaurs into modern-day London convincingly, but it's precisely the level of imagination *Doctor Who* was always about and just the sort of thing any child loves to see. Besides, the true meat of the story is a compelling conspiracy plot that has some shocks in store for the Doctor and audience alike.

DISC ONE

THE EPISODES

Episode one is restored from a 16mm black-and-white film copy of the original two-inch colour videotape recording, recovered by Roger Stevens in June 1983 and now held privately. Its mono soundtrack is remastered and the VidFIRE process is applied to studio-recorded shots to recapture the smoother motion of video (a part-coloured version is optional; see below). Episodes two to six are restored from digital duplicates of the original two-inch colour videotape recordings used for broadcast, with location scenes in episode five newly transferred from the original 16mm colour film, and their mono soundtracks remastered. The title sequences for all episodes are replaced by a modern transfer of the original 35mm film with credits remade to match the originals.

SPECIAL FEATURES

EPISODE 1 COLOUR Select **On** to play a partial-colour version of episode one when viewing via **Play All**, **Episode Selection** or **Scene Selection**. This is restored from the 16mm black-and-white film recording and recoloured from information in the mono images on the film that relates to the original colour of the video picture being filmed, using the Colour Recovery process. While this has been used on other releases to successfully restore full colour, here the technique wasn't completely effective owing to the quality of the film recording, so is offered as an option to the black-and-white version that plays by default.

AUDIO OPTIONS Select **Commentary** to play the audio commentary in place of the main soundtrack when watching the episodes. This is moderated by actor and comedian Toby Hadoke, talking with director Paddy Russell [eps 1,4,5], script editor Terrance Dicks [2,3], Richard Franklin (Yates) [2,3], Peter Miles (Whitaker) [2,3,6], designer Richard Morris [2,6] and Terence Wilton (Mark) [3,6].

— Select **Feature Audio** to reinstate the main soundtrack when watching the episodes.

INFO TEXT Select **On** to view subtitles when watching the episodes that provide information and anecdotes about the development, production, broadcast and history of *Invasion of the Dinosaurs*. Written by David Brunt.

COMING SOON (59s) Trailer for the DVD release of *The Sensorites*.

SUBTITLES

Select **On** to view subtitles for all episodes and the Coming Soon trailer (none for commentary).

DISC TWO

SPECIAL FEATURES

PEOPLE, POWER AND PUPPETRY (32m43s) Writer and broadcaster Matthew Sweet looks at the making of *Invasion of the Dinosaurs* to see if there's more to it than rubbery dinosaur puppets. He examines Malcolm Hulke's original script ideas, the social politics he liked to include and some of the contemporary concerns he was echoing; the questionable plausibility of Operation Golden Age; the choice of director and getting shots of a deserted Central London; Jon Pertwee's introduction of the Whomobile; designing the sets (and a genuinely rare instance of wobbling walls); the casting; the let-down of the dinosaur models; and the reasons behind shortening the title of episode one, to the disappointment of Hulke. With contributions from producer Barry

Letts (interviewed in 2008), script editor Terrance Dicks, director Paddy Russell, designer Richard Morris, and actors Jon Pertwee (interviewed in 1993), Peter Miles and Terence Wilton. Produced by Ed Stradling.

DELETED SCENES (4m48s) A scene cut from episode one, taken from a silent 16mm black-and-white film copy of the location footage, and extended scenes from episode three taken from an earlier edit.

NOW AND THEN (13m43s) Comparing the filming locations in Central and West London as they look today with how they appeared in late-September 1973 when used for *Invasion of the Dinosaurs*. Narrated and produced by Richard Bignell. *See Index iii for further editions*

DOCTOR WHO STORIES: ELISABETH SLADEN PART 1 (14m) Recorded in 2003 for BBC2's *The Story of Doctor Who*, actor Elisabeth Sladen recalls her experiences of playing companion Sarah Jane Smith from 1973 to 1976. *Part two is on* Terror of the Zygons

SUBTITLES Select **On** to view subtitles for all Special Features on disc two.

NEXT

JOHN LEVENE COMMENTARY (10m15s) The actor who played Sergeant Benton comments on the opening section of episode five and recalls his favourite moments from the story.

PHOTO GALLERY (6m12s) Slideshow of colour and black-and-white photos taken during production of *Invasion of the Dinosaurs*, including design department photos of the sets. Set to sound effects from the story. Compiled by Paul Shields.

BILLY SMART'S CIRCUS (1m42s) An appearance by Jon Pertwee in the Whomobile at Billy Smart's Children's Circus on Sunday 4 November 1973 and shown on BBC1 on Sunday 6 January 1974, before the car had appeared in *Doctor Who*.

PDF MATERIALS Accessible via a computer are the six episode listings from *Radio Times* for the original BBC1 broadcast of *Invasion of the Dinosaurs*, with illustrations by Peter Brookes and his dramatic artwork for episode one.

EASTER EGG
There is one hidden feature on these discs to find. *See Appendix 2 for details*

RELATED EXTRAS
Coming Soon trailer — Colony in Space
Paddy Russell - A Life in Television — Horror of Fang Rock
The UNIT Family — Terror of the Zygons

THE **INVASION OF TIME**

STORY No.97   SEASON No.15:6

Two discs with six episodes (150 mins) and 51 minutes of extras, plus optional CGI effects, commentary track, production subtitles and PDF items

TARDIS TEAM Fourth Doctor, Leela, K9
TIME AND PLACE Time Lord homeworld Gallifrey
ADVERSARIES Vardans; Sontarans (3rd appearance)
FIRST ON TV 4 February–11 March 1978
DVD RELEASE BBCDVD2586, 5 May 2008, PG (disc one and extras bar DVD trailer U)
COVER Photo illustration by Clayton Hickman, dark pink strip
ORIGINAL RRP £19.99
— Also released in Bred for War: The Sontaran Collection; BBCDVD2617, £39.99, 5 May 2008

STORY TEASER
Has the Doctor betrayed his own people? Returning to Gallifrey to claim his rightful place as Lord President of the Time Lords, he banishes Leela to the wilderness outside the Capitol, which he strips of its protective barriers and seems to invite invasion by the mysterious, shimmering Vardans. Only Leela trusts the Doctor has a reason for his seemingly treacherous actions, but it soon transpires that even he has been outwitted.

CONNECTIONS

This is the Doctor's second visit to his home planet in a little over a year, having been lured there by the Master in *The Deadly Assassin* (1976). Indeed, *The Invasion of Time* is almost a sequel to that story, with the Doctor enforcing his appointment as president (the only other candidate having died in *The Deadly Assassin*) and seemingly betraying the Time Lords as punishment for their earlier mistreatment of him. The only returning character is Borusa, regenerated (that is, played by a different actor) and promoted from cardinal to chancellor — he'll have made it to president himself by *Arc of Infinity* and *The Five Doctors* (both 1983) — although other offices are again represented, such as a castellan and the chancellery guard. The Sontarans make a surprise return (well, it was a surprise at the time), only their third appearance since their debut in *The Time Warrior* (1973/74) and the following season's *The Sontaran Experiment* (1975). Although it may seem their invasion of Gallifrey comes out of the blue and that the Sontarans were chosen just because their costumes were available from storage, they do have an ongoing association with time travel, Linx being able to transport people from the future in *The Time Warrior* and Stike seeking to gain a working time machine in *The Two Doctors* (1985). Gallifrey itself is first named on screen in *The Time Warrior*, in which Linx knows of the planet and its reported vulnerability to attack. More of the inside of the TARDIS is shown here than ever before; previously we'd seen a few antechambers to the control room in *The Edge of Destruction* (1964), and a boot cupboard and second control room in *The Masque of Mandragora* (1976). Here we see a lab, swimming pool, art gallery and more. There are cloisters, a zero room and lots of corridors on show in *Logopolis* (1981) and *Castrovalva* (1982) before we finally get to see more significant areas of the Ship in *Journey to the Centre of the TARDIS* (2013). The other surprise of the story is the rather sudden departure of Leela, who had been travelling with the Doctor since *The Face of Evil* (1977). The credited writer, David Agnew, is actually a pseudonym for producer Graham Williams and script editor Anthony Read, to avoid disapproval about writing for their own series, while director Gerald Blake's only other work on the show had been directing *The Abominable Snowmen* in 1967. Milton Johns (Castellan Kelner) makes his last of three appearances in *Doctor Who*, having played Benik in *The Enemy of the World* (1967/68) and Guy Crayford in *The Android Invasion* (1975), and Christopher Tranchell (Commander Andred) is Jenkins in *The Faceless Ones* (1967) and Roger Colbert in *The Massacre* (1966), in which Reginald Jessup (Lord Savar) also appears. Charles Morgan (Gold Usher) plays Abbott Songsten in *The Abominable Snowmen*, while Max Faulkner (Nesbin) plays several speaking stunt roles during the Third Doctor era and more significantly Corporal Adams in *The Android Invasion*.

WORTH WATCHING

Although *Doctor Who* had been finishing its seasons on a longer six-part story throughout the 1970s, *The Invasion of Time* at the end of the 1977/78 run, Graham Williams' first as producer, can be seen as the first true attempt at a grander season finale of the kind we're now familiar with. Not only does the Doctor return to his home planet Gallifrey, he's acting oddly and clearly there is much at risk. The reveal of the true enemy at the end of episode four — now sadly impossible not to have spoiled — was the sort of surprise the series rarely pulled off.

DISC ONE

THE EPISODES

All six episodes are restored from digital duplicates of the original two-inch colour videotape recordings used for broadcast, with location sequences newly transferred from the original 16mm colour film print used for broadcast (this was badly faded but has been restored, although some colours were mistakenly graded differently to how they appear in studio sequences). This has required shots that mix film and video elements to be recomposited and some video effects recreated. The episodes' mono soundtracks are remastered and the title sequences replaced by a modern transfer of the original 35mm film with credits remade to match the originals.

SPECIAL FEATURES

AUDIO OPTIONS Select **Commentary** to play the audio commentary in place of the main soundtrack when watching the episodes. With Louise Jameson (Leela), John Leeson (K9 voice), script editor Anthony Read and visual effects designer Mat Irvine on all six episodes.

— Select **Feature Audio** to reinstate the main soundtrack when watching the episodes.

CGI EFFECTS Select **CGI Effects On** to view updated computer-generated effects in place of some of the original visual effects when watching the episodes.

SUBTITLES

Select Subtitles **On** to view subtitles for all episodes (none for commentary).

— Select **Info Text On** to view subtitles when watching the episodes that provide information and anecdotes about the development, production, broadcast and history of *The Invasion of Time*. Written by Martin Wiggins.

DISC TWO

SPECIAL FEATURES

OUT OF TIME (16m52s) The making of *The Invasion of Time*, including the last-minute need to come up with a new season finale and choosing the Sontarans as a twist to extend the story; memories of director Gerald Blake; coping with tight budgets at a time of high inflation; the characters and cast; writing out Leela and Tom Baker's assuredness in his role; filming on location in a disused hospital; building the spaceship models and man-eating plants; realising the shimmering Vardans; and how Leela nearly came back. With contributions from script editor Anthony Read, visual effects designer Colin Mapson, and actors Louise Jameson, Milton Johns, John Leeson and Christopher Tranchell. Produced by Andrew Beech.

DELETED SCENES (5m55s) A selection of scenes from episodes five and six not used in the final programme, taken from the full location film footage.

THE RISE AND FALL OF GALLIFREY (9m59s) Discussion of the portrayal of the Doctor's people, the Time Lords, and their planet Gallifrey during the Classic Series. With contributions from script editors Terrance Dicks and Anthony Read, and former *Doctor Who Magazine* editors Alan Barnes and Gary Russell. Directed by Marcus Hearn.

THE ELUSIVE DAVID AGNEW (5m17s) A tongue-in-cheek probe into the mystery surrounding the credited writer of *The Invasion of Time*, whom no one seems ever to have met. With Terrance Dicks and Anthony Read.

CONTINUITY (3m26s) Continuity announcements from the original BBC1 broadcasts of all six episodes of *The Invasion of Time*, with a plug for the theme music single. Includes the BBC1 evening schedule for Saturday 11 March 1978.

SUBTITLES Select **On** to view subtitles for all Special Features on disc two.

NEXT

PHOTO GALLERY (7m5s) Slideshow of colour photos taken during production of *The Invasion of Time*, including design department photos of the sets. Set to sound effects from the story. Compiled by Derek Handley.

COMING SOON (1m16) Trailer for the DVD releases of *The Invisible Enemy* and *K9 and Company* in the K9 Tales boxset.

RADIO TIMES LISTINGS Accessible via a computer is a PDF file of the six episode listings for the original BBC1 broadcast of *The Invasion of Time*.

EASTER EGG

There is one hidden feature on these discs to find. *See Appendix 2 for details*

RELATED EXTRAS

Coming Soon trailer — The Five Doctors 25th Anniversary Edition

Built for War — The Sontaran Experiment

THE **INVISIBLE ENEMY**

STORY No.93   SEASON No.15:2

Released with **K9 AND COMPANY** in the **K9 TALES** boxset

One disc with four episodes (93 mins) and 73 minutes of extras, plus optional CGI effects, commentary track, production subtitles and PDF items

TARDIS TEAM Fourth Doctor, Leela, and introducing K9

TIME AND PLACE Saturn's moon Titan and Bi-Al medical facility in the asteroid belt

ADVERSARIES Mind-controlling virus

FIRST ON TV 1–22 October 1977

DVD RELEASE BBCDVD2799, 16 June 2008, 12 (episodes PG, extras bar commentary U)

● *The initial release of this disc had an error in which scenes at the end of episode three were out of order. A corrected disc was issued which was labelled 'BBCDVD2799 - A'*

COVER Photo illustration by Clayton Hickman, dark orange strip

ORIGINAL RRP £29.99 (boxset)

STORY TEASER

A space-borne sentient virus penetrates the TARDIS and infects the Doctor. He and Leela learn other victims are preparing a breeding ground on Titan where the Nucleus the Doctor now carries can incubate. He puts himself into a coma to prevent his mind being overcome, but first directs Leela to the medical facilities of the Bi-Al Foundation, where Professor Marius and his robot dog K9 strive to find a cure before the virus's servants can retrieve the Doctor. But their problems are about to get a whole lot bigger.

CONNECTIONS

Following the dark gothic feel of the preceding two years, *The Invisible Enemy* is the first clear sign that there's a new man in charge of the programme. It probably felt different and exciting at the time, but in retrospect it seems more of a throwback to the Third Doctor era and the likes of *The Mutants* (1972) and *Frontier in Space* (1973) in terms of its design and atmosphere. Spaceships, laser guns and clean white corridors position this firmly in the style of science fiction that was emerging from cinema of the time. And, of course, robots. Here we meet K9, a mobile computer shaped (vaguely) like a dog, who will join the Doctor in the TARDIS for the next three years (give or take the odd story). But no little people in costumes here: K9 is a genuine remote-controlled robot, although voiced by the very human John Leeson. Writers Bob Baker and Dave Martin obviously had their fingers on the pulse of the zeitgeist, although after some seven years of writing for the show, this is their penultimate script (*see Index v*). While it was director Derrick Goodwin's only work on *Doctor Who*, much of the main guest cast had previous roles. Michael Sheard (Lowe) first appeared in 1966's *The Ark*, returning as Dr Summers in *The Mind of Evil* (1971), Laurence Scarman in *Pyramids of Mars* (1975), Mergrave in *Castrovalva* (1982) and the Dalek-controlled headmaster in *Remembrance of the Daleks* (1988). Frederick Jaeger (Professor Marius) had similarly made his *Doctor Who* debut in 1966, as Jano in *The Savages*, and had more recently played another professor, Sorenson, in *Planet of Evil* (1975), while Brian Grellis (Safran) is the Vogan captain Sheprah in *Revenge of the Cybermen* (1975) and simply 'megaphone man' in *Snakedance* (1983).

WORTH WATCHING

The Invisible Enemy is often cited as the first instance of *Star Wars* having an effect on the production style of *Doctor Who*, given the story's impressive spaceship model work, laser-gun battles and introduction of a cute robot character in K9. And yet the show was made before *Star Wars* was even released, and it was broadcast two months before the movie reached UK cinemas. The greater influence on this story is the 1966 film *Fantastic Voyage*, in which scientists are miniaturised and injected into a human body, mirrored here by a journey into the Doctor's brain.

THE EPISODES

All four episodes are restored from digital duplicates of the original two-inch colour videotape recordings used for broadcast and their mono soundtracks remastered. The title sequences are replaced by a modern transfer of the original 35mm film with credits remade to match the originals.

SPECIAL FEATURES

DREAMS AND FANTASY (20m36s) The making of *The Invisible Enemy*, including producer Graham Williams' bid to lighten the tone of *Doctor Who*; writing the script, devising the character of K9 and working out his final design; the director's approach to the serial; problems with controlling K9 in the studio, as well as the struggles to achieve the complicated special effects required; and how the serial stands up today. Plus the original visual effects team visit K9 at his current home.

With contributions from writer Bob Baker, director Derrick Goodwin, visual effects designers Tony Harding and Mat Irvine, K9 operator Nigel Brackley, actors Louise Jameson and John Leeson, and fan journalist Gary Gillatt. Produced by Richard Higson.

STUDIO SWEEPINGS (20m33s) Footage from the full studio recording on Tuesday 12 April 1977 of scenes inside the Doctor's brain, including setups and retakes (and K9 going out of control). Features production assistant Norman Stewart helping set up the complex superimposition shots, which proved valuable experience when he came to direct *Underworld* six months later. Taken from a black-and-white video copy with on-screen time-code.

VISUAL EFFECT (16m26s) Mat Irvine meets with his former visual effects colleague Ian Scoones to discuss their work together creating and filming models for *Doctor Who*, in particular for *The Invisible Enemy*, looking through the extensive storyboard sketches that Scoones produced for the effects shooting and at Irvine's original space-shuttle models. Mat also shows his approach to building miniatures and how current *Doctor Who* still uses models mixed with CGI. Produced by Paul Vanezis.

BLUE PETER (4m32s) Extract from the Monday 10 October 1977 edition of the children's magazine programme in which Lesley Judd and John Noakes (and a rather excited Shep) meet K9. This was shown two days after episode two of *The Invisible Enemy* was broadcast, before K9 had been seen to join the TARDIS team.

CGI EFFECTS Select **CGI Effects On** to view updated computer-generated effects in place of some of the original visual effects when watching the episodes.

NEXT

AUDIO OPTIONS Select **Commentary** to play the audio commentary in place of the main soundtrack when watching the episodes. With Louise Jameson (Leela), John Leeson (K9 voice), writer Bob Baker and visual effects designer Mat Irvine on all four episodes.

— Select **Feature Audio** to reinstate the main soundtrack when watching the episodes.

INFO TEXT Select **On** to view subtitles when watching the episodes that provide information and anecdotes about the development, production, broadcast and history of *The Invisible Enemy*. Written by Richard Molesworth.

TRAILERS AND CONTINUITY (3m47s) Previews and continuity announcements from the original BBC1 broadcasts of all four episodes of *The Invisible Enemy*, with plugs for the *Doctor Who* exhibitions at Blackpool and Longleat and the theme music single, plus a preview of the following story, *Image of the Fendahl* (*also on* **Image of the Fendahl**).

PHOTO GALLERY (5m6s) Slideshow of colour and black-and-white photos taken during production of *The Invisible Enemy*, including shots of the model work and design department photos of the sets. Set to sound effects and music from the story. Compiled by Derek Handley.

COMING SOON (1m) Trailer for the DVD release of *The Brain of Morbius*.

RADIO TIMES LISTINGS Accessible via a computer is a PDF file of the four episode listings for the original BBC1 broadcast of *The Invisible Enemy*.

SUBTITLES

Select **On** to view subtitles for all episodes and Special Features (except commentary).

EASTER EGG

There is one hidden feature on this disc to find. *See Appendix 2 for details*

RELATED EXTRAS

Coming Soon trailer — The Invasion of Time

K9 AND COMPANY

The first ever spin-off from *Doctor Who*, featuring Sarah Jane Smith and K9 Mark III uniting to expose a druidic coven in the English countryside. Shown at Christmas in 1981 shortly after K9's departure from the main series, this pilot for a possible series is the only episode that was made.

● *See Appendix 1 for full details*

K9 TALES

Boxset of **THE INVISIBLE ENEMY** and **K9 AND COMPANY**

DVD RELEASE BBCDVD2439, 16 June 2008, 12
SLIPCASE Photo illustration by Clayton Hickman, silvered logo and title, blue background
ORIGINAL RRP £29.99

WHAT'S IN THE BOX

Two stories featuring popular late-70s companion K9, the robot dog who returned in the New Series and *The Sarah Jane Adventures*. *The Invisible Enemy* (1977) is K9's very first story in which he assists the Fourth Doctor and joins the TARDIS team. *K9 and Company* is the first ever spin-off from *Doctor Who*, shown Christmas 1981, in which Sarah Jane Smith discovers the Doctor has sent her K9 Mark III and together they uncover a druidic coven in an English village.

● *See individual stories for full contents*

KAMELION TALES

Boxset of **THE KING'S DEMONS** and **PLANET OF FIRE**

DVD RELEASE BBCDVD2738, 14 June 2010, PG
SLIPCASE Photo illustration by Clayton Hickman, silvered logo and title, blue background
ORIGINAL RRP £29.99

WHAT'S IN THE BOX

The two stories featuring the Fifth Doctor's short-lived android companion Kamelion. *The King's Demons* (1983) introduces the robot, which the Master is using to pervert English history. To defeat him, the Doctor takes Kamelion aboard the TARDIS but he doesn't appear again until *Planet of Fire* (1984) when the Master regains control of the android and uses him to hijack the TARDIS and bring it to the volcanic planet Sarn.

● *See individual stories for full contents*

THE **KEEPER OF TRAKEN**

STORY No.114   SEASON No.18:6

Released with **CASTROVALVA** and **LOGOPOLIS** in the **NEW BEGINNINGS** boxset
One disc with four episodes (98 mins) and 65½ minutes of extras, plus commentary and music—only tracks, production subtitles and PDF items

TARDIS TEAM Fourth Doctor, Adric, and introducing Nyssa
TIME AND PLACE Planet Traken
ADVERSARIES Second Master (2nd appearance); statue-like Melkur; its stooge Kassia
FIRST ON TV 31 January–21 February 1981
DVD RELEASE BBCDVD1331(A), 29 January 2007, PG (boxset 12)
COVER Photo illustration by Clayton Hickman, pale purple strip
ORIGINAL RRP £29.99 (boxset)

STORY TEASER

The powers of the Keeper have kept the Traken planetary system at peace for millennia. But some evil cannot be suppressed: although an apparently immobile stone statue, the malevolent Melkur is able to influence others, and the Keeper calls on the Doctor to help combat its menace. There is more to Melkur than anyone realises, however, and with the gullible council member Kassia under its control, its path to securing the Keeper's powers is clear.

CONNECTIONS

The Master returns in his decrepit form as seen in *The Deadly Assassin* (1976), still seeking a way to renew his lifecycle as he is on his last incarnation. The Doctor and Adric are travelling alone having left Romana and K9 in E-Space to help the Tharils in *Warriors' Gate*. This is the first story written by Johnny Byrne, who also scripted *Arc of Infinity* (1983) and *Warriors of the Deep* (1984), while John Black also directed *Four to Doomsday* (1982) and the spin-off *K9 and Company* in 1981 (*see Appendix 1*). Denis Carey (the Keeper) plays Professor Chronotis in the unfinished *Shada* (1980) but did appear in *Timelash* (1985); Margot van der Burgh (Katura) fell in love with the Doctor as Cameca in *The Aztecs* (1964); and John Woodnutt (Seron) makes his last of several appearances in *Doctor Who*, most notably as George Hibbert in *Spearhead from Space* (1970) and Broton in *Terror of the Zygons* (1975). Geoffrey Beevers (the Master) plays Private Johnson in *The Ambassadors of Death* (1970) and, without giving too much away, Anthony Ainley (Tremas) will be back.

WORTH WATCHING

A surprise for the audience at the time, it's now impossible not to approach *The Keeper of Traken* as the story in which the Master returns and gains a whole new lease of life. Last seen in *The Deadly Assassin* (1976) as a decayed figure on his last life, here he returns in the same form seeking the powers of the Traken Keepership to renew himself. The restored Master went on to be a recurring enemy during the Fifth, Sixth and Seventh Doctor eras. This story also introduces Nyssa, a young girl who helps the Doctor and Adric. Actress Sarah Sutton so impressed the production team that they chose to bring her back in the following story as an extra companion. *The Keeper of Traken* itself is a tale of courtly intrigue and betrayal that still works well even if you do know who the mysterious adversary turns out to be.

THE EPISODES

All four episodes are restored from digital duplicates of the original two-inch colour videotape recordings used for broadcast and their mono soundtracks remastered. The title sequences are replaced by a modern transfer of the original 35mm film with credits remade to match the originals.

SPECIAL FEATURES

SARAH SUTTON ON SWAP SHOP (11m16s) Extract from the 31 January 1981 edition of the BBC1 Saturday morning children's show in which Noel Edmonds interviews Sarah Sutton about her role in 1978 BBC children's drama *The Moon Stallion* and her casting as Nyssa, and they take viewers' questions on the phone, plus Sarah picks the winners for the previous week's competitions.

THE RETURN OF THE MASTER (9m40s) Geoffrey Beevers talks about his part in bringing back the Master, from the costume to his characterisation of the Doctor's arch enemy. With brief comments from director John Black and script editor Christopher H Bidmead.

BEING NICE TO EACH OTHER (30m2s) The making of *The Keeper of Traken*, including the steps the new production team took to restyle *Doctor Who*; the themes of this story, the original version before the Master was added and subsequent revisions to include the new adversary; the input of the director and designers, including costume and set ideas; the guest cast; recording the Keeper's appearances in the TARDIS and Kassia's effects make-up; and working with Tom Baker towards the end of his time as the Doctor. With contributions from script editor Christopher H Bidmead, writer Johnny Byrne, director John Black, and actors Geoffrey Beevers, Sheila Ruskin and Sarah Sutton. Narrated by George Williams, produced by Steve Broster and Paul Vanezis.

TRAILS AND CONTINUITIES (5m56s) Preview of episode one and continuity announcements from the original BBC1 broadcasts of all four episodes of *The Keeper of Traken*; plus the repeat showings on BBC1 in August 1981, with a plug for the upcoming *Five Faces of Doctor Who* run of repeats on BBC2 in November 1981. Includes the opening of the BBC1 early-evening News for Saturday 21 February 1981, and the BBC1 evening schedules for Monday 10, Tuesday 11, Wednesday 12 and Thursday 13 August 1981.

NEXT

PHOTO GALLERY (8m23s) Slideshow of colour and black-and-white photos taken during production of *The Keeper of Traken*, including design department photos of the sets. Set to music from the story. Compiled by Ralph Montagu.

INFO TEXT Select **On** to view subtitles when watching the episodes that provide information and anecdotes about the development, production, broadcast and history of *The Keeper of Traken*. Written by Martin Wiggins.

DOCTOR WHO ANNUAL Accessible via a computer is a PDF file of the 1982 *Doctor Who Annual*, published by World Distributors the autumn after *The Keeper of Traken* was broadcast. With stories featuring the Doctor, Adric and K9, plus science features and puzzles.

RADIO TIMES LISTINGS Accessible via a computer is a PDF file of the four episode listings for the original BBC1 broadcast of *The Keeper of Traken* and an article about Sarah Sutton.

— Also on the disc but not listed in the menus is a PDF file of BBC Enterprises' sales document for the 1980/81 season, describing its seven stories for potential overseas broadcasters.

AUDIO OPTIONS
Select **Commentary** to play the audio commentary in place of the main soundtrack when watching the episodes. With Matthew Waterhouse (Adric) and writer Johnny Byrne on all four episodes, joined from episode two by Anthony Ainley (Tremas) and Sarah Sutton (Nyssa).

— Select **Isolated Music** to hear only Roger Limb's music when watching the episodes.

— Select **Feature Audio** to reinstate the main soundtrack when watching the episodes.

SUBTITLES
Select **On** to view subtitles for all episodes and Special Features (except commentary).

EASTER EGG
There is one hidden feature on this disc to find. *See Appendix 2 for details*

THE **KEY TO TIME**

Boxset of **THE ANDROIDS OF TARA**, **THE ARMAGEDDON FACTOR**, **THE PIRATE PLANET**, **THE POWER OF KROLL**, **THE RIBOS OPERATION** and **THE STONES OF BLOOD**

DVD RELEASE BBCDVD2335, 24 September 2007, PG
SLIPCASE Photo illustration by Clayton Hickman, silvered logo and title, light purple background
ORIGINAL RRP £69.99

— Initial release limited edition of 15,000 copies. Rereleased with same packaging but white logo and title; BBCDVD2754, £69.99, 16 November 2009

WHAT'S IN THE BOX
The sixteenth season of *Doctor Who* in 1978/79 took a new approach by linking all of its six stories under the theme of the Doctor's search for the Key to Time. At the start of *The Ribos Operation* he is contacted by the White Guardian of Time and sent to find the six segments of the Key in order for them to be combined to restore universal balance. Each of the stories then sees the Doctor locating the segments and facing obstacles to their recovery, before at the conclusion of *The Armageddon Factor* he must prevent the Key falling into the hands of the Black Guardian. While this provided the ongoing motivation for the season, the individual stories are self-contained and can be watched without knowing anything about the earlier ones other than the Doctor's quest.

● *See individual stories for full contents*

THE **KEYS OF MARINUS**

STORY No.5   SEASON No.1:5

One disc with six episodes (147½ mins) and 19½ minutes of extras, plus commentary track, production subtitles and PDF items
Audio navigation of disc contents available by pressing Enter after the Doctor Who *DVDs promo*

TARDIS TEAM First Doctor, Barbara, Ian, Susan
TIME AND PLACE Various areas on the planet Marinus
ADVERSARIES Rubber-clad Voord; Morpho Brains; devious trapper Vasor
FIRST ON TV 11 April–16 May 1964
DVD RELEASE BBCDVD2616, 21 September 2009, PG (episodes U)
COVER Photo illustration by Clayton Hickman, pale blue strip

ORIGINAL RRP £19.56

STORY TEASER

On the planet Marinus, the Conscience Machine was built to keep the population at peace. But to prevent the Voord leader Yartek from using it to control everyone, it was disabled and its activating keys hidden while the machine was made safe from misuse. Now its keeper, Arbitan, is ready to reactivate it but everyone he has sent to recover the keys has not returned. When the TARDIS arrives, he coerces the Doctor and friends into a dangerous quest across the planet to find the keys before the Voord attack again.

CONNECTIONS

The Keys of Marinus is one of only two *Doctor Who* stories written by Terry Nation that don't feature his most famous creation the Daleks, the other being 1975's *The Android Invasion*. It did, however, establish a pattern he would use in later Dalek stories *The Chase* (1965) and *The Daleks' Master Plan* (1965/66) of having the action move to a new location each episode. Sending the Doctor on a quest to collect a number of artefacts was an idea used again for the sixteenth season in 1978/79, in which each story saw him seeking a segment of the Key to Time, and for the 2007 Tenth Doctor animated adventure *The Infinite Quest*. The travel dials worn on the wrist are an early television use of teleportation and prefigure the time ring Nation has a Time Lord give the Doctor in *Genesis of the Daleks* (1975) and the teleport bracelets featured in his late-70s science fiction series *Blake's 7*. Like the Morpho Brains, renegade Time Lord Morbius ends up as a bodiless brain in a jar in *The Brain of Morbius* (1976), as does Lady Cassandra after a few too many nips and tucks, as seen in *The End of the World* (2005) and *New Earth* (2006). The scene of the knights being freed from a block of ice is the earliest *Doctor Who* memory of Peter Davison, who had recently turned thirteen when it was shown on television. Edmund Warwick (Darrius) also plays the robot duplicate of the Doctor in *The Chase*, and Francis de Wolff (Vasor) is Agamemnon in *The Myth Makers* (1966). Martin Cort, seen here as Aydan, returns as Locke in *The Seeds of Death* (1969), Fiona Walker (Kala) is Lady Peinforte in *Silver Nemesis* (1988), Donald Pickering (Eyesen) plays Captain Blade in *The Faceless Ones* (1967) and Beyus in *Time and the Rani* (1987), while Stephen Dartnell (Yartek) can be seen two stories later as John in *The Sensorites* (1964).

WORTH WATCHING

With the success of the Daleks propelling *Doctor Who* into the limelight, Terry Nation was quickly approached to provide a second script for the still fledgling series, especially as he had proven himself a quick writer and the abandonment of another story meant a replacement was needed fast. To this end he devised a series of one-episode adventures that were easier to write than a longer storyline. While this left Raymond Cusick with less time to produce more sets, the results demonstrate what an inventive designer he was.

THE EPISODES

All six episodes are restored from 16mm film copies of the original black-and-white video recordings, recovered from BBC Enterprises in 1978. During restoration several short gaps were discovered in the archived films of episodes two and four, totalling seventeen seconds, and these have been filled with re-edited footage and audio recordings of the original soundtrack to make the story complete for the first time since its original broadcast. The episodes' mono soundtracks are remastered and the VidFIRE process is applied to studio-recorded shots to recapture the smoother motion of video. The title sequences are replaced by a modern transfer of the best surviving copy of the original 35mm film with end credits remade to match the originals.

SPECIAL FEATURES

THE SETS OF MARINUS (9m25s) Raymond Cusick talks about designing the sets, props and models for *The Keys of Marinus* under tougher than usual conditions, as a new setting was required for each episode, and his ingenious ways of saving money.

PHOTO GALLERY (7m25s) Slideshow of colour and black-and-white photos taken during production of *The Keys of Marinus*, including prop design drawings and contemporary publicity photos of Carole Ann Ford, plus shots of the commentary participants. Set to sound effects from the story. Compiled by Ralph Montagu.

AUDIO OPTIONS Select **Commentary** to play the audio commentary in place of the main soundtrack when watching the episodes. This is moderated by writer and journalist Clayton Hickman, talking with Carole Ann Ford (Susan), William Russell (Ian), director John Gorrie and designer Raymond Cusick on all six episodes.

— Select **Feature Audio** to reinstate the main soundtrack when watching the episodes.

INFO TEXT Select **On** to view subtitles when watching the episodes that provide information and anecdotes about the development, production, broadcast and history of *The Keys of Marinus*. Written by Richard Molesworth.

PDF MATERIALS Accessible via a computer are the six episode listings from *Radio Times* for the original BBC1 broadcast of *The Keys of Marinus* and an article introducing the story.

— Packaging and the full set of fifty sweet cigarette cards telling a story in pictures and text of 'Dr Who' versus the Daleks and Voord from Cadet Sweets' 1964 *Doctor Who* promotion.

COMING SOON (1m21s) Trailer for the DVD releases of *Frontier in Space* and *Planet of the Daleks* in the Dalek War boxset.

SUBTITLES
Select **On** to view subtitles for all episodes and Special Features (except commentary).

EASTER EGG
There is one hidden feature on this disc to find. *See Appendix 2 for details*

RELATED EXTRAS
Coming Soon trailer — The Twin Dilemma

KINDA

STORY No.118   SEASON No.19:3

Released with **SNAKEDANCE** in the **MARA TALES** boxset
One disc with four episodes (99 mins) and 84½ minutes of extras, plus optional CGI effect, commentary and music-only tracks, production subtitles and PDF items
Audio navigation of disc contents available by pressing Enter after the BBC ident

TARDIS TEAM Fifth Doctor, Adric, Nyssa, Tegan
TIME AND PLACE Planet Deva Loka
ADVERSARIES The Mara, a malevolent entity of the mind (1st appearance);
Hindle, a psychotic human
FIRST ON TV 1–9 February 1982
DVD RELEASE BBCDVD2871A, 7 March 2011, PG (episodes U)
COVER Photo illustration by Clayton Hickman, green strip; version with older BBC logo on reverse
ORIGINAL RRP £29.99 (boxset)

STORY TEASER
The members of a human expedition to Deva Loka are disappearing one by one, yet the only other life on this paradise planet is the peaceful Kinda tribe. Those who are left are becoming increasingly paranoid and are immediately suspicious of the Doctor and his friends when they arrive hoping to find some peace and quiet. When Tegan falls asleep beneath the windchimes in the Place of Dreaming she awakens the Mara, a malevolent force banished by the Kinda but which now uses Tegan to regain its physical form.

CONNECTIONS
The Buddhist themes behind much of *Kinda* are also an influence on this story's sequel, *Snakedance* (1983), and *Planet of the Spiders* (1974), which uses spiders rather than a snake to represent the darker aspects of the human mind. A human expedition encountering a telepathic race and being driven out of their minds forms the backstory to *The Sensorites* (1964), while other missions that find more than they bargained for and are tormented by it feature in *Planet of Evil* (1975) and *The Impossible Planet/The Satan Pit* (2006). Christopher Bailey also wrote *Snakedance*, while Peter Grimwade directed *Full Circle* (1980), *Logopolis* (1981) and *Earthshock* (1982).

Christopher Bailey's script for *Kinda* is arguably one of the most complex and adult in the series' history. While the themes have their roots in Buddhism, much of the on-screen iconography is Christian, creating a confusing yet intriguing mix of ideologies that's perhaps belied somewhat by the limitations of the production. And yet the scenes in Tegan's mind as she is tempted by the Mara are truly disturbing, and Simon Rouse's portrayal of Hindle's descent into madness is both convincing and terrifying.

THE EPISODES

All four episodes are restored from digital duplicates of the original two-inch colour videotape recordings used for broadcast and their mono soundtracks remastered. The title sequences are replaced by a modern transfer of the original 35mm film with credits remade to match the originals.

SPECIAL FEATURES

DREAM TIME (34m7s) The making of *Kinda*, including the themes and Buddhist influences in the script and its passage through three script editors; creating a jungle and the colonisers' dome in the studio; portraying the Kinda; the guest cast; playing Tegan's possession; the director's approach; and opinions of the giant snake. With contributions from script editors Christopher H Bidmead, Antony Root and Eric Saward, writer Christopher Bailey, director Peter Grimwade (interviewed in 1987), designer Malcolm Thornton, actors Janet Fielding, Nerys Hughes, Adrian Mills and Simon Rouse, and New Series writer Robert Shearman. Produced by Ed Stradling.

PETER GRIMWADE – DIRECTING WITH ATTITUDE (23m) Mark Strickson presents a profile of writer and director Peter Grimwade, who died in 1990, from his beginnings in television drama writing for *Z Cars* and as a production assistant and manager on programmes including *Doctor Who* in the 1970s, to moving into directing the show until his falling out with producer John Nathan-Turner when his next assignment was delayed by strike action. Subsequently he wrote three Fifth Doctor serials, which he novelised for Target, as well as writing original books. With contributions from Grimwade himself (interviewed in 1987), script editor Eric Saward, script consultant Ian Levine, writer Christopher Bailey, production assistant Margot Hayhoe, production secretary Jane Judge, designer Malcolm Thornton, actors Janet Fielding and Nerys Hughes, and Target Books editor Nigel Robinson. Produced by Keith Barnfather.

DELETED AND EXTENDED SCENES (14m38s) A selection of scenes from episodes one and two not used in the final programme, taken from a VHS copy of earlier edits with as-recorded sound and on-screen time-code.

CGI EFFECTS Select **CGI Effects On** to view a computer-generated version of the giant snake in place of the original visual effect when watching episode four.

CGI EFFECTS COMPARISON (1m37s) The climactic scene of the giant snake with the original and new CGI versions presented side by side.

NEXT

TRAILS AND CONTINUITY (4m16s) Continuity announcements from the original BBC1 broadcasts of all four episodes of *Kinda*, with a preview of episode four from earlier in the evening and plugs for the *Doctor Who* display at Madame Tussauds and for the following story, *The Visitation*. Includes the BBC1 evening schedules for Mondays 1 and 8 and Tuesday 9 February 1982.

PHOTO GALLERY (4m45s) Slideshow of colour and black-and-white photos taken during production of *Kinda*, including design department photos of the sets. Set to music and sound effects from the story. Compiled by Paul Shields.

AUDIO OPTIONS Select **Commentary** to play the audio commentary in place of the main soundtrack when watching the episodes. With Peter Davison, Janet Fielding (Tegan), Matthew Waterhouse (Adric) and Nerys Hughes (Todd) on all four episodes.

— Select **Isolated Score** to hear only Peter Howell's music when watching the episodes.

— Select **Feature Audio** to reinstate the main soundtrack when watching the episodes.

INFO TEXT Select **On** to view subtitles when watching the episodes that provide information and anecdotes about the development, production, broadcast and history of *Kinda*. Written by Jim Smith.

PDF MATERIALS Accessible via a computer are the four episode listings from *Radio Times* for the original BBC1 broadcast of *Kinda*.

COMING SOON (2m20s) Trailer for the Special Edition DVD releases of *Carnival of Monsters*, *Resurrection of the Daleks* and *The Seeds of Death* in the Revisitations 2 boxset.

SUBTITLES
Select **On** to view subtitles for all episodes and Special Features (except commentary).

RELATED EXTRAS
Coming Soon trailer — The Ark

THE **KING'S DEMONS**

STORY No.128   SEASON No.20:6

Released with **PLANET OF FIRE** in the **KAMELION TALES** boxset
One disc with two episodes (50 mins) and 43½ minutes of extras, plus music-only and two commentary tracks, production subtitles and PDF items
Audio navigation of disc contents available by pressing Enter after the BBC ident

TARDIS TEAM Fifth Doctor, Tegan, Turlough, and introducing Kamelion
TIME AND PLACE Northern England, 1215
ADVERSARIES Third Master (4th appearance)
FIRST ON TV 15–16 March 1983
DVD RELEASE BBCDVD2738(A), 14 June 2010, U (boxset PG)
COVER Photo illustration by Clayton Hickman, pale blue strip; version with older BBC logo on reverse

ORIGINAL RRP £29.99 (boxset)

STORY TEASER
The TARDIS arrives at the castle of Ranulf Fitzwilliam, where King John and his French champion are in residence to exact yet more war funds. Odd, then, that Ranulf's cousin has just returned from seeing the king in London. The Doctor discovers that neither of the royal visitors is who he seems but part of a plot to discredit the real king and destabilise the whole of British history.

CONNECTIONS
The Doctor encounters King John's elder brother, Richard I, some twenty years earlier during the Third Crusade in *The Crusade* (1965). Another instance of a renegade Time Lord attempting to disrupt the known course of English history occurs in *The Time Meddler* (1965), while a Sontaran tries to advance medieval technology in *The Time Warrior* (1973/74). The Master omce more tries to pervert Britain's past in *The Mark of the Rani* (1985). The Doctor is again knighted, this time by the genuine reigning monarch, in *Tooth and Claw* (2006). Frank Windsor (Ranulf) was the second major name from 1960s seminal police TV series *Z Cars* to appear in *Doctor Who*, following Stratford John as Monarch in *Four to Doomsday* (1982); colleagues Brian Blessed and James Ellis later appear in *The Trial of a Time Lord: Mindwarp* (1986) and *Battlefield* (1989) respectively, while Windsor returns as Inspector Mackenzie in *Ghost Light* (1989). Gerald Flood, here voicing Kamelion as well as playing King John, also voices the android for its return appearance in *Planet of Fire* (1984). A scene with Kamelion was recorded for *The Awakening* (1984) but cut before transmission; this is included on the DVD release of that story. The Doctor's only other purely robotic companion was K9, who first appeared in *The Invisible Enemy* (1977).

WORTH WATCHING
The prime motive for writing this story was a desire to use a genuine robot prop devised and created by Chris Padmore and Mike Power, and offered to the production team to promote their talents. In itself this wasn't a bad idea, and writer Terence Dudley wisely makes Kamelion central to the plot and uses the concept well. The Master is perhaps less effective, although there's fun to be had in his attempt at a French accent. There's also some good location filming at Bodiam Castle, lending the historical setting much authenticity.

Both episodes are restored from digital duplicates of the original two-inch colour videotape recordings used for broadcast and their mono soundtracks remastered. The title sequences are replaced by a modern transfer of the original 35mm film with credits remade to match the originals.

SPECIAL FEATURES

KAMELION – METAL MAN (13m54s) How a genuine computerised, mechanical robot came to be the Doctor's companion, from the initial approach to producer John Nathan-Turner by its creators, to its construction, problems with its performance, its dropped appearance in *The Awakening*, ongoing difficulties during *Planet of Fire*, and Kamelion's inevitable demise. With contributions from Kamelion co-creator Chris Padmore, script editor Eric Saward, and actors Nicola Bryant and Peter Davison. Produced by John Kelly.

MAGNA CARTA (22m26s) Medieval historians Dr Conrad Leyser of Oxford University and Dr Richard Goddard of Nottingham University discuss the society of England in the time of King John, his reputation then and subsequently, how he came into conflict with both the church and his own barons, leading to the signing of the Magna Carta to formalise the king's powers. With political advisor Michael McManus, they look at how this has influenced politics worldwide ever since. Written by David Harley, narrated by Sara Griffiths, produced by Stella Broster.

PHOTO GALLERY (5m56s) Slideshow of colour and black-and-white photos taken during production of *The King's Demons*, including design department photos of the sets. Set to music from the story. Compiled by Derek Handley.

NEXT

AUDIO OPTIONS Select **Commentary 1** to play the audio commentary in place of the main sound-track when watching the episodes. With Peter Davison, Isla Blair (Isabella) and script editor Eric Saward on both episodes.
— Select **Commentary 2** to play a commentary with director Tony Virgo on episode one only.
— Select **Isolated Score** to hear only Jonathan Gibbs' music when watching the episodes.
— Select **Feature Audio** to reinstate the main soundtrack when watching the episodes.

INFO TEXT Select **On** to view subtitles when watching the episodes that provide information and anecdotes about the development, production, broadcast and history of *The King's Demons*. Written by David Brunt.

PDF MATERIALS Accessible via a computer are the two episode listings from *Radio Times* for the original BBC1 broadcast of *The King's Demons*.

COMING SOON (1m3s) Trailer for the DVD release of *The Dominators*.

SUBTITLES

Select **On** to view subtitles for all episodes and Special Features (except commentary).

RELATED EXTRAS

Coming Soon trailer — The Creature from the Pit, Frontier in Space

THE **KROTONS**

STORY NO.47   SEASON NO.6:4

One disc with four episodes (90.5 mins) and 83½ minutes of extras, plus commentary track, production subtitles and PDF items
Audio navigation of disc contents available by pressing Enter after the BBC ident

TARDIS TEAM Second Doctor, Jamie, Zoe
TIME AND PLACE Homeworld of the Gonds
ADVERSARIES Krotons, robot-like creatures made of crystal
FIRST ON TV 28 December 1968–18 January 1969
DVD RELEASE BBCDVD3480, 2 July 2012, PG (episodes U)
COVER Photo illustration by Lee Binding (Kroton by Gavin Rymill), dark purple strip; version with older BBC logo on reverse

ORIGINAL RRP £20.42

STORY TEASER

The Gonds are held in thrall to the mysterious Krotons, relying on them for all knowledge but forced to submit their brightest students to servitude in the Dynatrope. When the Doctor discovers these victims are drained of all brain power and disposed of, he determines to help the Gonds overthrow their oppressors. Except that Zoe has demonstrated her intelligence and is summoned to the Dynatrope to join the Krotons.

CONNECTIONS

The idea of a population whose level of knowledge is limited by their unseen rulers, who feed on the people's essence, is used again in *State of Decay* (1980), while writer Robert Holmes himself reuses the idea of a small group ruled over by a robotic master in *The Trial of a Time Lord: The Mysterious Planet* (1986). The TARDIS's Hostile Action Displacement System, used here by the Doctor for the first time, is only ever used again on screen in *Cold War* (2013). This is the first *Doctor Who* story by Robert Holmes, who went on to become a prolific (and to many the best) writer for the series as well as its script editor from 1974 to 1977; similarly David Maloney, directing the second of three serials he handled in the 1968/69 season alone, worked on many of the most popular stories, including *The Deadly Assassin* (1976) and *The Talons of Weng-Chiang* (1977), also written by Holmes (*see Index v*). Philip Madoc, playing Eelek, returned later in the same season as the War Lord in *The War Games* (1969) and as Fenner in *The Power of Kroll* (1979), but his most fêted role is as crazed surgeon Mehendri Solon in *The Brain of Morbius* (1976). James Cairncross (Beta) is also Lemaitre in *The Reign of Terror* (1964).

WORTH WATCHING

The Krotons is seen as most notable among fans for being Robert Holmes' first script for *Doctor Who*, or because it was the first Second Doctor story they ever saw when it was repeated in the 1981 run *The Five Faces of Doctor Who*. There are more intrinsic delights, however, such as the deft characterisation of the three regulars and the way it mirrors contemporary social attitudes, with students rising up against an exploitative establishment (using acid). The design of the Krotons themselves is striking (at least from the waist up) while the soundscape produced by Brian Hodgson in place of conventional music still feels otherworldly.

THE EPISODES

Episode one is restored from the original 35mm black-and-white film onto which it was recorded in the studio, while episodes two, three and four are restored from 16mm film copies of the original black-and-white video recordings, the last returned to the BBC by the BFI in 1977, the two former still held by the BFI. Their mono soundtracks are remastered and the VidFIRE process is applied to studio-recorded shots to recapture the smoother motion of video. The title sequences are replaced by a modern transfer of the original 35mm film with credits remade to match the originals.

SPECIAL FEATURES

SECOND TIME AROUND (52m22s) An overview of the stories and changes during the three-year Second Doctor era of the programme, including the switchover from William Hartnell to Patrick Troughton and working out the new Doctor's look and character; the arrival of Jamie McCrimmon; the increasing focus on new monsters; grooming Peter Bryant to become producer; the junking of the original video recordings; Troughton's increasing tiredness with the production schedule; struggling to find workable scripts for the sixth season; and the game-changing elements of Troughton's epic finale *The War Games*. With contributions from script editor/producer Derrick Sherwin, script editor Terrance Dicks, writer Victor Pemberton, director Christopher Barry, companion actors Frazer Hines, Wendy Padbury, Deborah Watling and Anneke Wills, and fans Gary Russell and Robert Shearman. Narrated by Richard Heffer, produced by Ed Stradling.

DOCTOR WHO STORIES – FRAZER HINES (PART ONE) (17m27s) Recorded in 2003 for BBC2's *The Story of Doctor Who*, actor Frazer Hines recalls his experiences of playing companion Jamie McCrimmon from 1966 to 1969. *Part two is on* **The Ice Warriors**

THE DOCTOR'S STRANGE LOVE (7m17s) Writers Simon Guerrier and Joseph Lidster discuss the highs and lows of *The Krotons* from a fan's point of view. *See Index iii for further editions*

PHOTO GALLERY (5m26s) Slideshow of black-and-white photos taken during production of *The Krotons*, including design sketches for the Krotons and design department photos of the sets. Set to sound effects from the story. Compiled by Paul Shields.

NEXT

AUDIO OPTIONS Select **Commentary** to play the audio commentary in place of the main soundtrack when watching the episodes. This is moderated by actor and comedian Toby Hadoke, talking with Gilbert Wynne (Thara) [eps 1,2,4], Richard Ireson (Axus) [1,3], Philip Madoc (Eelek) [1,3,4], make-up supervisor Sylvia James [1,4], assistant floor manager David Tilley [2,3], costume designer Bobi Bartlett [2,3] and special sounds creator Brian Hodgson [2,4].

— Select **Feature Audio** to reinstate the main soundtrack when watching the episodes.

INFO TEXT Select **On** to view subtitles when watching the episodes that provide information and anecdotes about the development, production, broadcast and history of *The Krotons*. Written by Martin Wiggins.

PDF MATERIALS Accessible via a computer are the four episode listings from *Radio Times* for the original BBC1 broadcast of *The Krotons*.

COMING SOON (1m4s) Trailer for the DVD release of *The Greatest Show in the Galaxy*.

SUBTITLES

Select **On** to view subtitles for all episodes and Special Features (except commentary).

RELATED EXTRAS

Five Faces of Doctor Who Trailer — Carnival of Monsters (and Special Edition),
The Three Doctors (and Special Edition)

Coming Soon trailer — Death to the Daleks

THE **LEGACY COLLECTION**

Boxset of **SHADA** and **MORE THAN 30 YEARS IN THE TARDIS**

DVD RELEASE BBCDVD3388, 7 January 2013, PG

SLIPCASE Photo illustration by Clayton Hickman, silvered logo and title, blue background

ORIGINAL RRP £20.42

WHAT'S IN THE BOX

Shada was intended to be the final story of the 1979/80 season but was never finished owing to a strike at the BBC delaying its studio recordings, even though all the location filming had been completed. It's presented here in the form that was released on VHS in 1992 with links by Tom Baker filling in the unrecorded sections. *More Than 30 Years in the TARDIS* is the extended version of the documentary shown on BBC1 in November 1993 to celebrate the series' thirtieth anniversary, as released on VHS the following year.

● *See Appendix 1 for full contents*

THE **LEISURE HIVE**

STORY No.109   SEASON No.18:1

One disc with four episodes (87 mins) and 74½ minutes of extras, plus commentary, music-only and surround-sound tracks, and production subtitles

TARDIS TEAM Fourth Doctor, Second Romana, K9

TIME AND PLACE Desert planet Argolis

ADVERSARIES Reptilian Foamasi; Pangol, youngest of the Argolin

FIRST ON TV 30 August–20 September 1980

DVD RELEASE BBCDVD1351, 5 July 2004, PG

COVER Photo illustration by Clayton Hickman, yellow strip

ORIGINAL RRP £19.99

STORY TEASER

The Doctor wants a holiday. Romana suggests Argolis, where the Leisure Hive houses the last of the Argolin. They, like their planet, have been rendered sterile by the fallout of a nuclear war against the Foamasi and are on the verge of extinction. Tourism now funds their last hope: a human's experiment in using tachyonics to reverse time. But the youngest Argolin, Pangol, has his own plans for the technology and his people's survival.

CONNECTIONS

The idea of a species dying out as a result of nuclear war mirrors the origins of the Daleks, who were similarly confined within their city in *The Daleks* (1963/64), and the Kraals on Oseidon in *The Android Invasion* (1975), both by Terry Nation. The Doctor was again shown to age several hundred years without regenerating in *Last of the Time Lords* (2007) and *The Time of the Doctor* (2013), although it took him less time than that to next grow a beard in *Day of the Moon* (2011) and *The Wedding of River Song* (2011). This is the last story by David Fisher, who had written three previous stories — *The Stones of Blood* and *The Androids of Tara* in 1978 and *The Creature from the Pit* in 1979 — as well as the storyline on which *City of Death* (1979) was based. Laurence Payne (Morix) plays gunslinger Johnny Ringo in *The Gunfighters* (1966) and genetic scientist Dastari in *The Two Doctors* (1985), while David Allister (Stimson) returns as Bruchner in *The Trial of a Time Lord: Terror of the Vervoids* (1986).

WORTH WATCHING

This is the first story made under producer John Nathan-Turner and shows off all the changes he implemented on the programme in one fell swoop: new title graphics, theme arrangement and style of incidental music, a refined costume for the Doctor, and a stronger focus on the authenticity of the science in the story, thanks to new script editor Christopher H Bidmead. This is all tied together with panache by director Lovett Bickford, although his overspending meant this was the only *Doctor Who* serial he directed.

THE EPISODES

All four episodes are restored from digital duplicates of the original two-inch colour videotape recordings used for broadcast and their mono soundtracks remastered, with the opening location sequences newly transferred from the original 16mm colour film. The title sequences are replaced by a modern transfer of the original 35mm film with credits remade to match the originals.

SPECIAL FEATURES

A NEW BEGINNING (30m19s) How *Doctor Who*'s production was brought bang up to date in 1980 under a new producer, debuting with *The Leisure Hive*. From his desire to take things more seriously than the previous production team, to basing story ideas in genuine scientific principles; the problems with K9; reigning in some of the leading man's exuberance; updating the title sequence and theme; using the BBC Radiophonic Workshop for incidental music; redesigning the Doctor's outfit; and the input of the director. With contributions from producer John Nathan-Turner (interviewed in 1994), script editor Christopher H Bidmead, director Lovett Bickford, assistant floor manager Val McCrimmon, costume designer June Hudson, graphic designer Sid Sutton, composer Peter Howell, and actors Tom Baker and John Leeson. Produced by Ed Stradling.

FROM AVALON TO ARGOLIS (14m20s) Writer David Fisher and script editor Christopher H Bidmead talk about their collaboration over the script for *The Leisure Hive*, including handling the inputs of the executive producer, producer and director. With additional comments from producer John Nathan-Turner (interviewed in 1994). Produced by Richard Molesworth.

INFORMATION TEXT Select **On** to view subtitles when watching the episodes that provide information and anecdotes about the development, production, broadcast and history of *The Leisure Hive*. Written by Richard Molesworth.

SYNTHESIZING STARFIELDS (9m15s) Graphic designer Sid Sutton talks about the techniques he used when redesigning the title sequence, with film footage of the separate elements; while composer Peter Howell discusses his approach to rearranging the theme music, with extracts from BBC Schools programme *The Music Arcade* (shown on Tuesday 2 February 1982) demonstrating the process. Produced by Ed Stradling.

LEISURE WEAR (6m50s) Costume designer June Hudson talks about her work on *The Leisure Hive*, illustrated with many of her original design sketches.

BLUE PETER (3m58s) Extract from the Thursday 3 April 1980 edition of the BBC1 children's magazine programme in which Tina Heath visits the *Doctor Who* exhibition at Longleat House in Wiltshire, and chats with new producer John Nathan-Turner.

PICTURE GALLERY (6m1s) Slideshow of colour photos taken during production of *The Leisure Hive*, set to sound effects from the story. Compiled by Ralph Montagu.

AUDIO OPTIONS

Select **Commentary On** to play the audio commentary in place of the main soundtrack when watching the episodes. With Lalla Ward (Romana), script editor Christopher H Bidmead and director Lovett Bickford on all four episodes.

— Select **Isolated Music On** to hear only Peter Howell's music when watching the episodes.

— Select **Dolby Digital 5.1 Surround Audio** to hear the surround soundtrack when watching the episodes, newly remixed for this release.

SUBTITLES

Select **On** to view subtitles for all episodes and Special Features, or for the commentary.

EASTER EGG

There is one hidden feature on this disc to find. *See Appendix 2 for details*

LOGOPOLIS

STORY No.115   SEASON No.18:7

Released with **CASTROVALVA** and **THE KEEPER OF TRAKEN** in the **NEW BEGINNINGS** boxset
One disc with four episodes (98½ mins) and 80 minutes of extras, plus commentary and music-only tracks, production subtitles and PDF items

TARDIS TEAM   Fourth Doctor, Adric, re-meeting Nyssa, and introducing Tegan Jovanka
TIME AND PLACE   Contemporary England and planet Logopolis
ADVERSARIES   Third Master (1st appearance)
FIRST ON TV   28 February–21 March 1981
DVD RELEASE   BBCDVD1331(B), 29 January 2007, 12 (episodes U)
COVER   Photo illustration by Clayton Hickman, light purple strip
ORIGINAL RRP   £29.99 (boxset)
— Episodes released in the Regeneration box; BBCDVD3801, £61.27, 24 June 2013

STORY TEASER

The Doctor is horrified to discover the Master has renewed himself and has invaded the TARDIS itself. But an encounter with a mysterious white figure leads him to the planet Logopolis where a shocking discovery sets the stage for a battle that only one of the two Time Lords can survive.

CONNECTIONS

This is the middle section of a trilogy formed by the three stories in this boxset, in which the Master returns and gains a new body before causing the Doctor himself to regenerate. As such it's the first full appearance of Anthony Ainley as the third on-screen incarnation of the Master (after a brief glimpse at the end of *The Keeper of Traken*), who remained through to the end of the Classic Series and his final appearance in *Survival* (1989). It's revealed here that the Logopolitans created the CVEs, one of which the TARDIS falls through in *Full Circle* (1980) and escapes via in *Warriors' Gate* (1981). The Doctor again tries to repair the TARDIS's chameleon circuit, with limited success, in *Attack of the Cybermen* (1985). Here we see a new area of the TARDIS, its cloisters, following the addition of Romana's bedroom in *Full Circle* and the grand tour in *The Invasion of Time* (1978), not repeated until 2013's *Journey to the Centre of the TARDIS*. Christopher Bidmead rounded off his year of script editing the series by writing *Logopolis* and ended up writing its follow-up *Castrovalva* to open the next season, as well as *Frontios* (1984). Peter Grimwade directed *Full Circle* earlier in the season and returned the following year to helm *Kinda* and *Earthshock*. Tom Georgeson, playing the detective who tries to arrest the Doctor, had earlier appeared with Tom Baker in *Genesis of the Daleks* (1975). While Dolores Whiteman never returns as Tegan's aunt Vanessa, she was remembered by her niece, particularly in *Enlightenment* (1983) and *Resurrection of the Daleks* (1984).

WORTH WATCHING

After seven years as the Doctor, the longest of any actor to play the part, Tom Baker's departure needed to be marked with a momentous adventure and saving the entire universe fits the bill. Its overall tone, however, is sombre as befits the death of unarguably the most popular of the Classic Doctors, while the story itself ties up the strands of the 1980/81 season and brings its more scientific approach to storytelling to a climax.

THE EPISODES

All four episodes are restored from digital duplicates of the original two-inch colour videotape recordings used for broadcast and their mono soundtracks remastered. The title sequences are replaced by a modern transfer of the original 35mm film with credits remade to match the originals.

SPECIAL FEATURES

A NEW BODY AT LAST (50m23s) How the production team handled the changeover of Doctors after seven years of Tom Baker in the role, including Baker's decision finally to move on and the impact this had on his work and his personal relationship with Lalla Ward; the selection of Peter Davison as his successor; the inspirations behind the script for *Logopolis* and the origins of the Watcher; recording the regeneration (with footage from the full studio recording); and Davison's settling into the role in his first serial to be made, *Four to Doomsday*, before recording his actual debut story. With contributions from script editor and writer Christopher H Bidmead, directors John Black and Peter Moffatt, and actors Tom Baker, Peter Davison, Adrian Gibbs, Sarah Sutton and Matthew Waterhouse. Narrated by Denis Lawson, produced by Paul Vanezis.

NATIONWIDE – TOM BAKER (4m32s) Extract from the Friday 24 October 1980 edition of the BBC1 news magazine programme in which Sue Lawley announces Tom Baker's decision to relinquish the role of the Doctor and Sue Cook interviews him in the studio.

NATIONWIDE – PETER DAVISON (3m42s) Extract from the Wednesday 5 November 1980 edition of the BBC1 news magazine programme in which Sue Lawley announces the casting of Peter Davison (with much the same rundown of the Doctors to date as in the above extract), and interviews him in the studio. Includes a clip from *All Creatures Great and Small*.

PEBBLE MILL AT ONE PETER DAVISON (12m01s) Extract from the Wednesday 3 December 1980 edition of the BBC1 lunchtime magazine programme in which Donny MacLeod interviews Peter Davison and they look at viewers' costume suggestions for the Fifth Doctor, while studio guests give their ideas about his portrayal. Includes a clip from *Sink or Swim*.

NEWS ITEMS (1m57s) Three BBC News items in which Kenneth Kendall reports the wedding of Tom Baker to Lalla Ward (Saturday 13 December 1980); Jan Leeming announces the departure of Tom Baker, with a clip from the end of *Meglos* (Friday 24 October 1980); and Kendall reveals the casting of Peter Davison (Wednesday 5 November 1980).

NEXT

CONTINUITIES (2m23s) Continuity announcements from the original BBC1 broadcasts of episodes one, two and four of *Logopolis* (including full end credits for episode four with adapted title sequence), with plugs for the *Doctor Who* display at Madame Tussauds. Plus an announcement for the repeat of *Logopolis* under the *Five Faces of Doctor Who* banner in November 1981.

PHOTO GALLERY (5m07s) Slideshow of colour and black-and-white photos from *Logopolis*, including design department photos of the studio and model sets. Set to music from the story. Compiled by Ralph Montagu.

INFO TEXT Select **On** to view subtitles when watching the episodes that provide information and anecdotes about the development, production, broadcast and history of *Logopolis*. Written by Martin Wiggins.

DOCTOR WHO ANNUAL Accessible via a computer is a PDF file of the 1982 *Doctor Who Annual*, published by World Distributors the autumn after *Logopolis* was broadcast. With stories featuring the Doctor, Adric and K9, plus science features and puzzles.

RADIO TIMES LISTINGS Accessible via a computer is a PDF file of the four episode listings for the original BBC1 broadcast of *Logopolis*, and letters about the 1981 stories.

— Also on the disc but not listed in the menus is a PDF file of BBC Enterprises' sales document for the 1980/81 season, describing its seven stories for potential overseas broadcasters.

AUDIO OPTIONS
Select **Commentary** to play the audio commentary in place of the main soundtrack when watching the episodes. With Tom Baker, Janet Fielding (Tegan) and writer/script editor Christopher H Bidmead on all four episodes.

— Select **Isolated Music** to hear only Paddy Kingsland's music when watching the episodes.

— Select **Feature Audio** to reinstate the main soundtrack when watching the episodes.

SUBTITLES
Select **On** to view subtitles for all episodes and Special Features (except commentary).

RELATED EXTRAS
Five Faces of Doctor Who trailer — Carnival of Monsters (and Special Edition),
The Three Doctors (and Special Edition)
Peter Grimwade - Directing with Attitude — Kinda

LOST IN TIME

Collection of surviving episodes and clips from incomplete stories
Three discs with 18 full episodes (435 mins), four audio-only episodes (97½ mins) and 99½ minutes of extras, plus commentary tracks for six episodes

TARDIS TEAMS First Doctor, Barbara, Ian Susan, Steven, Katarina, Sara, Dodo; Second Doctor, Ben, Jamie, Polly, Victoria, Zoe

TIMES AND PLACES 12th Century Palestine; jungle planet Kembel, 51st Century Earth, swamp planet Mira, ancient Egypt; Toymaker's domain; contemporary Atlantis; the Moon; Gatwick airport; contemporary London, 19th Century mansion; 1930s Himalayan monastery; future Earth; London Underground; space station; space beacons and ships

ADVERSARIES Saracen emir El Akir; Daleks, ruler of solar system Mavic Chen, renegade Time Lord the Monk; the Toymaker; Professor Zaroff; Cybermen; body-snatching Chameleons; Daleks, Victorian magnate Theodore Maxtible; Yeti robots powered by the Great Intelligence; ruthless magnate (and the Doctor's double) Salamander; space pirate Caven

DVD RELEASE BBCDVD1353, 1 November 2004, PG

COVER Photo illustration by Clayton Hickman, light green strip

— Original release with cover sticker reading 'Over 7 Hours of Rare 1960s Episodes and Footage'

ORIGINAL RRP £29.99

WHAT'S IN THE BOX
During the 1960s and 70s it was standard practice at the BBC to reuse the expensive videotapes onto which programmes were recorded, thereby wiping what had previously been on them, including episodes of *Doctor Who*. In the days when repeats were unpopular and there was no home video market, it was assumed these programmes would never be needed again. Copies on film were often made, however, for sale to overseas broadcasters. While these lasted longer than the original videotapes, they too were eventually junked when their sales potential was deemed to have run out. By the late-70s attitudes were changing and the disposal of both formats was stopped, but that still left many programmes, particularly from the days of black-and-white television, missing from the newly formed archive. Since then efforts have been made to recover these shows (not just *Doctor Who*) from broadcasters around the world that had bought them on film and not yet returned or destroyed them. Most of the existing 1960s *Doctor Who* serials were retrieved this way, but sometimes all that was found were odd episodes rather than complete stories.

This set collects the surviving episodes that existed at the time of its release from otherwise incomplete stories. This was shortly after *The Daleks' Master Plan* episode two had been returned in January 2004, but since then further episodes have been found. In July 2011 *Galaxy 4* episode three was returned to the archive (subsequently released on The Aztecs Special Edition), followed two months later by *The Underwater Menace* episode two (expected to be released later in 2014). In 2013 *The Enemy of the World* was returned complete, along with all bar episode three of *The Web of Fear*, and these serials have both subsequently had individual DVD releases after initially being made available to download from iTunes.

Also on this set are numerous short clips from episodes that are missing in full. These are mainly from Australia and New Zealand, where the local television censors required cuts to be made in order for the programme to be shown to a family audience. Ironically, while the episodes themselves were subsequently junked, these censored segments survived and many are now the only visual material known to exist from some stories. Further short clips were filmed with an 8mm home-movie camera pointing at a television screen. While these are of poor quality, they again provide the only moving footage of some episodes.

WORTH WATCHING

These 'orphaned' episodes offer a different viewing experience compared to complete stories. For some people it's frustrating as they want to watch the rest of the story but can't, while for others it's thrilling to see at least something of these otherwise missing stories, many of which are considered classics of *Doctor Who*. It's undeniably better that we have them than not as they provide a valuable glimpse of what the whole serials might be like — although equally they can be deceptive. Now that *The Enemy of the World* has been recovered in its entirety, for example, the general opinion of the story is changing from that formed on the basis of the previously existing episode three alone. Either way, these episodes are a reminder of what's still missing, but that the search goes on. Even the short clips can be the sole indicator of what appeared on screen, and some behind-the-scenes footage represents the only colour record of these episodes.

DISC ONE

THE EPISODES ° OPTIONAL COMMENTARY

On this disc are six First Doctor episodes, plus the soundtracks for the two still-missing episodes of *The Crusade*. When selecting **Play All**, the introduction and links recorded by William Russell in character as Ian Chesterton for the July 1999 VHS release of *The Crusade* play before and after episodes one and three of that serial, and the audio-only episodes play in sequence.

THE CRUSADE episode one, 'The Lion', was restored for VHS release in July 1999 from a damaged 16mm film copy of the original black-and-white video recording, returned from Australia by film collector Bruce Grenville in January 1999, and its mono soundtrack remastered. Further clean-up was done for this release and the title sequence replaced by a modern transfer of the best surviving copy of the original 35mm film, but end credits are not remade and the VidFIRE motion-smoothing process is not applied owing to lower than optimum picture quality.

°**THE CRUSADE episode three**, 'The Wheel of Fortune', is restored from a 16mm film copy of the original black-and-white video recording that survived in the archive. Its mono soundtrack is remastered and the VidFIRE process is applied to studio-recorded shots to recapture the smoother motion of video. The title sequence is replaced by a modern transfer of the best surviving copy of original 35mm film but end credits are not remade.

The soundtracks for **THE CRUSADE episodes two and four**, 'The Knight of Jaffa' and 'The War-lords', are remastered from recordings made on audio tape by David Holman when the episodes were originally broadcast.

°**THE DALEKS' MASTER PLAN episode two**, 'Day of Armageddon', is restored from a 16mm film copy of the original black-and-white video recording, returned by Francis Watson in January 2004. Its mono soundtrack is remastered and the VidFIRE process is applied to studio-recorded shots to recapture the smoother motion of video. Film sequences are newly transferred from the original 35mm black-and-white footage. The title sequence is replaced by a modern transfer of the best surviving copy of original 35mm film and with credits remade to match the originals.

THE DALEKS' MASTER PLAN episodes five and ten, 'Counter Plot' and 'Escape Switch', are restored from 16mm film copies of the original black-and-white video recordings, recovered in October 1983 (found in a church basement). Their mono soundtracks are remastered and the VidFIRE process is applied to studio-recorded shots to recapture the smoother motion of video. The title sequences are replaced by a modern transfer of the best surviving copy of original 35mm film with end credits remade to match the originals.

THE CELESTIAL TOYMAKER episode one, 'The Final Test', is restored from a 16mm film copy of the original black-and-white video recording, returned by broadcaster ABC in Australia in February 1984. Its mono soundtrack is remastered and the VidFIRE process is applied to studio-recorded shots to recapture the smoother motion of video. The title sequence is replaced by a modern transfer of the best surviving copy of original 35mm film with end credits remade to match the originals. The missing 'Next episode' caption has also been recreated.

SPECIAL FEATURES

THE DALEKS' MASTER PLAN SURVIVING CLIPS (7m12s) Three clips from episode one and four from episode two, newly transferred from the original 35mm black-and-white film footage; a clip from episode three, taken from the Monday 25 October 1971 edition of *Blue Peter* in which it featured (*full extract is on* Day of the Daleks); and a clip from episode four, taken from the Monday 5 November 1973 edition of *Blue Peter* in which it featured (*full extract is on* The Tenth Planet *and* The Three Doctors Special Edition).

8MM OFF-SCREEN FOOTAGE FROM THE HARTNELL ERA (6m10s) Short clips from *The Reign of Terror* episodes four and five, *Galaxy 4* episode one, *The Myth Makers* episodes one, two and four, *The Savages* episodes three and four and *The Tenth Planet* episode four. These were recorded with an 8mm film camera aimed at the television screen by a viewer in Australia when the series was broadcast there in the 1960s. They are all silent but have been matched as closely as possible to soundtrack recordings made on audio tape when the episodes were originally broadcast.

THE TENTH PLANET SURVIVING CLIPS (1m23s) Some of the 8mm film clips as above leading up to the regeneration, which is taken from the 5 November 1973 edition of *Blue Peter* in which it featured (*full extract is on* The Tenth Planet *and* The Three Doctors Special Edition).

THE SMUGGLERS (3m58s) Select **Surviving Clips** to watch five clips from episodes one, three and four. These were sections cut from the 16mm black-and-white film copies of the episodes shown by Australian broadcaster ABC at the request of the Australian Film Censorship Board, but stored in the Board's archive long after the episodes themselves had been destroyed. They were discovered by Damian Shanahan in October 1996.

— Select **Location Film** to watch silent 16mm colour film footage shot by Donald Trewern, the owner of Trethewey Farm in Cornwall, during location filming there for *The Smugglers* on Wednesday 22 June 1966.

— Select **Play All** to watch both sets of footage.

AUDIOBOOK TRAILER (4m17s) An audio-only promotion for BBC Audio's series of missing story soundtrack releases.

SUBTITLES

Select **On** to view subtitles for all episodes and Special Features, or for the two commentaries.

COMMENTARY

Select **Commentary On** to play audio commentaries in place of the main soundtrack when watching selected episodes. On *The Crusade* episode three, 'The Wheel of Fortune', author and journalist Gary Russell talks with actor Julian Glover (King Richard). On *The Daleks' Master Plan* episode two, 'Day of Armageddon', are actors Peter Purves (Steven) and Kevin Stoney (Mavic Chen), and designer Raymond Cusick.

DISC TWO

THE EPISODES ° OPTIONAL COMMENTARY

On this disc are six Second Doctor episodes from his first year, plus the soundtracks for the two still-missing episodes of *The Moonbase*. When selecting **Play All**, these audio-only episodes also play in sequence.

THE UNDERWATER MENACE episode three is restored from a 16mm film copy of the original black-and-white video recording that survived in the archive. Its mono soundtrack is remastered and the VidFIRE process is applied to studio-recorded shots to recapture the smoother motion of video. The title sequence is replaced by a modern transfer of the best surviving copy of original 35mm film and with credits partly remade to match the originals.

The soundtracks for **THE MOONBASE episodes one and three** are remastered from recordings made on audio tape by Graham Strong when the episodes were originally broadcast.

THE MOONBASE episode two is restored from a 16mm film copy of the original black-and-white video recording that survived in the archive. Its mono soundtrack is remastered and the VidFIRE process is applied to studio-recorded shots to recapture the smoother motion of video. The title sequence is replaced by a modern transfer of the best surviving copy of original 35mm film with credits partly remade to match the originals.

THE MOONBASE episode four is restored from a 16mm film copy of the original black-and-white video recording, returned by Roger Stevens in 1981; this is missing the 'Next episode' caption, which is taken from a lower-quality 16mm film copy. Its mono soundtrack is remastered and the VidFIRE process is applied to studio-recorded shots to recapture the smoother motion of video. The title sequence is replaced by a modern transfer of the best surviving copy of original 35mm film with credits remade to match the originals.

THE FACELESS ONES episode one was restored for VHS release in October 2003 from a 16mm film copy of the original black-and-white video recording that survived in the archive, its mono soundtrack remastered and the VidFIRE process applied to studio-recorded shots to recapture the smoother motion of video. The title sequence is replaced by a modern transfer of the original 35mm film with end credits remade to match the originals.

THE FACELESS ONES episode three was restored for VHS release in October 2003 from an incomplete 16mm film copy of the original black-and-white video recording, returned by Gordon Hendry in April 1987. Missing sections were filled with edited shots from elsewhere in the episode and a recording of the soundtrack made on audio tape when the episode was originally broadcast. Its mono soundtrack is remastered and the VidFIRE process is applied to studio-recorded shots to recapture the smoother motion of video. The title sequence is replaced by a modern transfer of the original 35mm film with end credits remade to match the originals.

°**THE EVIL OF THE DALEKS episode two** is restored from a 16mm film copy of the original black-and-white video recording, returned by Gordon Hendry in May 1987. Its mono soundtrack is remastered and the VidFIRE process is applied to studio-recorded shots to recapture the smoother motion of video. The title sequence is replaced by a modern transfer of the original 35mm film with end credits remade to match the originals.

SPECIAL FEATURES

THE MACRA TERROR SURVIVING FOOTAGE (54s) Five clips from episodes two and three. These are sections cut from the 16mm black-and-white film copies of the episodes shown by Australian broadcaster ABC at the request of the Australian Film Censorship Board, but stored in the Board's archive long after the episodes themselves had been destroyed. They were discovered by Damian Shanahan in October 1996.

THE LAST DALEK – 8MM FILM (9m34s) Silent 8mm black-and-white footage shot by designer Tony Cornell during filming for *The Evil of the Daleks* episode seven at Ealing Studios on 16/17 May 1967, showing models being set up with explosive charges for their destruction in the final battle of the story and effects shots of Daleks in the Emperor's chamber. With a commentary by the serial's visual effects designers Peter Day and Michaeljohn Harris, who appear in the footage. *Also on* Resurrection of the Daleks Special Edition *and* The Seeds of Death

THE UNDERWATER MENACE SURVIVING FOOTAGE (1m23s) Six clips from episodes one, two and four. These are sections cut from the 16mm black-and-white film copies of the episodes shown by Australian broadcaster ABC at the request of the Australian Film Censorship Board, but stored in the Board's archive long after the episodes themselves had been destroyed. They were discovered by Damian Shanahan in October 1996.

THE HIGHLANDERS SURVIVING FOOTAGE (51s) An unused section from the location film footage showing production assistant Fiona Cumming cueing a shot, plus three clips from episode one. The latter are sections cut from the 16mm black-and-white film copies of the episode shown by Australian broadcaster ABC at the request of the Australian Film Censorship Board, but stored in the Board's archive long after the episode itself had been destroyed. They were discovered by Damian Shanahan in October 1996.

TROUGHTON ERA 8MM OFF–SCREEN FOOTAGE (3m20s) Short clips from *The Power of the Daleks* episodes one and two, *The Macra Terror* episode three and *The Faceless Ones* episode two. These were recorded with an 8mm film camera aimed at the television screen by a viewer in Australia when the series was broadcast there in the 1960s. They are all silent but have been matched as closely as possible to soundtrack recordings made on audio tape when the episodes were broadcast.

THE POWER OF THE DALEKS (2m47s) Select **Trailer** to watch an incomplete preview of episode one (including contemporary BBC1 globe ident) shown on Friday 4 November 1966, taken from the 16mm black-and-white film recording of another programme, which was discovered by archivist Andrew Martin in October 2003.

— Select **Surviving Footage** to watch six clips from episodes four, five and six. The first four are taken from a 16mm black-and-white film recording of the programme *Perspectives: C for Computer*, shown by ABC in Australia on Wednesday 29 May 1974 and recovered by Steve Roberts in August 1995. The fifth, longest clip is an extract from a 16mm black-and-white film recording of the Saturday 27 January 1968 edition of BBC2 documentary series *Whicker's World*, but was originally transferred for that programme from the 35mm film footage that still existed at the time. The last clip is taken from a 16mm black-and-white film recording of children's science programme *Tom Tom* shown on BBC1 on Tuesday 26 November 1968, discovered by Kevin Davies and Andrew Pixley in 1993.

— Select **Play All** to watch both sets of footage.

SUBTITLES

Select **On** to view subtitles for all episodes and Special Features, or for the commentary.

COMMENTARY

Select **Commentary On** to play the audio commentary in place of the main soundtrack when watching *The Evil of the Daleks* episode two, in which author and journalist Gary Russell talks with companion actress Deborah Watling (Victoria).

DISC THREE

THE EPISODES ° OPTIONAL COMMENTARY

On this disc are six Second Doctor episodes from his second and third years.

°**THE ABOMINABLE SNOWMEN episode two** is restored from a 16mm film copy of the original black-and-white video recording, returned by Roger Stevens in February 1982, with location sequences newly transferred from the original 16mm black-and-white film. The episode's mono soundtrack is remastered (a missing line of dialogue is recreated using sound clips from other episodes) and the VidFIRE process is applied to studio-recorded shots to recapture the smoother motion of video. The title sequence is replaced by a modern transfer of the original 35mm film and end credits remade to match the originals.

THE ENEMY OF THE WORLD episode three is restored from a 16mm film copy of the original black-and-white video recording that survived in the archive. Its mono soundtrack is remastered and the VidFIRE process is applied to studio-recorded shots to recapture the smoother motion of video. The title sequence is replaced by a modern transfer of the original 35mm film with end credits remade to match the originals.

°**THE WEB OF FEAR episode one** was restored for VHS release in October 2003 from a 16mm film copy of the original black-and-white video recording, recovered from BBC Enterprises in 1978. Its mono soundtrack is remastered and the VidFIRE process is applied to studio-recorded shots to recapture the smoother motion of video. The title sequence is replaced by a modern transfer of the original 35mm film while the end titles background footage of pulsing web is newly transferred from a 16mm black-and-white film copy with credits remade to match the originals.

THE WHEEL IN SPACE episode three is restored from a 16mm film copy of the original black-and-white video recording, returned by David Stead in April 1984. Its mono soundtrack is remastered and the VidFIRE process is applied to studio-recorded shots to recapture the smoother motion of video. The title sequence is replaced by a modern transfer of the original 35mm film with end credits remade to match the originals.

°**THE WHEEL IN SPACE episode six** is restored from the original 35mm black-and-white film onto which it was recorded in the studio. Its mono soundtrack is remastered and the VidFIRE process is applied to studio-recorded shots to recapture the smoother motion of video. The title sequence is replaced by a modern transfer of the original 35mm film with end credits remade to match the originals.

THE SPACE PIRATES episode two is restored from the original 35mm black-and-white film onto which it was recorded in the studio. Filmed and model sequences are newly transferred from the original silent 35mm black-and-white film footage, discovered by archivist Andrew Martin in 2004. The episode's mono soundtrack is remastered and the VidFIRE process is applied to studio-recorded shots to recapture the smoother motion of video. The title sequence is replaced by a modern transfer of the original 35mm film with end credits remade to match the originals.

SPECIAL FEATURES

THE WEB OF FEAR SURVIVING CLIPS (1m8s) Eight clips from episodes two, four and five. These are sections cut from the 16mm black-and-white film copies of the episodes shown by New Zealand broadcaster NZBC at the request of the government censor. They were discarded by NZBC and ended up in the possession of a film collector, where they were discovered by Graham Howard in April 2002. *Also on* The Seeds of Death

THE ABOMINABLE SNOWMEN (3m55s) Select **Surviving Clips** to watch two silent clips from episode four, taken from a 16mm black-and-white film recording of discussion programme *Late Night Line-Up* shown on BBC2 on Saturday 25 November 1967 (*full extract on* The Tomb of the Cybermen), discovered by Steve Roberts in 1993.

— Select **Location Film** to watch silent 8mm colour film footage shot by the serial's director Gerald Blake during location filming at Nant Ffrancon Pass in Snowdonia, Wales in September 1967.

— Select **Play All** to watch both sets of footage.

THE WHEEL IN SPACE SURVIVING CLIPS (33s) Four clips from episodes four and five. The first was cut from the 16mm black-and-white film copy of the episode shown by Australian broadcaster ABC at the request of the Australian Film Censorship Board, discovered by Damian Shanahan in October 1996. The rest are sections cut from the 16mm black-and-white film copies of the episodes shown by New Zealand broadcaster NZBC at the request of the government censor, discovered by Graham Howard in April 2002 (*also on* The Seeds of Death).

THE SPACE PIRATES FILM INSERTS + TRIMS (2m43s) Original silent 35mm black-and-white film footage of model work for episodes one and two, and sequences filmed at Ealing Studios on Friday 7 February 1969 for episode one, discovered by archivist Andrew Martin in 2004. Set to relevant sections from the episodes' soundtracks.

DOCUMENTARY THE MISSING YEARS (37m11s) Produced for *The Ice Warriors Collection* VHS release in November 1998, this feature looks at how *Doctor Who* recordings came to be junked and talks to some of the people involved in their recovery, including Gordon Hendry, Ian Levine, Sue Malden, Damian Shanahan, David Stead and Jan Vincent-Rudzki. It was the first time many of the clips on this DVD set had been released, along with a six-minute section of *Galaxy 4* episode one not included separately here. Presented by Frazer Hines and Deborah Watling. It is extended for this release to add discussion about the episodes found after 1998, including interviews with Bruce Grenville, Neil Lambess and Paul Scoones.

FURY FROM THE DEEP (11m12s) Select **8mm colour film** to watch silent footage shot by designer Tony Cornell during filming for episode six at Ealing Studios on Tuesday 5 March 1968, including the seaweed creature and lots of foam.

— Select **Raw Film Trims** to watch unused silent 16mm black-and-white film footage shot at Ealing Studios for episode six, showing setups and unused takes of the seaweed creature attack.

— Select **Surviving Clips** to watch eight clips from episodes one, two, four and five. The first is an extract that was later reused in *The War Games* episode ten and is taken from the 16mm black-and-white film recording of that episode. The rest are sections cut from the 16mm black-and-white film copies of the episodes shown by Australian broadcaster ABC at the request of the Australian Film Censorship Board, but stored in the Board's archive long after the episodes themselves had been destroyed. They were discovered by Damian Shanahan in October 1996. This ends with a 1m10s segment using footage from all the above sources set to the soundtrack of episode six to suggest how the climax might have looked in the broadcast episode.

— Select **Play All** to watch all three sets of footage.

SUBTITLES
Select **On** to view subtitles for all episodes and Special Features, or for the three commentaries.

COMMENTARY
Select **Commentary On** to play audio commentaries in place of the main soundtrack when watching selected episodes. On *The Abominable Snowmen* episode two, author and journalist Gary Russell talks with actress Deborah Watling (Victoria). On *The Web of Fear* episode one, Russell and Watling are joined by story editor Derrick Sherwin. On *The Wheel in Space* episode six are Sherwin and director Tristan de Vere Cole.

EASTER EGGS
There are three hidden features on these discs to find. *See Appendix 2 for details*

MANNEQUIN MANIA

Boxset of **SPEARHEAD FROM SPACE SPECIAL EDITION** and **TERROR OF THE AUTONS**

DVD RELEASE BBCDVD3135, 9 May 2011, PG

SLIPCASE Photo illustration by Clayton Hickman, silvered logo and title, pink/purple background

ORIGINAL RRP £35.73

WHAT'S IN THE BOX
The two Classic Series stories featuring the Nestene and their plastic automatons the Autons, which returned in the first New Series episode *Rose* (2005). *Spearhead from Space* (1970) is the first Third Doctor story in which he begins his exile on Earth and teams up with UNIT, headed by Brigadier Lethbridge-Stewart, to defeat the Nestene's first attempt at invading the planet. The version in this set is newly restored from higher quality sources than the serial's first release. In *Terror of the Autons* (1971) the Master makes his first appearance in the show, helping the Nestene with their second invasion bid, while UNIT recruit Jo Grant is assigned as the Doctor's new assistant.

◉ *See individual stories for full contents*

MARA TALES

Boxset of **KINDA** and **SNAKEDANCE**

DVD RELEASE BBCDVD2871, 7 March 2011, PG

SLIPCASE Photo illustration by Clayton Hickman, pink/purple background

ORIGINAL RRP £29.99

WHAT'S IN THE BOX
The two stories featuring the Mara, a malevolent force that dwells in the mind and seeks to return to its ophidian form. *Kinda* (1982) takes place on the planet Deva Loka where the peaceful telepathic locals have banished the Mara, but it finds a way back into the world through the mind of the Doctor's companion Tegan. In *Snakedance* (1983) the Mara reasserts its control over Tegan's mind and brings the TARDIS to the planet Manussa, which was once the centre of its empire, where it tries again to attain corporeal existence.

◉ *See individual stories for full contents*

THE **MARK OF THE RANI**

STORY No.139   SEASON No.22:3

One disc with two episodes (89½ mins) and 87 minutes of extras, plus commentary, music-only and alternative music tracks, production subtitles and PDF items

TARDIS TEAM Sixth Doctor, Peri

TIME AND PLACE Killingworth coalmine, 19th Century

ADVERSARIES Third Master (7th appearance); renegade Time Lord the Rani (1st appearance)

FIRST ON TV 2–9 February 1985

DVD RELEASE BBCDVD2224, 4 September 2006, U

COVER Photo illustration by Clayton Hickman, pale purple strip

ORIGINAL RRP £19.99

STORY TEASER

At the Killingworth mine, anti-industrialists are more violent than elsewhere, a condition the Doctor tracks down to a scheme of the Rani's, a fellow Time Lord banished from Gallifrey for her amoral experiments. Before he can act, however, he finds the Master is once again seeking to corrupt the course of English history. With the two old enemies at loggerheads, the Rani hopes to complete her plan unhindered.

CONNECTIONS

This is the Master's second attempt to divert known history, having tried to avert the signing of the Magna Carta in *The King's Demons* (1983), a tactic more fitting for that other renegade Time Lord the Monk (*The Time Meddler*, 1965). The Rani, again played by Kate O'Mara, returns in the debut Seventh Doctor story *Time and the Rani* (1987), also written by Pip and Jane Baker, who in between contributed to the final segments of *The Trial of a Time Lord* (1986). It's often assumed that the Doctor is always bumping into well-known historical figures on screen, but this is the first time he meets a genuine person — George Stephenson — since 1966's *The Gunfighters* (not counting the fake King John in *The King's Demons*). Shortly afterwards he encounters HG Wells in *Timelash* (1985) then, bar a brief chat with Einstein in *Time and the Rani*, doesn't do so again until bumping into Charles Dickens in *The Unquiet Dead* (2005). The TARDIS survives plummeting down a mine shaft in this story, as it does falling off cliffs in *The Romans* (1965) and *The Curse of Peladon* (1972), and down a ravine in *The Impossible Planet* (2006).

WORTH WATCHING

The Rani makes for an interesting villain, more unconcerned by the consequences of her actions than being outright evil. This could have made for a strong counterpoint to the Sixth Doctor's self-righteousness were it not for the presence of the Master, imposed on the writers by the production team. By now his plans were getting more frivolous and he adds little to the story beyond Anthony Ainley's performance. More impressive is the extensive location filming at Blists Hill, which provides great authenticity to the setting. This release also offers a rare chance to see how the incidental music can affect the feel of a programme, as original composer John Lewis' unused score for episode one can be heard as well as Jonathan Gibbs' replacement.

THE EPISODES

Both episodes are restored from digital duplicates of the original one-inch colour videotape recordings used for broadcast and their mono soundtracks remastered. The title sequences are replaced by a digital duplicate of the original one-inch colour videotape transfer of the 35mm film with credits remade to match the originals.

SPECIAL FEATURES

LORDS AND LUDDITES (43m20s) The making of *The Mark of the Rani*, including the beginnings of the Sixth Doctor's era; the origins of the story and the character of the Rani; the return of the Master; working with director Sarah Hellings; the casting of Kate O'Mara and her past working history with Colin Baker; the other guest cast; the location filming at Ironbridge Gorge Museum, with Baker doing his own stunts and people turning into trees; the studio recording and set design; and how the incidental music had to be redone at short notice after the untimely death of the original composer. With contributions from script editor Eric Saward, writers Pip and Jane Baker, composer Jonathan Gibbs, and actors Colin Baker, Nicola Bryant, Gary Cady and Kate O'Mara. Narrated by Louise Brady, produced by Steve Broster.

NOW AND THEN (4m6s) Comparing the filming locations in and around Blists Hill in Shropshire as they look today with how they appeared in late-October 1984 when used for *The Mark of the Rani*. Narrated by Louise Brady, produced by Steven Bagley. *See Index iii for further editions*

DELETED SCENES (8m40s) A selection of scenes from episode one not used in the final programme, taken from a copy of the initial edit with on-screen time-code. Sections without time-code are those used in the broadcast episode.

PLAYING WITH TIME (9m44s) Composer Jonathan Gibbs talks about working for the BBC Radio-phonic Workshop and scoring *The Mark of the Rani*, including selecting appropriate sounds, timing the music to the pictures, and writing the opening cue.

INFORMATION TEXT Select **On** to view subtitles when watching the episodes that provide information and anecdotes about the development, production, broadcast and history of *The Mark of the Rani*. Written by Richard Molesworth.

NEXT

RADIO TIMES LISTINGS Accessible via a computer is a PDF file of the two episode listings for the original BBC1 broadcast of *The Mark of the Rani*, an article about the location published the week of episode one, and letters about the increasing violence in the programme published the week of episode two (*also on* **Vengeance on Varos Special Edition**).

1985 DR WHO ANNUAL Accessible via a computer is a PDF file of the 1985 *Doctor Who Annual*, published by World Distributors the autumn before *The Mark of the Rani* was broadcast. With stories featuring the Doctor and Peri, plus behind-the-scenes features.

SATURDAY SUPERSTORE (2m3s) Extract from the 17 March 1984 edition of the BBC1 Saturday morning children's show in which Colin Baker and Nicola Bryant (in costume) take viewers' questions on the phone — and a surprise call from the Master. With host Mike Read. *Longer extract on* **Vengeance on Varos Special Edition**

PHOTO GALLERY (5m57s) Slideshow of colour and black-and-white photos taken during production of *The Mark of the Rani*, including design department photos of the sets. Set to sound effects from the story. Compiled by Derek Handley.

BLUE PETER (11m22s) Extract from the Thursday 16 February 1978 edition of the BBC1 children's magazine programme in which Peter Purves visits the Ironbridge Gorge Museum and relates its history in the development of the iron-making industry. Directed by Sarah Hellings, who later directed *The Mark of the Rani*.

AUDIO OPTIONS

Select **Commentary On** to play the audio commentary in place of the main soundtrack when watching the episodes. With Colin Baker, Nicola Bryant (Peri) and Kate O'Mara (the Rani) on both episodes.
— Select **Isolated Music Score On** to hear only Jonathan Gibbs' music when watching the episodes.
— Select **Alternative Soundtrack For Episode 1 On** to hear the soundtrack with John Lewis' original music, which was replaced before the serial was broadcast, when watching the episode.

SUBTITLES

Select **On** to view subtitles for all episodes and Special Features (except commentary).

EASTER EGG

There is one hidden feature on this disc to find. *See Appendix 2 for details*

THE **MASQUE OF MANDRAGORA**

STORY No.86   SEASON No.14:1

One disc with four episodes (99 mins) and 76 minutes of extras, plus commentary track, production subtitles and PDF items
Audio navigation of disc contents available by pressing Enter after the BBC ident

TARDIS TEAM Fourth Doctor, Sarah Jane
TIME AND PLACE San Martino, Northern Italy, late-15th Century
ADVERSARIES Mandragora Helix, a sentient form of energy; Count Federico and his court astrologer Hieronymous
FIRST ON TV 4–25 September 1976
DVD RELEASE BBCDVD2805, 8 February 2010, PG (episodes U)
COVER Photo illustration by Clayton Hickman, orange strip; version with older BBC logo on reverse
ORIGINAL RRP £19.99

STORY TEASER

When the TARDIS encounters the mysterious Mandragora Helix, the Doctor and Sarah believe they have made a narrow escape. But unknown to them the Helix has penetrated the Ship and directed it to Italy at the start of the Renaissance, where it finds a mind only too willing to help it keep the human race trapped by fear and superstition. While the Doctor finds an ally in the forward-thinking young duke, his uncle Count Federico is plotting a coup.

CONNECTIONS

The Fourth Doctor returns to Renaissance Italy in *City of Death* (1979), set just a few years later in 1505. He visits Rome during the reign of Emperor Nero in *The Romans* (1965), then narrowly survives the eruption of Vesuvius (*The Fires of Pompeii*, 2008) and a close encounter with fish-vampires (*The Vampires of Venice*, 2010). While the Doctor suggests the Mandragora Helix will be in position to attack the Earth again around the end of the 20th Century, it hasn't been encountered again on screen, although a suspiciously similar entity is fought off by Sarah Jane Smith and friends in *The Sarah Jane Adventures: Secrets of the Stars* (2008). Louis Marks wrote the previous season's *Planet of Evil* (1975), having earlier contributed single stories for the First and Third Doctors (*Planet of Giants*, 1964; *Day of the Daleks*, 1972). Rodney Bennett directed both *The Ark in Space* and *The Sontaran Experiment* in 1975, Tom Baker's first year as the Doctor. Norman Jones (Hieronymous) plays Khrisong in *The Abominable Snowmen* (1967) and Major Baker in *Doctor Who and the Silurians* (1970), while Robert James (High Priest) is Lesterson in *The Power of the Daleks* (1966). Tim Pigott-Smith (Marco) appears as Captain Harker in *The Claws of Axos* (1971).

WORTH WATCHING

This is a rarity in several respects for the Fourth Doctor: it's the furthest back of only four trips into Earth's history, and one of just two stories set entirely outside the UK. The feel of the period is suitably evoked by the location filming at the Italianate village of Portmeirion in North Wales, while Barry Newbery's authentic set designs maintain that illusion perfectly in the studio. He also redesigned the TARDIS control room in dark wood and brass for this season, and this is the best chance to see it as it was used only briefly in three other stories before the design reverted to the bright white of the original look.

THE EPISODES

All four episodes are restored from digital duplicates of the original two-inch colour videotape recordings used for broadcast and their mono soundtracks remastered. The title sequences are replaced by a modern transfer of the original 35mm film with credits remade to match the originals.

SPECIAL FEATURES

THE SECRET OF THE LABYRINTH (26m24s) Producer Philip Hinchcliffe, director Rodney Bennett, production unit manager Chris D'Oyly-John and John Laurimore (Federico) revisit Portmeirion to discuss the making of *The Masque of Mandragora*, including the inspirations for the setting; writing the scripts; the location filming; the guest cast; designing the costumes; handling horses and sword fights; redesigning the TARDIS inside and out, and creating the period sets; and recording the effects live in the studio. With contributions from designer Barry Newbery, actors Gareth Armstrong, Antony Carrick and Tim Pigott-Smith, television historian Jim Sangster, and fan journalist Steve O'Brien. Produced by Steve Broster.

BIGGER ON THE INSIDE (19m2s) Discussion of the design of the TARDIS, from the original concepts and influences to later adaptations and innovations, while children visiting the *Doctor Who* Experience exhibition give their ideas of what rooms could be included. With contributions from designer Barry Newbery, New Series designer Matthew Savage, writers Christopher H Bidmead and Robert Shearman, art writer Francesca Gavin, and Tom Baker (interviewed in 2003). Produced by James Goss.

NOW AND THEN (8m41s) Comparing the filming locations in and around Portmeirion in Wales as they look today with how they appeared in early-May 1976 when used for *The Masque of Mandragora*. Narrated and produced by Richard Bignell. *See Index iii for further editions*

BENEATH THE MASQUE (9m41s) Spoof documentary about the truth behind and legacy of 'The Mask of Mandragora'. Written by and featuring Clayton Hickman and Gareth Roberts, produced by James Goss.

TRAILS AND CONTINUITY (2m42s) Preview of episode one reconstructed by matching audio recordings made at the time of broadcast to clips from the episode, and continuity announcements from the original BBC1 broadcasts of episodes one, two and four of *The Masque of Mandragora*. Includes the BBC1 evening schedule for Saturday 4 September 1976.

NEXT

AUDIO OPTIONS Select **Commentary** to play the audio commentary in place of the main soundtrack when watching the episodes. With Tom Baker, producer Philip Hinchcliffe and production unit manager Chris D'Oyly-John on all four episodes, joined part-way into episode one by Gareth Armstrong (Giuliano).
— Select **Feature Audio** to reinstate the main soundtrack when watching the episodes.

INFO TEXT Select **On** to view subtitles when watching the episodes that provide information and anecdotes about the development, production, broadcast and history of *The Masque of Mandragora*. Written by Martin Wiggins.

PHOTO GALLERY (7m36s) Slideshow of colour and black-and-white photos taken during production of *The Masque of Mandragora*, including design department photos of the sets and behind-the-scenes shots of the location filming. Set to sound effects from the story. Compiled by Derek Handley.

PDF MATERIALS Accessible via a computer are the four episode listings from *Radio Times* for the original BBC1 broadcast of *The Masque of Mandragora*, a one-page article that introduced the 1976/77 season, and artwork by Roy Ellsworth that accompanied the billing for episode one.

COMING SOON (1m53s) Trailer for the DVD releases of *The Chase* and *The Space Museum*.

SUBTITLES

Select **On** to view subtitles for all episodes and Special Features (except commentary).

RELATED EXTRAS

Coming Soon trailer — The Curse of Peladon, The Monster of Peladon
Dressing Doctor Who — The Mutants
The Doctor's Composer — The Sun Makers

MAWDRYN UNDEAD

STORY No.125   SEASON No.20:3

Released with **ENLIGHTENMENT** and **TERMINUS** in **THE BLACK GUARDIAN TRILOGY** boxset
One disc with four episodes (98 mins) and 58½ minutes of extras, plus optional CGI effects, commentary and music-only tracks, production subtitles and PDF items
Audio navigation of disc contents available by pressing Enter after the BBC ident

TARDIS TEAM Fifth Doctor, Nyssa, Tegan, and introducing Vislor Turlough
TIME AND PLACE Brendon public school in 1977 and 1983, and orbiting spaceship
ADVERSARIES Alien scientist Mawdryn and his cohorts; the Black Guardian (2nd appearance)
FIRST ON TV 1–9 February 1983
DVD RELEASE BBCDVD2596A, 10 August 2009, PG
COVER Photo illustration by Clayton Hickman, pale brown strip
ORIGINAL RRP £39.14 (boxset)

STORY TEASER

The TARDIS avoids colliding with a spaceship orbiting the Earth by materialising aboard, but the vessel it seemingly deserted. When the Doctor and his companions take different routes down to the planet in search of the ship's crew, they become separated in time. While Tegan and Nyssa arrive in 1977 and find an injured man claiming to be a regenerated Doctor, the Doctor himself has arrived in 1983. He meets his old friend the Brigadier, now teaching at Brendon School, where student Turlough has just made a deadly pact to kill the Doctor.

CONNECTIONS

This story begins a trilogy in which the Black Guardian, again played by Valentine Dyall, seeks revenge on the Doctor for frustrating his attempt to gain the Key to Time at the conclusion of *The Armageddon Factor* (1979). As then, he can't act directly but selects an agent to do his dirty work, in this instance Turlough, a teenage alien unwillingly enrolled in a British public school. How he came to be there is revealed in *Planet of Fire* (1984). Also at the school, on the staff, is ex-Brigadier Lethbridge-Stewart, last seen on screen in *Terror of the Zygons* (1975) and, of course, in many earlier adventures (as seen in flashback here). He returns, still retired but no longer teaching, in *Battlefield* (1989) before making a final appearance in *The Sarah Jane Adventures: Enemy of the Bane* (2008). This is the only time he's seen without his trademark moustache, not counting his alternative-universe version in *Inferno* (1970). The Daleks were first to employ an assassin to rid themselves of the Doctor in *The Chase* (1965), in that case a robot duplicate of the First Doctor himself. Peter Grimwade wrote the previous season's *Time-Flight* (1982) and the following year's *Planet of Fire*, having previously been a director on the show. David Collings, playing Mawdryn, had previously been Vogan hothead Vorus in *Revenge of the Cybermen* (1975) and the fragile Poul in *The Robots of Death* (1977), while Angus Mackay (Headmaster) was the first actor to play Time Lord politician Borusa, in *The Deadly Assassin* (1976).

WORTH WATCHING

Any story featuring Nicholas Courtney as the Brigadier is, almost by definition, worth watching. Although here he's out of his usual purview he's undoubtedly the same character and works well with Peter Davison's softer Fifth Doctor. Also returning is the Black Guardian, an often mentioned but only once seen character who viewers might be forgiven for not recognising were it not for the unmistakable presence — and voice — of Valentine Dyall. This is the first story to feature Turlough, the reluctant assassin who goes on to be the Doctor's never-quite-trustworthy companion.

THE EPISODES

All four episodes are restored from digital duplicates of the original two-inch colour videotape recordings used for broadcast and their mono soundtracks remastered. The title sequences are replaced by a modern transfer of the original 35mm film with credits remade to match the originals.

SPECIAL FEATURES

AUDIO OPTIONS Select **Commentary** to play the audio commentary in place of the main soundtrack when watching the episodes. With Peter Davison, Mark Strickson (Turlough), Nicholas Courtney (the Brigadier) and script editor Eric Saward on all four episodes.

— Select **Isolated Music** to hear only Paddy Kingsland's music when watching the episodes.

— Select **Feature Audio** to reinstate the main soundtrack when watching the episodes.

INFO TEXT Select **On** to view subtitles when watching the episodes that provide information and anecdotes about the development, production, broadcast and history of *Mawdryn Undead*. Written by Richard Molesworth.

WHO WANTS TO LIVE FOREVER? (24m31s) Actors Lucy Benjamin, David Collings, Nicholas Courtney, Peter Davison and Mark Strickson, and script editor Eric Saward return to Trent Park in North London where much of *Mawdryn Undead* was filmed to recall the making of the serial, including the origins and ideas of the script; introducing Turlough; bringing back the Brigadier (after plans to use Ian Chesterton fell through) and the Black Guardian; the pains of Turlough's crystal prop; casting Mawdryn; rejuvenating Nyssa and Tegan; and the medical reality of extending life. With contributions from director Peter Moffatt (interviewed in 2003) and plastic surgeon Dr Simon Withey. Narrated by Floella Benjamin, produced by Brendan Sheppard.

LIBERTY HALL (7m20s) A fictionalised interview with the retired Brigadier Lethbridge-Stewart about his life after UNIT. With Nicholas Courtney and Simon Ockenden. Written by Karen Davies, directed by Brendan Sheppard.

DELETED AND EXTENDED SCENES (5m15s) A selection of scenes from episodes one and two not used in the final programme, taken from a copy of the 16mm colour film footage shot on location.

FILM TRIMS (3m33s) Silent 16mm colour film footage from the location shooting at Trent Park, Barnet in North London during late-August 1982, showing setups and takes not used in the final episodes. Includes the countdown clocks for the studio recordings of episodes one, two and three. Set to music from the story.

NEXT

OUT-TAKES (5m36s) Bloopers and fluffed lines taken from a copy of the 16mm colour film footage shot on location.

CGI EFFECTS Select **CGI Effects On** to view updated computer-generated effects in place of some of the original visual effects, including a new flashback sequence, when watching the episodes.

CONTINUITY (56s) Continuity announcements from the original BBC1 broadcasts of all four episodes of *Mawdryn Undead*, with plugs for the *Doctor Who The Music* album and for the following serial, *Terminus*.

PHOTO GALLERY (7m29s) Slideshow of colour and black-and-white photos taken during production of *Mawdryn Undead*, set to music from the story. Compiled by Derek Handley.

SET PHOTO GALLERY (1m26s) Slideshow of design department photos of the school, spaceship and transmat capsule sets from *Mawdryn Undead*. Set to dialogue extracts from the story.

PDF MATERIALS Accessible via a computer are the four episode listings from *Radio Times* for the original BBC1 broadcast of *Mawdryn Undead*, and a one-page article about the return of the Brigadier published the week of episodes one and two.

— Studio floorplans for three of the recording sessions in September 1982, showing the arrangement of sets including the TARDIS control room, Brigadier's hut, school and spaceship.

— Storyboard sketches by Russell Owen for some of the new CGI effects shots.

COMING SOON (1m2s) Trailer for the DVD release of *The Twin Dilemma*.

SUBTITLES

Select **On** to view subtitles for all episodes and Special Features (except commentary).

EASTER EGGS

There are two hidden features on this disc to find. *See Appendix 2 for details*

RELATED EXTRAS

Peter Grimwade - Directing with Attitude — Kinda

The UNIT Family — Terror of the Zygons

Directing Who — The Visitation (and Special Edition)

Coming Soon trailer — The War Games

MEGLOS

STORY No.110   SEASON No.18:2

One disc with four episodes (87 mins) and 54 minutes of extras, plus commentary and music-only tracks, production subtitles and PDF items
Audio navigation of disc contents available by pressing Enter after the BBC ident

TARDIS TEAM Fourth Doctor, Second Romana, K9

TIME AND PLACE Jungle planet Tigella and nearby desert planet Zolfa-Thura

ADVERSARIES Meglos, last of the Zolfa-Thurans; Lexa, devout Deon leader

FIRST ON TV 27 September–18 October 1980

DVD RELEASE BBCDVD2852, 10 January 2011, U

COVER Photo illustration by Lee Binding, dark purple strip; version with older BBC logo on reverse

ORIGINAL RRP £19.99

STORY TEASER

The society on Tigella is reliant of the mysterious power-giving Dodecahedron, but its output is failing. The scientific Savants want to examine the artefact, but the religious Deons seek to appease it, so their leader calls in the Doctor to arbitrate. On the nearby Zolfa-Thura, however, the last member of the species that built the Dodecahedron has his own uses for it. Trapping the Doctor in a time loop, Meglos takes on the Time Lord's appearance in order to steal the Dodecahedron as a power source for his ultimate weapon.

CONNECTIONS

While incarnations of the Doctor have had a few natural-born (as far as we know) doubles — the Abbot of Amboise in *The Massacre* (1966), Salamander in *The Enemy of the World* (1967/68), Commander Maxil in *Arc of Infinity* (1983) — he has also been the object of deliberate duplication. The Daleks build an android replica of the First Doctor to infiltrate and kill the TARDIS crew in *The Chase* (1965); similarly, the Kraals disguise one of their androids as the Fourth Doctor in *The Android Invasion* (1975); Omega bases his new body on the Fifth Doctor's in *Arc of Infinity*; Sharaz Jek creates another android copy of the Fifth Doctor in *The Caves of Androzani* (1984); and the Flesh grow a duplicate Eleventh Doctor in *The Rebel Flesh* (2011). Another double in this story, although strangely not remarked on by the Doctor, is Lexa, who is the exact likeness of early companion Barbara Wright — both characters played by Jacqueline Hill. Meglos in his natural state appears to be a sentient plant-based lifeform — cactus-like as are the Varga plants in *Mission to the Unknown* (1965). Other such vegetative life includes the Weed Creature (*Fury From the Deep*, 1968), the Krynoids (*The Seeds of Doom*, 1976), the Vervoids (*The Trial of a Time Lord: Terror of the Vervoids*, 1986) and the Forest of Cheem (*The End of the World*, 2005). Tigella has aggressive vegetation similar to that on Chloris (*The Creature from the Pit*, 1979), Eden (*Nightmare of Eden*, 1979), what the Doctor keeps in the TARDIS in *The Invasion of Time* (1978) and the Fungoids in *The Chase*. The Doctor traps Axos in a time loop in *The Claws of Axos* (1971) and tries to delay the Marshal in an unstable loop in *The Armageddon Factor* (1979), while the TARDIS holds River Song in a time loop to protect her from its destruction in *The Pandorica Opens/The Big Bang* (2010). The Gaztaks are a more effective bunch of incompetents than the scavengers in the previous season's *The Creature from the Pit* (1979), but just as easy for Romana to outwit. Bill Fraser (General Grugger) plays Commander Pollock a year later in the first *Doctor Who* spin-off *K9 and Company* (1981). That was written by this serial's director, Terence Dudley, who also wrote three Fifth Doctor stories: *Four to Doomsday* (1982), *Black Orchid* (1982) and *The King's Demons* (1983).

WORTH WATCHING

The key delight here is watching Tom Baker play the villain as the monomaniacal Meglos adopts the Doctor's appearance, a chance the actor relishes. It's also a pleasure to see Jacqueline Hill in the show again, although it was a long time since anyone had seen her as Barbara when *Meglos* was shown. While much is made of the new superimposition technique first used in this serial, it's the music that perhaps seemed the biggest innovation to viewers as the time. Calmer after the stridency of the BBC Radiophonic Workshop's debut on the preceding *The Leisure Hive*, it heralds the sound of the show for the remainder of the Classic Series.

THE EPISODES

All four episodes are restored from digital duplicates of the original two-inch colour videotape recordings used for broadcast and their mono soundtracks remastered (retaining the accidentally repitched theme music at the end of episode four). The title sequences are replaced by a modern transfer of the original 35mm film with credits remade to match the originals.

SPECIAL FEATURES

MEGLOS MEN (18m12s) Writers John Flanagan and Andrew McCulloch revisit some of their old London haunts to discuss how they came to be writing partners and get a commission for *Doctor Who*, their inspirations for the characters, and their views of the final production. They drop in on script editor Christopher H Bidmead at his home to recall their second script commission that was never made, 'Project Zeta-Sigma'. Produced by Chris Chapman.

THE SCENE SYNC STORY (11m4s) Explanation of the Scene Sync process, which allowed two cameras filming different scenes, such as actors and a model set, to track in unison so the shots could be combined with convincing movement. With cameramen Roger Bunce and Peter Leverick, and visual effects designer Stephen Drewett. Narrated by Philip Kelly, produced by John Kelly.

JACQUELINE HILL – A LIFE IN PICTURES (12m56s) Profile of the life and career of actor Jacqueline Hill, who died in 1993, best remembered for playing Barbara Wright, one of the very first companions in *Doctor Who*. With memories from Jacqueline's husband Alvin Rakoff, *Doctor Who* producer and friend Verity Lambert (interviewed in 1996), and actor friends Ann Davies and William Russell. Illustrated with photos and clips from Jacqueline's film and television work. Produced by Thomas Guerrier.

ENTROPY EXPLAINED (4m53s) Physics lecturer Dr Phillip Trwoga of Westminster University explains the scientific theories of entropy, which formed a theme for much of the 1980/81 season.

PHOTO GALLERY (4m18s) Slideshow of colour and black-and-white photos taken during production of *Meglos*, including design department photos of the sets and shots of the blue-screen work. Set to music from the story. Compiled by Paul Shields.

NEXT

AUDIO OPTIONS Select **Commentary** to play the audio commentary in place of the main soundtrack when watching the episodes. With composer Paddy Kingsland [eps 1,2*], Lalla Ward (Romana) [1,2,3,4], writer John Flanagan [1,2,4], Christopher Owen (Earthling/Meglos) [1,3,4] and composer Peter Howell [2*,3]. (* Howell takes over from Kingsland part-way into episode two.)

— Select **Isolated Score** to hear only Paddy Kingsland's and Peter Howell's music when watching the episodes.

— Select **Feature Audio** to reinstate the main soundtrack when watching the episodes.

INFO TEXT Select **On** to view subtitles when watching the episodes that provide information and anecdotes about the development, production, broadcast and history of *Meglos*. Written by Stephen James Walker.

PDF MATERIALS Accessible via a computer are the four episode listings from *Radio Times* for the original BBC1 broadcast of *Meglos*, and letters published the week of episode one.

COMING SOON (42s) Trailer for the DVD release of *The Mutants*.

SUBTITLES
Select **On** to view subtitles for all episodes and Special Features (except commentary).

EASTER EGG
There is one hidden feature on this disc to find. *See Appendix 2 for details*

RELATED EXTRAS
Coming Soon trailer — The Seeds of Doom

THE **MIND OF EVIL**

STORY No.56   SEASON No.8:2

Two discs with six episodes (147 mins) and 61 minutes of extras, plus commentary track, production subtitles and PDF items
Audio navigation of each disc's contents available by pressing Enter after the BBC ident

TARDIS TEAM Third Doctor, Jo, Brigadier and UNIT

TIME AND PLACE Contemporary London and Stangmoor Prison

ADVERSARIES First Master (2nd appearance); mind parasite

FIRST ON TV 30 January–6 March 1971

DVD RELEASE BBCDVD3269, 3 June 2013, U

COVER Photo illustration by Lee Binding, dark purple strip; version with older BBC logo on reverse

ORIGINAL RRP £20.42

STORY TEASER
A new technique for rehabilitating dangerous criminals raises the Doctor's suspicions and when he visits the prison where it's being demonstrated he soon learns the dreadful truth behind the

mind-altering method. Meanwhile UNIT are policing crucial peace talks while arranging the de-commission of a nuclear missile — a dangerous juggling act made worse when the Doctor discovers the Master has his own plans for the warhead.

CONNECTIONS

The Master makes an immediate return after the Doctor strands him on Earth too in the preceding story *Terror of the Autons* (1971) and turns up in the three following stories. Whereas in *The Mind of Evil* he takes over a prison, he soon finds himself incarcerated in one in *The Sea Devils* (1972). Although the Doctor has been locked up many times, the only time he's specifically sentenced to a spell in prison is in the 26th Century when he's jailed on the Moon (*Frontier in Space*, 1973). The way the mind parasite brings out people's negative emotions in order to feed on them is similar to the Mara's use of such feelings to reincarnate itself in *Kinda* (1982) and *Snakedance* (1983), although the placid state in which it leaves those it doesn't kill is reminiscent of the effects of the Kinda's Box of Jhana. Don Houghton wrote *Inferno* the previous year, while Timothy Combe also directed that year's *Doctor Who and the Silurians*. William Marlowe, playing Harry Mailer, returns as Lester in *Revenge of the Cybermen* (1975), while Neil McCarthy (Barnham) is Thawn in *The Power of Kroll* (1978/79). Michael Sheard (Dr Summers) is in *Doctor Who* several times, most notably as Laurence Scarman in *Pyramids of Mars* (1975) and Mergrave in *Castrovalva* (1982). Simon Lack, playing Professor Kettering, also appears as Zadek in *The Androids of Tara* (1978).

WORTH WATCHING

The Mind of Evil is perhaps as 'real' as Classic *Doctor Who* ever got, harking back to the grittier style of the previous year but having more in common with contemporary crime thrillers than science fiction. Indeed, the Master behaves as much like a gangland boss as he does an alien dissident, leading prison breaks and stealing nuclear weapons. Even his scheme with the alien mind parasite is a means to an end, helping him recruit the muscle he needs and keeping the Doctor off his back. UNIT too handles proper security intelligence work rather than shooting at monsters, giving the Brigadier in particular a chance to shine at what he does best. Given the episodes are only known to exist on black-and-white film, the chance to see this story in colour again is nothing short of miraculous and the results of the restoration are to be applauded even more than usual.

DISC ONE

THE EPISODES

This is the first release of the serial in complete colour since its original broadcast. All six episodes are restored from 16mm black-and-white film copies of the original two-inch colour videotape recordings, recovered from BBC Enterprises in 1978. Episodes two, three, four, five and six are recoloured from information in the mono images on the film that relates to the original colour of the video picture being filmed, using the Colour Recovery process. This information is not present in the film copy of episode one so this is recoloured manually, digitally painting in colour for key frames which is then extrapolated across further frames. The episodes' mono soundtracks are remastered and the VidFIRE process is applied to studio-recorded shots to recapture the smoother motion of video. The title sequences are replaced by a modern transfer of the original 35mm film with credits remade to match the originals.

SPECIAL FEATURES

AUDIO OPTIONS Select **Commentary** to play the audio commentary in place of the main soundtrack when watching the episodes. This is moderated by actor and comedian Toby Hadoke, talking with Fernanda Marlowe (Corporal Bell) [eps 1,2], Pik-Sen Lim (Chin Lee) [1,2,3], director Timothy Combe [1,2,3,4,5,6], script editor Terrance Dicks [1,3,4], producer Barry Letts [1,4,5,6], Katy Manning (Jo) [2,3,4,6] and stuntman Derek Ware [4,5].

— Select **Feature Audio** to reinstate the main soundtrack when watching the episodes.

INFO TEXT Select **On** to view subtitles when watching the episodes that provide information and anecdotes about the development, production, broadcast and history of *The Mind of Evil*. Written by Stephen James Walker and Martin Wiggins.

SUBTITLES

Select **On** to view subtitles for all episodes (none for commentary).

SPECIAL FEATURES

THE MILITARY MIND (22m44s) Producer Barry Letts, script editor Terrance Dicks, director Timothy Combe, and actors Nicholas Courtney, Pik-Sen Lim and Fernanda Marlowe revisit Dover Castle, where much of *The Mind of Evil* was filmed, to discuss the making of the serial, including the story's scripting; views of the director; finding the prison location and the hectic filming schedule, especially with a major action sequence to shoot; working with the RAF and a real missile; re-creating a prison wing in the studio; getting Jon Pertwee to speak Chinese; and a disappointing dragon. Narrated by Cameron McEwan, produced by Chris Chapman. (Recorded in 2009.)

NOW & THEN (7m6s) Comparing the filming locations in London and Dover Castle in Kent as they look today with how they appeared in late-October/early-November 1970 when used for *The Mind of Evil*. Narrated and produced by Richard Bignell. *See Index iii for further editions*

BEHIND THE SCENES: TELEVISION CENTRE (24m1s) Edition of the BBC1 children's documentary series broadcast on Wednesday 18 August 1971, in which reporter Norman Tozer spends a day at BBC Television Centre examining the various departments that contribute to making television programmes. Includes an interview with visual effects designer Michaeljohn Harris (with a glimpse of the Eye of Axos) and footage of the recording of *Cousin Bette* with Helen Mirren.

PHOTO GALLERY (4m55s) Slideshow of colour and black-and-white photos taken during production of *The Mind of Evil*, set to the Master's theme and sound effects from the story. Compiled by Derek Handley.

PDF MATERIALS Accessible via a computer are the six episode listings from *Radio Times* for the original BBC1 broadcast of *The Mind of Evil*.
— Packaging, adverts and the six badges from the 1971 *Doctor Who* promotion by Kellogg's Sugar Smacks breakfast cereal. *Also on* Terror of the Autons

SUBTITLES Select **On** to view subtitles for all Special Features on disc two.

COMING SOON (1m15s) Trailer for the Blu-ray release of *Spearhead from Space*.

EASTER EGG

There is one hidden feature on these discs to find. *See Appendix 2 for details*

RELATED EXTRAS

The UNIT Family — Day of the Daleks
Coming Soon trailer — Inferno Special Edition

M

THE **MIND ROBBER**

STORY No.45   SEASON No.6:2

One disc with five episodes (100 mins) and 77 minutes of extras, plus commentary track and production subtitles

TARDIS TEAM Second Doctor, Jamie, Zoe
TIME AND PLACE The Land of Fiction
ADVERSARIES White Robots; clockwork soldiers; the Master Brain
FIRST ON TV 14 September–12 October 1968
DVD RELEASE BBCDVD1358, 7 March 2005, PG (episodes U)
COVER Photo illustration by Clayton Hickman, dark orange strip
ORIGINAL RRP £19.99

STORY TEASER

To stop the TARDIS being buried in lava, the Doctor uses the Emergency Unit and takes it out of time and space altogether. He, Jamie and Zoe are each fooled into leaving the ship and find themselves in a strange land where the people seem strangely familiar. As the Doctor realises everything here is from a work of fiction, he must battle to prevent his friends from becoming imaginary too.

CONNECTIONS

The Land of Fiction is not dissimilar to the Toymaker's domain, where he too can make imaginary characters real (*The Celestial Toymaker*, 1966). The empty void is also like the Charged Vacuum Emboitment through which the TARDIS escapes E-Space in *Warriors' Gate* (1981), yet reminiscent of the TARDIS engine room too, as depicted in *Journey to the Centre of the TARDIS* (2013). The White Robots have chest units and square handles on their heads, like another popular monster of the period, recently encountered by the TARDIS team in *The Wheel in Space* (1968). The Doctor previously met fictional characters Dracula and Frankenstein's monster in what he (mistakenly) believed was a world of dreams in *The Chase* (1965), and meets the real Minotaur in *The Time Monster* (1972). The Doctor's trips into the Matrix in *The Deadly Assassin* (1976) and *The Trial of a Time Lord: The Ultimate Foe* (1986) also see him face threats conjured up by another's demented mind. The former serial is directed by David Maloney, who made his debut on *Doctor Who* with *The Mind Robber* (*see Index v*). Bernard Horsfall (Gulliver) appears in both stories too, and as Taron in the Maloney-directed *Planet of the Daleks* (1973). Christopher Robbie (the Karkus) returns as the Cyberleader in *Revenge of the Cybermen* (1975).

WORTH WATCHING

Doctor Who has always contained an element of the surreal — ever since the moment it was revealed that the TARDIS is vastly bigger on the inside than the outside — but *The Mind Robber* goes further than ever before or since. It becomes almost a story about the writing of stories, with the Doctor (a fictional character to us) fighting not be turned into a fictional character (to himself), a theme very much at the heart of Steven Moffat's approach to modern *Doctor Who*. In fact it has been suggested that the whole story is actually a dream of the Doctor's.

THE EPISODES

Episodes one, two, three and four are restored from 16mm film copies of the original black-and-white video recordings, recovered from BBC Enterprises in 1978, while episode five is restored from the original 35mm black-and-white film onto which it was recorded in the studio. Their mono soundtracks are remastered and the VidFIRE process is applied to studio-recorded shots to recapture the smoother motion of video. The title sequences are replaced by a modern transfer of the original 35mm film with credits remade to match the originals.

SPECIAL FEATURES

BASIL BRUSH SEGMENT (10m26s) Extract from the Saturday 25 October 1975 edition of BBC1 children's programme *The Basil Brush Show* (shown just before episode one of *Pyramids of Mars*) in which Basil (voiced by Ivan Owen) and Mr Roy (North) go climbing in the Himalayas and encounter a Yeti — one of the costumes from *The Web of Fear* (1968).

INFORMATION TEXT Select **On** to view subtitles when watching the episodes that provide information and anecdotes about the development, production, broadcast and history of *The Mind Robber*. Written by Martin Wiggins.

THE FACT OF FICTION (34m57s) The making of *The Mind Robber*, including trying out a new writer and director; adding an extra opening episode with no new sets, only the three regular cast and some old robot costumes; working around Frazer Hines being taken ill mid-production; realising the script's fantastical ideas like the clockwork soldiers, forest of words and unicorn; casting and performing Gulliver and the Karkus; inspirations for the Master (not *that* one); and designing the sets. With contributions from script editor Derrick Sherwin, writer Peter Ling, director David Maloney, designer Evan Hercules, and actors Frazer Hines, Wendy Padbury, Christopher Robbie and Hamish Wilson. Produced by Richard Molesworth.

HIGHLANDER (22m29s) Frazer Hines talks about getting the part of Jamie McCrimmon, adapting to becoming a regular companion, working with Patrick Troughton, the monsters he appeared with, Jamie's relationships with Victoria and Zoe, deciding to move on, his time on *Emmerdale Farm*, fitting in a brief return for *The Five Doctors* leading to a larger role in *The Two Doctors*, and getting on the *Doctor Who* convention circuit.

AUDIO OPTIONS Select **Commentary On** to play the audio commentary in place of the main soundtrack when watching the episodes. With Frazer Hines (Jamie), Wendy Padbury (Zoe) and director David Maloney on all five episodes, joined halfway through episode two by Hamish Wilson (replacement Jamie).

PHOTO GALLERY (6m52s) Slideshow of colour and black-and-white photos taken during production of *The Mind Robber*, plus shots from the *Out of the Unknown* episode 'The Prophet' in which the robot costumes were first used. Set to sound effects from the story. Compiled by Ralph Montagu.

SUBTITLES
Select **On** to view subtitles for all episodes and Special Features, or for the commentary.

EASTER EGG
There is one hidden feature on this disc to find. *See Appendix 2 for details*

RELATED EXTRAS
Sylvia James - In Conversation — The War Games

THE **MONSTER OF PELADON**

STORY No.73   SEASON No.11:4

Released with **THE CURSE OF PELADON** in the **PELADON TALES** boxset
Two discs with six episodes (146 mins) and 63 minutes of extras, plus commentary track, production subtitles and PDF items
Audio navigation of each disc's contents available by pressing Enter after the BBC ident

TARDIS TEAM Third Doctor, Sarah Jane
TIME AND PLACE Planet Peladon
ADVERSARIES Ice Warriors (4th appearance); militant miners
FIRST ON TV 23 March–27 April 1974
DVD RELEASE BBCDVD2744(B), 18 January 2010, PG (disc one U)
COVER Photo illustration by Clayton Hickman, dark orange strip;
          version with older BBC logo on reverse
ORIGINAL RRP £29.99 (boxset)

STORY TEASER
Returning to the planet Peladon fifty years after his previous visit, the Doctor finds membership of the Galactic Federation hasn't brought the population much benefit. Queen Thalira is little more than a puppet and the miners are being exploited for the minerals the planet contains. With rebellion brewing and the spirit of Aggedor seemingly angered, the Doctor is attempting to mediate when a squad of Ice Warriors arrives, supposedly to enforce the peace.

CONNECTIONS
The Doctor previously visited Peladon in *The Curse of Peladon* (1972), when he was influential in getting the planet accepted into the Federation. The Ice Warriors then were reformed characters, but here they revert to type for their last appearance in the show until *Cold War* (2013). Mines feature significantly in the previous year's *The Green Death* (1973), while another society exploited for its mineral wealth is seen in *Vengeance on Varos* (1985). *The Monster of Peladon* is writer Brian Hayles' final script for *Doctor Who*, having written all previous Ice Warrior stories, *The Smugglers* (1966) and initial drafts of *The Celestial Toymaker* (1966). Lennie Mayne directed one more serial after this, Sarah Jane's final story *The Hand of Fear* (1976), having already directed *The Three Doctors* (1973) and the previous Peladon tale. Returning from that story are Ysanne Churchman voicing Alpha Centauri, Ice Warrior actors Alan Bennion and Sonny Caldinez, and Nick Hobbs as Aggedor. Donald Gee (Eckersley) plays Major Ian Warne in *The Space Pirates* (1969), while Ralph Watson (Ettis) is Captain Knight in *The Web of Fear* (1968) and Ben Travers in *Horror of Fang Rock* (1977). Rex Robinson (Gebek) was a favourite of the director's, appearing in both *The Three Doctors* as Dr Tyler and *The Hand of Fear* as Dr Carter.

WORTH WATCHING
This is a rare instance in the Classic Series of the Doctor returning to a planet and witnessing the outcome of an earlier visit, as *The Curse of Peladon* had been popular with both audiences and the production team. As with that story, this drew on contemporary social issues, notably the miners' strikes and resulting power outages, which are less relevant to modern viewers but still recognisable

in the idea of political leaders taking advantage of the populace. It's also fun to see the Ice Warriors back to their old ways, even if the costumes are showing their age by now.

DISC ONE

THE EPISODES

All six episodes are restored from digital duplicates of the original two-inch colour videotape recordings used for broadcast and their mono soundtracks remastered (including the reinstatement of a missing line of dialogue). The title sequences are replaced by a modern transfer of the original 35mm film with credits remade to match the originals.

AUDIO OPTIONS

Select **Commentary** to play the audio commentary in place of the main soundtrack when watching the episodes. This is moderated by actor and comedian Toby Hadoke, talking with Nina Thomas (Thalira) [eps 1,2,3], Ralph Watson (Ettis) [1,2,3], Donald Gee (Eckersley) [1,2,3,5,6], producer Barry Letts [1,2,3,5,6], script editor Terrance Dicks [1,2,3,5,6] and Stuart Fell (Centauri) [5,6]. On episode four Hadoke talks with fellow fans Mark Aldridge, Kate Du-Rose, Philip Newman and Robert Shearman.

— Select **Feature Audio** to reinstate the main soundtrack when watching the episodes.

SUBTITLES

Select **Subtitles On** to view subtitles for all episodes (none for commentary).

— Select **Info Text On** to view subtitles when watching the episodes that provide information and anecdotes about the development, production, broadcast and history of *The Monster of Peladon*. Written by Martin Wiggins.

DISC TWO

SPECIAL FEATURES

THE PELADON SAGA – PART TWO (22m10s) Continuing the look at the making of *The Curse of Peladon* and *The Monster of Peladon*, including the realisation of the alien creatures in the stories; the portrayals of the Peladon inhabitants; the characterisation of Sarah Jane; Jon Pertwee's decision to leave and memories of the actor. With contributions from producer Barry Letts, script editor Terrance Dicks, production assistant Chris D'Oyly-John, make-up supervisor Elizabeth Moss, special sounds creator Brian Hodgson, and actors Sonny Caldinez, Stuart Fell, Donald Gee, Nick Hobbs, Katy Manning, Nina Thomas and Ralph Watson. Narrated by David Hamilton, produced by John Kelly. *Part one is on* The Curse of Peladon

DELETED SCENE (1m44s) A scene that was cut from episode one and which now only survives on a sound recording of the filming at Ealing Studios, reconstructed with stills and placed between the scenes where it was originally intended.

WHERE ARE THEY NOW? (2m28s) Extract from the Wednesday 17 September 1980 edition of the BBC1 interview programme in which David Jacobs talks to actress Ysanne Churchman about voicing Alpha Centauri.

ON TARGET – TERRANCE DICKS (21m27s) The Target range of *Doctor Who* novelisations was for years the only way to experience past stories, and its regular authors were very influential on their child readers. This examines the books of the range's most prolific author, Terrance Dicks. With contributions from Dicks, plus writers Alan Barnes, Paul Cornell, David J Howe and Gareth Roberts. Readings by Caroline John, Katy Manning and David Troughton, taken from the BBC Audiobook CD releases. Directed by Marcus Hearn.

PHOTO GALLERY (8m20s) Slideshow of colour and black-and-white photos taken during production of *The Monster of Peladon*, including design department photos of the sets. Set to sound effects from the story. Compiled by Derek Handley.

PDF MATERIALS Accessible via a computer are the six episode listings from *Radio Times* for the original BBC1 broadcast of *The Monster of Peladon*, with illustrations by Peter Brookes.

— Designer Gloria Clayton's blueprints for the citadel set (not studio floorplans as indicated in the menu).

— BBC Enterprises' sales document for *The Monster of Peladon*, describing the serial for potential overseas broadcasters.

COMING SOON (59s) Trailer for the DVD release of *The Masque of Mandragora*.

SUBTITLES Select **On** to view subtitles for all Special Features on disc two.

EASTER EGGS

There are two hidden features on these discs to find. *See Appendix 2 for details*

RELATED EXTRAS

Warriors of Mars — The Curse of Peladon

THE **MOONBASE**

STORY No.33   SEASON No.4:6

One disc with two original and two animated episodes (99½ mins) and 27 minutes of extras,
plus commentary track, production subtitles and PDF items
Audio navigation of disc contents available by pressing Enter after the BBC ident

TARDIS TEAM Second Doctor, Ben, Jamie, Polly

TIME AND PLACE The Moon, mid-21st Century

ADVERSARIES Cybermen (2nd appearance)

FIRST ON TV 11 February–4 March 1967

DVD RELEASE BBCDVD3698, 20 January 2014, PG

COVER Photo illustration by Lee Binding, dark grey strip; version with older BBC logo on reverse

ORIGINAL RRP £20.42

— Episodes two and four originally released in the Lost in Time set; BBCDVD1353, £29.99,
 1 November 2004

STORY TEASER

The TARDIS arrives on the Moon where Jamie injures himself while getting used to the lower gravity. Help is at hand from the nearby Moonbase, from which the Earth's weather is now controlled by the Gravitron device. The crew of the base are suspicious of the newcomers, however, as a mysterious illness is spreading and people have disappeared. The Doctor's investigations soon lead to the true culprits — the Cybermen — who are determined to take control of the Gravitron.

CONNECTIONS

The Doctor returns to the Moon in *The Seeds of Death* (1969), *Frontier in Space* (1973) and *Smith and Jones* (2007). The Cybermen here are of a more sleek design than in their first appearance, *The Tenth Planet* (1966), but stay more or less the same for *The Tomb of the Cybermen* (1967) and *The Wheel in Space* (1968). They use the Moon again, to hide their forces from detection, in *The Invasion* (1968), while infecting their victims is a tactic they repeat in *Revenge of the Cybermen* (1975). Writer Kit Pedler created the Cybermen with Gerry Davis and together they wrote *The Tenth Planet* and *The Tomb of the Cybermen*, while Pedler also provided story ideas for *The War Machines* (1966), *The Wheel in Space* and *The Invasion*. Morris Barry directed their next appearance in *The Tomb of the Cybermen*, as well as *The Dominators* (1968). Alan Rowe, playing Dr Evans, is Edward of Wessex in *The Time Warrior* (1973/74), Colonel Skinsale in *Horror of Fang Rock* (1977) and Decider Garif in *Full Circle* (1980), while Jon Rolfe (Sam Becket) plays an army captain in *The War Machines* and Ralph Fell in *The Green Death* (1973).

WORTH WATCHING

This is when the Cybermen become the more robot-like creatures we're now familiar with, rather than the nearer-human form they originated in, but still represent a horrifying vision of what a loss of emotion and empathy would do to us. It's also the first Second Doctor story where the action is centred in an isolated base that's under siege from the unknown, a model that would come to dominate the following year (and here positing a manned base on the Moon two years before we had been there in the real world). With much of Patrick Troughton's first year as the Doctor missing from the archive, this is a chance to see him when still settling into the role, as well as a sadly now rare appearance of Ben and Polly.

THE EPISODES

Episodes one and three, of which no film copies are known to exist, have been recreated with black-and-white animation by Planet 55 Studios with reference to surviving images from the serial and matched to a remastered recording of the soundtrack made on audio tape when the episodes were originally broadcast. Episodes two and four are newly restored from 16mm film copies of the original black-and-white video recordings, the former surviving in the archive while the latter was recovered by Roger Stevens in 1981 (its missing 'Next episode' caption is taken from a lower-quality film copy that was retained in the archive), using more advanced clean-up techniques than their previous release in the Lost in Time set. Their mono soundtracks are remastered and the VidFIRE process is applied to studio-recorded shots to recapture the smoother motion of video. The title sequences are replaced by a modern transfer of the original 35mm film with end credits remade to match the originals.

SPECIAL FEATURES

LUNAR LANDING (21m28s) The making of *The Moonbase*, including the speedy return of the Cybermen; accommodating the addition of Jamie to the TARDIS crew; refining Patrick Troughton's performance as the Doctor; casting the lead guest role; filming 'on the Moon' at Ealing Studios; dangerous sets and confusing Cybermen in the studio; devising the Cybermen's voices; and writing a good part for Polly. With contributions from production assistant Desmond McCarthy, and actors Frazer Hines, Reg Whitehead and Anneke Wills. Produced by Chris Chapman.

PHOTO GALLERY (4m25s) Slideshow of black-and-white photos taken during production of *The Moonbase*, including design department photos of the sets. Set to stock music used in the story. Compiled by Paul Shields.

PDF MATERIALS Accessible via a computer are the four episode listings from *Radio Times* for the original BBC1 broadcast of *The Moonbase* and an article that introduced the story.

AUDIO OPTIONS Select **Commentary** to play the audio commentary in place of the main soundtrack when watching the episodes. On episodes two and four, this is moderated by actor and comedian Toby Hadoke, talking with Frazer Hines (Jamie), Anneke Wills (Polly) and special sounds creator Brian Hodgson, joined on episode two by Edward Phillips (Bob). On episode one Hadoke presents extracts from an archive audio interview with producer Innes Lloyd and new interviews with Kit Pedler's daughters Carol Topolski and Lucy Pedler. On episode three Hadoke interviews assistant floor manager Lovett Bickford and Cybermen actors Derek Chaffer, Barry Noble and Reg Whitehead, and presents an archive interview with voice artist Peter Hawkins.

— Select **Feature Audio** to reinstate the main soundtrack when watching the episodes.

INFO TEXT Select **On** to view subtitles when watching episodes two and four that provide information and anecdotes about the development, production, broadcast and history of *The Moonbase*. Written by Martin Wiggins.

COMING SOON (59s) Trailer for the DVD release of *The Underwater Menace* (not yet released).

SUBTITLES

Select **On** to view subtitles for all episodes and Special Features (except commentary).

RELATED EXTRAS

The Cyber-Generations — Attack of the Cybermen

The Cyber Story — Attack of the Cybermen

Coming Soon trailer — The Tenth Planet, Terror of the Zygons

THE **MOVIE**

STORY No.156

One disc with one episode (86 mins) and 43½ minutes of extras, plus commentary and music-only tracks, production subtitles and image content

TARDIS TEAM Seventh and Eighth Doctors, and introducing Grace

TIME AND PLACE San Francisco, end of 1999

ADVERSARIES Fourth Master

FIRST ON TV 14 May 1996 (US); 27 May 1996 (UK)

DVD RELEASE BBCDVD1043, 13 August 2001, 12
COVER Photo montage, dark turquoise strip
ORIGINAL RRP £19.99
— Reissued in sleeve with orange logo and cover montage in a circle against dark purple
background; BBCDVD2473, £9.99, 2 July 2007

STORY TEASER

The Doctor is taking the exterminated remains of the Master back to their home planet. But the evil Time Lord is not as dead as he seems and in a mutated form he sabotages the TARDIS, forcing it to land on Earth at the end of the 20th Century. Emerging into an alleyway in San Francisco's Chinatown, the Doctor is shot by gang members and rushed to hospital, but his alien anatomy confuses surgeon Grace Holloway and he appears to die on the operating table. The Master takes possession of a human body but needs to track down the newly regenerated Doctor and absorb his remaining lives to stabilise the process, even if doing so means bringing about the end of the world.

CONNECTIONS

The Master features in the preceding televised story *Survival* (1989) although clearly much has happened to him in the time the programme has been away. This is the second time he has harassed the Doctor during one of the latter's regenerations, as he did in *Logopolis* (1981) and *Castrovalva* (1982). The Doctor also spends the early hours of his third incarnation in a hospital (*Spearhead from Space*, 1970), takes an injured Sarah Jane to one in *The Hand of Fear* (1976), is himself admitted to the Bi-Al medical facility in *The Invisible Enemy* (1977), visits the Albion Hospital in both *Aliens of London* and *The Empty Child/The Doctor Dances* (2005), spends time with a hospitalised Face of Boe in *New Earth* (2006), checks himself into the Royal Hope Hospital in *Smith and Jones* (2007), and defeats Patient Zero in Leadworth's hospital in *The Eleventh Hour* (2010). Like Grace, previous companion Harry Sullivan was a surgeon while Martha Jones was a trainee doctor, both of whom worked as medical officers for UNIT. The Doctor has experience of riding motorbikes, taking them for a spin in *The Dæmons* (1971), *Delta and the Bannermen* (1987), *Survival* (1989) and *The Bells of Saint John* (2013), as well as a moped in *The Idiot's Lantern* (2006). The Eye of Harmony is first mentioned and seen in *The Deadly Assassin* (1976), although then it's on Gallifrey. As *The Movie* was an American production, Sylvester McCoy is the only person who worked on it to have previously had any involvement with *Doctor Who*.

WORTH WATCHING

This looked like being Paul McGann's only ever appearance as the Eighth Doctor until his surprise return in the fiftieth anniversary online prequel *The Night of the Doctor* (2013). Nevertheless, *The Movie* is his prime outing and is sufficient to show what an interesting Doctor he would have made had a series followed. Despite the American production and somewhat overdone references to the past, this still fits with what went before (and came after) in terms of style and feel such that, while fans were initially unsure whether it counted as part of the series, it is now categorically a valid part of *Doctor Who*'s diverse history.

THE EPISODE

The movie was shot on 35mm colour film running at 24 frames per second (fps), which for editing was transferred to videotape in the standard format used in America: 60 interlaced fields per second, equivalent to 30fps. Instead of creating two video fields from each film frame (as is usual in the UK where 25fps film transfers neatly to 50-field-per-second videotape), this uses a process called 3:2 Pulldown to repeat certain video fields. For broadcast and VHS release in the UK in 1996, a conversion was supplied that removed these duplicate fields to produce a videotape that effectively has 48 fields per second, so when played at the usual 50 fields per second the programme is 4% shorter. The movie on this disc is restored from this original conversion, thereby retaining some shots that were cut before it was broadcast on BBC1 in 1996 (although this uncut version was shown on BBC2 in November 1999).

SPECIAL FEATURES *ALSO ON SPECIAL EDITION

*BBC TRAILER 1 (37s) Preview of the original BBC1 broadcast of *The Movie*.
*BBC TRAILER 2 (24s) Trailer shown on BBC1 the same day *The Movie* was broadcast.

*FOX PROMO (4m15s) Promotional video produced by US broadcaster Fox in 1996, featuring interviews with cast and crew, plus behind-the-scenes footage.

*INTERVIEWS (20m3s) Select to watch the full interviews from which extracts were used in the Fox promo above, with actors Sylvester McCoy (2m21s), Paul McGann (1m59s), Eric Roberts (52s) and Daphne Ashbrook (1m27s), executive producer Philip Segal (2m8s) and director Geoffrey Sax (2m16s). Plus a newly recorded interview with Philip Segal (9m).

*AUDIO OPTIONS Select **Commentary On** to play the audio commentary in place of the main soundtrack when watching the movie. With director Geoffrey Sax.

— Select **Isolated Music On** to hear only John Debney, Louis Febre and John Sponsler's music when watching the movie.

— Select **4 Audio Tracks** to listen individually to three songs heard in the movie — 'In a Dream', 'Ride into the Moonlight' and 'All Dressed Up' — and an arrangement of 'Auld Lang Syne' that was specially recorded but ultimately unused (9m56s).

PHOTO GALLERY Scroll through 48 colour photos taken during production of *The Movie*, plus publicity shots of Paul McGann taken at the Longleat *Doctor Who* exhibition when his casting was announced. Compiled by Ralph Montagu.

▶

INFORMATION TEXT Select **On** to view subtitles when watching the movie that provide information and anecdotes about its development, production, broadcast and history. Written by Richard Molesworth.

*BEHIND THE SCENES COMPILATION (4m47s) Footage of the shooting of *The Movie* on location and in the studio in January/February 1996, recorded by Fox for its promotional material.

*PHILIP SEGAL TOURS THE TARDIS SET (2m34s) The executive producer highlights some of the details in Richard Hudolin's impressive set for the TARDIS control room, recorded by Fox for its promotional material.

*ALTERNATE SCENE – "GIVE HIM THE KEYS!" (46s) A longer version of the scene in which the Doctor and Grace confront a motorcycle cop.

*ALTERNATE SCENE – "PUCCINI!" (17s) A different take of the newly regenerated Doctor meeting Grace in the hospital elevator.

Ⓜ

SUBTITLES
Select **On** to view subtitles for the episode and Special Features, or for the commentary.

EASTER EGG
There is one hidden feature on this disc to find. *See Appendix 2 for details*

THE **MOVIE** SPECIAL EDITION
STORY №.156

Released with **THE CAVES OF ANDROZANI SPECIAL EDITION** and **THE TALONS OF WENG-CHIANG SPECIAL EDITION** in the **REVISITATIONS 1** boxset
Two discs with one episode (86 mins) and 213½ minutes of extras, plus music-only and two commentary tracks, production subtitles and PDF items
Audio navigation of each disc's contents available by pressing Enter after the BBC ident

TARDIS TEAM Seventh and Eighth Doctors, and introducing Grace

TIME AND PLACE San Francisco, end of 1999

ADVERSARIES Fourth Master

FIRST ON TV 14 May 1996 (US); 27 May 1996 (UK)

DVD RELEASE BBCDVD2806(C), 4 October 2010, 12 (disc one extras and disc two PG)

COVER Photo illustration by Clayton Hickman, light blue strip;
version with older BBC logo on reverse

ORIGINAL RRP £39.99 (boxset)

— Episode released in the **Regeneration** box; BBCDVD3801, £61.27, 24 June 2013

STORY TEASER

The Doctor is taking the exterminated remains of the Master back to their home planet. But the evil Time Lord is not as dead as he seems and in a mutated form he sabotages the TARDIS, forcing it to land on Earth at the end of the 20th Century. Emerging into an alleyway in San Francisco's Chinatown, the Doctor is shot by gang members and rushed to hospital, but his alien anatomy confuses surgeon Grace Holloway and he appears to die on the operating table. The Master takes possession of a human body but needs to track down the newly regenerated Doctor and absorb his remaining lives to stabilise the process, even if doing so means bringing about the end of the world.

CONNECTIONS

The Master features in the preceding televised story *Survival* (1989) although clearly much has happened to him in the time the programme has been away. This is the second time he has harassed the Doctor during one of the latter's regenerations, as he did in *Logopolis* (1981) and *Castrovalva* (1982). The Doctor also spends the early hours of his third incarnation in a hospital (*Spearhead from Space*, 1970), takes an injured Sarah Jane to one in *The Hand of Fear* (1976), is himself admitted to the Bi-Al medical facility in *The Invisible Enemy* (1977), visits the Albion Hospital in both *Aliens of London* and *The Empty Child/The Doctor Dances* (2005), spends time with a hospitalised Face of Boe in *New Earth* (2006), checks himself into the Royal Hope Hospital in *Smith and Jones* (2007), and defeats Patient Zero in Leadworth's hospital in *The Eleventh Hour* (2010). Like Grace, previous companion Harry Sullivan was a surgeon while Martha Jones was a trainee doctor, both of whom worked as medical officers for UNIT. The Doctor has experience of riding motorbikes, taking them for a spin in *The Dæmons* (1971), *Delta and the Bannermen* (1987), *Survival* (1989) and *The Bells of Saint John* (2013), as well as a moped in *The Idiot's Lantern* (2006). The Eye of Harmony is first mentioned and seen in *The Deadly Assassin* (1976), although then it's on Gallifrey. As *The Movie* was an American production, Sylvester McCoy is the only person who worked on it to have previously had any involvement with *Doctor Who*.

WORTH WATCHING

This Special Edition features further clean-up of the episodes compared to the previous release and additional Special Features. *The Movie* looked like being Paul McGann's only ever appearance as the Eighth Doctor until his surprise return in the fiftieth anniversary online prequel *The Night of the Doctor* (2013). Nevertheless, it's his prime outing and is sufficient to show what an interesting Doctor he would have made had a series followed. Despite the American production and somewhat overdone references to the past, this still fits with what went before (and came after) in terms of style and feel such that, while fans were initially unsure whether it counted as part of the series, it is now categorically a valid part of *Doctor Who*'s diverse history.

DISC ONE

THE EPISODE

The movie was shot on 35mm colour film running at 24 frames per second (fps), which for editing was transferred to videotape in the standard format used in America: 60 interlaced fields per second, equivalent to 30fps. Instead of creating two video fields from each film frame (as is usual in the UK where 25fps film transfers neatly to 50-field-per-second videotape), this uses a process called 3:2 Pulldown to repeat certain video fields. For broadcast and VHS release in the UK in 1996, a conversion was supplied that removed these duplicate fields to produce a videotape that effectively has 48 fields per second, so when played at the usual 50 fields per second the programme is 4% shorter. The movie on this disc is restored from this original conversion, thereby retaining some shots that were cut before it was broadcast on BBC1 in 1996 (although this uncut version was shown on BBC2 in November 1999).

SPECIAL FEATURES *REPEATED FROM PREVIOUS RELEASE

THE SEVEN YEAR HITCH (53m54s) The story of how *Doctor Who* finally returned nearly seven years after the original series ended thanks to the persistence of American television producer Philip Segal, including the reasons behind the show's hiatus; UK-born Segal's fondness for the series and initial approach to the BBC; complications from the potential cinema movie; Segal's move to Amblin Entertainment and backing from Steven Spielberg; hope with the appointment of a *Who-*

friendly controller of BBC1; BBC Enterprises' plans for a VHS special, 'The Dark Dimension', and Segal's objection; the input of writer John Leekley to initial storyline ideas; early thoughts on casting the Doctor; interest from Fox as Amblin gets cold feet; finding a writer who could please all parties; dispute over bringing back Sylvester McCoy; appointing a director and finalising the main cast; last-minute script changes; and the movie's successes despite not going on to a full series. With contributions from BBC1 controller Alan Yentob, BBC head of drama series Peter Cregeen, executive producer Philip Segal, BBC executive producer Jo Wright, writer Matthew Jacobs and 'Dark Dimension' director Graeme Harper. Narrated by Amanda Drew, written and produced by Ed Stradling.

THE DOCTOR'S STRANGE LOVE (17m11s) Writers Simon Guerrier and Joseph Lidster and comedian Josie Long discuss the highs and lows of *The Movie* from a fan's point of view. *See Index iii for further editions*

PHOTO GALLERY (3m48s) Slideshow of colour and black-and-white photos taken during production of *The Movie*, set to music from the story. Compiled by Paul Shields.

AUDIO OPTIONS Select *Commentary 1 to play the audio commentary recorded for the previous release in place of the main soundtrack when watching the movie. With director Geoffrey Sax.

— Select **Commentary 2** to play the audio commentary recorded for this release when watching the movie. This is moderated by writer and actor Nicholas Briggs, talking with actors Sylvester McCoy and Paul McGann.

— Select *Isolated Music to hear only John Debney, Louis Febre and John Sponsler's music when watching the movie.

— Select *4 Audio Tracks to listen to three songs heard in the movie — 'In a Dream', 'Ride into the Moonlight' and 'All Dressed Up' — and an arrangement of 'Auld Lang Syne' that was specially recorded but ultimately unused (9m56s).

— Select **Feature Audio** to reinstate the main soundtrack when watching the movie.

INFO TEXT Select **On** to view subtitles when watching the movie that provide information and anecdotes about its development, production, broadcast and history, updated and expanded from the previous release. Written by Niall Boyce.

PDF MATERIALS Accessible via a computer is the listing from *Radio Times* for the original broadcast of *The Movie*, plus the cover of the 25 May 1996 edition (issue 3774), a piece previewing *The Movie* and a page of merchandise offers.

— The sixteen-page souvenir supplement from the above edition of *Radio Times* celebrating *The Movie* and charting the previous Doctors.

COMING SOON (51s) Trailer for the DVD release of *The Seeds of Doom*.

SUBTITLES

Select **On** to view subtitles for the episode and all Special Features on disc one (except commentaries).

DISC TWO

PRE-PRODUCTION

PAUL McGANN AUDITION (7m40s) VHS footage of Paul McGann performing extracts from John Leekley's script in a screen test for the part of the Doctor in September 1994.

VFX TESTS JUNE 1994 (50s) Test computer graphics by Amblin Imaging for the title sequence and a potential new form of Dalek.

VFX MARCH 1996 (2m33s) Computer graphics by Northwest Imaging for the final title sequence, TARDIS dematerialisation, Eye of Harmony, snake creature and other effects. Taken from a silent VHS copy with on-screen time-code.

PRODUCTION *REPEATED FROM PREVIOUS RELEASE

*EPK (15m24s) Promotional video produced by US broadcaster Fox in 1996, featuring interviews with cast and crew, plus behind-the-scenes footage; and the full interviews with actors Sylvester McCoy, Paul McGann, Eric Roberts and Daphne Ashbrook, executive producer Philip Segal and director Geoffrey Sax.

*BEHIND THE SCENES (4m47s) Footage of the shooting of *The Movie* on location and in the studio in January/February 1996, recorded by Fox for its promotional material.

*PHILIP SEGAL'S TOUR OF THE TARDIS SET (2m34s) The executive producer highlights some of the details in Richard Hudolin's impressive set for the TARDIS control room, recorded by Fox for its promotional material.

*ALTERNATE TAKES (1m4s) A different take of the newly regenerated Doctor meeting Grace in the hospital elevator, and a longer version of the scene in which the Doctor and Grace confront a motorcycle cop.

SPECIAL FEATURES *REPEATED FROM PREVIOUS RELEASE

*BBC TRAILS (1m2s) Two trailers for the original BBC1 broadcast of *The Movie*.

WHO PETER 1989-2009 (26m44s) BBC1 children's magazine programme *Blue Peter* has been a frequent promoter of *Doctor Who* throughout both series' histories. Gethin Jones presents a rundown of *Blue Peter*'s items about *Doctor Who* following the end of the Classic Series, keeping the programme in children's minds until it returned in 2005 and became a popular hit again. With contributions from *Blue Peter* editor Richard Marson, New Series showrunner Russell T Davies, brand executive Edward Russell, writers Clayton Hickman and Robert Shearman, and competition winners William Grantham, creator of the Abzorbaloff, and John Bell, who was cast as Creet in *Utopia* (2007). Written and produced by Chris Chapman. *Part one looking at the Classic Series years is on* The Horns of Nimon

THE WILDERNESS YEARS (23m31s) Even though *Doctor Who* was no longer on television after the 1989 season, stories about the Doctor's adventures proliferated across other media, including the comic strip in Marvel's *Doctor Who Magazine*, Virgin Books' New Adventures range of novels, BBV's and Reeltime Pictures' video dramas, and the 1993 documentary *30 Years in the TARDIS*. Then, following the one-off television movie, BBC Books ran its own range of novels telling new stories with the Eighth and earlier Doctors, and Big Finish began producing audio dramas on CD. With contributions from former BBC head of drama series Peter Cregeen, script editor Andrew Cartmel, *Doctor Who Magazine* editors John Freeman and Tom Spilsbury, Virgin Books editor Peter Darvill-Evans, video producers Bill Baggs and Keith Barnfather, director Kevin Davies, BBC Books consultant Justin Richards, and Big Finish producer Jason Haigh-Ellery. Narrated by Glen Allen, produced by Steve Broster and Richard Molesworth.

STRIPPED FOR ACTION – THE EIGHTH DOCTOR (19m47s) *Doctor Who* comic strips have run in various publications since the early days of the television series. This examines the Eighth Doctor's comic strip adventures in Marvel Comics UK's and later Panini Comics' *Doctor Who Magazine*, and briefly *Radio Times*. With contributions from magazine editors Alan Barnes and Clayton Hickman, comics writers Scott Gray and Gary Russell, artists Martin Geraghty, Roger Langridge and Lee Sullivan, and comics historians Jeremy Bentham and Paul Scoones. Directed by Marcus Hearn. *See Index iii for further editions*

TOMORROW'S TIMES THE EIGHTH DOCTOR (10m50s) Coverage in the national newspapers of the Eighth Doctor television movie in 1996. Presented by Nicholas Courtney, written and directed by Marcus Hearn. *See Index iii for further editions*

SUBTITLES
Select **On** to view subtitles for all Special Features on disc two.

EASTER EGGS
There are two hidden features on these discs to find. *See Appendix 2 for details*

RELATED EXTRAS
Coming Soon trailer — Time and the Rani

THE **MUTANTS**

STORY No.63   SEASON No.9:4

Two discs with six episodes (146 mins) and 91 minutes of extras, plus commentary track, production subtitles and PDF items
Audio navigation of each disc's contents available by pressing Enter after the BBC ident

TARDIS TEAM Third Doctor, Jo
TIME AND PLACE Planet Solos and orbiting Skybase, 30th Century
ADVERSARIES The Marshal, head of Skybase; Mutts, mutated Solonians
FIRST ON TV 8 April–13 May 1972
DVD RELEASE BBCDVD3042, 31 January 2011, PG
COVER Photo illustration by Lee Binding, purple strip; version with older BBC logo on reverse
ORIGINAL RRP £19.99

STORY TEASER

The Time Lords dispatch the Doctor to the planet Solos with a message box that will open only for the intended recipient, but don't tell him who that is. Is it one of the humans on the orbiting Skybase, who are preparing to withdraw their colonial plans against the brutal Marshal's wishes; or is it a Solonian native, long persecuted by the humans and violently seeking their independence, even though more of their people are mutating into hideous insect creatures?

CONNECTIONS

This is the third mission the Time Lords send the Doctor on during his supposed exile, after mediating on Uxarieus in *Colony in Space* (1971) and on Peladon in *The Curse of Peladon* (1972). Although his sentence is lifted shortly after (*The Three Doctors*, 1972/73), the Doctor is press-ganged again in *Genesis of the Daleks* (1975) and *The Brain of Morbius* (1976). Human involvement in other worlds is often at the expense of native inhabitants, including in *The Sensorites* (1964), *The Power of Kroll* (1978/79), *The Trial of a Time Lord: Terror of the Vervoids* (1986), *The Happiness Patrol* (1988), *Planet of the Ood* (2009) and *Forest of the Dead* (2009). Here humanoids evolve into an insectoid form, whereas in *The Ark in Space* (1975) they were forcibly mutated, while for the Vespiform it's a natural ability (*The Unicorn and the Wasp*, 2009). Bob Baker and Dave Martin wrote the previous year's *The Claws of Axos* and several later Third and Fourth Doctor stories, while Christopher Barry directed the very first Dalek story in 1963 and worked on *Doctor Who* on and off until 1979 (*see Index v*). Paul Whitsun-Jones (the Marshal) plays Squire Edwards in *The Smugglers* (1966), and Geoffrey Palmer (the Administrator) had more recently been seen as Edward Masters in *Doctor Who and the Silurians* (1970) and appears in the New Series as the Titanic's Captain Hardaker in *Voyage of the Damned* (2008). Christopher Coll (Stubbs) battles the Ice Warriors as Phipps in *The Seeds of Death* (1969); James Mellor (Varan) helps defeat the Cybermen as Flannigan in *The Wheel in Space* (1968); and as Castellan Spandrell, George Pravda (Jaeger) encounters the Master in *The Deadly Assassin* (1976), as well as playing Alexander Denes in *The Enemy of the World* (1967/68). Garrick Hagon (Ky) appears in the New Series as Abraham in *A Town Called Mercy* (2012).

WORTH WATCHING

Just two stories after analogising the European Economic Community, *Doctor Who* was back in the realm of contemporary politics with this parallel of the apartheid system then operating in South Africa, as well as earlier British withdrawals from colonised countries as its Empire shrank. Rather than sermonising, however, this is just background flavour to a typical Baker and Martin script that throws in ideas like there's no tomorrow yet brings them all together in an intriguing story.

DISC ONE

THE EPISODES

Episodes one and two are reverse-converted and restored from digital duplicates of conversions of the original two-inch colour videotape recordings in a lower-resolution format, recovered from a Canadian broadcaster in 1981. Episodes three, four, five and six are restored from digital duplicates of the original two-inch colour videotape recordings used for broadcast. All episodes' mono soundtracks are remastered and the title sequences replaced by a modern transfer of the original 35mm film with credits remade to match the originals.

SPECIAL FEATURES

AUDIO OPTIONS Select **Commentary** to play the audio commentary in place of the main soundtrack when watching the episodes. This is moderated by actor and writer Nicholas Pegg, talking with Katy Manning (Jo) [eps 1,2,4,6], script editor Terrance Dicks [1,3,5], director Christopher Barry [1,3,5,6], writer Bob Baker [1,5,6], special sounds creator Brian Hodgson [2,4], Garrick Hagon

(Ky) [2,4,6] and designer Jeremy Bear [3,5].

— Select **Feature Audio** to reinstate the main soundtrack when watching the episodes.

INFO TEXT Select **On** to view subtitles when watching the episodes that provide information and anecdotes about the development, production, broadcast and history of *The Mutants*. Written by Richard Bignell.

COMING SOON (1m4s) Trailer for the DVD release of *The Ark*.

SUBTITLES

Select **On** to view subtitles for all episodes and the Coming Soon trailer (none for commentary).

DISC TWO

SPECIAL FEATURES

MUTT MAD (20m39s) The making of *The Mutants*, including writing the script and its political allegories; the character of Ky and casting of Cotton; designing the sets (featuring design sketches) and the legacy of one particular piece of scenery; the location filming at Chislehurst Caves; James Acheson's Mutt costume design; staging the episode four cliffhanger and the transformation of Ky; and echoes of *Monty Python* in the opening scene. With contributions from producer Barry Letts (interviewed in 2008), script editor Terrance Dicks, writer Bob Baker, director Christopher Barry, designer Jeremy Bear and actor Garrick Hagon. Produced by Chris Chapman.

RACE AGAINST TIME (37m37s) How contemporary issues of imperialism and indigenous peoples are depicted in *Doctor Who*, particularly *The Mutants*, and the use of ethnic actors in the programme and British television generally. With contributions from writer and critic Bidisha, author Stephen Bourne, actor Fraser James and fan journalist Peter Ware. Written by Simon Guerrier, narrated by Noel Clarke, produced by Thomas Guerrier.

DRESSING DOCTOR WHO (27m5s) Costume designer James Acheson talks about his work on *Doctor Who* during the 1970s, which began with *The Mutants*, creating iconic costumes and monsters for this and *The Three Doctors* (1972/73), *Carnival of Monsters* (1973), *The Time Warrior* (1973/74), *Robot* (1974/75), *Terror of the Zygons* (1975), *The Masque of Mandragora* (1976) and *The Deadly Assassin* (1976). Narrated by Simon Ockenden.

BLUE PETER (1m36s) Extract from the Monday 27 November 1972 edition of the BBC1 children's magazine programme in which Peter Purves meets a Draconian (as yet unseen on screen), Oberon (sic, actually an Ogron) and Sea Devil to promote a BBC Visual Effects exhibition at the Science Museum which ran from 7 November 1972 until 10 June 1973.

PHOTO GALLERY (2m58s) Slideshow of colour and black-and-white photos taken during production of *The Mutants*, including design department photos of the sets. Set to music from the story. Compiled by Paul Shields.

PDF MATERIALS Accessible via a computer are the six episode listings from *Radio Times* for the original BBC1 broadcast of *The Mutants*, with illustrations by Frank Bellamy.

SUBTITLES Select **On** to view subtitles for all Special Features on disc two.

RELATED EXTRAS

Musical Scales — Doctor Who and the Silurians
Coming Soon trailer — Meglos

MYTHS AND LEGENDS

Boxset of **THE HORNS OF NIMON**, **THE TIME MONSTER** and **UNDERWORLD**

DVD RELEASE BBCDVD2851, 29 March 2010, 12

SLIPCASE Photo illustration by Clayton Hickman, silvered logo and title, pink/black background

ORIGINAL RRP £49.99

WHAT'S IN THE BOX

Three stories that contain elements relating to Greek mythology. In *The Time Monster* (1972) the Master is seeking to gain the power of the eponymous Kronos while the Third Doctor and Jo visit ancient Atlantis and meet the Minotaur. *Underworld* (1978) takes plot elements from the myth of Jason and the Argonauts and their quest for the golden fleece. *The Horns of Nimon* (1979/80) features the Minotaur-like Nimon which lives in a labyrinth demanding sacrifices.

● *See individual stories for full contents*

NEW BEGINNINGS

Boxset of **CASTROVALVA**, **THE KEEPER OF TRAKEN** and **LOGOPOLIS**

DVD RELEASE BBCDVD1331, 29 January 2007, 12

SLIPCASE Photo illustration by Clayton Hickman, silvered logo and title, green/black background

ORIGINAL RRP £29.99

WHAT'S IN THE BOX

Three consecutive stories from 1981/82 that feature the changeover from the Fourth Doctor (Tom Baker) to the Fifth (Peter Davison) as he does battle with a regenerated Master. In *The Keeper of Traken* the Doctor and Adric are summoned to the planet Traken to assist with the Keeper's own transition but find the statue Melkur inciting discord among his court. In *Logopolis* the Doctor learns the Master has gained a new body and is intent on ruling the universe by hijacking the Logopolitans' ability to control entropy. The Doctor saves the universe (of course) but in doing so is forced to regenerate. To recover from the process and the Master's ongoing vendetta, he retires to the peaceful city of Castrovalva but finds evil forces already at work there.

● *See individual stories for full contents*

NIGHTMARE OF EDEN

STORY No.107   SEASON No.17:4

One disc with four episodes (95½ mins) and 55½ minutes of extras, plus commentary track, production subtitles and PDF items

Audio navigation of disc contents available by pressing Enter after the BBC ident

TARDIS TEAM Fourth Doctor, Second Romana, K9

TIME AND PLACE Spaceliner Empress orbiting planet Azure, 22nd Century

ADVERSARIES Mandrels, swamp monsters from planet Eden; drug smugglers

FIRST ON TV 24 November–15 December 1979

DVD RELEASE BBCDVD3378, 2 April 2012, PG (episodes U)

COVER Photo illustration by Lee Binding, dark green strip; version with older BBC logo on reverse

ORIGINAL RRP £20.42

STORY TEASER

Two spaceships collide when emerging from hyperspace, leaving them interlocked with sections of unstable matter. Naturally the Doctor is the only one who can think how to undo the damage, but there are those aboard who have their reasons for keeping the ships fused together. Someone is smuggling the deadly drug Vraxoin, but what does it have to do with a zoologist's morally dubious method of collecting specimens?

CONNECTIONS

Passengers on cruise liners in *Doctor Who* don't have much luck: here they're mauled by Mandrels, in *The Trial of a Time Lord: Terror of the Vervoids* (1986) they're turned into compost, and in *Voyage of the Damned* (2009) they nearly crash into the Earth. The TARDIS almost collides with a ship in hyperspace in *Frontier in Space* (1973), while the same year's *Carnival of Monsters* features a device that's reminiscent of the Continuous Event Transmuter. The man-eating plants of Eden are akin to the Fungoids in *The Chase* (1965), the Sontaran-eating plant in *The Invasion of Time* (1978) and the bell plants on Tigella (*Meglos*, 1980). Although drugs are used medicinally throughout the series, Vraxoin is a rare instance of an addictive substance being featured, alongside Li H'Sen Chang's opium smoking in *The Talons of Weng-Chiang* (1977) and the mood drugs featured in *Gridlock*

(2007). This is writer Bob Baker's only solo script for the series, having previously written for the Third and Fourth Doctors with partner Dave Martin (*see Index v*), while Alan Bromly previously directed *The Time Warrior* (1973/74). That story also features David Daker, here playing Captain Rigg, while Geoffrey Hinsliff (Fisk) is Jack Tyler in *Image of the Fendahl* (1977), and Peter Craze (Costa) is Dako in *The Space Museum* (1965) and Du Pont *The War Games* (1969).

WORTH WATCHING

Drug taking may seem an inappropriate subject for a tea-time family adventure series, but arguably it's important for popular fiction to engage with such issues. Seven years later children's drama *Grange Hill* was giving familiar characters heroin addictions, whereas here the message is less graphic yet still delivered with conviction, especially by Tom Baker. Lightening the tone (deliberately or not) are the Mandrels, which seem to kill by cuddling, but even they are tied to the underlying theme in an ingenious way.

THE EPISODES

All four episodes are restored from digital duplicates of the original two-inch colour videotape recordings used for broadcast and their mono soundtracks remastered. The title sequences are replaced by a modern transfer of the original 35mm film with credits remade to match the originals.

SPECIAL FEATURES

THE NIGHTMARE OF TELEVISION CENTRE (13m23s) A look at the more troubled aspects of the production of *Nightmare of Eden*, including the unusual move of shooting models on video rather than film; the Mandrel costumes and making them crumble to dust; and problems with director Alan Bromly leading to his departure mid-recording. With contributions from visual effects designer Colin Mapson, assistant floor manager Val McCrimmon and video effects designer AJ Mitchell. Produced by Ed Stradling.

GOING SOLO (7m44s) Bob Baker talks about writing *Nightmare of Eden*, his first script without writing partner Dave Martin, including his inspirations in an earlier script they'd written for police drama series *Target* and scientific writings about hyperspace, and his views of the final production.

THE DOCTOR'S STRANGE LOVE (15m43s) Writers Simon Guerrier and Joseph Lidster and comedian Josie Long discuss the highs and lows of *Nightmare of Eden* from a fan's point of view. *See Index iii for further editions*

ASK ASPEL (11m2s) Extract from the Tuesday 15 July 1980 edition of the BBC1 children's clip-request show in which Michael Aspel talks to Lalla Ward about her career and her illustrations for the book *Astrology for Dogs*. Includes clips of Ward in *The Duchess of Duke Street* and *Hamlet*.

COMING SOON (1m59s) Trailer for the DVD releases of *Dragonfire* and *The Happiness Patrol* in the Ace Adventures boxset.

NEXT

PHOTO GALLERY (5m49s) Slideshow of colour photos taken during production of *Nightmare of Eden*, including design department photos of the sets. Set to sound effects from the story. Compiled by Paul Shields.

AUDIO OPTIONS Select **Commentary** to play the audio commentary in place of the main soundtrack when watching the episodes. This is moderated by actor and comedian Toby Hadoke, talking with writer Bob Baker [eps 1,2], Lalla Ward (Romana) [1,2,3,4], visual effects designer Colin Mapson [1,2,3,4], make-up supervisor Joan Stribling [2,4] and Peter Craze (Costa) [3,4].
— Select **Feature Audio** to reinstate the main soundtrack when watching the episodes.

INFO TEXT Select **On** to view subtitles when watching the episodes that provide information and anecdotes about the development, production, broadcast and history of *Nightmare of Eden*. Written by Nicholas Pegg.

PDF MATERIALS Accessible via a computer are the four episode listings from *Radio Times* for the original BBC1 broadcast of *Nightmare of Eden*.

SUBTITLES

Select **On** to view subtitles for all episodes and Special Features (except commentary).

RELATED EXTRAS

Coming Soon trailer — The Dæmons

PARADISE TOWERS

STORY No.145   SEASON No.24:2

One disc with four episodes (98½ mins) and 77 minutes of extras, plus commentary and alternative music tracks, production subtitles and PDF items
Audio navigation of disc contents available by pressing Enter after the BBC ident

TARDIS TEAM Seventh Doctor, Mel
TIME AND PLACE Future tower block
ADVERSARIES Caretakers and cleaning robots
FIRST ON TV 5–26 October 1987
DVD RELEASE BBCDVD3002, 18 July 2011, PG
COVER Photo illustration by Lee Binding, dark blue strip; version with older BBC logo on reverse
ORIGINAL RRP £20.42

STORY TEASER

Once a bold piece of architecture, Paradise Towers is now a rundown high-rise where yobbish youths and suspicious seniors are ruled over by tyrannical caretakers. But all are at risk from the robotic cleaners, which have been reprogrammed to kill by someone the Towers' original residents believed was long dead. In their search for the culprit, the Doctor and Mel must negotiate dangers everywhere, from the top-floor swimming pool to the spooky basement.

CONNECTIONS

The Doctor again faces dangers in the cellar of a domestic building in *Ghost Light* (1989), while the high-rise maintained by feared officers is similar to the county blocks on Starship UK in *The Beast Below* (2010). A society that has degenerated into tribalism features in *The Face of Evil* (1977), while another instance of people left to fend for themselves in a dangerous environment is seen in *Gridlock* (2007). That year's *Smith and Jones* sees the Doctor encounter another old lady who's more bloodthirsty than she appears. Stephen Wyatt also wrote *The Greatest Show in the Galaxy* the following year, while Nicholas Mallett also directed *The Trial of a Time Lord: The Mysterious Planet* (1986) and *The Curse of Fenric* (1989). Richard Briers (Chief Caretaker) plays Henry Parker in *Torchwood: A Day in the Death* (2008), while his deputy, Clive Merrison, is Jim Callum in *The Tomb of the Cybermen* (1967). Nisha Nayar, who plays a programmer on Satellite Five in *Bad Wolf/The Parting of the Ways* (2005), here has an early role as one of the non-speaking Red Kangs.

WORTH WATCHING

Coming from the troubled 1987 season, *Paradise Towers* is somewhat uneven in tone. The script is aiming for a dark tale of a broken-down society where people have reverted to more primitive states, with an interesting take on how this affects language. Yet the production, and especially the acting, appear to be going for a more comedic approach. That's not to say it doesn't work, in a surreal kind of way, and certainly the aspects of social commentary that new script editor Andrew Cartmel was introducing are something that has been continued in the New Series.

THE EPISODES

All four episodes are restored from digital duplicates of the original one-inch colour videotape recordings used for broadcast and their mono soundtracks remastered.

SPECIAL FEATURES

HORROR ON THE HIGH RISE (34m4s) Composer Mark Ayres examines the making of *Paradise Towers*, including the origins and development of the script; working with director Nicholas Mallett; characterising the kangs, caretakers, rezzies and Pex; the design of the sets and cleaning robots; shooting the swimming pool scenes on location; controversy over a moment of too realistic violence; and composing the original score and, at short notice, its replacement. With contributions from script editor Andrew Cartmel, writer Stephen Wyatt, composers Keff McCulloch and David Snell, and actors Richard Briers, Howard Cooke and Catherine Cusack. Produced by Steve Broster.

DELETED AND EXTENDED SCENES (7m54s) A selection of scenes from the last three episodes not used in the final programme, taken from earlier edits with as-recorded sound. The sections in black-and-white appear in the final episodes while those in colour are the unused scenes, to show where they would have fitted into the story.

CONTINUITY (3m54s) Preview of episode one and continuity announcements from the original BBC1 broadcasts of all four episodes of *Paradise Towers*, with previous-episode summaries and plugs for the next story, *Delta and the Bannermen*, and for *Doctor Who* on video.

GIRLS! GIRLS! GIRLS! THE EIGHTIES (21m44s) Three female companions from the 1980s discuss their time on *Doctor Who*, the portrayal of their characters and to what extent their experiences differed. With Sophie Aldred (Ace), Janet Fielding (Tegan) and Sarah Sutton (Nyssa). Introduced by Peter Purves, produced by Steve Broster.

CASTING SYLVESTER (3m47s) Former BBC director and producer Clive Doig talks about how he first came to work with Sylvester McCoy on *Vision On* and his role in getting the actor cast as the Doctor, as well as his interest in producing *Doctor Who* in the 1980s.

PHOTO GALLERY (4m35s) Slideshow of colour photos taken during production of *Paradise Towers*, set to music from the story. Compiled by Paul Shields.

NEXT

AUDIO OPTIONS Select **Commentary** to play the audio commentary in place of the main soundtrack when watching the episodes. This is moderated by composer and sound engineer Mark Ayres, talking with writer Stephen Wyatt on all four episodes, joined from episode two by actor Judy Cornwell (Maddy) and from episode three by special sounds creator Dick Mills.

— Select **Alternate Score** to hear the soundtrack with David Snell's original music, which was replaced before the serial was broadcast, when watching the episodes.

— Select **Feature Audio** to reinstate the main soundtrack when watching the episodes.

INFO TEXT Select **On** to view subtitles when watching the episodes that provide information and anecdotes about the development, production, broadcast and history of *Paradise Towers*. Written by David Brunt.

PDF MATERIALS Accessible via a computer are the four episode listings from *Radio Times* for the original BBC1 broadcast of *Paradise Towers*.

COMING SOON (1m10s) Trailer for the DVD release of *The Sun Makers*.

SUBTITLES

Select **On** to view subtitles for all episodes and Special Features (except commentary).

RELATED EXTRAS

Coming Soon trailer — The Awakening, The Gunfighters

PELADON TALES

Boxset of **THE CURSE OF PELADON** and **THE MONSTER OF PELADON**

DVD RELEASE BBCDVD2744, 18 January 2010, PG

SLIPCASE Photo illustration by Clayton Hickman, silvered logo and title, purple background

ORIGINAL RRP £29.99

WHAT'S IN THE BOX

The two Third Doctor stories in which he visits the medieval-like world of Peladon and encounters the Ice Warriors. In *The Curse of Peladon* (1972), the Doctor and Jo are sent by the Time Lords to assist with the planet's acceptance into the Galactic Federation, against some traditionalists' desires, and with rival forces seeking to secure Peladon's mineral wealth for themselves. The Doctor returns fifty years later, this time with Sarah Jane, in *The Monster of Peladon* (1974), only to find Federation membership has brought limited advancements and the mining class is on the verge of rebellion, while again enemy agents manipulate the political situation for their own ends.

● *See individual stories for full contents*

THE **PIRATE PLANET**

STORY No.99   SEASON No.16:2

Released with **THE ANDROIDS OF TARA, THE ARMAGEDDON FACTOR, THE POWER OF KROLL, THE RIBOS OPERATION** and **THE STONES OF BLOOD** in **THE KEY TO TIME** boxset
One disc with four episodes (102 mins) and 73½ minutes of extras, plus two commentary tracks, production subtitles and PDF items

TARDIS TEAM Fourth Doctor, First Romana, K9

TIME AND PLACE Planet Zanak

ADVERSARIES The Captain, a cyborg

FIRST ON TV 30 September–21 October 1978

DVD RELEASE BBCDVD2335(B), 24 September 2007, PG

COVER Photo illustration by Clayton Hickman, yellow strip

ORIGINAL RRP £69.99 (boxset)

STORY TEASER

The search for the Key to Time directs the TARDIS to the planet Calufrax, except when the Doctor and Romana emerge they inexplicably find themselves on Zanak. They learn how, periodically, the stars change position and the mineral wealth of the planet is miraculously renewed. Ruling over the meek inhabitants is the Captain, a bombastic bully who drains planets of their resources and energy. Calufrax has already fallen victim, and the Captain's next target is Earth. To stop him, the Doctor must uncover Zanak's secret and the real power behind the throne.

CONNECTIONS

This is the second story in the arc for the 1978/79 season, the quest for the Key to Time, and the first script for the series by Douglas Adams. He became *Doctor Who*'s script editor for the following season and wrote the final script for *City of Death* (1979), as well as the uncompleted *Shada* (1980). Zanak powers its own jumps across space, but in *The Stolen Earth/Journey's End* (2008) the Daleks use a Magnotron to shift planets into the Medusa Cascade, a device first used by the Time Lords in *The Trial of a Time Lord* (1986). The Daleks previously planned to remove the Earth's core and install an engine to pilot the planet (*The Dalek Invasion of Earth*, 1964), and the Tractators hoped to use their gravitational control to likewise steer a planet (*Frontios*, 1984). Owing to the cancellation of *Shada*, this was director Pennant Roberts' last broadcast work on *Doctor Who* until his return in the mid-80s (*see Index v*). The Doctor meets more traditional pirate types in *The Smugglers* (1966) and *The Curse of the Black Spot* (2011).

WORTH WATCHING

It's a Douglas Adams script so is full of his typical inventiveness and humour (and some lines that are awfully similar to ones in *The Hitchhiker's Guide to the Galaxy*, which he was writing around the same time). As such it prefigures the style of the following season, which Adams script-edited, with a more flippant Doctor and outrageous villain. Yet the ideas at the heart of the storyline are strong, and it's particularly good story for lovers of K9.

THE EPISODES

All four episodes are restored from digital duplicates of the original two-inch colour videotape recordings used for broadcast, with location sequences newly transferred from the original 16mm colour film negatives. This has required shots that mix film and video elements to be recomposited and some video effects recreated. The episodes' mono soundtracks are remastered and the title sequences replaced by a modern transfer of the original 35mm film with credits remade to match the originals.

SPECIAL FEATURES

PARROT FASHION (30m30s) The making of *The Pirate Planet*, including memories of the writer's early work and his first commission for *Doctor Who*; the characters and cast; filming in a genuine power station and on location in Gwent, Wales; similarities with *The Hitchhiker's Guide to the Galaxy*; and creating the visual effects, particularly the Polyphase Avatron. With contributions from writer Douglas Adams via an audio interview recorded in 1978 and a video interview from

1985, his half-brother James Thrift and biographer Nick Webb, script editor Anthony Read, director Pennant Roberts, film cameraman Elmer Cossey, visual effects designer Colin Mapson, and actors John Leeson, Rosalind Lloyd, Bruce Purchase, Mary Tamm and Primi Townsend. Produced by Kevin Davies.

FILM INSERTS, DELETED SCENES & OUTTAKES (13m57s) Footage from the 16mm colour film shot on location, including shots not used in the final programme (the silent portions). Plus fluffed lines taken from a VHS copy of the film footage with on-screen time-code, and two deleted scenes taken from a low-quality black-and-white video copy of the original studio recording in late-May 1978 with on-screen time-code.

WEIRD SCIENCE (17m26s) Spoof science show testing the accuracy of the science in *Doctor Who* circa 1978. With David Graham and Mat Irvine. Written and produced by Anthony Caulfield and Nicola Woodroff.

CONTINUITIES (3m43s) Continuity announcements from the original BBC1 broadcasts of episodes one and three of *The Pirate Planet* reconstructed by matching audio recordings made at the time of broadcast to clips from the episode, and for episodes two and four taken from a home video recording. Includes a trail for *Larry Grayson's Generation Game*, the BBC1 evening schedule for Saturday 21 October, and the UK weather for Sunday 22 October 1978.

NEXT

AUDIO OPTIONS Select **Commentary 1** to play the audio commentary recorded for an earlier US-only release of the story in place of the main soundtrack when watching the episodes. With director Pennant Roberts and Bruce Purchase (Captain) on all four episodes.

— Select **Commentary 2** to play the audio commentary recorded for this release when watching the episodes, with Tom Baker, Mary Tamm (Romana) and script editor Anthony Read on all four episodes.

— Select **Feature Audio** to reinstate the main soundtrack when watching the episodes.

INFO TEXT Select **On** to view subtitles when watching the episodes that provide information and anecdotes about the development, production, broadcast and history of *The Pirate Planet*. Written by Martin Wiggins.

PHOTO GALLERY (7m2s) Slideshow of colour and black-and-white photos taken during production of *The Pirate Planet*, set to sound effects from the story. Compiled by Derek Handley.

COMING SOON (1m) Trailer for the DVD release of *Planet of Evil*.

RADIO TIMES LISTINGS Accessible via a computer is a PDF file of the four episode listings for the original BBC1 broadcast of *The Pirate Planet*.

SUBTITLES

Select **On** to view subtitles for all episodes and Special Features (except commentaries).

RELATED EXTRAS

Coming Soon trailer — The Time Warrior

P

PLANET OF EVIL

STORY No.**81**   SEASON No.**13:2**

One disc with four episodes (94½ mins) and 61 minutes of extras, plus commentary track, production subtitles and PDF items
Audio navigation of disc contents available by pressing Enter after the BBC ident

TARDIS TEAM Fourth Doctor, Sarah Jane
TIME AND PLACE Jungle planet Zeta Minor
ADVERSARIES Anti-matter creatures
FIRST ON TV 27 September–18 October 1975
DVD RELEASE BBCDVD1814, 15 October 2007, PG
COVER Photo illustration by Lee Binding, red strip
ORIGINAL RRP £19.99

STORY TEASER

The TARDIS picks up a distress call but when it arrives at the remote planet of Zeta Minor the Doctor and Sarah find only an abandoned scientific base and a desiccated corpse. When a spaceship from the scientists' home planet arrives to investigate, the time travellers immediately fall under suspicion, even when the expedition leader Professor Sorenson is found alive. But when the ship tries to leave the planet, strange forces drag it back as the deaths continue to mount.

CONNECTIONS

The idea that a black hole leads to a universe of anti-matter was first seen in *The Three Doctors* (1972/73), and Omega's return from there in *Arc of Infinity* (1983) similarly threatens to destroy our universe by anti-matter annihilation. Although the Doctor pooh-poohs Sorenson's idea for using anti-matter as a power source, he's quite grateful for its use by 26th Century humans in *Earthshock* (1982). The professor's regression to a more primitive state is reminiscent of the Primords in *Inferno* (1970). Invisible creatures are encountered in *The Daleks' Master Plan* (1965/66), *The Ark* (1966), *Planet of the Daleks* (1973), *The Face of Evil* (1977) and *Vincent and the Doctor* (2010). The basic premise of a sentient object being mistaken for an astral body and possessing its tormentors when plundered for its energy is revisited in *42* (2007). Louis Marks also wrote *Planet of Giants* (1964) and *Day of the Daleks* (1972) before being invited back to the series by old pal Robert Holmes, contributing this and *The Masque of Mandragora* (1976). Director David Maloney was at the height of his work on *Doctor Who*, having most recently directed *Genesis of the Daleks* (1975) (*see Index v*). Frederick Jaeger (Sorenson) plays another professor — Marius, creator of K9 — in *The Invisible Enemy* (1977); he's also Jano in *The Savages* (1966) opposite Ewen Solon (Vishinksy) as Chal. Prentis Hancock appears as Vaber in *Planet of the Daleks* (1973), plus smaller roles in *Spearhead from Space* (1970) and *The Ribos Operation* (1978). Michael Wisher (Morelli) is most notable for playing Davros in *Genesis of the Daleks*, but can also be seen in *The Ambassadors of Death* (1970), *Terror of the Autons* (1971) and *Carnival of Monsters* (1973). Graham Weston (De Haan) is also Russell in *The War Games* (1969), while Louis Mahoney (Ponti) is a newsreader in *Frontier in Space* (1973) and appears in the New Series as the older Billy Shipton in *Blink* (2007).

WORTH WATCHING

This is where producer Philip Hinchcliffe and script editor Robert Holmes' unashamed lifting of ideas from classic horror literature and film really kicks in after their first season of stories were largely inherited from the previous production team. Here the inspiration of Robert Louis Stevenson's *Dr Jekyll and Mr Hyde* is obvious — a man alternates between respectable scientist and murderous brute, using a potion to restore himself — while visually the production draws on 1956 movie *Forbidden Planet*, particularly in the appearance of the anti-matter monster.

THE EPISODES

All four episodes are restored from digital duplicates of the original two-inch colour videotape recordings used for broadcast and their mono soundtracks remastered. The title sequences are replaced by a modern transfer of the original 35mm film with credits remade to match the originals.

SPECIAL FEATURES

A DARKER SIDE (25m52s) The making of *Planet of Evil*, including inspirations for the story; creating an alien jungle in Ealing Film Studios; replicating it in the studio and working with multiple-camera set-ups; creating believable sets; doing effects live in the studio; and memories of working with the director. With contributions from producer Philip Hinchcliffe, writer Louis Marks (interviewed in 2005), director David Maloney (interviewed in 2003), designer Roger Murray-Leach, and actors Tom Baker, Prentis Hancock and Elisabeth Sladen. Produced by Ed Stradling.

PLANETARY PERFORMANCE (13m32s) Actors talk about their experiences of rehearsing and recording *Planet of Evil*. With Tom Baker, Prentis Hancock, Tony McEwan, Elisabeth Sladen and Graham Weston. Produced by Steve Broster.

STUDIO SCENE (50s) All that survives of the original studio recording on Monday 30 June 1975 of the episode one cliffhanger.

CONTINUITIES (1m52s) Continuity announcements from the original BBC1 broadcasts of episode four of the preceding story, *Terror of the Zygons*, and episode four of *Planet of Evil* promoting the next story, *Pyramids of Mars*. Plus a trailer for the weekday repeats of *Planet of Evil* and *The Sontaran Experiment* in July 1976.

NEXT

AUDIO OPTIONS Select **Commentary** to play the audio commentary in place of the main soundtrack when watching the episodes. With Tom Baker, Elisabeth Sladen (Sarah Jane), Prentis Hancock (Salamar) and producer Philip Hinchcliffe on all four episodes.

— Select **Feature Audio** to reinstate the main soundtrack when watching the episodes.

INFO TEXT Select **On** to view subtitles when watching the episodes that provide information and anecdotes about the development, production, broadcast and history of *Planet of Evil*. Written by Richard Molesworth.

PHOTO GALLERY (7m5s) Slideshow of colour and black-and-white photos taken during production of *Planet of Evil*, including design department photos of the sets. Set to sound effects from the story. Compiled by Derek Handley.

COMING SOON (1m4s) Trailer for the DVD release of *Destiny of the Daleks*.

RADIO TIMES LISTINGS Accessible via a computer is a PDF file of the four episode listings for the original BBC1 broadcast of *Planet of Evil*, with an illustration by Frank Bellamy (cropped from a larger piece drawn for the repeat of *The Ark in Space* in August 1975).

SUBTITLES

Select **On** to view subtitles for all episodes and Special Features (except commentary).

EASTER EGG

There is one hidden feature on this disc to find. *See Appendix 2 for details*

RELATED EXTRAS

Coming Soon trailer — The Androids of Tara, The Armageddon Factor, The Pirate Planet, The Power of Kroll, The Ribos Operation, The Stones of Blood

Roger Murray-Leach Interview — The Ark in Space (and Special Edition)

PLANET OF FIRE

STORY No.134   SEASON No.21:5

Released with **THE KING'S DEMONS** in the **KAMELION TALES** boxset
Two discs with four episodes (97½ mins), a new 66½-minute Special Edition and 93½ minutes of extras, plus commentary and music-only tracks, production subtitles and PDF items
Audio navigation of each disc's contents available by pressing Enter after the BBC ident

TARDIS TEAM Fifth Doctor, Turlough, Kamelion, and introducing Peri Brown
TIME AND PLACE Contemporary Lanzarote and volcanic planet Sarn
ADVERSARIES Third Master (6th appearance)
FIRST ON TV 23 February–2 March 1984
DVD RELEASE BBCDVD2738(B), 14 June 2010, PG
COVER Photo illustration by Clayton Hickman, light turquoise strip; version with older BBC logo on reverse
ORIGINAL RRP £29.99 (boxset)

P

STORY TEASER

The TARDIS picks up a distress call from Earth just as an archaeologist brings up a strange object from the seabed off the coast of Lanzarote. While the Doctor and Turlough investigate, the Master regains control of shape-changing robot Kamelion and hijacks the TARDIS. With American student Peri Brown aboard, they arrive on the planet Sarn, where the locals worship the god of the nearby volcano, the flame from which can heal the sick. As Turlough's past catches up with him, Kamelion carries out the Master's plan at the risk of dooming the entire planet.

CONNECTIONS

Although Classic *Doctor Who* represented overseas locations at various times, it genuinely travelled abroad for filming only five times: to Paris for *City of Death* (1979), Amsterdam for *Arc of Infinity* (1983), Lanzarote for *Planet of Fire*, Seville for *The Two Doctors* (1985) and to Canada (from America) for *The Movie* (1996). The Master was last seen in the Middle Ages in *The King's Demons* (1983), in which Kamelion — again voiced by Gerald Flood — was snatched from him by the Doctor. His Tissue Compression Eliminator is first used to shrink people in *Terror of the Autons* (1971), then again in *The Deadly Assassin* (1976), *Logopolis* (1981) and *The Mark of the Rani* (1985). The TARDIS lands on the volcanic planet Tigus in *The Daleks' Master Plan* (1965/66) but the Doctor doesn't venture inside a volcano again until *The Fires of Pompeii* (2008). Other religious societies based on discarded technology include the Primitives on Uxaerius in *Colony in Space* (1971), the Exxilons in *Death to the Daleks* (1974), the Tesh in *The Face of Evil* (1977), the Deons in *Meglos* (1980) and the Tribe of the Free in *The Trial of a Time Lord: The Mysterious Planet* (1986). Peter Grimwade wrote Turlough's debut story *Mawdryn Undead* (1983) and the previous year's *Time-Flight*, while this was the last time Fiona Cumming worked on the programme, having earlier directed *Castrovalva* (1982), *Snakedance* (1983) and *Enlightenment* (1983).

WORTH WATCHING

Commissioned to write a story incorporating several cast changes — the departures of Turlough, Kamelion and, potentially, the Master, plus the introduction of new companion Peri — as well as accommodating the desired location filming in Lanzarote, Peter Grimwade manages to tie these all together in connected storylines, while also telling his own story about personal faith versus dogma.

DISC ONE

THE EPISODES

All four episodes are restored from digital duplicates of the original one-inch colour videotape recordings used for broadcast, with location sequences newly transferred from the original 16mm colour film negatives. Their mono soundtracks are remastered and the title sequences replaced by a modern transfer of the original 35mm film with credits remade to match the originals.

SPECIAL FEATURES

THE FLAMES OF SARN (25m36s) The making of *Planet of Fire*, including travelling to Lanzarote for the location filming; Turlough's departure; the problems with Kamelion; recording the demise of the Master; and casting the new companion and other characters. With contributions from director Fiona Cumming and designer Malcolm Thornton in Lanzarote, film cameraman John Walker, actors Nicola Bryant, Peter Davison and Mark Strickson, and producer John Nathan-Turner (taken from his 2000 audio reading of his memoirs). Narrated by Simon Ockenden, produced by Brendan Sheppard.

RETURN TO THE PLANET OF FIRE (12m37s) Fiona Cumming and Malcolm Thornton return to the story's locations on Lanzarote and recall their experiences of filming *Planet of Fire* there. Narrated by Simon Ockenden.

DESIGNS ON SARN (5m2s) Malcolm Thornton, in Lanzarote, talks about his set designs for *Planet of Fire* and their inspiration in the landscape of the island, adapting the Master's TARDIS and the sets for the miniaturised Master.

ALTERNATE EDITS, DELETED AND EXTENDED SCENES (15m25s) A selection of scenes not used in the final programme, including retakes, taken from the full location film footage and a copy of the studio recordings with as-recorded sound and on-screen time-code.

CONTINUITY (1m36s) Continuity announcements from the original BBC1 broadcasts of all four episodes of *Planet of Fire*, with a plug for producer John Nathan-Turner's live appearance on *Saturday Superstore* on 25 February 1984. Includes the BBC1 evening schedule for Thursday 23 February 1984.

PHOTO GALLERY (7m57s) Slideshow of colour photos taken during production of *Planet of Fire*, including design department photos of the sets. Set to music and sound effects from the story. Compiled by Derek Handley.

NEXT

AUDIO OPTIONS Select **Commentary** to play the audio commentary in place of the main soundtrack when watching the episodes. With Peter Davison, Nicola Bryant (Peri), Mark Strickson (Turlough) and director Fiona Cumming on all four episodes.

— Select **Isolated Score** to hear only Peter Howell's music when watching the episodes.
— Select **Feature Audio** to reinstate the main soundtrack when watching the episodes.

INFO TEXT Select **On** to view subtitles when watching the episodes that provide information and anecdotes about the development, production, broadcast and history of *Planet of Fire*. Written by Paul Scoones.

PDF MATERIALS Accessible via a computer are the four episode listings from *Radio Times* for the original BBC1 broadcast of *Planet of Fire*.

COMING SOON (1m3s) Trailer for the DVD release of *The Dominators*.

SUBTITLES
Select **On** to view subtitles for all episodes and Special Features on disc one (except commentary).

DISC TWO

SPECIAL EDITION
On this disc is a new edit of the story as a single 66½-minute episode in widescreen, with a newly recorded pre-titles scene, updated computer-generated visual effects, and stereo or Dolby 5.1 surround soundtrack.

PLAY WITH INTRODUCTION
Before the Special Edition plays, original director Fiona Cumming talks about her aims for the Special Edition (1m25s).

SPECIAL FEATURES
CALLING THE SHOTS (7m48s) How a programme like *Doctor Who* was produced in the television studio in the 1980s and the pressures involved, illustrated with behind-the-scenes footage from the full studio recording of *Planet of Fire*, taken from a copy with on-screen time-code. With comments from director Fiona Cumming, designer Malcolm Thornton and actors Nicola Bryant, Peter Davison and Mark Strickson. Narrated by Simon Ockenden, produced by Brendan Sheppard.

REMEMBERING ANTHONY AINLEY (12m35s) Profile of the life and career of actor Anthony Ainley, who died in 2004, best remembered for playing the Master during the 1980s, featuring footage of Ainley talking at a *Doctor Who* convention about his time on the series. With memories from the cast and crew of *Planet of Fire* interviewed for this DVD. Narrated by Simon Ockenden, produced by Brendan Sheppard.

AUDIO OPTIONS Select **Dolby Digital 5.1** or **Stereo** for the Special Edition soundtrack.

SUBTITLES
Select **On** to view subtitles for the Special Edition and Special Features on disc two.

EASTER EGGS
There are two hidden features on these discs to find. *See Appendix 2 for details*

RELATED EXTRAS
Coming Soon trailer — The Creature from the Pit, Frontier in Space
Peter Grimwade - Directing with Attitude — Kinda

P

PLANET OF GIANTS

STORY No.9   SEASON No.2:1

One disc with three episodes (73½ mins) and 95 minutes of extras, plus commentary and foreign dub tracks, production subtitles and PDF items
Audio navigation of disc contents available by pressing Enter after the BBC ident

TARDIS TEAM First Doctor, Barbara, Ian, Susan
TIME AND PLACE Contemporary England
ADVERSARIES Ruthless businessman Forester
FIRST ON TV 31 October–14 November 1964
DVD RELEASE BBCDVD3479, 20 August 2012, PG (episodes and extras bar DVD trailer U)
COVER Photo illustration by Lee Binding, purple strip; version with older BBC logo on reverse
ORIGINAL RRP £20.42

STORY TEASER

The Doctor finally gets Ian and Barbara back to their own time, but a fault during materialisation causes the TARDIS and its crew to shrink to tiny proportions. They must confront the now-giant creatures of an ordinary English garden to prevent a blinkered scientist and his callous associate from releasing an insecticide that will cause the destruction of all life on Earth.

CONNECTIONS

The Doctor is shrunk to a similar size in *The Armageddon Factor* (1979) but smaller still to operate the Teselecta in *The Wedding of River Song* (2011) (as Amy and Rory had been before him in *Let's Kill Hitler*), and a clone of him is reduced to microscopic size in order to enter the Doctor's own brain in *The Invisible Enemy* (1977). The Chameleons shrink the humans they kidnap in *The Faceless Ones* (1967), while the entire population of the far-future Earth is miniaturised for its trip to a new home in *The Ark* (1966). While the insects here just seem enormous to the diminished time travellers, they soon meet real giant insects on the planet Vortis in *The Web Planet* (1965), and the Doctor fights off a giant fly and maggots in *The Green Death* (1973), the insectoid Wirrn in *The Ark in Space* (1975), man-sized woodlice in *Frontios* (1984) and a waspish Vespiform in *The Unicorn and the Wasp* (2009). Louis Marks later wrote *Day of the Daleks* (1972), *Planet of Evil* (1975) and *The Masque of Mandragora* (1976), while director Mervyn Pinfield was the series' associate producer but also directed *The Space Museum* (1965) and episodes of *The Sensorites* (1964). The original episode four of this story was the first *Doctor Who* directed by Douglas Camfield, who went on to be a respected television director, including helming many of the best regarded *Doctor Who* serials (*see Index v*). This is also the first story to feature music by Dudley Simpson, who became the regular composer for the series throughout the 1970s.

WORTH WATCHING

The idea of having the TARDIS crew negotiate an everyday environment in reduced circumstances had been around ever since *Doctor Who* was conceived but it took a year of production before the producers got the script and studio facilities they needed to stage it with any chance of conviction. What really makes it succeed, however, are Raymond Cusick's clever sets, which totally sell the idea that the actors are only an inch high.

THE EPISODES

Episodes one and two are restored from 16mm film copies of the original black-and-white video recordings, recovered from BBC Enterprises in 1978; episode three is restored from a 16mm film copy of the 35mm film used for broadcast, itself an edited copy of the black-and-white video recordings of the original episodes three and four. Their mono soundtracks are remastered and the VidFIRE process is applied to studio-recorded shots to recapture the smoother motion of video. The title sequences are replaced by a modern transfer of the best surviving copy of the original 35mm film with end credits remade to match the originals.

SPECIAL FEATURES

EPISODE 3&4 RECONSTRUCTION (52m37s) Originally produced as a four-part serial, *Planet of Giants* had its last two episodes cut down into one before transmission to improve the pacing of the story. No copies of the original episodes three and four are known to exist, but the original script does, so for this DVD they have been reconstructed using the unrestored footage from the broadcast episode three with new footage and re-edited shots from other episodes to replace the cut scenes, while the missing dialogue has been re-recorded. Carole Ann Ford and William Russell recreate their roles of Susan and Ian, with John Guilor as the Doctor and Katherine Mount as Barbara, while the remaining parts are voiced by other actors. New material directed by Ian Levine, reconstruction produced by Ed Stradling.

REDISCOVERING THE URGE TO LIVE (8m29s) The producers and actors behind the reconstruction of the original episodes explain how they remade the missing material, while original actors Carole Ann Ford and William Russell recall recording the original serial. With John Guilor, Toby Hadoke, Paul Jones, Ian Levine and Ed Stradling.

SUDDENLY SUSAN (15m18s) Recorded in 2003 for BBC2's *The Story of Doctor Who*, actor Carole Ann Ford recalls her experiences of playing the first ever companion Susan from 1963 to 1964.

THE LAMBERT TAPES – THE DOCTOR (14m) Recorded in 2003 for BBC2's *The Story of Doctor Who*, the series' first producer Verity Lambert recalls her experiences on the programme, including the casting of William Hartnell as the Doctor and her hopes for the then-unbroadcast New Series. *Part one is on* More Than 30 Years in the TARDIS (*see Appendix 1*)
NEXT

PHOTO GALLERY (3m22s) Slideshow of colour and black-and-white photos taken during production of *Planet of Giants*, including design department photos of the 'giant' sets. Compiled by Paul Shields.

AUDIO OPTIONS Select **Commentary Audio** to play the audio commentary in place of the main soundtrack when watching the episodes. This is moderated by composer and sound engineer Mark Ayres, talking with vision mixer Clive Doig, special sounds creator Brian Hodgson, make-up supervisor Sonia Markham and studio floor assistant David Tilley on all three episodes.

— Select **Feature Arabic Audio** to hear the soundtrack with dialogue dubbed into Arabic when watching all three episodes, made for sales of the programme to Middle Eastern broadcasters. This also features different incidental music to that used in the UK broadcast.

— Select **Feature English Audio** to reinstate the main soundtrack when watching the episodes.

INFO TEXT Select **On** to view subtitles when watching the episodes that provide information and anecdotes about the development, production, broadcast and history of *Planet of Giants*. Written by Matthew Kilburn.

PDF MATERIALS Accessible via a computer are the three episode listings from *Radio Times* for the original BBC1 broadcast of *Planet of Giants*, a one-page article that introduced the 1964/65 season and a poetic letter anticipating its return.

— Designer Raymond Cusick's blueprints for the giant sink, briefcase and telephone receiver props to be constructed by Shawcraft Models.

COMING SOON (1m9s) Trailer for the Special Edition DVD release of *Vengeance on Varos*.
SUBTITLES
Select **On** to view subtitles for all episodes and Special Features (except commentary and Arabic soundtrack).
RELATED EXTRAS
Coming Soon trailer — The Greatest Show in the Galaxy
The Doctor's Composer — The War Games

PLANET OF THE DALEKS

STORY No.68   SEASON No.10:4

P

Released with **FRONTIER IN SPACE** in the **DALEK WAR** boxset
Two discs with six episodes (141 mins) and 96 minutes of extras, plus commentary track, production subtitles and PDF items
Audio navigation of each disc's contents available by pressing Enter after the BBC ident

TARDIS TEAM Third Doctor, Jo
TIME AND PLACE Jungle planet Spiridon
ADVERSARIES Daleks (9th appearance)
FIRST ON TV 7 April–12 May 1973
DVD RELEASE BBCDVD2614(B) [discs 2614(3) and 2614(4)], 5 October 2009, U (boxset PG)
COVER Photo illustration by Clayton Hickman, light green strip;
         version with older BBC logo on reverse
ORIGINAL RRP £34.26 (boxset)
STORY TEASER
The Doctor has discovered the Daleks are planning an invasion of the Earth's galaxy and tracks them to their base of operations on the planet Spiridon. Here the Daleks are experimenting to learn how the natives achieve their invisibility, an ability that would make their army invincible.

The Doctor meets a squad of Thals sent from Skaro to investigate but they're out of their depth, especially when they learn the full extent of the Dalek force.

CONNECTIONS

This story follows on directly from *Frontier in Space*, in which the Doctor learns the Daleks are behind the Master's plan to incite war between Earth and the neighbouring empire of Draconia. It's a common Dalek plan to weaken their enemies before swooping in to conquer them, as related in *The Dalek Invasion of Earth* (1964), *The Daleks' Master Plan* (1965/66), *Day of the Daleks* (1972) and *The Parting of the Ways* (2005). The Daleks also use germ warfare in *The Dalek Invasion of Earth*, *Death to the Daleks* (1974) and *Resurrection of the Daleks* (1984). Invisible creatures are a cheap way to create a monster and those encountered elsewhere include the Mirans in *The Daleks' Master Plan*, the Refusians in *The Ark* (1966), the anti-matter creature in *Planet of Evil* (1975), the projections of Xoanon in *The Face of Evil* (1977) and the Krafayis in *Vincent and the Doctor* (2010). The Doctor meets the Thals in *The Daleks* (1963), as recounted here, and in *Genesis of the Daleks* (1975). This was writer Terry Nation's first Dalek script since the 1960s and he would also write the next three, as well as *The Android Invasion* (1975) (*see Index v*); it was also director David Maloney's return to the series after directing three stories in the 1968/69 season (*see Index v*). Bernard Horsfall, playing Taron, was a favourite of Maloney's, also appearing as Gulliver in *The Mind Robber* (1968), a Time Lord in *The War Games* (1969) and Chancellor Goth in *The Deadly Assassin* (1976). Prentis Hancock (Vaber) has a small role as a reporter in *Spearhead from Space* (1970) and is Commander Salamar in *Planet of Evil* and the Shrieve captain in *The Ribos Operation* (1978).

WORTH WATCHING

Terry Nation returned to writing for *Doctor Who* as a result of the production team's remorse at having brought back the Daleks in *Day of the Daleks* (1972) without consulting him. His first attempt is something of a throwback to the style of storytelling from the 1960s, with straightforward action and uncomplicated morality, from which the show had arguably moved on. Yet that's part of what made the Daleks so engaging for children in the first place and it's here their 1970s renaissance really begins after their limited participation in the previous year's Dalek story. The Daleks are once more a massive, seemingly unstoppable force for destruction, not yet subservient to Davros or incapacitated by infighting as they will later become. Given episode three physically exists only on black-and-white film, the recolourisation is astounding and all but indistinguishable from an original video recording.

DISC ONE

THE EPISODES

This is the first release of the serial in complete colour since its original broadcast. Episodes one, two, four, five and six are restored from digital duplicates of the original two-inch colour videotape recordings used for broadcast and their mono soundtracks remastered. Episode three is restored from a 16mm black-and-white film copy of the original two-inch colour videotape recording, recovered from BBC Enterprises in 1978. Initially it was recoloured manually by Legend Films in California, digitally painting in colour for key frames which is then extrapolated across further sections. By the time this was completed, however, the Colour Recovery process had been sufficiently developed by Richard Russell to apply to the episode, using information in the mono images on the film that relates to the original colour of the video picture being filmed. The episode was ultimately recoloured using a combination of both colour sources, benefitting from the stability of the manual colourisation and the subtlety in variation of the recovered colour. The episode's mono soundtrack is remastered and the VidFIRE process is applied to studio-recorded shots to recapture the smoother motion of video. All episodes have the title sequences replaced by a modern transfer of the original 35mm film with credits remade to match the originals.

AUDIO OPTIONS

Select **Commentary** to play the audio commentary in place of the main soundtrack when watching the episodes. With Katy Manning (Jo), Tim Preece (Codal), producer Barry Letts and script editor Terrance Dicks on all six episodes, joined by Prentis Hancock (Vaber) up to episode five.

— Select **Feature Audio** to reinstate the main soundtrack when watching the episodes.

SUBTITLES

Select **Subtitles On** to view subtitles for all episodes (none for commentary).

— Select **Info Text On** to view subtitles when watching the episodes that provide information and anecdotes about the development, production, broadcast and history of *Planet of the Daleks*. Written by Martin Wiggins.

DISC TWO

SPECIAL FEATURES

THE PERFECT SCENARIO: THE END OF DREAMS (30m10s) Part two of a dramatised scenario in which hibernating humans of the 26th Century are kept entertained by stories projected into their sleeping minds. One of the official storytellers, Zed, is starting to run out of original plots and so accesses historical data about *Doctor Who*, specifically *Planet of the Daleks*, in order to get fresh ideas. His research covers influences of and connections to contemporary life in the writing and production of the story. With input from producer Barry Letts, script editor Terrance Dicks, and actors Janet Fielding, Bernard Horsfall, Jane How, Katy Manning and Tim Preece. Written by David Harley and featuring Rich Batsford, Mick Broster, Tony Broster and Paul Ewing; produced by Steve Broster. *Part one is on* Frontier in Space

THE RUMBLE IN THE JUNGLE (16m48s) The making of *Planet of the Daleks*, including filming on location in a cold quarry and 'ice tunnels' in Ealing Studios; creating a jungle in the television studio; and acting with invisible characters, the Daleks and Jon Pertwee. With contributions from director David Maloney (interviewed in 2005), designer John Hurst, and actors Bernard Horsfall, Jane How, Katy Manning and Tim Preece. Produced by Steve Broster.

MULTI-COLOURISATION (10m49s) Explanation of the complex processes required to return episode three to colour since the original videotape recording was wiped sometime around 1975. With contributions from video engineer James Insell and colourist Jonathan Wood, plus 1970s producer Barry Letts (interviewed in 2003) and Dan Hall, commissioning editor for the *Doctor Who* DVD range. Includes the countdown clock for the studio recording of episode one. Narrated by Glen Allen, produced by Ed Stradling.

STRIPPED FOR ACTION: THE DALEKS (13m55s) During the 1960s the Daleks held the unique claim of featuring in their own comic strip outside the Doctor's own adventures. This examines the Dalek stories in City Magazines' *TV Century 21*. With contributions from comics publisher Gerry Anderson, magazine editors Alan Barnes and Clayton Hickman, and comics historians Jeremy Bentham and Paul Scoones. Directed by Marcus Hearn. *See Index iii for further editions*

BLUE PETER (12m34s) Extract from the Thursday 7 June 1973 edition of the BBC1 children's magazine programme in which Peter Purves, John Noakes and Lesley Judd appeal for help finding two Daleks that were stolen from outside Television Centre two days earlier (in black and white); and the report from the following Monday 11 June edition about their recovery, in which Purves interviews police and public who helped (in colour).

PHOTO GALLERY (8m58s) Slideshow of colour and black-and-white photos taken during production of *Planet of the Daleks*, including some showing behind the scenes at the location filming and studio recording, plus shots of the commentary participants. Set to sound effects from the story. Compiled by Ralph Montagu.

PDF MATERIALS Accessible via a computer are the six episode listings from *Radio Times* for the original BBC1 broadcast of *Planet of the Daleks*, with illustrations by Frank Bellamy.

— Designer John Hurst's blueprints for the Dalek control room, corridor and cooling chamber, and the Thal shuttle sets.

SUBTITLES Select **On** to view subtitles for all Special Features on disc two.

EASTER EGGS

There are two hidden features on these discs to find. *See Appendix 2 for details*

RELATED EXTRAS

Terror Nation — Destiny of the Daleks

The Dalek Tapes — Genesis of the Daleks

Coming Soon trailer — The Keys of Marinus

PLANET OF THE SPIDERS

STORY No.74   SEASON No.11:5

Two discs with six episodes (147½ mins) and 186½ minutes of extras, plus commentary track, production subtitles and PDF items
Audio navigation of each disc's contents available by pressing Enter after the BBC ident

TARDIS TEAM Third Doctor, Sarah Jane, Brigadier and UNIT

TIME AND PLACE Contemporary England and planet Metebelis 3

ADVERSARIES Giant psychic spiders; bitter salesman Lupton

FIRST ON TV 4 May–8 June 1974

DVD RELEASE BBCDVD1809 [discs 1809A and 1809B], 18 April 2011, PG

COVER Photo illustration by Lee Binding, dark blue strip; version with older BBC logo on reverse

ORIGINAL RRP £19.99

— Episodes released in the Regeneration box; BBCDVD3801, £61.27, 24 June 2013

STORY TEASER

When the Doctor's former assistant Jo Grant returns the blue crystal he gave her as a wedding present, he discovers it's not unwanted by everyone. Giant spiders from the planet Metebelis 3 need the crystal and reach out to Earth with their mental powers, making contact with a group of resentful men at a meditation retreat and using them to recover it. If they succeed they will dominate the universe, but to stop them the Doctor must make a terrible sacrifice.

CONNECTIONS

Arachnophobes may wish to avoid this story, along with *Full Circle* (1980) and *The Runaway Bride* (2006). The blue crystal is taken from Metebelis by the Doctor and given to Jo in *The Green Death* (1973), in which its mind-affecting properties are also shown. By *Hide* (2013) the Doctor has acquired another. Mike Yates is dismissed from UNIT after the events of *Invasion of the Dinosaurs* (1974), which also sees the first appearance of the Doctor's new car, nicknamed the Whomobile. In *Battlefield* (1989) the Brigadier is seen to have eventually married the Doris who once gave him a watch in Brighton. An excessive dose of radiation also causes the Doctor's twelfth regeneration in *The End of Time* (2009/10). Robert Sloman also wrote *The Dæmons* (1971), *The Time Monster* (1972) and *The Green Death*, all in partnership with producer/director Barry Letts, who also directed *The Enemy of the World* (1967/68), *Terror of the Autons* (1971), *Carnival of Monsters* (1973) and *The Android Invasion* (1975), as well as later episodes of *Inferno* (1970) after original director Douglas Camfield was taken ill. John Dearth, playing Lupton, provided the voice of the computer BOSS in *The Green Death*, while of his entourage, Christopher Burgess (Barnes) is Swann in *The Enemy of the World* and Professor Philips in *Terror of the Autons*; Carl Forgione (Land) is Neanderthal Nimrod in *Ghost Light* (1989); Terence Lodge (Moss) is Medok in *The Macra Terror* (1967) and Orum in *Carnival of Monsters*; and Andrew Staines (Keaver) is Benik's sergeant in *The Enemy of the World*, Goodge in *Terror of the Autons* and captain of the SS Bernice in *Carnival of Monsters*. Cyril Shaps (Professor Clegg) also plays John Viner in *The Tomb of the Cybermen* (1967), Dr Lennox in *The Ambassadors of Death* (1970) and the Archimandrite in *The Androids of Tara* (1978); Kevin Lindsay (Cho-Je) portrays Sontarans in *The Time Warrior* (1973/74) and *The Sontaran Experiment* (1975); and George Cormack (K'anpo) is King Dalios in *The Time Monster* (1972), which also features the scene where the Doctor first mentions his old mentor. Providing spider voices are Ysanne Churchman, who voices Alpha Centauri in *The Curse of Peladon* (1972) and *The Monster of Peladon* (1974), and Kismet Delgado, widow of Roger Delgado who was the first actor to portray the Master.

WORTH WATCHING

It's Jon Pertwee's swan song as the Doctor and as such almost goes out of its way to be a greatest hits of the Third Doctor era, with references to past stories and characters, returning actors and, most noticeably, a last chance to give Pertwee as many unusual forms of transport to drive as possible. Being co-written, directed and produced by Barry Letts, *Planet of the Spiders* can be seen as the purest form of his vision for the programme, which had taken it to renewed heights of popularity over the previous five years.

THE EPISODES
All six episodes are restored from digital duplicates of the original two-inch colour videotape recordings used for broadcast and their mono soundtracks remastered. The title sequences are replaced by a modern transfer of the original 35mm film with credits remade to match the originals.

SPECIAL FEATURES
AUDIO OPTIONS Select **Commentary** to play the audio commentary in place of the main soundtrack when watching the episodes. With Elisabeth Sladen (Sarah), Richard Franklin (Yates), producer/writer/director Barry Letts and script editor Terrance Dicks on all six episodes, joined by Nicholas Courtney (the Brigadier) on episodes one, two and six.

— Select **Feature Audio** to reinstate the main soundtrack when watching the episodes.

INFO TEXT Select **On** to view subtitles when watching the episodes that provide information and anecdotes about the development, production, broadcast and history of *Planet of the Spiders*. Written by Nicholas Pegg.

COMING SOON (1m33s) Trailer for the Special Edition DVD release of *Spearhead from Space* and the first DVD release of *Terror of the Autons* in the Mannequin Mania boxset.

SUBTITLES
Select **On** to view subtitles for all episodes and the Coming Soon trailer (none for commentary).

SPECIAL FEATURES
THE FINAL CURTAIN (37m46s) The making of *Planet of the Spiders* as the conclusion of the Third Doctor era, including the reasons behind the departure of the key production team alongside the lead actor; the original plans for a final story with the Master; influences of Zen Buddhism in the eventual story; pulling together threads from earlier in the era; realising the giant spiders and their chamber; designing Metebelis and the limitations of the CSO (colour separation overlay) composition technique; filming the big chase; the character of Tommy; and the Doctor's death. With contributions from producer/writer/director Barry Letts (interviewed in 2008), script editor Terrance Dicks, designer Rochelle Selwyn, visual effects assistant Mat Irvine, actors Jon Pertwee (interviewed in 1995) and Richard Franklin, and New Series writer Mark Gatiss. Narrated by Glen Allen, produced by Ed Stradling.

JOHN KANE REMEMBERS... (12m45s) Actor John Kane talks about his experience playing Tommy in *Planet of the Spiders*, from a taxi ride that didn't go as planned, to working with Jon Pertwee and Elisabeth Sladen, memories of Barry Letts and the legacy of his appearance in *Doctor Who*.

DIRECTING WHO WITH BARRY LETTS (14m43s) Barry Letts talks about his move from being an actor to a director, starting out on *The Newcomers* and *Z Cars*, his first work on *Doctor Who* directing *The Enemy of the World*, and holding onto his director's hat while producing the series.

NOW & THEN (7m9s) Comparing the filming locations across southern England as they look today with how they appeared in mid-March 1974 when used for *Planet of the Spiders*. Narrated and produced by Richard Bignell. *See Index iii for further editions*

SUBTITLES Select **On** to view subtitles for all Special Features on disc two.

NEXT
'PLANET OF THE SPIDERS' OMNIBUS EDITION (105m17s) Version of the story edited down into a single episode, as repeated on BBC1 the afternoon of Friday 27 December 1974, the day before the first Fourth Doctor season began screening. Presented unrestored from the original two-inch colour videotape used for broadcast.

OMNIBUS TRAILER (1m40s) Preview of the omnibus repeat, shown on Thursday 26 December 1974. Includes the 1974 BBC1 Christmas globe.

PHOTO GALLERY (5m45s) Slideshow of colour and black-and-white photos taken during production of *Planet of the Spiders*, including design department photos of the sets. Set to music and sound effects from the story. Compiled by Paul Shields.

PDF MATERIALS Accessible via a computer are the six episode listings from *Radio Times* for the original BBC1 broadcast of *Planet of the Spiders*, with illustrations by Peter Brookes.

RELATED EXTRAS
Coming Soon trailer — Carnival of Monsters Special Edition, Resurrection of the Daleks Special Edition, The Seeds of Death Special Edition
The UNIT Family — Terror of the Zygons

THE **POWER OF KROLL**

STORY No.102　SEASON No.16:5

Released with **THE ANDROIDS OF TARA, THE ARMAGEDDON FACTOR, THE PIRATE PLANET, THE RIBOS OPERATION** and **THE STONES OF BLOOD** in **THE KEY TO TIME** boxset
One disc with four episodes (91½ mins) and 46 minutes of extras, plus commentary track, production subtitles and PDF items

TARDIS TEAM Fourth Doctor, First Romana
TIME AND PLACE Swampy moon of planet Delta Magna
ADVERSARIES Gunrunner Rohm-Dutt; native 'Swampies'; giant squid Kroll
FIRST ON TV 23 December 1978–13 January 1979
DVD RELEASE BBCDVD2335(E), 24 September 2007, PG
COVER Photo illustration by Clayton Hickman, green strip
ORIGINAL RRP £69.99 (boxset)

STORY TEASER
When Earth colonists settled on Delta Magna they moved the indigenous population to one of its moons where they could continue to worship their squid-like deity Kroll. Now vital resources have been discovered there and the 'Swampies' are in the way. Gunrunner Rohm-Dutt has brought them weapons with which to defend themselves, but gas refinery boss Thawn has his own plans for their eviction. Caught in the middle, the Doctor and Romana must avoid being shot or sacrificed while they seek the fifth Key to Time segment. And all have reckoned without the return of Kroll itself.

CONNECTIONS
Kroll is reminiscent of, if much bigger than, the undersea slime-dwelling Mire Beats in *The Chase* (1965). And despite the difficulties in representing such a large monster, the production team attempt it again the following season with Erato in *The Creature from the Pit* (1979); the New Series had more success with the Jagrafess in *The Long Game* (2005), although probably the largest is the planet-sized Akhaten in *The Rings of Akhaten* (2013). Aboriginals facing trouble from human colonists are also featured in *Colony in Space* (1971), *The Mutants* (1972), *Kinda* (1982), *The Happiness Patrol* (1988) and *Planet of the Ood* (2008). Gunrunners and their double-dealing backers crop up again in the same author's *The Caves of Androzani* (1984), while *Fury from the Deep* (1968) and *Terror of the Zygons* (1975) feature similar offshore rigs coming under attack from monsters. *The Power of Kroll* was writer Robert Holmes' last of many *Doctor Who* scripts during the 1970s, although he was persuaded to begin writing for the series again in 1983 (*see Index v*); director Norman Stewart handled the previous season's *Underworld* (1978). Neil McCarthy (Thawn) plays George Barnham, the first to undergo the Keller treatment in *The Mind of Evil* (1971), while John Leeson (Dugeen) was more commonly the voice of K9. Two long-time guest actors made their last appearances here: John Abineri (Ranquin) first appeared as Van Lutyens in *Fury from the Deep* and subsequently as General Carrington in *The Ambassadors of Death* (1970) and Richard Railton in *Death to the Daleks* (1974); and Philip Madoc (Fenner) plays Eelek in *The Krotons* (1969), the War Lord in *The War Games* (1969) and surgeon Mehendri Solon in *The Brain of Morbius* (1976).

WORTH WATCHING
It has been said that Robert Holmes' later highly regarded story *The Caves of Androzani* takes the ideas of *The Power of Kroll* and does them properly, but while there are some similarities between characters and motivations the comparison is a limited one: this is more a reworking of American Western themes than the political infighting that typifies the later story. This serial may not be as well remembered but the points of criticism are in the production rather than the script, and even

those are not as terrible as some people make out (one particular example of poor compositing has been much improved during the restoration for this release).

THE EPISODES

All four episodes are restored from digital duplicates of the original two-inch colour videotape recordings used for broadcast and their mono soundtracks remastered. The title sequences are replaced by a modern transfer of the original 35mm film with credits remade to match the originals.

SPECIAL FEATURES

IN STUDIO (11m27s) Footage from the first day's studio recording on Monday 9 October 1978 of scenes in the refinery, including retakes and shots unused in the final programme, taken from a low-quality black-and-white video copy with on-screen time-code.

VARIATIONS (6m26s) Report for BBC East local news programme broadcast on Friday 15 December 1978, covering the location filming for *The Power of Kroll* in Snape, Suffolk in late-September 1978. Featuring interviews with Tom Baker, Mary Tamm and one of the Swampie extras.

THERE'S SOMETHING ABOUT MARY (9m49s) Actress Mary Tamm recalls her experiences of playing the first incarnation of Romana during the 1978/79 season, including taking the role, working with Tom Baker and her decision not to stay for a second year.

PHILIP MADOC – A VILLAIN FOR ALL SEASONS (9m43s) Actor Philip Madoc talks about his various roles in *Doctor Who*, including the second Dalek movie *Daleks Invasion Earth: 2150AD*, working with Patrick Troughton and Tom Baker, and the idea of having played the Doctor himself.

CONTINUITIES (2m50s) Continuity announcements from the original BBC1 broadcasts of all four episodes of *The Power of Kroll*, some reconstructed by matching audio recordings made at the time of broadcast to clips from the episodes. Includes the BBC1 daytime schedule for Christmas Day 1978 (the Monday after episode one was shown).

NEXT

AUDIO OPTIONS Select **Commentary** to play the audio commentary, recorded for an earlier US-only release, in place of the main soundtrack when watching the episodes. With Tom Baker and John Leeson (Dugeen) on all four episodes.

— Select **Feature Audio** to reinstate the main soundtrack when watching the episodes.

INFO TEXT Select **On** to view subtitles when watching the episodes that provide information and anecdotes about the development, production, broadcast and history of *The Power of Kroll*. Written by Richard Molesworth.

PHOTO GALLERY (4m54s) Slideshow of colour and black-and-white photos taken during production of *The Power of Kroll*, including design department photos of the sets. Set to sound effects from the story. Compiled by Derek Handley.

COMING SOON (1M) Trailer for the DVD release of *Planet of Evil*.

RADIO TIMES LISTINGS Accessible via a computer is a PDF file of the four episode listings for the original BBC1 broadcast of *The Power of Kroll*.

SUBTITLES

Select **On** to view subtitles for all episodes and Special Features (except commentary).

RELATED EXTRAS

Coming Soon trailer — The Time Warrior

PYRAMIDS OF MARS

STORY No.82   SEASON No.13:3

One disc with four episodes (98½ mins) and 95 minutes of extras, plus commentary track and production subtitles

TARDIS TEAM Fourth Doctor, Sarah Jane

TIME AND PLACE England and Egypt, 1911

ADVERSARIES Sutekh, ancient Egyptian god; robot Mummies; Marcus Scarman, archaeologist possessed by Sutekh

FIRST ON TV 25 October–15 November 1975
DVD RELEASE BBCDVD1350, 1 March 2004, U
COVER Photo illustration by Clayton Hickman, light purple strip
ORIGINAL RRP £19.99
— Episodes released in *The Sarah Jane Adventures Complete Fourth Series* boxset; BBCDVD3503, £20.42, 31 October 2011

STORY TEASER

As eminent Egyptologist Professor Scarman breaks into the burial chamber of a long-lost pyramid, the TARDIS is invaded by an apparition and thrown off course. The Doctor and Sarah find themselves in the right place — the old priory on the remains of which UNIT HQ was built — but the wrong year: 1911. The priory is owned by Scarman, whose servants are preparing for his return. But the man who arrives is oddly different, seemingly unaware of his old friends or even his brother. The Doctor realises Scarman is reviving the powers of an alien being, held captive in the pyramid for millennia and who, if released, will spread darkness across the universe.

CONNECTIONS

The Doctor visits Egypt at the time of the building of the Great Pyramids in *The Daleks' Master Plan* (1965/66), and again some time later when he meets Queen Nefertiti (*Dinosaurs on a Spaceship*, 2012). In an alternative timeline where all of Earth history was happening at once, River Song has Silents imprisoned in an Egyptian pyramid (*The Wedding of River Song*, 2011). The planet-sized parasite Akhaten and its attendant pyramid-dwelling Mummy (*The Rings of Akhaten*, 2013) suggest a connection with the ancient Egyptian gods similar to the Osirans'. The Doctor doesn't set foot on Mars again until *The Waters of Mars* (2009), which doesn't turn out well for anyone involved. Sarah's comparison of Horus's tests to the city of the Exxilons refers to *Death to the Daleks* (1974), although as she doesn't enter the city herself she must be going by the Doctor's description. Paddy Russell also directed *The Massacre* (1966), *Invasion of the Dinosaurs* (1974) and *Horror of Fang Rock* (1977). Bernard Archard (Marcus Scarman) is the duplicitous Bragen in *The Power of the Daleks* (1966), while Michael Sheard, playing his brother Laurence, is also Rhos in *The Ark* (1966), Doctor Summers in *The Mind of Evil* (1971), Lowe in *The Invisible Enemy* (1977), Mergrave in *Castrovalva* (1982) and lastly the Dalek-controlled headmaster in *Remembrance of the Daleks* (1988). Gabriel Woolf (Sutekh) also voices the Beast in *The Impossible Planet/The Satan Pit* (2006).

WORTH WATCHING

Despite a troubled scripting process in which script editor Robert Holmes ended up totally rewriting Lewis Griefer's original submission, or perhaps because of that, *Pyramids of Mars* is highly regarded and cements the production team's style of drawing on classic horror themes with a *Who*-ish sci-fi twist. It's perhaps not the pinnacle of this approach owing to a switch in tone for the final episode, but with Tom Baker and Elisabeth Sladen established and comfortable in their partnership they keep the story believable and tense.

THE EPISODES

All four episodes are restored from digital duplicates of the original two-inch colour videotape recordings used for broadcast and their mono soundtracks remastered. The title sequences are replaced by a modern transfer of the original 35mm film with credits overlaid from the episode recordings.

SPECIAL FEATURES

OSIRIAN GOTHIC (22m11s) The making of *Pyramids of Mars*, including the need to rewrite the original script; working with the director; designing the sets; recording effects shots with the actors; casting Sutekh; and the degree of violence that could be portrayed. With contributions from producer Philip Hinchcliffe, director Paddy Russell, designer Christine Ruscoe, and actors Bernard Archard, Peter Copley, Michael Sheard, Elisabeth Sladen and Gabriel Woolf. Produced by Ed Stradling and Paul Vanezis.

SERIAL THRILLERS (41m56s) Examination of Philip Hinchcliffe's three years as producer of *Doctor Who*, from 1975 to 1977, and the stylistic and thematic changes he and script editor Robert Holmes introduced to build on the success they inherited from the Third Doctor era, making sure the scripts and production facilities were matched to achieve convincing stories, and taking the series in a more gothic direction that suited Tom Baker's early approach to the character of the Doctor. With contributions from Hinchcliffe, director David Maloney, writer Robert Banks Stewart, designers Roger Murray-Leach and Christine Ruscoe, companion actor Elisabeth Sladen, campaigner Mary Whitehouse (interviewed in 1993), and fans Alan Barnes, Andrew Beech, Gareth Roberts and Jim Sangster. Produced by Ed Stradling.

NOW AND THEN (7m51s) Comparing the filming locations at Stargrove Manor in Hampshire as they look today with how they appeared in April/May 1975 when used for *Pyramids of Mars*. Narrated by Michael Sheard, with dialogue readings by Jon Culshaw and Elisabeth Sladen. Accompanied by recreations of Dudley Simpson's music by Heathcliff Blair. Produced by Richard Bignell. *See Index iii for further editions*

DELETED SCENES (2m56s) Selection of scenes not used in the final programme, including model sequences taken from the original 16mm colour film, and scenes taken from a black-and-white video copy of the studio recording with on-screen time-code.

▶

INFORMATION TEXT Select **On** to view subtitles when watching the episodes that provide information and anecdotes about the development, production, broadcast and history of *Pyramids of Mars*. Written by Martin Wiggins.

OH MUMMY (6m44s) Spoof interview with Sutekh about his appearance in *Doctor Who* and his life and career since starring in the programme. With the voice of Gabriel Woolf, written by Robert Hammond, directed by Matt West.

AUDIO OPTIONS Select **Commentary On** to play the audio commentary in place of the main soundtrack when watching the episodes. With Elisabeth Sladen (Sarah), Michael Sheard (Laurence Scarman) and producer Philip Hinchcliffe on all four episodes, plus additional comments throughout from director Paddy Russell.

PICTURE GALLERY (10m46s) Slideshow of colour and black-and-white photos taken during production of *Pyramids of Mars*, including design department photos of the sets and pictures of the location filming visit by children of nearby St Martin's Primary School, plus shots of the commentary participants. Set to sound effects from the story. Compiled by Ralph Montagu.

SUBTITLES
Select **On** to view subtitles for all episodes and Special Features, or for the commentary.

EASTER EGG
There is one hidden feature on this disc to find. *See Appendix 2 for details*

RELATED EXTRAS
Paddy Russell - A Life in Television — Horror of Fang Rock
The Doctor's Composer — The Sun Makers

THE **REIGN OF TERROR**

R

STORY No.8   SEASON No.1:8

One disc with four original and two animated episodes (148½ mins) and 36½ minutes of extras, plus commentary track, production subtitles and PDF items
Audio navigation of disc contents available by pressing Enter after the BBC ident

TARDIS TEAM First Doctor, Barbara, Ian, Susan
TIME AND PLACE Paris, July 1794
ADVERSARIES French revolutionaries; Robespierre
FIRST ON TV 8 August–12 September 1964
DVD RELEASE BBCDVD3528, 28 January 2013, PG
COVER Photo illustration by Lee Binding (TARDIS by Gavin Rymill), dark purple strip; version with older BBC logo on reverse
ORIGINAL RRP £20.42

STORY TEASER

The TARDIS arrives in Revolutionary France at a turning point in the uprising. With Ian, Barbara and Susan captured, taken to Paris and quickly sentenced to death, the Doctor must follow them alone, gain an audience with the man in power and secure a reprieve for his friends. But with deception and betrayal the order of the day, they all face a trip to the dreaded guillotine.

CONNECTIONS

The Doctor arrives back in Paris at an earlier murderous point in its history in *The Massacre* (1966), at a more peaceful time in *City of Death* (1979), briefly in *The Girl in the Fireplace* (2006) and twice in *Vincent and the Doctor* (2010). This was the first *Doctor Who* script by Dennis Spooner, who also wrote *The Romans* (1965), *The Time Meddler* (1965) and parts of *The Daleks' Master Plan* (1965/66), as well as being story editor during the series' second season. James Cairncross, playing Lemaitre, appears again as Beta in *The Krotons* (1969), while Edward Brayshaw (Leon Colbert) returns as the War Chief in *The War Games* (1969). Dallas Cavell (Overseer) is also Bors in *The Daleks' Master Plan*, slaver Captain Trask in *The Highlanders* (1966/67), Sir James Quinlan in *The Ambassadors of Death* (1970) and the Pharos Project security chief in *Castrovalva* (1982).

WORTH WATCHING

At the end of its first season, *Doctor Who* was already beginning to relax its rules on how it handled stories set in Earth's history. This is the first to feature genuine recorded events and has the cast meeting known figures at pivotal points in their lives, if not yet going so far as to have them directly influence the course of events.

THE EPISODES

Episodes one and two are restored from 16mm film copies of the original black-and-white video-tape recordings, recovered from a broadcaster in Cyprus in 1984; episodes three and six are restored from 16mm film copies of the original black-and-white videotape recordings, recovered by Bruce Campbell in 1985 and 1982 respectively and now held by collectors Francis Niemczyk and Tim Hawtin. Their mono soundtracks are remastered and the VidFIRE process is applied to studio-recorded shots to recapture the smoother motion of video. The title sequences are replaced by a modern transfer of the best surviving copy of the original 35mm film with end credits remade to match the originals (except episode six). Episodes four and five, of which no film copies are known to exist, are recreated with black-and-white animation by Planet 55 Studios with reference to surviving clips and photos from the serial and matched to a remastered recording of the soundtrack made on audio tape when the episodes were originally broadcast.

SPECIAL FEATURES

DON'T LOSE YOUR HEAD (25m4s) The making of *The Reign of Terror*, including memories of director Henric Hirsch; selecting the cast; problems during rehearsals; shooting the series' first ever location filming and scenes at Ealing Studios; recording in Lime Grove Studios; and Hirsch's increasing difficulties, alleviated by a move to Television Centre. With contributions from production assistant Timothy Combe and actors Carole Ann Ford and William Russell. Produced by Chris Chapman.

ROBESPIERRE'S DOMAIN SET TOUR (2m44s) Planet 55's detailed set backgrounds created for the animated episodes, set to sound clips from the story.

PHOTO GALLERY (4m10s) Slideshow of colour and black-and-white photos taken during production of *The Reign of Terror*, including design department photos of the sets. Compiled by Paul Shields.

ANIMATION GALLERY (3m39s) Planet 55's character designs for and scenes from the animated episodes. Compiled by Paul Shields.

AUDIO OPTIONS Select **Commentary** to play the audio commentary in place of the main soundtrack when watching the episodes. This is moderated by actor and comedian Toby Hadoke, talking with Neville Smith (d'Argenson) [ep 1], Carole Ann Ford (Susan) [1,2,3,6], production assistant Timothy Combe [1,2,3,6], Jeffry Wickham (Webster) [2], Caroline Hunt (Danielle) [3] and Patrick Marley (Soldier) [6]. On episode four Hadoke talks with actor Ronald Pickup (Physician), and on episode five with missing episode hunters Philip Morris and Paul Vanezis (the latter having helped find these episodes in Cyprus in 1984).

— Select **Feature Audio** to reinstate the main soundtrack when watching the episodes.

INFO TEXT Select **On** to view subtitles when watching episodes one, two, three and six that provide information and anecdotes about the development, production, broadcast and history of *The Reign of Terror*. Written by Nicholas Pegg.

PDF MATERIALS Accessible via a computer are the six episode listings from *Radio Times* for the original BBC1 broadcast of *The Reign of Terror* and an article that introduced the story.

COMING SOON (1m1s) Trailer for the Special Edition DVD release of *The Ark in Space*.

SUBTITLES
Select **On** to view subtitles for all episodes and Special Features (except commentary).

RELATED EXTRAS
Coming Soon trailer — Shada

REMEMBRANCE OF THE DALEKS
STORY No.148   SEASON No.25:1

One disc with four episodes (98½ mins) and 21 minutes of extras, plus commentary and music-only tracks, production subtitles and image content

TARDIS TEAM Seventh Doctor, Ace

TIME AND PLACE Shoreditch, London, 1963

ADVERSARIES Daleks (15th appearance); Davros (5th appearance)

FIRST ON TV 5–26 October 1988

DVD RELEASE BBCDVD1040, 26 February 2001, PG

COVER Single photo, dark grey strip

ORIGINAL RRP £19.99

— Also released in Dalek Collector's Edition; BBCDVD1384, £39.99, 6 October 2003

— Also released in The Dalek Collection; BBCDVD2261, £79.99, 27 January 2007

— Reissued in sleeve with orange logo and new photo montage in a circle against dark purple background; BBCDVD2472, £9.99, 2 July 2007

STORY TEASER
When the Doctor returns to London in 1963 to wrap up some unfinished business, he discovers a group of Daleks have arrived before him in pursuit of the mysterious Time Lord device his first incarnation left behind. Their activity has attracted the attention of the Army, but faced with futuristic technology they can't begin to understand, Captain Gilmore's men are fighting a losing battle. With the unexpected arrival of a second faction of Daleks determined to exterminate the first and claim the prize themselves, the Doctor must play off the two sides without everyone getting caught in the crossfire.

CONNECTIONS
With this story kicking off the show's twenty-fifth anniversary season, it's appropriate the Doctor returns to locations featured in the first story *An Unearthly Child* in 1963, including the junkyard at Totter's Lane (also visited in *Attack of the Cybermen*, 1985) and Coal Hill School, where Clara is teaching by *The Day of the Doctor* (2013). The two factions of Daleks arise in *Revelation of the Daleks* (1985), when grey Daleks loyal to the Dalek Supreme arrest Davros and commandeer the white Daleks he has been breeding. Perhaps unsurprisingly, in the interim he evidently takes charge and becomes emperor, leaving the grey Daleks the weaker party. The origin of the Hand of Omega relates to events mentioned but not seen in *The Three Doctors* (1972/73), Omega being the Time Lord who converted a star into a black hole to use as an infinite energy source. The Army is again brought in to handle an alien incursion in London as in *The War Machines* (1966) and *The Web of Fear* (1968) before the formation of UNIT from *The Invasion* (1968). UNIT features in writer Ben Aaronovitch's next story, *Battlefield* (1989), while Andrew Morgan directed the Seventh Doctor's debut *Time and the Rani* (1987). Pamela Salem (Rachel Jensen) plays Toos in *The Robots of Death* (1977), while this was the last of several appearances by Michael Sheard (Headmaster), most notably

as Laurence Scarman in *Pyramids of Mars* (1975), Lowe in *The Invisible Enemy* (1977) and Mergrave in *Castrovalva* (1982). Peter Halliday (Vicar) also had several *Doctor Who* roles under his belt, especially Packer in *The Invasion* and Pletrac in *Carnival of Monsters* (1973), and William Thomas (Martin the undertaker) appears in the New Series as Mr Cleaver in *Boom Town* (2005) and later plays Gwen Cooper's father in *Torchwood*. Terry Molloy takes on the role of Davros in *Resurrection of the Daleks* (1984) and returns in *Revelation of the Daleks* (1985), while he's more recognisable as Russell in *Attack of the Cybermen*.

WORTH WATCHING

This is widely seen as where *Doctor Who* begins its late-80s renaissance after the turmoil of the reprieved cancellation in 1985 and subsequent production troubles. Script editor Andrew Cartmel has settled into the role and with his first full season to plan brings in new writers with new ideas, a new companion, and kicks off the show's silver anniversary season with the return of the Doctor's most famous enemy in the setting of the very first episode twenty-five years before.

THE EPISODES

All four episodes are restored from digital duplicates of the original one-inch colour videotape recordings used for broadcast, with some scenes recompiled from earlier, higher-quality edits (resulting in some video effects in the first two episodes being accidentally omitted). Their stereo soundtracks are as transmitted except for two songs by The Beatles, which are replaced with soundalikes as they couldn't be re-licensed.

● *Episodes begin playing automatically after one minute if no menu selection is made*

SPECIAL FEATURES   *ALSO ON SPECIAL EDITION

*EXTENDED AND DELETED SCENES (10m25s) A selection of scenes from all four episodes that weren't used in the final programme, taken from earlier edits of the episodes with original as-recorded sound. Includes the full versions of the Doctor's night-time café visit and his confrontation with Davros.

*BBC 1 TRAILER – EPISODE ONE (35s) Preview of the first episode of the new season beginning in October 1988.

*BBC 1 TRAILER – EPISODE TWO (34s) Preview of the second episode, shown on Wednesday 12 October 1988.

*AUDIO OPTIONS Select **Commentary On** to play the audio commentary in place of the main soundtrack when watching the episodes. With Sylvester McCoy and Sophie Aldred (Ace) on all four episodes.

— Select **Isolated Music On** to hear only Keff McCulloch's music when watching the episodes, including two cues unused in the final programme.

▶

*ALTERNATIVE ANGLES (5m30s) Two scenes originally shot with multiple cameras: of Ace attacking a Dalek in the science classroom, and of the Daleks bombarding the builder's yard. Select to view each camera angle with original as-recorded sound or the final edited scenes as they appeared in the programme.

*OUT-TAKES COMPILATION (4m7s) Bloopers and fluffed lines taken from the original studio and location recordings, some from a VHS copy with on-screen time-code.

*INFORMATION TEXT Select **On** to view subtitles when watching the episodes that provide information and anecdotes about the development, production, broadcast and history of *Remembrance of the Daleks*. Written by Richard Molesworth.

PHOTO GALLERY Scroll through 67 colour photos taken during production of *Remembrance of the Daleks*, including behind-the-scenes shots from the location recording. Compiled by Ralph Montagu.

SUBTITLES

Select **On** to view subtitles for all episodes and Special Features, or for the commentary.

RELATED EXTRAS

The Dalek Tapes — Genesis of the Daleks

Remembrance 'Demo' — The Greatest Show in the Galaxy

REMEMBRANCE OF THE DALEKS SPECIAL EDITION

STORY No.148 SEASON No.25:1

Two discs with four episodes (98½ mins) and 125 minutes of extras, plus commentary, music-only and surround-sound tracks, production subtitles and PDF items

TARDIS TEAM Seventh Doctor, Ace
TIME AND PLACE Shoreditch, London, 1963
ADVERSARIES Daleks (15th appearance); Davros (5th appearance)
FIRST ON TV 5–26 October 1988
DVD RELEASE BBCDVD2451, 20 July 2009, PG
COVER Photo illustration by Clayton Hickman, dark blue strip
SLEEVE Full version of cover illustration, silvered logo and title, dark blue background
ORIGINAL RRP £19.56
— First released in The Complete Davros Collection; BBCDVD2508, £99.99, 26 November 2007

STORY TEASER

When the Doctor returns to London in 1963 to wrap up some unfinished business, he discovers a group of Daleks have arrived before him in pursuit of the mysterious Time Lord device his first incarnation left behind. Their activity has attracted the attention of the Army, but faced with futuristic technology they can't begin to understand, Captain Gilmore's men are fighting a losing battle. With the unexpected arrival of a second faction of Daleks determined to exterminate the first and claim the prize themselves, the Doctor must play off the two sides without everyone getting caught in the crossfire.

CONNECTIONS

With this story kicking off the show's twenty-fifth anniversary season, it's appropriate the Doctor returns to locations featured in the first story *An Unearthly Child* in 1963, including the junkyard at Totter's Lane (also visited in *Attack of the Cybermen*, 1985) and Coal Hill School, where Clara is teaching by *The Day of the Doctor* (2013). The two factions of Daleks arise in *Revelation of the Daleks* (1985), when grey Daleks loyal to the Dalek Supreme arrest Davros and commandeer the white Daleks he has been breeding. Perhaps unsurprisingly, in the interim he evidently takes charge and becomes emperor, leaving the grey Daleks the weaker party. The origin of the Hand of Omega relates to events mentioned but not seen in *The Three Doctors* (1972/73), Omega being the Time Lord who converted a star into a black hole to use as an infinite energy source. The Army is again brought in to handle an alien incursion in London as in *The War Machines* (1966) and *The Web of Fear* (1968) before the formation of UNIT from *The Invasion* (1968). UNIT features in writer Ben Aaronovitch's next story, *Battlefield* (1989), while Andrew Morgan directed the Seventh Doctor's debut *Time and the Rani* (1987). Pamela Salem (Rachel Jensen) plays Toos in *The Robots of Death* (1977), while this was the last of several appearances by Michael Sheard (Headmaster), most notably as Laurence Scarman in *Pyramids of Mars* (1975), Lowe in *The Invisible Enemy* (1977) and Mergrave in *Castrovalva* (1982). Peter Halliday (Vicar) also had several *Doctor Who* roles under his belt, especially Packer in *The Invasion* and Pletrac in *Carnival of Monsters* (1973), and William Thomas (Martin the undertaker) appears in the New Series as Mr Cleaver in *Boom Town* (2005) and later plays Gwen Cooper's father in *Torchwood*. Terry Molloy takes on the role of Davros in *Resurrection of the Daleks* (1984) and returns in *Revelation of the Daleks* (1985), while he's more recognisable as Russell in *Attack of the Cybermen*.

WORTH WATCHING

This Special Edition features more advanced clean-up of the episodes compared to the previous release and additional Special Features. This is widely seen as where *Doctor Who* begins its late-80s renaissance after the turmoil of the reprieved cancellation in 1985 and subsequent production troubles. Script editor Andrew Cartmel has settled into the role and with his first full season to plan brings in new writers with new ideas, a new companion, and kicks off the show's silver anniversary season with the return of the Doctor's most famous enemy in the setting of the very first episode twenty-five years before.

DISC ONE

THE EPISODES

All four episodes are newly restored from digital duplicates of the original one-inch colour videotape recordings used for broadcast and their stereo soundtracks remastered (with original Beatles songs intact for the UK release). The computer-generated end title sequences are replaced by a digital duplicate of the original one-inch colour videotape recording with credits remade to match the originals.

SPECIAL FEATURES *REPEATED FROM PREVIOUS RELEASE

BACK TO SCHOOL (32m40s) Script editor Andrew Cartmel, writer Ben Aaronovitch, director Andrew Morgan, and actors Sophie Aldred, Karen Gledhill, Sylvester McCoy and Simon Williams return to St John's Junior School in Hammersmith, where much of *Remembrance of the Daleks* was recorded, to recall the making of the serial. Including the decision to bring back the Daleks; making the Doctor a more pro-active character; budgeting to make the production more impressive; working with the director; the cast; recording on location in London, including stunt work, lots of explosions and a full-size space shuttle; finally getting Daleks to go up stairs; and the story's commentary on racism. Featuring behind-the-scenes footage. With contributions from fan journalists Moray Laing and Paul Lang. Produced by Steve Broster.

REMEMBRANCES (15m17s) Cast and crew recall when they first saw *Doctor Who* and their memories of the Daleks, and discuss this story's references to earlier serials. With Ben Aaronovitch, Sophie Aldred, Andrew Cartmel, Karen Gledhill and Sylvester McCoy, plus Moray Laing and Paul Lang. Produced by Steve Broster.

EXTENDED AND DELETED SCENES (12m25s) A selection of scenes from all four episodes that weren't used in the final programme, taken from earlier edits of the episodes with original as-recorded sound. Includes the full versions of the Doctor's night-time café visit and his confrontation with Davros. As on previous release but with new introductions by Sophie Aldred and Sylvester McCoy.

***OUTTAKES** (4m13s) Bloopers and fluffed lines taken from the original studio and location recordings, some from a VHS copy with on-screen time-code.

***MULTI-ANGLE SEQUENCES** (3m40s) Two scenes originally shot with multiple cameras: of Ace attacking a Dalek in the science classroom, and of the Daleks bombarding the builder's yard. Select to view either camera shot with original as-recorded sound; press Angle on your remote to switch between them while watching.

NEXT

AUDIO OPTIONS Select *Commentary to play the audio commentary recorded for the previous release in place of the main soundtrack when watching the episodes. With Sylvester McCoy and Sophie Aldred (Ace) on all four episodes.

— Select *Isolated Music to hear only Keff McCulloch's music when watching the episodes, including two cues unused in the final programme. Remastered since the previous release.

— Select Feature Audio 5.1 to hear the Dolby Digital surround soundtrack when watching the episodes, newly remixed for this release.

— Select Feature Audio Stereo to reinstate the main soundtrack when watching the episodes.

***INFO TEXT** Select On to view subtitles when watching the episodes that provide information and anecdotes about the development, production, broadcast and history of *Remembrance of the Daleks*. Written by Richard Molesworth.

TRAILS AND CONTINUITY (5m) Previews and continuity announcements from the original BBC1 broadcasts of all four episodes of *Remembrance of the Daleks*, with plugs for *Doctor Who* on video and the 13 October and 27 October 1988 editions of *Radio Times* (issues 3385 and 3387). Includes the BBC1 evening schedules for 19 and 26 October 1988.

PHOTO GALLERY (8m37s) Slideshow of colour and black-and-white photos taken during production of *Remembrance of the Daleks*, including behind-the-scenes shots from the location recording. Set to music from the story. Compiled by Derek Handley.

RADIO TIMES LISTINGS Accessible via a computer is a PDF file of the four episode listings for the original BBC1 broadcast of *Remembrance of the Daleks* and a one-page article about the return of the Daleks published the week of episode one.

SUBTITLES
Select **On** to view subtitles for all episodes and Special Features on disc one (except commentary).

DISC TWO

DAVROS CONNECTIONS
This 43-minute history of the character of Davros, creator of the Daleks, examines his portrayal both on television and in fiction through *Doctor Who* itself and the Big Finish range of audio dramas, which go from his childhood and early life in the *I, Davros* series to further encounters with the Sixth and Eighth Doctors. With contributions from actors David Gooderson, Peter Miles, Terry Molloy and Michael Wisher (in an archive audio interview), writers Ben Aaronovitch, Gary Hopkins, Joseph Lidster and Eric Saward, television director Ken Grieve, and audio producer/director Gary Russell. Narrated by Terry Molloy, produced by Brendan Sheppard.

SUBTITLES
Select **On** to view subtitles for the documentary on disc two.

EASTER EGG
There is one hidden feature on these discs to find. *See Appendix 2 for details*

RELATED EXTRAS
The Dalek Tapes — Genesis of the Daleks
Remembrance 'Demo' — The Greatest Show in the Galaxy

THE **RESCUE**

STORY No.11   SEASON No.2:3

Released in a boxset with **THE ROMANS**
One disc with two episodes (50 mins) and 31 minutes of extras, plus commentary track, production subtitles and PDF items
Audio navigation of disc contents available by pressing Enter after the BBC ident

TARDIS TEAM First Doctor, Barbara, Ian, and introducing Vicki
TIME AND PLACE Planet Dido
ADVERSARIES Murderer Koquillion
FIRST ON TV 2–9 January 1965
DVD RELEASE BBCDVD2970, 23 February 2009, U (boxset BBCDVD2698)
COVER Photo illustration by Clayton Hickman, dark turquoise strip
ORIGINAL RRP £29.35 (boxset)

STORY TEASER
A spaceship from Earth has crash-landed on the planet Dido and its occupants killed by the local inhabitants. The only survivors are the crippled Bennett and orphaned teenager Vicki, held hostage in their ruined ship by the murderous Koquillion. When the TARDIS arrives, the crew are attacked by Koquillion. Barbara is rescued by Vicki while the Doctor and Ian must escape from a blocked-up cave. On meeting the two crash survivors, though, the Doctor soon realises Vicki's life is in greater danger than she suspects.

CONNECTIONS
Vicki is the first orphan taken in by the Doctor but not the last: he later takes Victoria and Nyssa with him as they have no one else to look after them. Writer David Whitaker had just finished his term as story editor for the first year of *Doctor Who*, during which he also wrote *The Edge of Destruction* (1964) and continued to write for the first two Doctors (*see Index v*). Christopher Barry directed many highly regarded *Doctor Who* serials (*see Index v*) and worked on both *The Rescue* and *The Romans* as a single six-episode production.

WORTH WATCHING
Although a slight story written to introduce a new companion, *The Rescue* is significant in that this is the first addition to the TARDIS crew since the very first story, as the Doctor's granddaughter

Susan stayed behind on Earth in the preceding *The Dalek Invasion of Earth*. In fact Vicki is given a more independent streak than Susan ever was, making her character far better suited to the Doctor's adventurous lifestyle.

THE EPISODES

Both episodes are restored from 16mm film copies of the original black-and-white video recordings, recovered from BBC Enterprises in 1978. Their mono soundtracks are remastered and the VidFIRE process is applied to studio-recorded shots to recapture the smoother motion of video. The title sequences are replaced by a modern transfer of the best surviving copy of the original 35mm film with credits remade to match the originals.

SPECIAL FEATURES

MOUNTING THE RESCUE (21m48s) The making of *The Rescue*, including the reasons behind Carole Ann Ford's departure and the upset it caused William Hartnell; initial ideas for a replacement character and selecting who to play her; working with the director; handling this and the next story as one production; creating the models and designing the sets; casting the main guest role; the costume for Koquillion; working with Hartnell; an accident with a special effect during recording and early techniques for picture composition; the importance of appropriate lighting; and keeping the story's twist a secret in *Radio Times*. With contributions from director Christopher Barry, designer Raymond Cusick, actors Ray Barrett, Maureen O'Brien and William Russell, and fan Ian McLachlan. Narrated by John Bowe, produced by Steve Broster.

PHOTO GALLERY (8m13s) Slideshow of black-and-white photos taken during production of *The Rescue*, including design department photos of the sets, the sand beast being made at Shawcraft's workshop, and publicity shots of Maureen O'Brien. Set to music from the story (composed for *The Daleks*). Plus Raymond Cusick's prop and monster design drawings. Compiled by Ralph Montagu.

AUDIO OPTIONS Select **Commentary** to play the audio commentary in place of the main soundtrack when watching the episodes. This is moderated by actor and comedian Toby Hadoke, talking with director Christopher Barry, designer Raymond Cusick and William Russell (Ian) on both episodes.
— Select **Feature Audio** to reinstate the main soundtrack when watching the episodes.

INFO TEXT Select **On** to view subtitles when watching the episodes that provide information and anecdotes about the development, production, broadcast and history of *The Rescue*. Written by Richard Molesworth.

PDF MATERIALS Accessible via a computer are the two episode listings from *Radio Times* for the original BBC1 broadcast of *The Rescue* and an article introducing the story.
— Designer Raymond Cusick's blueprints for the TARDIS and rocket ship sets, TARDIS model, props and sand beast.

COMING SOON (1m7s) Trailer for the DVD release of *Attack of the Cybermen*.

SUBTITLES

Select **On** to view subtitles for all episodes and Special Features (except commentary).

RELATED EXTRAS

Coming Soon trailer — Full Circle, State of Decay, Warriors' Gate

RESURRECTION OF THE DALEKS

STORY No.133   SEASON No.21:4

One disc with four episodes (98 mins) and 40½ minutes of extras, plus commentary, music-only and surround-sound tracks, and production subtitles

TARDIS TEAM Fifth Doctor, Tegan, Turlough

TIME AND PLACE Contemporary London and future prison space station

ADVERSARIES Daleks (13th appearance); Davros (3rd appearance); mercenary Lytton (1st appearance)

FIRST ON TV 8–15 February 1984

DVD RELEASE BBCDVD1100, 18 November 2002, PG

COVER Photo illustration by Clayton Hickman, dark turquoise strip
— Original release in black rubberised sleeve
ORIGINAL RRP £19.99
— Also released in Dalek Collector's Edition; BBCDVD1384, £39.99, 6 October 2003
— Also released in The Dalek Collection; BBCDVD2261, £79.99, 27 January 2007
— Also released in The Complete Davros Collection; BBCDVD2508, £99.99, 26 November 2007

STORY TEASER

When the TARDIS is caught in a time corridor, the Doctor discovers one end is in an old warehouse in London, 1984, where an army bomb disposal squad is guarding some unusual cylinders that could be far more deadly than bombs. The other end is on a Dalek battleship attacking a prison containing a very special inmate the Daleks need to release: their creator, Davros. But the Daleks have even bigger plans and, to stop Davros helping them, the Doctor is forced to take drastic action.

CONNECTIONS

This story follows on directly from the end of the preceding serial *Frontios*, with the TARDIS caught in the Daleks' time corridor. The Daleks are seen with similar time-travel abilities in *The Evil of the Daleks* (1967), *Day of the Daleks* (1972), *Remembrance of the Daleks* (1988), *Doomsday* (2006), *Evolution of the Daleks* (2007), *The Stolen Earth* (2008), *Victory of the Daleks* (2010) and *Asylum of the Daleks* (2012), and have actual TARDIS-like time machines in *The Chase* (1965) and *The Daleks' Master Plan* (1965/66). They also use germ warfare in *The Dalek Invasion of Earth* (1964), *Planet of the Daleks* (1973) and *Death to the Daleks* (1974). Davros is imprisoned at the end of *Destiny of the Daleks* (1979), in which the Daleks are first seen battling the Movellans. This is the first time the Doctor spends time battling monsters in contemporary Central London with help from the military since *Invasion of the Dinosaurs* (1974) (bar a brief face-off with a Skarasen in *Terror of the Zygons*, 1975) and doesn't do so again until *Aliens of London* (2005). Writer Eric Saward was script editor of the programme, during which time he also wrote *Earthshock* (1982) and *Revelation of the Daleks* (1985), while Matthew Robinson also directed *Attack of the Cybermen* (1985) in which Lytton returns, again played by Maurice Colbourne, along with Mike Braben and Michael Jeffries as his fake-police henchmen. Terry Molloy dons Davros's mask again in *Revelation of the Daleks* and *Remembrance of the Daleks*, and appears in person as Russell in *Attack of the Cybermen*.

WORTH WATCHING

Originally planned as the climax to the 1983 season in the show's twentieth year, *Resurrection of the Daleks* was delayed owing to strike action, so became part of Peter Davison's final season as the Doctor, and the last story for companion Tegan. Even then it was almost postponed once more due to coverage of the 1984 Winter Olympics, until producer John Nathan-Turner elected instead to re-edit its four parts into two 45-minute episodes that fitted the schedules better. The version on this disc is the original four-part edit. This is the Fifth Doctor's only televised confrontation with the Daleks and an action-packed return for the creatures.

THE EPISODES

All four episodes are restored from digital duplicates of the original one-inch colour videotape recordings initially prepared for broadcast, with location scenes reinserted from the original one-inch videotape transfer of the 16mm colour film. Their mono soundtracks are remastered and the opening title sequences replaced by a modern transfer of the original 35mm film with credits overlaid from the episode recordings.

SPECIAL FEATURES *ALSO ON SPECIAL EDITION

*ON LOCATION (18m32s) Producer John Nathan-Turner, writer Eric Saward and director Matthew Robinson return to Shad Thames, where much of *Resurrection of the Daleks* was filmed, to recall the making of the serial. Including how the director shot the opening scene; bringing back the Daleks and Davros; the level of violence in the story; Tegan's departure; selecting the location for filming; and how effects shots were filmed (illustrated with footage from the original filming). Produced by Paul Vanezis.

*BREAKFAST TIME (7m58s) Extracts from the BBC1 morning news magazine programme. The BBC Radiophonic Workshop's Brian Hodgson and Malcolm Clarke talk about creating the music and sound effects for *Doctor Who* using an example from *Resurrection of the Daleks* (from Thursday 15 March 1984); and Guy Michelmore introduces Janet Fielding, then Sally Magnusson interviews her and John Nathan-Turner about the role of the companions, tying in with the release of the latter's book *Doctor Who: The Companions* (Monday 20 October 1986).

*EXTENDED AND DELETED SCENES (7m5s) A selection of scenes not used in the final programme, taken from earlier edits with as-recorded sound, some from a VHS copy with on-screen time-code. Includes an alternative ending to episode two.

*BBC TRAILER (32s) Preview of the first episode, broadcast in February 1984.

▶

INFORMATION TEXT Select **On** to view subtitles when watching the episodes that provide information and anecdotes about the development, production, broadcast and history of *Resurrection of the Daleks*. Written by Richard Molesworth.

PHOTO GALLERY (3m13s) Slideshow of colour photos taken during production of *Resurrection of the Daleks*, set to sound effects from the story. Compiled by Ralph Montagu.

*AUDIO OPTIONS Select **Commentary On** to play the audio commentary in place of the main soundtrack when watching the episodes. With Peter Davison, Janet Fielding (Tegan) and director Matthew Robinson on all four episodes.

— Select **Isolated Music On** to hear only Malcolm Clarke's music when watching the episodes.

— Select **5.1 Dolby Digital** for feature to hear the surround soundtrack when watching the episodes, newly remixed for this release.

— Select **Mono for feature** to reinstate the main soundtrack when watching the episodes.

*TARDIS – CAM NO. 4 (43s) Short scene featuring the TARDIS, originally made for the BBCi *Doctor Who* website in 2001. The TARDIS arrives in an underwater base (model).

SUBTITLES

Select **On** to view subtitles for all episodes and Special Features, or for the commentary.

EASTER EGGS

There are two hidden features on this disc to find. *See Appendix 2 for details*

RELATED EXTRAS

The Dalek Tapes — Genesis of the Daleks

RESURRECTION OF THE DALEKS SPECIAL EDITION

STORY No.133   SEASON No.21:4

Released with **CARNIVAL OF MONSTERS SPECIAL EDITION** and **THE SEEDS OF DEATH SPECIAL EDITION** in the **REVISITATIONS 2** boxset

Two discs with two broadcast episodes (93½ mins), four original episodes (98 mins) and 157½ minutes of extras, plus two commentary, music-only and surround-sound tracks, production subtitles (four-part version only) and PDF items

Audio navigation of each disc's contents available by pressing Enter after the BBC ident

TARDIS TEAM Fifth Doctor, Tegan, Turlough

TIME AND PLACE Contemporary London and future prison space station

ADVERSARIES Daleks (13th appearance); Davros (3rd appearance); mercenary Lytton

FIRST ON TV 8–15 February 1984

DVD RELEASE BBCDVD2956C, 28 March 2011, PG

COVER Photo illustration by Clayton Hickman, purple strip; version with older BBC logo on reverse

ORIGINAL RRP £39.99 (boxset)

STORY TEASER

When the TARDIS is caught in a time corridor, the Doctor discovers one end is in an old warehouse in London, 1984, where an army bomb disposal squad is guarding some unusual cylinders that could be far more deadly than bombs. The other end is on a Dalek battleship attacking a prison containing a very special inmate the Daleks need to release: their creator, Davros. But the Daleks have even bigger plans and, to stop Davros helping them, the Doctor is forced to take drastic action.

CONNECTIONS

This story follows on directly from the end of the preceding serial *Frontios*, with the TARDIS caught in the Daleks' time corridor. The Daleks are seen with similar time-travel abilities in *The Evil of the Daleks* (1967), *Day of the Daleks* (1972), *Remembrance of the Daleks* (1988), *Doomsday* (2006), *Evolution of the Daleks* (2007), *The Stolen Earth* (2008), *Victory of the Daleks* (2010) and *Asylum of the Daleks* (2012), and have actual TARDIS-like time machines in *The Chase* (1965) and *The Daleks' Master Plan* (1965/66). They also use germ warfare in *The Dalek Invasion of Earth* (1964), *Planet of the Daleks* (1973) and *Death to the Daleks* (1974). Davros is imprisoned at the end of *Destiny of the Daleks* (1979), in which the Daleks are first seen battling the Movellans. This is the first time the Doctor spends time battling monsters in contemporary Central London with help from the military since *Invasion of the Dinosaurs* (1974) (bar a brief face-off with a Skarasen in *Terror of the Zygons*, 1975) and doesn't do so again until *Aliens of London* (2005). Writer Eric Saward was script editor of the programme, during which time he also wrote *Earthshock* (1982) and *Revelation of the Daleks* (1985), while Matthew Robinson also directed *Attack of the Cybermen* (1985) in which Lytton returns, again played by Maurice Colbourne, along with Mike Braben and Michael Jeffries as his fake-police henchmen. Terry Molloy dons Davros's mask again in *Revelation of the Daleks* and *Remembrance of the Daleks*, and appears in person as Russell in *Attack of the Cybermen*.

WORTH WATCHING

This Special Edition features the episodes in a previously unreleased format and additional Special Features. Originally planned as the climax to the 1983 season in the show's twentieth year, *Resurrection of the Daleks* was delayed owing to strike action, so became part of Peter Davison's final season as the Doctor, and the last story for companion Tegan. Even then it was almost postponed once more due to coverage of the 1984 Winter Olympics, until producer John Nathan-Turner elected instead to re-edit its four parts into two 45-minute episodes that fitted the schedules better. This release includes both versions of the serial. This is the Fifth Doctor's only televised confrontation with the Daleks and an action-packed return for the creatures.

DISC ONE

THE EPISODES

On this disc is the two-episode version of the story as broadcast on BBC1 in February 1984. Both episodes are restored from digital duplicates of the original one-inch colour videotape recordings used for broadcast, with location scenes reinserted from the original one-inch videotape transfer of the 16mm colour film. Their mono soundtracks are remastered and the title sequences replaced by a modern transfer of the original 35mm film with credits remade to match the originals.

SPECIAL FEATURES *REPEATED FROM PREVIOUS RELEASE

CASTING FAR AND WIDE (32m18s) Actor and comedian Toby Hadoke meets five actors who had one-off roles in *Resurrection of the Daleks* to discuss their careers and experiences of being in *Doctor Who*. With Roger Davenport (trooper), Del Henney (Colonel Archer), Leslie Grantham (Kiston), Jim Findley (Mercer) and William Sleigh (Galloway). Produced by Ed Stradling.

***ON LOCATION** (18m32s) Producer John Nathan-Turner, writer Eric Saward and director Matthew Robinson return to Shad Thames, where much of *Resurrection of the Daleks* was filmed, to recall the making of the serial. Including how the director shot the opening scene; bringing back the Daleks and Davros; the level of violence in the story; Tegan's departure; selecting the location for filming; and how effects shots were filmed (illustrated with footage from the original filming). Produced by Paul Vanezis.

***EXTENDED AND DELETED SCENES** (7m5s) A selection of scenes not used in the final programme, taken from earlier edits with as-recorded sound, some from a VHS copy with on-screen time-code. Includes an alternative ending to episode two.

***BREAKFAST TIME** (7m58s) Extracts from the BBC1 morning news magazine programme. The BBC Radiophonic Workshop's Brian Hodgson and Malcolm Clarke talk about creating the music and sound effects for *Doctor Who* using an example from *Resurrection of the Daleks* (from Thursday 15

R

March 1984); and Guy Michelmore introduces Janet Fielding, then Sally Magnusson interviews her and John Nathan-Turner about the role of the companions, tying in with the release of the latter's book *Doctor Who: The Companions* (Monday 20 October 1986).

*TRAILER (33s) Preview of the first episode, broadcast in February 1984.

NEXT

THE LAST DALEK (9m34s) Silent 8mm black-and-white footage shot by designer Tony Cornell during filming for *The Evil of the Daleks* episode seven at Ealing Studios on 16/17 May 1967, showing models being set up with explosive charges for their destruction in the final battle of the story and effects shots of Daleks in the Emperor's chamber. With a commentary by the serial's visual effects designers Peter Day and Michaeljohn Harris, who appear in the footage. *Also on* Lost in Time *and* The Seeds of Death

*TARDIS CAM NO.4 (43s) Short scene featuring the TARDIS, originally made for the BBCi *Doctor Who* website in 2001. The TARDIS arrives in an underwater base (model).

AUDIO OPTIONS Select **Commentary** to play the audio commentary recorded for this release in place of the main soundtrack when watching the episodes on this disc. This is moderated by actor and writer Nicholas Pegg, talking with Terry Molloy (Davros), writer/script editor Eric Saward and visual effects designer Peter Wragg on both episodes.

— Select **Isolated Music** to hear only Malcolm Clarke's music when watching the episodes.

— Select **Feature Audio 5.1** to hear the Dolby Digital surround soundtrack when watching the episodes, as remixed for the previous release then edited to fit this two-part version of the serial.

— Select **Feature Audio Mono** to reinstate the main soundtrack when watching the episodes.

PDF MATERIALS Accessible via a computer are the two episode listings from *Radio Times* for the original BBC1 broadcast of *Resurrection of the Daleks*, and a one-and-a-half-page article about the return of the Daleks published the week of episode one. The photo accompanying the article was intended for the cover to promote the Daleks' return, but lost out to Winter Olympics coverage.

COMING SOON (1m35s) Trailer for the DVD release of *Planet of the Spiders*.

SUBTITLES

Select **On** to view subtitles for all episodes and Special Features on disc one (except commentary).

DISC TWO

THE EPISODES

On this disc is the originally intended four-episode version of the story as previously released. All four episodes are restored from digital duplicates of the original one-inch colour videotape recordings initially prepared for broadcast, with location scenes reinserted from the original one-inch videotape transfer of the 16mm colour film. Their mono soundtracks are remastered and the title sequences replaced by a modern transfer of the original 35mm film with credits remade to match the originals.

SPECIAL FEATURES *REPEATED FROM PREVIOUS RELEASE

COME IN NUMBER FIVE (56m29s) David Tennant presents an examination of Peter Davison's three years as the Fifth Doctor, including the decisions behind casting him; changes among the production team through 1981 as John Nathan-Turner settled into his producership and resulting struggles to get scripts ready for the 1982 season; moving *Doctor Who* away from its traditional Saturday slot; coping with three companions by killing one off; the popular success of Davison's first season; Nathan-Turner's focus on well-known guest stars to gain publicity and his fondness for fan conventions; further companion changes in the 1983 season; ongoing script difficulties; finding directors suited to the style of the programme; facing a changing television environment; celebrating the twentieth anniversary; getting tougher in the stories for the 1984 season but too late to keep the cast; going out on a high; the effectiveness of Davison's Doctor; and returning in 2007 for *Time Crash*. With contributions from Davison, companion actors Janet Fielding and Mark Strickson, producer John Nathan-Turner (interviewed in 1999), BBC head of series and serials David Reid, executive producer Barry Letts (interviewed in 2008), script editors Christopher H Bidmead, Antony Root and Eric Saward, director Fiona Cumming and New Series executive producer Steven Moffat. Produced by Ed Stradling.

TOMORROW'S TIMES – THE FIFTH DOCTOR (12m18s) Coverage of *Doctor Who* in the national newspapers during the Fifth Doctor's era from 1982 to 1984. Presented by Frazer Hines, written and directed by Marcus Hearn. *See Index iii for further editions*

WALRUS (1m23s) Extract from the BBC Schools language programme ('Walrus' stood for Writing And Listening, Reading, Understanding, Speaking) first broadcast on Thursday 7 October 1982, in which a Dalek is baffled by the vocal inflections of a Welsh woman, played by Veronika Hyks. The Dalek featured is a surviving prop from the second Dalek movie *Daleks Invasion Earth: 2150AD*, originally given away by Sugar Puffs as part of its promotion for the film.

PHOTO GALLERY (5m18s) Slideshow of colour photos taken during production of *Resurrection of the Daleks*, including design department photos of the sets. Set to music and sound effects from the story. Compiled by Paul Shields.

*AUDIO OPTIONS Select **Commentary** to play the audio commentary recorded for the previous release in place of the main soundtrack when watching the episodes on this disc. With Peter Davison, Janet Fielding (Tegan) and director Matthew Robinson on all four episodes.

— Select **Feature Audio 5.1** to hear the Dolby Digital surround soundtrack when watching the episodes, as remixed for the previous release.

— Select **Feature Audio Mono** to reinstate the main soundtrack when watching the episodes.

INFO TEXT Select **On** to view subtitles when watching the episodes on this disc that provide information and anecdotes about the development, production, broadcast and history of *Resurrection of the Daleks*, updated and expanded from the previous release. Written by Paul Scoones.

COMING SOON (1m35s) Trailer for the DVD release of *Planet of the Spiders*.

SUBTITLES

Select **On** to view subtitles for all episodes and Special Features on disc two (except commentary).

EASTER EGGS

There are two hidden features on these discs to find. *See Appendix 2 for details*

RELATED EXTRAS

The Dalek Tapes — Genesis of the Daleks

Coming Soon trailer — Kinda, Snakedance

REVELATION OF THE DALEKS

STORY No.142   SEASON No.22:6

One disc with two episodes (90 mins) and 74 minutes of extras, plus optional CGI effects, commentary, music-only and surround-sound tracks, and production subtitles

TARDIS TEAM Sixth Doctor, Peri

TIME AND PLACE Tranquil Repose funerary service on planet Necros

ADVERSARIES Daleks (14th appearance); Davros (4th appearance); industrialist Kara

FIRST ON TV 23–30 March 1985

DVD RELEASE BBCDVD1357, 11 July 2005, PG

COVER Photo illustration by Clayton Hickman, light purple strip

ORIGINAL RRP £19.99

— Also released in The Dalek Collection; BBCDVD2261, £79.99, 27 January 2007

— Reissued in sleeve with orange logo and cover illustration in a circle against dark purple background; BBCDVD2475, £9.99, 2 July 2007

— Also released in The Complete Davros Collection; BBCDVD2508, £99.99, 26 November 2007

STORY TEASER

The Doctor is suspicious when he hears an old friend has checked in to Tranquil Repose, where the rich wait in deep freeze until their illnesses can be cured, so he arrives on Necros to investigate. He is right to be concerned. Tranquil Repose is funded by a ruthless industrialist whose profits are based on a very grisly secret, while in charge is Davros, who has his own use for the bodies there — one that involves a new breed of Daleks.

CONNECTIONS

The two groups of rival Daleks established here continue their antagonism in the next and last Classic Dalek story, *Remembrance of the Daleks* (1988). Post-Time War Daleks again use the remains of humans to rebuild their forces in *The Parting of the Ways* (2005), and successfully lure the Doctor into their clutches in *Asylum of the Daleks* (2012). The Doctor has seen his face is carved in stone before (but rather bigger than just a statue) in *The Face of Evil* (1977). Assassin-for-hire Orcini is reminiscent of writer Eric Saward's previous creation, the mercenary Lytton (*Resurrection of the Daleks*, 1984), who returns at the start of the 1985 season in *Attack of the Cybermen*, largely written uncredited by Saward. Graeme Harper also directed the Fifth Doctor's swan song *The Caves of Androzani* (1984) and returned for several Tenth Doctor stories, including directing the Daleks again in *Army of Ghosts/Doomsday* (2006) and Davros in *The Stolen Earth/Journey's End* (2008). Terry Molloy plays Davros for the second time after taking on the role in *Resurrection of the Daleks*, having appeared without a mask as Russell in *Attack of the Cybermen*, while Clive Swift (Jobel) returns as Mr Copper in *Voyage of the Damned* (2007). Eleanor Bron (Kara) has a cameo in *City of Death* (1979), while Hugh Walters (Vogel) appears briefly in *The Chase* (1965) and as the equally obsequious Runcible in *The Deadly Assassin* (1976). Alec Linstead (Stengos) is also Sergeant Osgood in *The Dæmons* (1971) and Arnold Jellicoe in *Robot* (1974/75), and Colin Spaull (Lilt) returns as Crane in *Rise of the Cybermen/The Age of Steel* (2006).

WORTH WATCHING

By the time *Revelation of the Daleks* was broadcast, it was known this would be the last *Doctor Who* story for some time, coming at the end of the 1985 season during which the show was cancelled then hurriedly reprieved following public outcry. The programme was criticised for becoming too violent, and there's some justification for that in the action and disturbing ideas featured here, and yet *Revelation of the Daleks* is considered by many to be the pinnacle of the Sixth Doctor era.

THE EPISODES

Both episodes are restored from digital duplicates of the original one-inch colour videotape recordings used for broadcast, with model shots newly transferred from the original 16mm colour film. Their mono soundtracks are remastered (one song by Jimi Hendrix is replaced with a soundalike as it couldn't be re-licensed) and the title sequences are replaced by a digital duplicate of the original one-inch colour videotape transfer of the 35mm film with credits remade to match the originals.

SPECIAL FEATURES

REVELATION EXHUMED (45m52s) The making of *Revelation of the Daleks*, including inspirations for the script; the characters and their portrayal; working with the Daleks; finding the location and matching it in model work and studio sets; surprise weather complicating the location filming; the director's vision; and composing the music. With contributions from writer/script editor Eric Saward, director Graeme Harper, designer Alan Spalding, costume designer Pat Godfrey, visual effects designer John Brace, composer Roger Limb, and actors Trevor Cooper, William Gaunt, Terry Molloy, Alexei Sayle (interviewed in 1993), Roy Skelton, Colin Spaull, Clive Swift and Hugh Walters. Produced by John Kelly.

BEHIND THE SCENES (15m37s) Footage from the full studio recording in late-January 1985 of scenes involving special effects, including destroying the glass Dalek, Orcini's attack on Davros, the Dalek shoot-out, scenes in Davros's lair, and the destruction of Tranquil Repose. With optional commentary by director Graeme Harper and actor Terry Molloy.

INFORMATION TEXT Select **On** to view subtitles when watching the episodes that provide information and anecdotes about the development, production, broadcast and history of *Revelation of the Daleks*. Written by Richard Molesworth.

CGI EFFECTS Select **CGI Effects On** to view updated computer-generated effects in place of some of the original visual effects when watching the episodes.

DELETED SCENES (2m15s) A selection of scenes not used in the final programme, taken from earlier edits of the episodes.

CONTINUITY (3m29s) Continuity announcements from the original BBC1 broadcasts of both episodes of *Revelation of the Daleks*, and from its four-part repeat (including unscripted cliff-hangers) on BBC2 in March/April 1993. Includes the fixtures for *Match of the Day* on Saturday 30 March 1985 and a plug for the Blackpool and Longleat *Doctor Who* exhibitions.

PHOTO GALLERY (5m56s) Slideshow of colour photos taken during production of *Revelation of the Daleks*, including shots of the model filming. Set to sound effects from the story. Compiled by Ralph Montagu.

AUDIO OPTIONS
Select **Commentary Feature and Behind the Scenes On** to play the audio commentary in place of the main soundtrack when watching the episodes. With Nicola Bryant (Peri), Terry Molloy (Davros), writer/script editor Eric Saward and director Graeme Harper on both episodes. This option also plays a commentary by Harper and Molloy when watching the behind-the-scenes footage.
— Select **Isolated Music On** to hear only Roger Limb's music when watching the episodes.
— Select **5.1 audio On** to hear the Dolby Digital surround soundtrack when watching the episodes, newly remixed for this release.

SUBTITLES
Select **On** to view subtitles for all episodes and Special Features (except commentary).

EASTER EGG
There is one hidden feature on this disc to find. *See Appendix 2 for details*

RELATED EXTRAS
The Dalek Tapes — Genesis of the Daleks

REVENGE OF THE CYBERMEN
STORY No.79   SEASON No.12:5

Released in a boxset with **SILVER NEMESIS**
One disc with four episodes (96½ mins) and 65½ minutes of extras, plus commentary track, production subtitles and PDF items
Audio navigation of disc contents available by pressing Enter after the BBC ident

TARDIS TEAM Fourth Doctor, Harry, Sarah Jane
TIME AND PLACE Space station Nerva near Jupiter, far future
ADVERSARIES Cybermen (6th appearance)
FIRST ON TV 19 April–10 May 1975
DVD RELEASE BBCDVD2854(A), 9 August 2010, U (boxset PG)
COVER Photo illustration by Clayton Hickman, blue strip; version with older BBC logo on reverse
ORIGINAL RRP £29.99 (boxset)

STORY TEASER
The Doctor, Sarah and Harry return to Nerva but arrive centuries before their previous visit, at a time when it's a navigation beacon warning spaceships of a new moon around Jupiter. A mysterious plague has killed most of the crew, but when the Doctor deduces its true cause the culprit is found to be working for the Cybermen. To them the beacon is a staging post to attacking the planetoid below, but its inhabitants have their own plans for repelling the Cybermen.

CONNECTIONS
The Doctor first arrives on Nerva when it's orbiting Earth, redeployed as a human refuge from solar flares that gets violated by Wirrn in *The Ark in Space* (1975). This is the first Cybermen story since *The Invasion* (1968), before which they were seen attacking a similar space station in *The Wheel in Space* (1968). That story and its predecessor, *The Tomb of the Cybermen* (1967), also feature Cybermats, which don't return until *Closing Time* (2011) and are superseded by Cybermites in *Nightmare in Silver* (2013). The Cybermen use infections to disable opposition in *The Moonbase* (1967), while gold is used against them in *Earthshock* (1982) and *Silver Nemesis* (1988). Writer Gerry Davis, who with Kit Pedler created the Cybermen in *The Tenth Planet* (1966), hadn't contributed a script since *The Tomb of the Cybermen*, whereas director Michael E Briant was a regular during the 1970s (*see*

Index v). Ronald Leigh-Hunt, playing Commander Stevenson, is also Commander Radnor in *The Seeds of Death* (1969), while William Marlow (Lester) is less sympathetic as Harry Mailer in *The Mind of Evil* (1971). Alex Wallis (Warner) plays Bowman in *The Sea Devils* and Christopher Robbie (Cyberleader) is the Karkus in *The Mind Robber* (1968). All four main Vogan actors appear more recognisably in other stories: David Collings (Vorus) as Poul in *The Robots of Death* and the title character in *Mawdryn Undead* (1983); Brian Grellis (Sheprah) as Safran in *The Invisible Enemy* (1977) and 'megaphone man' in *Snakedance* (1983); Kevin Stoney (Tyrum) plays chief villains Mavic Chen in *The Daleks' Master Plan* (1965/66) and Tobias Vaughan in *The Invasion*; and Michael Wisher (Magrik) is Rex Farrel in *Terror of the Autons* (1971), Kalik in *Carnival of Monsters* (1973) and Morelli in *Planet of Evil* (1975), as well as playing Davros in *Genesis of the Daleks* (1975).

WORTH WATCHING

Having been absent for the whole of the Third Doctor era, the return of the Cybermen is significant even if their storyline has little relation to their 1960s motives. Then they were perpetually seeking to convert humans into Cybermen in order to survive; here survival is still their aim but to be achieved by simply destroying their enemy, with none of the inherent horror of their earlier appearances. Without this return at one of the series' peaks in popularity, however, they may have been forgotten as a black-and-white era monster, given they don't surface again until the 1980s.

THE EPISODES

All four episodes are restored from digital duplicates of the original two-inch colour videotape recordings used for broadcast and their mono soundtracks remastered. The title sequences are replaced by a modern transfer of the original 35mm film with credits remade to match the originals.

SPECIAL FEATURES

THE TIN MEN AND THE WITCH (25m24s) The making of *Revenge of the Cybermen*, including the handover between producers during the 1975 season; getting the script up to scratch; saving money by reusing sets; strange events while on location at Wookey Hole caves in Somerset; revamping the Cybermen; realising the Vogans; the immediate impact of Tom Baker as the Doctor; the strengths of the director; and disagreements over the music score. With contributions from outgoing producer Barry Letts (interviewed in 2008), incoming producer Philip Hinchcliffe and director Michael E Briant. Produced by Ed Stradling.

LOCATION REPORT (5m56s) Report from the Friday 22 November 1974 edition of BBC local news programme *Points West*, shot on location at Wookey Hole, Somerset the day before and broadcast a few weeks before Tom Baker's first story was shown. Includes the first television interview with Baker since becoming the Doctor and behind-the-scenes footage of the location filming for *Revenge of the Cybermen*. Also on **The Ark in Space**

CHEQUES, LIES AND VIDEOTAPE (28m18s) Before *Doctor Who* stories began being regularly issued on VHS (of which *Revenge of the Cybermen* was the first), let alone DVD, fans had to find other means of rewatching their favourite show: exchanging videotapes recorded from a variety of illicit sources and duplicated for sometimes surprising amounts of money. Fans Dave Hankinson, Paul Jones, Alison Lawson, David Palfreyman, Damian Shanahan and Jamie Wells recall the early days of home video and their excitement (and sometimes disappointment) at getting to see past stories again. Written by Nicholas Pegg, narrated by Toby Longworth, produced by Ed Stradling.

PHOTO GALLERY (4m38s) Slideshow of colour and black-and-white photos taken during production of *Revenge of the Cybermen*, including design department photos of the sets. Set to sound effects from the story. Compiled by Derek Handley.

NEXT

AUDIO OPTIONS Select **Commentary** to play the audio commentary in place of the main soundtrack when watching the episodes. With Elisabeth Sladen (Sarah), David Collings (Vorus), producer Philip Hinchcliffe and designer Roger Murray-Leach on all four episodes.

— Select **Feature Audio** to reinstate the main soundtrack when watching the episodes.

INFO TEXT Select **On** to view subtitles when watching the episodes that provide information and anecdotes about the development, production, broadcast and history of *Revenge of the Cybermen*. Written by Nicholas Pegg.

PDF MATERIALS Accessible via a computer are the four episode listings from *Radio Times* for the original BBC1 broadcast of *Revenge of the Cybermen*.

COMING SOON (40s) Trailer for the DVD release of *Time and the Rani*.

SUBTITLES
Select **On** to view subtitles for all episodes and Special Features (except commentary).

EASTER EGG
There is one hidden feature on this disc to find. *See Appendix 2 for details*

RELATED EXTRAS
The Cyber-Generations — Attack of the Cybermen
Coming Soon trailer — The Dominators

REVISITATIONS 1

Boxset of **THE CAVES OF ANDROZANI SPECIAL EDITION**, **THE MOVIE SPECIAL EDITION** and **THE TALONS OF WENG-CHIANG SPECIAL EDITION**

DVD RELEASE BBCDVD2806, 4 October 2010, 12
SLIPCASE No illustration, silvered logo, turquoise background
ORIGINAL RRP £39.99

WHAT'S IN THE BOX
Three stories previously released on DVD early in the range, further restored using more advanced techniques and with more extensive Special Features. In *The Talons of Weng-Chiang* (1977) the Fourth Doctor and Leela arrive in Victorian London where young girls are going missing, Chinese gangs stalk the streets and at the Palace Theatre magician Li H'sen Chang's act includes a very suspicious ventriloquist's dummy. But all are in service to a much more dangerous master posing as an ancient Chinese god. *The Caves of Androzani* (1984) is the final Fifth Doctor story in which he and Peri are caught up in a war over the supply of a miraculous drug, which some people will go to any lengths to control. Infected with a fatal disease, can they survive everone's machinations long enough to find the cure? And *The Movie* (1996) is the American-produced one-off television movie in which the Seventh Doctor regenerates into the Eighth, played by Paul McGann, as the Master risks destroying the Earth in his bid to steal the Doctor's remaining lives.

● *See individual stories for full contents*

REVISITATIONS 2

Boxset of **CARNIVAL OF MONSTERS SPECIAL EDITION**, **RESURRECTION OF THE DALEKS SPECIAL EDITION** and **THE SEEDS OF DEATH SPECIAL EDITION**

DVD RELEASE BBCDVD2956, 28 March 2011, PG
SLIPCASE No illustration, silvered logo, red background
ORIGINAL RRP £39.99

WHAT'S IN THE BOX
Three stories previously released on DVD early in the range, further restored using more advanced techniques and with more extensive Special Features. *The Seeds of Death* (1969) features the Second Doctor's second encounter with the Ice Warriors as they take over the transmat control station on the Moon from which to launch their invasion of Earth. In *Carnival of Monsters* (1973) the Third Doctor and Jo find themselves trapped inside a kind of futuristic television in which the creatures on show are very real and very dangerous. And in *Resurrection of the Daleks* (1984) the Fifth Doctor is caught by the Daleks as they attack the prison holding Davros. They need their creator to find a cure for a disease that is wiping them out, and the Doctor finds himself left with one desperate option to prevent Davros saving the Daleks.

● *See individual stories for full contents*

REVISITATIONS 3

Boxset of **THE ROBOTS OF DEATH SPECIAL EDITION, THE THREE DOCTORS SPECIAL EDITION** and **THE TOMB OF THE CYBERMEN SPECIAL EDITION**

DVD RELEASE BBCDVD3003, 13 February 2012, PG

SLIPCASE No illustration, silvered logo, purple background

ORIGINAL RRP £35.74

WHAT'S IN THE BOX

Three stories previously released on DVD early in the range, further restored using more advanced techniques and with more extensive Special Features. In *The Tomb of the Cybermen* (1967) the Second Doctor arrives on the planet Telos and encounters an archaeological expedition that has unearthed the fabled city of the Cybermen, unaware that the creatures are not dead but merely in hibernation. *The Three Doctors* (1972/73) sees the Time Lords bring together the first three incarnations of the Doctor to help them reverse a power drain that's crippling their world. But the only way to do so is to venture into the very heart of a black hole. And in *The Robots of Death* (1977) the Fourth Doctor and Leela arrive on a mining vessel where robots do all the manual labour, overseen by a small group of humans, one of whom believes the robots should be free and has reprogrammed them to kill everyone aboard.

● *See individual stories for full contents*

THE **RIBOS OPERATION**

STORY No.98   SEASON No.16:1

Released with **THE ANDROIDS OF TARA, THE ARMAGEDDON FACTOR, THE PIRATE PLANET, THE POWER OF KROLL** and **THE STONES OF BLOOD** in **THE KEY TO TIME** boxset

One disc with four episodes (99½ mins) and 89½ minutes of extras, plus commentary track, production subtitles and PDF items

TARDIS TEAM Fourth Doctor, K9, and introducing First Romana

TIME AND PLACE Medieval planet Ribos

ADVERSARIES Ousted tyrant the Graff Vynda-K

FIRST ON TV 2–23 September 1978

DVD RELEASE BBCDVD2335(A), 24 September 2007, PG

COVER Photo illustration by Clayton Hickman, light turquoise strip

ORIGINAL RRP £69.99 (boxset)

STORY TEASER

Ribos is a medieval planet, completely unaware of the rest of the universe. But that doesn't stop deposed galactic despot the Graff Vynda-K from wanting to buy it, and con man Garron is only too happy to sell it to him, for the right price. He has convinced the Graff that Ribos is rich in the valuable mineral jethrik, and when the Doctor and Romana's search for the Key to Time leads them to Garron's sample of the rock, the hustler believes he can fleece both parties. But should the Graff realise the deception, he's mad enough to kill everyone on the planet in revenge.

CONNECTIONS

This story kicks off the Doctor's season-long hunt for the Key to Time, a mission he's sent on by the White Guardian, who returns in *Enlightenment* (1983), played again by Cyril Luckham. The society on Ribos is reminiscent of Peladon (*The Curse of Peladon*, 1972; *The Monster of Peladon*, 1974), with rituals and wild animals in catacombs, but less aware of other civilisations. Cheeky con-man Garron is not unlike Captain Jack Harkness when first seen in *The Empty Child* (2005) — as Garron claims to come from Earth, could he too be a time agent? The Graff, an outcast tyrant seeking to regain power with the help of some untrustworthy associates, is in a similar position to the eponymous character in *Meglos* (1980). This was Robert Holmes' first story for the series since relinquishing the role of script editor the year before; he also contributed *The Power of Kroll* to the

Key to Time season (*see Index v*). George Spenton-Foster also directed the previous season's *Image of the Fendahl* (1977). Of the mostly new cast, Prentis Hancock (Shrieve captain) returns for the last time since playing Salamar in *Planet of Evil* (1975), Vaber in *Planet of the Daleks* (1973) and a reporter in *Spearhead from Space* (1970), while Ann Tirard (the Seeker) is Locusta in episode three of *The Romans* (1965).

WORTH WATCHING

As well as setting up the search for the Key to Time, *The Ribos Operation* is a classic Robert Holmes story. While his previous contribution, *The Sun Makers*, depicted a population rising up against their oppressors, here an already deposed tyrant is given no sympathy as he's made a further fool of for trying to recapture what he's lost rather than learning any lesson. Holmes was always one for championing the common man trying to get by in a world run by the power-crazy, and here he makes us sympathise with Garron and Unstoffe despite their deceitful profession.

THE EPISODES

All four episodes are restored from digital duplicates of the original two-inch colour videotape recordings used for broadcast and their mono soundtracks remastered. The title sequences are replaced by a modern transfer of the original 35mm film with credits remade to match the originals.

SPECIAL FEATURES

A MATTER OF TIME (60m3s) Examination of Graham Williams' three years as producer of *Doctor Who*, from 1977 to 1980, when the programme came under new pressures from BBC management and the UK economy. Including changes to the style of storytelling to keep the level of violence in check and a greater influence from classic literature; the introduction of K9; the pressure on budgets from rocketing inflation; making the companion more intelligent and casting more women in main roles; giving the stories a connecting concept; regenerating Romana; the input of Douglas Adams; repeated strike action; and the rise of fandom. With contributions from Graham Williams (at conventions in 1985) and his widow Jackie; script editors Douglas Adams (interviewed in 1992) and Anthony Read; writers Bob Baker, David Fisher and Dave Martin; directors Christopher Barry, Darrol Blake, Ken Grieve, Michael Hayes and Pennant Roberts; designers Dick Coles and Richard McManan-Smith; visual effects designers Mat Irvine and Colin Mapson; actors Tom Baker (interviewed in 2003), Louise Jameson, John Leeson, Paul Seed, Mary Tamm and Lalla Ward; New Series writer Gareth Roberts; and fan Jeremy Bentham. Written by Nicholas Pegg, narrated by Toby Longworth, produced by Ed Stradling.

THE RIBOS FILE (19m39s) The making of *The Ribos Operation*, including the introduction of Romana; the set design; working with the director and with Tom Baker (and the actor's unfortunate encounter with a dog); the characters and cast; and realising the Shrivenzale. With contributions from actors Prentis Hancock, Nigel Plaskitt, Paul Seed and Mary Tamm, stuntman Stuart Fell, and fan journalist Clayton Hickman. Produced by Ed Stradling.

CONTINUITIES (2m8s) Continuity announcements from the original BBC1 broadcasts of all four episodes of *The Ribos Operation*, with plugs for the *Doctor Who* exhibitions at Blackpool and Longleat. Reconstructed by matching clips from the episodes to audio tape recordings made at the time of broadcast.

SEASON 16 TRAILER (42s) Preview of the new season shown on BBC1 in August 1978, featuring silent clips from *The Ribos Operation* and *The Pirate Planet* set to the *Doctor Who* theme music.

NEXT

AUDIO OPTIONS Select **Commentary** to play the audio commentary, recorded for an earlier US-only release, in place of the main soundtrack when watching the episodes. With Tom Baker and Mary Tamm (Romana) on all four episodes.

— Select **Feature Audio** to reinstate the main soundtrack when watching the episodes.

INFO TEXT Select **On** to view subtitles when watching the episodes that provide information and anecdotes about the development, production, broadcast and history of *The Ribos Operation*. Written by Martin Wiggins.

PHOTO GALLERY (6m3s) Slideshow of colour and black-and-white photos taken during production of *The Ribos Operation*, including design department photos of the sets. Set to sound effects from

R

the story. Compiled by Derek Handley.

COMING SOON (1m) Trailer for the DVD release of *Planet of Evil*.

RADIO TIMES LISTINGS Accessible via a computer is a PDF file of the four episode listings for the original BBC1 broadcast of *The Ribos Operation*.

SUBTITLES

Select **On** to view subtitles for all episodes and Special Features (except commentary).

EASTER EGG

There is one hidden feature on this disc to find. *See Appendix 2 for details*

RELATED EXTRAS

Coming Soon trailer — The Time Warrior

ROBOT

STORY No.75   SEASON No.12:1

One disc with four episodes (98½ mins) and 60 minutes of extras, plus commentary track, production subtitles and PDF items

TARDIS TEAM Fourth Doctor, Sarah Jane, Brigadier and UNIT, and introducing Harry Sullivan

TIME AND PLACE Contemporary Earth

ADVERSARIES Hilda Winters, head of Think Tank research group; K1 robot

FIRST ON TV 28 December 1974–18 January 1975

DVD RELEASE BBCDVD2332, 4 June 2007, U

COVER Photo illustration by Clayton Hickman, dark red strip

ORIGINAL RRP £19.99

STORY TEASER

No sooner has the Doctor undergone his third regeneration than Brigadier Lethbridge-Stewart and UNIT once more need his help. Plans and components for a powerful weapon have been stolen from supposedly impenetrable vaults and if the thieves get hold of the firing codes too they could hold the world to ransom. When Sarah discovers the work of robotics expert Professor Kettlewell is being continued in secret, the Doctor realises the culprits may be unstoppable.

CONNECTIONS

Six years after their first outing in *The Invasion* (1968) and having gradually featured in fewer stories each season throughout the Third Doctor era, UNIT make their last regular appearance as the new Doctor finds his feet. They return in *Terror of the Zygons* (1975), which had been planned as the last story of this season but was held over to begin the next; without the Brigadier in *The Android Invasion* (1975); briefly with all-new personnel in *The Seeds of Doom* (1976); and then not again until a one-off outing in *Battlefield* (1989). They do return in the New Series, however: fleetingly in *Aliens of London* (2005) then more centrally in *The Christmas Invasion* (2005), *The Sontaran Stratagem/The Poison Sky* (2008), *Planet of the Dead* (2009), *The Power of Three* (2012) and *The Day of the Doctor* (2013). The Doctor has met many robots, mostly of limited function, but more sophisticated examples like the K1, some of which were similarly manipulated to do harm, include the Super Voc in *The Robots of Death* (1977), K9 (temporarily controlled by the evil Shadow in *The Armageddon Factor*, 1979), Kamelion (*The King's Demons*, 1983; *Planet of Fire*, 1984), and Drathro (*The Trial of a Time Lord: The Mysterious Planet*, 1986). Terrance Dicks had just relinquished the role of script editor when he wrote *Robot*, having previously co-written *The War Games* (1969) and later scripting *Horror of Fang Rock* (1977), *State of Decay* (1980) and *The Five Doctors* (1983). Director Christopher Barry began working on *Doctor Who* with *The Daleks* (1963/64) and directs the Fourth Doctor again in *The Brain of Morbius* (1976) and *The Creature from the Pit* (1979) (*see Index v*). Edward Burnham (Professor Kettlewell) appears as another professor, Watkins, in *The Invasion*; Alec Linstead (Jellicoe) plays Sergeant Osgood in *The Dæmons* and Stengos in *Revelation of the Daleks* (1985); while Michael Kilgarriff as the robot of the title is also the Cyber Controller in *The Tomb of the Cybermen* (1967) and *Attack of the Cybermen* (1985).

WORTH WATCHING

It's Tom Baker's debut as the Doctor so a significant story in the history of the programme. After the popular Jon Pertwee, casting a relative unknown could be seen as risky, but Baker immediately makes the part his own and would quickly go on arguably to surpass Pertwee in popularity and memorability. The story itself is notable for the robot of its title, an impressive piece of costume design by future Oscar-winner James Acheson but importantly well characterised in Terrance Dicks' script. Often cited as a reworking of *King Kong*, that aspect only really plays in Sarah's sympathy towards the robot and at the end when it's accidentally swollen to giant size.

THE EPISODES

All four episodes are restored from digital duplicates of the original two-inch colour videotape recordings used for broadcast and their mono soundtracks remastered. The title sequences are replaced by a modern transfer of the original 35mm film with credits remade to match the originals.

SPECIAL FEATURES

ARE FRIENDS ELECTRIC? (38m58s) The making of *Robot*, including the change of production team in 1974; the process of casting a replacement for the departing Jon Pertwee and devising the portrayal of the Fourth Doctor; the concepts in the script; working with the director; the characters and cast; creating and portraying the robot; working with the CSO (colour separation overlay) composition technique and recording on location on videotape rather than film. With contributions from producers Philip Hinchcliffe and Barry Letts, writer Terrance Dicks, director Christopher Barry, production unit manager George Gallaccio, and actors Tom Baker, Edward Burnham, Michael Kilgarriff, Alec Linstead, Patricia Maynard and Elisabeth Sladen. Produced by Andrew Beech.

THE TUNNEL EFFECT (13m48s) Graphic designer Bernard Lodge talks about his career and how he devised the first title sequences for *Doctor Who* using the howlround technique. He subsequently designed the sequence introduced in the 1973/74 season — and reworked for the arrival of the Fourth Doctor in *Robot* — using the slit-scan technique, which he demonstrates using the original photographic elements. Produced by Brendan Sheppard.

BLUE PETER (2m14s) Extract from the Thursday 23 May 1974 edition of the children's magazine programme in which Lesley Judd, John Noakes and Peter Purves present from the sets for *Robot*, which had been left standing in the studio owing to a BBC scenery-shifters' strike. *Also on* The Talons of Weng-Chiang (*and* Special Edition)

PHOTO GALLERY (4m15s) Slideshow of colour and black-and-white photos taken during production of *Robot*, set to sound effects from the story. Compiled by Derek Handley.

RADIO TIMES LISTINGS Accessible via a computer is a PDF file of the four episode listings for the original BBC1 broadcast of *Robot*.

INFO TEXT Select **On** to view subtitles when watching the episodes that provide information and anecdotes about the development, production, broadcast and history of *Robot*. Written by Richard Molesworth.

AUDIO OPTIONS

Select **Commentary** to play the audio commentary in place of the main soundtrack when watching the episodes. With Tom Baker, Elisabeth Sladen (Sarah), producer Barry Letts and writer Terrance Dicks on all four episodes.

— Select **Feature Audio** to reinstate the main soundtrack when watching the episodes.

SUBTITLES

Select **On** to view subtitles for all episodes and Special Features (except commentary).

EASTER EGG

There is one hidden feature on this disc to find. *See Appendix 2 for details*

RELATED EXTRAS

Robot 8mm Location Film — The Ark in Space Special Edition

Dressing Doctor Who — The Mutants

The UNIT Family — Terror of the Zygons

THE **ROBOTS OF DEATH**

STORY No.90   SEASON No.14:5

One disc with four episodes (96 mins) and 9½ minutes of extras, plus commentary track and image content

TARDIS TEAM Fourth Doctor, Leela

TIME AND PLACE Sandmine crossing alien desert

ADVERSARIES Murderous robots; Taren Capel, campaigner for robot rights

FIRST ON TV 29 January–19 February 1977

DVD RELEASE BBCDVD1012, 13 November 2000, PG

COVER Single photo, dark grey strip

ORIGINAL RRP £19.99

STORY TEASER

Gliding over the surface of an alien desert, a mining vessel sucks up the rare minerals that the people aboard hope will make them rich. Yet someone seems unwilling to share this wealth, as one by one the crew are found strangled. The arrival of the Doctor and Leela provides an obvious pair of suspects, but the Doctor quickly identifies a possibility the others have fatally overlooked. Also aboard are dozens of robot servants, programmed never to harm humans — except someone is tampering with that programming. Hiding aboard the miner is a mad scientist who believes robots are better than people, and will kill to prove it.

CONNECTIONS

The Voc robots are paid homage to in *Voyage of the Damned* (2007) as the serene-looking servants the Heavenly Host are reprogrammed to go on a killing spree, similar to what happens to the clown and bus conductor robots in *The Greatest Show in the Galaxy* (1988/89). The Agatha Christie-like situation of a group of people in a confined location being killed off is common during the Second Doctor era, notably *The Moonbase* (1967) and *The Web of Fear* (1968), as well as *Pyramids of Mars* (1975), *Horror of Fang Rock* (1977), *Black Orchid* (1982), *The Trial of a Time Lord: Terror of the Vervoids* (1986), *The End of the World* (2005), *The Waters of Mars* (2009), *The Curse of the Black Spot* (2011), *The God Complex* (2011) and, of course, *The Unicorn and the Wasp* (2008), in which the Doctor meets Christie herself. Chris Boucher also wrote the preceding story that introduced Leela, *The Face of Evil*, and the following season's *Image of the Fendahl* (1977), while this was the last story directed by Michael E Briant (*see Index v*). Pamela Salem (Toos) returns as Professor Rachel Jensen in *Remembrance of the Daleks* (1988), while David Collings (Poul) is Vorus in *Revenge of the Cybermen* (1975) and the titular villain in *Mawdryn Undead* (1983).

WORTH WATCHING

This is a highly regarded story, frequently in the top ten of fan polls. The plot itself is a straightforward murder mystery — and it's often criticised that the identity of the murderer is obvious — but the twist of using the subservient robots to kill is well handled and the production as a whole raises the serial to a more engaging level, with nicely unified set and costume design, good model work and some impressive performances.

THE EPISODES

All four episodes are restored directly from the original two-inch colour videotape recordings used for broadcast.

● *Episodes begin playing automatically after 30 seconds if no menu selection is made*

SUBTITLE OPTIONS

Select **English** to view subtitles for all episodes and the featurette, **Commentary** to view subtitles for the audio commentary, or **Subs Off** to turn all subtitles off.

SPECIAL FEATURES *ALSO ON SPECIAL EDITION

*FEATURETTE (9m34s) A selection of footage from the production and transmission of *The Robots of Death*. The continuity announcement preceding the original BBC1 broadcast of episode one on Saturday 29 January 1977 (20s); a scene from episode one with the original as-recorded sound, including untreated robot voices (1m14s); silent model footage, much of it unused in the final programme, taken from a low-quality black-and-white video copy of the original 16mm colour film with on-screen time-code (7m38s); and the caption photo of the Doctor and Leela used for continuity announcements during 1977 (22s).

PHOTO GALLERY Scroll through 30 colour and black-and-white photos taken during production of *The Robots of Death*. Compiled by Ralph Montagu.

*STUDIO PLAN View three studio floorplans showing set arrangements and camera positions. The first is divided into four areas which can be selected for a closer view: the TARDIS control room, Sandmine crew room, captain's cabin and corridors, and control room (when zoomed in, select ◄ to return to the full plan). The second is a plan of the ore separation room; the third is of the dust scoop set.

*COMMENTARY Select **On** to play the audio commentary in place of the main soundtrack when watching the episodes. With writer Chris Boucher and producer Philip Hinchcliffe on all four episodes.

THE **ROBOTS OF DEATH** SPECIAL EDITION
STORY No.90   SEASON No.14:5

Released with **THE THREE DOCTORS SPECIAL EDITION** and **THE TOMB OF THE CYBERMEN SPECIAL EDITION** in the **REVISITATIONS 3** boxset
One disc with four episodes (96 mins) and 61½ minutes of extras, plus two commentary tracks, production subtitles, PDF items and image content
Audio navigation of disc contents available by pressing Enter after the BBC ident

TARDIS TEAM Fourth Doctor, Leela
TIME AND PLACE Sandmine crossing alien desert
ADVERSARIES Murderous robots; Taren Capel, campaigner for robot rights
FIRST ON TV 29 January–19 February 1977
DVD RELEASE BBCDVD3003C, 13 February 2012, PG
COVER Photo illustration by Clayton Hickman, purple strip; version with older BBC logo on reverse
ORIGINAL RRP £35.74 (boxset)

STORY TEASER
Gliding over the surface of an alien desert, a mining vessel sucks up the rare minerals that the people aboard hope will make them rich. Yet someone seems unwilling to share this wealth, as one by one the crew are found strangled. The arrival of the Doctor and Leela provides an obvious pair of suspects, but the Doctor quickly identifies a possibility the others have fatally overlooked. Also aboard are dozens of robot servants, programmed never to harm humans — except someone is tampering with that programming. Hiding aboard the miner is a mad scientist who believes robots are better than people, and will kill to prove it.

CONNECTIONS
The Voc robots are paid homage to in *Voyage of the Damned* (2007) as the serene-looking servants the Heavenly Host are reprogrammed to go on a killing spree, similar to what happens to the clown and bus conductor robots in *The Greatest Show in the Galaxy* (1988/89). The Agatha Christie-like situation of a group of people in a confined location being killed off is common during the Second Doctor era, notably *The Moonbase* (1967) and *The Web of Fear* (1968), as well as *Pyramids of Mars* (1975), *Horror of Fang Rock* (1977), *Black Orchid* (1982), *The Trial of a Time Lord: Terror of the Vervoids* (1986), *The End of the World* (2005), *The Waters of Mars* (2009), *The Curse of the Black Spot* (2011), *The God Complex* (2011) and, of course, *The Unicorn and the Wasp* (2008), in which the Doctor meets Christie herself. Chris Boucher also wrote the preceding story that introduced Leela, *The Face of Evil*, and the following season's *Image of the Fendahl* (1977), while this was the last story directed by Michael E Briant (*see Index v*). Pamela Salem (Toos) returns as Professor Rachel Jensen in *Remembrance of the Daleks* (1988), while David Collings (Poul) is Vorus in *Revenge of the Cybermen* (1975) and the titular villain in *Mawdryn Undead* (1983).

WORTH WATCHING

This Special Edition features more advanced clean-up of the episodes compared to the previous release and additional Special Features. This is a highly regarded story, frequently in the top ten of fan polls. The plot itself is a straightforward murder mystery — and it's often criticised that the identity of the murderer is obvious — but the twist of using the subservient robots to kill is well handled and the production as a whole raises the serial to a more engaging level, with nicely unified set and costume design, good model work and some impressive performances.

THE EPISODES

All four episodes are newly restored from digital duplicates of the original two-inch colour videotape recordings used for broadcast and their mono soundtracks remastered using more advanced techniques than the previous release. The title sequences are replaced by a modern transfer of the original 35mm film with credits remade to match the originals.

SPECIAL FEATURES   *REPEATED FROM PREVIOUS RELEASE

THE SANDMINE MURDERS (32m24s) The making of *The Robots of Death*, including the origins of the story and making amendments to the script during rehearsals; working with the director; the set and costume design, including the distinctive robots; and the characters and cast. With contributions from producer Philip Hinchcliffe, director Michael E Briant, costume designer Elizabeth Waller, and actors Tom Baker, David Collings, Brian Croucher, Louise Jameson and Pamela Salem. Produced by Steve Broster.

ROBOPHOBIA (11m48s) Comedian and writer Toby Hadoke takes a light-hearted look at the development of robots in the real world and the various forms that have been portrayed in *Doctor Who*. Written and produced by Richard Higson.

*STUDIO SOUND (1m24s) A scene from episode one with the original as-recorded sound, including untreated robot voices.

*MODEL SHOTS (7m47s) Silent model footage, much of it unused in the final programme, taken from a low-quality black-and-white video copy of the original 16mm colour film with on-screen time-code.

*STUDIO FLOOR PLAN View three studio floorplans showing set arrangements and camera positions. The first is divided into four areas which can be selected for a closer view: the TARDIS control room, Sandmine crew room, captain's cabin and corridors, and control room (when zoomed in, select ◀ to return to the full plan). The second is a plan of the ore separation room; the third is of the dust scoop set.

*CONTINUITY (53s) Continuity announcement from the original BBC1 broadcast of episode one of *The Robots of Death*, and the caption photo of the Doctor and Leela used for continuity announcements during 1977.

NEXT

PHOTO GALLERY (5m36s) Slideshow of colour and black-and-white photos taken during production of *The Robots of Death*, including design department photos of the sets. Set to sound effects from the story. Compiled by Paul Shields.

AUDIO OPTIONS Select *Commentary 1 to play the audio commentary recorded for the previous release in place of the main soundtrack when watching the episodes. With writer Chris Boucher and producer Philip Hinchcliffe on all four episodes.

— Select **Commentary 2** to play the audio commentary recorded for this release when watching the episodes. With Tom Baker, Louise Jameson (Leela), Pamela Salem (Toos) and director Michael E Briant on all four episodes.

— Select **Feature Audio** to reinstate the main soundtrack when watching the episodes.

INFO TEXT Select **On** to view subtitles when watching the episodes that provide information and anecdotes about the development, production, broadcast and history of *The Robots of Death*. Written by Martin Wiggins.

PDF MATERIALS Accessible via a computer are the four episode listings from *Radio Times* for the original BBC1 broadcast of *The Robots of Death*.

COMING SOON (1m26s) Trailer for the DVD release of *The Face of Evil*.

THE **ROMANS**

STORY No.12   SEASON No.2:4

Released in a boxset with **THE RESCUE**
*One disc with four episodes (97 mins) and 86½ minutes of extras, plus commentary track,
production subtitles and PDF items*
Audio navigation of disc contents available by pressing Enter after the BBC ident

TARDIS TEAM   First Doctor, Barbara, Ian, Vicki
TIME AND PLACE   Rome and environs, July 64AD
ADVERSARIES   Emperor Nero and his court; slave trader Sevcheria
FIRST ON TV   16 January–6 February 1965
DVD RELEASE   BBCDVD2971, 23 February 2009, U (boxset BBCDVD2698)
COVER   Photo illustration by Clayton Hickman, dark orange strip
ORIGINAL RRP   £29.35 (boxset)

STORY TEASER

The TARDIS crew have been taking a well-earned break in an Ancient Roman villa for a month, and before they leave the Doctor agrees to show Vicki nearby Rome. But an encounter with a murderous centurion en route leads to a potentially fatal audience with the emperor, Nero. Meanwhile Barbara and Ian are kidnapped by slave traders and separated, Ian sent to be a galley slave and Barbara sold into the emperor's court, where she catches Nero's wandering eye.

CONNECTIONS

The Caecilius family move to Rome in 79AD after being saved by the Doctor from the eruption of Vesuvius in *The Fires of Pompeii* (2008). The Doctor himself returns to what we now call Italy in *The Masque of Mandragora* (1976), *City of Death* (1979) and *The Vampires of Venice* (2010). He's present at the start of another Great Fire, that of London in September 1666, in *The Visitation* (1982), as well as the sacking of Troy in *The Myth Makers* (1965), while on a smaller scale he causes the priory home of Professor Scarman to burn down in *Pyramids of Mars* (1975). Barbara is earlier made to work as a slave for the Daleks in *The Dalek Invasion of Earth* (1964), as is Romana in *Destiny of the Daleks* (1979). Ben and Jamie are almost sold into slavery in *The Highlanders* (1966/67), while the Master makes all humans into slaves during his aborted year-long rule in *Last of the Time Lords* (2007). Humans traded Tharils in *Warriors' Gate* (1981), and happily let Ood serve them (*The Impossible Planet/The Satan Pit*, 2006) until the overthrow of the corrupt Ood Operations in *Planet of the Ood* (2008). The Sycorax planned to sell humans into slavery if their invasion had succeeded (*The Christmas Invasion*, 2005), while the Mentors of Thoros Beta enslaved people from its twin world Thoros Alpha (*The Trial of a Time Lord: Mindwarp*, 1986). Dennis Spooner wrote the previous season's *The Reign of Terror* as well as story-editing most of *Doctor Who*'s second season (*see Index v*). Christopher Barry directed both *The Romans* and preceding story *The Rescue*, and other serials throughout the 1960s and 70s (*see Index v*). Barry Jackson (Ascaris) appears again as Jeff Garvey in *Mission to the Unknown* (1965) and as ex-Time Lord Drax in *The Armageddon Factor* (1979), while Nicholas Evans (Didius) is hidden inside a Dalek and the Slyther in *The Dalek Invasion of Earth*. Gertan Klauber (Galley Master) has a more substantial role as Ola in *The Macra Terror* (1967), Kay Patrick (Poppaea) appears as Flower in *The Savages*, and Ann Tirard (Locusta) is the Seeker in *The Ribos Operation* (1978).

WORTH WATCHING

Commonly noted as an attempt to do all-out comedy in *Doctor Who*, *The Romans* is certainly more light-hearted than many stories of the time, but not hugely. Barbara's evasion of Nero's fumbled advances is played for laughs, as is the Doctor's emperor's-new-clothes approach to music. But the earlier storyline of Ian and Barbara's sale into slavery is played as seriously as usual, and in fact Ian's whole part in the story is as fraught with danger as ever. More notably it's the start of the Doctor having a more direct impact during his trips into Earth's history thanks to Spooner's desire to have more fun with the possibilities of time travel.

THE EPISODES

All four episodes are restored from 16mm film copies of the original black-and-white video recordings, recovered from BBC Enterprises in 1978. Their mono soundtracks are remastered and the VidFIRE process is applied to studio-recorded shots to recapture the smoother motion of video. The title sequences are replaced by a modern transfer of the best surviving copy of the original 35mm film with end credits remade to match the originals.

SPECIAL FEATURES

WHAT HAS 'THE ROMANS' EVER DONE FOR US? (33m59s) The making of *The Romans* and its faithfulness to known history, including the state of the Roman Empire in the First Century and the real Emperor Nero; memories of writer Dennis Spooner and his more comedic script for *The Romans*; Derek Francis' portrayal of Nero compared to others on film and television; designing the sets; arranging the fight scenes; the real Poppaea; the accuracy of the serial's representation of Christianity, slavery and the Great Fire of Rome; and referencing *The Romans* in the New Series. With contributions from director Christopher Barry, designer Raymond Cusick, actors Barry Jackson, Kay Patrick and William Russell, New Series writer James Moran, fan journalist Tom Spilsbury, and fan Ian McLachlan; plus historian Dr Mark Bradley of Nottingham University, and actors Anthony Andrews and Christopher Biggins who have played Nero in other productions. Narrated by John Bowe, produced by Steve Broster.

ROMA PARVA (2m33s) Director Christopher Barry describes how a studio recording session would be planned, using a surviving original studio floorplan and model of the sets for *The Romans* to demonstrate how camera positions were managed.

DENNIS SPOONER – WANNA WRITE A TELEVISION SERIES? (17m47s) Profile of the life and career of Dennis Spooner, who died in 1986, the writer for many popular television series of the 1960s and 1970s, including five *Doctor Who* stories as well as being the series' second story editor. With memories from friend and colleague Brian Clemens and his wife Janet, actors Peter Purves and William Russell, story editor Donald Tosh, and New Series writer Robert Shearman. Narrated by Anna Hope, produced by Robert Fairclough.

BLUE PETER (7m15s) Extract from the Thursday 4 January 1973 edition of the BBC1 children's magazine programme in which Valerie Singleton hosts a Roman banquet in the studio for Lesley Judd and Peter Purves, with John Noakes serving them.

NEXT

GIRLS! GIRLS! GIRLS! – THE 1960'S (17m40s) Overview of the changing roles and portrayals of the female companions over the course of the 1960s. With Carole Ann Ford (Susan), Jean Marsh (Sara), Anneke Wills (Polly) and Deborah Watling (Victoria), plus story editor Donald Tosh, director Christopher Barry, and actors Honor Blackman, Frazer Hines, Peter Purves and William Russell. Narrated by Dona Croll, produced by Robert Fairclough.

PHOTO GALLERY (6m7s) Slideshow of black-and-white photos taken during production of *The Romans*, including design department photos of the sets. Set to period music. Compiled by Ralph Montagu.

AUDIO OPTIONS Select **Commentary** to play the audio commentary in place of the main soundtrack when watching the episodes. This is moderated by actor and comedian Toby Hadoke, talking with Nick Evans (Didius) [ep 1], Barry Jackson (Ascaris) [1,2], William Russell (Ian) [1,2,3,4], director Christopher Barry [1,2,3,4] and designer Raymond Cusick [4].

— Select **Feature Audio** to reinstate the main soundtrack when watching the episodes.

INFO TEXT Select **On** to view subtitles when watching the episodes that provide information and anecdotes about the development, production, broadcast and history of *The Romans*. Written by Richard Molesworth.

PDF MATERIALS Accessible via a computer are the four episode listings from *Radio Times* for the original BBC1 broadcast of *The Romans* and an article that introduced the story.

COMING SOON (1m7s) Trailer for the DVD release of *Attack of the Cybermen*.

SUBTITLES
Select **On** to view subtitles for all episodes and Special Features (except commentary).

RELATED EXTRAS
Coming Soon trailer — Full Circle, State of Decay, Warriors' Gate

SCREAM OF THE SHALKA

In 2003 a bid was made to relaunch *Doctor Who* as an online animated series starring Richard E Grant. Shortly after, the New Series was announced and this one serial was all that was produced.
● *See Appendix 1 for full details*

THE **SEA DEVILS**

STORY No.62 SEASON No.9:3

Released with **DOCTOR WHO AND THE SILURIANS** and **WARRIORS OF THE DEEP** in the **BENEATH THE SURFACE** boxset
One disc with six episodes (148 mins) and 56½ minutes of extras, plus commentary and music-only tracks, production subtitles and PDF items

TARDIS TEAM Third Doctor, Jo

TIME AND PLACE Naval base, contemporary south England

ADVERSARIES First Master (6th appearance); aquatic Silurians (2nd appearance)

FIRST ON TV 26 February–1 April 1972

DVD RELEASE BBCDVD2438(B), 14 January 2008, PG

COVER Photo illustration by Clayton Hickman, pale blue strip

ORIGINAL RRP £39.99 (boxset)

STORY TEASER

When the Doctor and Jo visit the Master in his island prison they hear of mysterious attacks on local shipping and decide to investigate. Captain Hart of the nearby naval base refuses their help, until strange creatures are seen rising from the sea. Conscious of his last encounter with Earth's original civilisation, the Doctor is keen to negotiate a peace between humans and reptiles, but the Master is not as much a prisoner as he seems and is determined to foment all-out war.

CONNECTIONS

The so-called Sea Devils (a human nickname rather than their real name) are an underwater species of the cave-dwelling Silurians encountered in *Doctor Who and the Silurians* (1970), both of which return in *Warriors of the Deep* (1984). While the Silurians have appeared often in the New Series since *The Hungry Earth* (2010), their marine cousins have yet to resurface. The Master is said to have been tried and imprisoned following his capture at the end of *The Dæmons* (1971). He once more tries to instigate a war between humans and a race of reptile-men in *Frontier in Space* (1973). In place of UNIT, here the Doctor works with the Navy, who in real life were keen to contribute to the series, as the Army had done in *The Invasion* (1968) and the Air Force in *The Mind of Evil* (1971). Malcolm Hulke wrote the Silurians' earlier appearance, as well as *Frontier in Space* with its reptilian Draconians and *Invasion of the Dinosaurs* (1974) with, well, dinosaurs — plus a fake giant lizard in *Colony in Space* (1971). Coincidence or obsession? Director Michael E Briant had debuted on *Doctor Who* with *Colony in Space* and directed several Third and Fourth Doctor stories (*see Index v*). Edwin Richfield (Captain Hart) returns less recognisably as Mestor in *The Twin Dilemma* (1984), while Alex Wallis (Bowman) plays Warner in *Revenge of the Cybermen*, and Donald Sumpter (Ridgeway) is Enrico Casali in *The Wheel in Space* (1968).

S

WORTH WATCHING

In some ways this is a reworking of *Doctor Who and the Silurians*, certainly running through the same arguments about whether Man and Silurian can ever share the planet peacefully. But as befits this more action-oriented period of the show, it swaps scientific bases for battleships, submarines and hovercraft, and moral debates for the more black-and-white conflict of the Master versus the Doctor. The Sea Devil design is also more convincing that the rather rubbery Silurians, and their attack on the naval base is a real *tour de force*.

THE EPISODES

Episodes one, two and three are reverse-converted and restored from digital duplicates of conversions of the original two-inch colour videotape recordings in a lower-resolution format, recovered from a Canadian broadcaster in 1983. Episodes four, five and six are restored from digital duplicates of the original two-inch colour videotape recordings used for broadcast. Their mono soundtracks are remastered and the title sequences replaced by a modern transfer of the original 35mm film with credits remade to match the originals.

SPECIAL FEATURES

AUDIO OPTIONS Select **Commentary** to play the audio commentary in place of the main soundtrack when watching the episodes. This is moderated by late-80s script editor Andrew Cartmel, talking with producer Barry Letts, script editor Terrance Dicks and director Michael E Briant on all six episodes.

— Select **Isolated Music** to hear only Malcolm Clarke's music when watching the episodes.

— Select **Feature Audio** to reinstate the main soundtrack when watching the episodes.

INFO TEXT Select **On** to view subtitles when watching the episodes that provide information and anecdotes about the development, production, broadcast and history of *The Sea Devils*. Written by Martin Wiggins.

HELLO SAILOR (36m40s) The making of *The Sea Devils*, including the decision to bring back the Silurians in a marine setting and getting the cooperation of the Royal Navy; the input of the director and designing the Sea Devils; filming on location at Fraser Gunnery Range, Portsmouth (utilising genuine naval personnel and *Doctor Who*'s regular group of stuntmen), at No Man's Land Fort in the Solent, and at Norris Castle on the Isle of Wight; acting opposite monsters and arranging sword fights in the studio; and nearly getting into trouble over a model submarine. With contributions from producer Barry Letts, script editor Terrance Dicks, director Michael E Briant, stuntman Stuart Fell, actors Katy Manning and Donald Sumpter, Navy personnel David de Vere, Dave King and Steve Scholes who appeared in the location filming, and Digby Coventry, owner of Norris Castle. Narrated by David Cann, produced by George Williams.

8MM (3m53s) Silent colour film footage shot by Dave King, a sailor at Fraser Gunnery Range, during location filming for *The Sea Devils* on 22 October 1971. With commentary by Michael E Briant, Terrance Dicks and Barry Letts.

NEXT

TRAILS & CONTINUITY (6m20s) Continuity announcement from the original BBC1 broadcast of episode four of the preceding story, *The Curse of Peladon*; one-minute preview of *The Sea Devils* shown on Friday 25 February 1972, the day before episode one was broadcast; continuity announcements from episode two (including a two-and-a-half-minute précis of episode one, which many viewers had missed owing to widespread power cuts) and episode six; one-minute trail for the omnibus repeat of *The Sea Devils* on Wednesday 27 December 1972, and a following plug for the start of *The Three Doctors* on Saturday 30 December and its coverage in *Radio Times*; and a plug that followed episode four of *Planet of the Spiders* for the unscheduled repeat of the omnibus version of *The Sea Devils* on Monday 27 May 1974. All reconstructed by matching audio recordings made at the time of broadcast to clips from the episodes.

PHOTO GALLERY (8m39s) Slideshow of colour and black-and-white photos taken during production of *The Sea Devils*, including design department photos of the sets and shots taken for Portsmouth local newspaper *The News* (printed in its 22 October 1971 edition). Set to music from the story. Compiled by Ralph Montagu.

COMING SOON THE TIME MEDDLER (1m4s) Trailer for the DVD release of *The Time Meddler*.

RADIO TIMES LISTINGS Accessible via a computer is a PDF file of the six episode listings for the original BBC1 broadcast of *The Sea Devils*, with illustrations by Frank Bellamy; a one-page article published the week of episode one announcing the winners of the Win-a-Dalek competition; a piece by Katy Manning published the week of episode five; and the listing for the omnibus repeat on 27 December 1972, with artwork by Frank Bellamy.

PICCOLO BOOK – THE MAKING OF DOCTOR WHO Accessible via a computer is a PDF file of *The Making of Doctor Who* by Malcolm Hulke and Terrance Dicks, published by Pan Books under its Piccolo imprint on Thursday 20 April 1972. This early behind-the-scenes book examines the production of the programme and its history up to *The Sea Devils*, using that serial as an example of how a story is taken from script to screen.

SUBTITLES

Select **On** to view subtitles for all episodes and Special Features (except commentary).

RELATED EXTRAS

Coming Soon trailer — Destiny of the Daleks
Musical Scales — Doctor Who and the Silurians

THE **SEEDS OF DEATH**

STORY No.48   SEASON No.6:5

Two discs with six episodes (147 mins) and 42 minutes of extras, plus commentary track and production subtitles

TARDIS TEAM Second Doctor, Jamie, Zoe

TIME AND PLACE Earth and the Moon, mid-21st Century

ADVERSARIES Ice Warriors (2nd appearance)

FIRST ON TV 25 January–1 March 1969

DVD RELEASE BBCDVD1151, 17 February 2003, PG (episodes U)

COVER Photo illustration by Clayton Hickman, green strip
— Original release with cover sticker reading 'Doctor Who 40th Anniversary 1963–2003'

ORIGINAL RRP £19.99

STORY TEASER

T-Mat — a way to transport people and objects around the world in an instant — has made conventional forms of travel obsolete. Controlled from the Moon, it's fast and reliable. Yet when the Doctor, Jamie and Zoe arrive, T-Mat is behaving erratically and without it life on Earth is coming to a standstill. Travelling to the Moon in one of the last operable rockets, they soon find the cause of the problem: the Ice Warriors are in charge and have their own deadly use for T-Mat.

CONNECTIONS

The Martian warriors make their debut in the previous season's *The Ice Warriors* (1967) and return in two Third Doctor stories — *The Curse of Peladon* (1972) and *The Monster of Peladon* (1974) — before disappearing from our screens until the New Series episode *Cold War* (2013). Here they take over a base on the Moon controlling a vital function that affects everyone on Earth, much as the Cybermen do in *The Moonbase* (1967). Humans begin developing a matter transmission technique in *The Time Monster* (1972), and UNIT are still working on one in *The Stolen Earth* (2008). T-Mat is seemingly abandoned after this incident, or at least rocket ships make a return for venturing further into space, but by the time of *The Mutants* (1972) and *Revenge of the Cybermen* (1975) transmat systems are in use again, and by the year 4000 experiments are underway to vastly increase their range (*The Daleks' Master Plan*, 1965/66). The Doctor visits the Moon earlier in his second incarnation in *The Moonbase*, is briefly imprisoned there in *Frontier in Space* (1973) and is whisked there by the Judoon in *Smith and Jones* (2007). Brian Hayles wrote all four Ice Warrior stories from the Classic Series (*see Index v*), while Michael Ferguson also directed *The War Machines* (1966), *The Ambassadors of Death* (1970) and *The Claws of Axos* (1971). Ronald Leigh-Hunt (Commander

Radnor) returns as Commander Stevenson in *Revenge of the Cybermen*, while Harry Towb (Osgood) is the doomed McDermott in *Terror of the Autons* (1971). Christopher Coll (Phipps) plays Stubbs in *The Mutants*, while Martin Cort (Locke) has several roles in *The Keys of Marinus* (1964). Alan Bennion also plays Ice Lords in the two Peladon stories, while Sonny Caldinez dons an Ice Warrior's shell in all their Classic Series appearances.

WORTH WATCHING

After an increased variety in the style of stories during the 1968/69 season, in some ways *The Seeds of Death* harks back to the situations common the previous year when many bases were attacked by monsters (including in *The Ice Warriors*). It's not as formulaic as those earlier serials became, however, and adds new elements to the premise, such as a self-preserving coward being the cause of the tension rather than an obstinate boss. This is also the first major use of teleportation as a technology — now common in science fiction, but here appearing ahead of *Star Trek*'s transporters, at least on UK television.

DISC ONE

THE EPISODES

Episodes one, two, three, four and six are restored from 16mm film copies of the original black-and-white videotape recordings, recovered from BBC Enterprises in 1978, while episode five is restored from the 35mm black-and-white film onto which it was originally recorded in the studio. Their mono soundtracks are remastered and the VidFIRE process is applied to studio-recorded shots to recapture the smoother motion of video (and accidentally to a couple of filmed scenes at the end of episode five). The title sequences are replaced by a modern transfer of the original 35mm film with end credits remade to match the originals.

SPECIAL FEATURES *ALSO ON SPECIAL EDITION

*COMMENTARY Select **On** to play the audio commentary in place of the main soundtrack when watching the episodes. With director Michael Ferguson [eps 1,2,3,4,5,6], Frazer Hines (Jamie) [1,2,3,5,6], Wendy Padbury (Zoe) [1,2,3,5,6] and script editor/re-writer Terrance Dicks [3,4,5,6].

INFORMATION TEXT Select **On** to view subtitles when watching the episodes that provide information and anecdotes about the development, production, broadcast and history of *The Seeds of Death*. Written by Richard Molesworth.

SUBTITLES

Select **On** to view subtitles for all episodes, or for the commentary.

DISC TWO

SPECIAL FEATURES *ALSO ON SPECIAL EDITION

NEW ZEALAND CENSOR CLIPS (1m11s) Clips from the Second Doctor stories *The Web of Fear* (the full episodes of which were missing at the time this DVD was released) and *The Wheel in Space* that were cut from the 16mm black-and-white film copies of the episodes shown by New Zealand broadcaster NZBC at the request of the government censor. They were discarded by NZBC and ended up in the possession of a film collector, where they were discovered by Graham Howard in April 2002. *Also on* Lost in Time

THE LAST DALEK (9m34s) Silent 8mm black-and-white footage shot by designer Tony Cornell during filming for *The Evil of the Daleks* episode seven at Ealing Studios on 16/17 May 1967, showing models being set up with explosive charges for their destruction in the final battle of the story and effects shots of Daleks in the Emperor's chamber. With a commentary by the serial's visual effects designers Peter Day and Michaeljohn Harris, who appear in the footage. *Also on* Lost in Time *and* Resurrection of the Daleks Special Edition

*TARDIS CAM NO.5 (59s) Short scene featuring the TARDIS, originally made for the BBCi *Doctor Who* website in 2001. The TARDIS stands on a snowy planet (model).

*SSSOWING THE SSSEEDSSS (24m6s) Actors Alan Bennion and Sonny Caldinez recall their experiences of playing Ice Warriors, including getting to grips with the cumbersome costumes and how these affected their portrayals. With additional memories from make-up supervisor Sylvia James and comments from Bernard Bresslaw, who played Varga in *The Ice Warriors*, taken from an archive audio interview. Produced by Peter Finklestone.

PHOTO GALLERY (5m16s) Slideshow of black-and-white photos taken during production of *The Seeds of Death*, including shots of the models being filmed and behind-the-scenes photos of the filming at Ealing Studios. Set to sound effects from the story. Compiled by Ralph Montagu.

SUBTITLES Select **On** to view subtitles for all Special Features on disc two.

EASTER EGG

There is one hidden feature on these discs to find. *See Appendix 2 for details*

RELATED EXTRAS

Warriors of Mars — The Curse of Peladon

The Doctor's Composer — The War Games

Sylvia James - In Conversation — The War Games

THE **SEEDS OF DEATH** SPECIAL EDITION

STORY No.48   SEASON No.6:5

Released with **CARNIVAL OF MONSTERS SPECIAL EDITION** and **RESURRECTION OF THE DALEKS SPECIAL EDITION** in the **REVISITATIONS 2** boxset

Two discs with six episodes (147 mins) and 81½ minutes of extras, plus commentary track, production subtitles and PDF items

Audio navigation of each disc's contents available by pressing Enter after the BBC ident

TARDIS TEAM Second Doctor, Jamie, Zoe

TIME AND PLACE Earth and the Moon, mid-21st Century

ADVERSARIES Ice Warriors (2nd appearance)

FIRST ON TV 25 January–1 March 1969

DVD RELEASE BBCDVD2956A, 28 March 2011, PG (episodes and disc two U)

COVER Photo illustration by Clayton Hickman, light green strip; version with older BBC logo on reverse

ORIGINAL RRP £39.99 (boxset)

STORY TEASER

T-Mat — a way to transport people and objects around the world in an instant — has made conventional forms of travel obsolete. Controlled from the Moon, it's fast and reliable. Yet when the Doctor, Jamie and Zoe arrive, T-Mat is behaving erratically and without it life on Earth is coming to a standstill. Travelling to the Moon in one of the last operable rockets, they soon find the cause of the problem: the Ice Warriors are in charge and have their own deadly use for T-Mat.

CONNECTIONS

The Martian warriors make their debut in the previous season's *The Ice Warriors* (1967) and return in two Third Doctor stories — *The Curse of Peladon* (1972) and *The Monster of Peladon* (1974) — before disappearing from our screens until the New Series episode *Cold War* (2013). Here they take over a base on the Moon controlling a vital function that affects everyone on Earth, much as the Cybermen do in *The Moonbase* (1967). Humans begin developing a matter transmission technique in *The Time Monster* (1972), and UNIT are still working on one in *The Stolen Earth* (2008). T-Mat is seemingly abandoned after this incident, or at least rocket ships make a return for venturing further into space, but by the time of *The Mutants* (1972) and *Revenge of the Cybermen* (1975) transmat systems are in use again, and by the year 4000 experiments are underway to vastly increase their range (*The Daleks' Master Plan*, 1965/66). The Doctor visits the Moon earlier in his second incarnation in *The Moonbase*, is briefly imprisoned there in *Frontier in Space* (1973) and is whisked there by the Judoon in *Smith and Jones* (2007). Brian Hayles wrote all four Ice Warrior stories from the Classic Series (*see Index v*), while Michael Ferguson also directed *The War Machines* (1966), *The Ambassadors of Death* (1970) and *The Claws of Axos* (1971). Ronald Leigh-Hunt (Commander Radnor) returns as Commander Stevenson in *Revenge of the Cybermen*, while Harry Towb (Osgood) is the doomed McDermott in *Terror of the Autons* (1971). Christopher Coll (Phipps) plays Stubbs in *The Mutants*, while Martin Cort (Locke) has several roles in *The Keys of Marinus* (1964). Alan

Bennion also plays Ice Lords in the two Peladon stories, while Sonny Caldinez dons an Ice Warrior's shell in all their Classic Series appearances.

WORTH WATCHING

This Special Edition features more advanced clean-up of the episodes compared to the previous release and additional Special Features. After an increased variety in the style of stories during the 1968/69 season, in some ways *The Seeds of Death* harks back to the situations common the previous year when many bases were attacked by monsters (including in *The Ice Warriors*). It's not as formulaic as those earlier serials became, however, and adds new elements to the premise, such as a self-preserving coward being the cause of the tension rather than an obstinate boss. This is also the first major use of teleportation as a technology — now common in science fiction, but here appearing ahead of *Star Trek*'s transporters, at least on UK television.

DISC ONE

THE EPISODES

Episodes one, two, three, four and six are restored from 16mm film copies of the original black-and-white videotape recordings, recovered from BBC Enterprises in 1978, while episode five is restored from the 35mm black-and-white film onto which it was originally recorded in the studio. Their mono soundtracks are remastered and a more refined version of the VidFIRE process is applied to studio-recorded shots to recapture the smoother motion of video. The title sequences are replaced by a modern transfer of the original 35mm film with end credits remade to match the originals.

SPECIAL FEATURES *REPEATED FROM PREVIOUS RELEASE

*AUDIO OPTIONS Select **Commentary** to play the audio commentary recorded for the previous release in place of the main soundtrack when watching the episodes. With director Michael Ferguson [eps 1,2,3,4,5,6], Frazer Hines (Jamie) [1,2,3,5,6], Wendy Padbury (Zoe) [1,2,3,5,6] and script editor/re-writer Terrance Dicks [3,4,5,6].

— Select **Feature Audio** to reinstate the main soundtrack when watching the episodes.

INFO TEXT Select **On** to view subtitles when watching the episodes that provide information and anecdotes about the development, production, broadcast and history of *The Seeds of Death*, updated and expanded from the previous release. Written by Martin Wiggins.

COMING SOON (1m35s) Trailer for the DVD release of *Planet of the Spiders*.

SUBTITLES

Select **On** to view subtitles for all episodes and the Coming Soon trailer (none for commentary).

DISC TWO

SPECIAL FEATURES *REPEATED FROM PREVIOUS RELEASE

LORDS OF THE RED PLANET (28m32s) The making of *The Seeds of Death*, including Brian Hayles' original storyline for the Ice Warriors' return; problems with its replacement leading to a complete rewrite; working with the director; creating the look of Ice Lord Slaar (including early design sketches) and the sound of his Warriors; filming the model work, scenes at Ealing Studios amid lots of foam, and on location at Hamstead Heath; and the human cast and designing their outfits. With contributions from script editor Terrance Dicks, director Michael Ferguson, costume designer Bobi Bartlett, actors Frazer Hines and Wendy Padbury, and television historian Richard Bignell. Narrated by Katherine Mount, reading by Toby Hadoke, produced by Steve Broster.

*SSSOWING THE SSSEEDSSS (24m7s) Actors Alan Bennion and Sonny Caldinez recall their experiences of playing Ice Warriors, including getting to grips with the cumbersome costumes and how these affected their portrayals. With additional memories from make-up supervisor Sylvia James and comments from Bernard Bresslaw, who played Varga in *The Ice Warriors*, taken from an archive audio interview. Produced by Peter Finklestone.

MONSTER MASTERCLASS (3m46s) Director Michael Ferguson discusses the best ways to present monsters on screen to make them more frightening.

MONSTERS WHO CAME BACK FOR MORE! (16m28s) Fans Nicholas Briggs and Peter Ware discuss what gives certain monsters sufficient impact to warrant return appearances and how bringing them back allows for greater development of what made them frightening in the first place. Produced by Thomas Guerrier.

PHOTO GALLERY (4m32s) Slideshow of black-and-white photos taken during production of *The Seeds of Death*, including design department photos of the sets, shots of the models being filmed and behind-the-scenes photos of the filming at Ealing Studios. Set to music and sound effects from the story. Compiled by Paul Shields.

*TARDIS CAM NO.6 (1m) Short scene featuring the TARDIS, originally made for the BBCi *Doctor Who* website in 2001. The TARDIS stands on a snowy planet (model). *(This is the same as on the previous release, just numbered incorrectly.)*

PDF MATERIALS Accessible via a computer are the six episode listings from *Radio Times* for the original BBC1 broadcast of *The Seeds of Death*.

SUBTITLES Select **On** to view subtitles for all Special Features on disc two.

EASTER EGGS

There are two hidden features on these discs to find. *See Appendix 2 for details*

RELATED EXTRAS

Warriors of Mars — The Curse of Peladon

Coming Soon trailer — Kinda, Snakedance

The Doctor's Composer — The War Games

Sylvia James - In Conversation — The War Games

THE **SEEDS OF DOOM**

STORY No.85   SEASON No.13:6

Two discs with six episodes (145 mins) and 92 minutes of extras, plus commentary and music-only tracks, production subtitles and PDF items

Audio navigation of each disc's contents available by pressing Enter after the BBC ident

TARDIS TEAM Fourth Doctor, Sarah Jane

TIME AND PLACE Contemporary Antarctica and England

ADVERSARIES Krynoids, plant creatures that grow to enormous size; botanist Harrison Chase

FIRST ON TV 31 January–6 March 1976

DVD RELEASE BBCDVD3044, 25 October 2010, PG (all content bar menus U)

COVER Photo illustration by Clayton Hickman, green strip; version with older BBC logo on reverse

ORIGINAL RRP £19.99

STORY TEASER

When two alien seeds pods are found deep in the Antarctic ice, the Doctor flies out to take charge of them. But one of the scientists there is already infected and slowly he is consumed as Krynoid cells take over his body and mind. Word of the discovery has also been leaked to reclusive botanist Harrison Chase, who sends his henchmen to recover the seed pods for his collection. The Doctor desperately follows them back to England, knowing the danger to the world should a second Krynoid grow to full size and release its spores.

CONNECTIONS

The Doctor has encountered several forms of intelligent plant life, such as the Weed Creature in *Fury from the Deep* (1968), a Zolfa-Thuran in *Meglos* (1980), the genetically enhanced Vervoids in *The Trial of a Time Lord: Terror of the Vervoids* (1986) and the Forest of Cheem in *The End of the World* (2005). The Krynoids' method of propagation by consuming animal life is similar to the Wirrn's (*The Ark in Space*, 1975), infection by Pyrovile dust (*The Fires of Pompeii*, 2008) and a transfusion of Saturnyne blood (*The Vampires of Venice*, 2010). This is the Doctor's second on-screen trip to Antarctica, previously arriving at the South Pole just ahead of the Cybermen in *The Tenth Planet* (1966). Robert Bank Stewart also wrote *Terror of the Zygons* (1975), which was also directed by Douglas Camfield who had worked on *Doctor Who* from the beginning (*see Index v*). Hubert Rees, playing John Stevenson, is also the chief engineer in *Fury from the Deep* (1968) and Captain Ransom in *The War Games* (1969), while Seymour Green (Hargreaves) returns as the Jacondan chamberlain in *The Twin Dilemma* (1984).

WORTH WATCHING

The Seeds of Doom is a fascinating indication of the sort of programme *Doctor Who* could have been in the 1970s but never really was. It's more like *The Avengers*, with the Doctor being called in by the government to deal with a mad recluse in his country mansion. He even punches people and threatens them with guns. Yet the believability of the characters balances the usual fantasy of the situation in a way that makes the story thrilling and immediate, the danger seeming more real because of how the Doctor is forced to behave out of character at times. Douglas Camfield was known for being a dramatic director and he really pulls out all the stops for, as it turned out, his last *Doctor Who* story, proving as with *Terror of the Zygons* that he was the perfect match for Robert Banks Stewart's style of writing.

DISC ONE

THE EPISODES

All six episodes are restored from digital duplicates of the original two-inch colour videotape recordings used for broadcast and their mono soundtracks remastered. The title sequences are replaced by a modern transfer of the original 35mm film with credits remade to match the originals.

SPECIAL FEATURES

AUDIO OPTIONS Select **Commentary** to play the audio commentary in place of the main sound-track when watching the episodes. With Michael McStay (Moberley) [ep 1], Tom Baker [1,2,3,4,6], writer Robert Banks Stewart [1,4,5,6], the late-director's son Joggs Camfield [1,6], John Challis (Scorby) [2,3,4,5], producer Philip Hinchcliffe [2,3,4,5], designer Roger Murray-Leach [2,4,6] and Kenneth Gilbert (Dunbar) [3].

— Select **Isolated Score** to hear only Geoffrey Burgon's music when watching the episodes.

— Select **Feature Audio** to reinstate the main soundtrack when watching the episodes.

INFO TEXT Select **On** to view subtitles when watching the episodes that provide information and anecdotes about the development, production, broadcast and history of *The Seeds of Doom*. Written by Martin Wiggins.

SUBTITLES

Select **On** to view subtitles for all episodes (none for commentary).

DISC TWO

SPECIAL FEATURES

PODSHOCK (37m17s) The making of *The Seeds of Doom*, including writing the script; having to change designers after production had started; working with the director; the cast; shooting on location with video rather than film cameras; filming the model of the Antarctic base and recreating Antarctica in a sandpit; how the scene of the Doctor rescuing Sarah from the Krynoid pod was achieved; rescheduling the production owing to an actor falling ill; and orchestrating the incidental music. With contributions from producer Philip Hinchcliffe, writer Robert Banks Stewart, production assistant Graeme Harper, designer Jeremy Bear, design assistant Jan Spoc-zynski, visual effects designer Richard Conway, composer Geoffrey Burgon, and actors John Challis, Ian Fairbairn and Kenneth Gilbert. Produced by Steve Broster.

NOW AND THEN (8m58s) Comparing the filming locations at Athelhampton House in Dorset and the Buckland Sand & Silica Company quarry in Surrey as they look today with how they appeared in early-November and early-December 1975 when used for *The Seeds of Doom*. Narrated and produced by Richard Bignell. *See Index iii for further editions*

PLAYING IN THE GREEN CATHEDRAL (10m5s) Composer Geoffrey Burgon talks about writing the music for *Terror of the Zygons* and *The Seeds of Doom*, and how composing for television differs from concert music.

SO WHAT DO YOU DO EXACTLY? (6m24s) Graeme Harper, the production assistant on *The Seeds of Doom*, explains what the role involved, along with the director's assistant and production unit manager, ensuring everything runs smoothly when producing a television programme, as well as finding suitable filming locations.

SUBTITLES Select **On** to view subtitles for all Special Features on disc two.

NEXT

STRIPPED FOR ACTION – THE FOURTH DOCTOR (20m20s) *Doctor Who* comic strips have run in various publications since the early days of the television series. This examines the Fourth Doctor's adventures in Polystyle Publications' *TV Comic* and then Marvel Comics UK's *Doctor Who Weekly/Monthly*. With contributions from magazine editors Alan Barnes, Gary Russell and Dez Skinn, comics writer Pat Mills, artist Dave Gibbons, and comics historian Jeremy Bentham. Directed by Marcus Hearn. *See Index iii for further editions*

TRAIL AND CONTINUITY (1m25s) Preview of episode one shown earlier in the day on Saturday 31 January 1976, reconstructed by matching an audio recording made at the time of broadcast to clips from the episode; and continuity announcements from the original BBC1 broadcast of episode five. Includes the BBC1 evening schedule for Saturday 28 February 1976.

PHOTO GALLERY (4m48s) Slideshow of colour and black-and-white photos taken during production of *The Seeds of Doom*, including design department photos of the sets. Set to music and sound effects from the story. Compiled by Paul Shields.

PDF MATERIALS Accessible via a computer are the six episode listings from *Radio Times* for the original BBC1 broadcast of *The Seeds of Doom*, with an illustration by Frank Bellamy.
— The notes compiled by director Douglas Camfield of what he would cut to create a 90-minute omnibus of the serial for a planned repeat in December 1976 that was ultimately abandoned.

COMING SOON (1m7s) Trailer for the DVD release of *Meglos*.

EASTER EGGS
There are two hidden features on these discs to find. *See Appendix 2 for details*

RELATED EXTRAS
Coming Soon trailer — The Caves of Androzani Special Edition, The Movie Special Edition,
                              The Talons of Weng-Chiang Special Edition
The UNIT Family — Terror of the Zygons

THE **SENSORITES**

STORY No.7   SEASON No.1:7

One disc with six episodes (150 mins) and 37 minutes of extras, plus commentary track, production subtitles and PDF items
Audio navigation of disc contents available by pressing Enter after the BBC ident

TARDIS TEAM First Doctor, Barbara, Ian, Susan
TIME AND PLACE Planet Sense-Sphere and orbiting Earth spaceship, 28th Century
ADVERSARIES Sensorite City Administrator
FIRST ON TV 20 June–1 August 1964
DVD RELEASE BBCDVD3377, 23 January 2012, PG (episodes and extras bar DVD trailer U)
COVER Photo illustration by Lee Binding, blue strip; version with older BBC logo on reverse
ORIGINAL RRP £20.42

STORY TEASER
The Sensorites hold a spaceship from Earth in orbit around their planet, its crew unconscious or driven mad, and when the TARDIS arrives they steal its lock so the time travellers are unable to leave either. But their motives are far from malicious and the Doctor learns they have their reasons for distrusting humans. He offers to help investigate a disease that has been killing the Sensorites since an earlier human expedition visited the planet, but his efforts are hampered by those who would kill to preserve their isolation.

CONNECTIONS
The Sense-Sphere is later said to be in the same region of space as the Ood homeworld (*Planet of the Ood*, 2008). Its habitants use telepathy to communicate, as do the Ood, the giant spiders of Metebelis 3 (*Planet of the Spiders*, 1974), the people of Deva Loka (*Kinda*, 1982) and the Eternals (*Enlightenment*, 1983). The Doctor's disease-curing skills come in handy again in *The Ark* (1966), *Doctor Who and the Silurians* (1970), *The Green Death* (1973) and *New Earth* (2007), by which

time his methods have become more slapdash but no less effective. Mervyn Pinfield, who directed the first four episodes of *The Sensorites*, was the series' associate producer for its first year but also directed *Planet of Giants* (1964) and *The Space Museum* (1965); the director of the last two episodes, Frank Cox, also handled the last episode of *The Edge of Destruction* (1964). Stephen Dartnell, playing John, had been encased in rubber just a few weeks earlier as Yartek, leader of the Voord, in *The Keys of Marinus* (1964); John Bailey (Commander) plays Edward Waterfield in *The Evil of the Daleks* (1967) and Sezom in *The Horns of Nimon* (1979/80); and Martyn Huntley (Human survivor) is also a Roboman in *The Dalek Invasion of Earth* (1964) and Warren Earp in *The Gunfighters* (1966).

WORTH WATCHING

The Sensorites has some interesting ideas at play which make it stand out from the stories around it. It's the first time the programme presents an alien species that doesn't look human as not only benign but varied in character like we are. It's not just a simple twist of the 'monsters' really being nice, but that they're as likely to be trusting, devious, cowardly or honourable as any group of humans. It's the only story to make something of Susan being more than a naive teenager, utilising her latent telepathy and allowing her moments of maturity. And it's the first time the Doctor chooses to stay and help with a situation, even once he has regained access to the TARDIS, marking a shift in his motives away from pure exploration.

THE EPISODES

All six episodes are restored from 16mm film copies of the original black-and-white videotape recordings, recovered from BBC Enterprises in 1978. Their mono soundtracks are remastered and the VidFIRE process is applied to studio-recorded shots to recapture the smoother motion of video. The title sequences are replaced by a modern transfer of the best surviving copy of the original 35mm film with end credits remade to match the originals.

SPECIAL FEATURES

LOOKING FOR PETER (21m19s) Peter R Newman is generally remembered only for writing *The Sensorites* and the BBC television play *Yesterday's Enemy* in 1958, remade the year after by Hammer Films. Actor and writer Toby Hadoke finds out more about Newman's life and career, and tracks down his surviving family and even a recording of his voice. With help from television historian Richard Bignell and film historian Marcus Hearn. Produced by Chris Chapman.

VISION ON (7m4s) Former vision mixer Clive Doig talks about what the job involves and his work on the early years of *Doctor Who*, including what it was like recording television programmes in the early-60s.

SECRET VOICES OF THE SENSE SPHERE (2m4s) Clive Doig explains how the voices of production members could accidentally get recorded onto a programme's soundtrack, as happens in episode six of *The Sensorites* where the voice of the production assistant giving instructions to the camera operators is audible.

PHOTO GALLERY (4m36s) Slideshow of black-and-white photos taken during production of *The Sensorites*, including design department photos of the sets. Set to sound effects from the story. Compiled by Paul Shields.

NEXT

AUDIO OPTIONS Select **Commentary** to play the audio commentary in place of the main soundtrack when watching the episodes. This is moderated by actor and comedian Toby Hadoke, talking with Carole Ann Ford (Susan) [eps 1,2,3], William Russell (Ian) [1,2,4], designer Raymond Cusick [1,3,4], Joe Greig (Sensorite) [2,3,4,5], make-up supervisor Sonia Markham [4,5,6], director Frank Cox [5,6], Martyn Huntley (First Human) [6] and Giles Phibbs (Second Human) [6].

Select **Feature Audio** to reinstate the main soundtrack when watching the episodes.

INFO TEXT Select **On** to view subtitles when watching the episodes that provide information and anecdotes about the development, production, broadcast and history of *The Sensorites*. Written by Stephen James Walker.

PDF MATERIALS Accessible via a computer are the six episode listings from *Radio Times* for the original BBC1 broadcast of *The Sensorites*, a short article introducing the story and a profile of William Hartnell published the week of episode four.

— Designer Raymond Cusick's blueprints for props to be built by Shawcraft Models, including the Sensorite's mind-clearing helmet and the firing key for the disintegrator.

COMING SOON (1m49s) Trailer for the Special Edition DVD releases of *The Robots of Death*, *The Three Doctors* and *The Tomb of the Cybermen* in the **Revisitations 3** boxset.

SUBTITLES
Select **On** to view subtitles for all episodes and Special Features (except commentary).

RELATED EXTRAS
Coming Soon trailer — The Android Invasion, Invasion of the Dinosaurs

SHADA

This story was intended to be the last of the 1979/80 season but strike action at the BBC prevented its being completed so it was never broadcast. The material that was recorded was edited together and linked with in-person narration by Tom Baker for release on VHS in July 1992. This version has been reconstructed from restored footage for the DVD release.

● *See Appendix 1 for full details*

THE **SILURIANS**

STORY No.52   SEASON No.7:2

Released as **DOCTOR WHO AND THE SILURIANS** with **THE SEA DEVILS** and **WARRIORS OF THE DEEP** in the **BENEATH THE SURFACE** boxset

Although the title on screen for this story is clearly given as 'Doctor Who and the Silurians', there is some suggestion that this was a mistake made by the graphics people producing the caption and that the story was intended to be called just 'The Silurians'. While scripts and documents relating to the programme's production often included the words 'Doctor Who' or 'Dr Who' in the title, this was never meant to be used on screen. Sometimes during the 1960s the final episode of a story would end with a caption reading 'Next Week: Dr Who and the X' but when that story began the following week it was clearly titled just 'The X'. Then again, the 1970 season of *Doctor Who*, its first in colour, saw much experimentation, particularly with the opening title sequence. All four stories from this year play around with the titles: *Spearhead from Space* has the words begin small and then move towards the camera; *The Ambassadors of Death* initially reads 'The Ambassadors' and then 'of Death' is added with a ricochet sound; and *Inferno* has the title and writer credits slowly come into focus over footage of erupting volcanoes. So it's possible that including 'Doctor Who and' in the titles of *The Silurians* was a deliberate decision to try out different formats. Indeed, the story is credited in *Radio Times* as 'Dr Who and the Silurians', text that would have been provided by the production office. As the DVD release uses 'Doctor Who and the Silurians' on all its packaging, that is how the story is referred to in this book.

● *See* Doctor Who and the Silurians *for full contents*

S

SILVER NEMESIS

STORY No.150   SEASON No.25:3

Released in a boxset with **REVENGE OF THE CYBERMEN**
One disc with three episodes (73½ mins) and 70 minutes of extras, plus commentary, music-only and surround-sound tracks, production subtitles and PDF items
Audio navigation of disc contents available by pressing Enter after the BBC ident

TARDIS TEAM   Seventh Doctor, Ace
TIME AND PLACE   Contemporary and 17th Century Windsor

ADVERSARIES Cybermen (10th appearance); Lady Peinforte; neo-Nazis
FIRST ON TV 23 November–7 December 1988
DVD RELEASE BBCDVD2854(B), 9 August 2010, PG
COVER Photo illustration by Clayton Hickman, pale grey strip;
version with older BBC logo on reverse
ORIGINAL RRP £29.99 (boxset)

STORY TEASER

A silver statue of living metal, launched into space by the Doctor in 1638, orbits the Earth every 25 years bringing disaster in its wake. On the 23 November 1988 the Nemesis statue crash-lands in Windsor but awaiting its return are Lady Peinforte, who has used black magic to travel forward from the 17th Century; Herr de Flores, seeking to initiate the Fourth Reich; and the Cybermen. All want the statue's power, as does the Doctor, who has his own secret plans.

CONNECTIONS

The Cybermen return, appropriately enough (and given an apt shiny chrome finish), for the show's silver anniversary, having last been seen in *Attack of the Cybermen* (1985). Lady Peinforte isn't the only one to be transported from the mid-1600s to the modern day by time manipulation: Will Chandler slips through a crack caused by the Malus in *The Awakening* (1984), and the Master conjures forth a squad of Roundhead soldiers to battle UNIT in *The Time Monster* (1972). De Flores might have been better disposed towards the Doctor if he'd known his führer had met him, although perhaps not if he learned about the cupboard (*Let's Kill Hitler*, 2011). Statues that aren't really statues are, of course, the modus operandi of the Weeping Angels, first seen in *Blink* (2008); in *The Angels Take Manhattan* it's revealed metal statues like the Statue of Liberty can also be Weeping Angels. Most commonly noted is that *Silver Nemesis* has the same storyline as *Remembrance of the Daleks* just two stories prior, in both of which the Doctor plays off multiple adversaries against each other until just one remains to claim an ancient Gallifreyan weapon, only to find he's programmed it to destroy them instead. Chris Clough directed both three-part stories this season, handling them as if they were one production, as he had done for the previous two years (*see Index v*). Fiona Walker (Lady Peinforte) plays another murderous villain, Kala, in *The Keys of Marinus* (1964). David Banks plays Cyberleaders in *Earthshock* (1982), *The Five Doctors* (1983) and *Attack of the Cybermen*, while Mark Hardy is his Cyber deputy in the first two of those.

WORTH WATCHING

When the start of the 1988 season was pushed back a month, producer John Nathan-Turner re-arranged the running order to ensure *Silver Nemesis* still began on the show's twenty-fifth anniversary, so intrinsic was that date to the story. While *Remembrance of the Daleks* at the start of the season might seem a better fit for the celebration, that story is entirely concerned with the show's past, even drawing a line under it as the Daleks and their home world are obliterated as if to say that's all finished with now. *Silver Nemesis* tries to use the anniversary to set up a new era of the programme with the idea of the Doctor having a longer, darker history than we ever knew, much as the fiftieth anniversary special *The Day of the Doctor* (2013) does. Unfortunately, the cancellation of the programme the following year cut off that strand before it could be developed on television, although the Virgin series of novels that came after would take the idea and run with it.

THE EPISODES

All three episodes are restored from digital duplicates of the original one-inch colour videotape recordings used for broadcast and their stereo soundtracks remastered. The computer-generated title sequences are replaced by a digital duplicate of the original one-inch colour videotape recording with credits remade to match the originals.

SPECIAL FEATURES

INDUSTRIAL ACTION (33m31s) The making of *Silver Nemesis*, including incorporating the Cybermen, mystery about the Doctor and more humour in the script; the limited rehearsal time owing to delays on the previous story in production; selecting the cast; adding some live jazz; and shooting on location at Arundel Castle in place of Windsor and in undeveloped Docklands, including battle and stunt sequences. With contributions from script editor Andrew Cartmel, writer Kevin Clarke, director Chris Clough, stunt arranger Nick Gillard, musician Courtney Pine, and actors Sophie Aldred, Sylvester McCoy and Gerard Murphy. Narrated by Paul Ewing, produced by Steve Broster.

DELETED AND EXTENDED SCENES (22m33s) A selection of scenes from all three episodes not used in the final programme, taken from earlier edits.

TRAILS AND CONTINUITY (5m32s) Two-minute preview shown at the BBC Autumn Season press launch on Tuesday 16 August 1988, with specially recorded shots of the Doctor and Ace and music by Keff McCulloch (as released on *The Doctor Who 25th Anniversary Album*); trailer for episode one of *Silver Nemesis* featuring clips from *The Web Planet*; advert for the 19 November 1988 edition of *Radio Times* (issue 3390) with its *Doctor Who* coverage (see **PDF Materials**); and continuity announcements from the original BBC1 broadcasts of all three episodes of *Silver Nemesis*, with a plug for the *25th Anniversary Album.*

PHOTO GALLERY (7m38s) Slideshow of colour and black-and-white photos taken during production of *Silver Nemesis*, including costume department photos of Lady Peinforte and Ace in period dress, and behind-the-scenes shots of the location recording. Set to music from the story. Compiled by Derek Handley.

NEXT

AUDIO OPTIONS Select **Commentary** to play the audio commentary in place of the main soundtrack when watching the episodes. With script editor Andrew Cartmel and director Chris Clough on all three episodes, joined part-way into episode one by Sylvester McCoy and Sophie Aldred (Ace).
— Select **Isolated Soundtrack** to hear only Keff McCulloch's music when watching the episodes.
— Select **Dolby Digital 5.1 Mix** to hear the surround soundtrack when watching the episodes, newly remixed for this release.
— Select **Feature Audio** to reinstate the main soundtrack when watching the episodes.

INFO TEXT Select **On** to view subtitles when watching the episodes that provide information and anecdotes about the development, production, broadcast and history of *Silver Nemesis*. Written by Richard Molesworth.

PDF MATERIALS Accessible via a computer are the three episode listings from *Radio Times* for the original BBC1 broadcast of *Silver Nemesis*, plus a three-page article about the Doctor's companions, a column by Sylvester McCoy and an advert for the Who Dares 1989 *Doctor Who* calendar and *Cybermen* book, all published the week of episode one.

COMING SOON (40s) Trailer for the DVD release of *Time and the Rani*.

SUBTITLES
Select **On** to view subtitles for all episodes and Special Features (except commentary).

RELATED EXTRAS
The Cyber-Generations — Attack of the Cybermen
Coming Soon trailer — The Dominators

SNAKEDANCE

STORY No.124   SEASON No.20:2

Released with **KINDA** in the **MARA TALES** boxset
One disc with four episodes (98 mins) and 71 minutes of extras, plus commentary and music-only tracks, production subtitles and PDF items
Audio navigation of disc contents available by pressing Enter after the BBC ident

TARDIS TEAM Fifth Doctor, Nyssa, Tegan
TIME AND PLACE Planet Manussa
ADVERSARIES The Mara, a malevolent entity of the mind (2nd appearance);
         Lon, son of Manussa's ruler
FIRST ON TV 18–26 January 1983
DVD RELEASE BBCDVD2871B, 7 March 2011, PG (episodes U)
COVER Photo illustration by Clayton Hickman, purple strip; version with older BBC logo on reverse

ORIGINAL RRP £29.99 (boxset)

STORY TEASER

Tegan's mind is not free of the Mara after all and it uses her to direct the TARDIS to the planet Manussa, which it originally dominated and where preparations are underway for a ceremony celebrating the Mara's banishment. The Doctor tries to warn the authorities of the impending danger but they believe they are just playing out a tradition with no basis in historical truth. However, the possessed Tegan is preparing to usurp the ritual and bring about the Mara's resurrection.

CONNECTIONS

The Mara first attempts to revive itself through Tegan in *Kinda* (1982). The Doctor has faced several dangers long considered to be mere legend, such as the Devil-like Azal in *The Dæmons* (1971), the Minotaur in *The Time Monster* (1972), the Loch Ness Monster in *Terror of the Zygons* (1975), Egyptian god Sutekh in *Pyramids of Mars* (1975), the Fendahl in *Image of the Fendahl* (1977), the Great Vampire in *State of Decay* (1980), the Malus in *The Awakening* (1984), Fenric in *The Curse of Fenric* (1989), a werewolf in *Tooth and Claw* (2006), the Beast in *The Satan Pit* (2006) and Akhaten in *The Rings of Akhaten* (2013). In *The Pandorica Opens* (2010) the tables are turned and the Doctor is seen to be the dangerous reality of other planets' legends. Rituals thought to be meaningless tradition but deriving from real events also feature in *The Deadly Assassin* (1976), *The Face of Evil* (1977), *The Power of Kroll* (1978/79) and *Full Circle* (1980). The blue crystal that clears the mind of damaging thoughts is very similar to those from Metebelis 3 in *The Green Death* (1973), *Planet of the Spiders* (1974) and *Hide* (2013). Christopher Bailey also wrote the Mara's debut in *Kinda*, while Fiona Cumming also directed *Castrovalva* (1982), *Enlightenment* (1983) and *Planet of Fire* (1984). Brian Miller, playing Dugdale, provides voices for Daleks in *Resurrection of the Daleks* (1984) and *Remembrance of the Daleks*, while Brian Grellis (megaphone man) is Sheprah in *Revenge of the Cybermen* (1975) and Safran in *The Invisible Enemy* (1977).

WORTH WATCHING

Snakedance applies many of the same themes as its prequel *Kinda* but within a more straightforward adventure format, creating a more successful balance of emotional and intellectual engagement. In particular the characters are very strong and well acted. There's a notable early role for Martin Clunes as the immature Lon led into evil through his ennui, and John Carson impresses as Ambril, the head of antiquities who can't see beyond the physical attributes of artefacts to their meaning, making him blind to the lessons of history.

THE EPISODES

All four episodes are restored from digital duplicates of the original two-inch colour videotape recordings used for broadcast and their mono soundtracks remastered. The title sequences are replaced by a modern transfer of the original 35mm film with credits remade to match the originals.

SPECIAL FEATURES

SNAKE CHARMER (24m39s) The making of *Snakedance*, including the origins and themes of the script; the characters and cast; designing the sets and reusing scenery from *A Song for Europe* to save money; filming the desert scenes at Ealing Studios with live snakes; recording in the television studio; and what makes for good and bad cliffhangers. With contributions from script editor Eric Saward, writer Christopher Bailey, director Fiona Cumming, designer Jan Spoczynski, actors Peter Davison and Janet Fielding, and New Series writer Robert Shearman. Produced by Ed Stradling.

DELETED SCENES (3m6s) The original full ending of episode four, taken from a VHS copy of an earlier edit with as-recorded sound and on-screen time-code.

IN STUDIO (6m50s) Footage from the full studio recordings in April 1982 of scenes in the hall of mirrors and the demise of the Mara, including retakes and shots not used in the final programme.

SATURDAY SUPERSTORE (14m17s) Extract from the 20 November 1982 edition of the BBC1 Saturday morning children's show in which Mike Read asks Peter Davison about his love of cricket and they take viewers' questions on the phone, play a quick mini-cricket over with John Craven, and Peter picks the winners for the previous week's competitions.

NEXT

PHOTO GALLERY (5m22s) Slideshow of colour photos taken during production of *Snakedance*, including design department photos of the sets. Set to music from the story. Compiled by Paul Shields.

AUDIO OPTIONS Select **Commentary** to play the audio commentary in place of the main soundtrack when watching the episodes. With Peter Davison, Janet Fielding (Tegan) and Sarah Sutton (Nyssa) on all four episodes.

— Select **Isolated Score** to hear only Peter Howell's music when watching the episodes.

— Select **Feature Audio** to reinstate the main soundtrack when watching the episodes.

INFO TEXT Select **On** to view subtitles when watching the episodes that provide information and anecdotes about the development, production, broadcast and history of *Snakedance*. Written by Jim Smith.

PDF MATERIALS Accessible via a computer are the four episode listings from *Radio Times* for the original BBC1 broadcast of *Snakedance*.

COMING SOON (2m20s) Trailer for the Special Edition DVD releases of *Carnival of Monsters*, *Resurrection of the Daleks* and *The Seeds of Death* in the Revisitations 2 boxset.

SUBTITLES
Select **On** to view subtitles for all episodes and Special Features (except commentary).

EASTER EGG
There is one hidden feature on this disc to find. *See Appendix 2 for details*

RELATED EXTRAS
Coming Soon trailer — The Ark

THE **SONTARAN EXPERIMENT**

STORY No.77   SEASON No.12:3

One disc with two episodes (49½ mins) and 44½ minutes of extras, plus commentary track and production subtitles

TARDIS TEAM Fourth Doctor, Harry, Sarah Jane
TIME AND PLACE Earth in the far future
ADVERSARIES Sontarans (2nd appearance)
FIRST ON TV 22 February–1 March 1975
DVD RELEASE BBCDVD1811, 9 October 2006, PG
COVER Photo illustration by Lee Binding, orange strip
— Original release with cover sticker reading 'Special Value Edition'
ORIGINAL RRP £12.99
— Also released in Bred for War: The Sontaran Collection; BBCDVD2617, £39.99, 5 May 2008

STORY TEASER
Transmatting down to Earth from the Nerva ark, the Doctor, Sarah and Harry are surprised to discover the planet is not as lifeless as they had expected. A group of human colonists have returned to their home world, only to find themselves being killed off one by one as Sontaran field officer Styre runs sadistic tests of their resilience to physical attack. Sarah is also captured and tortured by the alien, while the Doctor discovers the reason behind Styre's experiments and finds himself facing an entire Sontaran invasion fleet.

CONNECTIONS
This story follows directly from *The Ark in Space*, with the Earth having recovered from the solar flares that sent the humans into hibernation aboard the Nerva ark. In *The Trial of a Time Lord: The Mysterious Planet* (1986) the Earth is similarly laid waste by a fireball, but the reason turns out to be a scheme of the Time Lords' not a natural event. A lone Sontaran debuts in the series in *The Time Warrior* (1973/74) while a larger group turns up in *The Invasion of Time* (1978), a pair in *The Two Doctors* (1985), then *en masse* in *The Sontaran Stratagem/The Poison Sky* (2008). Writers Bob Baker and Dave Martin contributed stories throughout the 1970s (*see Index v*), while Rodney Bennett also

directed *The Ark in Space* and later *The Masque of Mandragora* (1976). Kevin Lindsay (Styre) also plays fellow Sontaran Lynx in *The Time Warrior* and is more recognisable as Cho-Je in *Planet of the Spiders* (1974). Glyn Jones (Krans) wrote the 1965 story *The Space Museum*.

WORTH WATCHING

Something of a short breather before the epic *Genesis of the Daleks*, *The Sontaran Experiment* nevertheless tells a simple story with intrigue and excitement. Perhaps leaving the monster reveal until the end of the first episode, as often happens, is a mistake when there are only two episodes anyway, but it does allow for the weirdness of the empty planet to be heightened and for the focus to be on the three time travellers, two of whom were still relatively new to viewers at the time. All of Styre's plan has to be explained and foiled within half an hour, though, which is a pity as Kevin Lindsay is once more effectively menacing as a Sontaran.

THE EPISODES

Both episodes are restored from digital duplicates of the original two-inch colour videotape recordings used for broadcast and their mono soundtracks remastered. The title sequences are replaced by a modern transfer of the original 35mm film with credits remade to match the originals.

SPECIAL FEATURES

BUILT FOR WAR (39m49s) A history of the Sontarans' appearances in the original series of *Doctor Who*, running through each of their stories, plus how they were conceived by Robert Holmes; the making of *The Sontaran Experiment*; the one appearance of the Sontarans' enemy the Rutans; and their invasion of *Jim'll Fix It*. With contributions from script editors Terrance Dicks, Anthony Read and Eric Saward, writer Bob Baker, stuntman Stuart Fell, and actors Colin Baker, Nicola Bryant and Elisabeth Sladen. Produced by Steve Broster and Richard Molesworth.

PHOTO GALLERY (4m42s) Slideshow of colour and black-and-white photos taken during production of *The Sontaran Experiment*, including prop design sketches and behind-the-scenes shots of the location shooting. Set to sound effects from the story. Compiled by Derek Handley.

COMMENTARY Select **On** to play the audio commentary in place of the main soundtrack when watching the episodes. With Elisabeth Sladen (Sarah), producer Philip Hinchcliffe and writer Bob Baker on both episodes.

INFO TEXT Select **On** to view subtitles when watching the episodes that provide information and anecdotes about the development, production, broadcast and history of *The Sontaran Experiment*. Written by Martin Wiggins.

SUBTITLES

Select **On** to view subtitles for all episodes and Special Features (except commentary).

RELATED EXTRAS

Roger Murray-Leach Interview — The Ark in Space (and Special Edition)

THE **SPACE MUSEUM**

STORY No.15   SEASON No.2:7

Released in a boxset with **THE CHASE**
One disc with four episodes (91½ mins) and 39½ minutes of extras, plus commentary track, production subtitles and PDF items
Audio navigation of disc contents available by pressing Enter after the BBC ident

TARDIS TEAM First Doctor, Barbara, Ian Vicki

TIME AND PLACE Planet Xeros

ADVERSARIES Moroks, humanoid conquerors of the Xerons

FIRST ON TV 24 April–15 May 1965

DVD RELEASE BBCDVD2809(A), 1 March 2010, PG

COVER Photo illustration by Clayton Hickman, yellow strip; version with older BBC logo on reverse

ORIGINAL RRP £29.99 (boxset)

STORY TEASER

After a strange time slip, the TARDIS crew find they have arrived on the planet Xeros, home to the conquering Moroks' space museum. Or have they? They leave no footprints behind them and can't be seen or heard by anyone else. Then they discover themselves frozen as exhibits in the museum. As time gets back on track, the travellers become tangible, alerting the Moroks to their presence. With help from rebel Xerons they hide out in the museum, but how can they tell whether their actions will cause or avert the future they've seen?

CONNECTIONS

The Doctor lands in another museum of space exploration, this time on Earth, in *The Seeds of Death* (1969), comes across the Dulcian's museum of war in *The Dominators* (1968), finds Autons hiding their victims at Madame Tussauds in *Spearhead from Space* (1970), follows a distress call to Henry Van Statten's vault of alien artefacts in *Dalek* (2005) and is chased by a calcified Dalek around the National Museum in *The Big Bang* (2010). In *The Time of Angels* (2010) it's revealed he likes to visit museums in order to "keep score". The Doctor often topples corrupt regimes, of course, but he or his companions directly incite an uprising, as Vicki does here, in *The Ark* (1966), *The Savages* (1966), *The Underwater Menace* (1967), *The Evil of the Daleks* (1967), *Planet of the Spiders* (1974), *The Sun Makers* (1977), *The Pirate Planet* (1978), *State of Decay* (1980) and *The Happiness Patrol* (1988). This is writer Glyn Jones' only script for the series, although he later appeared as Krans in *The Sontaran Experiment* (1975), while director Mervyn Pinfield was the show's associate producer throughout its first year in production and also directed episodes of *The Sensorites* (1964) and *Planet of Giants* (1964). Richard Shaw (Lobos) plays Cross in *Frontier in Space* (1973) and Lakh in *Underworld* (1978), while Ivor Salter, playing his deputy commander, is Odysseus in *The Myth Makers* (1965) and Sergeant Markham in *Black Orchid* (1982). Of the young Xerons, Jeremy Bulloch (Tor) returns in *The Time Warrior* (1974) as Hal the archer, and Peter Craze (Dako) is Du Pont in *The War Games* (1969) and Landing Officer Costa in *Nightmare of Eden* (1979).

WORTH WATCHING

The Space Museum is generally only praised for its first episode, which is eerie and mysterious as the TARDIS crew try to work out how they can be somewhere yet not be tangible. After that it's often said to be dull, but it's the strongest story yet for Maureen O'Brien as Vicki, who gets to lead the main revolution plotline. The existential dilemma of trying to avoid a known future is maintained throughout, with the audience as unsure as the characters whether they've successfully changed the outcome until the end.

THE EPISODES

All four episodes are restored from 16mm film copies of the original black-and-white videotape recordings, recovered from BBC Enterprises in 1978. Their mono soundtracks are remastered and the VidFIRE process is applied to studio-recorded shots to recapture the smoother motion of video. The title sequences are replaced by a modern transfer of the best surviving copy of the original 35mm film with end credits remade to match the originals.

SPECIAL FEATURES

DEFENDING THE MUSEUM (9m28s) New Series writer Robert Shearman discusses his fondness for *The Space Museum* despite general fan dismissal of the story, and argues for its re-evaluation.

MY GRANDFATHER, THE DOCTOR (10m4s) Jessica Carney, William Hartnell's granddaughter, talks about what it was like growing up with his being the Doctor, a visit to the studio during production of *The Web Planet*, the popularity of the show, and Hartnell's approach to his acting roles.

A HOLIDAY FOR THE DOCTOR (14m1s) Comedy character Ida Barr (played by Christopher Green) takes a light-hearted look at the ways *Doctor Who* accommodated holidays for the regular cast in the days when the show was produced nearly all year round, from writing them out of certain episodes to pre-filming their scenes or using stand-ins (keeping their faces well hidden…usually). Produced by James Goss.

AUDIO OPTIONS Select **Commentary** to play the audio commentary in place of the main soundtrack when watching the episodes. This is moderated by actor and presenter Peter Purves, talking with Maureen O'Brien (Vicki) and writer Glyn Jones on all four episodes, joined by William Russell

S

(Ian) on episodes one, three and four.

— Select **Feature Audio** to reinstate the main soundtrack when watching the episodes.

NEXT

INFO TEXT Select **On** to view subtitles when watching the episodes that provide information and anecdotes about the development, production, broadcast and history of *The Space Museum*. Written by Jim Smith.

PHOTO GALLERY (4m26s) Slideshow of black-and-white photos taken during production of *The Space Museum*, including design department photos of the sets. Set to stock music used in the story. Compiled by Derek Handley.

PDF MATERIALS Accessible via a computer are the four episode listings from *Radio Times* for the original BBC1 broadcast of *The Space Museum* and an article introducing the story.

COMING SOON (1m34s) Trailer for the DVD releases of *The Horns of Nimon*, *The Time Monster* and *Underworld* in the Myths and Legends boxset.

SUBTITLES

Select **On** to view subtitles for all episodes and Special Features (except commentary).

RELATED EXTRAS

Coming Soon trailer — The Masque of Mandragora

THE **SPACE PIRATES**

STORY No.49   SEASON No.6:6

One surviving episode (part 2 of 6) released in the **LOST IN TIME** *set*

TARDIS TEAM Second Doctor, Jamie, Zoe

TIME AND PLACE Space beacons and ships

ADVERSARIES Space pirate Caven

FIRST ON TV 15 March 1969

DVD RELEASE BBCDVD1353, 1 November 2004, PG

● *See* Lost in Time *for full details*

SPEARHEAD FROM SPACE

STORY No.51   SEASON No.7:1

One disc with four episodes (97 mins) and 7½ minutes of extras, plus commentary track, production subtitles and image content

TARDIS TEAM Third Doctor, Brigadier and UNIT, and introducing Liz Shaw

TIME AND PLACE Contemporary England

ADVERSARIES Autons and Nestene (1st appearance)

FIRST ON TV 3–24 January 1970

DVD RELEASE BBCDVD1033, 29 January 2001, U

COVER Single photo, dark grey strip

ORIGINAL RRP £19.99

— Also released in The Third Doctor Collection; BBCDVD2263, £49.99, 6 November 2006

— Reissued in sleeve with orange logo and new photo montage in a circle against dark purple background; BBCDVD2470, £9.99, 2 July 2007

STORY TEASER

Investigating a suspicious meteorite shower, Brigadier Lethbridge-Stewart of UNIT instead finds a familiar Police Box, except its owner is not the man he expected — or is he? Meanwhile a nearby plastics factory has been taken over by a new proprietor and is producing some very deadly shop-window mannequins. The Doctor struggles to regain his senses and prove his identity in time to prevent an alien invasion.

CONNECTIONS

The Autons and their Nestene controller return for further attempts to take over the Earth in *Terror of the Autons* (1971) and *Rose* (2005), and are part of the alliance to trap the Doctor in *The Pandorica Opens* (2010). In fact, the iconic scene in *Spearhead from Space* in which mannequins smash their way out of a shop window is deliberately recreated in the New Series debut episode *Rose*. UNIT make the first of their regular appearances throughout the Third Doctor era, having already worked with the Second Doctor in the previous season's *The Invasion* (1968). As he drifts away from Earth in his fourth incarnation, the last appearance of UNIT is in *The Seeds of Doom* (1976) before a brief return in *Battlefield* (1989) and then again in the New Series. Writer Robert Holmes hits his *Doctor Who* stride here, having previously scripted two less fêted stories, *The Krotons* (1969) and *The Space Pirates* (1969). After this he becomes a regular and, to many fans, the ultimate series writer (*see Index v*). This is director Derek Martinus's last *Doctor Who* serial, having previously directed *Galaxy 4* and *Mission to the Unknown* (1965), *The Tenth Planet* (1966), *The Evil of the Daleks* (1967) and *The Ice Warriors* (1967). Nicholas Courtney as the Brigadier becomes a regular, having appeared in *The Web of Fear* (1968) and *The Invasion*; after leaving UNIT he appears in *Mawdryn Undead* (1983), *Battlefield* and *The Sarah Jane Adventures: Enemy of the Bane* (2008). John Woodnutt, playing George Hibbert, also appears as the Draconian emperor in *Frontier in Space* (1973), as the Duke of Forgill and Broton in *Terror of the Zygons* (1975) and as Consul Seron in *The Keeper of Traken* (1981), while Prentis Hancock, in an early role as a reporter, takes more significant parts in *Planet of the Daleks* (1973), *Planet of Evil* (1975) and *The Ribos Operation* (1978).

WORTH WATCHING

Spearhead from Space has so many firsts for *Doctor Who* that it almost feels like it has become another series entirely. There are the obvious changes like being in colour, the new Doctor, his being restricted to Earth, and new assistants in Liz Shaw and UNIT. But also the style of the programme is very different to what had gone before, being more recognisably set in the 'real' world, which makes the aliens more terrifying when they begin roaming the streets. Only once before had monsters been seen gunning down the general public, in 1966's *The War Machines*. Even in this new era's closest antecedents, *The Web of Fear* and *The Invasion*, the monsters were only seen battling the army in deserted spaces, whereas now the threat is brought much closer to home.

THE EPISODES

All four episodes were restored and their mono soundtracks remastered in 1999 (for a repeat showing on BBC2), episode one from the original 16mm colour film print used for broadcast and episodes two, three and four from new 16mm colour film prints made in 1990 as the original transmission prints for those episodes had since degraded. Further clean-up was done for this release and a Fleetwood Mac song removed from the soundtrack as it was too expensive to re-license.

● *Episodes begin playing automatically after one minute if no menu selection is made*

SPECIAL FEATURES *ALSO ON SPECIAL EDITION

*BBC 2 TRAILER– EPISODES1&2 COMBINED(1999) (33s) Previews of the first two episodes' repeat on BBC2 on Tuesday 16 November 1999.

*BBC 2 TRAILER– EPISODE 3 (1999) (23s) Preview of the episode's repeat on BBC2 on Tuesday 23 November 1999. Note, the broadcast version used a Led Zeppelin song that couldn't be re-licensed and is replaced with a soundalike.

*BBC 2 TRAILER– 'DOCTOR WHO NIGHT'(1999) (43s) Preview of the evening of programmes about *Doctor Who* on BBC2 on Saturday 13 November 1999.

INFORMATION TEXT Select **On** to view subtitles when watching the episodes that provide information and anecdotes about the development, production, broadcast and history of *Spearhead from Space*. Written by Richard Molesworth.

▶

PHOTO GALLERY Scroll through 56 colour and black-and-white photos taken during production of *Spearhead from Space*, plus publicity shots of Jon Pertwee — from the press call announcing his casting and in costume for *Radio Times* — and Caroline John. Compiled by Ralph Montagu.

*COMMENTARY Select **On** to play the audio commentary in place of the main soundtrack when watching the episodes. With Nicholas Courtney (the Brigadier) and Caroline John (Liz) on all four episodes.

*UNIT RECRUITING FILM (4m48s) Spoof recruitment promo for UNIT broadcast on BBC1 on Friday 17 December 1993 under the banner 'Doctor Who and the Daleks' preceding the repeat of *Planet of the Daleks* episode six. With story clips, voiceover by Nicholas Courtney and Dexter Fletcher, and music by Mark Ayres. When broadcast this ended with a telephone number that viewers could call to hear a recorded message by Courtney about the upcoming repeat of *The Green Death* in January 1994.

SUBTITLES
Select **On** to view subtitles for all episodes and Special Features, or for the commentary.

EASTER EGG
There is one hidden feature on this disc to find. *See Appendix 2 for details*

SPEARHEAD FROM SPACE SPECIAL EDITION

STORY No.51   SEASON No.7:1

Released with **TERROR OF THE AUTONS** in the **MANNEQUIN MANIA** boxset
One disc with four episodes (97 mins) and 53½ minutes of extras, plus two commentary tracks, production subtitles and PDF items
Audio navigation of disc contents available by pressing Enter after the BBC ident

TARDIS TEAM Third Doctor, Brigadier and UNIT, and introducing Liz Shaw
TIME AND PLACE Contemporary England
ADVERSARIES Autons and Nestene (1st appearance)
FIRST ON TV 3–24 January 1970
DVD RELEASE BBCDVD3135A, 9 May 2011, PG (episodes U)
COVER Photo illustration by Clayton Hickman, purple strip; version with older BBC logo on reverse
ORIGINAL RRP £35.73 (boxset)

STORY TEASER
Investigating a suspicious meteorite shower, Brigadier Lethbridge-Stewart of UNIT instead finds a familiar Police Box, except its owner is not the man he expected — or is he? Meanwhile a nearby plastics factory has been taken over by a new proprietor and is producing some very deadly shop-window mannequins. The Doctor struggles to regain his senses and prove his identity in time to prevent an alien invasion.

CONNECTIONS
The Autons and their Nestene controller return for further attempts to take over the Earth in *Terror of the Autons* (1971) and *Rose* (2005), and are part of the alliance to trap the Doctor in *The Pandorica Opens* (2010). In fact, the iconic scene in *Spearhead from Space* in which mannequins smash their way out of a shop window is deliberately recreated in the New Series debut episode *Rose*. UNIT make the first of their regular appearances throughout the Third Doctor era, having already worked with the Second Doctor in the previous season's *The Invasion* (1968). As he drifts away from Earth in his fourth incarnation, the last appearance of UNIT is in *The Seeds of Doom* (1976) before a brief return in *Battlefield* (1989) and then again in the New Series. Writer Robert Holmes hits his *Doctor Who* stride here, having previously scripted two less fêted stories, *The Krotons* (1969) and *The Space Pirates* (1969). After this he becomes a regular and, to many fans, the ultimate series writer (*see Index v*). This is director Derek Martinus's last *Doctor Who* serial, having previously directed *Galaxy 4* and *Mission to the Unknown* (1965), *The Tenth Planet* (1966), *The Evil of the Daleks* (1967) and *The Ice Warriors* (1967). Nicholas Courtney as the Brigadier becomes a regular, having appeared in *The Web of Fear* (1968) and *The Invasion*; after leaving UNIT he appears in *Mawdryn Undead* (1983), *Battlefield* and *The Sarah Jane Adventures: Enemy of the Bane* (2008). John Woodnutt, playing George Hibbert, also appears as the Draconian emperor in *Frontier in Space* (1973), as the Duke of Forgill and Broton in *Terror of the Zygons* (1975) and as Consul Seron in *The Keeper of Traken* (1981), while

Prentis Hancock, in an early role as a reporter, takes more significant parts in *Planet of the Daleks* (1973), *Planet of Evil* (1975) and *The Ribos Operation* (1978).

WORTH WATCHING

This Special Edition features more advanced clean-up of the episodes compared to the previous release and additional Special Features. *Spearhead from Space* has so many firsts for *Doctor Who* that it almost feels like it has become another series entirely. There are the obvious changes like being in colour, the new Doctor, his being restricted to Earth, and new assistants in Liz Shaw and UNIT. But also the style of the programme is very different to what had gone before, being more recognisably set in the 'real' world, which makes the aliens more terrifying when they begin roaming the streets. Only once before had monsters been seen gunning down the general public, in 1966's *The War Machines*. Even in this new era's closest antecedents, *The Web of Fear* and *The Invasion*, the monsters were only seen battling the army in deserted spaces, whereas now the threat is brought much closer to home.

THE EPISODES

All four episodes are newly restored from a modern print of the original 16mm colour film negatives and their mono soundtracks newly remastered (with original Fleetwood Mac song intact).

SPECIAL FEATURES   *REPEATED FROM PREVIOUS RELEASE

DOWN TO EARTH: FILMING SPEARHEAD FROM SPACE (22m40s) The making of the Third Doctor's debut, including the need to revamp *Doctor Who* in the face of falling ratings at the end of the 1960s; casting the new Doctor and designing his look; devising the new companion; filming the planned location scenes; and moving the interior scenes to location when strike action made the studios unavailable. With contributions from producers Barry Letts (interviewed in 2008) and Derrick Sherwin, script editor Terrance Dicks, assistant script editor Robin Squire, costume designer Christine Rawlins, and Jon Pertwee (interviewed in 1995). Narrated by Carl Kennedy, produced by Chris Chapman.

REGENERATIONS: FROM BLACK AND WHITE TO COLOUR (18m42s) What technical and production changes were required for the BBC's move to colour television at the end of the 1960s, reworking *Doctor Who*'s opening titles in colour, and the advantages for new effects that were introduced. With memories from producer Derrick Sherwin, script editor Terrance Dicks, directors Christopher Barry, Timothy Combe and Michael Ferguson, designer Roger Cheveley, graphic designer Bernard Lodge, and actors Frazer Hines and Wendy Padbury. Narrated and produced by Steve Broster.

*UNIT RECRUITMENT FILM (4m49s) Spoof recruitment promo for UNIT broadcast on BBC1 on Friday 17 December 1993 under the banner 'Doctor Who and the Daleks' preceding the repeat of *Planet of the Daleks* episode six. With story clips, voiceover by Nicholas Courtney and Dexter Fletcher, and music by Mark Ayres. When broadcast this ended with a telephone number that viewers could call to hear a recorded message by Courtney about the upcoming repeat of *The Green Death* in January 1994.

*TRAILERS (1m40s) Two previews of the 16–30 November 1999 repeat of *Spearhead from Space* on BBC2, and one for the evening of programming about *Doctor Who* on BBC2 on Saturday 13 November 1999.

PHOTO GALLERY (3m51s) Slideshow of colour and black-and-white photos taken during production of *Spearhead from Space*, plus publicity shots of Jon Pertwee — from the press call announcing his casting and in costume for *Radio Times* — and Caroline John. Set to sound effects from the story. Compiled by Paul Shields.

NEXT

AUDIO OPTIONS Select ***Commentary with Caroline John & Nicholas Courtney** to play the audio commentary recorded for the previous release in place of the main soundtrack when watching all four episodes.

— Select **Commentary with Derrick Sherwin (producer) & Terrance Dicks (script editor)** to play the audio commentary recorded for this release in place of the main soundtrack when watching all four episodes.

— Select **Feature Audio** to reinstate the main soundtrack when watching the episodes.

INFO TEXT Select **On** to view subtitles when watching the episodes that provide information and anecdotes about the development, production, broadcast and history of *Spearhead from Space*, updated and expanded from the previous release. Written by Richard Bignell.

PDF MATERIALS Accessible via a computer are the four episode listings from *Radio Times* for the original BBC1 broadcast of *Spearhead from Space*; a short article about Caroline John and preview of the story published the week before episode one; the cover of the 1 January 1970 edition (issue 2408) and a two-page article about the New Year's stars including Jon Pertwee; and the four episode listings for the 9–30 July 1971 repeat of the serial, with illustration by Frank Bellamy.

COMING SOON (1m1s) Trailer for the DVD release of *Frontios*.

SUBTITLES
Select **On** to view subtitles for all episodes and Special Features (except commentaries).

EASTER EGG
There is one hidden feature on this disc to find. *See Appendix 2 for details*

RELATED EXTRAS
Coming Soon trailer — Planet of the Spiders

STATE OF DECAY

STORY No.112   **SEASON No.18:4**

Released with **FULL CIRCLE** and **WARRIORS' GATE** in **THE E-SPACE TRILOGY** boxset
One disc with four episodes (95 mins) and 67 minutes of extras, plus commentary and music-only tracks, production subtitles and PDF items
Audio navigation of disc contents available by pressing Enter after the BBC ident

TARDIS TEAM Fourth Doctor, Second Romana, Adric, K9
TIME AND PLACE Unnamed planet in E-Space
ADVERSARIES Vampire overlords Aukon, Camilla and Zargo
FIRST ON TV 22 November–13 December 1980
DVD RELEASE BBCDVD1835(B), 26 January 2009, PG
COVER Photo illustration by Clayton Hickman, dark orange strip
ORIGINAL RRP £34.99 (boxset)

STORY TEASER
Seeking a way out of E-Space, the Doctor and Romana arrive on a planet where K9 has detected technology that may help them. What they find is a single village where all learning is forbidden by the sinister Three Who Rule, immortals from whose tower no one ever returns. The Doctor encounters a band of rebels who have found remnants of spaceship hardware that reveals the truth about the three rulers, but with Romana and stowaway Adric in their clutches, their master is now ready to rise again.

CONNECTIONS
The TARDIS is still in the alternative universe of E-Space into which it was pulled in *Full Circle*. While these are the closest the Doctor comes on television to the classic vampires of Gothic literature, he does meet other creatures with similar traits, notably the Haemovores from Earth's polluted future in *The Curse of Fenric* (1989) and the Plasmavore the Judoon are tracking in *Smith and Jones* (2007). Disguised Saturnyne are mistaken for vampires in *The Vampires of Venice* (2010) but actually transfuse their blood into humans to convert them. Other species that drink blood include the Ogri (*The Stones of Blood*, 1978) and the Tetraps (*Time and the Rani*, 1987). The Animus (*The Web Planet*, 1965) and Axos (*The Claws of Axos*, 1971) suck the life force out of whole planets as the Great Vampires are said to have done. Like the Three Who Rule, the Krotons keep the people of a planet in ignorance of knowledge that could threaten their dominion (*The Krotons*, 1968/69), while a society that has forgotten the technology it once used features in *The Face of Evil* (1977). Writer Terrance Dicks first worked on the series as assistant script editor from 1968 (*see Index v*) and

originally submitted 'The Vampire Mutations' as this was originally titled for the 1977/78 season, replacing it with *Horror of Fang Rock* when it was vetoed by the BBC. This was the first of six serials directed in the early-80s by Peter Moffatt (*see Index v*). Arthur Hewlett (Kalmar) also plays Kimber in *The Trial of a Time Lord: Terror of the Vervoids* (1986), while Clinton Greyn (Ivo) returns as Sontaran group marshal Stike in *The Two Doctors* (1985).

WORTH WATCHING

It's well recorded that this serial was originally written for the 1977/78 season but was initially shelved owing to worries it might be seen as undermining the BBC's production of *Bram Stoker's Dracula*, shown in December 1977. The script was ultimately dusted off in 1980 when new stories were scarce. Passing through the scientific focus of then-script editor Christopher Bidmead gave the story an intriguing mix of Gothic horror and social science. Ultimately under director Peter Moffatt the aesthetic of the former wins through and leaves *State of Decay* a melodramatic tale in an otherwise clinical season.

THE EPISODES

All four episodes are restored from digital duplicates of the original two-inch colour videotape recordings used for broadcast and their mono soundtracks remastered. The title sequences are replaced by a modern transfer of the original 35mm film with credits remade to match the originals.

SPECIAL FEATURES

AUDIO OPTIONS Select **Commentary** to play the audio commentary in place of the main soundtrack when watching the episodes. With Matthew Waterhouse (Adric), writer Terrance Dicks and director Peter Moffatt on all four episodes.

— Select **Isolated Score** to hear only Paddy Kingsland's music when watching the episodes.

— Select **Feature Audio** to reinstate the main soundtrack when watching the episodes.

INFO TEXT Select **On** to view subtitles when watching the episodes that provide information and anecdotes about the development, production, broadcast and history of *State of Decay*. Written by Nicholas Pegg.

THE VAMPIRE LOVERS (20m25s) The making of *State of Decay*, including the origins of the story and changes made by the script editor and director; working with the director and guest cast; influences from Hammer horror films; designing the sets; and realising the Great Vampire. With contributions from script editor Christopher H Bidmead, writer Terrance Dicks, director Peter Moffatt, designer Christine Ruscoe, and actors Clinton Greyn, John Leeson and Lalla Ward. Produced by Steve Broster.

FILM TRIMS (5m33s) Silent colour 35mm film footage of the model effects work, comprising shots of the Great Vampire's demise and the tower that weren't used in the final programme.

LEAVES OF BLOOD (17m5s) Actor Nicholas Briggs presents an examination of the portrayal of vampires in literature from Victorian popular fiction to variations in the late-20th Century. With authors Ramsey Campbell, Simon Clark, Pete Crowther, Alison LR Davies, Chris Fowler, Stephen Gallagher and Kim Newman, and vampire fiction specialist Dr Tina Rath. Readings by Nick Scovell, produced by Keith Barnfather.

THE BLOOD SHOW (10m30s) The cultural significances of blood, especially in cooking. With butcher Frank Baker, haematologist Simon Clare, cultural historian Sir Christopher Frayling, food writer Stefan Gates, chef Fergus Henderson, anthropologist Dr Lola Martinez and club promoter Emily Richards. Produced by Ann Kelly.

NEXT

THE FRAYLING READING (4m37s) Cultural historian Sir Christopher Frayling discusses the themes of *State of Decay* and its relation to the vampire myth.

CONTINUITY (3m33s) Continuity announcements from the original BBC1 broadcasts of all four episodes of *State of Decay*, with plugs for the *Doctor Who* display at Madame Tussauds, and an invitation for comments to be put to Peter Davison in his appearance on *Pebble Mill at One* on 3 December 1980 (*included on* Logopolis).

PHOTO GALLERY (4m3s) Slideshow of colour and black-and-white photos taken during production of *State of Decay*, including model shots. Set to music from the story. Compiled by Derek Handley.

— Select **Info Text On** before selecting **Play Gallery** to view descriptive captions while watching the photo slideshow.

RADIO TIMES LISTINGS Accessible via a computer is a PDF file of the four episode listings for the original BBC1 broadcast of *State of Decay*, plus a short item about upcoming cast changes published the week of episode one.

COMING SOON (1m14s) Trailer for the DVD releases of *The Rescue* and *The Romans*.

SUBTITLES
Select **On** to view subtitles for all episodes and Special Features (except commentary).

RELATED EXTRAS
Directing Who — The Visitation (and Special Edition)
Coming Soon trailer — Battlefield

THE **STONES OF BLOOD**

STORY No.100   SEASON No.16:3

Released with **THE ANDROIDS OF TARA, THE ARMAGEDDON FACTOR, THE PIRATE PLANET, THE POWER OF KROLL** and **THE RIBOS OPERATION** in **THE KEY TO TIME** boxset
One disc with four episodes (96 mins) and 80 minutes of extras, plus two commentary tracks, production subtitles and PDF items

TARDIS TEAM Fourth Doctor, First Romana, K9
TIME AND PLACE Contemporary Cornwall
ADVERSARIES Celtic goddess the Cailleach; Ogri, mobile blood-sucking monoliths; escaped convict Cessair of Diplos
FIRST ON TV 28 October–18 November 1978
DVD RELEASE BBCDVD2335(C), 24 September 2007, PG
COVER Photo illustration by Clayton Hickman, dark pink strip
ORIGINAL RRP £69.99 (boxset)

STORY TEASER
Their search for the third segment of the Key to Time leads the Doctor and Romana to a stone circle on present-day Earth, where they meet eccentric academic Amelia Rumford and her friend Vivien Fay, who are performing a fresh survey of the site. For some reason historical accounts of the number of stones vary, but surely standing stones can't come and go? As local druids assemble to call on their goddess, the Cailleach, the Doctor begins to suspect the source of her power and the connection to a long line of women who have owned the circle.

CONNECTIONS
The Doctor visits England's most famous stone circle, Stonehenge, in *The Pandorica Opens* (2010). Other stone-based lifeforms like the Ogri include the Kastrians (*The Hand of Fear*, 1976) and the Pyroviles (*The Fires of Pompeii*, 2008). A druidic cult worshipping Hecate is uncovered by Sarah Jane Smith in *K9 and Company* (1981). Ships that travel through hyperspace are also featured in *Frontier in Space* (1973) and *Nightmare of Eden* (1979). David Fisher also wrote the following story, *The Androids of Tara*, plus *The Creature from the Pit* (1979), *The Leisure Hive* (1980) and the initial storyline that became *City of Death* (1979). Of the guest cast only Shirin Taylor, playing one of the doomed campers, appears again in the series, in 1987's *Dragonfire*.

WORTH WATCHING
The only story of the Key to Time season set on Earth, *The Stones of Blood* initially harkens back to the Fourth Doctor's early years, with apparitions and an ancient goddess set to rise again. And while the explanation for these is not as mystical as it seems, as is typical for *Doctor Who*, the second half of the story becomes a sci-fi courtroom drama and loses much of the atmosphere it has built. Particularly notable is Beatrix Lehmann as Professor Rumford, who gives merit to Tom Baker's flippant notion that the Doctor could have an elderly companion — at the end you're willing her to join the Doctor and Romana on their travels.

THE EPISODES

All four episodes are restored from digital duplicates of the original two-inch colour videotape recordings: those used for broadcast of episodes one, three and four, and a higher-quality earlier edit for episode two. Their mono soundtracks are remastered and the title sequences replaced by a modern transfer of the original 35mm film with credits remade to match the originals.

SPECIAL FEATURES

GETTING BLOOD FROM THE STONES (26m34s) The making of *The Stones of Blood*, including the origins of the story; creating the Ogri props and model stone circle; shooting on location with video rather than film cameras; casting the villain; working with Tom Baker, Beatrix Lehmann and K9; the cut birthday scene; matching the spaceship model to the full-size sets; realising the Megara; and a grisly death for a pair of campers. With contributions from script editor Anthony Read, writer David Fisher, director Darrol Blake, visual effects designer Mat Irvine, actors Susan Engel, John Leeson and Mary Tamm, and fan journalists Clayton Hickman and Steve O'Brien. Produced by Ed Stradling.

HAMMER HORROR (13m7s) The influence of Hammer Films' classic horror movies on much of 1970s *Doctor Who*, especially under script editor Robert Holmes. With Tom Baker, script editors Terrance Dicks and Anthony Read, journalist David Miller, and author Jonathan Rigby. Narrated by Kate Brown, directed by Marcus Hearn.

STONES FREE (9m3s) Mary Tamm returns to the Rollright Stones in Oxfordshire, where much of *The Stones of Blood* was recorded, to unearth the history of the stone circle and the folklore that surrounds it. With site trustee Karin Attwood, druid Veronica Hammond and archaeologist George Lambrick. Written and directed by Richard Adamson.

DELETED SCENES (2m13s) Two scenes from episode two not used in the final programme, taken from an earlier edit of the episode.

CONTINUITIES (2m25s) Continuity announcements from the original BBC1 broadcasts of all four episodes of *The Stones of Blood*, with a plug for the *BBC Space Themes* album. Some reconstructed by matching audio recordings made at the time of broadcast to clips from the episodes.

MODEL WORLD (2m42s) Extract from *The Model World of Robert Symes* broadcast on BBC2 on Monday 1 January 1979, in which visual effects designer Mat Irvine demonstrates his work on the hyperspace vessel model from *The Stones of Blood*.

NEXT

AUDIO OPTIONS Select **Commentary 1** to play the audio commentary recorded for an earlier US-only release in place of the main soundtrack when watching the episodes. With Mary Tamm (Romana) and director Darrol Blake on all four episodes.

— Select **Commentary 2** to play the audio commentary recorded for this release when watching the episodes. With Tom Baker, Mary Tamm (Romana) and Susan Engel (Vivien Fay) on all four episodes, joined from episode two by a laconic David Fisher, writer.

— Select **Feature Audio** to reinstate the main soundtrack when watching the episodes.

INFO TEXT Select **On** to view subtitles when watching the episodes that provide information and anecdotes about the development, production, broadcast and history of *The Stones of Blood*. Written by Martin Wiggins.

BLUE PETER (6m5s) Extract from the Thursday 23 November 1978 edition of the children's magazine programme in which Simon Groom and Lesley Judd mark the fifteenth anniversary of *Doctor Who* with a look through past clips (using largely the same script as the tenth anniversary edition from 1973, *included on* The Tenth Planet *and* The Three Doctors).

NATIONWIDE (8m51s) Extract from the Wednesday 22 November 1978 edition of the news magazine programme in which Frank Bough discusses *Doctor Who*'s fifteenth anniversary with original companion Carole Ann Ford, latest companion Mary Tamm and Tom Baker. Features a clip from *The Edge of Destruction* dubbed into Arabic.

PHOTO GALLERY (8m2s) Slideshow of colour and black-and-white photos taken during production of *The Stones of Blood*, including design department photos of the sets and shots of the models. Set to sound effects from the story and the stereo version of the original theme music that was released on a single in 1973 and reissued in 1978. Compiled by Derek Handley.

COMING SOON (1m) Trailer for the DVD release of *Planet of Evil*.

RADIO TIMES LISTINGS Accessible via a computer is a PDF file of the four episode listings for the original BBC1 broadcast of *The Stones of Blood*.

SUBTITLES

Select **On** to view subtitles for all episodes and Special Features (except commentaries).

RELATED EXTRAS

Coming Soon trailer — The Time Warrior

THE **SUN MAKERS**

STORY No.95   SEASON No.15:4

One disc with four episodes (100 mins) and 49½ minutes of extras, plus commentary track, production subtitles and PDF items
Audio navigation of disc contents available by pressing Enter after the BBC ident

TARDIS TEAM Fourth Doctor, Leela, K9

TIME AND PLACE Far-future Pluto

ADVERSARIES Chief banker the Collector; his underling Gatherer Hade

FIRST ON TV 26 November–17 December 1977

DVD RELEASE BBCDVD2955, 1 August 2011, U

COVER Photo illustration by Lee Binding, dark red strip; version with older BBC logo on reverse

ORIGINAL RRP £20.42

STORY TEASER

The Doctor and Leela arrive on a Pluto made habitable by a series of artificial suns. But they soon discover life there is no picnic when they meet a worker prepared to commit suicide to escape the unshakeable burden of extortionate taxation. The people are under the thumb of the Collector, who runs the economy purely for the profit of the controlling Company. But he has reckoned without the Doctor's unique approach to financial management.

CONNECTIONS

Human colonies oppressed by monomaniacal rulers include the subjects of crazed computer Xoanon in *The Face of Evil* (1977), the survivors of Earth's relocation by the Time Lords kept underground by Drathro in *The Trial of a Time Lord: The Mysterious Planet* (1986), the occupants of a dilapidated tower block kept in check by the Chief Caretaker in *Paradise Towers* (1987), and the population of Terra Alpha forced to stay happy by Helen A in *The Happiness Patrol* (1988). Societies in thrall to the profit motives of corporate entities include any on a world where the Interplanetary Mining Corporation wants to dig, as in *Colony in Space* (1971), and that on Androzani Major where business magnate Morgus has excessive political influence (*The Caves of Androzani*, 1984). Writer Robert Holmes had just relinquished his role as script editor when he wrote *The Sun Makers* (*see Index v*), while this was the second serial directed by Pennant Roberts following *The Face of Evil* the previous season (*see Index v*).

WORTH WATCHING

This is perhaps Robert Holmes at his most scathing (having just returned to being a freelance writer) in a blatant parody of the economic policies of the time, when inflation and income tax were high and public service unions went on strike regularly. And things haven't changed so much that we can't still see the satire and join in the wishful thinking of overthrowing a corrupt government. Sadly those very economic factors were impinging on *Doctor Who*'s budgets and the production, while full of humour and imagination, suffers in its realisation.

THE EPISODES

All four episodes are restored from digital duplicates of the original two-inch colour videotape recordings used for broadcast and their mono soundtracks remastered. The title sequences are replaced by a modern transfer of the original 35mm film with credits remade to match the originals.

RUNNING FROM THE TAX MAN (24m50s) The making of *The Sun Makers*, including the origins of the story in the economic situation of the time; current astronomical understanding of Pluto; filming on location atop a tobacco factory in Bristol; the time and budgetary constraints on the production; the guest cast; an uncomfortable moment for Louise Jameson; and the story's attitude to violence. With contributions from director Pennant Roberts (interviewed in 2005), actors Louise Jameson and Michael Keating, astronomer Marek Kukula, and historian Dominic Sandbrook. Produced by Thomas Guerrier.

TRAILER (43s) Preview of *The Sun Makers* broadcast the week before episode one.

THE DOCTOR'S COMPOSER – PART 2 (18m5s) Composer Dudley Simpson talks about his extensive contribution to the incidental music for *Doctor Who*, interviewed in his home town of Sydney. This part covers his role as regular composer throughout the 1970s, working closely with the BBC Radiophonic Workshop and later his own band of musicians. Narrated by Simon Ockenden, produced by Brendan Sheppard. *Part one is on* The War Games

OUTTAKES (34s) A blooper from the recording of episode four in which actor Roy Macready has problems with a troublesome gun prop.

PHOTO GALLERY (4m6s) Slideshow of colour and black-and-white photos taken during production of *The Sun Makers*, including design department photos of the sets. Set to sound effects and music from the story. Compiled by Paul Shields.

NEXT

AUDIO OPTIONS Select **Commentary** to play the audio commentary in place of the main soundtrack when watching the episodes. With Tom Baker [eps 1,2,3,4], Louise Jameson (Leela) [1,2,4], director Pennant Roberts [1,3,4] and Michael Keating (Goudry) [2,3].

— Select **Feature Audio** to reinstate the main soundtrack when watching the episodes.

INFO TEXT Select **On** to view subtitles when watching the episodes that provide information and anecdotes about the development, production, broadcast and history of *The Sun Makers*. Written by Jim Smith.

PDF MATERIALS Accessible via a computer are the four episode listings from *Radio Times* for the original BBC1 broadcast of *The Sun Makers*.

COMING SOON (1m22s) Trailer for the DVD release of *Day of the Daleks*.

Select **On** to view subtitles for all episodes and Special Features (except commentary).

Coming Soon trailer — Paradise Towers

SURVIVAL

STORY No.155   SEASON No.26:4

Two discs with three episodes (73 mins) and 193½ minutes of extras, plus two commentaries, music-only and surround-sound tracks, production subtitles and PDF items

S

TARDIS TEAM Seventh Doctor, Ace

TIME AND PLACE Contemporary London and planet of the Cheetah people

ADVERSARIES Third Master (9th appearance); Cheetah people

FIRST ON TV 22 November–6 December 1989

DVD RELEASE BBCDVD1834, 16 April 2007, PG

COVER Photo illustration by Lee Binding, light orange strip

— Original release with cover sticker reading 'The Final Classic Adventure'

ORIGINAL RRP £19.99

The Doctor takes Ace home to Perivale to catch up with her friends, only to find most of them have recently disappeared. As the Doctor's suspicions are aroused by the number of stray black cats about, Ace revisits her old haunts. But when she too vanishes, the Doctor must follow her to an alien world where indulging one's animal nature is attractive but highly dangerous — as his old enemy the Master has discovered.

CONNECTIONS

Survival is often said to be closer in style to the New Series than the Classic Series it capped. Certainly it's the first time a contemporary suburban street is featured since Sarah Jane Smith's departure in *The Hand of Fear* (1976), and the first time the Doctor visits a council estate of the sort he'll spend a lot of time on after *Rose* (2005). While many species, including humans, develop some form of teleportation technology, only the Kitlings and giant spiders of Metebelis 3 (*Planet of the Spiders*, 1974) are seen to do so naturally, although the Sisterhood of Karn could use their psychic powers to teleport others (*The Brain of Morbius*, 1976). It appears to be the planet itself that changes people into Cheetahs, but other species that propagate in a similar transforming manner include the Vargas (*Mission to the Unknown*, 1965), the Cybermen (*The Tenth Planet*, 1966 *et seq*), the Wirrn (*The Ark in Space*, 1975), the Krynoids (*The Seeds of Doom*, 1976), the Haemovores (*The Curse of Fenric*, 1989) and the Flood (*The Waters of Mars*, 2009). This incarnation of the Master is first encountered in *Logopolis* (1981) and returns each year up to his previous appearance in *The Trial of a Time Lord: The Ultimate Foe* (1986). The Doctor rides motorbikes more safely in *The Dæmons* (1971), *Delta and the Bannermen* (1987), *The Movie* (1996) and *The Bells of Saint John* (2013), and a moped in *The Idiot's Lantern* (2006). Alan Wareing also directed *Ghost Light* the same year, having handled *The Greatest Show in the Galaxy* the season before.

WORTH WATCHING

As indicated above, *Survival* brings *Doctor Who* right into the audience's everyday lives like never before or, arguably, since. It's concerned with the disassociation felt by young people at the end of ten years of Thatcherism, the 'every man for himself' credo of which is represented in Sergeant Paterson's misappropriation of 'survival of the fittest'. While the early years of the New Series contrast the Doctor's adventures with Rose's humdrum life, it uses only her and a few family friends to represent a whole strand of society, whereas *Survival* shows different members of the same community facing a threatening situation in their own ways. How typical this story would have become had the series continued is impossible to say, but *Doctor Who* was clearly finding a new relevance that it would have to wait fifteen years to fulfil.

DISC ONE

THE EPISODES

All three episodes are restored from digital duplicates of the original one-inch colour videotape recordings used for broadcast and their stereo soundtracks remastered.

SPECIAL FEATURES

CAT FLAP PART 1 (28m5s) The making of *Survival*, this part covering its pre-production. Including the development of Ace throughout the 1989 season and adding to the Doctor's mystery; writing the script; ties to the New Series; working with the director; choosing the guest cast; reintroducing the Master; and designing the Cheetah people. With contributions from script editor Andrew Cartmel, director Alan Wareing, costume designer Ken Trew, visual effects assistant Mike Tucker, and actors Sophie Aldred, Will Barton, Lisa Bowerman, Sylvester McCoy and Sakuntala Ramanee. Narrated by Paul Ewing, produced by Steve Broster.

CAT FLAP PART 2 (34m) The making of *Survival*, this part covering its production. Including the start of recording on location in Perivale, West London; coping with cat's-eye contact lenses; casting comedy duo Hale & Pace; working with animals, real and fake; staging the motorbike crash; recording at Warmwell Quarry, Dorset in hot weather; augmenting the alien planet scenes with video and visual effects; composing the score; and preparing for the end. With contributions from those above plus composer Dominic Glynn and actor Adele Silva. Narrated by Paul Ewing, produced by Steve Broster.

DELETED AND EXTENDED SCENES (9m18s) A selection of scenes not used in the final programme and sections that were initially sequenced differently, taken from earlier edits of the episodes with as-recorded sound and no video effects.

OUT-TAKES (16m26s) Bloopers and fluffed lines, compiled in 1989 from the original video recordings to show at the post-production party.

NEXT

CONTINUITIES (3m4s) Previews and continuity announcements from the original BBC1 broadcasts of all three episodes of *Survival* (plus episode two on BBC1 Scotland). Includes the BBC1 evening schedules for Wednesdays 22 and 29 November and 6 December 1989, and a plug for the BBC's *Fast Forward* magazine.

PHOTO GALLERY (8m38s) Slideshow of colour and black-and-white photos taken during production of *Survival*, set to music from the story. Compiled by Ralph Montagu.

INFO TEXT Select **On** to view subtitles when watching the episodes that provide information and anecdotes about the development, production, broadcast and history of Survival. Written by Richard Molesworth.

RADIO TIMES LISTINGS Accessible via a computer is a PDF file of the three episode listings for the original BBC1 broadcast of *Survival*, with an illustration by Christian Adams, plus letters published the week of episode two about the series' cancellation and a reassurance by BBC head of drama series Peter Cregeen that *Doctor Who* would return.

AUDIO OPTIONS

Select **Main Commentary** to play the audio commentary in place of the main soundtrack when watching the episodes. With Sylvester McCoy, Sophie Aldred (Ace) and script editor Andrew Cartmel on all three episodes.

— Select **Fan Commentary – Episode 3** to play an audio commentary by three winners of a *Doctor Who Magazine* competition when watching episode three. This is moderated by then-*DWM* editor Clayton Hickman, talking with Niall Boyce, Erykah Brackenbury and Tim Kittel.

— Select **Isolated Music** to hear only Dominic Glynn's music when watching the episodes.

— Select **Episode 5.1** to hear the Dolby Digital surround soundtrack when watching the episodes, newly remixed for this release.

— Select **Episode Stereo Audio** to reinstate the main soundtrack when watching the episodes.

SUBTITLES

Select **On** to view subtitles for all episodes and Special Features on disc one (except commentary).

DISC TWO

SPECIAL FEATURES

ENDGAME (44m22s) Plans for the future of *Doctor Who* after the 1989 season, the growing hints that the programme wouldn't be recommissioned, and the BBC management's reasons for taking it off air for an indefinite period. Includes a rundown of what story ideas might have featured had a 1990 season gone ahead, including a likely new companion. With contributions from BBC head of drama series Peter Cregeen, script editor Andrew Cartmel, writer Ben Aaronovitch, visual effects assistant Mike Tucker, composer Mark Ayres, actors Sophie Aldred and Sylvester McCoy, and *EastEnders* script editor Colin Brake. Narrated by Paul Ewing, illustrations by Robert Hammond, produced by Richard Molesworth.

SEARCH OUT SCIENCE (19m20s) An edition of the BBC Schools programme first broadcast on BBC2 on Wednesday 21 November 1990, in which Sylvester McCoy as the Doctor puts questions about astronomy to Ace (Sophie Aldred), K9 (voiced by John Lesson) and Cedric from Glurk (Stephen Johnson).

LITTLE GIRL LOST (16m33s) Examination of the character and portrayal of Seventh Doctor companion Ace. With actress Sophie Aldred, script editor Andrew Cartmel and writer Ian Briggs, who created the character. Produced by John Kelly.

DESTINY OF THE DOCTORS (13m51s) Footage recorded by Anthony Ainley, in his last appearance as the Master, for the 1997 PC video game *Destiny of the Doctors*, in which the player had to rescue each incarnation of the Doctor from the Master's trap. Links written by Terrance Dicks.

SUBTITLES Select **On** to view subtitles for all Special Features on disc two.

THE **TALONS OF WENG-CHIANG**

STORY No.91   SEASON No.14:6

Two discs with six episodes (144 mins) and 128½ minutes of extras, plus commentary track and production subtitles

TARDIS TEAM Fourth Doctor, Leela
TIME AND PLACE Victorian London
ADVERSARIES Magician Li H'sen Chang; his dummy Mr Sin; fugitive Magnus Greel
FIRST ON TV 26 February–2 April 1977
DVD RELEASE BBCDVD1152, 28 April 2003, PG
COVER Photo illustration by Clayton Hickman, red strip
— Original release with cover sticker reading 'Doctor Who 40th Anniversary 1963–2003'
ORIGINAL RRP £19.99

STORY TEASER

In the dark streets of 1890s London, girls are going missing, a corpse is found floating in the Thames half eaten by some giant animal, and something is lurking in the sewers beneath the Palace Theatre, where the Chinese magician Li H'Sen Chang and his sinister ventriloquist's dummy Mr Sin perform nightly. With help from theatre owner Henry Gordon Jago and police pathologist Professor George Litefoot, the Doctor and Leela must link these seemingly unconnected events and uncover Weng-Chiang, head of the deadly Tong of the Black Scorpion.

CONNECTIONS

The Doctor was last in Victorian Britain when kidnapped through time by Edward Waterfield at the behest of the Daleks in *The Evil of the Daleks* (1967). He briefly lands in Scotland, 1885 in *Timelash* (1985), takes Ace back to the house Gabriel Chase when it was still inhabited in *Ghost Light* (1989), accidentally arrives in Cardiff, 1869 in *The Unquiet Dead* (2005), happens across Cybermen in Victorian London in *The Next Doctor* (2008), hides out there after losing the Ponds in *The Snowmen* (2012) and challenges Mrs Gillyflower's Victorian attitudes in *The Crimson Horror* (2013). He meets Queen Victoria herself, travelling in Scotland, in *Tooth and Claw* (2006). The era is also conjured up by the Valeyard to trap the Doctor in the Matrix in *The Trial of a Time Lord: The Ultimate Foe* (1986). While the disappearances of young women in *The Talons of Weng-Chiang* evokes the crimes of Jack the Ripper, we now know him to have been eaten by Madam Vastra (*A Good Man Goes to War*, 2011). Chang smokes opium to dull his pain much as people will take Vraxoin (*Nightmare of Eden*, 1979) and mood drugs (*Gridlock*, 2007). The Doctor visits the theatre again in *The Unquiet Dead*, where he meets Charles Dickens, and *The Shakespeare Code* (2007), where he meets (you guessed it) William Shakespeare. This was a late submission by script editor Robert Holmes when another script didn't work out, as were *The Ark in Space* (1975), *Pyramids of Mars* (1975) and, to some degree, *The Brain of Morbius* (1976). It was director David Maloney's last *Doctor Who* serial, having worked on the series since 1969 (*see Index v*), after which he became the first producer of *Blake's 7*. John Bennett (Chang) also appears as General Finch in *Invasion of the Dinosaurs* (1974), Michael Spice (Greel) voices Morbius in *The Brain of Morbius*, and Christopher Benjamin (Jago) plays Sir Keith Gold in *Inferno* (1970) and appears in the New Series as Colonel Hugh Curbishley in *The Unicorn and the Wasp* (2008).

WORTH WATCHING

Frequently topping fan polls, this is the culmination of the Gothic era of producer Philip Hinchcliffe and script editor Robert Holmes, and arguably the peak of Tom Baker's time as the Fourth Doctor. Everything comes together to create as perfect a show as it's possible to get given the way the programme was made. Even the one iffy monster that's often cited as a problem is brief and barely enough to dent enjoyment of the adventure as a whole. In recent times it has been criticised for its portrayal of the Chinese (indeed, one Canadian broadcaster refused to show it for this reason) and by modern standards this is uncomfortable, but watched as a product of its time this can be pardoned if not condoned.

THE EPISODES

All six episodes are restored from digital duplicates of the original two-inch colour videotape recordings used for broadcast and their mono soundtracks remastered. The title sequences are replaced by a modern transfer of the original 35mm film with credits overlaid from the episode recordings.

SPECIAL FEATURES *ALSO ON SPECIAL EDITION

*COMMENTARY Select **On** to play the audio commentary in place of the main soundtrack when watching the episodes. With director David Maloney [eps 1,2,3,5,6], John Bennett (Chang) [1,2,4,5*], Christopher Benjamin (Jago) [1,2,4,5,6], Louise Jameson (Leela) [1,3,4,5,6] and producer Philip Hinchcliffe [2,3,5,6]. (* John Bennett also comments on the last four minutes of episode six.)

INFORMATION TEXT Select **On** to view subtitles when watching the episodes that provide information and anecdotes about the development, production, broadcast and history of *The Talons of Weng-Chiang*. Written by Martin Wiggins.

SUBTITLES

Select **On** to view subtitles for all episodes, or for the commentary.

SPECIAL FEATURES *ALSO ON SPECIAL EDITION

*WHOSE DOCTOR WHO (58m44s) The first documentary about *Doctor Who*, part of the *Lively Arts* strand presented by Melvyn Bragg, broadcast on BBC2 on Sunday 3 April 1977. Featuring many clips from the series and specially recorded interviews with Tom Baker and Philip Hinchcliffe, it examines the series' history, the nature of its monsters, its impact on children, and the character and morality of the Doctor. It also goes behind the scenes of *The Talons of Weng-Chiang*.

*BEHIND THE SCENES (24m) Footage from the full studio recording in early-February 1977 of scenes for episodes five and six, including retakes and shots unused in the final programme, taken from a low-quality black-and-white video copy with on-screen time-code.

*BLUE PETER THEATRE (26m) Extract from the Thursday 23 May 1974 edition of the BBC1 children's magazine programme in which Lesley Judd, John Noakes and Peter Purves present from the sets for *Robot*, which had been left standing in the studio owing to a BBC scenery-shifters' strike (*also on* **Robot**). Then extracts from the Thursday 28 April, Thursday 5 May and Thursday 19 May 1977 editions in which the presenters show how to make a model theatre, scenery and *Doctor Who* figures, and sound effects with help from Dick Mills of the BBC Radiophonic Workshop.

SUBTITLES Select **On** to view subtitles for all Special Features on disc two.

▶

*PHILIP HINCHCLIFFE INTERVIEW (11m30s) Extract from the Thursday 31 March 1977 edition of the BBC1 lunchtime magazine programme *Pebble Mill at One* in which David Seymour interviews producer Philip Hinchcliffe to promote the upcoming *Whose Doctor Who* documentary. Introduced by Donny MacLeod.

*TRAILS AND CONTINUITY (2m28s) Continuity announcements from the original BBC1 broadcasts of episode four of the preceding story, *The Robots of Death*, plugging "The Talons of Wang-Cheng" (sic); of episodes one and six of *The Talons of Weng-Chiang*; and trailers for the *Whose Doctor Who* documentary. Includes the BBC2 evening schedule for Sunday 3 April 1977.

*TARDIS CAM NO.6 (1m43s) Short scene featuring the TARDIS, originally made for the BBCi *Doctor Who* website in 2001. The TARDIS floats among a school of space whales (CGI).

*PHOTO GALLERY (3m25s) Slideshow of colour and black-and-white photos taken during production of *The Talons of Weng-Chiang*, including design department photos of the sets. Set to sound effects from the story. Compiled by Ralph Montagu.

EASTER EGGS

There are two hidden features on these discs to find. *See Appendix 2 for details*

RELATED EXTRAS

Roger Murray-Leach Interview — The Ark in Space (and Special Edition)
The Doctor's Composer — The Sun Makers

T

THE **TALONS OF WENG-CHIANG** SPECIAL EDITION

STORY No.91   SEASON No.14:6

Released with **THE CAVES OF ANDROZANI SPECIAL EDITION** and **THE MOVIE SPECIAL EDITION** in the **REVISITATIONS 1** boxset

Three discs with six episodes (144 mins) and 241½ minutes of extras, plus commentary track, production subtitles and PDF items

Audio navigation of each disc's contents available by pressing Enter after the BBC ident

TARDIS TEAM Fourth Doctor, Leela

TIME AND PLACE Victorian London

ADVERSARIES Magician Li H'sen Chang; his dummy Mr Sin; fugitive Magnus Greel

FIRST ON TV 26 February–2 April 1977

DVD RELEASE BBCDVD2806(A), 4 October 2010, PG (boxset 12)

COVER Photo illustration by Clayton Hickman, orange strip; version with older BBC logo on reverse

ORIGINAL RRP £39.99 (boxset)

STORY TEASER

In the dark streets of 1890s London, girls are going missing, a corpse if found floating in the Thames half eaten by some giant animal, and something is lurking in the sewers beneath the Palace Theatre, where the Chinese magician Li H'Sen Chang and his sinister ventriloquist's dummy Mr Sin perform nightly. With help from theatre owner Henry Gordon Jago and police pathologist Professor George Litefoot, the Doctor and Leela must link these seemingly unconnected events and uncover Weng-Chiang, head of the deadly Tong of the Black Scorpion.

CONNECTIONS

The Doctor was last in Victorian Britain when kidnapped through time by Edward Waterfield at the behest of the Daleks in *The Evil of the Daleks* (1967). He briefly lands in Scotland, 1885 in *Timelash* (1985), takes Ace back to the house Gabriel Chase when it was still inhabited in *Ghost Light* (1989), accidentally arrives in Cardiff, 1869 in *The Unquiet Dead* (2005), happens across Cybermen in Victorian London in *The Next Doctor* (2008), hides out there after losing the Ponds in *The Snowmen* (2012) and challenges Mrs Gillyflower's Victorian attitudes in *The Crimson Horror* (2013). He meets Queen Victoria herself, travelling in Scotland, in *Tooth and Claw* (2006). The era is also conjured up by the Valeyard to trap the Doctor in the Matrix in *The Trial of a Time Lord: The Ultimate Foe* (1986). While the disappearances of young women in *The Talons of Weng-Chiang* evokes the crimes of Jack the Ripper, we now know him to have been eaten by Madam Vastra (*A Good Man Goes to War*, 2011). Chang smokes opium to dull his pain much as people will take Vraxoin (*Nightmare of Eden*, 1979) and mood drugs (*Gridlock*, 2007). The Doctor visits the theatre again in *The Unquiet Dead*, where he meets Charles Dickens, and *The Shakespeare Code* (2007), where he meets (you guessed it) William Shakespeare. This was a late submission by script editor Robert Holmes when another script didn't work out, as were *The Ark in Space* (1975), *Pyramids of Mars* (1975) and, to some degree, *The Brain of Morbius* (1976). It was director David Maloney's last *Doctor Who* serial, having worked on the series since 1969 (*see Index v*), after which he became the first producer of *Blake's 7*. John Bennett (Chang) also appears as General Finch in *Invasion of the Dinosaurs* (1974), Michael Spice (Greel) voices Morbius in *The Brain of Morbius*, and Christopher Benjamin (Jago) plays Sir Keith Gold in *Inferno* (1970) and appears in the New Series as Colonel Hugh Curbishley in *The Unicorn and the Wasp* (2008).

WORTH WATCHING

This Special Edition features further clean-up of the episodes compared to the previous release and additional Special Features. Frequently topping fan polls, this is the culmination of the Gothic era of producer Philip Hinchcliffe and script editor Robert Holmes, and arguably the peak of Tom Baker's time as the Fourth Doctor. Everything comes together to create as perfect a show as it's possible to get given the way the programme was made. Even the one iffy monster that's often cited as a problem is brief and barely enough to dent enjoyment of the adventure as a whole. In recent times it has been criticised for its portrayal of the Chinese (indeed, one Canadian broadcaster refused to show it for this reason) and by modern standards this is uncomfortable, but watched as a product of its time this can be pardoned if not condoned.

DISC ONE

THE EPISODES

All six episodes are restored from digital duplicates of the original two-inch colour videotape recordings used for broadcast and their mono soundtracks newly remastered. The title sequences are replaced by a modern transfer of the original 35mm film with credits remade to match the originals.

SPECIAL FEATURES *REPEATED FROM PREVIOUS RELEASE

*AUDIO OPTIONS Select **Commentary** to play the audio commentary recorded for the previous release in place of the main soundtrack when watching the episodes. With director David Maloney [eps 1,2,3,5,6], John Bennett (Chang) [1,2,4,5*], Christopher Benjamin (Jago) [1,2,4,5,6], Louise Jameson (Leela) [1,3,4,5,6] and producer Philip Hinchcliffe [2,3,5,6]. (* John Bennett also comments on the last four minutes of episode six.)

— Select **Feature Audio** to reinstate the main soundtrack when watching the episodes.

INFO TEXT Select **On** to view subtitles when watching the episodes that provide information and anecdotes about the development, production, broadcast and history of *The Talons of Weng-Chiang*, updated and expanded from the previous release. Written by Martin Wiggins.

COMING SOON (51s) Trailer for the DVD release of *The Seeds of Doom*.

SUBTITLES

Select **On** to view subtitles for all episodes and the Coming Soon trailer (none for commentary).

DISC TWO

SPECIAL FEATURES

THE LAST HURRAH (33m34s) Producer Philip Hinchcliffe discusses with actors Tom Baker and Louise Jameson, designer Roger Murray-Leach and costume designer John Bloomfield their memories of making *The Talons of Weng-Chiang*, including the characterisation of Leela; working out the production requirements as the script was still being written; working with the director; the characters and cast; filming on location in Wapping and at a real theatre in Northampton; designing the costumes and sets; and the final studio recording. With contributions from director David Maloney (interviewed in 2003), and actors Trevor Baxter and Christopher Benjamin. Produced by Steve Broster.

MOVING ON (4m35s) Producer Philip Hinchcliffe talks about his early ideas for the 1977/78 season had he not been moved to producing police series *Target* instead.

THE FOE FROM THE FUTURE (6m46s) Writer Robert Banks Stewart talks about his original storyline for the concluding serial of the 1976/77 season, which ultimately wasn't written as he was offered another job, and dispels the myth that *The Talons of Weng-Chiang* reworked any of his ideas. With producer Philip Hinchcliffe.

NOW & THEN (11m3s) Comparing the filming locations in Bankside, Twickenham and Wapping in London, and at the Royal Theatre and other locations in Northampton as they look today with how they appeared in mid-December 1976 and early-January 1977 when used for *The Talons of Weng-Chiang*. Narrated and produced by Richard Bignell. *See Index iii for further editions*

LOOK EAST (3m39s) Report from the Friday 14 January 1977 edition of the BBC local news programme on the location recording at the Royal Theatre in Northampton, in which reporter David Cass interviews Tom Baker.

SUBTITLES Select **On** to view subtitles for all Special Features on disc two.

NEXT

VICTORIANA AND CHINOISERIE (8m8s) The use of ideas from Victorian society and literature in *The Talons of Weng-Chiang*. With producer Philip Hinchcliffe and literature lecturer Dr Anne Witchard. Produced by Stella Broster.

MUSIC HALL (21m44s) Author Michael McManus presents a history of the music hall tradition in the UK and some its biggest performers, recorded at the Hoxton Hall theatre which began as MacDonald's Music Hall in 1863. With British Music Hall Society co-founder Gerald Glover, actor

Johnny Dennis, and variety stars Pamela Cundell and Victor Spinetti. Songs sung by Katy Baker, produced by Steve Broster.

LIMEHOUSE – A VICTORIAN CHINATOWN (19m21s) Writer and broadcaster Matthew Sweet presents a history of the district of East London by the river Thames that developed alongside the city's growing importance as an international port, and its representation in literature and popular myth. With historian Dr John Seed, museum curator Dr Tom Wareham and literature lecturer Dr Anne Witchard. Produced by Stella Broster.

PHOTO GALLERY (3m19s) A new slideshow of colour and black-and-white photos taken during production of *The Talons of Weng-Chiang*, including design department photos of the sets. Set to sound effects from the story. Compiled by Paul Shields.

PDF MATERIALS Accessible via a computer are the six episode listings from *Radio Times* for the BBC1 broadcast of *The Talons of Weng-Chiang* and that for the *Whose Doctor Who* documentary (with illustration by Bill Tidy), plus letters about the lack of monsters in the series (and a reply from incoming producer Graham Williams) published the weeks of episodes two and five.

DISC THREE

SPECIAL FEATURES *REPEATED FROM PREVIOUS RELEASE

*WHOSE DOCTOR WHO (58m44s) The first documentary about *Doctor Who*, part of the *Lively Arts* strand presented by Melvyn Bragg, broadcast on BBC2 on Sunday 3 April 1977. Featuring many clips from the series and specially recorded interviews with Tom Baker and Philip Hinchcliffe, it examines the series' history, the nature of its monsters, its impact on children, and the character and morality of the Doctor. It also goes behind the scenes of *The Talons of Weng-Chiang*.

*BLUE PETER THEATRE (26m) Extract from the Thursday 23 May 1974 edition of the BBC1 children's magazine programme in which Lesley Judd, John Noakes and Peter Purves present from the sets for *Robot*, which had been left standing in the studio owing to a BBC scenery-shifters' strike (*also on* **Robot**). Then extracts from the Thursday 28 April, Thursday 5 May and Thursday 19 May 1977 editions in which the presenters show how to make a model theatre, scenery and *Doctor Who* figures, and sound effects with help from Dick Mills of the BBC Radiophonic Workshop.

*BEHIND THE SCENES (24m) Footage from the full studio recording in early-February 1977 of scenes for episodes five and six, including retakes and shots unused in the final programme, taken from a low-quality black-and-white video copy with on-screen time-code.

SUBTITLES Select **On** to view subtitles for all Special Features on disc three.

NEXT

*PHILIP HINCHCLIFFE INTERVIEW (11m30s) Extract from the Thursday 31 March 1977 edition of the BBC1 lunchtime magazine programme *Pebble Mill at One* in which David Seymour interviews producer Philip Hinchcliffe to promote the upcoming *Whose Doctor Who* documentary. Introduced by Donny MacLeod.

*TRAILS AND CONTINUITY (2m28s) Continuity announcements from the original BBC1 broadcasts of episode four of the preceding story, *The Robots of Death*, plugging "The Talons of Wang-Cheng" (sic); of episodes one and six of *The Talons of Weng-Chiang*; and trailers for the *Whose Doctor Who* documentary. Includes the BBC2 evening schedule for Sunday 3 April 1977.

*PHOTO GALLERY (3m25s) Slideshow of colour and black-and-white photos taken during production of *The Talons of Weng-Chiang*, including design department photos of the sets. Set to sound effects from the story. Compiled by Ralph Montagu.

*TARDIS–CAM NO.6 (1m43s) Short scene featuring the TARDIS, originally made for the BBCi *Doctor Who* website in 2001. The TARDIS floats among a school of space whales (CGI).

EASTER EGGS

There are two hidden features on these discs to find. *See Appendix 2 for details*

RELATED EXTRAS

Roger Murray-Leach Interview — The Ark in Space (and Special Edition)

The Doctor's Composer — The Sun Makers

Coming Soon trailer — Time and the Rani

THE **TENTH PLANET**

STORY No.**29**   SEASON No.**4:2**

Two discs with three original and one animated episodes (94½ mins) and 144 minutes of extras,
plus commentary track, production subtitles and PDF items
Audio navigation of each disc's contents available by pressing Enter after the BBC ident

TARDIS TEAM First Doctor, Ben, Polly
TIME AND PLACE South Pole, 1986
ADVERSARIES Cybermen (1st appearance)
FIRST ON TV 8–29 October 1966
DVD RELEASE BBCDVD3382, 14 October 2013, PG
COVER Photo illustration by Lee Binding, light blue strip; version with older BBC logo on reverse
ORIGINAL RRP £20.42
— Episodes first released in the Regeneration box; BBCDVD3801, £61.27, 24 June 2013

STORY TEASER

The scientists headed by General Cutler at the South Pole Space Tracking Station are shocked when they discover the rocket they're guiding back down to Earth is way off course. The reason is soon discovered to be a rogue planet that has entered the solar system and is affecting the gravitational field. As it approaches the Earth, the energy of first the rocket and then the whole planet starts draining away, and then horrifying metal-men arrive at the base… Even the Doctor finds himself weakened and able to do little as he faces his own apotheosis.

CONNECTIONS

This is the debut of the Cybermen who, although they return often during the Second Doctor's era, are never seen in this form again. By *The Moonbase* (1967) they have become more robotic in appearance, rather than the clearly augmented humans they are here. The events of *Attack of the Cybermen* (1985) are closely related, as future Cybermen return to Earth before its encounter with Mondas with the intention of changing the outcome of this story. The Doctor returns to Antarctica in *The Seeds of Doom* (1976), and is again involved in helping a tracking station recover stranded astronauts in *The Ambassadors of Death* (1970). A scientific military outpost whose commander goes to pieces under the pressure of an alien assault becomes a frequent circumstance for the Second Doctor, most notably in *The Ice Warriors* (1967), *Fury from the Deep* (1968) and *The Wheel in Space* (1968), the last also featuring the Cybermen. Writers Kit Pedler and Gerry Davis collaborated again on *The Moonbase* and *The Tomb of the Cybermen* (both 1967), while the latter wrote *Revenge of the Cybermen* (1975). Derek Martinus also directed *Galaxy 4* and *Mission to the Unknown* (1965), *The Evil of the Daleks* (1967), *The Ice Warriors* and *Spearhead from Space* (1970).

WORTH WATCHING

All the reasons that now make this a landmark story in the history of *Doctor Who* were unknown to the audience at the time. They might have read that William Hartnell was leaving the series and Patrick Troughton was set to replace him, but the nature of the switch, and certainly the unique move of directly transforming one into the other, would have been a complete surprise. Publicity also showed the Cybermen but didn't reveal their nature, and of course no one could know they would return and become second in popularity to the Daleks. We watch it now as the origin of much of the Second Doctor era, but to dedicated viewers at the time it must have felt like the world really was coming to an end.

DISC ONE

THE EPISODES

Episodes one, two and three were restored for VHS release in November 2000 from 16mm film copies of the original black-and-white videotape recordings that survived in the archives. Further picture restoration was done for this release, the episodes' mono soundtracks remastered and the VidFIRE process applied to studio-recorded shots to recapture the smoother motion of video. The title sequences are replaced by a modern transfer of the best surviving copy of the original 35mm film with credits remade to match the originals. Episode four, of which no film copy is known to exist, is recreated with black-and-white animation by Planet 55 Studios with reference to surviving images from the serial and matched to a remastered recording of the soundtrack made on audio tape when the episode was originally broadcast.

SPECIAL FEATURES

FROZEN OUT (29m10s) The making of *The Tenth Planet*, including the growing need to replace William Hartnell; writing the script; working with director Derek Martinus; creating the look of the Cybermen; recreating Antarctica in Ealing Studios; casting a multi-cultural future society; designing the sets; coping with Hartnell's sudden absence from episode three; recording the regeneration; and the legacy of that first changeover. With contributions from designer Peter Kindred, vision mixer Shirley Coward, and actors Earl Cameron, Reg Whitehead and Anneke Wills. Produced by Chris Chapman.

EPISODE 4 VHS RECONSTRUCTION (24m22s) The recreation of episode four produced for the story's release on VHS in November 2000, composed of off-screen images, clips and the surviving footage of the regeneration matched to a recording of the soundtrack made on audio tape when the episode was originally broadcast.

PHOTO GALLERY (3m39s) Slideshow of black-and-white photos taken during production of *The Tenth Planet*, including design department photos of the sets. Set to stock music and sound effects from the story. Compiled by Paul Shields.

PDF MATERIALS Accessible via a computer are the four episode listings from *Radio Times* for the original BBC1 broadcast of *The Tenth Planet*, an article introducing the story and a preview of the return of the Daleks in the next story.

AUDIO OPTIONS Select **Commentary** to play the audio commentary in place of the main soundtrack when watching the first three episodes. This is moderated by actor and comedian Toby Hadoke, talking with Alan White (Schultz) [eps 1,2], Earl Cameron (Williams) [1,2], Donald van der Maaten aka Gregg Palmer (Cybermen) [1,2,3], Christopher Matthews (Radar technician) [1,2,3], Anneke Wills (Polly) [1,2,3] and Christopher Dunham (Radio technician) [3], plus additional comments from an interview with designer Peter Kindred during episodes two and three.

— Select **Feature Audio** to reinstate the main soundtrack when watching the episodes.

INFO TEXT Select **On** to view subtitles when watching the first three episodes that provide information and anecdotes about the development, production, broadcast and history of *The Tenth Planet*. Written by Stephen James Walker.

COMING SOON (1m3s) Trailer for the DVD release of *The Moonbase*.

SUBTITLES

Select **On** to view subtitles for all episodes and Special Features on disc one (except commentary).

DISC TWO

SPECIAL FEATURES

WILLIAM HARTNELL INTERVIEW (3m18s) The Christmas after relinquishing the role of the Doctor, William Hartnell appeared in panto as Buskin the fairy cobbler in *Puss in Boots*. The show toured the UK and at the end of its run in Taunton local BBC News programme *Points West* reporter Roger Mills interviewed the actor in his dressing room, broadcast on Tuesday 17 January 1967. This is the film shot of Hartnell for what is now his only surviving television interview.

DOCTOR WHO STORIES – ANNEKE WILLS (13m39s) Recorded in 2003 for BBC2's *The Story of Doctor Who*, actor Anneke Wills recalls her experiences of playing companion Polly from 1966 to 1967.

THE GOLDEN AGE (15m49s) Historian and writer Dominic Sandbrook examines the idea that *Doctor Who* was better in the past, an argument that has come up regularly in each era of the show and has more basis in childhood nostalgia than public popularity. Written by Simon Guerrier, produced by Thomas Guerrier.

BOYS! BOYS! BOYS! (19m33s) Three male companions discuss their time on *Doctor Who*, the portrayal of their characters and to what extent their experiences differed. With Frazer Hines (Jamie), Peter Purves (Steven) and Mark Strickson (Turlough). Produced by Steve Broster.

COMPANION PIECE (24m24s) What role the companion plays in *Doctor Who*, what travelling with the Doctor says about their personalities, and what it's like to play the companion. With contributions from companion actors Nicola Bryant, Arthur Darvill, Louise Jameson, William Russell and Elisabeth Sladen, writers Nev Fountain and Joseph Lidster, and psychologist Dr Tomas Chamorro-Premuzic. Produced by James Goss and Tim Kittel.

BLUE PETER (9m5s) Extract from the Monday 5 November 1973 edition of the children's magazine programme in which Peter Purves, Lesley Judd and John Noakes mark the tenth anniversary of *Doctor Who* with a look through past clips. This is the source of the surviving clip of the first regeneration. *Also on* The Three Doctors *(and* Special Edition*)*

SUBTITLES Select **On** to view subtitles for all Special Features on disc two.

RELATED EXTRAS

The Cyber-Generations — Attack of the Cybermen

The Cyber Story — Attack of the Cybermen

TERMINUS

STORY No.126   SEASON No.20:4

Released with **ENLIGHTENMENT** and **MAWDRYN UNDEAD** in **THE BLACK GUARDIAN TRILOGY** boxset

One disc with four episodes (99 mins) and 46½ minutes of extras, plus optional CGI effects, commentary and music-only tracks, production subtitles and PDF items

Audio navigation of disc contents available by pressing Enter after the BBC ident

TARDIS TEAM Fifth Doctor, Nyssa, Tegan, Turlough

TIME AND PLACE Terminus space station and transport ship

ADVERSARIES Victims of Lazar's disease; Vanir, human guards of the infected; the Black Guardian (3rd appearance)

FIRST ON TV 15–23 February 1983

DVD RELEASE BBCDVD2596B, 10 August 2009, PG

COVER Photo illustration by Clayton Hickman, pale turquoise strip

ORIGINAL RRP £39.14 (boxset)

STORY TEASER

Still under the command of the Black Guardian to assassinate the Doctor, Turlough has joined the TARDIS crew and one of his first acts is to sabotage the Ship, causing it to lock on to a passing space-craft to avoid destruction. But this takes it to Terminus, where those with the incurable Lazar's disease are brought to die. With Nyssa infected and the overseeing Vanir hunting the Doctor, he has little time to find a cure for his friend, but does discover that Terminus's continued running is crucial to the existence of the entire universe.

CONNECTIONS

Usually the TARDIS is the Doctor's safe haven but can be the cause of danger itself, as in *The Edge of Destruction* (1964), *The Wheel in Space* (1968), *The Mind Robber* (1968), *Castrovalva* (1982), *The Doctor's Wife* (2010) and *Journey to the Centre of the TARDIS* (2013). In *Castrovalva* the TARDIS is sent hurtling back in time towards the start of the universe, the origin of which is speculated on in *Terminus*. The Ship also ends up at almost the very end of the universe when trying to shake off the immortal Jack Harkness in *Utopia* (2007). The Fifth Doctor is ultimately forced to regenerate after contracting a disease, spectrox toxaemia, in *The Caves of Androzani* (1984), and in his fourth incarnation he was infected by the space-borne virus the Swarm (*The Invisible Enemy*, 1977). Of his companions, Steven is almost fatally infected by Dodo's common cold in *The Ark* (1966), Jo is sprayed with fungal spores in *Planet of the Daleks* (1973), Sarah Jane gets a mild dose of distronic toxaemia in *Genesis of the Daleks* (1975) and shortly after is infected by a Cybermat in *Revenge of the Cybermen* (1975), and Peri also contracts spectrox toxaemia in *The Caves of Androzani*. Steve Gallagher also wrote *Warriors' Gate* (1981). Valentine Dyall plays the Black Guardian in the other two stories of this trilogy, having first appeared in *The Armageddon Factor* (1979), while Tim Munro (Sigurd) is Ainu in *The Creature from the Pit* (1979).

T

WORTH WATCHING

Stephen Gallagher is now a respected novelist as well as television script writer, and had written *Warriors' Gate* for the 1980/81 season, which is well regarded by fans. Sadly *Terminus* doesn't receive as much praise. This is perhaps due more to the quality of the production rather than the script, although the writer struggles to come up with enough for all the companions to do and the pace of the direction is very leisurely. The focus is rightly on Nyssa, this being her last story, and the reasons for her departure arise naturally from her character.

THE EPISODES

All four episodes are restored from digital duplicates of the original two-inch colour videotape recordings used for broadcast and their mono soundtracks remastered. The title sequences are replaced by a modern transfer of the original 35mm film with credits remade to match the originals.

SPECIAL FEATURES

AUDIO OPTIONS Select **Commentary** to play the audio commentary in place of the main soundtrack when watching the episodes. With Peter Davison, Mark Strickson (Turlough), Sarah Sutton (Nyssa) and writer Stephen Gallagher on all four episodes.

— Select **Isolated Music** to hear only Roger Limb's music when watching the episodes.

— Select **Feature Audio** to reinstate the main soundtrack when watching the episodes.

INFO TEXT Select **On** to view subtitles when watching the episodes that provide information and anecdotes about the development, production, broadcast and history of *Terminus*. Written by Richard Molesworth.

BREAKING POINT (22m52s) The making of *Terminus*, including the origins of the story and juggling all the characters; working with director Mary Ridge; delays from cancelled recording days and problems in the studio; coping with the Vanir's noisy armour and realising the Garm; casting the main guest role; and the departure of Nyssa. With contributions from writer Stephen Gallagher, designer Dick Coles, camera supervisor Alec Wheal, sound supervisor Scott Talbott, actors Peter Davison, Martin Potter, Mark Strickson and Sarah Sutton, and fellow director Fiona Cumming. Narrated by Floella Benjamin, produced by Brendan Sheppard.

ORIGINS OF THE UNIVERSE (6m29s) Astronomers Sir Patrick Moore and Dr John Mason expound the current theories about how the universe may have started.

ORIGINAL STORYBOARDS (1m18s) Design sketches by visual effects designer Peter Pegrum for the model effects work in *Terminus*, alongside the shots as seen in the final programme.

UNUSED MODEL SHOTS (3m29s) Silent video footage of the model recording, including shots not used in the final episodes, taken from a VHS copy with on-screen time-code. Set to music from the story.

NEXT

CGI EFFECTS Select **CGI Effects On** to view updated computer-generated effects in place of some of the original visual effects when watching the episodes.

CONTINUITY (1m51s) Continuity announcements from the original BBC1 broadcasts of all four episodes of *Terminus*, with a plug for the Longleat celebration weekend in April 1983.

PHOTO GALLERY (8m16s) Slideshow of colour and black-and-white photos taken during production of *Terminus*, including design department photos of the sets. Set to music from the story. Compiled by Derek Handley.

PDF MATERIALS Accessible via a computer are the four episode listings from *Radio Times* for the original BBC1 broadcast of *Terminus*.

— Storyboard sketches by Russell Owen for some of the new CGI effects shots.

COMING SOON (1m2s) Trailer for the DVD release of *The Twin Dilemma*.

SUBTITLES

Select **On** to view subtitles for all episodes and Special Features (except commentary).

EASTER EGGS

There are two hidden features on this disc to find. *See Appendix 2 for details*

RELATED EXTRAS

Coming Soon trailer — The War Games

TERROR OF THE AUTONS

STORY No.55   SEASON No.8:1

Released with **SPEARHEAD FROM SPACE SPECIAL EDITION** in the **MANNEQUIN MANIA** boxset

One disc with four episodes (95½ mins) and 73 minutes of extras, plus commentary track, production subtitles and PDF items

Audio navigation of disc contents available by pressing Enter after the BBC ident

TARDIS TEAM Third Doctor, Brigadier and UNIT, and introducing Jo Grant

TIME AND PLACE Contemporary England

ADVERSARIES First Master (1st appearance); Autons and Nestene (2nd appearance)

FIRST ON TV 2–23 January 1971

DVD RELEASE BBCDVD3135B, 9 May 2011, PG (episodes U)

COVER Photo illustration by Clayton Hickman, pink strip; version with older BBC logo on reverse

ORIGINAL RRP £35.73 (boxset)

— Episodes released in The Monster Collection: The Master; BBCDVD3814, £9.99, 30 September 2013

STORY TEASER

The Time Lords warn the Doctor that his old acquaintance the Master has come to Earth. He has already stolen the one surviving Nestene energy unit from its first invasion attempt and is using its ability to animate plastic objects with deadly results. Even as the Brigadier and UNIT begin searching for factories the Master could be using as his base of operations, he is seeking out the Doctor, determined to end their feud once and for all.

CONNECTIONS

The Autons and their controlling Nestene first appear in *Spearhead from Space* (1970) and return only in the New Series, first *Rose* in 2005, a brief appearance in *Love & Monsters* (2006), then again in *The Pandorica Opens* (2010). This incarnation of the Master becomes the regular villain for the rest of the 1971 season, appearing in all five stories, then less frequently for the following two years until his final scheme in *Frontier in Space* (1973). The character was resurrected in 1976's *The Deadly Assassin* and again in 1981's *The Keeper of Traken* before once more becoming a regular villain through to the end of the Classic Series. He was brought back for *The Movie* in 1996 and returned in the New Series in 2007's *Utopia*. The Nestene take over a factory from which to produce the Autons and launch their invasion, as do the Sontarans in *The Sontaran Stratagem* (2008), whereas Cybus Industries in *Rise of the Cybermen/The Age of Steel* (2006) and Mrs Gillyflower in *The Crimson Horror* (2013) build their own factories to produce their vision for the world. Robert Holmes also wrote the Autons' debut, having contributed scripts to the 1968/69 season before that. He went on to write *Carnival of Monsters* (1973) and *The Time Warrior* (1973/74) for the Third Doctor before becoming script editor for the first three years of the Fourth Doctor's era (*see Index v*). Director Barry Letts was the producer throughout the Third Doctor's era but kept his hand in at directing having previously handled *The Enemy of the World* (1967/68) and taken over on *Inferno* (1970) when original director Douglas Camfield was taken ill (*see Index v*). This is the first major role in *Doctor Who* for Michael Wisher, playing Rex Farrel, after a small part in *The Ambassadors of Death* (1970); he later played Kalik in *Carnival of Monsters* and Magrik in *Revenge of the Cybermen* (1975) before being cast as the first Davros in *Genesis of the Daleks* (1975). Harry Towb (McDermott) is Osgood in *The Seeds of Death* (1969), while David Garth (Time Lord) is seedy Solicitor Grey in *The Highlanders* (1966/67), and Roy Stewart (Tony) is Toberman in *The Tomb of the Cybermen* (1967). Christopher Burgess (Professor Phillips) and Andrew Staines (Goodge) were often cast by Letts, including in *The Enemy of the World* and *Planet of the Spiders* (1974).

WORTH WATCHING

In some ways this is a rehash of *Spearhead from Space*, as the Nestene's plan is pretty much the same despite its previous defeat, including failing to control their human stooge. But of course it's greatly enhanced by Roger Delgado's masterly performance as the Doctor's new nemesis. He instantly marks the character as someone to be reckoned with and whose appearance on screen you look forward to. He's perfectly cast against Jon Pertwee's Doctor and really the rest of the story plays second fiddle to the anticipation of a confrontation between these two. There'll be plenty of those in this season, but the first time is always the best.

THE EPISODES

All four episodes are restored from 16mm black-and-white film copies of the original two-inch colour videotape recordings and recoloured using copies of lower-resolution home-video recordings made when the serial was broadcast in America in 1977. Their mono soundtracks are remastered and the VidFIRE process is applied to studio-recorded shots to recapture the smoother motion of video. A scene in episode one is replaced with a two-inch colour videotape copy that survives as part of the 22 June 1973 edition of *Nationwide*. The title sequences are replaced by a modern transfer of the original 35mm film with credits remade to match the originals.

SPECIAL FEATURES

LIFE ON EARTH (33m41s) The making of *Terror of the Autons*, including the introduction of a new regular villain and casting two new companions; building a cordial company of actors; bringing back the Autons, in 1971 and 2005; writing the script; and filming on location. Also how characterisation and violence in the show differ between the 1970s and 2000s, and how television production has changed. With contributions from producer/director Barry Letts (interviewed in 2008), script editor Terrance Dicks, actors Richard Franklin, Katy Manning and Jon Pertwee (interviewed in 1995), and New Series producer Phil Collinson. Produced by Ed Stradling.

THE DOCTOR'S MORIARTY (18m55s) The contrasts between the Doctor and the Master, the latter's character and his enduring appeal. With producer Barry Letts, script editors Christopher H Bidmead and Terrance Dicks, New Series writers Joseph Lidster and Robert Shearman, and actor Katy Manning. Illustrations by Daryl Joyce, produced by James Goss.

PLASTIC FANTASTIC (11m3s) The social impact of the development of plastic products and how attitudes to them made plastic an ideal source of horror for television science-fiction series like *Doctor Who* and *Doomwatch*. With script editor Terrance Dicks, art critic Francesca Gavin, New Series designer Matthew Savage and writer Robert Shearman. Produced by James Goss.

PHOTO GALLERY (8m32s) Slideshow of colour and black-and-white photos taken during production of *Terror of the Autons*, set to the Master's theme and sound effects. Compiled by Derek Handley.

NEXT

AUDIO OPTIONS Select **Commentary** to play the audio commentary in place of the main soundtrack when watching the episodes. With Katy Manning (Jo), Nicholas Courtney (the Brigadier) and producer/director Barry Letts on all four episodes.

— Select **Feature Audio** to reinstate the main soundtrack when watching the episodes.

INFO TEXT Select **On** to view subtitles when watching the episodes that provide information and anecdotes about the development, production, broadcast and history of *Terror of the Autons*. Written by Martin Wiggins.

PDF MATERIALS Accessible via a computer are the four episode listings from *Radio Times* for the original BBC1 broadcast of *Terror of the Autons*, plus the cover of the 31 December 1970 edition (issue 2460) and half-page article introducing the new series.

— Chocolate bar display packaging and the fifteen wrappers featuring the full story of 'Doctor Who Fights Masterplan "Q"', from the 1971 Nestlé *Doctor Who* promotion.

— Packaging, adverts and the six badges from the 1971 *Doctor Who* promotion by Kellogg's Sugar Smacks breakfast cereal. *Also on* The Mind of Evil

COMING SOON (1m1s) Trailer for the DVD release of *Frontios*.

SUBTITLES

Select **On** to view subtitles for all episodes and Special Features (except commentary).

RELATED EXTRAS

The UNIT Family — Day of the Daleks

Coming Soon trailer — Planet of the Spiders

The Doctor's Composer — The Sun Makers

TERROR OF THE ZYGONS

STORY No.80   SEASON No.13:1

Two discs with four episodes (96½ mins or 98mins with extended episode one) and 164 minutes of extras, plus commentary, music-only and surround-sound tracks, production subtitles and PDF items
Audio navigation of each disc's contents available by pressing Enter after the BBC ident

TARDIS TEAM Fourth Doctor, Harry, Sarah Jane, Brigadier and UNIT
TIME AND PLACE Contemporary Scotland and London
ADVERSARIES Shape-shifting Zygons; their pet monster the Skarasen
FIRST ON TV 30 August–20 September 1975
DVD RELEASE BBCDVD3482, 30 September 2013, PG
COVER Photo illustration by Lee Binding, dark green strip; version with older BBC logo on reverse
ORIGINAL RRP £20.42
— Episodes first released in The Fourth Doctor Time Capsule; BBCDVD3800, £62.99, 29 July 2013

STORY TEASER

The Brigadier recalls the Doctor to Earth to help him investigate the destruction of oil rigs off the Scottish coast. Examination of the wreckage reveals giant tooth marks: could the nearby Loch Ness really house a monster? When Harry is shot, Sarah attacked and the Brigadier gassed, the Doctor realises not everyone is who they appear to be, while deep beneath the loch alien forces are plotting their takeover of the world.

CONNECTIONS

The TARDIS also lands in Scotland in *The Highlanders* (1966/67), *Timelash* (1985) and *Tooth and Claw* (2006), as well as *The Hand of Fear* (1976)È it later transpired. The Doctor deals with trouble at sea in *Fury from the Deep* (1968), *The Sea Devils* (1972), *Warriors of the Deep* (1984) and *Cold War* (2013). The Zygons — which make their long-awaited return in *The Day of the Doctor* (2013) — join other shape-shifters (whether naturally or through technology) in the series such as the Chameleons in *The Faceless Ones* (1967), the Axons in *The Claws of Axos* (1971), the Rutan in *Horror of Fang Rock* (1977), the titular villain in *Meglos* (1980), the Navarino in *Delta and the Bannermen* (1987) and Prisoner Zero in *The Eleventh Hour* (2010). Of course, the most notable shape-shifter is the Doctor himself (and all Time Lords), whose own regenerations can be doubles of existing people: we know the First, Second, possibly Sixth, and Twelfth Doctors are. While some of these species also mimic the Doctor or his companions, further confusion is caused by some enemies constructing duplicates, such as the Daleks in *The Chase* (1965) and *Resurrection of the Daleks* (1984), the Kraals in *The Android Invasion* (1975), the Tarans in *The Androids of Tara* (1978), Sharaz Jek in *The Caves of Androzani* (1984) and the Nestene in *Rose* (2005) and *The Pandorica Opens* (2010), while the Tesselecta in *Let's Kill Hitler* (2011) can be made to look like anyone. Omega also takes on the Doctor's appearance in *Arc of Infinity* (1983), while the Sontarans clone Martha in *The Sontaran Stratagem* (2008). Robert Banks Stewart also wrote this season's finale *The Seeds of Doom* (1976), which like *Terror of the Zygons* was directed by Douglas Camfield, his last two *Doctor Who* stories (*see Index v*). John Woodnutt, playing both Broton and the Duke of Forgill (and Broton impersonating the Duke), is George Hibbert in *Spearhead from Space*, the Draconian emperor in *Frontier in Space* (1973) and Consul Seron in *The Keeper of Traken* (1981), while Angus Lennie (pub landlord Angus McRanald) is also Storr in *The Ice Warriors* (1967).

WORTH WATCHING

As the final major outing for UNIT, with the Brigadier's last regular appearance and Harry leaving the TARDIS crew, *Terror of the Zygons* makes the perfect conclusion to Tom Baker's first season as the Doctor, which saw him shaking off the trappings of his predecessor leaving him free to strike out into the universe in the following season. As it happens, this serial was held back to kick off the new run when the start was pulled back from January to the preceding autumn, so some of the sense of symmetry is lost. But watching it on its own, its quality is not diminished, thanks to an intriguing story, strong direction, top-notch performances and the striking design of the Zygons. This release is especially interesting for the reinsertion of a cut scene from episode one of the TARDIS's arrival that was included in the Target novelisation but long thought lost on film. Its discovery and restoration finally allows the episode to be presented as it was originally intended.

DISC ONE

THE EPISODES

All four episodes are restored from digital duplicates of the original two-inch colour videotape recordings used for broadcast, with location sequences in episodes three and four and some in episode two newly transferred from the original 16mm colour film. The episodes' mono soundtracks are remastered and the title sequences replaced by a modern transfer of the original 35mm film with credits remade to match the originals.

SPECIAL FEATURES

EPISODE 1 DIRECTOR'S CUT Select **On** to play an extended version of episode one when viewing via **Play All**, **Episode Selection** or **Scene Selection**. This includes a 1m40s scene of the TARDIS team arriving that was cut from the broadcast episode after it had been edited and scored due to technical problems, and was subsequently thought lost. A silent 16mm film copy of the missing material, only partly in colour, was discovered in 2012 and is reinserted into the episode, with the black-and-white sections recoloured manually, digitally painting in colour for key frames which is then extrapolated across further frames. The sound is restored from an existing audio recording of the location filming.

AUDIO OPTIONS Select **Commentary** to play the audio commentary in place of the main soundtrack when watching the episodes (including extended episode one). This is moderated by composer and sound engineer Mark Ayres, talking with writer Robert Banks Stewart [eps 1,2,3], production unit manager George Gallaccio [1,2,4], special sounds creator Dick Mills [1,2,4], producer Philip Hinchcliffe [2,3,4] and make-up supervisor Sylvia James [3,4].

— Select **Isolated Score** to hear only Geoffrey Burgon's music when watching the episodes (including extended episode one).

— Select **5.1 Audio** to hear the Dolby Digital surround soundtrack when watching the episodes, newly remixed for this release (including extended episode one).

— Select **Mono Audio** to reinstate the main soundtrack when watching the episodes.

INFO TEXT Select **On** to view subtitles when watching the episodes (including extended episode one) that provide information and anecdotes about the development, production, broadcast and history of *Terror of the Zygons*. Written by Martin Wiggins.

SUBTITLES

Select **On** to view subtitles for all episodes (none for commentary).

DISC TWO

SPECIAL FEATURES

SCOTCH MIST IN SUSSEX (31m24s) The making of *Terror of the Zygons*, including the origins of the story in the Loch Ness myth and contemporary boom in North Sea oil drilling; creating the feel of Scotland when filming on location in West Sussex; the model filming; designing the Zygon ship interior and other sets; realising the look of the Zygons; animating the Skarasen; the cast; phasing out UNIT; coping with complexity in the studio; and seeing off the competition from *Space: 1999* on ITV. With contributions from producer Philip Hinchcliffe, writer Robert Banks Stewart, designer Nigel Curzon, costume designer James Acheson, visual effects assistant Steve Bowman, actors John Levene and John Woodnutt (interviewed in 1993), and television historian Simon Farquhar. Produced by Ed Stradling.

REMEMBERING DOUGLAS CAMFIELD (30m3s) Profile of director Douglas Camfield, who died in 1984, from his early work on the first years of *Doctor Who* to directing many of the most popular and successful television series of the 1970s. With memories from his son Joggs and colleagues Graeme Harper, Philip Hinchcliffe, Celia Imrie, John Levene, Jonathan Newth, Peter Purves and Robert Banks Stewart. Narrated by Glen Allen, produced by Ed Stradling.

THE UNIT FAMILY – PART THREE (28m28s) Examination of the UNIT era story by story, by the people involved in creating it. This edition covers *The Time Warrior* to *The Seeds of Doom* (1974–76) plus *Mawdryn Undead* (1983), *The Five Doctors* (1983) and *Battlefield* (1989), including the introduction of Sarah Jane Smith, the treachery of Captain Yates, the changeover from Jon Pertwee to Tom Baker, the addition of Harry Sullivan, the phasing out of UNIT from the series under a new production team, and the enduring popularity of the Brigadier. With contributions from producers Philip Hinchcliffe and Barry Letts (interviewed in 2005), script editor Terrance Dicks, and actors Tom Baker, Nicholas Courtney (the Brigadier), Richard Franklin (Yates) and John Levene (Benton). Produced by Richard Molesworth. *Part one is on* Inferno *(and* Special Edition*); part two is on* Day of the Daleks

DOCTOR WHO STORIES – TOM BAKER (22m56s) Recorded in 2003 for BBC2's *The Story of Doctor Who*, actor Tom Baker recalls his experiences of playing the Doctor from 1974 to 1981.

DOCTOR WHO STORIES – ELISABETH SLADEN (19m45s) Recorded in 2003 for BBC2's *The Story of Doctor Who*, actor Elisabeth Sladen recalls her experiences of playing companion Sarah Jane Smith from 1974 to 1976. *Part one is on* Invasion of the Dinosaurs

SUBTITLES Select On to view subtitles for all Special Features on disc two.

NEXT

MERRY–GO–ROUND – THE FUEL FISHERS (19m39s) Edition of the BBC Schools programme, first broadcast on BBC2 on Monday 9 May 1977, in which Elisabeth Sladen visits a North Sea drilling rig to find out how oil is prospected for and drilled.

SOUTH TODAY (3m10s) Report from the Monday 17 March 1975 edition of the BBC local news programme on the location filming at Climping Beach in West Sussex, including an interview with Tom Baker.

PHOTO GALLERY (5m8s) Slideshow of colour and black-and-white photos taken during production of *Terror of the Zygons*, including design department photos of the sets and shots of the Zygon spaceship model. Set to music and sound effects from the story. Compiled by Paul Shields.

PDF MATERIALS Accessible via a computer are the four episode listings from *Radio Times* for the original BBC1 broadcast of *Terror of the Zygons*, with artwork by Frank Bellamy, and a two-page article about the Loch Ness monster with colour illustration by Bellamy published the week of episode one.

COMING SOON (1m3s) Trailer for the DVD release of *The Moonbase*.

EASTER EGGS

There are two hidden features on these discs to find. *See Appendix 2 for details*

RELATED EXTRAS

Dressing Doctor Who — The Mutants

Coming Soon trailer — Scream of the Shalka

Playing in the Green Cathedral — The Seeds of Doom

THE **THIRD DOCTOR COLLECTION**

Boxset of **CARNIVAL OF MONSTERS, THE CLAWS OF AXOS, THE GREEN DEATH, INFERNO, SPEARHEAD FROM SPACE** and **THE THREE DOCTORS**

DVD RELEASE BBCDVD2263, 6 November 2006, PG

SLIPCASE Photo illustration by Clayton Hickman, silvered logo and title, purple/black background

ORIGINAL RRP £49.99

This set was released exclusively by Amazon.co.uk in a limited edition. Each story has the same contents and packaging as the individual releases — at the time all the Third Doctor stories that were out on DVD — held in a cardboard slipcase. All six have since been re-released as Special Edition versions with more advanced restoration and additional features.

● *See individual stories for full contents*

THE **THREE DOCTORS**

STORY No.65   SEASON No.10:1

One disc with four episodes (98½ mins) and 86½ minutes of extras, plus commentary track and production subtitles

TARDIS TEAM Third Doctor, Jo, Brigadier and UNIT

TIME AND PLACE Contemporary England and inside a black hole

ADVERSARIES Omega (1st appearance); anti-matter Gel creatures

FIRST ON TV 30 December 1972–20 January 1973

DVD RELEASE BBCDVD1144, 24 November 2003, PG

COVER Photo illustration by Clayton Hickman, purple strip
— Original release with cover sticker reading 'Doctor Who 40th Anniversary 1963–2003'

ORIGINAL RRP £19.99
— Also issued in a Gift Set with Corgi die-cast model of Bessie
— Also released in The Third Doctor Collection; BBCDVD2263, £49.99, 6 November 2006

STORY TEASER

An impossible light ray emanating from a black hole brings a strange energy creature to Earth intent on hunting the Doctor. Unable to neutralise it, he seeks held from the Time Lords, but even their great power is being drained by the black hole and they must resort to desperate measures to give the Doctor the assistance he needs. His first two incarnations are plucked from his past and brought forward to help, if they can stop arguing. When the Doctor ventures into the black hole itself he finds a world of anti-matter and a legendary Time Lord bent on revenge.

CONNECTIONS

It transpires in *The Deadly Assassin* (1976) that the Time Lords' power derives from a singularity held in stasis beneath their city, which their founder Rassilon retrieved from a black hole that is assumed to be the one created by Omega. Yet the black hole featured here is suggested to be in deep space and still has its singularity, so perhaps it was Omega's work that enabled Rassilon to later harness a different black hole. In *The Satan Pit* (2006) when flying the TARDIS out of a black hole the Doctor asserts his people invented them in the first place. In *The Horns of Nimon* (1979/80) artificial black holes are used to warp space-time and create an entrance to hyperspace. The Doctor has further trouble with anti-matter in *Planet of Evil* (1975) and *Arc of Infinity* (1983) — the latter being Omega's second attempt to return home — although it proves helpful for trapping Cybermen in doors in *Earthshock* (1982). Multiple incarnations of the Doctor are brought together again in *The Five Doctors* (1983) and *The Day of the Doctor* (2013), but they can also happen across each other by chance, as in *The Two Doctors* (1985) and *Time Crash* (2007). Writers Bob Baker and Dave Martin began on *Doctor Who* with *The Claws of Axos* (1971) and continued contributing scripts throughout the 1970s (*see Index v*), while Lennie Mayne also directed *The Curse of Peladon* (1972), *The Monster of Peladon* (1974) and *The Hand of Fear* (1976). As well as reappearances by William Hartnell and Patrick Troughton, Stephen Thorne (Omega) returns, having played Azal in *The Dæmons*; he's also an Ogron in *Frontier in Space* (1973) and Eldrad in *The Hand of Fear*. Rex Robinson (Dr Tyler) was a favourite of Mayne's and also appears in *The Monster of Peladon* and *The Hand of Fear*, while Clyde Pollitt (Time Lord Chancellor) is one of the Time Lords who sentences the Doctor to exile in *The War Games* (1969), possibly the same character.

WORTH WATCHING

It's the first time different incarnations of the Doctor are brought together, something that's now thought of as *de rigueur* for anniversary specials, even though it has since happened as often on other occasions (and strictly speaking this isn't an anniversary tale, coming nearer the start of the show's tenth year than its end). That viewers had written to the production team suggesting the idea is a sign of the growing fan audience, not just aware of the show's history but wanting to see at least elements of it again. The story is equally pivotal to the future of the programme, however, ending the Doctor's exile on Earth and establishing aspects of the Time Lords' history and society that will be picked up by later writers.

THE EPISODES

All four episodes are restored from digital duplicates of the original two-inch colour videotape recordings used for broadcast and their mono soundtracks remastered. The opening title sequences are replaced by a modern transfer of the original 35mm film with title captions overlaid from the episode recordings.

SPECIAL FEATURES *ALSO ON SPECIAL EDITION

***40TH ANNIVERSARY CELEBRATION** (3m) Compilation of clips from all eras of Classic *Doctor Who*, set to Orbital's version of the theme music, included on all releases in 2003.

***PEBBLE MILL AT ONE** (20m44s) Extract from the Friday 21 December 1973 edition of the BBC1 lunchtime magazine programme introduced by Bob Langley, in which David Seymour talks to Bernard Wilkie of the BBC Visual Effects department about *Doctor Who's* monsters and demonstrates some special effects techniques, while Marian Foster interviews Patrick Troughton.

***BLUE PETER** (13m40s) Extract from the Monday 5 November 1973 edition of the BBC1 children's magazine programme in which Jon Pertwee drives his Whomobile into the studio to give Peter Purves a rundown of its features and explains its construction. Purves, Lesley Judd and John Noakes then mark the tenth anniversary of *Doctor Who* with a look through past clips. *Clips section also on* The Tenth Planet

***BSB HIGHLIGHTS** (10m15s) Trailers, links and interviews from the British Satellite Broadcasting channel Galaxy's '31 Who' *Doctor Who* weekend on 22/23 September 1990. Debbie Flint talks to Nicholas Courtney and Terrance Dicks about *The Three Doctors*; John Nathan-Turner interviews writers Bob Baker and Dave Martin about their creation of K9; and Shyama Perera talks to Jon Pertwee about his time on the show.

PANOPTICON '93 (29m45s) Jon Pertwee on stage at the *Doctor Who* convention in London on Saturday 4 September 1993, talking to Steve Wickham about the Third Doctor radio serial *The Paradise of Death* then being broadcast on BBC Radio 5, his career and time in *Doctor Who*, and what happened to the Whomobile. They're joined by Katy Manning, who recalls her one and only argument with Pertwee, and briefly by Nicholas Courtney.

▶

***FIVE FACES OF DOCTOR WHO TRAIL** (4m12s) Trailer for the series of repeats on BBC2 in November 1981 that included *The Three Doctors*, along with *An Unearthly Child* (1963), *The Krotons* (1968/69), *Carnival of Monsters* (1973) and *Logopolis* (1981). *Also on* Carnival of Monsters *(and* Special Edition*)*

INFORMATION TEXT Select **On** to view subtitles when watching the episodes that provide information and anecdotes about the development, production, broadcast and history of *The Three Doctors*. Written by Richard Molesworth.

***COMMENTARY** Select **On** to play the audio commentary in place of the main soundtrack when watching the episodes. With Nicholas Courtney (the Brigadier), Katy Manning (Jo) and producer Barry Letts on all four episodes.

***PHOTO GALLERY** (3m55s) Slideshow of colour and black-and-white photos taken during production of *The Three Doctors*, including publicity shots of the three lead actors, plus the photo shoot for *Radio Times*, the cover of the 28 December 1972 edition (issue 2564) and Frank Bellamy's illustrations for the episode billings. Set to sound effects from the story. Compiled by Ralph Montagu.

***BBC 1 TRAIL** (49s) Preview of *The Three Doctors* broadcast on BBC1 on Friday 29 December 1972, reconstructed by matching clips from the first episode to an audio recording of the trailer made at the time of broadcast. Features the unused 'Delaware' version of the theme music.

SUBTITLES

Select **On** to view subtitles for all episodes and Special Features, or for the commentary.

RELATED EXTRAS

The Omega Factor — Arc of Infinity
The UNIT Family — Day of the Daleks
Dressing Doctor Who — The Mutants

THE **THREE DOCTORS** SPECIAL EDITION

STORY No.65   SEASON No.10:1

Released with **THE ROBOTS OF DEATH SPECIAL EDITION** and **THE TOMB OF THE CYBERMEN SPECIAL EDITION** in the **REVISITATIONS 3** boxset

Two discs with four episodes (98½ mins) and 116½ minutes of extras, plus commentary track, production subtitles and PDF items

Audio navigation of each disc's contents available by pressing Enter after the BBC ident

TARDIS TEAM Third Doctor, Jo, Brigadier and UNIT

TIME AND PLACE Contemporary England and inside a black hole

ADVERSARIES Omega (1st appearance); anti-matter Gel creatures

FIRST ON TV 30 December 1972–20 January 1973

DVD RELEASE BBCDVD3003B, 13 February 2012, PG (disc two U)

COVER Photo illustration by Clayton Hickman, dark orange strip; version with older BBC logo on reverse

ORIGINAL RRP £35.74 (boxset)

STORY TEASER

An impossible light ray emanating from a black hole brings a strange energy creature to Earth intent on hunting the Doctor. Unable to neutralise it, he seeks held from the Time Lords, but even their great power is being drained by the black hole and they must resort to desperate measures to give the Doctor the assistance he needs. His first two incarnations are plucked from his past and brought forward to help, if they can stop arguing. When the Doctor ventures into the black hole itself he finds a world of anti-matter and a legendary Time Lord bent on revenge.

CONNECTIONS

It transpires in *The Deadly Assassin* (1976) that the Time Lords' power derives from a singularity held in stasis beneath their city, which their founder Rassilon retrieved from a black hole that is assumed to be the one created by Omega. Yet the black hole featured here is suggested to be in deep space and still has its singularity, so perhaps it was Omega's work that enabled Rassilon to later harness a different black hole. In *The Satan Pit* (2006) when flying the TARDIS out of a black hole the Doctor asserts his people invented them in the first place. In *The Horns of Nimon* (1979/80) artificial black holes are used to warp space-time and create an entrance to hyperspace. The Doctor has further trouble with anti-matter in *Planet of Evil* (1975) and *Arc of Infinity* (1983) — the latter being Omega's second attempt to return home — although it proves helpful for trapping Cybermen in doors in *Earthshock* (1982). Multiple incarnations of the Doctor are brought together again in *The Five Doctors* (1983) and *The Day of the Doctor* (2013), but they can also happen across each other by chance, as in *The Two Doctors* (1985) and *Time Crash* (2007). Writers Bob Baker and Dave Martin began on *Doctor Who* with *The Claws of Axos* (1971) and continued contributing scripts throughout the 1970s (*see Index v*), while Lennie Mayne also directed *The Curse of Peladon* (1972), *The Monster of Peladon* (1974) and *The Hand of Fear* (1976). As well as reappearances by William Hartnell and Patrick Troughton, Stephen Thorne (Omega) returns, having played Azal in *The Dæmons*; he's also an Ogron in *Frontier in Space* (1973) and Eldrad in *The Hand of Fear*. Rex Robinson (Dr Tyler) was a favourite of Mayne's and also appears in *The Monster of Peladon* and *The Hand of Fear*, while Clyde Pollitt (Time Lord Chancellor) is one of the Time Lords who sentences the Doctor to exile in *The War Games* (1969), possibly the same character.

WORTH WATCHING

This Special Edition features further clean-up of the episodes compared to the previous release and additional Special Features. It's the first time different incarnations of the Doctor are brought together, something that's now thought of as *de rigueur* for anniversary specials, even though it has since happened as often on other occasions (and strictly speaking this isn't an anniversary tale, coming nearer the start of the show's tenth year than its end). That viewers had written to the production team suggesting the idea is a sign of the growing fan audience, not just aware of the show's history but wanting to see at least elements of it again. The story is equally pivotal to the future of the programme, however, ending the Doctor's exile on Earth and establishing aspects of the Time Lords' history and society that will be picked up by later writers.

DISC ONE

THE EPISODES

All four episodes are restored from digital duplicates of the original two-inch colour videotape recordings used for broadcast and their mono soundtracks remastered. The title sequences are replaced by a modern transfer of the original 35mm film with credits remade to match the originals.

SPECIAL FEATURES   *REPEATED FROM PREVIOUS RELEASE

*PEBBLE MILL AT ONE (20m44s) Extract from the Friday 21 December 1973 edition of the BBC1 lunchtime magazine programme introduced by Bob Langley, in which David Seymour talks to Bernard Wilkie of the BBC Visual Effects department about *Doctor Who*'s monsters and demonstrates some special effects techniques, while Marian Foster interviews Patrick Troughton.

*BLUE PETER 5/11/73 (13m40s) Extract from the Monday 5 November 1973 edition of the BBC1 children's magazine programme in which Jon Pertwee drives his Whomobile into the studio to give Peter Purves a rundown of its features and explains its construction. Purves, Lesley Judd and John Noakes then mark the tenth anniversary of *Doctor Who* with a look through past clips. *Clips section also on* The Tenth Planet

*BSB HIGHLIGHTS (10m15s) Trailers, links and interviews from the British Satellite Broadcasting channel Galaxy's '31 Who' *Doctor Who* weekend on 22/23 September 1990. Debbie Flint talks to Nicholas Courtney and Terrance Dicks about *The Three Doctors*; John Nathan-Turner interviews writers Bob Baker and Dave Martin about their creation of K9; and Shyama Perera talks to Jon Pertwee about his time on the show.

*'FIVE FACES OF DOCTOR WHO' TRAIL (4m12s) Trailer for the series of repeats on BBC2 in November 1981 that included *The Three Doctors*, along with *An Unearthly Child* (1963), *The Krotons* (1968/69), *Carnival of Monsters* (1973) and *Logopolis* (1981). *Also on* Carnival of Monsters *(and* Special Edition*)*

*BBC1 TRAIL (49s) Preview of *The Three Doctors* broadcast on BBC1 on Friday 29 December 1972, reconstructed by matching clips from the first episode to an audio recording of the trailer made at the time of broadcast. Features the unused 'Delaware' version of the theme music.

NEXT

*40TH ANNIVERSARY PROMO (3m) Compilation of clips from all eras of Classic *Doctor Who*, set to Orbital's version of the theme music, included on all releases in 2003.

*AUDIO OPTIONS Select **Commentary** to play the audio commentary recorded for the previous release in place of the main soundtrack when watching the episodes. With Nicholas Courtney (the Brigadier), Katy Manning (Jo) and producer Barry Letts on all four episodes.

— Select **Feature Audio** to reinstate the main soundtrack when watching the episodes.

INFO TEXT Select **On** to view subtitles when watching the episodes that provide information and anecdotes about the development, production, broadcast and history of *The Three Doctors*, updated and expanded from the previous release. Written by David Brunt.

PDF MATERIALS Accessible via a computer are the four episode listings from *Radio Times* for the original BBC1 broadcast of *The Three Doctors*, with illustrations by Frank Bellamy; the cover of the 28 December 1972 edition (issue 2564) and a two-page article about the Doctor's companions, featuring interviews with Carole Ann Ford, Frazer Hines and Katy Manning; and a preview of that issue from the week before.

COMING SOON (1m26s) Trailer for the DVD release of *The Face of Evil*.

SUBTITLES

Select **On** to view subtitles for all episodes and Special Features on disc one (except commentary).

DISC TWO

SPECIAL FEATURES   *REPEATED FROM PREVIOUS RELEASE

HAPPY BIRTHDAY TO WHO (23m12s) The making of *The Three Doctors*, including the decision to bring back the past Doctors for the season debut; writing the script and having to cut back on William Hartnell's involvement; working with the director; portraying Omega; the contrasting personalities of Jon Pertwee and Patrick Troughton; and filming on location (plus how the sites look today). With contributions from producer Barry Letts (interviewed in 2008), script editor Terrance Dicks, writer Bob Baker, and actors Katy Manning and Stephen Thorne. Narrated by Toby Hadoke, produced by Richard Higson.

WAS DOCTOR WHO RUBBISH? (14m1s) Fans defend the series against the common misconceptions and unrealistic expectations some people have, from wobbly sets to the prevalence of quarries, cheap monsters, bad acting, unrealistic effects, and a lack of emotion. With Katreena Dare, Karen Davies, Thomas Guerrier and Joseph Lidster. Produced by Chris Chapman and Richard Higson.

GIRLS, GIRLS, GIRLS – 1970S (21m16s) Three female companions from the 1970s discuss their time on *Doctor Who*, the portrayal of their characters and to what extent their experiences differed. With Louise Jameson (Leela), Caroline John (Liz) and Katy Manning (Jo). Introduced by Peter Purves, produced by Steve Broster.

*****PHOTO GALLERY** (3m55s) Slideshow of colour and black-and-white photos taken during production of *The Three Doctors*, including publicity shots of the three lead actors, plus the photo shoot for *Radio Times*, the cover of the 28 December 1972 edition (issue 2564) and Frank Bellamy's illustrations for the episode billings. Set to sound effects from the story. Compiled by Ralph Montagu.

SUBTITLES Select **On** to view subtitles for all Special Features on disc two.

RELATED EXTRAS

The Omega Factor — Arc of Infinity
The UNIT Family — Day of the Daleks
Dressing Doctor Who — The Mutants
Coming Soon trailer — The Sensorites

TIME AND THE RANI

STORY No.144   SEASON No.24:1

One disc with four episodes (98½ mins) and 73 minutes of extras, plus commentary track, production subtitles and PDF items
Audio navigation of disc contents available by pressing Enter after the BBC ident

TARDIS TEAM Seventh Doctor, Mel
TIME AND PLACE Planet Lakertya
ADVERSARIES The Rani (2nd appearance); man-sized bat-like Tetraps
FIRST ON TV 7–28 September 1987
DVD RELEASE BBCDVD2808, 13 September 2010, PG
COVER Photo illustration by Clayton Hickman, pink strip; version with older BBC logo on reverse
ORIGINAL RRP £19.99
— Episodes released in the Regeneration box; BBCDVD3801, £61.27, 24 June 2013

STORY TEASER

The Rani hijacks the TARDIS, causing the Doctor to regenerate. His disoriented state makes it easier for her to gain his unwitting help in her latest diabolical experiment on the planet Lakertya, where she has the locals in thrall and a rocket aimed at an approaching asteroid. As the Doctor gradually regains his senses, he must uncover the Rani's plans while keeping himself and Mel out of the clutches of the blood-guzzling Tetraps.

CONNECTIONS

This was the first regeneration to occur at the start rather than the end of a story (coming before the opening titles even), and only the next change from the Seventh into the Eighth Doctors follows suit, occurring a quarter of the way through *The Movie* (1996). Even when we eventually get to see the Eighth and War Doctors' regenerations, they come at the end of their episodes. Kate O'Mara as the Rani debuts in *The Mark of the Rani* (1985), also written by Pip and Jane Baker, who scripted five episodes of the fourteen-part *The Trial of a Time Lord* (1986) too. Director Andrew Morgan returned the following year to helm *Remembrance of the Daleks* (1988). Donald Pickering (Beyus) plays Millennian lawyer Eyesen in *The Keys of Marinus* (1964) and Captain Blade in *The Faceless Ones* (1967), the latter also featuring Wanda Ventham (Faroon) as Jean Rock, while she plays Thea Ransome in *Image of the Fendahl* (1977).

WORTH WATCHING

Time and the Rani is much derided among fans and would likely be totally ignored were it not a regeneration story. To be fair it's hard to pin down specifically what's amiss. The plot is arguably no dafter than some more respected stories, the production is slick, making effective use of the burgeoning digital video effects technology of the time, and the monsters are well realised. Perhaps in combination, though, it's rather too garish: the predominantly pink colouring, the camp portrayal of the Rani — a popular character when she first appeared and the series is no stranger to over-the-top villains, but making her dress up as Mel was perhaps going too far — and a new actor as the Doctor trying to find his feet. As ever with received wisdom, however, it's better to watch for yourself and come to your own conclusions.

THE EPISODES

All four episodes are restored from digital duplicates of the original one-inch colour videotape recordings used for broadcast, with model shots newly transferred from the original 35mm colour film. Their mono soundtracks are remastered and the computer-generated title sequences are replaced by a digital duplicate of the original one-inch colour videotape recording (retaining the earlier version mistakenly used on episode four) and credits remade to match the originals.

SPECIAL FEATURES

THE LAST CHANCE SALOON (28m39s) The making of *Time and the Rani* at a time when *Doctor Who* was at a low ebb in the opinions of BBC management, its production team and fans alike. Including the decision to keep the show on air given the furore caused by the last attempt to cancel it; insisting the producer stay but recasting the lead actor; finding a new script editor; reworking the script to include the regeneration; working out the character of the new Doctor; bringing back the Rani and impersonating Bonnie Langford; moving into the digital era with the video effects and title sequence; and a failure to re-grab the audience. With contributions from BBC head of series and serials Jonathan Powell, producer John Nathan-Turner (interviewed in 1994), script editor Andrew Cartmel, writers Pip and Jane Baker, director Andrew Morgan, graphic designer Oliver Elmes, and actors Sylvester McCoy and Kate O'Mara. Written by Nev Fountain, narrated by Richard Heffer, produced by Ed Stradling.

7D FX (11m22s) How the visual effects for *Time and the Rani* were realised by combining practical, video and model effects for greater realism, including the bubble traps, the Rani's citadel and rocket, and the Tetrap lair. Includes footage from the model shooting not used in the final episodes. With video effects designer Dave Chapman, visual effects designer Colin Mapson and visual effects assistant Mike Tucker. Produced by John Kelly.

HELTER–SKELTER (9m17s) Graphic designer Oliver Elmes and CGI animator Gareth Edwards talk about how they conceived and created the Seventh Doctor title sequence using the then-latest in computer graphics technology. Includes Elmes' original storyboard sketches.

LAKERTYA (2m4s) How the conception of the planet Lakertya changed from the writers' intention of a forest world to become yet another rocky quarry to accommodate the director's practical requirements. With Pip and Jane Baker and Andrew Morgan.

HOT GOSSIP (2m28s) Actors Sylvester McCoy and Kate O'Mara recall the fun of working with Donald Pickering and Wanda Ventham on *Time and the Rani*. With director Andrew Morgan.

ON LOCATION (4m6s) Report from the Tuesday 5 May 1987 edition of the BBC1 morning news magazine programme *Breakfast Time* about the location recording for *Time and the Rani* in Cloford Quarry, Somerset on 7 April, in which reporter Guy Michelmore talks to Sylvester McCoy, Kate O'Mara and producer John Nathan-Turner.

NEXT

BLUE PETER (1m22s) Extract from the Monday 2 March 1987 edition of the BBC1 children's magazine programme in which Janet Ellis meets the newly cast Sylvester McCoy.

PHOTO GALLERY (8m16s) Slideshow of colour photos taken during production of *Time and the Rani*, set to music from the story. Compiled by Derek Handley.

AUDIO OPTIONS Select **Commentary** to play the audio commentary in place of the main soundtrack when watching the episodes. With Sylvester McCoy, Bonnie Langford (Mel) and writers Pip and Jane Baker on all four episodes.

— Select **Feature Audio** to reinstate the main soundtrack when watching the episodes.

INFO TEXT Select **On** to view subtitles when watching the episodes that provide information and anecdotes about the development, production, broadcast and history of *Time and the Rani*. Written by Stephen James Walker.

PDF MATERIALS Accessible via a computer are the four episode listings from *Radio Times* for the original BBC1 broadcast of *Time and the Rani*, a one-page article promoting the new season and a mention of available merchandise.

COMING SOON (2m8s) Trailer for the Special Edition DVD releases of *The Caves of Androzani*, *The Movie* and *The Talons of Weng-Chiang* in the **Revisitations** 1 boxset.

SUBTITLES

Select **On** to view subtitles for all episodes and Special Features (except commentary).

EASTER EGGS

There are three hidden features on this disc to find. *See Appendix 2 for details*

RELATED EXTRAS

Coming Soon trailer — Revenge of the Cybermen, Silver Nemesis

THE **TIME MEDDLER**

STORY No.17   SEASON No.2:9

One disc with four episodes (97½ mins) and 28 minutes of extras, plus commentary track, production subtitles, PDF items and text content

TARDIS TEAM First Doctor, Steven, Vicki

TIME AND PLACE North England, 1066

ADVERSARIES Renegade Time Lord the Monk (1st appearance); Viking marauders

FIRST ON TV 3–24 July 1965

DVD RELEASE BBCDVD2331, 4 February 2008, PG

COVER Photo illustration by Clayton Hickman, dark turquoise strip

ORIGINAL RRP £12.99

STORY TEASER

Newly arrived aboard the TARDIS, Steven Taylor doesn't believe the Doctor's claim that it's a time machine. Its next landing on a beach apparently on Earth doesn't clarify the issue, especially as the travellers find both a Viking helmet and a wristwatch. While the Doctor learns they're in England, 1066, Steven and Vicki discover further futuristic items at a nearby monastery. How can the lone monk there have such technology in this century, and what are his plans for the invading Vikings?

CONNECTIONS

This is the first time the Doctor encounters one of his own people on screen, although not named as a Time Lord, a designation that isn't coined until *The War Games* (1969) when he next has a confrontation with a fellow renegade, the War Chief. Other rebel Time Lords who mess around in Earth's history include the Master in *The King's Demons* (1983) and the Rani in *The Mark of the Rani* (1985). The Monk himself, played again by Peter Butterworth, returns in *The Daleks' Master Plan* (1965/66) to take his revenge on the Doctor. Aliens finding themselves on Earth in our past inevitably risk altering the future as we know it, if only by taking over, but those seeking deliberately to rewrite time include the Great Intelligence (*The Abominable Snowmen*, 1967; *The Snowmen*, 2012), Sutekh (*Pyramids of Mars*, 1975), the Mandragora Helix (*The Masque of Mandragora*, 1976), the Terileptils (*The Visitation*, 1982), Fenric (*The Curse of Fenric*, 1989), the Gelth (*The Unquiet Dead*, 2005), the Carrionites (*The Shakespeare Code*, 2007), the Pyroviles (*The Fires of Pompeii*,

2008), the Cybermen (*The Next Doctor*, 2008), the Saturnyne (*The Vampires of Venice*, 2010), and the Silents (*The Impossible Astronaut/Day of the Moon*, 2011). Dennis Spooner had just finished being the series' story editor when he wrote *The Time Meddler*, having previously written historical stories *The Reign of Terror* (1964) and *The Romans* (1965), while it was the second full story directed by Douglas Camfield after *The Crusade* (1965); he went on to direct many of the most admired *Doctor Who* stories (*see Index v*). Alethea Charlton (Edith) plays Hur in the very first *Doctor Who* story, *An Unearthly Child* (1963), while David Anderson (Sven) is the Aztec guard captain in *The Aztecs* (1964) and Sir Reynier de Marun in *The Crusade* (1965). Geoffrey Cheshire (Viking leader), Michael Guest (Hunter) and Norman Hartley (Ulf) all have small roles in later Camfield-directed stories *The Daleks' Master Plan* and *The Invasion* (1968), while Ronald Rich (Gunnar) plays Trantis in the former's prelude *Mission to the Unknown* (1965).

WORTH WATCHING

Long before we knew of Time Lords and Gallifrey, the Doctor's first meeting with another of his own people feels like a significant moment, and yet little is suggested about their common heritage. Their similarity is defined purely in terms of each possessing a TARDIS, and although the Doctor sets out to scupper the Monk's plan to change the outcome of the Battle of Hastings, this is perhaps hypocritical coming weeks after he happily started the Great Fire of Rome in *The Romans* (by the same writer). This story seems to clarify the Doctor's insistence to Barbara in *The Aztecs* that she couldn't rewrite history as a matter of morality rather than ability.

THE EPISODES

Episode one is restored from an edited 16mm film copy of the original black-and-white videotape recording, returned from a Nigerian broadcaster in January 1985, with cut sections reinstated from a transfer made in 1994 of a complete 16mm film copy of the episode then held by Ian Levine, having been acquired from a collector by Ian Sheward in 1981. Episode two was restored for VHS release in 2002 from a 16mm film copy of the original black-and-white videotape recording that survived in the archive; further picture restoration was done for this release and the news footage of a replica Viking ship is retransferred from the original 35mm black-and-white film. Episodes three and four were restored for VHS release in 2002 from edited 16mm film copies of the original black-and-white videotape recordings, returned from Nigeria in January 1985; further picture restoration was done for this release and cut sections in episode three reinstated from a transfer made in 1994 of a complete 16mm film copy then held by Ian Levine, having been recovered by Ian Sheward in 1981, but a 12-second cut in episode four was unable to be replaced (see **Special Features**). The episodes' mono soundtracks are remastered, the title sequences replaced by a modern transfer of the best surviving copy of the original 35mm film and end credits remade to match the originals. The VidFIRE motion-smoothing process is not applied owing to lower than optimum picture quality.

SPECIAL FEATURES

VERITY LAMBERT OBITUARY Verity Lambert OBE, the very first and groundbreaking producer of *Doctor Who*, died on 22 November 2007 and the commentary on this disc was her last contribution to the DVD releases. Scroll through a written eulogy covering her extensive contribution to British television over five decades.

VERITY LAMBERT PHOTO GALLERY (2m12s) Slideshow of colour and black-and-white photos of Verity taken throughout her career.

AUDIO OPTIONS Select **Commentary** to play the audio commentary in place of the main soundtrack when watching the episodes. This is moderated by writer and journalist Clayton Hickman, talking with Peter Purves (Steven), producer Verity Lambert, story editor Donald Tosh and designer Barry Newbery on all four episodes.

— Select **Feature Audio** to reinstate the main soundtrack when watching the episodes.

INFO TEXT Select **On** to view subtitles when watching the episodes that provide information and anecdotes about the development, production, broadcast and history of *The Time Meddler*. Written by Richard Molesworth.

STRIPPED FOR ACTION – THE FIRST DOCTOR (16m5s) *Doctor Who* comic strips have run in various publications since the early days of the television series. This examines the First Doctor's comic strip adventures in Polystyle Publications' *TV Comic*. With contributions from magazine editors Alan Barnes and Gary Russell, artist Bill Mevin, and comics historians John Ainsworth and Jeremy Bentham. Directed by Marcus Hearn. *See Index iii for further editions*

NEXT

THE LOST TWELVE SECONDS (1m5s) A section of episode four of *The Time Meddler* from which a cut made by an overseas broadcaster is filled using descriptions of the action from the script and a recording of the soundtrack made on audio tape when the episode was originally broadcast.

RESTORATION (4m55s) Comparisons of picture and sound quality before and after restoration, demonstrating the techniques used on this and other black-and-white episodes. Includes more of the news footage of the replica Viking ship taken from *The Landing of the Vikings* broadcast on Tuesday 28 June 1949. With explanatory captions.

PHOTO GALLERY (2m39s) Slideshow of black-and-white photos taken during production of *The Time Meddler*, including design department photos of the sets. Set to stock music. Compiled by Derek Handley.

COMING SOON (1m13s) Trailer for the 25th Anniversary Edition DVD release of *The Five Doctors*.

RADIO TIMES LISTINGS Accessible via a computer is a PDF file of the four episode listings for the original BBC1 broadcast of *The Time Meddler* and an article introducing the story.

SUBTITLES

Select **On** to view subtitles for all episodes and Special Features (except commentary).

RELATED EXTRAS

Coming Soon trailer — Doctor Who and the Silurians, The Sea Devils, Warriors of the Deep

THE **TIME MONSTER**

STORY No.64   SEASON No.9:5

Released with **THE HORNS OF NIMON** and **UNDERWORLD** in the **MYTHS AND LEGENDS** boxset

One disc with six episodes (148 mins) and 35½ minutes of extras, plus commentary track, production subtitles and PDF items
Audio navigation of disc contents available by pressing Enter after the BBC ident

TARDIS TEAM Third Doctor, Jo, Brigadier and UNIT

TIME AND PLACE Contemporary England and ancient Atlantis

ADVERSARIES First Master (7th appearance); Kronos the Chronovore

FIRST ON TV 20 May–24 June 1972

DVD RELEASE BBCDVD2851(A), 29 March 2010, PG (episodes and extras bar DVD trailer U; boxset 12)

COVER Photo illustration by Clayton Hickman, light blue strip; version with older BBC logo on reverse

ORIGINAL RRP £49.99 (boxset)

STORY TEASER

What links the time experiments of an obscure Cambridge professor with seismic activity in the Mediterranean? When UNIT are brought in to view a demonstration of the former, the Doctor quickly realises his nemesis the Master is up to no good again. With a mysterious crystal, he is attempting to control Kronos, a creature that can manipulate and consume time itself. But in ancient Atlantis the crystal co-exists and draws both the Master and the Doctor on an epic journey that only one of them can survive.

CONNECTIONS

This is the first rematch with the Master following his escape from prison earlier in the season (*The Sea Devils*, 1972) and the penultimate appearance of Roger Delgado owing to his untimely death the following year. Another professor experimenting with time features in *City of Death* (1979) but with more benign motives (not so his boss), while both the Argolin and a human scientist attempt to use tachyonics to rejuvenate people in *The Leisure Hive* (1980). Kartz and Reimer have developed a partially working time capsule in *The Two Doctors* (1985), and in *The Lazarus Experiment* (2007) the titular professor uses sound waves to make himself young again. Theodore Maxtible and Edward Waterfield were trying to manipulate time with mirrors but only succeeded in attracting the attention of Daleks in *The Evil of the Daleks* (1967). In *The Dæmons* (1971) it's suggested Atlantis was destroyed by Azal, while the Doctor finds himself in its modern-day remains in *The Underwater Menace* (1967). He encounters an image of the Minotaur in the Land of Fiction in *The Mind Robber* (1968) at which point he believes the creature to be a myth but meets the real thing here. He later meets the Minotaur-like Nimon in *The Horns of Nimon* (1979/80) and a related species in *The God Complex* (2011). Robert Sloman also wrote, with an uncredited Barry Letts, *The Dæmons*, *The Green Death* (1973) and *Planet of the Spiders* (1974), while Paul Bernard also directed *Day of the Daleks* (1972) and *Frontier in Space* (1973). Ian Collier, playing Stewart Hyde, returns as Omega in *Arc of Infinity* (1983), while Neville Barber (Dr Cook) appears as Howard Baker in *K9 and Company* (1981), and Barry Ashton (Proctor) is Franz in *The Moonbase* (1967) and Lieutenant Kemp in *Frontier in Space*. George Cormack (Dalios) returns as the Doctor's mentor K'anpo in *Planet of the Spiders*, and Ingrid Pitt (Galleia) plays karate-kicking Dr Solow in *Warriors of the Deep* (1984).

WORTH WATCHING

This is the quintessential Third Doctor story and the pinnacle of the UNIT era. There are scientific experiments, military battles, a raging monster threatening the world and the Master seeking to control a power that ultimately turns against him. Although UNIT continue to appear over the next three seasons, plans were already afoot to give control of the TARDIS back to the Doctor and take him away from Earth more often. *The Time Monster* is the last hurrah for the format that once more made *Doctor Who* a popular success.

THE EPISODES

Episodes one, two, three, four and five are reverse-converted and restored from digital duplicates of conversions of the original two-inch colour videotape recordings in a lower-resolution format, recovered from a Canadian broadcaster in 1981. Episode six is restored from a two-inch desaturated video copy of the original two-inch colour videotape recording, with full colour added using a reverse-converted copy of the episode recovered from Canada. The episodes' mono soundtracks are remastered and the title sequences replaced by a modern transfer of the original 35mm film with credits remade to match the originals.

SPECIAL FEATURES

BETWEEN NOW...AND NOW! (23m39s) Producer and co-writer Barry Letts discusses his inspirations for the story, while physics professor Jim Al-Khalili examines the plausibility of the ideas about the nature of time featured in *The Time Monster*. With actors Richard Franklin and Katy Manning. Produced by Steve Broster.

RESTORATION COMPARISON (3m23s) Comparisons of picture quality before and after restoration demonstrating the reverse-conversion from the North American NTSC standard back to the UK PAL system. With explanatory captions.

PHOTO GALLERY (8m1s) Slideshow of colour and black-and-white photos taken during production of *The Time Monster*, including design department photos of the sets and behind-the-scenes shots during rehearsals. Set to sound effects and the Master's theme. Compiled by Derek Handley.

AUDIO OPTIONS Select **Commentary** to play the audio commentary in place of the main soundtrack when watching the episodes. On episodes one, five and six this is moderated by actor and comedian Toby Hadoke, talking with producer/writer Barry Letts and production assistant Marion McDougall, joined on episode five by Susan Penhaligon (Lakis). On episodes two and four John Levene (Benton) comments alone. On episode three Hadoke talks with fellow fans and writers Graham Duff, Phil Ford, Joseph Lidster and James Moran.

— Select **Feature Audio** to reinstate the main soundtrack when watching the episodes.

INFO TEXT Select **On** to view subtitles when watching the episodes that provide information and anecdotes about the development, production, broadcast and history of *The Time Monster*. Written by Martin Wiggins.

PDF MATERIALS Accessible via a computer are the six episode listings from *Radio Times* for the original BBC1 broadcast of *The Time Monster*, with illustrations by Dennis Curran (and two — the Doctor and the Master — by Frank Bellamy, reused from earlier serials).

COMING SOON (41s) Trailer for the DVD release of *The Creature from the Pit*.

SUBTITLES

Select **On** to view subtitles for all episodes and Special Features (except commentary).

RELATED EXTRAS

Coming Soon trailer — The Chase, The Space Museum

The UNIT Family — Day of the Daleks

THE **TIME WARRIOR**

STORY No.70   SEASON No.11:1

One disc with four episodes (97 mins) and 44½ minutes of extras, plus optional CGI effects, commentary track, production subtitles and PDF items

TARDIS TEAM Third Doctor, Brigadier and UNIT, and introducing Sarah Jane Smith

TIME AND PLACE Contemporary and 12th Century England

ADVERSARIES Sontaran (1st appearance); medieval ruffian Irongron

FIRST ON TV 15 December 1973–5 January 1974

DVD RELEASE BBCDVD2334, 3 September 2007, PG

COVER Photo illustration by Clayton Hickman, light orange strip

— Original release with cover sticker reading 'Sarah Jane's First Adventure'

ORIGINAL RRP £19.99

— Also released in Bred for War: The Sontaran Collection; BBCDVD2617, £39.99, 5 May 2008

— Episodes released in The Monster Collection: The Sontarans; BBCDVD3812, £9.99, 30 September 2013

STORY TEASER

A spaceship lands in medieval England and local villain Irongron claims it for himself. In the present day, UNIT investigates the disappearance of prominent scientists. The Doctor tracks them back in time and finds stranded Sontaran Linx giving modern weapons to Irongron in return for shelter while he repairs his ship, with help from the kidnapped scientists. As Irongron prepares to wipe out his enemies with technology he shouldn't have, the Doctor must face Linx in combat.

CONNECTIONS

This is the first appearance of the Sontarans, which feature again in *The Sontaran Experiment* (1975), *The Invasion of Time* (1978) and *The Two Doctors* (1985), returning in the New Series in *The Sontaran Stratagem* (2008). Not all aliens the Doctor encounters in Earth's past risk rewriting its future, but those that do include the Monk (*The Time Meddler*, 1965), the Great Intelligence (*The Abominable Snowmen*, 1967; *The Snowmen*, 2012), Sutekh (*Pyramids of Mars*, 1975), the Mandragora Helix (*The Masque of Mandragora*, 1976), the Terileptils (*The Visitation*, 1982), Fenric (*The Curse of Fenric*, 1989), the Gelth (*The Unquiet Dead*, 2005), the Wire (*The Idiot's Lantern*, 2006), the Carrionites (*The Shakespeare Code*, 2007), the Pyroviles (*The Fires of Pompeii*, 2008), the Cybermen (*The Next Doctor*, 2008) and the Saturnyne (*The Vampires of Venice*, 2010). The Doctor is back in the Middle Ages in *The King's Demons* (1983) as well as *The Time Meddler*, joins King Richard himself in Palestine in *The Crusade* (1965) and travels across 13th Century China in *Marco Polo* (1964). This is the sixth of Robert Holmes' stories for *Doctor Who* after which he became script editor for the following three years (*see Index v*), while director Alan Bromly returned to the series for *Nightmare of Eden* (1979). Kevin Lindsay, playing Linx, dons the mask again for *The Sontaran Experiment* but appears himself as Cho-Je in *Planet of the Spiders* at the end of the 1973/74 season. David Daker (Irongron) plays Captain Rigg in *Nightmare of Eden*; Alan Rowe (Edward) is Dr Evans in *The Moonbase* (1967), Colonel Skinsale in *Horror of Fang Rock* (1977) and Decider Garif in *Full Circle* (1980); while a young Jeremy Bulloch (Hal) appears as Tor in *The Space Museum* (1965).

WORTH WATCHING

Despite not being keen on historical settings — or perhaps because of it — Robert Holmes essentially creates a new style of story here that has since become synonymous with *Doctor Who*. Whereas the series' earliest trips into history tried to be accurate to known facts and feature only human villains, here we get the first monster stomping around in the past. There were precursors, *The Time Meddler* (1965) being the first to mix history with science fiction, but that had no monster, while the likes of *The Evil of the Daleks* (1967) and *The Abominable Snowmen* (1967) made little relevance of their historical settings. From hereon it became the default mode for stories set in Earth's past to feature a monster, a style that has continued into the New Series. And of course the monster Holmes created, the Sontaran, became one of the series' top rank, despite relatively few appearances, thanks to a well-realised and striking look and excellent portrayal by Kevin Lindsay.

THE EPISODES

All four episodes are restored from digital duplicates of the original two-inch colour videotape recordings used for broadcast and their mono soundtracks remastered. The opening title sequences are replaced by a modern transfer of the original 35mm film with credits remade to match the originals (although one caption slide is accidentally omitted from episode one).

SPECIAL FEATURES

BEGINNING THE END (30m15s) Producer Barry Letts, script editor Terrance Dicks, designer Keith Cheetham, and actors Jeremy Bulloch, Donald Pelmear and Elisabeth Sladen return to Peckforton Castle, Cheshire where much of *The Time Warrior* was filmed to recall the making of the story, including Jon Pertwee's decision to leave *Doctor Who*; conceiving the story and writing the script; devising and casting the new companion; Kevin Lindsay's portrayal of Linx; casting the other guest roles; working with director Alan Bromly; designing the sets and the Sontaran spaceship; and dissatisfaction with the original effects work. Narrated by Simon Ockenden, produced by Brendan Sheppard.

TRAILS AND CONTINUITY (1m11s) Preview of *The Time Warrior* and the edition of *Radio Times* covering the week of episode one, and continuity announcements from the original BBC1 broadcasts of episodes one and four, including a plug for the following story 'Invasion' and the *Radio Times 10th Anniversary Special* magazine. Reconstructed by matching clips from the episodes to audio tape recordings made at the time of broadcast.

CGI EFFECTS Select **CGI Effects On** to view updated computer-generated effects in place of some of the original visual effects when watching the episodes.

PHOTO GALLERY (9m16s) Slideshow of colour and black-and-white photos taken during production of *The Time Warrior*, including behind-the-scenes shots of the location filming, plus the photo shoot for *Radio Times* and publicity shots of Jon Pertwee and Elisabeth Sladen. Set to the theme music and sound effects from the story. Compiled by Derek Handley.

NEXT

AUDIO OPTIONS Select **Commentary** to play the audio commentary in place of the main soundtrack when watching the episodes. With Elisabeth Sladen (Sarah Jane), producer Barry Letts and script editor Terrance Dicks on all four episodes.

— Select **Feature Audio** to reinstate the main soundtrack when watching the episodes.

INFO TEXT Select **On** to view subtitles when watching the episodes that provide information and anecdotes about the development, production, broadcast and history of *The Time Warrior*. Written by Richard Molesworth.

"COMING SOON" TRAILER (1m32s) Trailer for the DVD release of The Key to Time boxset.

DOCTOR WHO ANNUAL Accessible via a computer is a PDF file of the 1974 *Doctor Who Annual*, published by World Distributors the autumn before *The Time Warrior* was broadcast. With stories featuring the Doctor, Jo, the Brigadier and Captain Yates, plus science features, puzzles and games.

RADIO TIMES LISTINGS Accessible via a computer is a PDF file of the four episode listings for the original BBC1 broadcast of *The Time Warrior*, with illustrations by Peter Brookes, the cover of the 13 December 1973 edition (issue 2614), and a two-page article about the new series published the week of episode one.

SUBTITLES
Select **On** to view subtitles for all episodes and Special Features (except commentary).

EASTER EGGS
There are two hidden features on this disc to find. *See Appendix 2 for details*

RELATED EXTRAS
Coming Soon trailer — Arc of Infinity, Time-Flight
Dressing Doctor Who — The Mutants
Built for War — The Sontaran Experiment
The UNIT Family — Terror of the Zygons

TIME-FLIGHT

STORY No.122   SEASON No.19:7

Released in a boxset with **ARC OF INFINITY**
One disc with four episodes (98 mins) and 64½ minutes of extras, plus commentary track, production subtitles and PDF items

TARDIS TEAM Fifth Doctor, Nyssa, Tegan
TIME AND PLACE Contemporary Heathrow airport and primeval Earth
ADVERSARIES Third Master (3rd appearance)
FIRST ON TV 22–30 March 1982
DVD RELEASE BBCDVD2327A, 6 August 2007, PG
COVER Photo illustration by Dan Budden, red strip
ORIGINAL RRP £29.99 (boxset)

STORY TEASER
The Doctor finally gets Tegan back to Heathrow — by accident, of course — just as a Concorde flight mysteriously vanishes. Detecting a time contour, he has the TARDIS loaded aboard the next flight to track the source, only to find the plane whisked into prehistory, where an old enemy is trapped but on the verge of breaking free.

CONNECTIONS
Throughout the 1982 season the Doctor is trying to return Tegan to Earth in time for the flight she was meant to be boarding in *Logopolis* (1981), notably failing to in *Four to Doomsday* and *The Visitation*. The TARDIS had earlier landed at London's second airport, Gatwick, in *The Faceless Ones* (1967), while the Doctor also visits prehistoric Earth in *City of Death* (1979) to deal with another crashed spaceship. This is the first return of the Master after his reincarnation in the trilogy of stories that spanned the crossover from the Fourth to the Fifth Doctors: *The Keeper of Traken* (1981), *Logopolis* and *Castrovalva* (1982). In his next story, *The King's Demons* (1983), the Xeraphin are said to have created the shape-shifting robot Kamelion which the Doctor adopts as a companion. Writer Peter Grimwade had previously been a production assistant on *Doctor Who* in the 1970s and directed *Full Circle* (1980), *Logopolis*, *Kinda* (1982) and *Earthshock* (1982) before turning to writing; *Time-Flight* was followed by *Mawdryn Undead* (1983) and *Planet of Fire* (1984). Newly qualified director Ron Jones had just completed *Black Orchid* (1982) and directs further stories over the subsequent four years (*see Index v*). John Flint, playing Captain Urquhart in episode one, appears as William des Preaux in *The Crusade* (1965).

WORTH WATCHING
Time-Flight draws all the short straws, coming at the end of a season, when money was always at its tightest, with a script that had passed through three script editors while the writer was busy directing other serials the same year, and being assigned to an inexperienced director. Its initial reputation perhaps also suffered from following the much more dynamic and impressively directed *Earthshock*, with its shock climax — *Time-Flight*'s own attempt at a surprise ending pales in comparison. While the use of Concorde is an impressive coup, the filming at Heathrow during a freezing winter looks as uncomfortable as it doubtless was for the actors (although the fresh transfer

of the original film for this release makes it look a lot better than it did in 1982).

THE EPISODES

All four episodes are restored from digital duplicates of the original two-inch colour videotape recordings used for broadcast, with location sequences newly transferred from the original 16mm colour film. This has required shots that mix film and video elements to be recomposited. The episodes' mono soundtracks are remastered and the title sequences replaced by a modern transfer of the original 35mm film with credits remade to match the originals.

SPECIAL FEATURES

MOUTH ON LEGS (13m38s) Janet Fielding talks about getting the part of companion Tegan Jovanka; working with Tom Baker, Peter Davison and producer John Nathan-Turner; her costumes; deciding to leave after three years; and her work at improving the status of women in television.

DELETED SCENES (3m44s) A selection of scenes not used in the final programme, taken from a VHS copy of the original studio recordings with on-screen time-code.

JURASSIC LARKS (19m33s) Footage from the full studio recording sessions in mid-January and early-February 1982 including retakes and effects setups with as-recorded sound, some from a copy with on-screen time-code. With explanatory captions.

OUT-TAKES (13m52s) Bloopers and fluffed lines, taken from the studio recordings, some with on-screen time-code.

PETER GRIMWADE INTERVIEW (4m12s) An interview with the director and writer about how the two roles relate, from 1987. Recorded by Keith Barnfather, interviewer Nicholas Briggs.

NEXT

AUDIO OPTIONS Select **Commentary** to play the audio commentary in place of the main soundtrack when watching the episodes. With Peter Davison, Janet Fielding (Tegan), Sarah Sutton (Nyssa) and script editor Eric Saward on all four episodes.

— Select **Feature Audio** to reinstate the main soundtrack when watching the episodes.

INFO TEXT Select **On** to view subtitles when watching the episodes that provide information and anecdotes about the development, production, broadcast and history of *Time-Flight*. Written by Martin Wiggins.

PHOTO GALLERY (8m22s) Slideshow of colour and black-and-white photos taken during production of *Time-Flight*, including design department photos of the sets and behind-the-scenes shots of the studio recording. Set to music from the story. Compiled by Ralph Montagu.

DOCTOR WHO ANNUAL Accessible via a computer is a PDF file of the 1983 *Doctor Who Annual*, published by World Distributors the autumn after *Time-Flight* was broadcast. With stories featuring the Doctor, Adric, Nyssa and Tegan, plus behind-the-scenes and science features.

RADIO TIMES LISTINGS Accessible via a computer is a PDF file of the four episode listings for the original BBC1 broadcast of *Time-Flight*.

COMING SOON TRAILER (1m) Trailer for the DVD release of *The Time Warrior*.

SUBTITLES

Select **On** to view subtitles for all episodes and Special Features (except commentary).

RELATED EXTRAS

Peter Grimwade - Directing with Attitude — Kinda

Coming Soon trailer — Timelash

TIMELASH

STORY No.141   SEASON No.22:5

One disc with two episodes (89½ mins) and 35 minutes of extras, plus commentary track, production subtitles and PDF items

TARDIS TEAM Sixth Doctor, Peri

TIME AND PLACE Planet Karfel and Scotland 1885

ADVERSARIES The Borad, mutant ruler of Karfel; Tekker, his chief minister

FIRST ON TV 9–16 March 1985
DVD RELEASE BBCDVD2333, 9 July 2007, PG
COVER Photo illustration by Lee Binding, light blue strip
ORIGINAL RRP £12.99

STORY TEASER

The apparition of a woman in the TARDIS leads the Doctor and Peri to the planet Karfel, whose leader implores them to help recover the woman who accidentally fell into their time tunnel, the Timelash. The Doctor finds her, and an aspiring author, on 19th Century Earth and returns with them to Karfel, only to find Peri kidnapped and the planet's true ruler — the hideous Borad — intent on destroying all life on the planet to repopulate it with mutants like himself. As interplanetary war looms, the Doctor must save Peri from a fate worse than death.

CONNECTIONS

Although this story relates a previous trip to Karfel by the Third Doctor and Jo, this is never seen on screen, although Jo does mention the planet in her appearance in *The Sarah Jane Adventures: Death of the Doctor* (2010). The Doctor spies on Shakespeare through his Time and Space Visualiser in *The Chase* (1965) but this is the first time he is seen to meet a well-known author, something that becomes more commonplace in the New Series, as with Charles Dickens in *The Unquiet Dead* (2005), a younger William Shakespeare in *The Shakespeare Code* (2007) and Agatha Christie in *The Unicorn and the Wasp* (2008). The Karfelons' kontron tunnel is similar to the time corridor used by the Daleks in *Resurrection of the Daleks* (1984) and *Victory of the Daleks* (2010), and Sutekh's in *Pyramids of Mars* (1975). This was the last *Doctor Who* story directed by Pennant Roberts (*see Index v*). Paul Darrow (Tekker) plays UNIT Captain Hawkins in *Doctor Who and the Silurians* (1970), while Dean Hollingsworth is another android, the Bus Conductor, in *The Greatest Show in the Galaxy* (1988/89). Denis Carey (Old Man) also appears as the eponymous character in *The Keeper of Traken* (1981) having not made into onto the screen as Professor Chronotis in the unfinished *Shada*, also directed by Pennant Roberts.

WORTH WATCHING

Timelash is most notable for teaming up the Doctor with one of the fathers of science fiction, HG Wells, with the conceit being that the author got many of his story ideas from this adventure, particularly elements of his novel *The Time Machine*. It's an idea reused in *The Shakespeare Code*, in which the Doctor quotes to the playwright several lines we now ascribe to him. *Timelash* and the same season's *The Mark of the Rani*, which features Robert Stephenson, are the first time we've seen the Doctor meet famous people from history since the historical adventures in the 1960s, latterly Wyatt Earp and company in *The Gunfighters* (1966), although he drops plenty of names in the interim. *Timelash* also features a fun performance by Paul Darrow, who makes an otherwise standard villain much more watchable.

THE EPISODES

Both episodes are restored from digital duplicates of the original one-inch colour videotape recordings used for broadcast and their mono soundtracks remastered. The title sequences are replaced with a digital duplicate of the original one-inch colour videotape transfer of the 35mm film with credits remade to match the originals.

SPECIAL FEATURES

THE GOOD, THE BAD AND THE UGLY (25m3s) The making of *Timelash*, including the development of the 1985 season; writing the script; working with director Pennant Roberts; the characterisation of the Doctor and Peri; the portrayals of Tekker, the Borad and HG Wells; the impact on rehearsals of the regular cast's appearances in pantomime and at conventions; views on the design aspects; padding out short episodes; and the serial's reputation. With contributions from script editor Eric Saward, writer Glen McCoy, actors Robert Ashby, Colin Baker, Nicola Bryant, David Chandler and Paul Darrow, and fan journalist Paul Lang. Narrated by Terry Molloy, produced by John Kelly.

PHOTO GALLERY (8m52s) Slideshow of colour and black-and-white photos taken during production of *Timelash*, including design department photos of the sets and shots of the Borad make-up. Set to music from the story. Compiled by Ralph Montagu.

COMING SOON (1m15s) Trailer for the DVD releases of *Arc of Infinity* and *Time-Flight*.

RADIO TIMES LISTINGS Accessible via a computer is a PDF file of both episode listings for the original BBC1 broadcast of *Timelash*.

INFO TEXT Select **On** to view subtitles when watching the episodes that provide information and anecdotes about the development, production, broadcast and history of *Timelash*. Written by Martin Wiggins.

AUDIO OPTIONS

Select **Commentary** to play the audio commentary in place of the main soundtrack when watching the episodes. With Colin Baker, Nicola Bryant (Peri) and Paul Darrow (Tekker) on both episodes.
— Select **Feature Audio** to reinstate the main soundtrack when watching the episodes.

SUBTITLES

Select **On** to view subtitles for all episodes and Special Features (except commentary).

EASTER EGG

There is one hidden feature on this disc to find. *See Appendix 2 for details*

THE **TOMB OF THE CYBERMEN**

STORY No.37   SEASON No.5:1

One disc with four episodes (96½ mins) and 48½ minutes of extras, plus commentary track, production subtitles and image content

TARDIS TEAM Second Doctor, Jamie, Victoria

TIME AND PLACE Planet Telos

ADVERSARIES Cybermen (3rd appearance); Klieg and Kaftan

FIRST ON TV 2–23 September 1967

DVD RELEASE BBCDVD1032, 14 January 2002, PG

COVER Photo illustration by Clayton Hickman, light blue strip

ORIGINAL RRP £19.99

— Also released in The Cybermen Collection; BBCDVD2262, £39.99, 6 November 2006

STORY TEASER

The TARDIS arrives on the planet Telos just as a group of archaeologists unearth the long-lost tombs of the Cybermen. Inside they find a complex system of controls that require the highest intelligence to decode, and beneath is the entire Cyberman army in frozen hibernation. When the expedition's rocket is sabotaged it becomes clear that some of the party are intent on reviving them, and soon the Doctor and his friends face being converted into Cybermen themselves.

CONNECTIONS

After this story the Cybermen are often found in a dormant state, awaiting the call to attack, such as in *The Wheel in Space* (1968), *The Invasion* (1968), *Earthshock* (1982), *Attack of the Cybermen* (1985) and *Rise of the Cybermen/The Age of Steel* (2006). *Attack of the Cybermen* sees a return to the Telosian tombs (although they look very different) while trying to reverse the destruction of their original home Mondas, as seen in *The Tenth Planet* (1966); it also features a resurrected Cyber Controller (again played by Michael Kilgarriff) and is the only other time we see people partly converted into Cybermen. This is the first appearance of Cybermats, which the Cybermen use again in *The Wheel in Space*, *Revenge of the Cybermen* (1975) and *Closing Time* (2011) before switching to Cybermites in *Nightmare in Silver* (2013). Writers Kit Pedler and Gerry Davis also collaborated on *The Tenth Planet* and *The Moonbase* (1966), while the latter wrote *Revenge of the Cybermen*; Morris Barry also directed *The Moonbase* and *The Dominators* (1968). Cyril Shaps (Viner) keeps gaining seniority in his *Doctor Who* roles, as Dr Lennox in *The Ambassadors of Death* (1970), Professor Clegg in *Planet of the Spiders* (1974) and the Archimandrite in *The Androids of Tara* (1978). Clive Merrison (Callum) returns as the deputy chief caretaker in *Paradise Towers* (1987), Bernard Holley (Haydon) is the face of Axos in *The Claws of Axos* (1971), and Roy Stewart (Toberman) plays another taciturn strongman in *Terror of the Autons* (1971).

WORTH WATCHING

Until film prints of this story were discovered in Hong Kong in 1992, opinion was based on that of people who had seen it on broadcast and the Target novelisation. Both perhaps gave a better account than the episodes themselves, but to many this remains the pinnacle of the 1960s Cybermen stories. Certainly the presentation of their tombs is impressive and their awakening is ominous, even if their strategy is as suspect as ever. The addition of human villains adds a welcome layer to the usual us-against-them plot of previous Cybermen stories.

THE EPISODES

All four episodes are restored from 16mm film copies of the original black-and-white videotape recordings, recovered from a Hong Kong broadcaster in 1992. Their mono soundtracks are remastered and title sequences replaced by a modern transfer of the original 35mm film.

SPECIAL FEATURES *ALSO ON SPECIAL EDITION

*TITLE SEQUENCE TESTS (3m27s) Graphics footage shot for the Second Doctor title sequence, including elements not used in the final titles, created by Bernard Lodge. Set to an extended version of the remixed *Doctor Who* theme music produced by Delia Derbyshire of the BBC Radiophonic Workshop in 1967.

*LATE NIGHT LINE-UP: 'SPECIAL EFFECTS' (2m50s) Extract from the Saturday 25 November 1967 edition of the BBC2 critical discussion programme in which Jack Kine of BBC Visual Effects talks to Joan Bakewell about the department's work. Featuring footage of Cybermen and Cybermats, and two clips from *The Abominable Snowmen* episode four that are now the only known footage from that episode.

PHOTO GALLERY Scroll through 25 colour and black-and-white photos taken during production of *The Tomb of the Cybermen*, including behind-the-scenes shots of director Morris Barry at work, plus the cover of the 31 August 1967 edition of *Radio Times* (issue 2286) publicising the story. Compiled by Ralph Montagu.

*THE FINAL END (1m20s) Parts of the silent 8mm black-and-white footage shot by designer Tony Cornell during filming for *The Evil of the Daleks* episode seven at Ealing Studios on 16/17 May 1967, set to a recording of the episode's soundtrack made on audio tape when it was originally broadcast, giving an indication of how the climax of that missing story may have appeared on screen. *The full footage shot by Cornell is on* Lost in Time, The Seeds of Death *and* Resurrection of the Daleks Special Edition

TOMBWATCH (28m43s) Highlights from interview panels featuring cast and crew who worked on *The Tomb of the Cybermen* held at a screening of the recently recovered episodes at BAFTA in London on Sunday 26 April 1992. With producer Peter Bryant, story editor Victor Pemberton, director Morris Barry, and actors Shirley Cooklin, Frazer Hines, Michael Kilgarriff, Clive Merrison, George Roubicek and Deborah Watling. Presented by Andrew Beech.

▶

REMASTERING FOR DVD (5m18s) Comparisons of picture and sound quality before and after restoration, demonstrating the techniques used on this and other black-and-white episodes. With explanatory captions.

*MORRIS BARRY INTRO (3m7s) The introduction to the story recorded by director Morris Barry for the May 1992 VHS release of *The Tomb of the Cybermen*, in which he recalls the casting of Michael Kilgarriff as the Cyber Controller and receiving audience complaints about the grisly effect used for a dying Cyberman.

INFORMATION TEXT Select On to view subtitles when watching the episodes that provide information and anecdotes about the development, production, broadcast and history of *The Tomb of the Cybermen*. Written by Richard Molesworth.

*AUDIO OPTIONS Select Commentary On to play the audio commentary in place of the main soundtrack when watching the episodes. With Frazer Hines (Jamie) and Deborah Watling (Victoria) on all four episodes.

SUBTITLES

Select On to view subtitles for all episodes and Special Features, or for the commentary.

EASTER EGGS
There are three hidden features on this disc to find. *See Appendix 2 for details*
RELATED EXTRAS
The Cyber-Generations — Attack of the Cybermen
The Cyber Story — Attack of the Cybermen

THE **TOMB OF THE CYBERMEN** SPECIAL EDITION

STORY No.37   SEASON No.5:1

Released with **THE ROBOTS OF DEATH SPECIAL EDITION** and **THE THREE DOCTORS SPECIAL EDITION** in the **REVISITATIONS 3** boxset

Two discs with four episodes (96½ mins) and 98½ minutes of extras, plus two commentary tracks, production subtitles and PDF items

Audio navigation of each disc's contents available by pressing Enter after the BBC ident

TARDIS TEAM Second Doctor, Jamie, Victoria

TIME AND PLACE Planet Telos

ADVERSARIES Cybermen (3rd appearance); Klieg and Kaftan

FIRST ON TV 2–23 September 1967

DVD RELEASE BBCDVD3003A, 13 February 2012, PG (disc two U)

COVER Photo illustration by Clayton Hickman, pale blue strip;
        version with older BBC logo on reverse

ORIGINAL RRP £35.74 (boxset)

— Episodes released in The Monster Collection: The Cybermen; BBCDVD3809, £9.99,
    30 September 2013

STORY TEASER

The TARDIS arrives on the planet Telos just as a group of archaeologists unearth the long-lost tombs of the Cybermen. Inside they find a complex system of controls that require the highest intelligence to decode, and beneath is the entire Cyberman army in frozen hibernation. When the expedition's rocket is sabotaged it becomes clear that some of the party are intent on reviving them, and soon the Doctor and his friends face being converted into Cybermen themselves.

CONNECTIONS

After this story the Cybermen are often found in a dormant state, awaiting the call to attack, such as in *The Wheel in Space* (1968), *The Invasion* (1968), *Earthshock* (1982), *Attack of the Cybermen* (1985) and *Rise of the Cybermen/The Age of Steel* (2006). *Attack of the Cybermen* sees a return to the Telosian tombs (although they look very different) while trying to reverse the destruction of their original home Mondas, as seen in *The Tenth Planet* (1966); it also features a resurrected Cyber Controller (again played by Michael Kilgarriff) and is the only other time we see people partly converted into Cybermen. This is the first appearance of Cybermats, which the Cybermen use again in *The Wheel in Space*, *Revenge of the Cybermen* (1975) and *Closing Time* (2011) before switching to Cybermites in *Nightmare in Silver* (2013). Writers Kit Pedler and Gerry Davis also collaborated on *The Tenth Planet* and *The Moonbase* (1966), while the latter wrote *Revenge of the Cybermen*; Morris Barry also directed *The Moonbase* and *The Dominators* (1968). Cyril Shaps (Viner) keeps gaining seniority in his *Doctor Who* roles, as Dr Lennox in *The Ambassadors of Death* (1970), Professor Clegg in *Planet of the Spiders* (1974) and the Archimandrite in *The Androids of Tara* (1978). Clive Merrison (Callum) returns as the deputy chief caretaker in *Paradise Towers* (1987), Bernard Holley (Haydon) is the face of Axos in *The Claws of Axos* (1971), and Roy Stewart (Toberman) plays another taciturn strongman in *Terror of the Autons* (1971).

WORTH WATCHING

This Special Edition features further clean-up of the episodes compared to the previous release and additional Special Features. Until film prints of this story were discovered in Hong Kong in 1992, opinion was based on that of people who had seen it on broadcast and the Target novelisation. Both

T

perhaps gave a better account than the episodes themselves, but to many this remains the pinnacle of the 1960s Cybermen stories. Certainly the presentation of their tombs is impressive and their awakening is ominous, even if their strategy is as suspect as ever. The addition of human villains adds a welcome layer to the usual us-against-them plot of previous Cybermen stories.

DISC ONE

THE EPISODES

All four episodes are restored from 16mm film copies of the original black-and-white videotape recordings, recovered from a Hong Kong broadcaster in 1992. Their mono soundtracks are remastered and the VidFIRE process is applied to studio-recorded shots to recapture the smoother motion of video. The title sequences are replaced by a modern transfer of the original 35mm film with credits remade to match the originals.

SPECIAL FEATURES *REPEATED FROM PREVIOUS RELEASE

*MORRIS BARRY INTRODUCTION (3m7s) The introduction to the story recorded by director Morris Barry for the May 1992 VHS release of *The Tomb of the Cybermen*, in which he recalls the casting of Michael Kilgarriff as the Cyber Controller and receiving audience complaints about the effect used for a dying Cyberman.

*TITLE SEQUENCE TESTS (3m27s) Graphics footage shot for the Second Doctor title sequence, including elements not used in the final titles, created by Bernard Lodge. Set to an extended version of the remixed *Doctor Who* theme music produced by Delia Derbyshire of the BBC Radiophonic Workshop in 1967.

*LATE NIGHT LINE-UP (2m50s) Extract from the Saturday 25 November 1967 edition of the BBC2 critical discussion programme in which Jack Kine of BBC Visual Effects talks to Joan Bakewell about the department's work. Featuring footage of Cybermen and Cybermats, and two clips from *The Abominable Snowmen* episode four that are now the only known footage from that episode.

*THE FINAL END (1m20s) Parts of the silent 8mm black-and-white footage shot by designer Tony Cornell during filming for *The Evil of the Daleks* episode seven at Ealing Studios on 16/17 May 1967, set to a recording of the episode's soundtrack made on audio tape when it was originally broadcast, giving an indication of how the climax of that missing story may have appeared on screen. *The full footage shot by Cornell is on* Lost in Time, The Seeds of Death *and* Resurrection of the Daleks Special Edition

AUDIO OPTIONS Select ***Commentary 1** to play the audio commentary recorded for the previous release in place of the main soundtrack when watching the episodes. With Frazer Hines (Jamie) and Deborah Watling (Victoria) on all four episodes.

— Select **Commentary 2** to play the audio commentary recorded for this release when watching the episodes. This is moderated by actor and comedian Toby Hadoke, talking with story editor Victor Pemberton [ep 1], Bernard Holley (Haydon) [1], Shirley Cooklin (Kaftan) [2,3,4], Frazer Hines [2,3,4], Deborah Watling [2,3,4] and Reg Whitehead (Cyberman) [3,4].

— Select **Feature Audio** to reinstate the main soundtrack when watching the episodes.

INFO TEXT Select **On** to view subtitles when watching the episodes that provide information and anecdotes about the development, production, broadcast and history of *The Tomb of the Cybermen*, updated and expanded from the previous release. Written by Martin Wiggins.

COMING SOON (1m26s) Trailer for the DVD release of *The Face of Evil*.

SUBTITLES

Select **On** to view subtitles for all episodes and Special Features on disc one (except commentaries).

DISC TWO

SPECIAL FEATURES

THE LOST GIANTS (26m53s) The making of *The Tomb of the Cybermen*, including memories of producer Peter Bryant, writers Gerry Davis and Kit Pedler, and director Morris Barry; the guest cast; creating the tomb set; portraying the Cyber Controller; operating the Cybermats; filming on location at Gerrards Cross quarry; and recording in Lime Grove Studios. With contributions from story editor Victor Pemberton, visual effects designer Peter Day, and actors Shirley Cooklin, Frazer Hines, Bernard Holley, Michael Kilgarriff and Deborah Watling. Produced by Steve Broster.

THE CURSE OF THE CYBERMEN'S TOMB (14m26s) Similarities between *The Tomb of the Cybermen* and Howard Carter's discovery of King Tutankhamun's tomb in 1922 and its cultural impact. With cultural historian Sir Christopher Frayling and Dr Debbie Challis from the Petrie Museum of Egyptian Archaeology. Produced by James Goss.

CYBERMEN EXTENDED EDITION (32m27s) Writer and broadcaster Matthew Sweet presents an examination of the origins and natures of the Cybermen as presented in both the Classic and New Series. Produced by Thomas Guerrier. *First released in* The Cybermen Collection *in April 2009*

SUBTITLES Select **On** to view subtitles for all Special Features on disc two.

NEXT

THE MAGIC OF VIDFIRE (5m57s) Explanation of the process used on the DVD releases of black-and-white *Doctor Who* stories that restores the smoother motion of 50-field-per-second video recordings to programmes copied onto 25-frame-per-second film. With fan Jonathan Way. Narrated by Philip Kelly, produced by John Kelly.

SKY RAY ADVERT (31s) Television commercial from 1967 for Wall's Sky Ray ice lolly *Doctor Who* promotion, featuring two genuine Dalek props (see **PDF Materials** for more).

PHOTO GALLERY (3m25s) Slideshow of colour and black-and-white photos taken during production of *The Tomb of the Cybermen*, including design department photos of the sets and behind-the-scenes shots of the filming. Set to stock music used in the story. Compiled by Paul Shields.

PDF MATERIALS Accessible via a computer are the four episode listings from *Radio Times* for the original BBC1 broadcast of *The Tomb of the Cybermen*, the cover of the 31 August 1967 edition (issue 2286) and an article introducing the story, and a small preview item published the week before.
— Packaging and promotional material from the 1967 Wall's Sky Ray ice lolly *Doctor Who* promotion, including the full set of thirty-six cards telling a story of Dr Who's battle against the Daleks, aided by the Zaons and the Sky Ray Space Raiders; the 28-page *Dr Who's Space Adventure Book* into which the cards could be pasted; storyboard sketches for the television advert (see above); and design sketches for the book with the initial outline for the 'Dr Who on Zaos' story.

EASTER EGGS

There are three hidden features on these discs to find. *See Appendix 2 for details*

RELATED EXTRAS

The Cyber-Generations — Attack of the Cybermen

The Cyber Story — Attack of the Cybermen

Coming Soon trailer — The Sensorites

THE TRIAL OF A TIME LORD

STORY No.143   SEASON No.23:1

Boxset of the fourteen-episode story on four discs each in its own case

DVD RELEASE BBCDVD2422, 29 September 2008, PG

SLIPCASE Photo illustration by Clayton Hickman, silvered logo and title, pink/black background

ORIGINAL RRP £49.99

WHAT'S IN THE BOX

After the attempt by the BBC to cancel *Doctor Who* in 1985 was revoked owing to fan-fuelled public outcry, the series was recommissioned to return in the autumn of 1986 but reduced to fourteen 25-minute episodes. The production team decided they would tell a single story over the whole season, of the Doctor on trial by the Time Lords, with three sections of evidence from his past, present and future and a concluding judgement. The series ran into many problems during its development but was ultimately produced in three blocks, each with a different director and crew, covering four scripts by three writers, then presented on screen as a single story in fourteen parts. Overall, then, the story is known as *The Trial of a Time Lord*, but the four component scripts have since been given their own titles (mainly based on the writers' working titles) which are used for the four discs in this release, the contents of which are detailed individually below.

Parts 1 to 4 'THE MYSTERIOUS PLANET'

One disc with four episodes (98½ mins) and 83 minutes of extras, plus two commentary tracks and production subtitles

TARDIS TEAM Sixth Doctor, Peri

TIME AND PLACE Planet Ravolox

ADVERSARIES Drathro, a robot

FIRST ON TV 6–27 September 1986

DVD RELEASE BBCDVD2422(A), 29 September 2008, PG

COVER Photo illustration by Clayton Hickman, light blue strip

— Original release with cover sticker reading 'Parts One to Four 'The Mysterious Planet''

ORIGINAL RRP £49.99 (boxset)

STORY TEASER

The Time Lords pluck the TARDIS out of time and bring the Doctor to a massive courtroom in space to face an inquiry into his actions. Accusing him of irresponsible interference is the Valeyard, who presents as evidence the Doctor's visit to Ravolox, a planet oddly similar to Earth but which records say was devastated by a solar fireball. There is life there, however. On the surface live the primitive Tribe of the Free who worship a totem that is clearly technological, while in tunnels are more advanced survivors ruled over by the robot Drathro. With his power system on the verge of failure both groups are at risk of destruction, but Drathro is programmed to protect a secret at all costs, a secret the Doctor must never discover.

CONNECTIONS

This is the first appearance of the Time Lords since *The Five Doctors* (1983) and the third time the Doctor has faced a legal hearing, following his capture in *The War Games* (1969) and trial for murder in *The Deadly Assassin* (1976) — neither really matches the situation here so the Doctor's claim to have "been through several such inquiries before" probably means generally rather than specifically by the Time Lords. The Matrix is first featured in *The Deadly Assassin* and again in *Arc of Infinity* (1983). A colony dominated by robotic rulers claiming the environment is unsafe features in Robert Holmes' *The Krotons* (1968/69), while nefarious duo Glitz and Dibber are reminiscent of *The Ribos Operation's* (1978) Garron and Unstoffe and *The Caves of Androzani's* (1984) Stotz and Krelper. The Doctor ventures into the working London Underground in *The Web of Fear* (1968) and *Invasion of the Dinosaurs* (1974), and possibly its long-disused tunnels in *The Sontaran Experiment* (1975) at a time when the planet has similarly recovered from fiery devastation. While he has faced many forms of robot, more sophisticated, individual examples like Drathro include the K1 (*Robot*, 1975), Super Voc 7 in *The Robots of Death* (1977), K9, the Terileptil android in *The Visitation* (1982), and Kamelion (*The King's Demons*, 1983; *Planet of Fire*, 1984). After being a regular writer for the series throughout the 1970s, Holmes wrote four more scripts in the mid-80s of which this was the penultimate (*see Index v*). He was set to write the final two episodes of *The Trial of a Time Lord* but died after completing only the first. Nicholas Mallett also directed *Paradise Towers* (1987) and *The Curse of Fenric* (1989). Tony Selby plays Sabalom Glitz again at the end of the season and in *Dragonfire* (1987), while Tom Chadbon (Merdeen) is Duggan in *City of Death* (1979).

WORTH WATCHING

This is *Doctor Who* stalwart Robert Holmes' last full story and, while arguably not one of his absolute best, features enough of his familiar character types and witty dialogue to be enjoyable for that reason alone. The opening model shot is justifiably renowned — a stunning achievement given the resources the programme was afforded at this time — and the production as a whole is slick and inventive.

THE EPISODES

All four episodes are restored from digital duplicates of the original one-inch colour videotape recordings used for broadcast, with the spaceship model sequences newly transferred from the original 35mm colour film. Their mono soundtracks are remastered and the title sequences replaced by a modern transfer of the original 35mm film with credits remade to match the originals.

SPECIAL FEATURES

THE MAKING OF THE MYSTERIOUS PLANET (25m2s) The production of the first segment of *The Trial of a Time Lord*, including the decision to put the Doctor on trial, mirroring the real-life situation of the programme itself; writing the script; rearranging the theme music; filming and scoring the opening model shot; the characters and cast; and building the two robots. With contributions from script editor Eric Saward, visual effects designer Mike Kelt, composer Dominic Glynn, actors Colin Baker, Nicola Bryant, Michael Jayston and Tony Selby, fan journalist Clayton Hickman and television historian Jim Sangster. Produced by Steve Broster.

DELETED AND EXTENDED SCENES (8m30s) A selection of scenes not used in the final programme, taken from earlier edits of the episodes with as-recorded sound.

TRAILS AND CONTINUITY (9m59s) Previews and continuity announcements from the original BBC1 broadcasts of episodes one to four of *The Trial of a Time Lord*, with preview page from Ceefax, episode one continuity from BBC1 Wales, previous-episode summaries, plugs for *Doctor Who* on video and the Longleat exhibition, and the BBC1 evening schedules for Saturdays 6 and 20 September 1986. Plus extracts from the Saturday 13 September 1986 edition of *Roland Rat: The Series* featuring Colin Baker.

35MM FILM SEQUENCE (1m15s) The full silent 35mm colour film footage of the Time Lord spaceship model.

MUSIC VIDEOS Select **Clean Titles** (2m18s) to watch the full opening and closing title sequences with Dominic Glynn's theme arrangement from the 1986 season, in original mono, newly mixed in stereo, or newly mixed in Dolby Digital 5.1 surround sound.
— Select **Theme Music Remix** (3m8s) to hear the full version of Dominic Glynn's theme arrangement, in original mono as released on single, or newly remixed and enhanced in either stereo or Dolby Digital 5.1 surround sound.
— Select **The Trial Theme** (2m49s) to hear a new composition by Glynn based on cues from 'The Mysterious Planet', in stereo or Dolby Digital 5.1 surround. Set to clips from all four segments of *The Trial of a Time Lord*.

NEXT

AUDIO OPTIONS Select **Commentary 1** to play the audio commentary in place of the main soundtrack when watching the episodes. With Colin Baker (solo for the first five minutes), Nicola Bryant (Peri) and Tony Selby (Glitz) on all four episodes, joined from the end of episode one by Adam Blackwood (Balazar).
— Select **Commentary 2** to play an alternative audio commentary when watching episode one. With script editor Eric Saward.
— Select **Feature Audio** to reinstate the main soundtrack when watching the episodes.

INFO TEXT Select **On** to view subtitles when watching the episodes that provide information and anecdotes about the development, production, broadcast and history of 'The Mysterious Planet'. Written by Richard Molesworth.

WOGAN (14m24s) Extract from the Monday 25 August 1986 edition of the BBC1 early-evening chat show in which Terry Wogan interviews Colin Baker and Lynda Bellingham (and encounters a Mandrel and a Sea Devil).

BLUE PETER (6m52s) Extract from the Thursday 18 September 1986 edition of the BBC1 children's magazine programme in which Janet Ellis talks to L1 operator Mike Ellis (her dad) and Drathro operator Paul McGuinness; Peter Duncan meets Nabil Shaban in costume as Sil; and Ellis and Mark Curry talk to Colin Baker and Bonnie Langford on the TARDIS set.

POINTS OF VIEW (2m23s) Extract from the Wednesday 17 September 1986 edition of the BBC1 viewer feedback programme in which Anne Robinson introduces letters about the return of *Doctor Who* and the new theme arrangement.

PHOTO GALLERY (6m31s) Slideshow of colour photos taken during production of 'The Mysterious Planet', set to music from the story. Compiled by Derek Handley.

SUBTITLES

Select **On** to view subtitles for all episodes and Special Features (except commentary).

Parts 5 to 8 'MINDWARP'

One disc with four episodes (99 mins) and 71 minutes of extras, plus commentary track and production subtitles

TARDIS TEAM Sixth Doctor, Peri

TIME AND PLACE Planet Thoros Beta

ADVERSARIES Sil (2nd appearance); Kiv, leader of his fellow Mentors; human scientist Crozier

FIRST ON TV 4–25 October 1986

DVD RELEASE BBCDVD2422(B), 29 September 2008, PG

COVER Photo illustration by Clayton Hickman, red strip

— Original release with cover sticker reading 'Parts Five to Eight 'Mindwarp''

ORIGINAL RRP £49.99 (boxset)

STORY TEASER

The inquiry has become a trial and the Valeyard's prosecution of the Doctor continues with his most recent adventure: a visit to Thoros Beta, home of the slimy financier Sil, whose boss Kiv is taking unnatural measures to prolong his life. His brain is developing too fast for his amphibian body so Kiv has employed genetic surgeon Crozier to find a way of transplanting it into a new head. The arrival of the Doctor and Peri provide two new potential donors.

CONNECTIONS

Sil makes his debut in *Vengeance on Varos* (1985), again played by Nabil Shaban. Another surgeon working to transplant a brain into a suitable body features in *The Brain of Morbius* (1976), whom the Time Lords also direct the Doctor to stop. Other amphibious species like the Mentors and the Raak include the Aridians (*The Chase*, 1965), some Silurians (*The Sea Devils*, 1972; *Warriors of the Deep*, 1984), the Rutans (*Horror of Fang Rock*, 1977), the Marshmen (*Full Circle*, 1980), the Terileptils (*The Visitation*, 1982), the Myrka (*Warriors of the Deep*), the Hath (*The Doctor's Daughter*, 2008) and the Saturnyne (*The Vampires of Venice*, 2010). Philip Martin previously wrote *Vengeance on Varos*, which was also directed by Ron Jones (*see Index v*). Christopher Ryan, playing Kiv, appears in the New Series as Sontarans General Staal in T*he Sontaran Stratagem/The Poison Sky* (2008) and Commander Stark in *The Pandorica Opens* (2010), while Trevor Laird (Frax) plays Martha Jones' father Clive in the 2007 series.

WORTH WATCHING

Sil was a popular villain from the 1985 season and his return was planned for the following year even before the show's postponement threw things into disarray. Rather than playing sidekick to the Ice Warriors, we instead get to see more of his home world and people, which allows for greater development of the character. Also unmissable (in every sense) is Brian Blessed as King Yrcanos, who out-bombasts even the Sixth Doctor. And the story builds strongly to a shocking ending that still packs a punch despite later developments.

THE EPISODES

All four episodes are restored from digital duplicates of the original one-inch colour videotape recordings used for broadcast, with the spaceship model sequences newly transferred from the original 35mm colour film. Their mono soundtracks are remastered and the title sequences replaced by a modern transfer of the original 35mm film with credits remade to match the originals.

SPECIAL FEATURES

THE MAKING OF MINDWARP (20m22s) The production of the second segment of *The Trial of a Time Lord*, including recording the beach scenes; the portrayals of Yrcanos, Crozier and Sil; the set design; deciphering the script; and writing out Peri. With contributions from script editor Eric Saward, writer Philip Martin, actors Colin Baker, Brian Blessed, Nicola Bryant, Michael Jayston and Patrick Ryecart, fan journalist Clayton Hickman and television historian Jim Sangster. Produced by Steve Broster.

DELETED AND EXTENDED SCENES (9m4s) A selection of scenes not used in the final programme, taken from earlier edits of the episodes with as-recorded sound.

NOW AND THEN – ON THE TRAIL OF A TIME LORD (21m2s) The changes in how location scenes were shot during Classic *Doctor Who*'s history, and comparison of the recording locations at Telscombe Cliffs near Brighton, Camber Sands near Rye and Gladstone Pottery Museum in Staffordshire as they look today with how they appeared in June and early-July 1986 when used for *The Trial of a Time Lord*. With footage of the location recording for 'Mindwarp' without the recolouring video effects. Narrated by Simon Ockenden, produced by Richard Bignell. *See Index iii for further editions*

A FATE WORSE THAN DEATH? (2m23s) Colin Baker and Nicola Bryant provide an audio commentary for the closing moments of episode fourteen in which Peri's true fate is revealed.

TRAILS AND CONTINUITY (3m32s) Continuity announcements from the original BBC1 broadcasts of episodes five to eight of *The Trial of a Time Lord*, with previous-episode summaries, and plugs for *Doctor Who* on video and the Longleat exhibition.

NEXT

AUDIO OPTIONS Select **Commentary** to play the audio commentary in place of the main soundtrack when watching the episodes. With Colin Baker, Nicola Bryant (Peri) and writer Philip Martin on all four episodes.

— Select **Feature Audio** to reinstate the main soundtrack when watching the episodes.

INFO TEXT Select **On** to view subtitles when watching the episodes that provide information and anecdotes about the development, production, broadcast and history of 'Mindwarp'. Written by Richard Molesworth.

CHILDREN IN NEED (3m16s) Extracts from the BBC's charity telethon on Friday 22 November 1985 in which Colin Baker and Nicola Bryant visit the *Doctor Who* exhibition at Blackpool, and many Doctors and companions emerge from the TARDIS to present Terry Wogan and Patrick Moore with cheques from fans' fundraising.

LENNY HENRY (4m36s) Sketch from the Thursday 3 October 1985 edition of *The Lenny Henry Show* with Henry as the Doctor and Jadie Rivas as Perry confronting Cyber-leader Thatchos.

PHOTO GALLERY (6m58s) Slideshow of colour and black-and-white photos taken during production of 'Mindwarp', set to sound effects from the story. Compiled by Derek Handley.

SUBTITLES

Select **On** to view subtitles for all episodes and Special Features (except commentary).

Parts 9 to 12 'TERROR OF THE VERVOIDS'

One disc with four episodes (98½ mins) and 89½ minutes of extras, plus commentary track and production subtitles

TARDIS TEAM Sixth Doctor, and introducing Mel Bush

TIME AND PLACE Space liner Hyperion III

ADVERSARIES Vervoids, genetically modified humanoid plants

FIRST ON TV 1–22 November 1986

DVD RELEASE BBCDVD2422(C), 29 September 2008, PG

COVER Photo illustration by Clayton Hickman, yellow strip

— Original release with cover sticker reading 'Parts Nine to Twelve 'Terror of the Vervoids''

ORIGINAL RRP £49.99 (boxset)

STORY TEASER

The Doctor is given access to the Matrix from which to select his defence, choosing an incident from his own future. A space liner on its way from Mogar to Earth sends a distress call to the TARDIS. The Doctor and new companion Melanie are soon caught snooping, but fortunately know the ship's commander and are given a free reign to help solve a man's murder. The deaths begin piling up, however, when a covert genetic experiment gets out of hand. The culprit must be found before the ship is pulled straight into a black hole.

CONNECTIONS

The Doctor is the last person you want to spend a space cruise with: shortly after he arrives on the Empress it's overrun with monsters in *Nightmare of Eden* (1979), while no sooner has he come aboard the Titanic on its way from Sto than it's plunging towards the Earth in *Voyage of the Damned* (2007). The Agatha Christie-like situation of a group of people in a confined location being killed off is common during the Second Doctor era, notably *The Moonbase* (1967) and *The Web of Fear* (1968), as well as in *Pyramids of Mars* (1975), *The Robots of Death* (1977), *Horror of Fang Rock* (1977), *The End of the World* (2005), *The Waters of Mars* (2009), *The Curse of the Black Spot* (2011), *The God Complex* (2011) and, of course, *The Unicorn and the Wasp* (2008), in which the Doctor meets Christie herself. He has trouble with black holes in *The Three Doctors* (1972/73), *The Horns of Nimon* (1979/80) and *The Impossible Planet/The Satan Pit* (2006), and has encountered several forms of intelligent plant life, such as the Weed Creature in *Fury from the Deep* (1968), the Krynoids in *The Seeds of Doom* (1976), a Zolfa-Thuran in *Meglos* (1980), and the Forest of Cheem in *The End of the World*. Pip and Jane Baker also wrote *The Mark of the Rani* (1985) and *Time and the Rani* (1987), as well as the final part of *The Trial of a Time Lord*. Chris Clough directed this and the final two episodes, as well as *Delta and the Bannermen* and *Dragonfire* in 1987, and *The Happiness Patrol* and *Silver Nemesis* in 1988. David Allister (Bruchner) plays Stimson in *The Leisure Hive* (1980), while Arthur Hewlett appears as Kalmar in *State of Decay* (1980).

WORTH WATCHING

The basic story is fairly straightforward but with an interesting twist on the whodunnit format. However, by now the court scenes are getting intrusive and the arc plot detracts from the adventure. There are some good guest stars and the Vervoid design isn't as bad as some people claim — the heads and hands are effective, the torso less so. The half-human version is nicely creepy, though.

THE EPISODES

All four episodes are restored from digital duplicates of the original one-inch colour videotape recordings used for broadcast and their mono soundtracks remastered. The title sequences are replaced by a modern transfer of the original 35mm film with credits remade to match the originals.

SPECIAL FEATURES

THE MAKING OF TERROR OF THE VERVOIDS (19m18s) The production of the third segment of *The Trial of a Time Lord*, including the origins and concepts of the script; the look of the Vervoids; the introduction of Mel; the characters and cast; working with the director; cliffhanger close-ups; and the design of the sets. With contributions from script editor Eric Saward, writers Pip and Jane Baker, director Chris Clough, actors Colin Baker, Michael Craig and Malcolm Tierney, fan journalist Clayton Hickman and television historian Jim Sangster. Produced by Steve Broster.

DELETED AND EXTENDED SCENES (14m6s) A selection of scenes not used in the final programme, taken from earlier edits of the episodes with as-recorded sound.

TRAILS AND CONTINUITY (3m14s) Continuity announcements from the original BBC1 broadcasts of episodes nine to twelve of *The Trial of a Time Lord*, with previous-episode summaries and the BBC2 morning schedule for Sunday 16 November 1986.

THE LOST SEASON (10m58s) The original plans for the 1986 season that were abandoned following the attempted cancellation of *Doctor Who* in 1985, including the return of the Toymaker in Graham Williams' 'The Nightmare Fair'; Wally K Daly's 'The Ultimate Evil'; a Robert Holmes script set in Singapore; the return of the Ice Warriors and of Sil in Philip Martin's 'Mission to Magnus'; and possible scripts by Christopher H Bidmead and Michael Feeney Callan. With contributions from script editor Eric Saward and writer Philip Martin. Narrated by Colin Baker, illustrations by Robert Hammond, produced by Richard Molesworth.

NEXT

AUDIO OPTIONS Select **Commentary** to play the audio commentary in place of the main soundtrack when watching the episodes. With Colin Baker, Michael Craig (Commodore), writers Pip and Jane Baker, and director Chris Clough on all four episodes.

— Select **Feature Audio** to reinstate the main soundtrack when watching the episodes.

INFO TEXT Select **On** to view subtitles when watching the episodes that provide information and anecdotes about the development, production, broadcast and history of 'Terror of the Vervoids'. Written by Richard Molesworth.

NOW, GET OUT OF THAT (28m20s) Discussion of *Doctor Who*'s different types of episode cliffhanger, from monster reveals to threats to the Doctor's life, unexpected events, cheat endings and some of the weaker examples. With writers Nev Fountain, Joseph Lidster and Robert Shearman, plus comments from actors Sophie Aldred, Colin Baker, Tom Baker, Peter Davison and Anneke Wills. Produced by James Goss.

SATURDAY PICTURE SHOW (7m32s) Extract from the 6 September 1986 edition of the BBC1 Saturday morning children's show in which Mark Curry talks to Bonnie Langford about her stage role in *Peter Pan* and joining *Doctor Who*.

PHOTO GALLERY (5m55s) Slideshow of colour photos taken during production of 'Terror of the Vervoids', set to music from the story. Compiled by Derek Handley.

SUBTITLES

Select **On** to view subtitles for all episodes and Special Features (except commentary).

Parts 13 to 14 'THE ULTIMATE FOE'

One disc with two episodes (54½ mins) and 114 minutes of extras, plus two commentary tracks, production subtitles and PDF items

TARDIS TEAM Sixth Doctor, Mel

TIME AND PLACE Trial courtroom and inside the Matrix

ADVERSARIES Valeyard; Third Master (8th appearance)

FIRST ON TV 29 November–6 December 1986

DVD RELEASE BBCDVD2422(D), 29 September 2008, PG

COVER Photo illustration by Clayton Hickman, black strip

— Original release with cover sticker reading 'Parts Thirteen to Fourteen 'The Ultimate Foe''

ORIGINAL RRP £49.99 (boxset)

STORY TEASER

When the Master interrupts the proceedings from within the Matrix itself, all hope seems lost for the Doctor. A shocking revelation puts his very future in turmoil and he too must venture inside the Matrix to flush out his enemies. But nothing is as it seems in this world of the imagination, and the truth behind the trial is revealed.

CONNECTIONS

The Doctor's previous trips into the Matrix have been only mentally, connecting his mind to it in *The Deadly Assassin* (1976) and *Arc of Infinity* (1983). The Master was last seen trapped in the Rani's out-of-control TARDIS in *The Mark of the Rani* (1985), and has escaped from his fate here by the time of *Survival* (1989). The Valeyard's true nature is similar to that of the Dream Lord in *Amy's Choice* (2010). Tony Selby returns as Glitz from the opening segment, 'The Mysterious Planet', and appears again in *Dragonfire* (1987). James Bree (the Keeper) also plays the Security Chief in *The War Games* (1969) and Decider Nefred in *Full Circle* (1980).

WORTH WATCHING

If you've got this far through *The Trial of a Time Lord* then you have to see its conclusion, even though problems with the scripting process meant it wasn't as climactic as initially planned. Given Robert Holmes' health at the time, episode thirteen is tremendous, building on ideas from *The Deadly Assassin* but heightening the danger by making the threat physical rather than mental. Episode fourteen by Pip and Jane Baker was a rushed replacement yet manages to maintain the atmosphere and provide a more or less coherent ending.

THE EPISODES

Both episodes are restored from digital duplicates of the original one-inch colour videotape recordings used for broadcast, with the spaceship model sequences newly transferred from the original 35mm colour film. Their mono soundtracks are remastered and the title sequences replaced by a modern transfer of the original 35mm film with credits remade to match the originals.

SPECIAL FEATURES

THE MAKING OF THE ULTIMATE FOE (15m15s) The production of the final segment of *The Trial of a Time Lord*, including the troubled scripting process; recording on location at Camber Sands and overnight at Gladstone Pottery Museum in Staffordshire; the concept of the Matrix; the villains; justifying the jargon; and unfortunate last words. With contributions from script editor Eric Saward, writers Pip and Jane Baker, director Chris Clough, actors Colin Baker, Michael Jayston and Tony Selby, fan journalist Clayton Hickman and television historian Jim Sangster. Produced by Steve Broster.

DELETED AND EXTENDED SCENES (4m37s) A selection of scenes not used in the final programme, taken from earlier edits of the episodes with as-recorded sound.

TRAILS AND CONTINUITY (1m13s) Previews and continuity announcements from the original BBC1 broadcasts of episodes thirteen and fourteen of *The Trial of a Time Lord*, with previous-episode summaries.

TRIALS AND TRIBULATIONS (55m6s) Examination of Colin Baker's unsettled time as the Sixth Doctor, including his casting; establishing his character; *that* costume; the struggle to find suitable writers; the positivity when recording the 1985 season; BBC management's attempt to cancel the show, commuted to a postponement after fan outcry (spurred on by the producer); recording the charity single 'Doctor in Distress'; the decision to keep the same production team; the radio serial *Slipback*; setting the trial theme for the next season and building a writing team; killing the companion and controversy over her replacement; the producer's focus on fandom; the resignation of the script editor leaving the trial without a conclusion and resultant tensions with the producer; and the edict to sack Baker. With contributions from BBC heads of series and serials Jonathan Powell and David Reid, producer John Nathan-Turner (interviewed in 1994), script editor Eric Saward, writers Pip and Jane Baker and Philip Martin, actors Colin Baker and Nicola Bryant, continuity advisor Ian Levine, and fan publisher Gary Leigh. Produced by Ed Stradling.

1985 HIATUS (3m55s) Reports from BBC News programmes on Wednesday 27 February 1985 about the postponement of the next season, from BBC *Breakfast Time* the following morning with Frank Bough and actress Gwen Taylor, and an extract from BBC1 chat show *Wogan* on Friday 1 March featuring the Cyber Controller (David Banks).

DOCTOR IN DISTRESS (3m45s) The full music video for the charity single released on Friday 15 March 1985 to raise awareness of *Doctor Who*'s hiatus, featuring pop stars and members of the programme's cast.

OPEN AIR (10m29s) Extract from the Monday 8 December 1986 edition of the BBC1 viewer feedback programme in which Pattie Coldwell talks to fans (including future New Series writer Chris Chibnall) in the studio about their disappointments with the 1986 season, puts their concerns to writers Pip and Jane Baker, and talks to producer John Nathan-Turner on the phone.

NEXT

AUDIO OPTIONS Select **Commentary 1** to play the audio commentary in place of the main soundtrack when watching the episodes. With Colin Baker, Tony Selby (Glitz) and director Chris Clough on both episodes, joined on episode fourteen by writers Pip and Jane Baker.

— Select **Commentary 2** to play an alternative audio commentary when watching episode thirteen. With script editor Eric Saward.

— Select **Feature Audio** to reinstate the main soundtrack when watching the episodes.

INFO TEXT Select **On** to view subtitles when watching the episodes that provide information and anecdotes about the development, production, broadcast and history of 'The Ultimate Foe'. Written by Richard Molesworth.

SATURDAY SUPERSTORE (13m32s) Extract from the 29 November 1986 edition of the BBC1 Saturday morning children's show in which Mike Read talks to Colin Baker and presents him with a TARDIS cake, and they take viewers' questions on the phone. With Sarah Greene.

PHOTO GALLERY (5m2s) Slideshow of colour and black-and-white photos taken during production of 'The Ultimate Foe', set to music from the story. Compiled by Derek Handley.

PDF MATERIALS Accessible via a computer are the fourteen episode listings from *Radio Times* for the original BBC1 broadcast of *The Trial of a Time Lord*, a two-page article and item on merchandise published the week of episode one, and a one-page article published the week of episode nine introducing Bonnie Langford.

— BBC press release with quotes from cast members of *The Trial of a Time Lord*.

— Magazine produced for the BBC Schools programme *Zig Zag* looking at the production process of *Doctor Who*, using the last production block of *The Trial of a Time Lord* as an example.

COMING SOON (57s) Trailer for the DVD release of *Four to Doomsday*.

SUBTITLES

Select **On** to view subtitles for all episodes and Special Features (except commentary).

RELATED EXTRAS

Coming Soon trailer — Black Orchid, The Brain of Morbius

THE **TWIN DILEMMA**

STORY No.136   SEASON No.21:7

One disc with four episodes (99½ mins) and 72 minutes of extras, plus commentary track, production subtitles and PDF items
Audio navigation of disc contents available by pressing Enter after the BBC ident

TARDIS TEAM Sixth Doctor, Peri
TIME AND PLACE Asteroid Titan 3 and planet Jaconda
ADVERSARIES Mestor the Gastropod
FIRST ON TV 22–30 March 1984
DVD RELEASE BBCDVD2598, 7 September 2009, PG (episodes U)
COVER Photo illustration by Clayton Hickman, green strip
ORIGINAL RRP £19.56

STORY TEASER

The newly regenerated Doctor is behaving erratically and, in a fit of remorse after attacking Peri, he decides they must both become hermits on Titan 3. But they find they are not alone: an old friend of the Doctor's, retired Time Lord Azmael, is holding twins he has been forced to kidnap. Their mathematical genius is needed for an astronomical plan by Mestor, the slug-like creature who has taken control of Azmael's adopted home world Jaconda. And he's likely to succeed if the Doctor can't pull himself together in time.

CONNECTIONS

There's a common assumption that the Doctor is disoriented and behaves out of character after a regeneration but this story sees the only extended instance of this. After his first he's mysterious but lucid (*The Power of the Daleks*, 1966); he sleeps off his second and is then fine (*Spearhead from Space*, 1970); likewise his third even if his new personality is more manic than most anyway (*Robot*, 1974/75); after his fourth regeneration he's weakened but coherent once he's found his way to the peacefulness of the zero room (*Castrovalva*, 1982); after his sixth he's just a little unsteady on his feet before the Rani messes with his perceptions (*Time and the Rani*, 1987); he briefly forgets who he is after his seventh (*The Movie*, 1996); seems determined from what little we see of him after his eighth (*Night of the Doctor*, 2013); is manic after his tenth before again sleeping it off (Children In Need special and *The Christmas Invasion*, 2005); his eleventh simply heals his injuries without changing his face (*Journey's End*, 2008); and his twelfth merely leaves his taste buds awry (*The Eleventh Hour*, 2010). Indeed, given the nature of his sixth persona, even strangling Peri and forcing her to become a hermit doesn't seem that out of character. Most Time Lords the Doctor encounters away from Gallifrey are renegades up to no good, but some like Azmael are less despicable, such as K'anpo in *Planet of the Spiders* (1974), Drax in *The Armageddon Factor* (1979), Professor Chronotis (*Shada*, 1980) and the Corsair mentioned in *The Doctor's Wife* (2011). Peter Moffatt directed several *Doctor Who* stories during the early-80s of which this was his penultimate (*see Index v*). Edwin Richfield (Mestor) is more recognisable as Captain Hart in *The Sea Devils* (1972), Dennis Chinnery (Professor Sylvest) plays Richardson, first mate of the Mary Celeste, in *The Chase* (1965) and Gharman in *Genesis of the Daleks* (1975), and Seymour Green (Jacondan chamberlain) is Harrison Chase's butler Hargreaves in *The Seeds of Doom* (1976).

THE EPISODES

All four episodes are restored from digital duplicates of the original one-inch colour videotape recordings used for broadcast, with location sequences newly transferred from the original 16mm colour film. Their mono soundtracks are remastered and the title sequences replaced by a modern transfer of the original 35mm film with credits remade to match the originals.

SPECIAL FEATURES

AUDIO OPTIONS Select **Commentary** to play the audio commentary in place of the main soundtrack when watching the episodes. With Colin Baker, Nicola Bryant (Peri) and Kevin McNally (Hugo Lang) on all four episodes.

— Select **Feature Audio** to reinstate the main soundtrack when watching the episodes.

INFO TEXT Select **On** to view subtitles when watching the episodes that provide information and anecdotes about the development, production, broadcast and history of *The Twin Dilemma*. Written by Jim Smith.

THE STAR MAN (6m4s) Graphic designer Sid Sutton talks about the adaptations for the arrival of the Sixth Doctor he and camera operator Terry Handley made to the 'starfield' title sequence they had created in 1980.

LOOK 100 YEARS YOUNGER (11m46s) Colin Baker and style icon Amy Lamé discuss the Doctor's outfit selections throughout his first seven incarnations, and what Baker would have preferred to wear as the Sixth Doctor. Produced by James Goss.

STRIPPED FOR ACTION – THE SIXTH DOCTOR (17m46s) *Doctor Who* comic strips have run in various publications since the early days of the television series. This examines the Sixth Doctor's comic strip adventures in Marvel Comics UK's *Doctor Who Magazine*. With contributions from magazine editors Alan Barnes, Alan McKenzie and Gary Russell, comics writer Simon Furman, and artist John Ridgway. Directed by Marcus Hearn. *See Index iii for further editions*

BREAKFAST TIME (9m54s) Extracts from the Thursday 22 March 1984 edition of the BBC1 morning news magazine programme in which Frank Bough and Selina Scott talk to Colin Baker (in costume) and Nicola Bryant.

NEXT

BLUE PETER (10m2s) Extract from the Thursday 15 March 1984 edition of the BBC1 children's magazine programme in which Janet Ellis talks to Colin Baker in costume, with a clips compilation of the Doctor's past regenerations and preview clips of *The Twin Dilemma*. (The *Saturday Superstore* appearance mentioned at the end is on **Vengeance on Varos Special Edition**.)

CONTINUITY (3m13s) Continuity announcements from the original BBC1 broadcasts of episode four of the preceding story, *The Caves of Androzani*, and all four episodes of *The Twin Dilemma*, with plugs for the very first video release of *Revenge of the Cybermen* and the *Doctor Who The Music* album. Includes an advert for the 22 March 1984 edition of the BBC's *The Listener* magazine, and the BBC1 evening schedule for Thursday 29 March 1984.

PHOTO GALLERY (8m5s) Slideshow of colour photos taken during production of *The Twin Dilemma*, including design department photos of the sets. Set to music from the story. Compiled by Derek Handley.

PDF MATERIALS Accessible via a computer are the four episode listings from *Radio Times* for the original BBC1 broadcast of *The Twin Dilemma*, and a one-page article about the new Doctor published the week of episodes one and two.

COMING SOON (1m11s) Trailer for the DVD release of *The Keys of Marinus*.

SUBTITLES

Select **On** to view subtitles for all episodes and Special Features (except commentary).

EASTER EGG

There is one hidden feature on this disc to find. *See Appendix 2 for details*

RELATED EXTRAS

Coming Soon trailer — Enlightenment, Mawdryn Undead, Terminus

Directing Who — The Visitation (and Special Edition)

THE **TWO DOCTORS**

STORY No.140   SEASON No.22:4

Two discs with three episodes (134 mins) and 190½ minutes of extras, plus commentary and music-only tracks, and production subtitles

TARDIS TEAM Sixth Doctor, Peri; Second Doctor, Jamie

TIME AND PLACE Space station Camera and contemporary Seville

ADVERSARIES Sontarans (4th appearance); Androgums Chessene and Shockeye

FIRST ON TV 16 February–2 March 1985

DVD RELEASE BBCDVD1213, 8 September 2003, PG

COVER Photo illustration by Clayton Hickman, dark orange strip

— Original release with cover sticker reading 'Doctor Who 40th Anniversary 1963–2003'

ORIGINAL RRP £19.99

— Also released in Bred for War: The Sontaran Collection; BBCDVD2617, £39.99, 5 May 2008

STORY TEASER

Investigating a scientific institute's dangerous experiments into time travel, the Doctor discovers unsavoury other parties have been waiting for a Time Lord to arrive as they need to examine one's genetic make-up to complete their time machine, and he will do very nicely. When his later incarnation chances upon evidence of his earlier death, he must find and rescue himself before he's carved up and past events swallow his future.

CONNECTIONS

While other stories have featured various incarnations of the Doctor being deliberately brought together, notably *The Three Doctors* (1973), *The Five Doctors* (1983) and *The Day of the Doctor* (2013), this is the only time he has crossed his own path by chance (unless you also count the 2007 Children In Need episode *Time Crash*). The Sontarans make their last appearance in the Classic Series, having debuted in *The Time Warrior* (1973/74), followed by *The Sontaran Experiment* (1975) and *The Invasion of Time* (1978); they return in the New Series in *The Sontaran Stratagem* (2008). The time-travel experiments of Kartz and Reimer perhaps build on the work of Edward Waterfield and Theodore Maxtible in *The Evil of the Daleks* (1967), Professor Thascales in *The Time Monster* (1972), Professor Kerensky in *City of Death* (1979), Hardin in *The Leisure Hive* (1980) and Professor Lazarus in *The Lazarus Experiment* (2007). Other time capsules seen in the series (excepting TARDISes) include the Daleks' time machine in *The Chase* (1965) and *The Daleks' Master Plan* (1965/66), the SIDRATs in *The War Games* (1969), Magnus Greel's Time Cabinet in *The Talons of Weng-Chiang* (1977), the vessel acquired by the Cybermen in *Attack of the Cybermen* (1985), and the Silents' time ship seen in *The Lodger* (2010) and *Day of the Moon* (2011). This is the Doctor's only on-screen trip to Spain, although he visits the Spanish Canary Islands in *Planet of Fire* (1984). Writer Robert Holmes had returned to the series with the previous season's well-regarded *The Caves of Androzani* (1984) having not contributed since 1979, while this was director Peter Moffatt's last *Doctor Who* serial, having first worked on 1980's *State of Decay* (*see Index v*). Laurence Payne, playing Dastari, is also gunslinger Johnny Ringo in *The Gunfighters* (1966) and Argolin leader Morix in *The Leisure Hive* (1980), while Clinton Greyn (Stike) appears as Ivo in *State of Decay*.

WORTH WATCHING

After the critical success of *The Caves of Androzani*, Robert Holmes was once again the golden boy of *Doctor Who* writers and *The Two Doctors* sees him being given full reign to indulge his dark and sometimes grisly sense of humour. Often this is fun but sometimes it's uncomfortably close to the bone, and some of the more flippant moments are decidedly distasteful. Holmes was asked to include the Sontarans but is clearly more interested in his new creations, the Androgums, and the monsters are sadly underused for their last Classic Series appearance.

DISC ONE

THE EPISODES

All three episodes are restored from digital duplicates of the original one-inch colour videotape recordings used for broadcast and their mono soundtracks remastered. The title sequences are replaced by a digital duplicate of the original one-inch colour videotape transfer of the 35mm film with credits overlaid from the episode recordings.

SPECIAL FEATURES

A FIX WITH SONTARANS (9m18s) *Doctor Who* mini-episode written by script editor Eric Saward from the Saturday 2 March 1985 edition of BBC1 viewer requests show *Jim'll Fix It*, starring Colin Baker as the Doctor, Janet Fielding as Tegan, the Sontarans, and Gareth Jenkins in his home-made Sixth Doctor costume. With Jimmy Saville.

INFORMATION TEXT Select **On** to view subtitles when watching the episodes that provide information and anecdotes about the development, production, broadcast and history of *The Two Doctors*. Written by Richard Molesworth.

AUDIO OPTIONS

Select **Commentary On** to play the audio commentary in place of the main soundtrack when watching the episodes. With Colin Baker, Nicola Bryant (Peri), Frazer Hines (Jamie), Jacqueline Pearce (Chessene) and director Peter Moffatt on all three episodes.

— Select **Isolated Score On** to hear only Peter Howell's music when watching the episodes.

SUBTITLES

Select **On** to view subtitles for all episodes and *A Fix with Sontarans*, or for the commentary.

DISC TWO

SPECIAL FEATURES

BEHIND THE SOFA ROBERT HOLMES & DOCTOR WHO (45m29s) Profile of television writer Robert Holmes, who died in 1986, from how he started contributing to *Doctor Who*, to becoming the series' script editor during one of its most popular periods, and writing many of its most lauded stories. With memories from colleagues director/producer Barry Letts, producer Philip Hinchcliffe, script editors Terrance Dicks and Eric Saward, and writer Chris Boucher. Produced by Richard Molesworth.

BENEATH THE LIGHTS (27m57s) Footage from the full studio recording on Friday 31 August 1984 of three scenes on the space station from episodes one and two, including retakes and shots unused in the final programme.

BENEATH THE SUN (36m15s) Footage from the location filming between Thursday 9 and Sunday 12 August 1984 at the hacienda and surrounding countryside near Seville, Spain, including retakes and shots unused in the final programme. Taken from a VHS recording of the film's projection.

40TH ANNIVERSARY CELEBRATION (3m) Compilation of clips from all eras of Classic *Doctor Who*, set to Orbital's version of the theme music, included on all releases in 2003.

ADVENTURES IN TIME AND SPAIN (29m26s) Production manager Gary Downie talks about the process of finding and filming at locations in and around Seville for *The Two Doctors*. Produced by Peter Finklestone.

WAVELENGTH (29m) Edition of the BBC Schools Radio programme broadcast on BBC Radio 4 on Thursday 20 September 1984, going behind the scenes of *Doctor Who* during production of *The Two Doctors*. Featuring interviews with actors Colin Baker, Nicola Bryant, Tim Raynham, John Stratton and Patrick Troughton, director Peter Moffatt, designer Tony Burroughs, costume designer Jan Wright, make-up supervisor Catherine Davies, studio sound recordist Keith Bowden, special sounds creator Dick Mills, production manager Gary Downie, production secretary Sarah Lee, and producer John Nathan-Turner. Presented by Andy Peebles, reporter Jackie Rowley, produced by Sarah McNeill.

PHOTO GALLERY (8m5s) Slideshow of colour photos taken during production of *The Two Doctors*. Set to sound effects from the story. Compiled by Ralph Montagu.

SUBTITLES Select **On** to view subtitles for all Special Features on disc two.

EASTER EGG

There is one hidden feature on these discs to find. *See Appendix 2 for details*

RELATED EXTRAS

Built for War — The Sontaran Experiment

Directing Who — The Visitation (and Special Edition)

THE **UNDERWATER MENACE**

STORY No.32   SEASON No.4:5

One surviving episode (part 3 of 4) released in the **LOST IN TIME** *set*

TARDIS TEAM Second Doctor, Ben, Jamie, Polly
TIME AND PLACE Contemporary Atlantis
ADVERSARIES Professor Zaroff
FIRST ON TV 28 January 1967
DVD RELEASE BBCDVD1353, 1 November 2004, PG
● *See* Lost in Time *for full details*

Since the Lost in Time set was released, episode two of *The Underwater Menace* has been recovered, returned to the archive in September 2011 by film collector Terry Burnett, who bought the film at a school fête in the 1980s. He also acquired episode three of *Galaxy 4* (1965), which he subsequently returned in July 2011 and was included, fully restored, on the Special Edition release of *The Aztecs* in March 2013. It has been reported that *The Underwater Menace* will be issued on DVD sometime in 2014, although no specific date has been announced. Along with the existing third episode that has always survived in the archive, it's expected the two remaining missing episodes will be animated by Planet 55 Studios, although this has not been confirmed. Special features including a documentary on the making of the serial, produced by Russell Minton, are known to have been made, and at least the standard features of commentary, production subtitles and a photo gallery are likely, as is part two of The Television Centre of the Universe, part one of which is on The Visitation Special Edition.

RELATED EXTRAS
Coming Soon trailer — The Moonbase
The Doctor's Composer — The War Games

UNDERWORLD

STORY No.96   SEASON No.15:5

Released with **THE HORNS OF NIMON** and **THE TIME MONSTER** in the **MYTHS AND LEGENDS** boxset

One disc with four episodes (89½ mins) and 55 minutes of extras, plus commentary track, production subtitles and PDF items
Audio navigation of disc contents available by pressing Enter after the BBC ident

TARDIS TEAM Fourth Doctor, Leela, K9
TIME AND PLACE Minyan spaceship the R1C and planetoid around sister ship the P7E
ADVERSARIES Oracle computer and its attendant Seers
FIRST ON TV 7–28 January 1978
DVD RELEASE BBCDVD2851(B), 29 March 2010, 12 (episodes and commentaries PG)
COVER Photo illustration by Clayton Hickman, dark pink strip;
          version with older BBC logo on reverse
ORIGINAL RRP £49.99 (boxset)

STORY TEASER
The Doctor and Leela encounter the crew of a spaceship from Minyos that has been travelling for millennia in search of its sister ship the P7E. To survive the quest they have been perpetually regenerating, but ship are crew are on their last legs. Entering a region of space where planets spontaneously form, they narrowly avoid being buried by crushing rocks. The P7E has suffered that very fate, however, and the survivors subjugated by the very thing the Minyans hope will save them.

CONNECTIONS
Events on Minyos are given as the reason for the Time Lords' policy of non-intervention, for the transgression of which the Doctor was tried in both *The War Games* (1969) and *The Trial of a Time Lord* (1986). Another group that tried to mimic the Time Lords' regenerative abilities, resulting in

perpetual renewal, were the scientists in *Mawdryn Undead* (1983). This story is explicitly a rewriting of the Greek story of Jason and the Argonauts' quest for the Golden Fleece; similarly *The Horns of Nimon* (1979/80) reworks elements of the legend of the minotaur. The Doctor meets some real Greeks we only know from legend in *The Myth Makers* (1965). Writers Bob Baker and Dave Martin contributed stories throughout the 1970s, from *The Claws of Axos* in 1971 to *The Armageddon Factor* in 1979 (*see Index v*), while Norman Stewart also directed *The Power of Kroll* the following season. Richard Shaw (Lakh) also appears as Lobos in *The Space Museum* (1965) and Cross in *Frontier in Space* (1973), Frank Jarvis (Ankh) is an army corporal in *The War Machines* (1966) and Skart in *The Power of Kroll*, and Jimmy Gardner (Idmon) plays Chenchu in *Marco Polo* (1964).

WORTH WATCHING

Doctor Who has taken many old familiar stories and given them a science-fiction rewrite, so it's perhaps surprising it took fifteen years to get its take on a Greek myth. Spotting the references to the legend of Jason can be fun, although these days they're well catalogued by fans. The script itself spends a little too much time squeezing in as many allusions as it can and less on constructing an engaging story, but it's the production that really lets the serial down. While some might argue it's an innovative attempt at using virtual sets, now *de rigueur* in filmmaking, in actuality it's hard to watch and maintain suspension of one's disbelief.

THE EPISODES

All four episodes are restored from digital duplicates of the original two-inch colour videotape recordings used for broadcast and their mono soundtracks remastered. The title sequences are replaced by a modern transfer of the original 35mm film with credits remade to match the originals.

SPECIAL FEATURES

INTO THE UNKNOWN (30m43s) The making of *Underworld*, including the origins of the script; elements of the story of Jason and the Argonauts and other Greek legends that are referenced; coping with a minimal budget; deciding to try using model sets and choosing a suitable director; the difficulties of acting without scenery; working with actor Alan Lake; adding the video effects; and the model work. With contributions from producer Graham Williams (at a convention in 1985), script editor Anthony Read, writers Bob Baker and Dave Martin (interviewed in 2006), director Norman Stewart (from a 1995 audio interview), designer Dick Coles, video effects designer AJ Mitchell, and actors Jonathan Newth and Norman Tipton. Narrated by Richard Heffer, produced by Ed Stradling.

UNDERWORLD – IN STUDIO (17m30s) Footage from the full studio recordings in October 1977 showing the difficulty of the blue-screen process, including retakes and shots unused in the final programme, some taken from a low-quality black-and-white copy with on-screen time-code, some from a colour VHS copy. Narrated by Philip Kelly.

PHOTO GALLERY (5m55s) Slideshow of colour and black-and-white photos taken during production of *Underworld*, including design department photos of the sets. Set to sound effects from the story. Compiled by Derek Handley.

AUDIO OPTIONS Select **Commentary** to play the audio commentary in place of the main soundtrack when watching the episodes. With Tom Baker, Louise Jameson (Leela) and writer Bob Baker on all four episodes.

— Select **Feature Audio** to reinstate the main soundtrack when watching the episodes.

INFO TEXT Select **On** to view subtitles when watching the episodes that provide information and anecdotes about the development, production, broadcast and history of *Underworld*. Written by Jim Smith.

PDF MATERIALS Accessible via a computer are the four episode listings from *Radio Times* for the original BBC1 broadcast of *Underworld*.

COMING SOON (41s) Trailer for the DVD release of *The Creature from the Pit*.

SUBTITLES

Select **On** to view subtitles for all episodes and Special Features (except commentary).

RELATED EXTRAS

Coming Soon trailer — The Chase, The Space Museum

U.N.I.T FILES

Boxset of **THE ANDROID INVASION** and **INVASION OF THE DINOSAURS**

DVD RELEASE BBCDVD3376, 9 January 2012, PG

SLIPCASE Photo illustration by Clayton Hickman, silvered logo and title, orange/brown background

ORIGINAL RRP £30.63

WHAT'S IN THE BOX

Two stories featuring the United Nations Intelligence Taskforce, the military group led by Brigadier Lethbridge-Stewart tasked with investigating strange and alien activities, and to which the Doctor was scientific advisor. In *Invasion of the Dinosaurs* (1974) the Third Doctor and Sarah Jane return to find London evacuated, dinosaurs roaming the city, and a conspiracy that goes to the heart of UNIT. And in *The Android Invasion* (1975) the Fourth Doctor and Sarah think they're back on Earth but their UNIT friends are behaving oddly and hideous Kraals are in charge.

● *See individual stories for full contents*

VENGEANCE ON VAROS

STORY No.138   SEASON No.22:2

One disc with two episodes (89½ mins) and 19½ minutes of extras, plus commentary and studio-sound tracks, production subtitles and image content

TARDIS TEAM Sixth Doctor, Peri

TIME AND PLACE Planet Varos

ADVERSARIES Sil (1st appearance); colony rulers the Chief and Quillam

FIRST ON TV 19–26 January 1985

DVD RELEASE BBCDVD1044, 15 October 2001, PG

COVER Photo montage, green strip

ORIGINAL RRP £19.99

STORY TEASER

The population of Varos is struggling to survive, selling its only natural resource, Zeiton-7, exclusively to the Galatron Mining Corporation for a pitiful price, unaware that it's one of the rarest minerals in the universe. So rare that when the TARDIS runs out, the Doctor is forced to use up its last ounce of power in a bid to reach Varos. But the planet's rulers have found a new source of income — selling videos of torture and death — and the Doctor and Peri find themselves with starring roles in the next show.

CONNECTIONS

The TARDIS loses all power when it lands on the planet Exxilon in *Death to the Daleks* (1974). Human colonies struggling to sustain themselves feature in *Colony in Space* (1971) and *Frontios* (1984), while the former also sees them being exploited by a ruthless mining corporation. In *The Macra Terror* (1967) the head of a colony is similarly convinced aliens are misusing his people but is opposed by his security chief. Sil returns, along with others of his species, in *The Trial of a Time Lord: Mindwarp* (1986), while his business practices are reminiscent of those of the Usurian Collector in *The Sun Makers* (1977). Philip Martin also wrote Sil's return, which was directed by Ron Jones too, having first worked on *Doctor Who* in 1982 (*see Index v*). Martin Jarvis (the Governor) plays the Menoptra Hilio in *The Web Planet* (1965) and Butler in *Invasion of the Dinosaurs* (1974), Stephen Yardley (Arak) is Sevrin in *Genesis of the Daleks* (1975), while Sheila Reid (Etta) returns as Clara's gran in *The Time of the Doctor* (2013).

WORTH WATCHING

In 1985 there was much concern over the ready availability on VHS of so-called 'video nasties', particularly the risk of children seeing them, and *Vengeance on Varos* offered a timely take on the impact of treating gruesome images as entertainment. It's ironic, then, that it should coincide with one of the regular backlashes against the degree of violence presented in the show itself. While the production might be trying to have its cake and eat it in terms of its critique of how violence is portrayed on television, *Vengeance on Varos* is a strong story with a memorable monster villain.

THE EPISODES

Both episodes are restored from digital duplicates of the original one-inch colour videotape recordings used for broadcast.

SPECIAL FEATURES *ALSO ON SPECIAL EDITION

*BBC ONE TRAILER EPISODE 1 (23s) Preview broadcast fifteen minutes ahead of the episode on Saturday 19 January 1985.

*BBC ONE TRAILER EPISODE 2 (18s) Preview broadcast fifteen minutes ahead of the episode on Saturday 26 January 1985.

*EXTENDED/DELETED SCENES (10m21s) A selection of scenes from both episodes not used in the final programme, taken from a VHS copy of earlier edits with as-recorded sound and on-screen time-code.

*BEHIND THE SCENES (4m42s) Footage from the full studio recording on Wednesday 1 August 1984 of a scene in the prison control centre, including retakes and shots unused in the final programme.

*AUDIO OPTIONS Select **Commentary On** to play the audio commentary in place of the main soundtrack when watching the episodes. With Colin Baker, Nicola Bryant (Peri) and Nabil Shaban (Sil) on both episodes.

— Select **Production Audio On** to watch the episodes with sound as recorded in the studio, before the addition of music and sound effects.

▶

INFORMATION TEXT Select **On** to view subtitles when watching the episodes that provide information and anecdotes about the development, production, broadcast and history of *Vengeance on Varos*. Written by Richard Molesworth.

- ● *On the initial UK release of this disc the production subtitles stop ten minutes into episode two due to an error in authoring. This was corrected for the Region 4 (Australasia/South America) release, which is playable in the UK.*

PHOTO GALLERY Scroll through 71 colour photos taken during production of *Vengeance on Varos*. Compiled by Ralph Montagu.

*OUTTAKES (3m6s) Bloopers and fluffed lines taken from the original studio recording.

*CONTINUITY ANNOUNCEMENTS (35s) Continuity announcements from the original BBC1 broadcasts of both episodes of *Vengeance on Varos*.

SUBTITLES

Select **On** to view subtitles for all episodes and Special Features, or for the commentary.

VENGEANCE ON VAROS SPECIAL EDITION

STORY No.138   SEASON No.22:2

Two discs with two episodes (89½ mins) and 116 minutes of extras, plus commentary, studio-sound, music-only and surround-sound tracks, production subtitles and PDF items
Audio navigation of each disc's contents available by pressing Enter after the BBC ident

TARDIS TEAM Sixth Doctor, Peri

TIME AND PLACE Planet Varos

ADVERSARIES Sil (1st appearance); colony rulers the Chief and Quillam

FIRST ON TV 19–26 January 1985

DVD RELEASE BBCDVD3512, 10 September 2012, PG

COVER Photo illustration by Lee Binding, light purple strip; version with older BBC logo on reverse

ORIGINAL RRP £20.42

STORY TEASER

The population of Varos is struggling to survive, selling its only natural resource, Zeiton-7, exclusively to the Galatron Mining Corporation for a pitiful price, unaware that it's one of the rarest minerals in the universe. So rare that when the TARDIS runs out, the Doctor is forced to use up its last ounce of power in a bid to reach Varos. But the planet's rulers have found a new source of income — selling videos of torture and death — and the Doctor and Peri find themselves with starring roles in the next show.

CONNECTIONS

The TARDIS loses all power when it lands on the planet Exxilon in *Death to the Daleks* (1974). Human colonies struggling to sustain themselves feature in *Colony in Space* (1971) and *Frontios* (1984), while the former also sees them being exploited by a ruthless mining corporation. In *The Macra Terror* (1967) the head of a colony is similarly convinced aliens are misusing his people but is opposed by his security chief. Sil returns, along with others of his species, in *The Trial of a Time Lord: Mindwarp* (1986), while his business practices are reminiscent of those of the Usurian Collector in *The Sun Makers* (1977). Philip Martin also wrote Sil's return, which was directed by Ron Jones too, having first worked on *Doctor Who* in 1982 (*see Index v*). Martin Jarvis (the Governor) plays the Menoptra Hilio in *The Web Planet* (1965) and Butler in *Invasion of the Dinosaurs* (1974), Stephen Yardley (Arak) is Sevrin in *Genesis of the Daleks* (1975), while Sheila Reid (Etta) returns as Clara's gran in *The Time of the Doctor* (2013).

WORTH WATCHING

This Special Edition features more advanced clean-up of the episodes compared to the previous release and additional Special Features. In 1985 there was much concern over the ready availability on VHS of so-called 'video nasties', particularly the risk of children seeing them, and *Vengeance on Varos* offered a timely take on the impact of treating gruesome images as entertainment. It's ironic, then, that it should coincide with one of the regular backlashes against the degree of violence presented in the show itself. While the production might be trying to have its cake and eat it in terms of its critique of how violence is portrayed on television, *Vengeance on Varos* is a strong story with a memorable monster villain.

DISC ONE

THE EPISODES

Both episodes are newly restored from digital duplicates of the original one-inch colour videotape recordings used for broadcast and their mono soundtracks remastered. The title sequences are replaced by a modern transfer of the original 35mm colour film with credits remade to match the originals.

SPECIAL FEATURES *REPEATED FROM PREVIOUS RELEASE

AUDIO OPTIONS Select ***Commentary** to play the audio commentary recorded for the previous release in place of the main soundtrack when watching the episodes. With Colin Baker, Nicola Bryant (Peri) and Nabil Shaban (Sil) on both episodes.

— Select ***Mono Production Audio** to watch the episodes with sound as recorded in the studio, before the addition of music and sound effects.

— Select **5.1 Audio** to hear the Dolby Digital surround soundtrack when watching the episodes, newly remixed for this release.

— Select **Isolated Score** to hear only Jonathan Gibbs' music when watching the episodes.

— Select **Isolated Score in 5.1** to hear only Jonathan Gibbs' music in Dolby Digital surround when watching the episodes, newly remixed for this release.

— Select **Mono Audio** to reinstate the main soundtrack when watching the episodes.

INFO TEXT Select **On** to view subtitles when watching the episodes that provide information and anecdotes about the development, production, broadcast and history of *Vengeance on Varos*, updated and expanded from the previous release. Written by Paul Scoones.

SUBTITLES

Select **On** to view subtitles for both episodes (none for commentary).

DISC TWO

SPECIAL FEATURES *REPEATED FROM PREVIOUS RELEASE

NICE OR NASTY (29m39s) Writer and broadcaster Matthew Sweet presents a look at the making of *Vengeance on Varos* to gauge if it really matches its grisly reputation. He examines the origins and concepts of the script; portraying the audience within the story; the creation and realisation of Sil; composing the incidental music; the impact of the move to 45-minute episodes; and the validity of the claim of excessive violence as a reason to cancel *Doctor Who*. Sweet talks to script editor Eric Saward, writer Philip Martin, composer Jonathan Gibbs, and actors Sheila Reid and Nabil Shaban. Produced by Thomas Guerrier.

THE IDIOT'S LANTERN (7m31s) Journalist and broadcaster Samira Ahmed examines the uses of the formats and medium of television itself within the narrative of the Classic and New Series. Written by Simon Guerrier, produced by Thomas Guerrier.

EXTENDED AND DELETED SCENES (17m43s) A selection of scenes from both episodes not used in the final programme, taken from a VHS copy of earlier edits with as-recorded sound and on-screen time-code. Expanded from the previous release.

ACID BATH SCENE WITH ALTERNATIVE MUSIC (1m37s) The scene from episode two with a music cue that was rewritten for the broadcast episode.

*BEHIND THE SCENES (4m42s) Footage from the full studio recording on Wednesday 1 August 1984 of a scene in the prison control centre, including retakes and shots unused in the final programme.

SUBTITLES Select **On** to view subtitles for all Special Features on disc two.

NEXT

*OUTTAKES (3m6s) Bloopers and fluffed lines taken from the original studio recording.

*TRAILERS (43s) Previews of the episodes broadcast fifteen minutes ahead of each on Saturdays 19 and 26 January 1985.

*CONTINUITIES (35s) Continuity announcements from the original BBC1 broadcasts of both episodes of *Vengeance on Varos*.

TOMORROW'S TIMES – THE SIXTH DOCTOR (12m55s) Coverage of *Doctor Who* in the national newspapers during the Sixth Doctor's era from 1984 to 1987. Presented by Sarah Sutton, written and directed by Marcus Hearn. *See Index iii for further editions*

NEWS (1m8s) Item from the BBC1 *Nine O'Clock News* on Friday 19 August 1983, in which John Humphrys introduces a report by Frances Coverdale on the casting of Colin Baker as the Doctor.

BREAKFAST TIME (5m43s) Extract from the Monday 22 August 1983 edition of the BBC1 morning news programme in which Frank Bough talks to Colin Baker about his casting as the Doctor.

NEXT

SATURDAY SUPERSTORE (15m7s) Extract from the 17 March 1984 edition of the BBC1 Saturday morning children's show in which Mike Read talks to Colin Baker and Nicola Bryant (in costume), and they take viewers' questions on the phone — including a surprise call from the Master. John Craven and graphologist Diane Simpson examine Baker's handwriting to determine his personality traits. *Shorter extract also on* The Mark of the Rani

FRENCH & SAUNDERS (7m33s) Unbroadcast sketch from the comedy duo's 1987 series (recorded on Sunday 25 January but dropped from the Monday 13 April show) with George Layton as the Doctor, Joanna Bowen as the Questioner, Jim Hopper as Oliver, and Dawn and Jennifer as Silurian guards. Recorded on the courtroom set from *The Trial of a Time Lord*.

PHOTO GALLERY (6m40s) Slideshow of colour photos taken during production of *Vengeance on Varos*, set to music from the story. Compiled by Paul Shields.

PDF MATERIALS Accessible via a computer are the two episode listings from *Radio Times* for the original BBC1 broadcast of *Vengeance on Varos*, and letters about the increasing violence in the programme published in the 7 February 1985 edition (also on The Mark of the Rani).

— BBC Enterprises' sales document for *Vengeance on Varos*, describing the serial for potential overseas broadcasters.

COMING SOON (1m6s) Trailer for the DVD release of *The Ambassadors of Death*.

RELATED EXTRAS

Coming Soon trailer — Planet of Giants

THE **VISITATION**

STORY No.119   SEASON No.19:4

One disc with four episodes (96½ mins) and 67½ minutes of extras, plus commentary and music-only tracks, and production subtitles

TARDIS TEAM Fifth Doctor, Adric, Nyssa, Tegan

TIME AND PLACE Outskirts of London, September 1666

ADVERSARIES Reptilian Terileptils; their jewelled android

FIRST ON TV 15–23 February 1982

DVD RELEASE BBCDVD1329, 19 January 2004, PG (episodes U)

COVER Photo illustration by Clayton Hickman (amended by in-house designer), turquoise strip

ORIGINAL RRP £19.99

STORY TEASER

Fear of the plague makes strangers unwelcome in 17th Century England, as the TARDIS crew discover when they are attacked by the inhabitants of a village where ominous lights in the sky have heralded the appearance of the Grim Reaper himself. Seeking sanctuary at the local manor house, they discover they are not the only new arrivals. Escaped alien convicts are hiding in the cellar and planning a contagion that will eradicate the human race.

CONNECTIONS

The Doctor revisits 17th Century England on the trail of Lady Peinforte in *Silver Nemesis* (1988), and encounters both real and recreational Roundheads from the period in *The Time Monster* (1972) and *The Awakening* (1984) respectively. The Earth has been visited by several monster species in its past, including the Daleks (*The Daleks' Master Plan*, 1965/66; *The Evil of the Daleks*, 1967; *Remembrance of the Daleks*, 1988; *Daleks in Manhattan*, 2007; *Victory of the Daleks*, 2010), the Great Intelligence and its Yeti (*The Abominable Snowmen*, 1967), the Sontarans (*The Time Warrior*, 1973/74), the Zygons (*Terror of the Zygons*, 1975; *The Day of the Doctor*, 2013), the Osirans (*Pyramids of Mars*, 1975), the Rutans (*Horror of Fang Rock*, 1977), the Jagaroth (*City of Death*, 1979), the Malus (*The Awakening*), the Carrionites (*The Shakespeare Code*, 2007), the Pyroviles (*The Fires of Pompeii*, 2008), the Vespiform (*The Unicorn and the Wasp*, 2008), the Cybermen (*The Next Doctor*, 2008), the Saturnyne (*The Vampires of Venice*, 2010), the Krafayis (*Vincent and the Doctor*, 2010), and the Ice Warriors (*Cold War*, 2013). Writer Eric Saward went on to become script editor for the following four years and also wrote *Earthshock* (1982), *Resurrection of the Daleks* (1984) and *Revelation of the Daleks* (1985), as well as much of *The Twin Dilemma* (1984) and *Attack of the Cybermen* (1985), while this was the second of several serials directed by Peter Moffatt (*see Index v*).

WORTH WATCHING

While the early historical adventures featured only human adversaries, and today's ventures into Earth's past always include an alien presence, the monster-in-history style of story — dubbed 'pseudo-historical' — is less prevalent in the Classic Series than is commonly assumed. *The Visitation* is one of the better examples, with the alien plot arising from and relevant to the period. The Terileptils are also a notable early use of animatronic masks, while the two main guest stars — Michaels Melia and Robbins — impress. It even builds to a twist of the sort that people assume is common in *Doctor Who* but again is actually rare.

THE EPISODES

All four episodes are restored from digital duplicates of the original two-inch colour videotape recordings used for broadcast, with location sequences newly transferred from the original print of the 16mm colour film. Their mono soundtracks are remastered and the opening title sequences replaced by a modern transfer of the original 35mm film with title credits overlaid from the episode recordings.

SPECIAL FEATURES   *ALSO ON SPECIAL EDITION

*DIRECTING WHO – PETER MOFFATT (26m14s) Peter Moffatt talks about his work on *Doctor Who*, directing the serials *State of Decay* (1980), *The Visitation*, *Mawdryn Undead* (1983), *The Five Doctors* (1983), *The Twin Dilemma* (1984) and *The Two Doctors* (1985).

V

*SCORING THE VISITATION (16m19s) Composer Paddy Kingsland talks to fellow musician Mark Ayres about the ideas and processes behind scoring the incidental music for this serial.

*FILM TRIMS (5m32s) Unused 16mm colour film footage from the location filming at Black Park in Buckinghamshire, Hurley Tithe Barn in Berkshire and Ealing Studios in early-May 1981. Plus silent footage for use on monitors in the story, set to music from the serial.

*AUDIO OPTIONS Select **Commentary On** to play the audio commentary in place of the main soundtrack when watching the episodes. With Peter Davison and director Peter Moffatt on all four episodes, joined part-way into episode one by Janet Fielding (Tegan), Sarah Sutton (Nyssa) and Matthew Waterhouse (Adric).

— Select **Isolated Music On** to hear only Paddy Kingsland's music when watching the episodes.

▶

*WRITING A FINAL VISITATION (12m51s) Eric Saward talks about scripting his first *Doctor Who* serial, including the origins of his Richard Mace character, conceiving the Terileptils and destroying the sonic screwdriver.

*PHOTO GALLERY (5m12s) Slideshow of colour photos taken during production of *The Visitation*, with sound effects from the story. Compiled by Ralph Montagu.

INFORMATION TEXT Select **On** to view subtitles when watching the episodes that provide information and anecdotes about the development, production, broadcast and history of *The Visitation*. Written by Richard Molesworth.

SUBTITLES
Select **On** to view subtitles for all episodes and Special Features, or for the commentary.

EASTER EGG
There is one hidden feature on this disc to find. *See Appendix 2 for details*

THE **VISITATION** SPECIAL EDITION

STORY No.119   SEASON No.19:4

Two discs with four episodes (96½ mins) and 173½ minutes of extras, plus commentary and music-only tracks, production subtitles and PDF items
Audio navigation of each disc's contents available by pressing Enter after the BBC ident

TARDIS TEAM Fifth Doctor, Adric, Nyssa, Tegan
TIME AND PLACE Outskirts of London, September 1666
ADVERSARIES Reptilian Terileptils; their jewelled android
FIRST ON TV 15–23 February 1982
DVD RELEASE BBCDVD3690, 6 May 2013, PG (episodes U)
COVER Photo illustration by Lee Binding, dark red strip; version with older BBC logo on reverse
ORIGINAL RRP £20.42

STORY TEASER
Fear of the plague makes strangers unwelcome in 17th Century England, as the TARDIS crew discover when they are attacked by the inhabitants of a village where ominous lights in the sky have heralded the appearance of the Grim Reaper himself. Seeking sanctuary at the local manor house, they discover they are not the only new arrivals. Escaped alien convicts are hiding in the cellar and planning a contagion that will eradicate the human race.

CONNECTIONS
The Doctor revisits 17th Century England on the trail of Lady Peinforte in *Silver Nemesis* (1988), and encounters both real and recreational Roundheads from the period in *The Time Monster* (1972) and *The Awakening* (1984) respectively. The Earth has been visited by several monster species in its past, including the Daleks (*The Daleks' Master Plan*, 1965/66; *The Evil of the Daleks*, 1967; *Remembrance of the Daleks*, 1988; *Daleks in Manhattan*, 2007; *Victory of the Daleks*, 2010), the Great Intelligence and its Yeti (*The Abominable Snowmen*, 1967), the Sontarans (*The Time Warrior*, 1973/74), the Zygons (*Terror of the Zygons*, 1975; *The Day of the Doctor*, 2013), the Osirans (*Pyramids of Mars*,

1975), the Rutans (*Horror of Fang Rock*, 1977), the Jagaroth (*City of Death*, 1979), the Malus (*The Awakening*), the Carrionites (*The Shakespeare Code*, 2007), the Pyroviles (*The Fires of Pompeii*, 2008), the Vespiform (*The Unicorn and the Wasp*, 2008), the Cybermen (*The Next Doctor*, 2008), the Saturnyne (*The Vampires of Venice*, 2010), the Krafayis (*Vincent and the Doctor*, 2010), and the Ice Warriors (*Cold War*, 2013). Writer Eric Saward went on to become script editor for the following four years and also wrote *Earthshock* (1982), *Resurrection of the Daleks* (1984) and *Revelation of the Daleks* (1985), as well as much of *The Twin Dilemma* (1984) and *Attack of the Cybermen* (1985), while this was the second of several serials directed by Peter Moffatt (*see Index v*).

WORTH WATCHING

This Special Edition features further clean-up of the episodes compared to the previous release and additional Special Features. While the early historical adventures featured only human adversaries, and today's ventures into Earth's past always include an alien presence, the monster-in-history style of story — dubbed 'pseudo-historical' — is less prevalent in the Classic Series than is commonly assumed. *The Visitation* is one of the better examples, with the alien plot arising from and relevant to the period. The Terileptils are also a notable early use of animatronic masks, while the two main guest stars — Michaels Melia and Robbins — impress. It even builds to a twist of the sort that people assume is common in *Doctor Who* but again is actually rare.

DISC ONE

THE EPISODES

All four episodes are restored from digital duplicates of the original two-inch colour videotape recordings used for broadcast and their mono soundtracks remastered, with location sequences newly transferred from the original 16mm colour film negatives. The title sequences are replaced by a modern transfer of the original 35mm film with credits remade to match the originals.

SPECIAL FEATURES *REPEATED FROM PREVIOUS RELEASE

*FILM TRIMS (5m32s) Unused 16mm colour film footage from the location filming at Black Park in Buckinghamshire, Hurley Tithe Barn in Berkshire and Ealing Studios in early-May 1981. Plus silent footage for use on monitors in the story, set to music from the serial.

*DIRECTING WHO – PETER MOFFATT (26m14s) Peter Moffatt talks about his work on *Doctor Who*, directing the serials *State of Decay* (1980), *The Visitation*, *Mawdryn Undead* (1983), *The Five Doctors* (1983), *The Twin Dilemma* (1984) and *The Two Doctors* (1985).

*WRITING A FINAL VISITATION (12m51s) Eric Saward talks about scripting his first *Doctor Who* serial, including the origins of his Richard Mace character, conceiving the Terileptils and destroying the sonic screwdriver.

*SCORING THE VISITATION (16m19s) Composer Paddy Kingsland talks to fellow musician Mark Ayres about the ideas and processes behind scoring the incidental music for this serial.

NEXT

*PHOTO GALLERY (5m12s) Slideshow of colour photos taken during production of *The Visitation*, with sound effects from the story. Compiled by Ralph Montagu.

INFO TEXT Select **On** to view subtitles when watching the episodes that provide information and anecdotes about the development, production, broadcast and history of *The Visitation*, updated and expanded from the previous release. Written by Nicholas Pegg.

*AUDIO OPTIONS Select **Commentary** to play the audio commentary recorded for the previous release in place of the main soundtrack when watching the episodes. With Peter Davison and director Peter Moffatt on all four episodes, joined part-way into episode one by Janet Fielding (Tegan), Sarah Sutton (Nyssa) and Matthew Waterhouse (Adric).

— Select **Isolated Music** to hear only Paddy Kingsland's music when watching the episodes.

— Select **Feature Audio** to reinstate the main soundtrack when watching the episodes.

SUBTITLES

Select **On** to view subtitles for all episodes and Special Features on disc one (except commentary).

DISC TWO

SPECIAL FEATURES

GRIM TALES (45m10s) Peter Davison, Janet Fielding and Sarah Sutton return to the filming locations used in *The Visitation* to discuss with Mark Strickson the making of the serial, including coping with the noise of aeroplanes when filming near Heathrow; their opinions of the script; setting up a full-size escape pod on location; staging the fights; the guest cast; realising the Terileptils and their android; working with actor Michael Robbins and director Peter Moffatt; and staging the Great Fire of London at Ealing Studios. With contributions from writer Eric Saward, designer Ken Starkey, costume designer Odile Dicks-Mireaux, make-up supervisor Carolyn Perry, actors Michael Melia and Peter Van Dissel, and Howard and Jennifer Leigh, owners of filming location Tithecote Manor. Produced by Russell Minton.

THE TELEVISION CENTRE OF THE UNIVERSE – PART ONE (32m12s) Presenter Yvette Fielding takes actors Peter Davison, Janet Fielding and Mark Strickson on a tour through BBC Television Centre to recall working at the iconic studio complex in the 1980s. With contributions from production assistant Jane Ashford, costume designer Odile Dicks-Mireaux, assistant floor manager Sue Hedden, producer Richard Marson, make-up artists Carolyn Perry and Joan Stribling, and film traffic supervisor Neville Withers. Produced by Russell Minton. *Part two has yet to be released*

DOCTOR FOREVER – THE APOCALYPSE ELEMENT (27m30s) Examining how *Doctor Who* has spread beyond the television screen, this edition looks at the audio adventures that have been produced by Big Finish since 1999 starring all the surviving Classic Series Doctors, and the BBC's readings of Target novelisations. With contributions from New Series showrunner Russell T Davies, BBC Worldwide range editor Steve Cole, Big Finish executive producers Nicholas Briggs, Jason Haigh-Ellery and Gary Russell and producer David Richardson, AudioGo commissioning editor Michael Stevens, writers Paul Cornell, Mark Gatiss, Joseph Lidster, Justin Richards and Robert Shearman, and actors Colin Baker, Lisa Bowerman and William Russell. Presented by Ayesha Antoine, produced by James Goss. *See Index iii for further editions*

PDF MATERIALS Accessible via a computer are the four episode listings from *Radio Times* for the original BBC1 broadcast of *The Visitation*.

— BBC Enterprises' sales document for *The Visitation*, describing the serial for potential buyers.

SUBTITLES Select **On** to view subtitles for all Special Features on disc two.

COMING SOON (1m4s) Trailer for the Special Edition DVD release of *Inferno*.

EASTER EGG

There is one hidden feature on these discs to find. *See Appendix 2 for details*

THE **WAR GAMES**

STORY No.50   SEASON No.6:7

Three discs with ten episodes (241 mins) and 213 minutes of extras, plus commentary track, production subtitles and PDF items
Audio navigation of each disc's contents available by pressing Enter after the BBC ident

TARDIS TEAM Second Doctor, Jamie, Zoe

TIME AND PLACE Alien planet with Earth war zones

ADVERSARIES War Lords posing as human generals

FIRST ON TV 19 April–21 June 1969

DVD RELEASE BBCDVD1800, 6 July 2009, PG

COVER Photo illustration by Clayton Hickman, blue strip

ORIGINAL RRP £24.46

— Episodes released in the Regeneration box; BBCDVD3801, £61.27, 24 June 2013

STORY TEASER

The TARDIS lands in the No-Man's Land of World War One, or so it seems. Both English and German soldiers are behaving oddly and their generals have a hypnotic control over them. When the Doctor and his friends suddenly find themselves facing a Roman legion, then men from the American Civil War, they realise someone is kidnapping soldiers from different times — someone who has access to their own TARDISes and with whom the Doctor is strangely familiar.

CONNECTIONS

Shortly before the onset of the First World War a humanised Doctor is teaching history at an English public school, from which several of the boys end up in the trenches (*Human Nature/The Family of Blood*, 2007), while in *Silver Nemesis* (1988) the passing of the Nemesis comet is said to have heralded the start of the war. The Doctor visits Rome during its empire in *The Romans* (1965) and Pompeii in *The Fires of Pompeii* (2008) but avoids any military conflict, and the closest he is seen to get to the American Civil War is watching Abraham Lincoln's Gettysburg Address on the Time and Space Visualiser in *The Chase* (1965). The War Chief is only the second of his own people the Doctor encounters on screen after the Monk in *The Time Meddler* (1965) and *The Daleks' Master Plan* (1965/66), although he soon meets more, of course, as we're introduced to the Time Lords, who will make return appearances most notably in *The Three Doctors* (1973), *The Deadly Assassin* (1976), *The Invasion of Time* (1978), *Arc of Infinity* (1983), *The Five Doctors* (1983), *The Trial of a Time Lord* (1986), *The End of Time* (2009/10) and *The Day of the Doctor* (2013). The Doctor is again tried for interference in *The Trial of a Time Lord*, and for murder in *The Deadly Assassin*, while his sentence here is played out over the following three years of the programme. The Second Doctor, Jamie and Zoe appear again in *The Five Doctors*, while in *The Two Doctors* (1985) Jamie seems to have rejoined the Second Doctor for further adventures. Terrance Dicks was just moving up to become full script editor when writing *The War Games*, a post he would hold throughout the Third Doctor era, to which his co-writer Malcolm Hulke would contribute several scripts (*see Index v*). David Maloney had already directed *The Mind Robber* and *The Krotons* earlier in the 1968/69 season, and would later direct many well-regarded serials (*see Index v*). David Savile (Lieutenant Carstairs) plays Dr Winser in *The Claws of Axos* (1971) and Colonel Crichton in *The Five Doctors*, Terence Bayler (Major Barrington) appears as Yendom in *The Ark* (1966), and Hubbert Rees (Captain Ransom) is the chief engineer in *Fury from the Deep* (1968) and Stevenson in *The Seeds of Doom* (1976). Gregg Palmer (Lucke) plays Cybermen in their first appearance in *The Tenth Planet* (1966), while David Garfield (Von Weich) is also in *The Face of Evil* (1977), as is Leslie Schofield (Leroy), playing Neeva and Calib respectively. Michael Lynch (Spencer) is a Thal in *Genesis of the Daleks* (1975), Graham Weston (Sergeant Russell) plays De Haan in *Planet of Evil* (1975), Peter Craze (Du Pont) is Dako in *The Space Museum* (1965) and Costa in *Nightmare of Eden* (1979), while David Troughton (Private Moor) has more substantial roles as King Peladon in *The Curse of Peladon* (1972) and Professor Hobbes in *Midnight* (2008). James Bree (Security Chief) returns as Decider Nefred in *Full Circle* (1980) and the Keeper of the Matrix in *The Trial of a Time Lord: The Ultimate Foe* (1986), Edward Brayshaw (War Chief) plays Leon Colbert in *The Reign of Terror* (1964), and Philip Madoc (War Lord) is Eelek in *The Krotons* (1969), Solon in *The Brain of Morbius* (1976) and Fenner in *The Power of Kroll* (1978/79). Time Lords Bernard Horsfall and Clyde Pollitt return in *The Deadly Assassin* and *The Three Doctors* respectively, possibly as the same characters.

WORTH WATCHING

Although its length was down to a lack of other scripts, *The War Games* feels suitably epic for not only the end of the Second Doctor's era but also the end of the first phase of *Doctor Who*. Different producers put their own stamps on the first six years but it was always the same show; after this it would still be *Doctor Who* but demonstrably different, not only by being in colour and tied to Earth but also in its style and sophistication of storytelling. And even at ten episodes *The War Games* barely drags, each additional war zone adding something new to the plot or the Doctor's understanding, until the climactic final episode that changes the character's nature for ever.

DISC ONE

THE EPISODES

To maximise their quality on the DVDs, episodes one to five are on disc one and episodes six to ten are on disc two. All five episodes on this disc are restored from 16mm film copies of the original black-and-white videotape recordings, held by the BFI. Their mono soundtracks are remastered and the VidFIRE process is applied to studio-recorded shots to recapture the smoother motion of video. The title sequences are replaced by a modern transfer of the original 35mm film with end credits remade to match the originals.

AUDIO OPTIONS

Select **Commentary** to play the audio commentary in place of the main soundtrack when watching the episodes. With Frazer Hines (Jamie) [eps 1,2,3,4,5], Wendy Padbury (Zoe) [1,2,3,5], writer Terrance Dicks [1,2,4,5], Jane Sherwin (Lady Jennifer) [1,3,4,5] and producer Derrick Sherwin [2,3,4].

— Select **Feature Audio** to reinstate the main soundtrack when watching the episodes.

SUBTITLES

Select **Subtitles On** to view subtitles for all episodes on disc one (none for commentary).

— Select **Info Text On** to view subtitles when watching the episodes that provide information and anecdotes about the development, production, broadcast and history of *The War Games*. Written by Martin Wiggins.

DISC TWO

THE EPISODES

Episodes six to ten on this disc are restored from 16mm film copies of the original black-and-white videotape recordings, held by the BFI. Their mono soundtracks are remastered and the VidFIRE process is applied to studio-recorded shots to recapture the smoother motion of video. The title sequences are replaced by a modern transfer of the original 35mm film with end credits remade to match the originals.

AUDIO OPTIONS

Select **Commentary** to play the audio commentary in place of the main soundtrack when watching the episodes. With Graham Weston (Russell) [eps 6,7,8,9], Wendy Padbury (Zoe) [6,7,8,10], Frazer Hines (Jamie) [6,8,10], producer Derrick Sherwin [6,9,10], Philip Madoc (War Lord) [7,8,9,10] and writer Terrance Dicks [7,9,10].

— Select **Feature Audio** to reinstate the main soundtrack when watching the episodes.

SUBTITLES

Select **Subtitles On** to view subtitles for all episodes on disc two (none for commentary).

— Select **Info Text On** to view subtitles when watching the episodes that provide information and anecdotes about the development, production, broadcast and history of *The War Games*. Written by Martin Wiggins.

DISC THREE

PLAY ALL

Plays each of the Special Features in turn

SPECIAL FEATURES

WAR ZONE (36m24s) The making of *The War Games*, including the origins of the script and keeping the story going for ten weeks; working with the director; the characters and cast; filming on location at a rubbish tip; designing the sets; the creation of the Time Lords; and the departures of all the regular cast. With contributions from producer Derrick Sherwin, writer Terrance Dicks, director David Maloney (interviewed in 2003), designer Roger Cheveley, actors Frazer Hines, Bernard Horsfall, Wendy Padbury, Jane Sherwin and Graham Weston, New Series writers Paul Cornell, Joseph Lidster and James Moran, and fan journalist Tom Spilsbury. Narrated by Gerard Murphy, produced by Steve Broster.

SHADES OF GREY (21m46s) Examination of the process and style of television production, design and performance in the 1960s when television was in made in black and white, discussion of whether this was an advantage or a limitation, and how *Doctor Who* differed from other pro-grammes of the era. With memories from producer Derrick Sherwin, script editor Terrance Dicks, director Timothy Combe, set designer Roger Cheveley, sound designer Brian Hodgson, graphic designer Bernard Lodge, and actors Frazer Hines, Wendy Padbury and Jane Sherwin. Narrated by Gerard Murphy, produced by Steve Broster.

NOW AND THEN (9m35s) Comparing the filming locations in the area around Brighton and Eastbourne as they look today with how they appeared in late-March 1969 when used for *The War Games*. With colour photos from the location recce of Sheepcote Rubbish Tip in Brighton and Birling Manor Farm in East Sussex, and cuttings from local press reports. Narrated and produced by Richard Bignell. *See Index iii for further editions*

THE DOCTOR'S COMPOSER (17m32s) Composer Dudley Simpson talks about his extensive contribution to the incidental music for *Doctor Who*, interviewed in his home town of Sydney. This part covers his early career, his first work on *Doctor Who* for *Planet of Giants* (1964), *The Crusade* (1965) and *The Chase* (1965), and using more electronic sounds in collaboration with the BBC Radiophonic Workshop for later scores like *The Underwater Menace* (1967), *The Evil of the Daleks* (1967) and *The Seeds of Death* (1969). Narrated by Simon Ockenden, produced by Brendan Sheppard. *Part two covering the 1970s is on* The Sun Makers

SYLVIA JAMES – IN CONVERSATION (8m27s) Make-up supervisor Sylvia James talks about her regular work during the Second Doctor era, creating the make-up and hair styles for each story from *The Abominable Snowmen* (1967) to *The War Games*.

TALKING ABOUT REGENERATION (24m24s) Discussion of the Doctor's regenerations (up the *The Parting of the Ways*, 2005) and how each is presented on screen. With fan writers Clayton Hickman, Joseph Lidster, Gareth Roberts and Robert Shearman, plus actors Peter Davison and Kate O'Mara. Produced by James Goss.

TIME ZONES (15m22s) Historians discuss the real histories of the First World War and American Civil War, plus the sophistication of the Roman army. With classical archaeologist Lindsay Allison-Jones, political historian Dr Martin Farr, author Professor Susan-Mary Grant and military historian Crispin Swayne. Produced by Chris Chapman.

NEXT

STRIPPED FOR ACTION – THE SECOND DOCTOR (13m46s) *Doctor Who* comic strips have run in various publications since the early days of the television series. This examines the Second Doctor's adventures in Polystyle Publications' *TV Comic*. With contributions from magazine editors Alan Barnes and Gary Russell, and comics historians John Ainsworth and Jeremy Bentham. Directed by Marcus Hearn. *See Index iii for further editions*

ON TARGET – MALCOLM HULKE (20M) The Target range of *Doctor Who* novelisations was for years the only way to experience past stories, and its regular authors were very influential on their child readers. This examines the books of Malcolm Hulke, including the first behind-the-scenes book *The Making of Doctor Who* in 1972 (included on The Sea Devils) and his work for Target which greatly expanded on his own television scripts. With contributions from fellow author Terrance Dicks, writers Alan Barnes, David J Howe and Gary Russell, and artist Chris Achilleos. Readings by Katy Manning and Peter Miles, directed by Marcus Hearn.

DEVIOUS (12m17s) Footage from a 1990s fan video project charting the adventures of the Doctor between his second and third incarnations, as played by Tony Garner. This sequence features Jon Pertwee in his last recorded performance as the Third Doctor. Select to hear optional commentary by its creators David Clarke, Stephen Cranford and Ashley Nealfuller.

PHOTO GALLERY (6m33s) Slideshow of colour and black-and-white photos taken during production of *The War Games*, including design department photos of the sets and locations, plus shots of the commentary participants. Set to sound effects from the story. Compiled by Derek Handley.

PDF MATERIALS Accessible via a computer are the ten episode listings from *Radio Times* for the original BBC1 broadcast of *The War Games* and an article that introduced the story.
— Designer Roger Cheveley's blueprints for the SIDRAT prop.
— BBC Enterprises' sales document for *The War Games*, describing the serial for potential overseas broadcasters.

COMING SOON (1m10s) Trailer for the DVD releases of *Enlightenment*, *Mawdryn Undead* and *Terminus* in The Black Guardian Trilogy boxset.

SUBTITLES

Select **On** to view subtitles for all Special Features on disc three.

EASTER EGGS

There are three hidden features on these discs to find. *See Appendix 2 for details*

RELATED EXTRAS

Coming Soon trailer — Delta and the Bannermen
The Rise and Fall of Gallifrey — The Invasion of Time

THE **WAR MACHINES**

STORY No.27   SEASON No.3:10

One disc with four episodes (95½ mins) and 46 minutes of extras, plus commentary track, production subtitles and PDF items

TARDIS TEAM First Doctor, Dodo, and introducing Bcn Jackson and Polly
TIME AND PLACE London, 1966
ADVERSARIES Advanced computer WOTAN; War Machines, computer-controlled tanks
FIRST ON TV 25 June–16 July 1966
DVD RELEASE BBCDVD2441, 25 August 2008, PG
COVER Photo illustration by Clayton Hickman, red strip
ORIGINAL RRP £19.99

STORY TEASER

Construction of the imposing Post Office Tower has just been completed and installed at the very top is WOTAN, a thinking computer that's set to link with others to create the first global computer network. But WOTAN has plans of its own, taking over the minds of its creators and ordering them to construct powerful War Machines to replace humans as the rulers of the Earth. As the machines go on the rampage, the army is powerless to stop them and soon realise it is the Doctor who is required to defeat this menace.

CONNECTIONS

This is the first story explicitly set in contemporary London since the TARDIS left the Totter's Lane junkyard in *An Unearthly Child* (1963) and it won't return until *The Faceless Ones* (1967), which it transpires takes place on the same day as *The War Machines*. The Doctor faces further crazed computers such as BOSS in *The Green Death* (1973), Xoanon in *The Face of Evil* (1977), the Oracle in *Underworld* (1978) and Mentalis in *The Armageddon Factor* (1979). Following this and the evac-uation in 1963 (*Remembrance of the Daleks*, 1988), London comes under increased attack from monstrous forces, including the Yeti in *The Web of Fear* (1968), leading to the creation of the special investigation team UNIT. They save London from the Cybermen in *The Invasion* (1968), Autons in *Spearhead from Space* (1970) and dinosaurs in *Invasion of the Dinosaurs* (1974). However, they don't appear to be around for later Auton and Cybermen invasions in *Rose* (2005) and *The Army of Ghosts/Doomsday* (2006). *The War Machines* is the first story based on ideas suggested by scientist Kit Pedler, who would help create the Cybermen and contribute to their appearances throughout the remainder of the 1960s, while script writer Ian Stuart Black also wrote *The Savages* (1966) and *The Macra Terror* (1967). Michael Ferguson returned to direct *The Seeds of Death* (1969), *The Ambassadors of Death* (1970) and *The Claws of Axos* (1971). John Harvey (Professor Brett) plays Officia in *The Macra Terror*, which also features Sandra Bryant (Kitty). John Rolfe (Army Captain) appears as Sam Becket in *The Moonbase* (1967) and Ralph Fell in *The Green Death*, Frank Jarvis (Corporal) is Ankh in *Underworld* (1978) and Skart in *The Power of Kroll* (1978/79), and Ric Felgate (Reporter) is cast by Ferguson again as Brent in *The Seeds of Death* and astronaut Charles Van Leyden in *The Ambassadors of Death*.

WORTH WATCHING

A sea change in *Doctor Who* occurs here. Prior to this the series is about adventures in weird and wonderful places across the universe or dangerous times in Earth's past; afterwards it will increasingly be about protecting the present day from attack by superior forces, sometimes homegrown, mostly alien. The threat here may be somewhat clunky, but it represents a more realistic style of storytelling that will become the series' norm by the end of the decade.

THE EPISODES

All four episodes are restored from 16mm film copies of the original black-and-white videotape recordings, recovered from a Nigerian broadcaster in January 1985. Episode one is complete but these copies of episodes two, three and four are edited. The cuts from episode two are restored from a lower-quality 16mm film copy returned from Australia by Donald Gee in 1978; some gaps in episode three are restored from footage cut at the request of the Australian Film Censorship

Board but stored in the Board's archive long after the episodes themselves had been destroyed and discovered by Damian Shanahan in October 1996; and a cut from episode four (plus two existing shots) is restored from a 35mm film copy used in the 20 June 1966 edition of *Blue Peter*. Further missing sections are filled with edited shots from elsewhere in the episode matched to a recording of the soundtrack made on audio tape when the episodes were originally broadcast. A section of Ealing Studio filming in episode three is newly transferred from the original 35mm black-and-white film. The episodes' mono soundtracks are remastered and the VidFIRE process is applied to studio-recorded shots to recapture the smoother motion of video. The title sequences are replaced by a modern transfer of the best surviving copy of the original 35mm film with credits remade to match the originals.

SPECIAL FEATURES

NOW AND THEN (6m40s) Comparing the filming locations in Central London as they look today with how they appeared in late-May 1966 when used for *The War Machines*. Narrated by Simon Ockenden, produced by Richard Bignell. *See Index iii for further editions*

BLUE PETER (16m15s) Extracts from the BBC1 children's magazine programme. From the Monday 11 October 1965 edition, Valerie Singleton shows two stamps marking the opening of the Post Office Tower while Christopher Trace visits the building itself, then shows how to make your own model of the tower. From the Monday 20 June 1966 edition, Trace previews *The War Machines* and he and Singleton encounter the real thing in the studio. From the Monday 27 June 1966 edition, Trace shows pictures of a Dalek built by the children of Forches Cross Primary School in Barnstaple, Devon, and in the studio talks to viewer Philip Campbell about the working Dalek made by him and his brother Simon.

ONE FOOT IN THE PAST (7m32s) Extract from the Tuesday 19 May 1998 edition of the BBC2 history programme in which ex-MP Tony Benn revisits the Post Office Tower and recalls its opening in 1965 when he was Postmaster General.

WOTAN ASSEMBLY (9m14s) Detailing the recovery of the episodes of *The War Machines* and the complex restoration undertaken for this release using all the footage that survives. With episode hunter Ian Levine (interviewed in 1998). Narrated by Anneke Wills.

COMING SOON (1m13s) Trailer for the DVD release of *Battlefield*.

NEXT

AUDIO OPTIONS Select **Commentary** to play the audio commentary in place of the main soundtrack when watching the episodes. With Anneke Wills (Polly) and director Michael Ferguson on all four episodes.

— Select **Feature Audio** to reinstate the main soundtrack when watching the episodes.

INFO TEXT Select **On** to view subtitles when watching the episodes that provide information and anecdotes about the development, production, broadcast and history of *The War Machines*. Written by Richard Bignell.

PHOTO GALLERY (4m12s) Slideshow of black-and-white photos taken during production of *The War Machines*, including publicity shots of new companions Ben and Polly, and design department photos of the sets. Set to pop music tracks used in the story. Compiled by Ralph Montagu.

— Select **Info Text On** before selecting **Play Gallery** to view descriptive captions while watching the slideshow.

PDF MATERIALS Accessible via a computer are the four episode listings from *Radio Times* for the original BBC1 broadcast of *The War Machines*, and an article introducing the story with illustration by Victor Reinganum.

— Designer Raymond London's blueprints for the War Machine prop.

SUBTITLES

Select **On** to view subtitles for all episodes and Special Features (except commentary).

EASTER EGG

There is one hidden feature on this disc to find. *See Appendix 2 for details*

RELATED EXTRAS

Coming Soon trailer — Four to Doomsday

WARRIORS OF THE DEEP

STORY No.130   SEASON No.21:1

Released with **DOCTOR WHO AND THE SILURIANS** and **THE SEA DEVILS** in the **BENEATH THE SURFACE** boxset

One disc with four episodes (97½ mins) and 68 minutes of extras, plus commentary and music-only tracks, production subtitles and PDF items

TARDIS TEAM Fifth Doctor, Tegan, Turlough

TIME AND PLACE Earth, 2084

ADVERSARIES Silurians and Sea Devils (3rd appearance); human infiltrators

FIRST ON TV 5–13 January 1984

DVD RELEASE BBCDVD2438(C), 14 January 2008, PG

COVER Photo illustration by Clayton Hickman, pale green strip

ORIGINAL RRP £39.99 (boxset)

STORY TEASER

Making an emergency landing on Earth in 2084, when the world is on the brink of nuclear war, the TARDIS arrives in a military Sea Base on the ocean floor that is the first line of defence, or attack. The crew suspect the Doctor, Tegan and Turlough of being enemy agents, unaware that real spies are already working to gain control of the base's missiles. But the real enemy is outside, in the dark waters, awakening from a long sleep and only too happy to help Man destroy himself.

CONNECTIONS

The Silurians debut in *Doctor Who and the Silurians* (1970) and their underwater cousins in *The Sea Devils* (1972). A different species of the former appears in the New Series in *The Hungry Earth/ Cold Blood* (2010). Strangely the Myrka has not been revived. Being trapped in a base under siege from reptilian monsters with mutually destructive weapons under unstable computer control is reminiscent of *The Ice Warriors* (1967). Johnny Byrne also wrote *The Keeper of Traken* (1981) and *Arc of Infinity* (1983), while director Pennant Roberts helmed four Fourth Doctor serials in the late-70s before returning for this and the following year's *Timelash* (*see Index v*). Ingrid Pitt (Dr Solow) plays Queen Galleia in *The Time Monster* (1972), while Stuart Blake (Scibus) appears as Zoldaz in *State of Decay* (1980) and the Chancellery Guard captain in *The Five Doctors* (1983).

WORTH WATCHING

Opinion of *Warriors of the Deep* is generally pretty low but it's one of those serials where ambitions and expectations exceeded the realities of mid-80s television production (not helped in this instance by a shortened time in which to make the episodes). The script asked for a run-down underwater base being stormed by an army of reptile-men; it got brightly lit corridors with rubber monsters ambling along them. This is a common occurrence throughout *Doctor Who*'s history, though, and arguably should be its default starting point: aim high and see how close you can get. When it hits the target the results are amazing, but even when it doesn't there's at least some virtue in the attempt.

THE EPISODES

All four episodes are restored from digital duplicates of the original one-inch colour videotape recordings used for broadcast and their mono soundtracks remastered. The title sequences are replaced by a modern transfer of the original 35mm film with credits remade to match the originals.

SPECIAL FEATURES

AUDIO OPTIONS Select **Commentary** to play the audio commentary in place of the main soundtrack when watching the episodes. With Peter Davison, Janet Fielding (Tegan), script editor Eric Saward and visual effects designer Mat Irvine on all four episodes.

— Select **Isolated Music** to hear only Jonathan Gibbs' music when watching the episodes.

— Select **Feature Audio** to reinstate the main soundtrack when watching the episodes.

INFO TEXT Select **On** to view subtitles when watching the episodes that provide information and anecdotes about the development, production, broadcast and history of *Warriors of the Deep*. Written by Martin Wiggins.

THE DEPTHS (31m44s) The making of *Warriors of the Deep*, including the decision to bring back and team up the Silurians and Sea Devils; reflections of the Cold War and the story's morality; the guest cast; losing production time owing to General Election coverage; designing and lighting the sets; realising the Myrka; staging the battles and shooting underwater scenes; and the legacy of *Warriors of the Deep*. With contributions from writer Johnny Byrne, continuity advisor Ian Levine, director Pennant Roberts, visual effects designer Mat Irvine, actors John Asquith, James Coombes, Peter Davison, Janet Fielding and Ian McCulloch, and fan Ed Stradling. Narrated by David Harley, produced by Steve Broster.

NEXT

THEY CAME FROM BENEATH THE SEA (12m56s) The realisation of the Silurians, Sea Devils and Myrka as they appeared in *Warriors of the Deep*. With writer Johnny Byrne, director Pennant Roberts, visual effects designer Mat Irvine, Myrka operators John Asquith and William Perrie, and actor Peter Davison. Produced by Steve Broster.

SCIENCE IN ACTION (5m59s) Extract from the BBC Schools science programme first broadcast on BBC2 on Monday 14 March 1988, in which presenter Kjartan Poskitt visits Mat Irvine in the BBC Visual Effects department to look at the materials and techniques used in effects work. Features a Silurian mask and submarine from *Warriors of the Deep*, a Tetrap head from *Time and the Rani* (1987) and the Biomechanoid from *Dragonfire* (1987).

TRAILS & CONTINUITIES (3m58s) Preview of the 1984 season, with clips from *Warriors of the Deep*, *The Awakening*, *Frontios* and *Resurrection of the Daleks*; and trailers and continuity announcements from the original BBC1 broadcasts of all four episodes of *Warriors of the Deep*.

NEXT

PHOTO GALLERY (7m42s) Slideshow of colour photos taken during production of *Warriors of the Deep*, including design department photos of the sets. Set to music from the story. Compiled by Ralph Montagu.

COMING SOON: THE TIME MEDDLER (1m4s) Trailer for the DVD release of *The Time Meddler*.

RADIO TIMES LISTINGS Accessible via a computer is a PDF file of the four episode listings for the original BBC1 broadcast of *Warriors of the Deep*.

SUBTITLES
Select **On** to view subtitles for all episodes and Special Features (except commentary).

EASTER EGG
There is one hidden feature on this disc to find. *See Appendix 2 for details*

RELATED EXTRAS
Coming Soon trailer — Destiny of the Daleks

WARRIORS' GATE

STORY No.113   SEASON No.18:5

Released with **FULL CIRCLE** and **STATE OF DECAY** in **THE E-SPACE TRILOGY** boxset
One disc with four episodes (94 mins) and 79 minutes of extras, plus commentary and music-only tracks, production subtitles and PDF items
Audio navigation of disc contents available by pressing Enter after the BBC ident

TARDIS TEAM Fourth Doctor, Second Romana, Adric, K9
TIME AND PLACE Void between E-Space and N-Space
ADVERSARIES Human slave traders; Gundan robots
FIRST ON TV 3–24 January 1981
DVD RELEASE BBCDVD1835(C), 26 January 2009, PG
COVER Photo illustration by Clayton Hickman, pale blue strip
ORIGINAL RRP £34.99 (boxset)

STORY TEASER
The TARDIS and a slave trading ship are both marooned in a void, each brought there by the time-sensitive Tharil Biroc. His people are exploited for their ability to navigate through time, but they

hope to escape to their home in E-Space via the only structure in this void: a crumbling stone gateway. While the Doctor passes through a mirror inside the gateway and experiences the Tharils' ignoble past, Romana is captured by the human slavers who realise she too is time-sensitive and might be able to get them out of there, little realising that their very presence is collapsing the void around them.

CONNECTIONS

The origin of the CVEs, the pathways into E-Space, is revealed at the end of the season in *Logopolis* (1981). The Doctor has previously found himself in blank dimensions in *The Celestial Toymaker* (1966) and *The Mind Robber* (1968), although those had controlling intelligences. This is different to the Void through which the TARDIS falls in *Rise of the Cybermen* (2006) and from which the Daleks emerge in *Army of Ghosts* (2006), but looks oddly similar to the engine room of the TARDIS (*Journey to the Centre of the TARDIS*, 2013). Dwarf star alloy is used again to build a prison for the Doctor in *Day of the Moon* (2011). Writer Stephen Gallagher also scripted *Terminus* (1983), while David Weston (Biroc) plays Nicholas Muss in *The Massacre* (1966).

WORTH WATCHING

Doctor Who can and does tell many strange and wonderful stories, but this is one that's like no other. With complex concepts and events occurring in different times in a non-linear fashion, it's more abstruse than a Steven Moffat script. Yet there are clear, strong characters and morals that keep it grounded and accessible. The result is a *tour de force* of ideas and imagery that, in terms of storytelling and direction, is decades ahead of its time.

THE EPISODES

All four episodes are restored from digital duplicates of the original two-inch colour videotape recordings used for broadcast and their mono soundtracks remastered. Model sequences are newly transferred from the original 16mm and 35mm colour film. The title sequences are replaced by a modern transfer of the original 35mm film with credits remade to match the originals.

SPECIAL FEATURES

AUDIO OPTIONS Select **Commentary** to play the audio commentary in place of the main soundtrack when watching the episodes. With Lalla Ward (Romana), John Leeson (K9 voice), script editor Christopher H Bidmead, director Paul Joyce and visual effects designer Mat Irvine on all four episodes.

— Select **Isolated Score** to hear only Peter Howell's music when watching the episodes.

— Select **Feature Audio** to reinstate the main soundtrack when watching the episodes.

INFO TEXT Select **On** to view subtitles when watching the episodes that provide information and anecdotes about the development, production, broadcast and history of *Warriors' Gate*. Written by Martin Wiggins.

THE DREAMING (27m10s) The making of *Warriors' Gate*, including thrashing out the script among writer, script editor and director; conceiving the Tharils; portraying the villain; the model filming, creating an empty void and realising the Tharils' realm; the director's approach to the studio recording and resultant problems; and the departure of Romana and K9. With contributions from script editor Christopher H Bidmead, writer Stephen Gallagher, director Paul Joyce, visual effects designer Mat Irvine, and actors John Leeson, Clifford Rose, Lalla Ward and David Weston. Narrated by Stephen Greif, produced by Andrew Beech.

THE BOY WITH THE GOLDEN STAR (19m42) Matthew Waterhouse recalls his experiences of playing companion Adric from 1980 to 1982, including his casting and character, his fellow companions, working with a new Doctor, and the manner of his departure.

LALLA'S WARDROBE (18m59s) Lalla Ward looks back at the costumes she wore as Romana, those she liked most and least, and which were the most controversial. With costume designers June Hudson and Louise Page, and writers Nev Fountain and Jonathan Morris, plus opinions from the general public. Produced by James Goss.

NEXT

EXTENDED & DELETED SCENES (4m12s) A selection of scenes from episode two not used in the final programme, taken from an earlier edit of the episode with as-recorded sound.

CONTINUITY (2m) Continuity announcements from the original BBC1 broadcasts of all four episodes of *Warriors' Gate*, with plugs for the theme music single and *Doctor Who* display at Madame Tussauds. Includes a Ceefax Dalek.

PHOTO GALLERY (4m46s) Slideshow of colour and black-and-white photos taken during production of *Warriors' Gate*, including the design sketch for the gateway and shots of the models being filmed. Set to music and sound effects from the story. Compiled by Derek Handley.

— Select **Info Text On** before selecting **Play Gallery** to view descriptive captions while watching the slideshow.

RADIO TIMES LISTINGS Accessible via a computer is a PDF file of the four episode listings for the original BBC1 broadcast of *Warriors' Gate*.

COMING SOON (1m14s) Trailer for the DVD releases of *The Rescue* and *The Romans*.

SUBTITLES
Select **On** to view subtitles for all episodes and Special Features (except commentary).

EASTER EGG
There is one hidden feature on this disc to find. *See Appendix 2 for details*

RELATED EXTRAS
Coming Soon trailer — Battlefield

THE **WEB OF FEAR**

STORY No.41   SEASON No.5:5

One disc with five original and one reconstructed episodes (148 mins) and 1 minute of extras
Audio navigation of disc contents available by pressing Enter after the BBC ident

TARDIS TEAM Second Doctor, Jamie, Victoria
TIME AND PLACE Contemporary London
ADVERSARIES Great Intelligence and its Yeti robots (2nd appearance)
FIRST ON TV 3 February–9 March 1968
DVD RELEASE BBCDVD3867, 24 February 2014, PG
COVER Full-cover photo illustration by Lee Binding (TARDIS by Gavin Rymill); version with
standard cover style, dark blue strip, on reverse
ORIGINAL RRP £20.42
— Limited Edition sold by BBCShop.com in a sleeve with alternative illustration by Binding
— Episode one (with commentary) first released in the Lost in Time set; BBCDVD1353, £29.99,
1 November 2004

STORY TEASER
When the TARDIS lands in the London Underground, the Doctor, Jamie and Victoria head for the surface but find themselves locked in and only a dead news vendor by the gates. Seeking an exit, the Doctor encounters robot Yeti while his friends are caught by the army, who are battling to keep the tunnels clear of a web-like substance that's deadly to any who touch it. Their efforts are failing, however, and even with backup from the Doctor and Colonel Lethbridge-Stewart, the web, the Yeti and the controlling Great Intelligence are closing in.

CONNECTIONS
Such was the tight production schedule then that the Yeti and Great Intelligence returned only twelve weeks after they debuted in *The Abominable Snowmen* (1967). A planned third encounter with the Second Doctor never happened but the Intelligence eventually returned in *The Snowmen* (2012), *The Bells of Saint John* (2013) and *The Name of the Doctor* (2013). A lone Yeti roamed the Death Zone on Gallifrey in *The Five Doctors* (1983). The Doctor ventures into the London Underground again in *Invasion of the Dinosaurs* (1974) and, when long disused, in *The Trial of a Time Lord: The Mysterious Planet* (1986). He assists the army to defeat earlier alien menaces to London in *Remembrance of the Daleks* (1988) and *The War Machines* (1966), while Lethbridge-Stewart, promoted to Brigadier but still played by Nicholas Courtney, returns to help him do

W

so again in *The Invasion* (1968) and becomes a regular from *Spearhead from Space* (1970) until *Terror of the Zygons* (1975). Once retired, he appears in *Mawdryn Undead* (1983), *The Five Doctors*, *Battlefield* (1989) and finally *The Sarah Jane Adventures: Enemy of the Bane* (2008). Writers Mervyn Haisman and Henry Lincoln wrote the Yeti's debut serial and *The Dominators* (1968). This was director Douglas Camfield's fourth full serial, having most recently helmed the epic *The Daleks' Master Plan* (1965/66), and he directed four more stories, all featuring UNIT (*see Index v*). Jack Watling returns as Professor Travers from *The Abominable Snowmen*, while Ralph Watson (Captain Knight) plays a different Travers in *Horror of Fang Rock* (1977) and is Ettis in *The Monster of Peladon* (1974). Derek Pollitt (Evans) is also Private Wright in *Doctor Who and the Silurians* (1970) and Professor Caldera in the unfinished *Shada* (1980), while Richardson Morgan (Corporal Blake) is Rogin in *The Ark in Space* (1975).

WORTH WATCHING
Highly regarded when it was missing all but episode one, *The Web of Fear* can now be better evaluated since its near-complete rediscovery in Nigeria in 2013. The weight of forty-five years of fan wisdom declaring it an unimpeachable classic won't be shifted easily. Certainly the direction is as taught as one would expect from Douglas Camfield's other work, and the Tube tunnels are suitably spooky and impressively recreated in the studio. But are the Yeti really any less cuddly than in their debut, do some of the cast go a little over the top in their performances, does the story hold up? Well now, at last, we can all watch and decide for ourselves.

THE EPISODES
Episodes one, two, four, five and six are restored from 16mm film copies of the original black-and-white videotape recordings, recovered from a Nigerian broadcaster by Philip Morris and returned in May 2013. Their mono soundtracks are remastered and the VidFIRE process is applied to studio-recorded shots to recapture the smoother motion of video. The title sequences are replaced by a modern transfer of the original 35mm film with credits remade to match the originals. Episode three, of which no film copy is known to exist, is recreated using surviving images from the serial matched to a remastered recording of the soundtrack made on audio tape when the episode was originally broadcast.

SUBTITLES
Select **On** to view subtitles for all episodes and the trailer.

AVAILABLE NOW
Trailer for the DVD release of *The Enemy of the World* (56s).

RELATED EXTRAS
Coming Soon trailer — The Enemy of the World
Sylvia James - In Conversation — The War Games

THE **WEB PLANET**

STORY No.13   SEASON No.2:5

One disc with six episodes (146½ mins) and 101½ minutes of extras, plus commentary and foreign-dub tracks, production subtitles, PDF items and image content

TARDIS TEAM First Doctor, Barbara, Ian, Vicki
TIME AND PLACE Planet Vortis
ADVERSARIES Squid-like Animus controlling man-sized ant-like Zarbi
FIRST ON TV 13 February–20 March 1965
DVD RELEASE BBCDVD1355, 3 October 2005, U
COVER Photo illustration by Clayton Hickman, purple strip
ORIGINAL RRP £19.99

STORY TEASER
The once-lush plains of Vortis have been turned to dust by the parasitic Animus, the planet's inhabitants the Menoptra — peaceful butterfly-people — driven away by the ant-like Zarbi and

their venom-shooting larvae. The arrival of the TARDIS coincides with a last-ditch attempt by the Menoptra to regain their home, but the advance guard are caught and without their signal the main force cannot land. With the Zarbi holding the TARDIS and the Doctor, the only option is to breach their fortress and face the insidious Animus itself.

CONNECTIONS

Other species that resemble giant Earth insects include the Wirrn in *The Ark in Space* (1975), the Tractators in *Frontios* (1984), the Vespiform in *The Unicorn and the Wasp* (2008) and the Time Beetle in *Turn Left* (2008), while normal maggots are mutated to huge size by the pollution from Global Chemical in *The Green Death* (1973). The Solonians in *The Mutants* (1972) and Josiah in *Ghost Light* (1989) also evolve through insectoid stages. Richard Martin also directed *The Dalek Invasion of Earth* (1964), *The Chase* (1965) and episodes of *The Daleks* (1963/64) and *The Edge of Destruction* (1964). Martin Jarvis (Hilio) plays Butler in *Invasion of the Dinosaurs* (1974) and the Governor in *Vengeance on Varos* (1985), while Roslyn de Winter (Vrestin) and Arne Gordon (Hrostar) are more recognisable in *The Chase*.

WORTH WATCHING

The Web Planet is like no *Doctor Who* story before or since, and some might say that's a good thing. To have a story where all the guest cast play non-human-looking aliens was certainly innovative for the time, especially when some are in cumbersome giant-ant costumes. The story of a people trying to recapture their home from an invading force is interesting in its application to another planet and there is curious use of metaphor in the speech of the underground Optera, but the production arguably attempts to be too ambitious on a 1960s *Doctor Who* budget. Points for trying, though.

THE EPISODES

All six episodes are restored from 16mm film copies of the original black-and-white videotape recordings, recovered from BBC Enterprises in 1978. Their mono soundtracks are remastered (including reducing the level of unwanted noise from sets and costumes) and the VidFIRE process is applied to studio-recorded shots to recapture the smoother motion of video. The title sequences are replaced by a modern transfer of the best surviving copy of the original 35mm film and end credits remade to match the originals.

SPECIAL FEATURES

LAIR OF ZARBI SUPREMO (AUDIO ONLY) (56m44s) William Russell reads this story about the Doctor's return to Vortis, from the first *Doctor Who Annual* published in September 1965 (see **Doctor Who Annual PDF's**).

INFORMATION TEXT Select **On** to view subtitles when watching the episodes that provide information and anecdotes about the development, production, broadcast and history of *The Web Planet*. Written by Martin Wiggins.

DOCTOR WHO ANNUAL PDF'S Accessible via a computer is a PDF file of the very first *Doctor Who Annual*, published by World Distributors the autumn after *The Web Planet* was broadcast. With stories featuring the Doctor against Zarbi, Voord and Sensorites, plus features and puzzles.

GIVE-A-SHOW SLIDES Scroll through 14 slides from the 1965 *Doctor Who* Give-A-Show Slide Projector toy made by Chad Valley, telling a shorter version of the story of *The Web Planet*. *Full set of slides on* **The Chase**

TALES OF ISOP (37m50s) The making of *The Web Planet*, including the ideas in the script; the input of the design team; using innovative camera techniques; designing Vortis; realising the Zarbi, larvae guns, Menoptra and Optera; producing the visual effects; working with William Hartnell and Jacqueline Hill; the guest cast; filming the flying scenes at Ealing Studios; and recording the episodes in Riverside Studios. With contributions from producer Verity Lambert, director Richard Martin, designer John Wood, make-up supervisor Sonia Markham, and actors Martin Jarvis, Maureen O'Brien and William Russell. Produced by Andrew Beech.

PHOTO GALLERY (6m45s) Slideshow of black-and-white photos taken during production of *The Web Planet*, including shots of the mask-less Menoptra and photos of the Zarbi and other monsters at Shawcraft Models. Set to music by Les Structures Sonores and sound effects from the story. Compiled by Ralph Montagu.

AUDIO OPTIONS

Select **Commentary On** to play the audio commentary in place of the main soundtrack when watching the episodes. This is moderated by author and journalist Gary Russell, talking with producer Verity Lambert [eps 1,2,3,6], director Richard Martin [1,2,4,5,6], William Russell (Ian) [1,3,5,6] and Martin Jarvis (Hilio) [4,5,6].

— Select **Alternative Spanish Sound Track Episode 6 On** to hear the soundtrack with dialogue dubbed into Spanish when watching episode six, made for sales of the programme to South American broadcasters.

SUBTITLES

Select **On** to view subtitles for all episodes and Special Features (except commentary and Spanish soundtrack).

THE **WHEEL IN SPACE**

STORY No.43   SEASON No.5:7

Two surviving episodes (parts 3 and 6 of 6) released in the **LOST IN TIME** *set*

TARDIS TEAM Second Doctor, Jamie, and introducing Zoe Heriot

TIME AND PLACE Space station, mid-21st Century

ADVERSARIES Cybermen (4th appearance)

FIRST ON TV 11 May and 1 June 1968

DVD RELEASE BBCDVD1353, 1 November 2004, PG

● *See* Lost in Time *for full details*

RELATED EXTRAS

The Cyber-Generations — Attack of the Cybermen

APPENDIX 1 **RELATED RELEASES**

The following discs were released as part of the main range but are not broadcast Doctor Who *serials, or are special sets that combine Classic episodes with other material*

THE **FIVE DOCTORS** SPECIAL EDITION

One disc with one episode (101 mins) and 32½ minutes of extras

DVD RELEASE BBCDVD1006, 1 November 1999, U
COVER Painted illustration by Colin Howard
ORIGINAL RRP £19.99

— Reissued in sleeve with orange logo and photo montage in a circle against dark purple background; BBCDVD2468, £9.99, 2 July 2007

WHAT'S ON THE DISC

This is the very first release of *Doctor Who* on DVD, part of a batch of programmes to test the demand for BBC material in the early days of the UK DVD market. The other releases in this initial group were *The Black Adder, Noddy in Toyland, Jane Austen's Persuasion* and *The Best of Monty Python's Flying Circus volume one*, followed by *The Planets* in January 2000. *The Five Doctors* was chosen to represent *Doctor Who* because an extended Special Edition had been produced for VHS in 1995, re-edited and remastered from the original videotape recordings with new computer-generated video effects and the soundtrack remixed in Dolby Surround. It was therefore felt this cleaned-up version would best showcase the qualities of DVD to help persuade consumers of its benefits over VHS. These six early releases had covers in the same format, with the top half having the title on a silvery background and the bottom half an image from the programme; *The Five Doctors* features a cropped version of the illustration used for the cover of the VHS release. The standard range began the following year, with a new cover design (still based on a similar half-and-half layout) and matching menus, although the TARDIS-in-vortex opening animation was retained. Eventually the broadcast version of *The Five Doctors* was released in March 2008 as the 25th Anniversary Edition (see main section) and included this Special Edition on a second disc.

STORY TEASER

One by one the first five incarnations of the Doctor are plucked out of time and deposited in a barren wasteland that he soon learns is the Death Zone on Gallifrey, an arena where the ancient Time Lords placed lesser species to fight. With several formidable adversaries also roaming the Zone, the Doctors must work together to discover who has revived the deadly Game of Rassilon.

WORTH WATCHING

As this is one of the few *Doctor Who* stories for which all the original footage survives, and given its special nature, it was an obvious candidate for an extended reworking and updated effects — an idea that has carried over into the DVD range, with several stories being similarly reworked (*see Index i*). As well as an opportunity to see unused material edited back into the episode, it demonstrated how far video effects technology had come in the twelve years since the original programme was made, although the irony now of course is that the 'new' effects look dated themselves given how much further techniques have developed in the last two decades.

THE EPISODE

The Special Edition was first produced for VHS release in November 1995, featuring extra scenes originally cut from the broadcast version, plus updated visual effects and new music cues. It was recompiled from digital duplicates of the original two-inch colour videotape recordings and further clean-up work has been done for this release. The soundtrack is remixed in Dolby Digital 5.1. Credits are remade with Special Edition producers added.

● *Episode begins playing automatically after one minute if no menu selection is made*

SPECIAL MUSIC

Select to listen to eight suites of Peter Howell's music from the episode, including the new cues composed for the extended scenes. Each plays in sequence without returning to the menu, and cycles back to the first track after playing the last. Pressing Menu or Return on your keypad reloads the main menu, not the music menu.

● *Due to an authoring error the music plays slower than it should and is thus lower in pitch.*

LANGUAGE SELECTION
Select to view menus and programme subtitles in English, Dutch, French, Italian, Portugese or Spanish. This selection also appears when the disc is loaded.

SUBTITLES
Select to view subtitles when watching the episode.

THE **FOURTH DOCTOR TIME CAPSULE**

Box of Fourth Doctor memorabilia including three discs (182 mins), book, toys and postcards
DVD RELEASE BBCDVD3800, 29 July 2013, PG
ORIGINAL RRP £62.99

WHAT'S IN THE BOX
With the approaching fiftieth anniversary special featuring the return of the Zygons, and their debut story scheduled to be released on DVD for the first time in September, this box celebrating the era of the Fourth Doctor was released in a limited edition of 5,000 numbered copies. Inside are: a DVD featuring a new interview with Tom Baker about his time playing the Fourth Doctor (25m57s); a DVD of 1975's *Terror of the Zygons* (four episodes, 96m31s), restored and with an optional Dolby Digital 5.1 soundtrack, but without the extra scene included on the individual release and no other special features (see main section); a CD of the 2011 AudioGo release of *Genesis of the Daleks* (59m45s), a cut-down version of the 1975 story's soundtrack with linking narration by Tom Baker, based on the 1979 BBC Records LP; the novel *Tomb of Valdemar* by Simon Messingham, originally published by BBC Books in 2000, featuring the Fourth Doctor and First Romana; a five-inch action figure of the Fourth Doctor, still in the Third Doctor's costume after regenerating, produced exclusively for this release by Character Options; the same company's Fourth Doctor sonic screwdriver toy, which plays appropriate sound effects; an A5 colour print of the Fourth Doctor (a photo taken during location filming for *Terror of the Zygons*); nine monochrome postcards featuring photos of each of the Fourth Doctor's companions; and a letter written by Tom Baker himself. Each of the three discs is in its own DVD-style case with obscured titles on the covers that require the enclosed red filter to read them.

K9 AND COMPANY

Released with **THE INVISIBLE ENEMY** in the **K9 TALES** boxset
One disc with one episode (50 mins) and 24 minutes of extras, plus commentary track, production subtitles and PDF items

FIRST ON TV 28 December 1981
DVD RELEASE BBCDVD2798, 16 June 2008, PG (boxset 12)
COVER Full-cover photo illustration by Clayton Hickman; version with standard cover style, dark blue strip, on reverse
ORIGINAL RRP £29.99 (boxset)

WHAT'S ON THE DISC
When it was announced that K9 would be written out of *Doctor Who* during its 1980/81 season there was a minor public outcry (*The Sun* newspaper even launched a Save K9 campaign). With an ambitious new producer having just taken charge of the series, consideration was given to the robot dog starring in his own spin-off and a pilot episode was commissioned. Being an infamously unreliable prop, however, K9 on his own was not going to be a viable lead so John Nathan-Turner

approached Elisabeth Sladen, who had played popular 1970s companion Sarah Jane Smith, to co-star in the vehicle. Despite healthy viewing figures, a new controller of BBC1 was less sympathetic to the project than his predecessor and the hoped-for series never materialised.

STORY TEASER

It has been years since Sarah Jane Smith travelled with the Doctor. So when she comes to the village of Moreton Harwood to spend Christmas with her aunt Lavinia, she is astonished to find waiting for her a present from the Time Lord, in the form of K9 Mark III. But Lavinia herself has departed suddenly for America, leaving her ward Brendan to be looked after by Sarah. Could there be more to her aunt's absence, however, given her accusations of witchcraft being practised in the village? As Sarah meets some very odd villagers and other people begin to disappear — including Brendan — she and K9 must race against time to expose the mysterious goings-on in Moreton Harwood.

CONNECTIONS

This is the first (and only during the Classic years) spin-off from *Doctor Who*, uniting Third/Fourth Doctor companion Sarah Jane Smith (Elisabeth Sladen) with robot dog K9 (voiced by John Leeson) in a pilot for a possible series that was never commissioned. However, the pairing was upheld for their appearance in *The Five Doctors* (1983) and subsequently their returns in the New Series episodes *School Reunion* (2006) and *The Stolen Earth/Journey's End* (2008), and ultimately Elisabeth Sladen's own series *The Sarah Jane Adventures* (2007–11). Their investigation here of witchery and sacrifices to an ancient goddess is reminiscent of *The Stones of Blood* (1978). It's written by Terence Dudley, who also wrote *Four to Doomsday* (1982), *Black Orchid* (1982) and *The King's Demons* (1983), and directed *Meglos* (1980), while director John Black also handled *Four to Doomsday* and *The Keeper of Traken* (1981). Bill Fraser (Commander Pollock) also plays General Grugger in *Meglos*, Colin Jeavons (George Tracey) is Damon in *The Underwater Menace* (1967), and Neville Barber (Howard Baker) is Dr Cook in *The Time Monster* (1972).

WORTH WATCHING

As a pilot for a series, this doesn't inspire much confidence. The story is rather light and uncomplicated, and a country village seems an odd milieu for a robot dog — he always worked better on smooth studio floors, not outdoors — so a series along similar lines would probably have been unwise (just look at the stories in the one and only K9 annual, included on this disc [see **PDF Materials**], which took this episode as its template). Yet the concept and the pairing of Sarah and K9 has since been proven to be more workable than this first attempt suggests. Their return in *School Reunion* was not just a nostalgic hit but reiterated what strong characters they are, and they went on to huge success in *The Sarah Jane Adventures*. In that context, *K9 and Company* can now be seen as a hesitant start to something really rather good.

THE EPISODE

Restored from a digital duplicate of the original two-inch colour videotape recording used for broadcast and its mono soundtrack remastered.

SPECIAL FEATURES

THE K-9 FILES (11m42s) Cast and crew recall the making of *K9 and Company*, and the continued popularity of K9. With contributions from director John Black, visual effects designer Mat Irvine, actors John Leeson and Elisabeth Sladen, K9 co-creator Dave Martin (interviewed in 2006), writer Terrance Dicks, and fan journalist Moray Laing. Directed by Marcus Hearn.

K-9 – A DOG'S TALE (3m27s) A light-hearted interview with K9 himself about his time on *Doctor Who*. Written by Hamish Logie.

PEBBLE MILL AT ONE (2m41s) Extract from the Wednesday 23 December 1981 edition of the BBC1 lunchtime magazine show in which David Freeman talks to K9 Mark III to promote the broadcast of *K9 and Company* and its theme single.

TRAILS AND CONTINUITIES (2m11s) Previews and continuity announcements from the original BBC1 broadcast of *K9 and Company* (with a plug for the upcoming *Doctor Who* season) and its BBC2 repeat on Friday 24 December 1982. Includes the BBC1 evening schedule for Monday 28 December 1981.

NEXT

AUDIO OPTIONS Select **Commentary** to play the audio commentary in place of the main soundtrack when watching the episodes. With Elisabeth Sladen, John Leeson, Linda Polan (Juno Baker) and script editor Eric Saward.
— Select **Feature Audio** to reinstate the main soundtrack when watching the episodes.

INFO TEXT Select **On** to view subtitles when watching the episode that provide information and anecdotes about the development, production, broadcast and history of *K9 and Company*. Written by Martin Wiggins.

PHOTO GALLERY (3m2s) Slideshow of colour photos taken during production of *K9 and Company*, including design department photos of the sets. Set to the theme music, written by Ian Levine and Fiachra Trench, arranged by Peter Howell. Compiled by Derek Handley.

PDF MATERIALS Accessible via a computer is the episode listing from *Radio Times* for the original BBC1 broadcast of K9 and Company.
— The 1983 *K9 Annual*, published by World Distributors the autumn after *K9 and Company* was first broadcast. With stories featuring K9, Sarah and Brendan, plus features about the characters.
— Separate PDFs of the four children's illustrated storybooks written by K9 co-creator Dave Martin, published by Sparrow Books in 1980: *K9 and the Time Trap*, *K9 and the Beasts of Vega*, *K9 and the Zeta Rescue* and *K9 and the Missing Planet*.

COMING SOON (1m) Trailer for the DVD release of *The Brain of Morbius*.

SUBTITLES
Select **On** to view subtitles for all episodes and Special Features (except commentary).

RELATED EXTRAS
Coming Soon trailer — The Invasion of Time

THE **MONSTER COLLECTION: DAVROS**

Two discs with six Classic episodes (143 mins) and two New Series episodes (108½ mins)
Audio navigation of each disc's contents available by pressing Enter after the BBC ident

DVD RELEASE BBCDVD3810, 30 September 2013, PG
COVER AND SLEEVE Photo illustration by Stuart Crouch
ORIGINAL RRP £9.99

WHAT'S ON THE DISCS
The Monster Collection showcases six adversaries from the Classic Series that have been revived in the New Series, pairing one adventure from each. For Davros, the creator of the Daleks, these are his debut in 1975's *Genesis of the Daleks* (see main section), and his return in *The Stolen Earth/Journey's End* (2008), in which he prepares a bomb for the Daleks to wipe out all of reality itself. The Classic episodes are the fully restored versions but the discs feature no extras.

THE **MONSTER COLLECTION: THE CYBERMEN**

One disc with four Classic episodes (96½ mins) and two New Series episodes (92 mins)
Audio navigation of disc contents available by pressing Enter after the BBC ident

DVD RELEASE BBCDVD3809, 30 September 2013, PG
COVER AND SLEEVE Photo illustration by Stuart Crouch
ORIGINAL RRP £9.99

WHAT'S ON THE DISC
The Monster Collection showcases six adversaries from the Classic Series that have been revived in the New Series, pairing one adventure from each. For the Cybermen, the technologically augmented humans, these are an early appearance in 1967's *The Tomb of the Cybermen* (see main section), and their return in *Rise of the Cybermen/The Age of Steel* (2006), in which they are created on a parallel Earth. The Classic episodes are the fully restored versions but the discs feature no extras.

THE **MONSTER COLLECTION: THE DALEKS**

Two discs with seven Classic episodes (171½ mins) and one New Series episode (49 mins)
Audio navigation of each disc's contents available by pressing Enter after the BBC ident

DVD RELEASE BBCDVD3813, 30 September 2013, PG

COVER AND SLEEVE Photo illustration by Stuart Crouch

ORIGINAL RRP £9.99

WHAT'S ON THE DISCS

The Monster Collection showcases six adversaries from the Classic Series that have been revived in the New Series, pairing one adventure from each. For the Daleks, the xenophobic exterminators, these are their debut in 1963/64's *The Daleks* (see main section), and their appearance in *Asylum of the Daleks* (2012), in which they kidnap the Doctor to help them keep their maddest prisoners contained. The Classic episodes are the fully restored versions but the discs feature no extras.

THE **MONSTER COLLECTION: THE MASTER**

Two discs with four Classic episodes (95½ mins) and two New Series episodes (132 mins)
Audio navigation of each disc's contents available by pressing Enter after the BBC ident

DVD RELEASE BBCDVD3814, 30 September 2013, PG

COVER AND SLEEVE Photo illustration by Stuart Crouch

ORIGINAL RRP £9.99

WHAT'S ON THE DISCS

The Monster Collection showcases six adversaries from the Classic Series that have been revived in the New Series, pairing one adventure from each. For the Master, the renegade Time Lord, these are his debut in 1971's *Terror of the Autons* (see main section), and his appearance in *The End of Time* (2009/10), in which he's brought back to life and turns the population of the world into copies of himself. The Classic episodes are the fully restored versions but the discs feature no extras.

THE **MONSTER COLLECTION: THE SILURIANS**

Two discs with seven Classic episodes (167 mins) and two New Series episodes (89 mins)
Audio navigation of each disc's contents available by pressing Enter after the BBC ident

DVD RELEASE BBCDVD3811, 30 September 2013, PG

COVER AND SLEEVE Photo illustration by Stuart Crouch

ORIGINAL RRP £9.99

WHAT'S ON THE DISCS

The Monster Collection showcases six adversaries from the Classic Series that have been revived in the New Series, pairing one adventure from each. For the Silurians, the reptilian bipeds who populated the Earth before Mankind evolved, these are their debut in 1970's *Doctor Who and the Silurians* (see main section), and their return in *The Hungry Earth/Cold Blood* (2010), in which a drilling project in Wales disturbs the hibernation of a group of Silurians. The Classic episodes are the fully restored versions but the discs feature no extras.

THE **MONSTER COLLECTION: THE SONTARANS**

One disc with four Classic episodes (97 mins) and two New Series episodes (89 mins)
Audio navigation of disc contents available by pressing Enter after the BBC ident

DVD RELEASE BBCDVD3812, 30 September 2013, PG

COVER AND SLEEVE Photo illustration by Stuart Crouch

ORIGINAL RRP £9.99

WHAT'S ON THE DISC

The Monster Collection showcases six adversaries from the Classic Series that have been revived in the New Series, pairing one adventure from each. For the Sontarans, the dome-headed warmongers, these are their debut in 1973/74's *The Time Warrior* (see main section), and their return in *The Sontaran Stratagem/The Poison Sky* (2008), in which they attempt to transform the Earth into a cloning world for their troops. The Classic episodes are the fully restored versions but the discs feature no extras.

MORE THAN 30 YEARS IN THE TARDIS

Released with **SHADA** in **THE LEGACY COLLECTION** boxset
One disc with one programme (88 mins) and 80½ minutes of extras, plus PDF item
Audio navigation of disc contents available by pressing Enter after the BBC ident

DVD RELEASE BBCDVD3388B, 7 January 2013, U (cover wrongly labelled PG)
COVER Photo illustration by Clayton Hickman, light purple strip;
version with older BBC logo on reverse
ORIGINAL RRP £20.42 (boxset)

WHAT'S ON THE DISC

In 1993, with *Doctor Who* having been off the air for less than four years, there was still hope among fans and even some areas of the BBC that it could be revived (indeed, talks were already underway with Philip Segal, who would eventually produce *The Movie* in 1996). As the thirtieth anniversary approached, plans for a one-off drama, 'The Dark Dimension', fell through and thoughts turned instead to a documentary about the history and legacy of *Doctor Who*. Kevin Davies, a budding drama director, had made *The Making of The Hitchhiker's Guide to the Galaxy* (having worked as an animator on the television adaptation) for BBC Video and proposed various ways to commemorate *Doctor Who*'s anniversary, involving clips from episodes within a newly recorded dramatic framework, and interviews with past contributors and celebrity fans. His ideas were refined into *30 Years in the TARDIS*, a fifty-minute programme directed by Davies and produced by the team on the BBC2 arts series *The Late Show*, broadcast on BBC1 on Monday 29 November 1993. The following year an extended version, *More Than 30 Years in the TARDIS*, adding further interview footage and reinstating many of Davies' dramatic recreations of classic scenes from past episodes, was released on VHS on Monday 7 November 1994.

WORTH WATCHING

Before all surviving episodes were restored to their best possible quality and released on DVD, when less than half the then-archived stories had been issued on VHS, *Doctor Who* fans were hungry for any morsel of their favourite show on television. After the insipid Children In Need skit *Dimensions in Time*, this extensive documentary was a more satisfying celebration of the thirtieth anniversary. And not just clips from old episodes, but untransmitted scenes, behind-the-scenes footage, extracts from other programmes — in fact, exactly the sort of thing that now makes up much of the extra material on the DVD range (and some that never made it onto disc). This documentary was a rare, and at the time the only, chance to see it again. Now we can watch any episode whenever we want, but watching *More Than 30 Years in the TARDIS* more than twenty years on is a reminder of the days when seeing *Doctor Who*'s past was a rare dish to be savoured.

MORE THAN THIRTY YEARS IN THE TARDIS

The programme is transferred from the original digital videotape. All clips are unrestored as in the original documentary, providing a reminder of how the material can look without the careful restoration performed for the DVD releases. As well as archive footage, the programme features specially recorded or recent interviews with Doctors Colin Baker, Sylvester McCoy and Jon Pertwee; companions Sophie Aldred, Nicola Bryant, Nicholas Courtney, Carole Ann Ford, Frazer Hines, Elisabeth Sladen and Deborah Watling; movie companions Jennie Linden and Roberta Tovey;

1

producers Philip Hinchcliffe, Verity Lambert, Barry Letts and John Nathan-Turner; script editors Douglas Adams, Terrance Dicks and Eric Saward; writers Ben Aaronovitch and Terry Nation; designer Raymond Cusick; visual effects designer Mat Irvine; continuity advisor Ian Levine; William Hartnell's granddaughter Jessica Carney; fan journalist Gary Russell; television campaigner Mary Whitehouse; and celebrities Gerry Anderson, Stephen Bayley, Mike Gatting, Ken Livingstone, Lowrie Turner and Toyah Wilcox. Narrated by Nicholas Courtney, directed by Kevin Davies.

SPECIAL FEATURES

REMEMBERING NICHOLAS COURTNEY (25m58s) Author Michael McManus examines the life and career of actor Nicholas Courtney, who died in 2011, best remembered for playing Brigadier Lethbridge-Stewart. Featuring extracts from past interviews with Courtney about his *Doctor Who* work (from 1999 and 2003), and a new interview conducted by his biographer McManus in 2010, to which Tom Baker pops along. Produced by Ed Stradling.

DOCTOR WHO STORIES – PETER PURVES (13m31s) Recorded in 2003 for BBC2's *The Story of Doctor Who*, actor Peter Purves recalls his experiences of playing companion Steven Taylor from 1965 to 1966.

THE LAMBERT TAPES – PART ONE (10m35s) Recorded in 2003 for BBC2's *The Story of Doctor Who*, the series' first producer Verity Lambert recalls her experiences on the programme, including getting her first producing role, coping with the structures of the BBC, and making the early serials. *Part two is on* Planet of Giants

THOSE DEADLY DIVAS (22m38s) Rundown of some of the Doctor's female adversaries, from the more glamorous — like Lady Adrasta, Yvonne Hartman, Kara, Lady Peinforte, the Rani, Timmin and Captain Wrack — to what happens when female companions are turned bad; the Master's conquests such as Queen Galleia, Kassia and Lucy Saxon; and those who marry for power like Kala and Countess Scarlioni. With contributions from actors Camille Coduri, Tracy-Ann Oberman and Kate O'Mara, and writers Clayton Hickman and Gareth Roberts. Produced by James Goss.

PHOTO GALLERY (6m6s) Slideshow of colour photos taken during production of *30 Years in the TARDIS*, set to music composed by Mark Ayres for the documentary. Compiled by Paul Shields.

PDF MATERIALS Accessible via a computer is the listing from *Radio Times* for the original BBC1 broadcast of *30 Years in the TARDIS*.

SUBTITLES

Select **On** to view subtitles for all features.

EASTER EGG

There is one hidden feature on this disc to find. See Appendix 2 for details.

RELATED EXTRAS

Coming Soon trailer — The Claws of Axos Special Edition

REGENERATION

Box of commemorative book and six discs with 37 episodes (1,086 mins)
Audio navigation of each disc's contents available by pressing Enter after the BBC ident

DVD RELEASE BBCDVD3801, 24 June 2013, 12 (all episodes U or PG except *The Movie*)
ORIGINAL RRP £61.27

WHAT'S IN THE BOX

With the news that Matt Smith would be leaving the show and speculation rife about his successor, this box collecting each story in which the Doctor regenerates was released in a limited edition of 10,000 numbered copies. Inside is an A4 twelve-leaf board book with photos and text detailing the circumstances of his regenerations, plus six DVDs containing the stories *The Tenth Planet* (with animated episode four; 1966), *The War Games* (1969), *Planet of the Spiders* (1974), *Logopolis* (1981), *The Caves of Androzani* (1984), *Time and the Rani* (1987), *The Movie* (1996), *Bad Wolf/Parting of the Ways* (2005) and *The End of Time* (2009/10). The Classic episodes are the fully restored versions but the discs feature no extras. Each disc is held in a pocket within the thickness of the book's pages.

SCREAM OF THE SHALKA

One disc with six episodes (79½ mins) and 88 minutes of extras, plus commentary track and production subtitles

FIRST ONLINE 13 November–18 December 2003
DVD RELEASE BBCDVD3858, 16 September 2013, PG
COVER Composition by Lee Binding (artwork by Cosgrove Hall), dark red strip;
version with older BBC logo on reverse
ORIGINAL RRP £20.42

WHAT'S ON THE DISC

By the turn of the century, *Doctor Who* seemed well and truly dead on screen. *The Movie* had come and gone, leaving uncertainty over who even held the rights to produce a television series any more. One area where the show was still going strong, however, was BBC Interactive's website, as sci-fi fans were an obvious adopter of the then-fledging internet. Those working on the site gained confidence in presenting new dramatic material when in 2002 they backed the failed radio series pilot *Death Comes to Time* and broadcast it instead via the site with accompanying illustrations. The success of this at bringing in new site visitors led to them commissioning Big Finish — who were having success with their range of CD audio dramas — to produce *Real Time*, a six-part webcast featuring the Sixth Doctor and the Cybermen. Again the imagery was simple camera-animated artwork as connection speeds at the time were low, but by their next project in early 2003 the animation was getting more sophisticated (see Shada, below). Buoyed by their success and with the show's fortieth anniversary imminent, BBCi went all out with an attempt to relaunch *Doctor Who* as an online series of animated adventures, starring a new Doctor. They commissioned Cosgrove Hall to produce the Flash-based animation for a story written by fan author Paul Cornell and cast Richard E Grant as the Doctor, Sophie Okonedo as companion Alison Cheney and Derek Jacobi as the Master (there was even a small part for a little-known actor called David Tennant). Such was the enthusiasm for the project that the BBC announced this was an 'official' continuation of the series with the genuine Ninth Doctor. Ironically, by the time *Scream of the Shalka* was broadcast the new television series had been announced, as a result of which further online animations never happened and Grant's position as the Ninth Doctor was usurped.

STORY TEASER

The Doctor unwillingly finds himself in the Lancashire town of Lannet, where everyone is trying to live a quiet life — quite literally, as screeching cobra-like creatures erupt from the ground in response to any loud noise. These are the Shalka, which live beneath the surface and can manipulate anything through the sonic control of their screams. Their plans extend beyond the domination of one small town, however, and the entire population of the world is powerless to stop them.

CONNECTIONS

Scream of the Shalka eschewed links to the television series as it wished to be seen as a new, accessible take on *Doctor Who*, featuring just the Doctor and the TARDIS (and the sonic screwdriver). He does travel with a robotic embodiment of the Master, however, who was last seen on television being sucked into the Eye of Harmony in the TARDIS's cloisters (*The Movie*, 1996) and curiously is next seen in the New Series in the guise of Professor Yana (*Utopia*, 2007), played by Derek Jacobi, who voices the animated Master here. At the conclusion of *Last of the Time Lords* the Doctor even suggests taking on the Master as his companion, so perhaps *Scream of the Shalka* is an alternative timeline where things turned out differently. The TARDIS is pulled into the ground by subsurface creatures, as in *Frontios* (1984), although here it survives intact. The Shalka, beings of molten rock in a crusty shell, are reminiscent in that regard of the Pyroviles in *The Fires of Pompeii* (2008). Richard E Grant previously played an incarnation of the Doctor (the tenth) in the 1999 Comic Relief parody *The Curse of Fatal Death*, and appears in the New Series as Dr Simeon in *The Snowmen* (2012), whose form is subsequently adopted by the Great Intelligence in *The Bells of Saint John* and *The Name of the Doctor* (both 2013). Sophie Okonedo (Alison) plays Liz Ten, the future queen of Starship UK, in *The Beast Below* (2010).

1

WORTH WATCHING

Restricted to a stuttering, compressed video stream when first shown online, *Scream of the Shalka* can now at least be viewed properly. The story is an interesting take on how to relaunch *Doctor Who* in the early 2000s and although it didn't take as radical and arguably risky an approach as the eventual new television series, it does prefigure some of what was to come, such as a solitary, spiky Doctor who meets a spirited London girl with a blasé boyfriend and a dead-end job, and rediscovers his connection with humanity. The animation is simple but stylish, and led the way for the recreation of missing episodes, as featured on several DVDs, and even the 2007 Tenth Doctor animation *The Infinite Quest*.

THE EPISODE

The episodes are transferred from the archived digital videotape transfer of the original Flash animation files.

SPECIAL FEATURES

CARRY ON SCREAMING (26m52s) BBCi executive producer James Goss presents the making of *Scream of the Shalka*, including getting the project off the ground; writing the script; balancing the old with the new; casting the Doctor; recording in the studio; reaction to the announcement of the webcast; adapting the animation for streaming online; figuring out who owned the rights to *Doctor Who*; and learning of the series' return to television. With contributions from BBCi's executive producer Martin Trickey, producers Jelena Djordjevic and Muirinn Lane Kelly, and researcher Daniel Judd, writer Paul Cornell, and Cosgrove Hall producer Jon Doyle. Directed by James Brailsford.

THE SCREAMING SESSION (7m19s) Interviews with the cast of *Scream of the Shalka* recorded during production in 2003, including actors Anna Calder-Marshall (Mathilda), Craig Kelly (Joe), Jim Norton (Kennet), Sophie Okonedo (Alison) and Diana Quick (Shalka Prime), and director Wilson Milam. With footage from the studio recording.

INTERWEB OF FEAR (23m47s) History of the BBC's online coverage of *Doctor Who* in the early days of the internet, from its treatment as a cult programme from the past, to developing original drama productions that pushed the limits of media streaming, and building a community via images from missing episodes, ebooks and a controversial message board. With contributions from former BBCi digital staff Martin Belam, Ian Garrard, James Goss, Ann Kelly, Ben Lavender (the man who invented the iPlayer) and Martin Trickey, and New Series showrunner Russell T Davies. Narrated by Zeb Soanes, produced by James Brailsford and James Goss.

PHOTO GALLERY (2m4s) Slideshow of colour photos of the cast taken during production of *Scream of the Shalka* and publicity artwork, set to music from the story. Compiled by James Goss.

SOUNDTRACK ALBUM (26m58s) Composer Russell Stone's full score for *Scream of the Shalka*, plus Creation Music's theme remix.

AUDIO OPTIONS Select **Commentary** to play the audio commentary in place of the main soundtrack when watching the episodes. This is moderated by actor and comedian Toby Hadoke, talking with writer Paul Cornell [eps 1,4,6], director Wilson Milam [2,5] and executive producer James Goss [3].
 — Select **Feature Audio** to reinstate the main soundtrack when watching the episodes.

INFORMATION TEXT Select **On** to view subtitles when watching the episodes that provide information and anecdotes about the development, production, webcast and history of *Scream of the Shalka*. Written by Paul Scoones.

COMING SOON (1m10s) Trailer for the DVD release of *Terror of the Zygons*.

SUBTITLES

Select **On** to view subtitles for all episodes and Special Features (except commentary).

RELATED EXTRAS

Coming Soon trailer — The Ice Warriors

SHADA

Released with **MORE THAN 30 YEARS IN THE TARDIS** in **THE LEGACY COLLECTION** boxset
Two discs with six part-narrated episodes (109½ mins) and 242½ minutes of extras, plus production subtitles
Audio navigation of each disc's contents available by pressing Enter after the BBC ident

TARDIS TEAM Fourth Doctor, Second Romana, K9
TIME AND PLACE Contemporary Earth
ADVERSARIES Skagra; mind-draining sphere; Krargs
DVD RELEASE BBCDVD3388A, 7 January 2013, PG (episodes U)
COVER Photo illustration by Clayton Hickman, dark orange strip;
　　　　　version with older BBC logo on reverse
ORIGINAL RRP £20.42 (boxset)

WHAT'S ON THE DISCS

The BBC of the late-70s was beset by union strike action and while this had been making things difficult for *Doctor Who* in previous years, by the time of the 1979/80 season it finally became impossible. *Shada* was intended to be broadcast in January/February 1980 as the concluding six-part story of the season, but after completing all the location filming and the first of three planned studio recording sessions, another strike began and studios were unavailable to finish the serial. Once the union dispute was resolved, BBC management prioritised shooting programmes for the Christmas period and *Shada* had to be abandoned as part of that season. Some attempt was made to rework it as a four-part story within the 1980/81 season under new producer John Nathan-Turner but this ultimately fell through and so *Shada* was never broadcast, although all the material that had been shot was retained in the archive. Jump ahead to the 1990s and, following the cancellation of the television series, Nathan-Turner was working with BBC Video on ideas for special VHS releases. One such was *Shada*, an edit of what material existed with newly recorded links by Tom Baker to cover the missing sections. The BBC Radiophonic Workshop's Dick Mills created sound effects and composer Keff McCulloch scored new incidental music. The VHS was released on Monday 6 July 1992 bundled with a book of the full script, and the same edit of the story is on this DVD.

STORY TEASER

The Doctor and Romana visit Professor Chronotis, a retired Time Lord who is living out his days in obscurity at Cambridge University. Elsewhere scientist Skagra is seeking an ancient Gallifreyan book that reveals the location of Shada, the Time Lord's prison planet and last known location of the renowned criminal Salyavin. It transpires Chronotis took the book when he left Gallifrey but is now too absent-minded to locate it. But should it fall into the wrong hands, if Shada is found and Salyavin released, then nothing will stop Skagra from imposing his will on all of creation.

CONNECTIONS

Despite the wealth of Gallifreyan lore revealed here, none of it relates to existing knowledge about the Doctor's homeworld, beyond the fact that Time Lord society is capable of producing criminals, such as the Master and Morbius (and by Time Lord standards the Doctor himself). During the Time War the Time Lords constructed a dimensionally transcendental prison to contain Daleks, which the Daleks captured and christened the Genesis Ark (*Doomsday*, 2006). Part of the footage of the Doctor and Romana punting is used in *The Five Doctors* (1983) to represent the Fourth Doctor's participation after Tom Baker declined to take part. *Shada* was Douglas Adams' last contribution to *Doctor Who*, having written *The Pirate Planet* (1978) and the final scripts for *City of Death* (1979), and been the show's script editor for the 1979/80 season; he repurposed some of his ideas in later works. *Shada*'s cancellation was also a disappointing end to producer Graham Williams' producership of *Doctor Who*, and even his planned return as a writer was scuppered when his script for the 1986 season, 'The Nightmare Fair', was dropped just before going into production because the series was suspended. Pennant Roberts had directed serials for the previous three seasons but also moved on from the show after *Shada* was abandoned, although he did return for two more stories in the 1980s (*see Index v*). Dennis Carey, playing Professor Chronotis, appears as the title

1

character in *The Keeper of Traken* (1981) and as the Borad's public face in *Timelash* (1985), while Derek Pollitt (Professor Caldera) is Driver Evans in *The Web of Fear* (1968) and Private Wright in *Doctor Who and the Silurians* (1970).

WORTH WATCHING

We can never really know what *Shada* would have been like had it been finished and broadcast. Despite the footage that does exist, this was never fully edited into a final form at the time and had no effects or music scored, all of which can affect how a programme is viewed. And even though we have the script for the sections that weren't recorded, these were still being rehearsed and would undoubtedly have changed to some degree before going in front of the cameras (especially once Tom Baker had been through them), and again the actors' performances are key to a story's reception. Some people believe we were robbed of the crowning glory of producer Graham Williams' time on the show and a definitive statement of writer Douglas Adams' approach to *Doctor Who*; others feel we were spared a cheap-looking series finale that would be of little interest were it not for the prestige of Adams. This version does at least allow us to see the early episodes in a mostly complete form, and while there is less original material as the serial progresses, Tom Baker's links have an appeal all their own.

DISC ONE

THE EPISODES

Original story content is restored from digital duplicates of the original two-inch colour videotape recordings and edited to match the VHS release, with location sequences newly transferred from the original 16mm colour film. The linking sequences and other material produced for the VHS release are transferred from the digital videotape masters made in 1992. The episodes' mono soundtracks are remastered and the title sequences newly created from a modern transfer of the original 35mm colour film with credits made in a contemporary style.

SPECIAL FEATURES

SHADA – BBCi / BIG FINISH VERSION (140m38s) Accessible via a computer is an HTML file that can be opened in a web browser to watch the version of *Shada* that was produced by Big Finish and webcast on the BBCi *Doctor Who* site in May/June 2003. The story was reworked to feature the Eighth Doctor, played by Paul McGann, remembering an adventure that was interrupted by his being kidnapped in *The Five Doctors*. He collects Romana (Lalla Ward) and K9 (John Leeson) from Gallifrey, and goes to Cambridge in 1979 to meet Professor Chronotis (James Fox) and defeat Skagra (Andrew Sachs). The soundtrack is accompanied by Flash-animated artwork by Lee Sullivan.

INFO TEXT Select **On** to view subtitles when watching the episodes that provide information and anecdotes about the development, production and history of *Shada*. Written by Nicholas Pegg.

COMING SOON (1m) Trailer for the DVD release of *The Reign of Terror*.

SUBTITLES

Select **On** to view subtitles for all episodes and the Coming Soon trailer.

DISC TWO

SPECIAL FEATURES

TAKEN OUT OF TIME (25m37s) Actor Daniel Hill, director's assistant Olivia Bazalgette, production assistant Ralph Watson, assistant designer Les McCallum and chorister Angus Smith return to Cambridge, where *Shada* was filmed, to recall the making of the serial. Including writing the script; working with the director; the location filming; recording the first studio session, finding the second hit by strike action, then learning the planned remount had been cancelled by BBC management; and the interest generated by its incompletion. With contributions from director Pennant Roberts (interviewed in 2005) and Tom Baker. Produced by Chris Chapman.

NOW & THEN (12m43s) Comparing the filming locations in and around Cambridge as they look today with how they appeared in mid-October 1979 when used for *Shada*. Produced and narrated by Richard Bignell. *See Index iii for further editions*

STRIKE! STRIKE! STRIKE! (27m47s) How industrial action throughout the 1970s and early-80s impacted the production of several *Doctor Who* serials, and sometimes even benefitted the series.

With contributions from politician Lord Addington, actors Nicola Bryant and Peter Purves, former entertainment industry union president Tony Lennon, producers Barry Letts (interviewed in 2008) and Derrick Sherwin, directors Richard Martin and Paul Seed, and fan writer Gary Russell. Presented by BBC political reporter Shaun Ley, produced by James Goss.

BEING A GIRL (30m10s) The portrayal of women throughout the history of *Doctor Who*, including the developing complexity in the characterisation of the Doctor's female companions, how the male assistants compare, women adversaries, and the impact of the predominance on men among the key production members. With contributions from journalist and broadcaster Samira Ahmed and fan Emma Price. Written by Simon Guerrier, narrated by Louise Jameson, produced by Thomas Guerrier.

PHOTO GALLERY (4m47s) Slideshow of colour photos taken during production of *Shada*, including design department photos of the sets. Set to Keff McCulloch's music for the VHS release of the story. Compiled by Paul Shields.

SUBTITLES Select On to view subtitles for all Special Features on disc two.

RELATED EXTRAS
Coming Soon trailer — The Claws of Axos Special Edition

SPEARHEAD FROM SPACE BLU-RAY

One disc with four episodes (97 mins) and 97½ minutes of extras
Audio navigation of disc contents available by pressing Enter after the BBC ident

TARDIS TEAM Third Doctor, Brigadier and UNIT, and introducing Liz Shaw

TIME AND PLACE Contemporary England

ADVERSARIES Autons and Nestene (1st appearance)

FIRST ON TV 3–24 January 1970

BLU-RAY RELEASE BBCBD0230, 15 July 2013, PG (episodes U)

COVER Photo illustration by Lee Binding, silvered logo and title; version with standard cover style, blue strip, on reverse

— Original release with cover sticker reading 'The Third Doctor in High Definition for the First Time'

ORIGINAL RRP £20.52

WHAT'S ON THE DISC
By a fluke of circumstances, *Spearhead from Space* was the only Classic *Doctor Who* story recorded entirely on film, and thus the only candidate for a true high-definition Blu-ray release. (*The Movie* was also shot on film but transferred to videotape before editing and post-production, and it's not known if the original film footage survives.) Even though the film stock used was 16mm rather than 35mm (which, being larger, can capture more detail and has relatively finer grain), it still has more detail than can be seen at standard definition and so benefits from high-resolution scanning. All Special Features except the Coming Soon trailer are also in high definition.

STORY TEASER
Investigating a suspicious meteorite shower, Brigadier Lethbridge-Stewart of UNIT instead finds a familiar Police Box, except its owner is not the man he expected — or is he? Meanwhile a nearby plastics factory has been taken over by a new proprietor and is producing some very deadly shop-window mannequins. The Doctor struggles to regain his senses and prove his identity in time to prevent an alien invasion.

WORTH WATCHING
As televisions move towards ever higher screen resolutions, *Spearhead from Space* is the only opportunity we have to view a *Doctor Who* story in genuine high definition. While video material in standard definition can be 'upscaled' the extra resolution is computer-estimated and not true detail. Video needs to be shot in high definition in the first place (as the New Series has been since 2009's *Planet of the Dead*), while film can be rescanned at any resolution. In practice, however, film stock

1

has a grain that limits the image quality so it's unlikely that any higher magnification of *Spearhead from Space*'s 16mm negatives would yield any greater detail. This, then, is the clearest, sharpest way to view the episodes.

THE EPISODES

Episodes one, two and four are newly scanned in high definition and restored from the original 16mm colour film negatives, while episode three is scanned and restored from the print made in 2010 as the original negative was found to have been damaged at that time. Their mono soundtracks are as remastered for the Special Edition DVD release (with the as-broadcast TARDIS materialisation sound effect in episode one reinstated) and the opening title sequences replaced by an upscale of the restored versions from the Special Edition DVD release.

SPECIAL FEATURES

A DANDY AND A CLOWN (42m19s) Profile of the life and career of Jon Pertwee, who died in 1996, from his time in the Navy to radio stardom, becoming the Doctor, and even greater success as Worzel Gummidge. With memories from script editor Terrance Dicks, actors Geoffrey Bayldon, Judy Cornwell, Kenneth Earle and Katy Manning, and friends David Jacobs and Stuart Money. Produced by Chris Chapman.

CARRY ON: THE LIFE OF CAROLINE JOHN (29m7s) Profile of actress Caroline John, who died in 2012, including her time playing the Third Doctor's companion Liz Shaw and later embracing of *Doctor Who* fandom through convention appearances. With memories from husband Geoffrey Beevers, daughter Daisy Ashford, sister Priscilla John, brother Seb John, and friends Jennie Heslewood and Patricia Merrick. Produced by Chris Chapman.

TITLE SEQUENCE MATERIAL (22m38s) Silent 16mm colour film footage shot for the first Third Doctor titles, including material not used in the final sequence.

RESTORATION COMPARISON (2m13s) Comparing the mastering of this release in high definition against previous standard-definition versions, and some of the problems encountered when scanning forty-year-old film.

COMING SOON (1m22s) Trailer for the Special Edition DVD release of *The Green Death*.

SUBTITLES

Select **On** to view subtitles for all episodes and Special Features.

RELATED EXTRAS

Coming Soon trailer — The Mind of Evil

APPENDIX 2 **EASTER EGGS**

On many discs are items only accessible by using your remote to find a hidden Doctor Who *logo and selecting it. The idea is that they're slightly obscure extras that don't warrant listing in the menus but are fun for viewers to stumble across. The main entries indicate if there are any easter eggs on a release and how many, so you can search for them without being spoiled if you want. But if you can't find any or just want to know where and what they are, they are listed here.*

THE ANDROID INVASION

Go to the first page of **Special Features**, scroll down to **Weetabix Advert**, press right and select the revealed *Doctor Who* logo
— *Sound recordings from the location filming on Monday 21 July 1975 at the National Radiological Protection Board in Harwell, Oxfordshire of scenes in episodes two and four (7m50s)*

ARC OF INFINITY

When watching on a TV via a DVD player, go to the second page of **Special Features**, then on your remote enter **1 9 7 5** (you may need to press Enter between each number). If watching on a computer, go to title 14
— *Teaser for* The Complete Davros Collection *(13s)*

THE ARK IN SPACE

Keep watching after the end titles of episode four when viewing via **Play All** or **Episode Selection**
— *A promo for the Blackpool* Doctor Who *Exhibition featuring Tom Baker (14s)*
Go to the **Episode Selection** page, press up to highlight the *Doctor Who* logo and select
— *Countdown clock for the studio recording of episode two (32s)*
Go to the first page of **Special Features**, scroll down to **Tom Baker Interview**, press left and select the revealed *Doctor Who* logo
— *Another promo by Tom Baker for the Blackpool* Doctor Who *Exhibition (15s)*

THE ARK IN SPACE SPECIAL EDITION

On disc one, keep watching after the end titles of episode four
— *A promo for the Blackpool* Doctor Who *Exhibition featuring Tom Baker (14s)*
On disc one, go to **Play All**, press left to highlight the *Doctor Who* logo and select
— *Countdown clock for the studio recording of episode two (32s)*
On disc one, go to the second page of **Special Features**, scroll down to **Photo Gallery**, press left and select the revealed *Doctor Who* logo
— *Another promo by Tom Baker for the Blackpool* Doctor Who *Exhibition (15s)*

THE ARMAGEDDON FACTOR

On disc two, go to the second page of **Special Features**, scroll down to **Continuities**, press right and select the revealed *Doctor Who* logo
— *The transmission interruption that occurred during the original broadcast of episode five on Saturday 17 February 1979 owing to a technical fault. The music played is 'Gotcha', the theme to* Starsky and Hutch, *by Tom Scott (1m25s)*

ATTACK OF THE CYBERMEN

Go to the second page of **Special Features**, scroll down to **The Cyber-Generations**, press left and select the revealed *Doctor Who* logo
— *Professor Kevin Warwick presents his Cybernetic Autonomous Dalek (1m6s)*

THE AZTECS

Go to the first page of **Special Features**, scroll down to **Intro Sequences**, press left and select the revealed *Doctor Who* logo

— *The BBC Enterprises globe that was added to the start of film copies of programmes sold abroad (12s)*

THE AZTECS SPECIAL EDITION

On disc one, go to the second page of **Special Features**, scroll down to **Photo Gallery**, press left and select the revealed *Doctor Who* logo

— *The BBC Enterprises globe that was added to the start of film copies of programmes sold abroad (12s)*

BLACK ORCHID

Go to the second page of **Special Features**, scroll down to **Points of View**, press left and select the revealed *Doctor Who* logo

— *Continuity announcements from the original BBC1 broadcasts of both episodes of* Black Orchid *(50s)*

THE BRAIN OF MORBIUS

Go to **Episode Selection**, scroll to **Main Menu**, press left and select the revealed *Doctor Who* logo
— *Trivia about* The Brain of Morbius *(1m43s)*
Go to the first page of **Special Features**, scroll down to **Set Tour**, press left and select the revealed *Doctor Who* logo

— *Reading of a letter to the writer of* The Brain of Morbius *from a young viewer, and script editor Robert Holmes' reply (1m13s)*

CARNIVAL OF MONSTERS

Go to the first page of **Special Features**, scroll down to **Delaware Opening Titles**, press left and select the revealed *Doctor Who* logo

— *Full opening title sequence with Delia Derbyshire's remixed theme arrangement used for Third Doctor episodes from 1970 to 1973 (44s)*
Go to the **Subtitles** page, scroll to **Feature On/Off**, press left to highlight the *Doctor Who* logo and select

— *Countdown clock for the studio recording of episode two (30s)*

CARNIVAL OF MONSTERS SPECIAL EDITION

On disc one, go to the first page of **Special Features**, scroll down to **Director's Amended Ending**, press left and select the revealed *Doctor Who* logo

— *Full opening title sequence with Delia Derbyshire's remixed theme arrangement used for Third Doctor episodes from 1970 to 1973 (44s)*

CASTROVALVA

On the main menu, scroll down to **Audio Options**, press left to highlight the *Doctor Who* logo and select

— *Footage of the* Doctor Who *float at the Lord Mayor's Show in London on Saturday 14 November 1981, Peter Davison's first public appearance in costume (32s)*

THE CAVES OF ANDROZANI SPECIAL EDITION

On disc one, go to **Episode Selection**, scroll to **Part One**, press left to highlight the *Doctor Who* logo and select

— *The opening of episode one with the original unstable matte effect as broadcast, which director Graeme Harper requested be corrected for the DVD release (4m3s)*

THE CHASE

On disc two, on the first page of **Special Features**, scroll down to **Daleks Beyond the Screen**, press right and select the revealed *Doctor Who* logo
— *Participants in the documentary features discuss the limitations of the Mechonoids (2m49s)*

CITY OF DEATH

On disc one, keep watching after the end titles of episode four when viewing via **Play All** or **Episode Selection**
— *Continuity announcement for the next story,* The Creature from the Pit *(18s)*

On disc two, scroll to **Paris in Springtime**, press left and select the revealed *Doctor Who* logo
— *Spoof electronic sales brochure for the Mk III Jagaroth Battlecruiser (2m2s)*

On disc two, scroll to down **Prehistoric Landscapes**, press left and select the revealed *Doctor Who* logo
— *Extract from a 1985 interview with Douglas Adams in which he recalls a spontaneous trip to Paris with* Destiny of the Daleks *director Ken Grieve during filming for* City of Death *(6m33s)*

On disc two, scroll to down **Photo Gallery**, press left and select the revealed *Doctor Who* logo
— *Unused material from the 'Eye on…Blatchford' extra, featuring actor Gabriel Woolf (1m44s)*

On disc two, scroll down to **Doctor Who Annual**, press left and select the revealed *Doctor Who* logo
— *Comedy sketch featuring Tom Baker and John Cleese, recorded for the 1979 BBC staff Christmas video (18s)*

THE CLAWS OF AXOS

Go to **Special Features**, select **Information Text**, then select **On** for **Claws of Axos Information Text**
— *When playing episode one, a caption at the start shows the* Radio Times *description for the episode*

THE CLAWS OF AXOS SPECIAL EDITION

On disc one, go to **Special Features**, scroll down to **Audio Options**, press left and select the revealed *Doctor Who* logo
— *The explanation of the Reverse Standards Conversion process, presented by Jack Pizzey, repeated from the previous release of* The Claws of Axos *(10m10s)*

THE CURSE OF FENRIC

On disc one, go to **Special Features** and turn on **Information Text**, then use **Play All** to watch the episodes
— *The Haemovores' nicknames are revealed in captions after episodes two and three*

On disc one, go to **Special Features**, scroll down to **Claws and Effect**, press left and select the revealed *Doctor Who* logo
— *Continuity announcements from the original BBC1 broadcasts of all four episodes of* The Curse of Fenric *(1m49s)*

On disc two, scroll down to **Recutting the Runes**, press left and select the revealed *Doctor Who* logo
— *Composer Mark Ayres talks about how he developed the themes and instrumentation for his original score, and the changes he made for the Special Edition (6m11s)*

THE DALEK INVASION OF EARTH

On disc two, go to the first page of **Special Features**, scroll down to **Talking Daleks**, press left and select the revealed *Doctor Who* logo
— *A short clip featuring Sid the Slyther (28s)*

On disc two, go to the second page of **Special Features**, scroll down to **Photo Gallery**, press left and select the revealed *Doctor Who* logo
— *Sid the Slyther looks forward to a date (47s)*

THE DEADLY ASSASSIN

Go to the first of page of **Special Features**, scroll down to **Photo Gallery**, press left and select the revealed *Doctor Who* logo

— *Continuity announcement from the original BBC1 broadcast of* The Hand of Fear *episode four on Saturday 23 October 1976 (26s)* Also on The Hand of Fear

DEATH TO THE DALEKS

Go to the first of page of **Special Features**, scroll down to **Photo Gallery**, press right and select the revealed *Doctor Who* logo

— *Full opening and closing title sequences with Delia Derbyshire's remixed theme arrangement used for Third Doctor episodes in 1974 (1m27s)*

DESTINY OF THE DALEKS

Go to the second of page of **Special Features**, scroll to **Audio Options**, press left and select the revealed *Doctor Who* logo

— *Countdown clocks for the studio recordings of all four episodes (24s)*

DOCTOR WHO AND THE SILURIANS

On disc two, keep watching after the end titles of episode seven when playing via **Episode Selection** or **Scene Selection** (but not **Play All**)

— *Trailer for the following story,* The Ambassadors of Death, *shown after episode seven of* The Silurians, *combining clips with specially shot footage of Jon Pertwee as the Doctor. Reconstructed by matching an audio recording made at the time of broadcast to footage from the episodes and a manually recoloured black-and-white film copy of the Doctor sections. Note, the episode audio commentary continues during the trailer (1m34s)* Also on The Ambassadors of Death

THE DOMINATORS

Go to the first of page of **Special Features**, scroll down to **Photo Gallery**, press right and select the revealed *Doctor Who* logo

— *Comedy sketch by the Scottish Falsetto Sock Puppet Theatre. The socks struggle with Classic episode story codes (2m36s)*

EARTHSHOCK

Go to the first page of **Special Features**, scroll down to **40th Anniversary Celebration**, press left and select the revealed *Doctor Who* logo

— *Extract from the Friday 14 May 1993 edition of comedy sketch show* The Real McCoy, *featuring a clip from* Earthshock *dubbed into Jamaican patois (1m)*

ENLIGHTENMENT

On disc one, go to the first page of **Special Features**, scroll down to **Singe Write Female**, press left and select the revealed *Doctor Who* logo

— *Trivia about* Enlightenment *(1m20s)*

On disc one, go to the second page of **Special Features**, scroll down to **Coming Soon**, press left and select the revealed *Doctor Who* logo

— *Janet Fielding and Peter Davison recall a prank the latter played on the former in her tight costume (1m17s)*

On disc two, go to the first page of **Special Features**, scroll down to **Finding Mark Strickson**, press left and select the revealed *Doctor Who* logo

— *Photo gallery of behind-the-scenes shots from the production of the Special Features for* The Black Guardian Trilogy *boxset, set to the 'Milonga' music from* Enlightenment *(2m)*

THE FIVE DOCTORS 25TH ANNIVERSARY EDITION

On disc one, go to **Special Features**, select **Audio Options**, scroll down to **Companions Commentary**, press right and select the revealed *Doctor Who* logo

— *The episode will play with a special commentary by David Tennant (Tenth Doctor), New Series producer Phil Collinson and New Series writer Helen Raynor.*

On disc two, go to the second page of **Special Features**, scroll down to **Nationwide**, press left and select the revealed *Doctor Who* logo

— *The BBC Video ident from the original Special Edition VHS release in November 1995 (22 secs)*

FRONTIER IN SPACE

On disc two, select **Subtitles**, scroll down to **Special Features**, press down to highlight the *Doctor Who* logo and select

— *Countdown clock for the studio recording of episode five plus the unrestored opening and closing title sequences featuring the unused 'Delaware' version of the theme music (1m42s)*

GHOST LIGHT

On the main menu, scroll down to **Episode Selection**, press left and select the revealed *Doctor Who* logo

— *The full recording of Katharine Schlesinger singing 'That's the Way to the Zoo' (1m3s)*

Go to **Special Features**, scroll down to **Writer's Question Time**, press left and select the revealed *Doctor Who* logo

— *Continuity announcements from the original BBC1 broadcasts of all three episodes of* Ghost Light, *with the as-broadcast misspelling of Katharine Schlesinger's name on episode one and a plug for the following story,* The Curse of Fenric. *Includes the line-up for BBC1's* Sportsnight *on Wednesday 4 October 1989, and an advert for the first issue of* BBC Good Food *magazine (3m33s)*

THE GREATEST SHOW IN THE GALAXY

Go to the first page of **Special Features**, scroll down to **Deleted and Extended Scenes**, press right and select the revealed *Doctor Who* logo

— *A clip of the 'Psychic Circus' music video, edited to look like it was part of an off-air home video recording (intended for use as viral marketing for the DVD) (53s)*

THE GREEN DEATH

On the main menu, scroll to **Play All**, press left and select the revealed *Doctor Who* logo

— *Continuity announcements from the original BBC1 broadcasts of episode six of the preceding story,* Planet of the Daleks, *and episodes one, five and six of* The Green Death *(reconstructed from audio recordings made at the time of broadcast); and from the repeat of* The Green Death *on BBC2 in January 1994 (4m9s)*

THE GREEN DEATH SPECIAL EDITION

On disc two, go to the first page of **Special Features**, scroll down to **Visual Effects**, press left to highlight the *Doctor Who* logo and select

— *Continuity announcements from the original BBC1 broadcasts of episode six of the preceding story,* Planet of the Daleks, *and episodes one, five and six of* The Green Death *(reconstructed from audio recordings made at the time of broadcast); and from the repeat of* The Green Death *on BBC2 in January 1994 (4m9s)*

On disc two, go to the second page of **Special Features**, scroll down to **Photo Gallery**, press left and select the revealed *Doctor Who* logo

— *Outtake from the* **Global Conspiracy?** *spoof (40s)*

THE HAND OF FEAR

On the main menu, scroll to **Play All**, press left twice to highlight the *Doctor Who* logo and select

— *Extract from the Thursday 13 May 1976 edition of news magazine programme* Nationwide *in which Dilys Morgan interviews Elisabeth Sladen about her decision to leave* Doctor Who. *With Michael Barratt and a Dalek (1m41s)*

THE HORNS OF NIMON

Go to the first page of **Special Features**, scroll down to **Read the Writer**, press right and select the revealed *Doctor Who* logo

— *Comedy sketch by the Scottish Falsetto Sock Puppet Theatre. The socks offer a handy tip for remembering the names of the actors to play the Doctor (1m20s)*

HORROR OF FANG ROCK

Go to **Special Features**, scroll down to **The Antique Doctor Who Show**, press left and select the revealed *Doctor Who* logo

— *Countdown clock for the studio recording of episode three (10s)*

IMAGE OF THE FENDAHL

Go to the first page of **Special Features**, scroll down to **Trailer**, press left and select the revealed *Doctor Who* logo

— *Louise Jameson discusses the Denys Fisher doll of Leela (37s)*

INFERNO

On disc one, when playing the episodes, at the start of episode seven press rewind or skip back to the start of the chapter

— *Countdown clock for the studio recording of episode seven (26s)*

On disc two, go to the first page of **Special Features**, scroll down to **Next**, press left and select the revealed *Doctor Who* logo

— *Full opening title sequence for* Inferno *including the footage of volcanoes and lava (1m2s)*

INFERNO SPECIAL EDITION

On disc one, when playing the episodes, at the start of episode seven press rewind or skip back to the start of the chapter

— *Countdown clock for the studio recording of episode seven (26s)*

On disc two, go to the first page of **Special Features**, scroll down to **Next**, press left and select the revealed *Doctor Who* logo

— *Full opening title sequence for* Inferno *including the footage of volcanoes and lava (1m2s)*

On disc two, go to the second page of **Special Features**, scroll down to **Pertwee Years Intro**, press left and select the revealed *Doctor Who* logo

— *Actor David Burton recalls recording what was hoped to be a pilot for a new* Doctor Who *series in the early 1990s (5m21s)*

INVASION OF THE DINOSAURS

On disc two, go to the first page of **Special Features**, scroll down to **Now and Then**, press left and select the revealed *Doctor Who* logo

— *Countdown clock for the studio recording of episode five (29s)*

THE INVASION OF TIME

On disc two, go to the second page of **Special Features**, scroll down to **Radio Times Listings**, press left and select the revealed *Doctor Who* logo

— *Visual effects designer Colin Mapson examines the original prop of the Matrix coronet and describes how it was made (1m5s)*

THE INVISIBLE ENEMY
Go to the first page of **Special Features**, scroll down to **Visual Effect**, press left and select the revealed *Doctor Who* logo
— *K9 appears on* Larry Grayson's Generation Game *on Saturday 14 October 1978 (1m15s)*

THE KEEPER OF TRAKEN
Keep watching after the end titles of episode four
— *A dedication to Anthony Ainley, who died in 2004, with a clip from the material he recorded for the* Destiny of the Doctors *video game in 1997 (19s). All his footage from the game is on* **Survival**

THE KEYS OF MARINUS
Go to **Special Features** and select **PDF Materials** then, on the caption page, press left to highlight the *Doctor Who* logo and select
— *Silent 8mm colour film footage of the sound gallery for Studio D at Lime Grove shot by grams operator Patrick Heigham (1m9s)*

THE LEISURE HIVE
On the main menu, scroll down to **Episode Selection**, press left and select the revealed *Doctor Who* logo
— *Trailers and continuity announcements from the original BBC1 broadcasts of all four episodes of* The Leisure Hive. *Includes a plug for* Doctor Who *'Picture Packs' photo postcards, and* Match of the Day *Sunday football line-ups for 31 August and 7 September 1980 (3m36s)*

LOST IN TIME
On the main menu of disc one, scroll to **Play All**, wait for the rotating symbols to align and chimes to sound over the music, then press up to highlight the *Doctor Who* logo and select
— *BBC1 405-line test card, followed by the countdown clock for the studio recording of episode three of* The Crusade, *'The Wheel of Fortune' (30s)*
On the main menu of disc two, scroll to **Play All**, wait for the rotating symbols to align and chimes to sound over the music, then press up to highlight the *Doctor Who* logo and select
— *Frazer Hines' introduction to* The Underwater Menace *episode 3, recorded for its VHS release in* The Ice Warriors Collection *in November 1998 (36s)*
On disc three, play *The Wheel in Space* episode six with commentary
— *After the end titles is a snippet of the original studio sound from the end of recording (5s)*

THE MARK OF THE RANI
On the main menu, scroll down to **Special Features**, press left and select the revealed *Doctor Who* logo
— *Continuity announcements from the final episode of the preceding story,* Vengeance on Varos, *and both episodes of* The Mark of the Rani, *including a trail for episode two (1m39s)*

MAWDRYN UNDEAD
Go to the first page of **Special Features**, scroll down to **Deleted And Extended Scenes**, press left and select the revealed *Doctor Who* logo
— *Trivia about* Mawdryn Undead *(50s)*
Go to the second page of **Special Features**, scroll down to **Set Photo Gallery**, press left and select the revealed *Doctor Who* logo
— *Studio floorplans (also on the disc as a PDF) (35s)*

MEGLOS

Go to the second page of **Special Features**, scoll to **Audio Options**, press left and select the revealed *Doctor Who* logo
— *Full opening and closing title sequences with Peter Howell's theme arrangement used for Fourth Doctor episodes from 1980 to 1981 (1m57s)*

THE MIND OF EVIL

On disc one, select **Episode Selection**
— *Sound recording of a trailer for* The Mind of Evil, *with voiceover by Richard Bebb, broadcast on BBC1 on Saturday 23 January 1971 after episode four of* Terror of the Autons *(1m10s)*

THE MIND ROBBER

On the main menu, scroll down to **Episode Selection**, press left and select the revealed *Doctor Who* logo
— *Continuity announcements for all five episodes of* The Mind Robber *from the repeat showings on BBC2 in February 1992 (showing the poor state of the film prints used) (2m5s)*

THE MONSTER OF PELADON

On disc two, scroll down to **Where Are They Now?**, press left and select the revealed *Doctor Who* logo
— *16mm colour film footage shot by BBC News of Jon Pertwee driving a traction engine in a race with Lord Montagu of Beaulieu – a village in Hampshire, home to the National Motor Museum – at a steam engine rally on Sunday 27 May 1973 (31s)*
On disc two, select **PDF Materials** then, on the caption page, press right to highlight the *Doctor Who* logo and select
— *Sound recordings from the filming at Ealing Studios during the third week of January 1974 (the film footage of which is now lost), including retakes and a scene not used in the final episodes (5m7s)*

THE MOVIE

On the main menu, scroll to **Play All**, press left to highlight the *Doctor Who* logo and select
— *The dedication to Jon Pertwee shown before the original UK broadcast on BBC1 on Monday 27 May 1996, as the actor had died just seven days before (6s)*

THE MOVIE SPECIAL EDITION

On disc two, go to **Production**, scroll down to **Alternate Takes**, press right and select the revealed *Doctor Who* logo
— *Writer Matthew Jacobs recalls his earliest memory of* Doctor Who: *a studio visit during production of* The Gunfighters *in April 1966, in which his father Anthony Jacobs played Doc Holliday (2m3s)*
On disc two, go to **Special Features**, scroll down to **Who Peter 1989-2009**, press left and select the revealed *Doctor Who* logo
— *The interview with Philip Segal recorded in 2001 for the previous release (9m)*

PLANET OF EVIL

Go to the first page of **Special Features**, scroll down to **Continuities**, press left and select the revealed *Doctor Who* logo
— *Producer Philip Hinchcliffe peruses the BBC's production documentation for* Planet of Evil *(10m42s)*

PLANET OF FIRE

On disc one, go to the first page of **Special Features**, scroll to **The Flames of Sarn**, press left and select the revealed *Doctor Who* logo
— *Countdown clocks for the studio recordings of all four episodes, showing the switch from blackboards to an electronic clock from episode three (29s)*

On disc one, go to the second page of **Special Features**, select **Audio Options**, select **Isolated Score** then scroll back to **Isolated Score**, press right to highlight the *Doctor Who* logo and select
— *Trivia about* Planet of Fire *(1m51s)*

2

PLANET OF THE DALEKS
On disc one, keep watching after the end titles of episode six
— *Continuity announcement for the following story,* The Green Death, *and a plug for the theme music single (12s)*
On disc two, scroll down to **Multi-Colourisation**, press right and select the revealed *Doctor Who* logo
— *The opening section of episode three in black-and-white with the commentary participants discussing why it no longer exists in colour, recorded in case the recolourisation of the episode hadn't been completed successfully (2m49)*

PYRAMIDS OF MARS
Go to the second page of **Special Features**, scroll down to **Oh Mummy**, press left and select the revealed *Doctor Who* logo
— *Continuity announcements from the original BBC1 broadcasts of episode four of the preceding story,* Planet of Evil; *episodes one and four of* Pyramids of Mars, *the latter promoting the next story,* The Android Invasion; *and from the four-part repeat of* Pyramids on Mars *on BBC2 in March 1994 (2m27s)*

REMEMBRANCE OF THE DALEKS SPECIAL EDITION
On disc one, go to the first page of **Special Features**, scroll down to **Remembrances**, press left and select the revealed *Doctor Who* logo
— *Outtake from Sophie Aldred's deleted scenes introduction (13s)*

RESURRECTION OF THE DALEKS
Go to the first page of **Special Features**, scroll down to **BBC1 Trailer**, press left and select the revealed *Doctor Who* logo
— *Countdown clock for the studio recording of the original episode two (14s)*
Go to the second page of **Special Features**, scroll down to **Photo Gallery**, press left and select the revealed *Doctor Who* logo
— *Full opening and closing title sequences with Peter Howell's theme arrangement used for Fifth Doctor episodes from 1982 to 1984 (2m8s)*

RESURRECTION OF THE DALEKS SPECIAL EDITION
On disc one, go to **Episode Selection**, scroll across to **Part Two**, press right to highlight the *Doctor Who* logo and select
— *Full opening and closing title sequences with Peter Howell's theme arrangement used for Fifth Doctor episodes from 1982 to 1984 (2m6s)*
On disc one, go to the second page of **Special Features**, select **Audio Options**, scroll to **Feature Audio Mono**, press left and select the revealed *Doctor Who* logo
— *Countdown clock for the studio recording of the original episode two (14s)*

REVELATION OF THE DALEKS
On the main menu, scroll down to **Episode Selection**, press left and select the revealed *Doctor Who* logo
— *Cast members re-recording dialogue for the disc's new Dolby 5.1 soundtrack (48s)*

REVENGE OF THE CYBERMEN

Go to the first page of **Special Features**, scroll down to **Cheques, Lies and Videotape**, press left and select the revealed *Doctor Who* logo
— *The BBC Video ident from early-80s VHS releases (22s)*

THE RIBOS OPERATION

Go to the second page of **Special Features** and select **Info Text On**
— *When playing episode one, a caption at the start reveals how consideration was given to moving* Doctor Who *from its traditional Saturday slot for the 1978/79 season*

ROBOT

On the main menu, scroll down to **Special Features**, press left to highlight the *Doctor Who* logo and select
— *Continuity announcements from the original BBC1 broadcasts of the first and last episodes of* Robot, *the latter plugging the following story,* The Ark in Space *(40s)*

THE SEEDS OF DEATH

On disc two, scroll down to **Tardis Cam No.5**, press left and select the revealed *Doctor Who* logo
— *Footage of the commentary recording for the scene in episode six where Wendy Padbury accidentally laughs on camera (59s)*

THE SEEDS OF DEATH SPECIAL EDITION

On disc one, from the main menu select **Episode Selection**
— *Sound recording of a trailer for* The Seeds of Death *narrated by Richard Bebb, broadcast on BBC1 on Saturday 18 January 1969 after the final episode of the previous story,* The Krotons *(46s)*
On disc two, scroll to **Lords of the Red Planet**, press right and select the revealed *Doctor Who* logo
— *Footage of the commentary recording for the scene in episode six where Wendy Padbury accidentally laughs on camera (58s)*

THE SEEDS OF DOOM

On disc two, go to the first page of **Special Features**, scroll down to **Playing in the Green Cathedral**, press right and select the revealed *Doctor Who* logo
— *An outtake from the climax of episode five, taken from the BBC2 programme* Festival 40: What Do You Think of it So Far? *marking forty years of broadcasting, shown on Sunday 29 August 1976 (10s)*
On disc two, go to the second page of **Special Features**, scroll down to **Photo Gallery**, press left and select the revealed *Doctor Who* logo
— *John Challis tells an anecdote about a later encounter with Tom Baker (1m16s)*

SNAKEDANCE

Go to the second page of **Special Features**, select **Audio Options**, select **Isolated Score**, then scroll back to **Isolated Score**, press left to highlight the *Doctor Who* logo and select
— *Writer Christopher Bailey discusses his two* Doctor Who *stories and the experience of writing them with New Series writer Robert Shearman (14m18s)*

SPEARHEAD FROM SPACE

On the main menu, scroll to **Play All**, press left to highlight the *Doctor Who* logo and select
— *Unused version of the opening title sequence (45s)*

SPEARHEAD FROM SPACE SPECIAL EDITION

On the main menu, scroll to **Play All**, press left to highlight the *Doctor Who* logo and select
— *Unused version of the opening title sequence (45s)*

THE TALONS OF WENG-CHIANG

Play the episodes with commentary switched on
— *Continuity announcements from the original BBC1 broadcasts can be heard during the closing titles of episodes one, two and five*

On disc two, go to the second page of **Special Features**, scroll down to **Trails and Continuity**, press left and select the revealed *Doctor Who* logo
— *Full opening title sequence with Delia Derbyshire's remixed theme arrangement used for Fourth Doctor episodes from 1975 to 1980 (42s)*

THE TALONS OF WENG-CHIANG SPECIAL EDITION

Play the episodes with commentary switched on
— *Continuity announcements from the original BBC1 broadcasts can be heard during the closing titles of episodes one, two and five*

On disc three, go to the second page of **Special Features**, scroll down to **Trails and Continuity**, press right and select the revealed *Doctor Who* logo
— *Full opening title sequence with Delia Derbyshire's remixed theme arrangement used for Fourth Doctor episodes from 1975 to 1980 (42s)*

TERMINUS

Go to the first page of **Special Features**, scroll to **Audio Options**, press up and select the revealed *Doctor Who* logo
— *Countdown clocks for the studio recordings of all four episodes (31s)*

Go to the second page of **Special Features**, scroll down to **Menu**, press down and select the revealed *Doctor Who* logo
— *Trivia about* Terminus *(53s)*

TERROR OF THE ZYGONS

On disc two, go to the first page of **Special Features**, scroll down to **Remembering Douglas Camfield**, press left and select the revealed *Doctor Who* logo
— *Clip from the Monday 25 August 1975 edition of* Disney Time*, which Tom Baker presented in costume as the Doctor (36s)*

On disc two, go to the second page of **Special Features**, scroll down to **South Today**, press left and select the revealed *Doctor Who* logo
— *The unrestored film footage of the scene cut from episode one and rediscovered in 2012 in the collection of the serial's film editor Ian McKendrick (1m49s)*

TIME AND THE RANI

Go to the first page of **Special Features**, scroll down to **7D FX**, press left and select the revealed *Doctor Who* logo
— *A CGI remake of the regeneration to include Colin Baker's face (35s)*

Go to the second page of **Special Features**, scroll to **Blue Peter**, press right and select the revealed *Doctor Who* logo
— *Director Andrew Morgan, writer Pip Baker and Kate O'Mara recall a problem caused by hanging the actress upside down (1m40s)*

Go to the second page of **Special Features**, scroll down to **PDF Material**, press left and select the revealed *Doctor Who* logo
— *Sylvester McCoy relates how he was cast at the Doctor just as Timothy Dalton was being cast as James Bond (1m14s)*

THE TIME WARRIOR

On the main menu, scroll down to **Special Features**, press left to highlight the *Doctor Who* logo and select

— *Trivia about* The Time Warrior *(1m32)*

Go to the second page of **Special Features**, scoll down to **Back**, press left and select the revealed *Doctor Who* logo

— *Terrance Dicks reminisces about a photograph of him, Barry Letts and Jon Pertwee (39s)*

TIMELASH

On the main menu, scroll down to **Special Features**, press left to highlight the *Doctor Who* logo and select

— *Continuity announcements from the original BBC1 broadcasts of both episodes. Includes the BBC1 evening schedule for Saturday 16 March 1985 (1m30s)*

THE TOMB OF THE CYBERMEN

On the main menu, scroll to **Play All**, press up to highlight the *Doctor Who* logo and select

— *Full opening title sequence with Delia Derbyshire's remixed theme arrangement used for Second Doctor episodes from 1967 to 1969 (38s)*

On the main menu, scroll to **Play All**, press up to highlight the *Doctor Who* logo, then right (Cyber logo appears over second picture), then left so a green circle appears over the first picture, and select

— *A clip from episode three treated with the then-new VidFIRE motion-smoothing process, which wasn't developed in time to process the whole serial for this release (2m30s)*

Go to the second page of **Special Features**, select **Audio Options**, then press left to highlight the *Doctor Who* logo and select

— *Sound recording of a trailer for the following story,* The Abominable Snowmen, *broadcast on BBC1 on Saturday 23 September 1967 after episode four of* The Tomb of the Cybermen *(52s)*

THE TOMB OF THE CYBERMEN SPECIAL EDITION

On disc one, from the main menu select **Episode Selection**

— *Sound recording of a trailer for the following story,* The Abominable Snowmen, *broadcast on BBC1 on Saturday 23 September 1967 after episode four of* The Tomb of the Cybermen *(52s)*

On disc one, go to **Special Features**, scroll down to **Title Sequence Tests**, press left and select the revealed *Doctor Who* logo

— *Full opening title sequence with Delia Derbyshire's remixed theme arrangement used for Second Doctor episodes from 1967 to 1969 (38s)*

On disc two, on the first page of **Special Features**, scroll to **The Lost Giants**, press left and select the revealed *Doctor Who* logo

— *CGI recreations by Rob Semenoff of the TARDIS control room and Cybermen tomb sets (1m10s)*

THE TWIN DILEMMA

Go to the first page of **Special Features**, scroll down to **Breakfast Time**, press left and select the revealed *Doctor Who* logo

— *Silent 16mm colour film footage of the location filming at Gerrards Cross quarry in Buckinghamshire on Wednesday 8 February 1984 for scenes set on the surface of Jaconda (3m58s)*

THE TWO DOCTORS

On disc one, on the main menu scroll down to **Episode Selection**, press left and select the revealed *Doctor Who* logo

— *Full opening and closing title sequences with Peter Howell's remixed theme arrangement used for Sixth Doctor episodes from 1984 to 1985 (2m3s)*

THE VISITATION
Go to the second page of **Special Features**, scroll to **Writing a Final Visitation**, press left and select the revealed *Doctor Who* logo
— *Continuity announcements from the original BBC1 broadcasts of all four episodes of* The Visitation, *including plugs for the Blackpool and Longleat exhibitions (1m27s)*

THE VISITATION SPECIAL EDITION
On disc one, go to the second page of **Special Features**, scroll to **Photo Gallery**, press left and select the revealed *Doctor Who* logo
— *Continuity announcements from the original BBC1 broadcasts of all four episodes of* The Visitation, *including plugs for the Longleat and Blackpool exhibitions (1m27s)*

THE WAR GAMES
On disc one, on the main menu scroll down to **Subtitles**, press left to highlight the *Doctor Who* logo and select
— *Sound recordings from the location filming on Monday 31 March 1969 of scenes in episode three and dialogue for the end of episode nine. This was discovered among the tapes kept by Delia Derbyshire of the BBC Radiophonic Workshop after her death in 2001 (19m15s)*
On disc two, select **Subtitles**, scroll down to **Info Text On/Off**, press right and select the revealed *Doctor Who* logo
— *Comedy sketch by the Scottish Falsetto Sock Puppet Theatre. The socks re-enact the Doctor's trial (5m51s)*
On disc three, on the main menu scroll down to **Subtitles**, press left to highlight the *Doctor Who* logo and select
— *Original 16mm black-and-white film footage for the forcefield effect used in episode ten (43s)*

THE WAR MACHINES
Go to **Episode Selection**, scroll to **Episode Two**, press right and select the revealed *Doctor Who* logo
— *Silent 35mm black-and-white film footage from episode three of soldiers battling War Machine 3, including the operators evacuating as the prop catches fire. Filmed at Ealing Studios on Wednesday 25 May 1966 (1m4s)*

WARRIORS OF THE DEEP
Go to the second page of **Special Features**, scroll down to **Science in Action**, press left and select the revealed *Doctor Who* logo
— *Visual effects designer Mat Irvine shows the models, masks and props he made for* Warriors of the Deep *as they are today and talks about their construction (4m34s)*

WARRIORS' GATE
Go to the second page of **Special Features**, scroll down to **Continuity**, press right and select the revealed *Doctor Who* logo
— *Visual effects designer Mat Irvine talks about making the Gundan axe props (1m4s)*

MORE THAN 30 YEARS IN THE TARDIS
On the main menu, scroll down to **Photo Gallery**, press left to highlight the *Doctor Who* logo and select
— *Director Richard Martin remembers working with producer Verity Lambert (1m49s)*

APPENDIX 3 UK RELEASE ORDER

All UK releases of Classic Doctor Who *in the order they were issued, with cover details and notes on packaging differences. Notes in brackets refer only to the next listed DVD (or indicated group of DVDs), otherwise they apply to all subsequent releases. Titles in bold are boxsets; those in quote marks weren't featured on packaging (only the story titles making up the set) but are used here to indicate the connection of the contents*

	RELEASE DATE	BBC DVD	CERT	No. DISC	RRP	COVER ARTIST	BOOKLET WRITER
White BBC and DVD Video logos and certificate on front and spine; silver discs							
The Five Doctors SE	1/11/99	1006	U	1	£19.99	Colin Howard	no booklet
The Robots of Death	13/11/00	1012	PG	1	£19.99	photo	Richard Molesworth
Spearhead from Space	29/1/01	1033	U	1	£19.99	photo	Richard Molesworth
Remembrance of the Daleks	26/2/01	1040	PG	1	£19.99	photo	Richard Molesworth
The Caves of Androzani	18/6/01	1042	PG	1	£19.99	photo montage	Richard Molesworth
The Movie	13/8/01	1043	12	1	£19.99	photo montage	Richard Molesworth
Vengeance on Varos	15/10/01	1044	PG	1	£19.99	photo montage	Richard Molesworth
(No certificate on spine)							
The Tomb of the Cybermen	14/1/02	1032	PG	1	£19.99	Clayton Hickman	Richard Molesworth
DVD Video logo on front reduced and moved to below certificate							
The Ark in Space	8/4/02	1097	U	1	£19.99	Clayton Hickman	Richard Molesworth
Carnival of Monsters	15/7/02	1098	U	1	£19.99	Clayton Hickman	Richard Molesworth
No certificate on spine							
The Aztecs	21/10/02	1099	U	1	£19.99	Clayton Hickman	Richard Molesworth
(Case in black rubberised sleeve)							
Resurrection of the Daleks	18/11/02	1100	PG	1	£19.99	Clayton Hickman	Richard Molesworth
The Seeds of Death	17/2/03	1151	PG*	2	£19.99	Clayton Hickman	Richard Molesworth
The Talons of Weng-Chiang	28/4/03	1152	PG	2	£19.99	Clayton Hickman	Richard Molesworth
The Dalek Invasion of Earth	16/6/03	1156	PG	2	£19.99	Clayton Hickman	Richard Molesworth
Earthshock	18/8/03	1153	PG	2	£19.99	Clayton Hickman	Richard Molesworth
The Two Doctors	8/9/03	1213	PG	2	£19.99	Clayton Hickman	Richard Molesworth
The Curse of Fenric	6/10/03	1154	PG	2	£19.99	Clayton Hickman	Richard Molesworth
Dalek Collector's Edition	6/10/03	1384	PG	4	£39.99	Andrew Skilleter	
The Three Doctors	24/11/03	1144	PG	1	£19.99	Clayton Hickman	Richard Molesworth
BBC DVD logo added on front							
The Visitation	19/1/04	1329	PG*	1	£19.99	Clayton Hickman[1]	Richard Molesworth
Pyramids of Mars	1/3/04	1350	U	1	£19.99	Clayton Hickman	Richard Molesworth
The Green Death	10/5/04	1142	U	1	£19.99	Clayton Hickman	Richard Molesworth
The Leisure Hive	5/7/04	1351	PG	1	£19.99	Clayton Hickman	Richard Molesworth
Ghost Light	20/9/04	1352	PG	1	£19.99	Clayton Hickman	Richard Molesworth
(Certificate on spine); discs printed with cover artwork							
Lost in Time	1/11/04	1353	PG	3	£29.99	Clayton Hickman	Richard Molesworth
Horror of Fang Rock	17/1/05	1356	U	1	£19.99	Clayton Hickman	Richard Molesworth
BBC logo removed from front							
The Mind Robber	7/3/05	1358	PG*	1	£19.99	Clayton Hickman	Richard Molesworth
The Claws of Axos	25/4/05	1354	U	1	£19.99	Clayton Hickman	Richard Molesworth
Black 2 entertain logo added to spine; commentary subtitles dropped							
Revelation of the Daleks	11/7/05	1357	PG	1	£19.99	Clayton Hickman	Richard Molesworth
The Web Planet	3/10/05	1355	U	1	£19.99	Clayton Hickman	Richard Molesworth
City of Death	7/11/05	1664	PG*	2	£19.99	Clayton Hickman	Richard Molesworth
The Beginning	30/1/06	1882	12	3	£29.99	Clayton Hickman	
— An Unearthly Child	30/1/06	1882(A)	U	1	—	Clayton Hickman	Richard Molesworth
— The Daleks	30/1/06	1882(B)	12*	1	—	Clayton Hickman	Richard Molesworth
— The Edge of Destruction	30/1/06	1882(C)	PG	1	—	Clayton Hickman	Richard Molesworth
Genesis of the Daleks	10/4/06	1813	PG	2	£19.99	Clayton Hickman	Richard Molesworth
Inferno	19/6/06	1802	PG	2	£19.99	Clayton Hickman	Richard Molesworth
The Hand of Fear	24/7/06	1829	PG	1	£19.99	Lee Binding	Richard Molesworth
The Mark of the Rani	4/9/06	2224	U	1	£19.99	Clayton Hickman	Sue Cowley
The Sontaran Experiment	9/10/06	1811	PG	1	£12.99	Lee Binding	Sue Cowley
The Invasion	6/11/06	1829	PG	2	£19.99	Clayton Hickman	Sue Cowley
The Cybermen Collection	6/11/06	2262	PG	4	£39.99	Clayton Hickman	

	RELEASE DATE	BBC DVD	CERT	No. DISC	RRP	COVER ARTIST	BOOKLET WRITER
The Third Doctor Collection	6/11/06	2263	PG	7	£49.99	Clayton Hickman	
The Dalek Collection	27/1/07	2261	PG	7	£79.99	Clayton Hickman	
(New Beginnings covers have Black DVD Video logo on spine)							
New Beginnings	29/1/07	1331	12	3	£29.99	Clayton Hickman	
— The Keeper of Traken	29/1/07	1331(A)	PG	1	—	Clayton Hickman	Richard Molesworth
— Logopolis	29/1/07	1331(B)	12*	1	—	Clayton Hickman	Moray Laing
— Castrovalva	29/1/07	1331(C)	U	1	—	Clayton Hickman	Richard Molesworth
(Black DVD Video logo on spine and none on front)							
Survival	16/4/07	1834	PG	2	£19.99	Lee Binding	Richard Molesworth
Robot	4/6/07	2332	U	1	£19.99	Clayton Hickman	Sue Cowley
(Following reissues have standard cases in sleeve with orange logo, cover art in a circle against dark purple background)							
The Five Doctors SE reissue	2/7/07	2468	U	1	£9.99	photo montage	Richard Molesworth
Genesis of the Daleks reissue	2/7/07	2469	PG	2	£9.99	Richard Molesworth	Richard Molesworth
Spearhead from Space reissue	2/7/07	2470	U	1	£9.99	photo montage	Richard Molesworth
Earthshock reissue	2/7/07	2471	PG	1	£9.99	Clayton Hickman	Richard Molesworth
Remembrance of the Daleks reissue	2/7/07	2472	PG	1	£9.99	photo montage	Richard Molesworth
The Movie reissue	2/7/07	2473	12	1	£9.99	photo montage	Richard Molesworth
The Hand of Fear reissue	2/7/07	2474	PG	1	£9.99	Lee Binding	Richard Molesworth
Revelation of the Daleks reissue	2/7/07	2475	PG	1	£9.99	Richard Molesworth	Richard Molesworth
Timelash	9/7/07	2333	PG	1	£12.99	Lee Binding	Moray Laing
"Tegan boxset"	6/8/07	2327	PG	2	£29.99	Clayton Hickman	
— Time-Flight	6/8/07	2327A	PG	1	—	Dan Budden	Moray Laing
— Arc of Infinity	6/8/07	2327B	PG	1	—	Dan Budden	Sue Cowley
The Time Warrior	3/9/07	2334	PG	1	£19.99	Clayton Hickman	Richard Molesworth
(Key to Time discs printed with picture of Key rather than cover artwork)							
The Key to Time	24/9/07	2335	PG	7	£69.99	Clayton Hickman	
— The Ribos Operation	24/9/07	2335(A)	PG	1	—	Clayton Hickman	Niall Boyce/ Richard Molesworth
— The Pirate Planet	24/9/07	2335(B)	PG	1	—	Clayton Hickman	Tim Kittel/ Richard Molesworth
— The Stones of Blood	24/9/07	2335(C)	PG	1	—	Clayton Hickman	Sue Cowley
— The Androids of Tara	24/9/07	2335(D)	PG	1	—	Clayton Hickman	Sue Cowley
— The Power of Kroll	24/9/07	2335(E)	PG	1	—	Clayton Hickman	Moray Laing
— The Armageddon Factor	24/9/07	2335(F)	PG*2	2	—	Clayton Hickman	Moray Laing
Planet of Evil	15/10/07	1814	PG	1	£19.99	Lee Binding	Richard Molesworth[3]
White 2 entertain logo on spine							
Destiny of the Daleks	26/11/07	2434	PG	1	£19.99	Lee Binding	Evye Onians
The Complete Davros Collection	26/11/07	2508	PG	8	£99.99	Clayton Hickman	Niall Boyce/Tim Kittel
Beneath the Surface	14/1/08	2438	PG	4	£39.99	Clayton Hickman	
— Doctor Who and the Silurians	14/1/08	2438(A)	PG	2	—	Clayton Hickman	Sue Cowley
— The Sea Devils	14/1/08	2438(B)	PG	1	—	Clayton Hickman	Sue Cowley
— Warriors of the Deep	14/1/08	2438(C)	PG	1	—	Clayton Hickman	Sue Cowley
The Time Meddler	4/2/08	2331	PG	1	£12.99	Clayton Hickman	Sue Cowley
(Case in sleeve with full-cover illustration and orange logo)							
The Five Doctors 25th Anniversary Edition	3/3/08	2450	PG*	2	£19.99	Clayton Hickman	Sue Cowley
Black Orchid	14/4/08	2432	PG	1	£12.99	Clayton Hickman	Moray Laing
The Invasion of Time	5/5/08	2586	PG*	2	£19.99	Clayton Hickman	Stewart Sheargold
Bred for War: The Sontaran Collection	5/5/08	2617	PG	6	£39.99	Clayton Hickman	
K9 Tales	16/6/08	2439	12	2	£29.99	Clayton Hickman	
(Full-cover illustration, standard design printed on reverse; both use 'K9 and Company' logo)							
— K9 and Company	16/6/08	2798	PG	1	—	Clayton Hickman	Richard Molesworth
(BBC DVD logo on front black instead of usual white)							
— The Invisible Enemy	16/6/08	2799	12*	1	—	Clayton Hickman	Stewart Sheargold
The Brain of Morbius	21/7/08	1816	PG	1	£19.99	Clayton Hickman	Niall Boyce
The War Machines	25/8/08	2441	PG	1	£19.99	Clayton Hickman	Moray Laing
Four to Doomsday	15/9/08	2431	PG	1	£19.99	Clayton Hickman	Niall Boyce
(Trial of a Time Lord covers have episode numbers on spine)							
The Trial of a Time Lord	29/9/08	2422	PG	4	£49.99	Clayton Hickman	
— The Mysterious Planet	29/9/08	2422(A)	PG	1	—	Clayton Hickman	Niall Boyce
— Mindwarp	29/9/08	2422(B)	PG	1	—	Clayton Hickman	Stewart Sheargold
— Terror of the Vervoids	29/9/08	2422(C)	PG	1	—	Clayton Hickman	Tim Kittel
— The Ultimate Foe	29/9/08	2422(D)	PG	1	—	Clayton Hickman	Stewart Sheargold

3

	RELEASE DATE	BBC DVD	CERT	No. DISC	RRP	COVER ARTIST	BOOKLET WRITER
Audio navigation of disc contents introduced							
Battlefield	29/12/08	2440	PG	2	£19.99	Clayton Hickman	Sue Cowley
The E-Space Trilogy	26/1/09	1835	PG	3	£34.99	Clayton Hickman	
— Full Circle	26/1/09	1835(A)	U	1	—	Clayton Hickman	Sue Cowley
— State of Decay	26/1/09	1835(B)	PG	1	—	Clayton Hickman	Moray Laing
— Warriors' Gate	26/1/09	1835(C)	PG	1	—	Clayton Hickman	Moray Laing
"Vicki boxset"	23/2/09	2698	U	2	£29.35	Clayton Hickman	
— The Rescue	23/2/09	2970	U	1	—	Clayton Hickman	Moray Laing
— The Romans	23/2/09	2971	U	1	—	Clayton Hickman	Sue Cowley
Attack of the Cybermen	16/3/09	2436	U	1	£19.56	Clayton Hickman	Stewart Sheargold
Image of the Fendahl	20/4/09	1820	PG	1	£19.56	Clayton Hickman	Tim Kittel
The Deadly Assassin	11/5/09	2430	PG	1	£19.56	Clayton Hickman	Tom Kelly
Delta and the Bannermen	22/6/09	2599	PG	1	£19.56	Clayton Hickman	Niall Boyce
The War Games	6/7/09	1800	PG	3	£24.46	Clayton Hickman	Niall Boyce
(Case in sleeve with full-cover illustration; 'Special Edition' on front but not spine; no audio navigation)							
Remembrance of the Daleks SE	20/7/09	2451	PG	2	£19.56	Clayton Hickman	Sue Cowley
The Black Guardian Trilogy	10/8/09	2596	PG	4	£39.14	Clayton Hickman	
— Mawdryn Undead	10/8/09	2596A	PG	1	—	Clayton Hickman	Moray Laing
— Terminus	10/8/09	2596B	PG	1	—	Clayton Hickman	Sue Cowley
— Enlightenment	10/8/09	2596C	PG	2	—	Clayton Hickman	Sue Cowley
The Twin Dilemma	7/9/09	2598	PG*	1	£19.56	Clayton Hickman	Moray Laing
The Keys of Marinus	21/9/09	2616	PG*	1	£19.56	Clayton Hickman	Richard Molesworth
New purple BBC logo on front and spine; version with previous white logo printed on reverse							
Dalek War	5/10/09	2614	PG	4	£34.26	Clayton Hickman	
— Frontier in Space	5/10/09	2614(A)	PG*	2	—	Clayton Hickman	Sue Cowley
— Planet of the Daleks	5/10/09	2614(B)	U	2	—	Clayton Hickman	Moray Laing
The Key to Time reissue	16/11/09	2754	PG	7	£69.99	Clayton Hickman	as original releases
Peladon Tales	18/1/10	2744	PG	3	£29.99	Clayton Hickman	
— The Curse of Peladon	18/1/10	2744(A)	PG	1	—	Clayton Hickman	Sue Cowley
— The Monster of Peladon	18/1/10	2744(B)	PG*	2	—	Clayton Hickman	Moray Laing
The Masque of Mandragora	8/2/10	2805	PG*	1	£19.99	Clayton Hickman	Niall Boyce
"First Doctor boxset"	1/3/10	2809	PG	3	£29.99	Clayton Hickman	
— The Space Museum	1/3/10	2809(A)	PG	1	—	Clayton Hickman	Sue Cowley
— The Chase	1/3/10	2809(B)	PG	2	—	Clayton Hickman	Moray Laing
Myths and Legends	29/3/10	2851	12	3	£49.99	Clayton Hickman	
— The Time Monster	29/3/10	2851(A)	PG*	1	—	Clayton Hickman	Sebastian J Brook
— Underworld	29/3/10	2851(B)	12*	1	—	Clayton Hickman	Sue Cowley
— The Horns of Nimon	29/3/10	2851(C)	PG*	1	—	Clayton Hickman	Moray Laing
The Creature from the Pit	3/5/10	2849	PG	1	£19.99	Clayton Hickman	John Daly/Tom Kelly
Kamelion Tales	14/6/10	2738	PG	3	£29.99	Clayton Hickman	
— The King's Demons	14/6/10	2738(A)	U	1	—	Clayton Hickman	Sue Cowley
— Planet of Fire	14/6/10	2738(B)	PG	2	—	Clayton Hickman	Sue Cowley
The Dominators	12/7/10	2807	PG*	1	£19.99	Clayton Hickman	Niall Boyce
"Cybermen boxset"	9/8/10	2854	PG	2	£29.99	Clayton Hickman	
— Revenge of the Cybermen	9/8/10	2854(A)	U	1	—	Clayton Hickman	Niall Boyce
— Silver Nemesis	9/8/10	2854(B)	PG	1	—	Clayton Hickman	Tim Kittel
Time and the Rani	13/9/10	2808	PG	1	£19.99	Clayton Hickman	Tim Kittel
(Revisitation 1 covers have 'Special Edition' on front but not spine, same on reverse)							
Revisitations 1	4/10/10	2806	12	7	£39.99	none	
— The Talons of Weng-Chiang SE	4/10/10	2806(A)	PG	3	—	Clayton Hickman	Niall Boyce
— The Caves of Androzani SE	4/10/10	2806(B)	PG	2	—	Clayton Hickman	Tim Kittel
— The Movie SE	4/10/10	2806(C)	12	2	—	Clayton Hickman	Sue Cowley
The Seeds of Doom	25/10/10	3044	PG*	2	£19.99	Clayton Hickman	Tim Kittel
Meglos	10/1/11	2852	U	1	£19.99	Lee Binding	Sue Cowley
The Mutants	31/1/11	3042	PG	2	£19.99	Lee Binding	Moray Laing
The Ark	14/2/11	2957	PG*	1	£19.99	Lee Binding	Niall Boyce
Mara Tales	7/3/11	2871	PG	2	£29.99	Clayton Hickman	
— Kinda	7/3/11	2871A	PG*	1	—	Clayton Hickman	Niall Boyce
— Snakedance	7/3/11	2871B	PG*	1	—	Clayton Hickman	Sue Cowley

	RELEASE DATE	BBC DVD	CERT	No. DISC	RRP	COVER ARTIST	BOOKLET WRITER
(Revisitation 2 covers have 'Special Edition' on front but not spine, same on reverse)							
Revisitations 2	28/3/11	2956	PG	6	£39.99	none	
— The Seeds of Death SE	28/3/11	2956A	PG*	2	—	Clayton Hickman	Sue Cowley
— Carnival of Monsters SE	28/3/11	2956B	PG*	2	—	Clayton Hickman	Sue Cowley
— Resurrection of the Daleks SE	28/3/11	2956C	PG*	2	—	Clayton Hickman	Moray Laing
Planet of the Spiders	18/4/11	1809	PG	2	£19.99	Lee Binding	Sue Cowley
Mannequin Mania	9/5/11	3135	PG	2	£35.73	Clayton Hickman	
('Special Edition' on front but not spine, same on reverse)							
— Spearhead from Space SE	9/5/11	3135A	PG*	1	—	Clayton Hickman	Sebastian J Brook
— Terror of the Autons	9/5/11	3135B	PG*	1	—	Clayton Hickman	Moray Laing
Frontios	30/5/11	3004	PG	1	£20.42	Lee Binding	Tim Kittel
Earth Story	20/6/11	3380	PG	2	£30.63	Clayton Hickman	
— The Gunfighters	20/6/11	3380A	PG	1	—	Clayton Hickman	Niall Boyce
— The Awakening	20/6/11	3380B	PG	1	—	Clayton Hickman	Moray Laing
Paradise Towers	18/7/11	3002	PG	1	£20.42	Lee Binding	Sue Cowley/ Mike Tucker
The Sun Makers	1/8/11	2955	U	1	£20.42	Lee Binding	Moray Laing
(Irish certificate on front and spine but not on reverse for next two releases)							
Day of the Daleks	12/9/11	3043	PG*	2	£20.42	Lee Binding	Moray Laing
Colony in Space	3/10/11	3381	PG*	1	£20.42	Lee Binding	Moray Laing
U.N.I.T Files	9/1/12	3376	PG	3	£30.63	Clayton Hickman	
— Invasion of the Dinosaurs	9/1/12	3376A	PG	2	—	Clayton Hickman	Tim Kittel
— The Android Invasion	9/1/12	3376B	PG	1	—	Clayton Hickman	Stewart Sheargold
The Sensorites	23/1/12	3377	PG*	1	£20.42	Lee Binding	Niall Boyce
(Revisitation 3 covers have 'Special Edition' on front but not spine, same on reverse)							
Revisitations 3	13/2/12	3003	PG	5	£35.74	none	
— The Tomb of the Cybermen SE	13/2/12	3003A	PG	2	—	Clayton Hickman	Sue Cowley
— The Three Doctors SE	13/2/12	3003B	PG	2	—	Clayton Hickman	Pete McTighe
— The Robots of Death SE	13/2/12	3003C	PG	1	—	Clayton Hickman	Moray Laing
The Face of Evil	5/3/12	3379	PG	1	£20.42	Lee Binding	Moray Laing
(Irish certificate on front but not spine or reverse)							
The Dæmons	19/3/12	3383	PG	2	£20.42	Lee Binding	Moray Laing
Nightmare of Eden	2/4/12	3378	PG*	1	£20.42	Lee Binding	Stewart Sheargold
2 entertain logo removed from spine, certificate added; reverse kept as before							
Ace Adventures	7/5/12	3387	PG	2	£30.63	Clayton Hickman	
— Dragonfire	7/5/12	3387A	PG	1	—	Clayton Hickman	Tim Kittel
— The Happiness Patrol	7/5/12	3387B	PG	1	—	Clayton Hickman	Tim Kittel
Death to the Daleks	18/6/12	3483	PG*	1	£20.42	Lee Binding	Moray Laing
The Krotons	2/7/12	3480	PG*	1	£20.42	Lee Binding	Moray Laing
The Greatest Show in the Galaxy	30/7/12	3481	PG	1	£20.42	Lee Binding	Moray Laing
Planet of Giants	20/8/12	3479	PG*	1	£20.42	Lee Binding	Moray Laing
('Special Edition' on front and spine, same on reverse)							
Vengeance on Varos SE	10/9/12	3512	PG	2	£20.42	Lee Binding	Pete McTighe
The Ambassadors of Death	1/10/12	3484	PG*	2	£20.42	Lee Binding	Moray Laing
('Special Edition' on front and spine, on front but not spine on reverse)							
The Claws of Axos SE	22/10/12	3670	PG*	2	£20.42	Lee Binding	Moray Laing
The Legacy Collection	7/1/13	3388	PG	3	£20.42	Clayton Hickman	
— Shada	7/1/13	3388A	PG*	2	—	Clayton Hickman	Pete McTighe
— More Than 30 Years in the TARDIS	7/1/13	3388B	U⁴	1	—	Clayton Hickman	Moray Laing
The Reign of Terror	28/1/13	3528	PG	1	£20.42	Lee Binding	Pete McTighe
(Next four releases have 'Special Edition' on front and spine, on front but not spine on reverse)							
The Ark in Space SE	25/2/13	3672	PG*	2	£20.42	Lee Binding	Pete McTighe
The Aztecs SE	11/3/13	3689	PG*	2	£20.42	Lee Binding	Moray Laing
The Visitation SE	6/5/13	3690	PG*	2	£20.42	Lee Binding	Pete McTighe
Inferno SE	27/5/13	3671	PG	2	£20.42	Lee Binding	Moray Laing
The Mind of Evil	3/6/13	3269	U	2	£20.42	Lee Binding	Moray Laing
Regeneration	24/6/13	3801	12*	6	£61.27	photo	none
(Full-cover illustration, standard design printed on reverse)							
Spearhead from Space Blu-ray	15/7/13	0230†	PG*	1	£20.52	Lee Binding	Moray Laing
Fourth Doctor Time Capsule	29/7/13	3800	PG		£62.99	none	none

	RELEASE DATE	BBC DVD	CERT	No. DISC	RRP	COVER ARTIST	BOOKLET WRITER
('Special Edition' on front and spine, same on reverse)							
The Green Death SE	5/8/13	3778	PG*	2	£20.42	Lee Binding	Moray Laing
(Black BBC logo on reverse spine instead of usual white)							
The Ice Warriors	26/8/13	3558	PG	2	£20.42	Lee Binding	Pete McTighe
Scream of the Shalka	16/9/13	3858‡	PG	1	£20.42	Lee Binding	Pete McTighe
Terror of the Zygons	30/9/13	3482	PG	2	£20.42	Lee Binding	Sue Cowley[3]
(Monster Collection single-sided covers)							
The Monster Collection: The Cybermen	30/9/13	3809	PG	1	£9.99	Stuart Crouch	Moray Laing
The Monster Collection: Davros	30/9/13	3810	PG	2	£9.99	Stuart Crouch	Moray Laing
The Monster Collection: The Silurians	30/9/13	3811	PG	2	£9.99	Stuart Crouch	Moray Laing
The Monster Collection: The Sontarans	30/9/13	3812	PG	1	£9.99	Stuart Crouch	Moray Laing
The Monster Collection: The Daleks	30/9/13	3813	PG	2	£9.99	Stuart Crouch	Moray Laing
The Monster Collection: The Master	30/9/13	3814	PG	2	£9.99	Stuart Crouch	Moray Laing
(Black BBC logo on reverse spine instead of usual white)							
The Tenth Planet	14/10/13	3382	PG	2	£20.42	Lee Binding	Moray Laing
(Full-cover illustration, standard design printed on reverse)							
The Enemy of the World	25/11/13	3866	PG	1	£20.42	Lee Binding	Pete McTighe
The Moonbase	20/1/14	3698	PG	1	£20.42	Lee Binding	Moray Laing
(Full-cover illustration, standard design printed on reverse)							
The Web of Fear	24/2/14	3867	PG	1	£20.42	Lee Binding	Moray Laing

* Episodes lower certificate

1 Artwork amended by unknown designer

2 Cover wrongly labelled U; disc two PG

3 Credit on cover incorrect

4 Cover wrongly labelled PG

† BBCBD number

‡ Originally scheduled in 2004 as BBCDVD2131

APPENDIX 4 **DOCTOR WHO DVDs OVERSEAS**

AMERICA/CANADA

Doctor Who first aired in the US on 21 August 1972 on WPHL in Philadelphia, Pennsylvania, one of sixteen stations that bought the first three Third Doctor seasons (except *Spearhead from Space*) then being distributed by Time-Life Films under licence from BBC Enterprises. Attempts in the 1960s to market the series in the US had failed, but its move into colour made it a more appealing prospect. Although colour television had been available there as early as 1954, it wasn't until the mid-60s that most commercial networks' primetime programming was in colour, and 1972 was the first year that colour televisions outsold black-and-white sets. *Doctor Who* was shown in eleven States over the next five years but made little impact, and most stations dropped it before airing all of the thirteen serials they had bought. That's not to say it went completely unnoticed, however, and the home-video recordings made by the first wave of American fans would be crucial to the restoration of some of these episodes years later.

Then in 1977 a certain movie set in a galaxy far, far away reinvigorated the public's interest in science fiction. Keen to engage this post-*Star Wars* audience, BBC Enterprises remembered it had a science fiction series of its own that it could sell, and struck a new deal with Time-Life Television to distribute the first four Fourth Doctor seasons in the US. In 1978 Time-Life heavily promoted the show in industry magazines and by the end of the year was reporting sales to some seventy-five stations. The first to start showing these episodes was WTEV in New Bedford, Massachusetts on Monday 28 August 1978. This time the programme tapped into the growing science fiction and fantasy fan network and began to develop a dedicated following — sufficient that the first US *Doctor Who* convention held in West Hollywood, California on Saturday 1 December 1979 expected some 300 attendees, but had more than 1,000 once it was known Tom Baker would be appearing.

Broadcasts in the most northern States could be picked up by fans in neighbouring Canada, even though the programme was being shown there by local stations. The Canadian Broadcasting Corporation had actually bought the first five serials and aired them from January to July 1965, but then never showed the programme again (until the New Series). In 1976 stations CKVU in Vancouver, British Columbia and TVOntario in Toronto separately acquired groups of Third Doctor serials, including several from his last two seasons that had never been shown in the US. Both stations began their runs on Saturday 18 September 1976, which for CKVU was just two weeks after the station had launched. These purchases would prove invaluable as both stations were later able to return colour copies of several stories that were otherwise missing from the archives.

TVOntario subsequently began showing Fourth Doctor episodes from Saturday 16 September 1978 and continued broadcasting through to the end of the Classic Series, as did stations across the US. *Doctor Who* soon had an established audience in North America and when BBC Video started releasing the series on VHS in the UK, distribution in the US and Canada soon followed, initially by CBS/Fox Video and from 2000 by Warner Home Video. This concluded in October 2003 with *The End of the Universe Collection*, a boxset mopping up the last eleven unreleased stories.

By then the market for VHS was dwindling as DVD became the home media of choice. With the UK releases beginning in earnest in November 2000, North Americans were able to start their collections later the next year. Initially BBC Worldwide Americas supplemented the content from the UK discs with short text biographies of the main cast (for American viewers less familiar with British actors), in a few cases the narration by Howard da Silva that had been added to broadcasts of that first batch of Fourth Doctor episodes (indicative of the nostalgia felt by those who first discovered *Doctor Who* through its late-70s airings), and even commissioned its own commentary track for *The Five Doctors Special Edition*. The releases also had different covers, designed at BBC Worldwide in the US. These additions came to be considered an unnecessary cost, however, and from 2003 the contents matched the UK releases. The unique covers continued for longer but were heavily criticised by fans for being less accomplished than the UK's, so from 2007 the same artwork was used on both. In fact, the US design came to be preferred by many as it used the full illustration across the cover, rather than confining it to the bottom half as the UK design did.

Sometimes the US lost out compared to the UK, usually in cases where commercial music used in the episodes couldn't be licensed for worldwide use. The US release of *The Chase* has two minutes of footage featuring a Beatles performance cut out, while the Special Edition of *Remembrance of the Daleks* still has Beatles tracks replaced even though the UK version is now intact thanks to revised usage permissions. Ironically, for many years the US-produced *The Movie* wasn't actually available in North America because the distribution rights lay with Universal rather than the BBC. When the story was given the Special Edition treatment and re-released in the UK, 2 entertain was able to negotiate a deal to also sell it in the US and it finally appeared in February 2011. One other downside for American fans was that, whereas UK releases of individual stories were priced the same irrespective of how many discs they contained, in the US multi-disc releases cost more, generally $10 per extra disc above the standard price for single-disc releases.

For the most part, however, the US was limited to serials that were already on sale in the UK, although the delay between the two regions meant the release order could be altered. Whereas the UK had individual releases approximately every two months, BBC Worldwide Americas chose to issue two stories every three months, picking pairings from what was available that best suited its market. This allowed it to back up anticipated weaker-selling stories — essentially anything without Tom Baker in, but particularly the 1960s serials — with a more popular title. Except in one instance, every pair of releases during the first two years of the schedule included either a Fourth Doctor or a Dalek story, and until the very end of the range no black-and-white story was ever released without a colour one at the same time.

Even so, the distributor was struggling to get the DVDs onto store shelves as the US market was heavily geared towards boxsets of complete series, the norm for modern television series. The range was very nearly cancelled in 2002 but instead BBCWA decided to produce its own boxset to get the series into stores and provide an anchor that the individual releases could sit beside. They chose the six stories from the 1978/79 season, which formed the Doctor's search for the Key to Time, again building on the familiarity with Tom Baker's Doctor thanks to those early broadcasts. The episodes had some basic restoration done by the team working on the releases in the UK, while BBCWA organised the production of commentaries, information subtitles and photo galleries. The strategy succeeded in getting the range shelf space, helped later by the UK doing its own boxsets and the return of the series to television. The Key to Time season was released in the UK in September 2007, fully restored from scratch and with a host of new special features, plus the commentaries from the US set, and these upgraded versions were reissued in the US labelled as Special Editions.

Boxsets continued to be a point of difference between the UK and US releases, however. Despite its preference for such bundles, BBCWA did also release the titles separately (presumably in the interests of consumer choice), whereas once the UK started selling sets these were the only way to buy the stories contained. At least 2 entertain in the UK was consistent, with boxsets always containing the individual stories in their own cases and covers, so collectors could place them on their shelves in the order of their choice. While the US generally did the same, to allow for selling the box contents separately, there were exceptions. The first UK set, The Beginning, containing the first three stories from 1963/64, was packaged in two cases instead of three in the US, partly because the stories were linked anyway but mainly because the third disc contained most of the extras, making the three discs uneven as individual titles. The stories in the New Beginnings, Beneath the Surface and re-released Key to Time sets were all available separately, yet the E-Space Trilogy, Black Guardian Trilogy and Dalek War sets weren't. (Nor was *The Trial of a Time Lord*, an obvious exception given its unique nature as one story composed of four sections.) Indeed, two story pairings that had been released as boxsets in the UK — *The Rescue/The Romans* and *The Space Museum/The Chase* — were combined in single cases in the US. As these are black-and-white stories, this was to keep the price more attractive by packaging them as multi-disc sets rather than boxsets.

After those, however, the US saw no Classic *Doctor Who* boxsets, even though they continued in the UK. The main reason for this is that these later UK sets contained non-sequential stories —

mixes from different eras, perhaps featuring the same monster or remastered stories from early in the range — which BBCWA was less keen on. The rise in online shopping and the decline of physical stores, particularly for products like DVDs, may have influenced a move away from boxsets too. Also by then the UK schedule had been accelerated to monthly releases, allowing the US to raise its release rate to six pairs a year. These still generally lagged behind by several months, however, and BBC Worldwide began to worry that the gap created potential for the UK discs to be pirated online, tempting eager American viewers away from buying the DVDs. Thus from 2011 a concerted effort was made to bring the two release schedules closer together. BBCWA still issued two or three stories at a time, but these were usually within a month or less of the most recent UK release date, and in the last few years of the range it managed a rate of almost two a month.

Most recently the US saw two Classic Series releases that haven't been issued in the UK. Each month during 2013, BBC America built anticipation for the fiftieth anniversary by broadcasting new half-hour documentaries about each of the Doctors followed by one of their stories, unrestored and edited into a single omnibus version framed in widescreen. These have since been released on DVD in sets covering Doctors one to four, five to eight and nine to eleven. The first two releases contain the relevant documentaries, the edited stories as broadcast, but also the fully restored episodic originals, plus new introductions by showrunner Steven Moffat. The stories on The Doctors Revisited 1–4 are *The Aztecs*, *The Tomb of the Cybermen*, *Spearhead from Space* and *Pyramids of Mars*, while on The Doctors Revisited 5–8 are *Earthshock*, *Vengeance on Varos*, *Remembrance of the Daleks* and *The Movie*. The third set also has the documentaries, introductions by Moffat but only one version of the episodes — *Bad Wolf/The Parting of the Ways*, *The Stolen Earth/Journey's End* and *The Impossible Astronaut/Day of the Moon* — and on 3 June 2014 all three sets were reissued together in a single giftset. Also released in the US alone is a Blu-ray/DVD 'combo pack' of *An Adventure in Space and Time*, the dramatised account of William Hartnell's time as the Doctor. As well as extras relating to the drama, this includes the first story, *An Unearthly Child*.

REGION 1 RELEASE SCHEDULE

All releases of Classic Doctor Who *in the US and Canada in the order they were issued, with notes on differences from the UK. Notes in brackets refer only to the next listed DVD (or indicated group of DVDs), otherwise they apply to all subsequent releases. Titles in bold are boxsets. Where boxset contents weren't also issued separately, refer to the UK schedule (Appendix 3) for the titles contained. Note, dates are in the UK format of day/month/year*

	RELEASE DATE	No. DISCS	ORIGINAL US SRP	ORIGINAL CAN SRP		RELEASE DATE	No. DISCS	ORIGINAL US SRP	ORIGINAL CAN SRP
Full-cover photo illustration different to UK					Resurrection of the Daleks	1/7/03	1	$24.98	$30.98
Spearhead from Space	11/9/01	1	$24.98	$32.98	The Dalek Invasion of Earth	7/10/03	2	$34.98	$43.98
The Robots of Death	11/9/01	1	$24.98	$32.98	The Talons of Weng-Chiang	7/10/03	2	$34.98	$43.98
The Five Doctors SE	11/9/01	1	$24.98	$32.98	The Seeds of Death	2/3/04	2	$34.98	$43.98
The Caves of Androzani	2/4/02	1	$24.98	$32.98	The Three Doctors	2/3/04	1	$24.98	$30.98
Remembrance of the Daleks	2/4/02	1	$24.98	$32.98	The Two Doctors	1/6/04	2	$34.98	$43.98
The Tomb of the Cybermen	6/8/02	1	$24.98	$29.98	The Curse of Fenric	1/6/04	2	$34.98	$43.98
The Ark in Space	6/8/02	1	$24.98	$29.98	Pyramids of Mars	7/9/04	1	$24.98	$30.98
(Key to Time set and individuals not released in UK)					Earthshock	7/9/04	1	$24.98	$30.98
The Key to Time	1/10/02	6	$124.98	$149.98	Lost in Time	2/11/04	3	$49.98	$62.48
The Ribos Operation	1/10/02	1	$24.98	$29.98	Lost in Time: Hartnell Years	2/11/04	1	$24.98	$30.98
The Pirate Planet	1/10/02	1	$24.98	$29.98	Lost in Time: Troughton Years	2/11/04	2	$34.98	$43.98
The Stones of Blood	1/10/02	1	$24.98	$29.98	The Green Death	1/3/05	1	$24.98	$30.98
The Androids of Tara	1/10/02	1	$24.98	$29.98	The Visitation	1/3/05	1	$24.98	$30.98
The Power of Kroll	1/10/02	1	$24.98	$29.98	The Leisure Hive	7/6/05	1	$24.98	$30.98
The Armageddon Factor	1/10/02	1	$24.98	$29.98	Ghost Light	7/6/05	1	$24.98	$30.98
The Aztecs	4/3/03	1	$24.98	$30.98	The Mind Robber	6/9/05	1	$24.98	$30.98
Vengeance on Varos	4/3/03	1	$24.98	$30.98	Horror of Fang Rock	6/9/05	1	$24.98	$30.98
Carnival of Monsters	1/7/03	1	$24.98	$30.98	The Claws of Axos	8/11/05	1	$24.98	$30.98

	RELEASE DATE	No. DISCS	ORIGINAL US SRP	ORIGINAL CAN SRP
City of Death	8/11/05	2	$34.98	$43.98
The Beginning	28/3/06	3	$49.98	$62.48
Genesis of the Daleks	6/6/06	2	$34.98	$43.98
Revelation of the Daleks	6/6/06	1	$24.98	$30.98
The Web Planet	5/9/06	1	$24.98	$30.98
Inferno	5/9/06	2	$34.98	$43.98
The Hand of Fear	7/11/06	1	$24.98	$30.98
The Mark of the Rani	7/11/06	1	$24.98	$30.98
The Invasion	6/3/07	2	$34.98	$43.98
The Sontaran Experiment	6/3/07	1	$14.98	$19.98
New Beginnings	5/6/07	3	$49.98	$62.48
The Keeper of Traken	5/6/07	1	$24.98	$30.98
Logopolis	5/6/07	1	$24.98	$30.98
Castrovalva	5/6/07	1	$24.98	$30.98
Same artwork as UK but over full cover				
Robot	14/8/07	1	$24.98	$30.98
Survival	14/8/07	2	$34.98	$43.98
Time-Flight	6/11/07	1	$24.98	$30.98
Arc of Infinity	6/11/07	1	$24.98	$30.98
Planet of Evil	4/3/08	1	$24.98	$30.98
Destiny of the Daleks	4/3/08	1	$24.98	$30.98
(UK artwork adapted to suit full cover for next two releases)				
The Time Warrior	1/4/08	1	$24.98	$30.98
Timelash	1/4/08	1	$24.98	$30.98
(Cover adapted from UK slipcase artwork)				
Beneath the Surface	3/6/08	4	$59.98	$74.98
Doctor Who and the Silurians	3/6/08	2	$34.98	$43.98
The Sea Devils	3/6/08	1	$24.98	$30.98
Warriors of the Deep	3/6/08	1	$24.98	$30.98
The Time Meddler	5/8/08	1	$24.98	$30.98
Black Orchid	5/8/08	1	$14.98	$19.98
(Cover same as UK sleeve artwork)				
The Five Doctors 25th AE	5/8/08	2	$34.98	$43.98
The Invisible Enemy[1]	2/9/08	2	$34.98	$43.98
The Invasion of Time	2/9/08	2	$34.98	$43.98
The Brain of Morbius	7/10/08	1	$24.98	$30.98
The Trial of a Time Lord	7/10/08	4	$59.98	$74.98
The War Machines	6/1/09	1	$24.98	$30.98
Four to Doomsday	6/1/09	1	$24.98	$30.98
(Artwork same as UK on black background)				
The Key to Time	3/3/09	7	$99.98	$124.98
(Key to Time SEs same content as UK non-SE releases)				
The Ribos Operation SE	3/3/09	1	$24.98	$30.98
The Pirate Planet SE	3/3/09	1	$24.98	$30.98
The Stones of Blood SE	3/3/09	1	$24.98	$30.98
The Androids of Tara SE	3/3/09	1	$24.98	$30.98
The Power of Kroll SE	3/3/09	1	$24.98	$30.98
The Armageddon Factor SE	3/3/09	2	$34.98	$43.98
Battlefield	5/5/09	2	$34.98	$43.98
The E-Space Trilogy	5/5/09	3	$49.98	$62.48
Attack of the Cybermen	7/7/09	1	$24.98	$30.98
(Cover adapted from UK slipcase artwork)				
The Rescue/The Romans	7/7/09	2	$34.98	$43.98
The Deadly Assassin	1/9/09	1	$24.98	$30.98
Image of the Fendahl	1/9/09	1	$24.98	$30.98
Delta and the Bannermen	1/9/09	1	$24.98	$30.98
The War Games	3/11/09	3	$49.98	$62.48
The Black Guardian Trilogy	3/11/09	4	$59.98	$74.98
The Keys of Marinus	5/1/10	1	$24.98	$30.98
The Twin Dilemma	5/1/10	1	$24.98	$30.98

	RELEASE DATE	No. DISCS	ORIGINAL US SRP	ORIGINAL CAN SRP
(Cover adapted from UK sleeve artwork)				
Remembrance of the Daleks SE	2/3/10	2	$24.98	$30.98
(Cover adapted from UK slipcase artwork)				
Dalek War	2/3/10	4	$59.98	$74.98
The Curse of Peladon	4/5/10	1	$24.98	$30.98
The Monster of Peladon	4/5/10	2	$34.98	$43.98
The Masque of Mandragora	4/5/10	1	$24.98	$30.98
The Time Monster	6/7/10	1	$24.98	$30.98
Underworld	6/7/10	1	$24.98	$30.98
The Horns of Nimon	6/7/10	1	$24.98	$30.98
(Cover adapted from UK slipcase artwork)				
The Space Museum/The Chase	6/7/10	3	$49.98	$62.48
The Creature from the Pit	7/9/10	1	$24.98	$30.98
The King's Demons	7/9/10	1	$14.98	$18.74
Planet of Fire	7/9/10	2	$24.98	$30.98
Revenge of the Cybermen	2/11/10	1	$24.98	$30.98
Silver Nemesis	2/11/10	1	$24.98	$30.98
The Dominators	11/1/11	1	$24.98	$30.98
Meglos	11/1/11	1	$24.98	$30.98
The Mutants	8/2/11	2	$34.98	$43.98
The Movie SE	8/2/11	2	$34.98	$43.98
The Ark	8/3/11	1	$24.98	$30.98
The Seeds of Doom	8/3/11	2	$34.98	$43.98
Kinda	12/4/11	1	$24.98	$30.98
Snakedance	12/4/11	1	$24.98	$30.98
Terror of the Autons	10/5/11	1	$24.98	$30.98
(UK artwork adapted to suit full cover)				
Planet of the Spiders	10/5/11	2	$34.98	$43.98
Frontios	14/6/11	1	$24.98	$30.98
Time and the Rani	14/6/11	1	$24.98	$30.98
The Gunfighters	12/7/11	1	$24.98	$30.98
The Awakening	12/7/11	1	$14.98	$30.98
The Sun Makers	9/8/11	1	$24.98	$30.98
Paradise Towers	9/8/11	1	$24.98	$30.98
Day of the Daleks	13/9/11	2	$34.98	$30.98
The Talons of Weng-Chiang SE	11/10/11	3	$34.98	$43.98
Colony in Space	8/11/11	1	$24.98	$30.98
Invasion of the Dinosaurs	10/1/12	2	$34.98	$43.98
The Android Invasion	10/1/12	1	$24.98	$30.98
The Sensorites	14/2/12	1	$24.98	$30.98
The Caves of Androzani SE	14/2/12	2	$34.98	$43.98
The Tomb of the Cybermen SE	13/3/12	2	$34.98	$43.98
The Three Doctors SE	13/3/12	2	$34.98	$43.98
The Face of Evil	13/3/12	1	$24.98	$30.98
The Robots of Death SE	13/3/12	1	$24.98	$30.98
The Dæmons	10/4/12	2	$34.98	$43.98
Carnival of Monsters SE	10/4/12	2	$34.98	$43.98
Nightmare of Eden	8/5/12	1	$24.98	$30.98
Dragonfire	8/5/12	1	$24.98	$30.98
The Happiness Patrol	8/5/12	1	$24.98	$30.98
The Seeds of Death SE	12/6/12	2	$34.98	$43.98
Resurrection of the Daleks SE	12/6/12	2	$34.98	$43.98
The Krotons	10/7/12	1	$24.98	$30.98
Death to the Daleks	10/7/12	1	$24.98	$30.98
Spearhead from Space SE	14/8/12	1	$24.98	$30.98
Greatest Show in the Galaxy	14/8/12	1	$24.98	$30.98
Planet of Giants	11/9/12	1	$24.98	$30.98
Vengeance on Varos SE	11/9/12	2	$34.98	$43.98
The Ambassadors of Death	9/10/12	2	$34.98	$43.98
The Claws of Axos SE	13/11/12	2	$34.98	$43.98

	RELEASE DATE	No. DISCS	ORIGINAL US SRP	ORIGINAL CAN SRP
Shada[2]	8/1/13	3	$39.98	$49.98
The Reign of Terror	12/2/13	1	$24.98	$30.98
The Aztecs SE	12/3/13	2	$34.98	$43.98
The Ark in Space SE	12/3/13	2	$34.98	$43.98
The Visitation SE	14/5/13	2	$34.98	$43.98
Inferno SE	11/6/13	2	$34.98	$43.98
The Mind of Evil	11/6/13	2	$34.98	$43.98
(Photo-montage cover; not released in UK)				
The Doctors Revisited 1-4	16/7/13	4	$39.98	$49.98
Spearhead from Space Blu-ray	13/8/13	1	$29.98	$37.48
The Green Death SE	13/8/13	2	$34.98	$43.98
The Ice Warriors	17/9/13	2	$34.98	$43.98
Scream of the Shalka	17/9/13	1	$24.98	$30.98

	RELEASE DATE	No. DISCS	ORIGINAL US SRP	ORIGINAL CAN SRP
(Photo-montage cover; not released in UK)				
The Doctors Revisited 5-8	1/10/13	4	$39.98	$49.98
Terror of the Zygons	8/10/13	2	$34.98	$43.98
The Tenth Planet	19/11/13	2	$34.98	$43.98
The Moonbase	11/2/14	1	$24.98	$30.98
The Web of Fear	22/4/14	1	$19.98	$24.98
The Enemy of the World[3]	20/5/14	1	$19.98	$24.98
(Not released in UK)				
An Adventure in Space and Time[4]	27/5/14	3	$24.98	$30.98
(Not released in UK)				
The Doctors Revisited Giftset	3/6/14	11	$125.92	$141.58

1 With *K9 and Company: A Girl's Best Friend*

2 With *More Than 30 Years in the TARDIS*

3 First released in Canada 10/12/13 exclusive to Best Buy stores, $19.99

DVD/Blu-ray combo pack, includes *An Unearthly Child*

AUSTRALIA/NEW ZEALAND

Doctor Who has been on air in Australia almost as long as in the UK. ABC, the country's national broadcaster, was a major buyer of BBC programmes and was first to be offered *Doctor Who* as early as March 1964. It bought the initial thirteen episodes, which it planned to start showing in May, but had to delay broadcast until the following year when the Australian Film Censorship Board didn't give them the rating that ABC needed for an early-evening showing. The series ultimately debuted in Perth, Western Australia at 7.30pm on Tuesday 12 January 1965, airing three days later in Sydney and Canberra, and the following week in Brisbane and Melbourne. This began what would go on to be a complete run of Classic *Doctor Who* in Australia over the next twenty-five years.

Well, almost complete. To meet the censor's requirements for a general audience rating, some episodes had to have moments of strong violence cut out, and sometimes whole stories were dropped if they required too many cuts or were given an adult rating outright. *Mission to the Unknown* and *The Daleks' Master Plan* were thus never broadcast in Australia, while four Third Doctor stories — *Inferno*, *The Mind of Evil*, *The Dæmons* and *Invasion of the Dinosaurs* — weren't aired until much later in the 1980s when they could be reclassified (the last excluding its first episode, which was by then missing from the BBC's archive). In a quirk of fate, while many of the 1960s episodes are now missing, those sections physically cut from the film copies by the Australian censors have survived and are now the only footage in the archive for several stories.

The initial delay in ABC's showing of the first three serials meant that New Zealand became the first country to broadcast *Doctor Who* outside the UK, with *An Unearthly Child* episode one airing in Christchurch on Friday 18 September 1964, Auckland on 30 October and Wellington a week later (viewers in Dunedin didn't get to see it until March 1965). The New Zealand censors were stricter than those in Australia, however, and all three stories were classified as unsuitable for children. Broadcaster NZBC thus showed them at just before 8pm but was unhappy that a supposed family series couldn't be transmitted earlier in the evening and so it declined further episodes. *Marco Polo* was broadcast in late 1966, but it wasn't until 1968 that NZBC really tried the series again. This time it was determined to show it earlier, so any stories that had episodes classified as unsuitable for children were dropped. The broadcast of *Doctor Who* in New Zealand during the 1970s was therefore more erratic than in Australia, although eventually all surviving episodes were shown when the BBC resold them during the 1980s. And again we have the censors to thank for retaining footage that was cut from the episodes and which is now our only glimpse of some long-lost serials.

With both countries being long-term *Doctor Who* buyers, the region was a prime market for the series on VHS and subsequently DVD, licensed by ABC DVD and distributed by Roadshow

Entertainment. As Australia and New Zealand use the same PAL video standard as the UK, the content doesn't need converting and so the discs are the same (except printed with the circles pattern from the covers rather than the artwork), and indeed most of the UK releases are dual-coded for Regions 2 and 4. This changed in 2009 when ABC DVD requested the Coming Soon trailers be removed, so the two regions got their own pressings. The release order stuck closely to the UK's, with Australia generally only two or three months behind, although as with North America, from 2011 an effort was made to shorten this gap and for the last two years releases were a month or less after their UK debut. The most notable difference between the DVDs in the UK and Australia is on their covers, as the latter is required to give more prominence to the rating certificate. So while they use the same design and artwork, the Australian covers have a smaller *Doctor Who* logo to allow for a wider strip across the bottom where the certificate is positioned. This allowed for other occasional differences, such as using the fortieth-anniversary logo on releases in 2003, whereas in the UK this was on a sticker. Also, in place of the booklet that comes in UK releases, the Australian covers have information about the special features printed on the reverse, visible through the clear case.

REGION 4 RELEASE SCHEDULE

All releases of Classic Doctor Who *in Australia and New Zealand in the order they were issued, with notes on differences from the UK. Notes in brackets refer only to the next listed DVD (or indicated group of DVDs), otherwise they apply to all subsequent releases. Titles in bold are boxsets; refer to the UK schedule (Appendix 3) for titles contained. New Zealand releases initially followed a month or two behind Australia, but caught up to about a week behind from 2011, and the same day from 2012. New Zealand suggested retail prices were around the same numeric value in NZ$.*

	RELEASE DATE	CERT	No. DISCS	ORIGINAL AUS SRP		RELEASE DATE	CERT	No. DISCS	ORIGINAL AUS SRP
The Five Doctors SE	9/10/00	PG	1	$34.95	City of Death	1/12/05	PG*	2	$39.95
The Robots of Death	5/3/01	PG*	1	$34.95	**The Beginning**	2/3/06	PG	3	$69.95
Spearhead from Space	3/9/01	G	1	$34.95	Genesis of the Daleks	4/5/06	PG	2	$39.95
The Caves of Androzani	7/1/02	PG	1	$34.95	Inferno	6/7/06	PG	2	$39.95
Vengeance on Varos	7/1/02	PG	1	$34.95	The Hand of Fear	7/9/06	G	1	$29.95
The Tomb of the Cybermen	1/4/02	PG	1	$34.95	The Mark of the Rani	1/11/06	G	1	$29.95
Remembrance of the Daleks	13/5/02	PG	1	$34.95	The Sontaran Experiment	6/12/06	PG	1	$29.95
The Ark in Space	3/6/02	G	1	$34.95	The Invasion	3/1/07	PG	2	$39.95
Carnival of Monsters	2/9/02	G†	1	$34.95	**New Beginnings**	7/3/07	PG	3	$69.95
The Aztecs	2/12/02	G	1	$34.95	Survival	6/6/07	PG	2	$39.95
(Covers for 2003 releases use 40th Anniversary logo)					Robot	4/7/07	PG	1	$29.95
Resurrection of the Daleks	3/2/03	PG	1	$34.95	Timelash	1/8/07	PG	1	$29.95
The Seeds of Death	5/5/03	G	2	$49.95	Time-Flight/Arc of Infinity	5/9/07	PG	2	$39.95
The Talons of Weng-Chiang	23/6/03	PG*	2	$49.95	The Time Warrior	3/10/07	PG	1	$29.95
The Dalek Invasion of Earth	13/8/03	PG	2	$49.95	**The Key to Time**	7/11/07	PG¹	7	$145.95
Earthshock	1/10/03	PG	1	$34.95	Planet of Evil	5/12/07	PG	1	$29.95
(Also in Collector's Edition with Corgi model Bessie for $49.95)					Destiny of the Daleks	6/2/08	PG	1	$29.95
The Three Doctors	12/11/03	PG	1	$34.95	**Complete Davros Collection**	6/2/08	PG	8	$149.95
The Two Doctors	7/1/04	G	2	$49.95	**Beneath the Surface**	6/3/08	PG	4	$59.95
The Curse of Fenric	11/2/04	PG	2	$49.95	The Time Meddler	3/4/08	PG	1	$29.95
The Visitation	7/4/04	PG	1	$34.95	*(Cover uses UK sleeve artwork)*				
Pyramids of Mars	9/6/04	G	1	$34.95	The Five Doctors 25th AE	8/5/08	PG	2	$39.95
The Green Death	4/8/04	G	1	$34.95	Black Orchid	5/6/08	PG	1	$29.95
The Leisure Hive	6/10/04	PG	1	$34.95	The Invasion of Time	3/7/08	PG	2	$39.95
Lost in Time	1/12/04	PG	3	$69.95	**Bred for War**	7/8/08	PG	6	$99.95
Ghost Light	3/2/05	PG	1	$29.95	**K9 Tales**	4/9/08	PG	2	$39.95
Horror of Fang Rock	7/4/05	G	1	$29.95	The Brain of Morbius	2/10/08	PG	1	$29.95
The Mind Robber	5/5/05	G	1	$29.95	The War Machines	6/11/08	PG	1	$29.95
The Claws of Axos	2/6/05	PG	1	$29.95	Four to Doomsday	4/12/08	PG	1	$29.95
Revelation of the Daleks	1/9/05	PG	1	$29.95	**The Trial of a Time Lord**	2/1/09	PG	4	$69.95
The Web Planet	3/11/05	G	1	$29.95	Battlefield	5/2/09	PG	2	$39.95

	RELEASE DATE	CERT	No. DISCS	ORIGINAL AUS SRP
The E–Space Trilogy	5/3/09	PG	3	$59.98
The Rescue/The Romans	2/4/09	G†	2	$39.98
Attack of the Cybermen	7/5/09	M	1	$29.98
Image of the Fendahl	4/6/09	PG	1	$29.98
The Deadly Assassin	2/7/09	PG	1	$29.98
Delta and the Bannermen	6/8/09	PG	1	$29.98
The War Games	3/9/09	PG	3	$49.98
(Released in sleeve with same artwork as UK)				
Remembrance of the Daleks SE	1/10/09	PG	2	$39.98
The Black Guardian Trilogy	5/11/09	PG	4	$59.98
The Twin Dilemma	3/12/09	G	1	$29.98
The Keys of Marinus	7/1/10	PG	1	$29.98
Dalek War	4/2/10	PG	4	$79.98
Peladon Tales	4/3/10	PG	3	$59.98
The Masque of Mandragora	1/4/10	G	1	$29.98
The Space Museum/ The Chase	6/5/10	PG	3	$49.98
Myths and Legends	3/6/10	PG	3	$49.99
The Creature from the Pit	1/7/10	PG	1	$29.98
Lost in Time reissue	1/7/10	PG	3	$39.99
Kamelion Tales	5/8/10	PG	3	$49.98
The Dominators	2/9/10	PG	1	$29.98
Revenge of the Cybermen/ Silver Nemesis	7/10/10	G	2	$39.98
Time and the Rani	4/11/10	PG	1	$29.98
The Seeds of Doom	2/12/10	G	2	$39.98
Revisitations 1	2/12/10	M²	7	$89.98
Meglos	20/1/11	PG	1	$29.98
The Mutants	3/2/11	PG	2	$39.98
The Ark	3/3/11	PG	1	$29.98
The Movie SE	3/3/11	M	2	$39.98
Mara Tales	7/4/11	G	2	$39.98
Revisitations 2	5/5/11	PG	6	$89.98
Planet of the Spiders	2/6/11	G	2	$39.98
Mannequin Mania	2/6/11	PG	2	$39.98
Frontios	7/7/11	PG	1	$29.98
Earth Story	4/8/11	PG‡	2	$39.98

	RELEASE DATE	CERT	No. DISCS	ORIGINAL AUS SRP
The Sun Makers	1/9/11	PG	1	$29.98
Paradise Towers	1/9/11	PG	1	$29.98
Day of the Daleks	6/10/11	G†	2	$39.98
Colony in Space	1/12/11	PG	1	$29.98
U.N.I.T Files	5/1/12	G†	3	$49.98
The Sensorites	2/2/12	PG	1	$29.98
Revisitations 3	1/3/12	G†	5	$69.99
The Dæmons	19/4/12	PG	2	$29.99
Nightmare of Eden	3/5/12	PG	1	$29.99
Ace Adventures	7/6/12	PG	2	$29.99
Death to the Daleks	5/7/12	PG*	1	$29.99
The Krotons	2/8/12	G†	1	$29.99
The Greatest Show in the Galaxy	16/8/12	PG	1	$29.99
Planet of Giants	5/9/12	PG	1	$29.98
Vengeance on Varos SE	5/9/12	PG	2	$29.99
The Ambassadors of Death	3/10/12	M	2	$29.98
The Claws of Axos SE	7/11/12	PG	2	$29.99
The Legacy Collection	9/1/13	PG	3	$34.99
The Reign of Terror	6/2/13	PG	1	$29.99
The Ark in Space SE	20/2/13	G	2	$29.99
The Aztecs SE	20/3/13	G	2	$29.99
The Visitation SE	15/5/13	PG	2	$29.99
Inferno SE	5/6/13	PG	2	$29.99
The Mind of Evil	5/6/13	PG	2	$29.99
Spearhead from Space Blu-ray	17/7/13	G	1	$29.99
The Green Death SE	7/8/13	PG	2	$29.99
The Ice Warriors	28/8/13	G†	2	$29.99
Regeneration³	4/9/13	PG	6	$89.99
Scream of the Shalka	18/9/13	PG	1	$29.99
Terror of the Zygons	2/10/13	PG	2	$29.99
The Tenth Planet	30/10/13	PG	2	$29.99
(Revisited covers same as US)				
The Doctors Revisited 1–4	20/11/13	PG	4	$39.99
The Doctors Revisited 5–8	20/11/13	M	4	$39.99
The Enemy of the World	27/11/13	PG	1	$19.99
The Moonbase	29/1/14	PG	1	$29.99
The Web of Fear	26/2/14	PG	1	$19.99

* Rated G in New Zealand
† Rated PG in New Zealand
‡ Rated M in New Zealand

1 *The Pirate Planet* rated G, others PG
2 Only *The Movie* rated M, others PG
3 Not released in New Zealand

ITALY

Italy's national public broadcaster Radiotelevisione Italiana (RAI) aired seven early Fourth Doctor stories in 1980/81, beginning on Wednesday 6 February 1980 with *Robot*, followed by *The Ark in Space*, *The Sontaran Experiment*, *Revenge of the Cybermen*, *Planet of Evil* and *Pyramids of Mars*. These were repeated in 1981 along with *Terror of the Zygons*. The episodes were dubbed by an Italian cast who were credited in the closing titles, while the opening titles were suitably translated (such as 'La Vendetta dei Ciberniani'). So it's perhaps unusual that the only Classic *Doctor Who* DVD releases in Italy have been of 1960s stories.

On 26 September 2007, DNC Entertainment issued Doctor Who: Gli Inizi, a boxset containing the first three stories of the series: *An Unearthly Child*, *The Daleks* and *The Edge of Destruction* — the equivalent of the UK set The Beginning. Priced at €39.99 for four discs (*The Daleks* is split over discs two and three), this features English and Italian soundtracks, and Italian subtitles. Most of the special features from the UK release are included (except for the commentaries, information subtitles and PDF items), all dubbed in Italian. The cover is unique to this set, depicting the TARDIS on the Paleolithic plain with the familiar circles pattern behind. The disc menus are also an original design, with animated photos of the TARDIS console and Daleks in their city.

Five months later, on 14 February 2008, DNC released a second boxset of First Doctor episodes. I Dalek Invadono la Terra is a unique set containing *The Aztecs*, *The Dalek Invasion of Earth* and *The Web Planet*. These are again over four discs (the Dalek story split in half, whereas the equal length *The Web Planet* is on one disc but with no extras) but this time priced at €44.99. Although episodes and special features are again both dubbed into Italian, and with Italian subtitles, there are fewer extras from the UK releases. *The Aztecs* is accompanied by the interview with designer Barry Newbery, the animated item on how to make cocoa the Aztec way, and the short feature on the restoration of the story. *The Dalek Invasion of Earth* includes the interviews with actors, Carole Ann Ford's 8mm film of rehearsals and the photo gallery on disc two, while disc three has the piece on how the Dalek voices were created and the location feature. Also contained in the set, however, is a sixteen-page booklet by Marcello Rossi detailing the dates, casts and plots of all the First Doctor's adventures. The set's cover is adapted from the UK cover for The Dalek Invasion of Earth.

Finally, on 11 June 2008 DNC issued L'Invasione, another four-disc set this time of Second Doctor stories *The Mind Robber*, *The Invasion* and *The Seeds of Death*. Priced €44.99, with Italian dubbing and subtitles, this again contains a booklet describing the Second Doctor's adventures, but special features are reduced even further. *The Mind Robber* disc includes just the making-of feature; *The Invasion* episodes one to four are on disc two along with the Flash Frames and Character Design items about the animation; episode five to eight are paired with the documentary about fans' off-air audio recordings; and lastly on disc four are *The Seeds of Death* and the interviews with Ice Warrior actors. This set's cover is adapted from the UK release of The Mind Robber.

NETHERLANDS

The Netherlands' public broadcaster Televisie en Radio Omroep Stichting (TROS) was the first Continental European country to show *Doctor Who* when it broadcast most of the first two Fourth Doctor seasons from Monday 28 July 1975 through to September 1976, also making it the first to air these stories outside the UK. The episodes were in English with Dutch subtitles. Of the eleven serials, *Genesis of the Daleks* and *Pyramids of Mars* were not shown, probably deemed too violent, a concern that was reported as being the reason for such few sales of the programme to Europe in the 1970s. Nevertheless, the Netherlands' brief flirtation with *Doctor Who* at this time extended beyond television, with Dutch translations of the first eight Target novelisations and the 1975 *Dr Who Annual* being published while the programme was on air.

TROS next broadcast the series in 1985/86. Again it kicked off with a new Doctor, thanks to Peter Davison's profile in the country from showings of *All Creatures Great and Small*, airing *Four to Doomsday* from Monday 30 September 1985. The episodes were again in English with Dutch subtitles, and continued with the rest of the 1982 season (except *Castrovalva*) and the first three stories of the 1983 run, although not in their UK broadcast order.

Unsurprisingly, then, when Dutch publisher Memphis Belle International licensed *Doctor Who* for DVD release, it chose a selection of Fourth and Fifth Doctor stories, although only a few were among the serials broadcast the previous century. In January 2006 it issued *The Ark in Space*, *Horror of Fang Rock*, *Pyramids of Mars* and *The Robots of Death*, each on a single disk priced at €7.99. The covers feature the same design and artwork as the UK releases, and the serials are rated as suitable for children aged six and over (as are the later releases). The episodes themselves have Dutch subtitles, but not the special features, which match the UK releases except for losing the information subtitles (and the studio plans from *The Robots of Death*).

A further batch was issued on 30 April 2007, this time four Fifth Doctor serials: *Earthshock*, *The Five Doctors Special Edition*, *Resurrection of the Daleks* and *The Visitation*. Again priced at €7.99 for single discs with UK-based covers, these are missing not only the information subtitles but also any audio options — that is, commentaries and music-only tracks. *Earthshock* also has no alternative CGI effects option. The remaining extras again have no subtitles, only the episodes themselves.

It was back to the Fourth Doctor for the last set of releases on 21 May 2008, with single-disc releases of *City of Death*, *Genesis of the Daleks*, *The Leisure Hive* and *The Talons of Weng-Chiang*, each at €7.99. Only the last's cover differs from the UK's, being slightly adapted to feature just the Doctor. Again only the episodes have subtitles, and more extras were dropped. As with the last batch, *City of Death* and *The Leisure Hive* are missing information subtitles and audio options, as well as the Annual PDF from the former. (*The Leisure Hive* menu lists Synthesizing Starfields twice, but the first instance does actually play the From Avalon to Argolis feature.) *Genesis of the Daleks* and *The Talons of Weng-Chiang*, however, are harder hit having had the luxury of two discs' worth of material for their UK releases. The former has just a photo gallery, the *Blue Peter* extract and continuities (odd given they're from the original UK broadcast and this story was never shown in the Netherlands), while the latter features only the photo gallery, producer Philip Hinchcliffe's appearance on *Pebble Mill At One* and the TARDIS-Cam.

APPENDIX 5 DOCTOR WHO DVD FILES

In January 2009, partwork publisher GE Fabbri launched *Doctor Who DVD Files*, a fortnightly magazine and DVD combination that would build into a complete collection. Initially it focused on the New Series (although an early incentive for subscribers was a special issue with *The Movie*), with each disc containing two episodes — beginning with *Rose* and *The End of the World* — while the 24-page magazine provided information, photos and artwork about the characters, enemies, technology and production of the series, including some coverage of the Classic Series. Issues cost £6.99 (£5.99 for subscribers), and in March 2009 the publisher began offering online subscriptions to just the magazine content for £3 a month or £25 a year, although this service ended in early 2011 when GE Fabbri was bought out by Eaglemoss Publications.

By issue 28 in January 2010 the publication had covered the first four series (up to *The Next Doctor*, the 2008 Christmas Special) and was catching up with the transmitted episodes, so it switched to releasing Classic stories. The magazine continued to offer a mix of New and Classic Series material while each DVD contained a single Classic serial, fully restored but with none of the special features from the main release range. The four 2009 New Series Specials were released in issues 55 and 56 in February 2011, after which the Classic releases continued until November, when the first Eleventh Doctor series (*The Eleventh Hour* to *A Christmas Carol*) was issued.

All subsequent editions have featured Classic story DVDs and at the time of writing the run was recently extended to at least issue 152 (due 29 October 2014). If it continues with Classic releases until then (rather than switching back to New Series Six), there will be twenty-five available stories unreleased in the *DVD Files* series (mostly 1960s serials, although only the Sixth and Seventh Doctors have had all their stories issued).

ISSUE	STORY	DATE	MAIN COVER IMAGE
1–28	*Rose–Next Doctor 14/1/09–27/1/10*		
Subscriber special: The Movie 3/09			
29	Remembrance of the Daleks	10/2/10	Special Weapons Dalek
30	The Three Doctors	24/2/10	Omega
31	Genesis of the Daleks	10/3/10	Davros
32	Earthshock	24/3/10	Cyberman
33	Pyramids of Mars	7/4/10	Sutekh
34	Resurrection of the Daleks	21/4/10	Davros *(four-episode version)*
35	Spearhead from Space	5/5/10	Doctor
36	The Caves of Androzani	19/5/10	Sharaz Jek
37	City of Death	2/6/10	Scaroth
38	Revelation of the Daleks	16/6/10	Davros
39	The Curse of Fenric	30/6/10	Haemovore
40	The Brain of Morbius	14/7/10	Doctor, Solon
41	The Talons of Weng-Chiang	28/7/10	Doctor
42	The Visitation	11/8/10	Terileptil
43	The Hand of Fear	25/8/10	Eldrad, Sarah
44	Inferno	8/9/10	Primord
45	The Two Doctors	22/9/10	Sontaran Stike, Doctors
46	Logopolis	6/10/10	Master
47	Castrovalva	20/10/10	Doctor, Master, Portreeve
48	The Green Death	3/11/10	Maggots
49	Robot	17/11/10	K1 robot
50	Mawdryn Undead	1/12/10	Mawdryn
51	Survival	15/12/10	Master
52	The Deadly Assassin	29/12/10	Doctor
53	The Time Warrior	12/1/11	Lynx
54	The Robots of Death	26/1/11	Voc robot
55–56	*Planet of the Dead–The End of Time 4/2/11–23/2/11*		
57	Enlightenment	9/3/11	Tegan, Doctor
58	Destiny of the Daleks	23/3/11	Dalek
59	Battlefield	6/4/11	Morgaine, Destroyer

ISSUE	STORY	DATE	MAIN COVER IMAGE
60	Carnival of Monsters	20/4/11	Doctor, Drashig
61	Horror of Fang Rock	4/5/11	Doctor
62	Delta and the Bannermen	18/5/11	Gavrok, Delta
63	The Mark of the Rani	1/6/11	Rani, Master
64	The Masque of Mandragora	15/6/11	Hieronymous
65	Doctor Who and the Silurians	29/6/11	Silurian, Doctor
66	The Sea Devils	13/7/11	Sea Devil
67	The Stones of Blood	27/7/11	Cailleach
68	Vengeance on Varos	10/8/11	Sil
69	The Keeper of Traken	24/8/11	Melkur
70	Image of the Fendahl	7/9/11	Fendahl
71	The Curse of Peladon	21/9/11	Ice Lord Izlyr, Alpha Centauri, Arcturus
72	The Androids of Tara	5/10/11	Wood Beast
73	The Tomb of the Cybermen	19/10/11	Cyberman
74–80	The Eleventh Hour–A Christmas Carol	2/11/11–25/1/12	
81	Planet of the Daleks	8/2/12	Dalek
82	Attack of the Cybermen	22/2/12	Cyberman
83	Warriors of the Deep	7/3/12	Silurian
84	The Mind Robber	21/3/12	Soldiers, Medusa, Unicorn
85	Full Circle	4/4/12	Marshman
86	State of Decay	18/4/12	Aukon
87	Warriors' Gate	2/5/12	Doctor
88	The Invasion 1-4	16/5/12	Cyberman
89	The Invasion 5-8	30/5/12	Cybermen
90	The Ark in Space	13/6/12	Wirrn
91	The Daleks	27/6/12	Dalek
92	Day of the Daleks	11/7/12	Daleks
93	Kinda	25/7/12	Panna
94	Planet of Evil	8/8/12	Sorenson
95	The Dalek Invasion of Earth	22/8/12	Dalek
96	Ghost Light	5/9/12	Light
97	The Claws of Axos	19/9/12	Axons
98	The Leisure Hive	3/10/12	Pangol
99	Time and the Rani	17/10/12	Tetrap
100	Frontios	31/10/12	Gravis
101	Terror of the Autons	14/11/12	Doctor
102	Silver Nemesis	28/11/12	Cybermen
103	Snakedance	12/12/12	Lon, Mara
104	Frontier in Space	26/12/12	Dalek
105	Four to Doomsday	9/1/13	Monarch
106	Paradise Towers	23/1/13	Tabby, Tilda
107	The Ribos Operation	6/2/13	Romana, Doctor
108	Arc of Infinity	20/2/13	Omega
109	Meglos	6/3/13	Meglos
110	Planet of the Spiders	20/3/13	Doctor
111	Revenge of the Cybermen	3/4/13	Doctor, Cyberman
112	The Pirate Planet	17/4/13	Captain
113	The Greatest Show in the Galaxy	1/5/13	Chief Clown
114	Death to the Daleks	15/5/13	Dalek
115	The Seeds of Death	29/5/13	Ice Lord Slaar
116	Planet of Fire	12/6/13	Master
117	The Dæmons	26/6/13	Azal
118	The Invasion of Time	10/7/13	Sontaran Stor
119	The Happiness Patrol	24/7/13	The Kandyman
120	The Seeds of Doom	7/8/13	Krynoid
121	Invasion of the Dinosaurs	21/8/13	Doctor *(includes colour episode one)*
122	The Aztecs	4/9/13	Barbara
123	Dragonfire	18/9/13	Doctor, Ace
124	The Face of Evil	2/10/13	Doctor
125	The Monster of Peladon	16/10/13	Alpha Centauri
126	The Android Invasion	30/10/13	Chedaki
127	The Twin Dilemma	13/11/13	Mestor

5

ISSUE	STORY	DATE	MAIN COVER IMAGE
128	An Unearthly Child	27/11/13	Doctor
129	The Mysterious Planet	11/12/13	Drathro
130	Mindwarp	25/12/13	Kiv
131	Terror of the Vervoids	8/1/14	Vervoid
132	The Ultimate Foe	22/1/14	Doctor
133	The Invisible Enemy	5/2/14	Doctor, Leela
134	Nightmare of Eden	19/2/14	Mandrel
135	Time-Flight	5/3/14	Doctor, Kalid
136	The Armageddon Factor	19/3/14	Doctor, Romana, Astra
137	The Time Monster	2/4/14	Kronos
138	The Chase	16/4/14	Daleks
139	The Horns of Nimon	30/4/14	Nimon, Romana
140	Terminus	14/5/14	Doctor, Garm
141	Timelash	28/5/14	Borad
142	The War Machines	11/6/14	War Machine
143	The Mind of Evil	25/6/14	Doctor
144	The Awakening	9/7/14	Malus

5

Checklist of commonly included Special Features. Brackets indicate item is an easter egg (see Appendix 2)

	COMMENTARY	INFO SUBTITLES	PHOTO GALLERY	RT LISTINGS	MAKING OF	MUSIC TRACK	DELETED SCENES	RAW FOOTAGE	CONTINUITIES	SPECIAL EDIT	NEW EFFECTS	5.1 AUDIO
Ambassadors of Death, The	●	●	●	●	●				●			
An Unearthly Child	●	●	●	1				●				
Android Invasion, The	●	●	●	●	●							
Androids of Tara, The	●	●	●	●	●							
Arc of Infinity	●	●	●	●	●	●	●	●	●		●	
Ark, The	●	●	●	●								
Ark in Space, The	●	●	●					●	●		●	
Ark in Space Special Edition, The	●	●	●					●	●		●	
Armageddon Factor, The	❷	●	●	●	●		●		●			
Attack of the Cybermen	●	●	❷	●	●	●			●			
Awakening, The	●	●	●	●	●	●	●	●	●			
Aztecs, The	●	●	●		2							
Aztecs Special Edition, The	●	●	●	●	2							
Battlefield	●	●	●	●	●	●		●	●	●	●	●
Black Orchid	●	●	●	●			●		(●)			
Brain of Morbius, The	●	●	❷	●	●							
Carnival of Monsters	●	●	●					●	●			
Carnival of Monsters Special Edition	❷	●	●	●	●			●	●			
Castrovalva	●	●	●			●		●	●			
Caves of Androzani, The	●	●	●			●		●	●			
Caves of Androzani Special Edition, The	●	●	●	●	●	●	●	●	●			
Chase, The	●	●	●	●								
City of Death	●	●	●		●				●	(●)		
Claws of Axos, The	●	●	●					●	●			
Claws of Axos Special Edition, The	●	●	●	●	●			●	●			
Colony in Space	●	●	●	●	●			●				
Creature from the Pit, The	●	●	●	●			●					
Curse of Fenric, The	●	●	●			●		●	(●)	●	●	●
Curse of Peladon, The	●	●	●	●	●							
Dæmons, The	●	●	●	●	●		●					
Dalek Invasion of Earth, The	●	●	●		2			●	●		●	
Daleks, The	●	●	●	1								
Day of the Daleks	●	●	●	●	●					●	●	
Deadly Assassin, The	●	●	●	●	●				(●)			
Death to the Daleks	●	●	●	●	●	●		●				
Delta and the Bannermen	●	●	●	●			●	●	●			
Destiny of the Daleks	●	●	●						●		●	
Doctor Who and the Silurians	●	●	●	●	●	●			(●)			
Dominators, The	●	●	●	●	●							
Dragonfire	●	●	●	●	●	●	●					
Earthshock	●	●	●		●	●		●			●	

	COMMENTARY	INFO SUBTITLES	PHOTO GALLERY	RT LISTINGS	MAKING OF	MUSIC TRACK	DELETED SCENES	RAW FOOTAGE	CONTINUITIES	SPECIAL EDIT	NEW EFFECTS	5.1 AUDIO
Edge of Destruction, The		●	●	●	●							
Enemy of the World, The												
Enlightenment	●	●	●	●	●	●		●	●	●	●	●
Face of Evil, The	●	●	●	●	●			●				
Five Doctors Special Edition, The						●[3]						
Five Doctors 25th Anniversary Edition, The	❷	❷	●	●	●	●		●	●	●	●	●
Four to Doomsday	●	●	●	●				●				
Frontier in Space	●	●	●	●	●							
Frontios	●	●	●	●	●	●	●					
Full Circle	●	●	●[4]	●	●	●			●			
Genesis of the Daleks	●	●	●	●	●				●			
Ghost Light	●	●	●		●	●	●	●	(●)			●
Greatest Show in the Galaxy, The	●	●	●	●	●	●	●	●				●
Green Death, The	●	●	●						(●)			
Green Death Special Edition, The	❷	●	●	●	●			●	(●)			
Gunfighters, The	●	●	●	●								
Hand of Fear, The	●	●	●	●	●				●			
Happiness Patrol, The	●	●	●	●	●	●	●					
Horns of Nimon, The	●	●	●	●								
Horror of Fang Rock	●	●	●									
Ice Warriors, The	●	●[5]	●	●	●				●			
Image of the Fendahl	●	●	●	●	●			●	●			
Inferno	●	●	●	●	●			●				
Inferno Special Edition	●	●	●	●	●			●				
Invasion, The	●	●	●	[6]	●							
Invasion of the Dinosaurs	●	●	●	●	●			●				
Invasion of Time, The	●	●	●	●	●			●			●	
Invisible Enemy, The	●	●	●	●	●			●	●		●	
K9 and Company	●	●	●	●	●				●			
Keeper of Traken, The	●	●	●	●	●	●			●			
Keys of Marinus, The	●	●	●	●								
Kinda	●	●	●	●	●	●	●		●		●	
King's Demons, The	❷	●	●	●		●						
Krotons, The	●	●	●	●								
Leisure Hive, The	●	●	●			●			(●)			●
Logopolis	●	●	●	●		●			●			
Mark of the Rani, The	●	●	●	●	●	●	●		(●)			
Masque of Mandragora, The	●	●	●	●	●				●			
Mawdryn Undead	●	●	❷	●	●	●	●	●	●		●	
Meglos	●	●	●	●		●						
Mind of Evil, The	●	●	●	●	●				(●)			
Mind Robber, The	●	●	●		●				(●)			
Monster of Peladon, The	●	●	●	●	●		●					
Moonbase, The	●	●[5]	●	●	●							
More Than 30 Years in the Tardis		●	●									

	COMMENTARY	INFO SUBTITLES	PHOTO GALLERY	RT LISTINGS	MAKING OF	MUSIC TRACK	DELETED SCENES	RAW FOOTAGE	CONTINUITIES	SPECIAL EDIT	NEW EFFECTS	5.1 AUDIO
Movie, The	●	●	●			●	●	●	●			
Movie Special Edition, The	❷	●	●	●		●	●	●	●			
Mutants, The	●	●	●	●	●							
Nightmare of Eden	●	●	●	●	●							
Paradise Towers	●	●	●	●	●		●		●			
Pirate Planet, The	❷	●	●	●	●		●	●	●			
Planet of Evil	●	●	●	●				●	●			
Planet of Fire	●	●	●	●	●	●	●	●	●	●	●	●
Planet of Giants	●	●	●	●								
Planet of the Daleks	●	●	●	●	●				(●)			
Planet of the Spiders	●	●	●	●	●				●			
Power of Kroll, The	●	●	●	●				●	●			
Pyramids of Mars	●	●	●		●			●	(●)			
Reign of Terror, The	●	●[5]	❷	●	●							
Remembrance of the Daleks	●	●	●			●	●	●	●			
Remembrance of the Daleks Special Edition	●	●	●	●	●	●	●	●	●			●
Rescue, The	●	●	●	●	●							
Resurrection of the Daleks	●	●	●			●	●		●			●
Resurrection of the Daleks Special Edition	❷	●[7]	●	●	●	●	●		●			●
Revelation of the Daleks	●	●	●		●	●	●	●	●		●	●
Revenge of the Cybermen	●	●	●	●	●							
Ribos Operation, The	●	●	●	●					●			
Robot	●	●	●	●	●			[8]	(●)			
Robots of Death, The	●		●					●	●			
Robots of Death Special Edition, The	❷	●	●	●	●			●	●			
Romans, The	●	●	●	●	●							
Scream of the Shalka	●	●	●		●	●[3]						
Sea Devils, The	●	●	●	●	●	●		●	●			
Seeds of Death, The	●	●	●									
Seeds of Death Special Edition, The	●	●	●	●	●				(●)			
Seeds of Doom, The	●	●	●	●	●	●			●			
Sensorites, The	●	●	●	●								
Shada		●	●	[9]	●							
Silurians, Doctor Who and the	●	●	●	●	●	●			(●)			
Silver Nemesis	●	●	●	●	●	●	●		●			●
Snakedance	●	●	●	●	●	●	●	●				
Sontaran Experiment, The	●	●	●		●							
Space Museum, The	●	●	●	●								
Spearhead from Space	●	●	●						●			
Spearhead from Space Special Edition	❷	●	●	●	●				●			
Spearhead from Space Blu-ray												
State of Decay	●	●	●[4]	●	●	●		●	●			
Stones of Blood, The	❷	●	●	●	●		●		●			
Sun Makers, The	●	●	●	●	●			●	●			
Survival	❷	●	●	●	●	●	●	●	●			●

	COMMENTARY	INFO SUBTITLES	PHOTO GALLERY	RT LISTINGS	MAKING OF	MUSIC TRACK	DELETED SCENES	RAW FOOTAGE	CONTINUITIES	SPECIAL EDIT	NEW EFFECTS	5.1 AUDIO
Talons of Weng-Chiang, The	●	●	●					●	●			
Talons of Weng-Chiang Special Edition, The	●	●	❷	●	●			●	●			
Tenth Planet, The	●	●[5]	●	●	●							
Terminus	●	●	●	●	●	●		●	●	●		
Terror of the Autons	●	●	●	●	●							
Terror of the Zygons	●	●	●	●	●	●						●
Three Doctors, The	●	●	●						●			
Three Doctors Special Edition, The	●	●	●	●	●				●			
Time and the Rani	●	●	●	●	●							
Time Meddler, The	●	●	❷	●								
Time Monster, The	●	●	●									
Time Warrior, The	●	●	●	●	●				●		●	
Time-Flight	●	●	●	●			●	●				
Timelash	●	●	●	●	●				(●)			
Tomb of the Cybermen, The	●	●	●						(●)			
Tomb of the Cybermen Special Edition, The	❷	●	●	●	●				(●)			
Trial of a Time Lord: The Mysterious Planet	❷	●	●	[10]	●			●	●	●		
Trial of a Time Lord: Mindwarp	●	●	●	[10]	●			●		●		
Trial of a Time Lord: Terror of the Vervoids	●	●	●	[10]	●			●		●		
Trial of a Time Lord: The Ultimate Foe	❷	●	●	●	●			●		●		
Twin Dilemma, The	●	●	●	●					(●)	●		
Two Doctors, The	●	●	●			●		●				
Underworld	●	●	●	●	●			●				
Vengeance on Varos	●	●	●				●	●	●			
Vengeance on Varos Special Edition	●	●	●	●	●	●[11]	●	●	●			●
Visitation, The	●	●	●			●		●	(●)			
Visitation Special Edition, The	●	●	●	●	●	●		●	(●)			
War Games, The	●	●	●	●	●							
War Machines, The	●	●	●[4]	●						(●)		
Warriors of the Deep	●	●	●	●	●	●				●		
Warriors' Gate	●	●	●[4]	●	●	●	●			●		
Web of Fear, The	[12]											
Web Planet, The	●	●	●		●							

1 Included on The Edge of Destruction
2 Cast interviews cover production aspects
3 Music included as suites
4 With optional captions
5 Not on animated episodes
6 Included on Attack of the Cybermen
7 On four-part version (disc two) only
8 Included on The Ark in Space Special Edition
9 Mock-up listings printed in booklet
10 Included on The Ultimate Foe
11 Also in Dolby 5.1
12 Commentary for episode one on Lost in Time

INDEX ii **KEY COMMENTATORS**

Notable participants in audio commentary tracks. Only releases that include commentaries are listed, in broadcast order

	DOCTOR	COMPANION(S)	WRITER	SCRIPT EDITOR	DESIGNER	DIRECTOR	PRODUCER	OTHER(S)	MODERATOR
An Unearthly Child (eps 1, 4 & pilot only)		●				●	●		GR
The Daleks (eps 2, 4 & 7 only)		●				●	●		GR
The Keys of Marinus		●			●	●			CH
The Aztecs		●					●		
The Aztecs Special Edition		●					●		
The Sensorites		●			●	●		●	TH
The Reign of Terror		●						●	TH
Planet of Giants								●	MA
The Dalek Invasion of Earth		●				●	●		GR
The Rescue		●			●	●			TH
The Romans		●			●	●		●	TH
The Web Planet		●				●	●	●	GR
The Crusade (Lost in Time, ep 3 only)		●						●	GR
The Space Museum	●	●							PP
The Chase		●				●			PP
The Time Meddler		●	●	●			●		CH
The Daleks' Master Plan (Lost in Time, ep 2 only)		●		●				●	
The Ark		●				●			TH
The Gunfighters		●						●	TH
The War Machines		●				●			
The Tenth Planet (eps 1, 2 & 3 only)		●			●			●	TH
The Moonbase		●					●	●	TH
The Evil of the Daleks (Lost in Time, ep 2 only)		●							GR
The Tomb of the Cybermen		●							
The Tomb of the Cybermen Special Edition 1		●							
2		●	●					●	TH
The Abominable Snowmen (Lost in Time, ep 2 only)		●							GR
The Ice Warriors		●	●		●			●	TH
The Web of Fear (Lost in Time, ep 1 only)		●	●						GR
The Wheel in Space (Lost in Time, ep 6 only)			●			●			
The Dominators		●						●	TH
The Mind Robber		●				●	●		
The Invasion		●					●		
The Krotons		●						●	TH
The Seeds of Death		●	●			●			
The Seeds of Death Special Edition		●	●			●			
The War Games		●	●				●	●	
Spearhead from Space		●							
Spearhead from Space Special Edition 1		●							
2				●			●		

MODERATORS **AC** Andrew Cartmel **GR** Gary Russell **NB** Nicholas Briggs **PP** Peter Purves
CH Clayton Hickman **MA** Mark Ayres **NP** Nicholas Pegg **TH** Toby Hadoke

	DOCTOR	COMPANION(S)	WRITER	SCRIPT EDITOR	DESIGNER	DIRECTOR	PRODUCER	OTHER(S)	MODERATOR
Doctor Who and the Silurians		●	●			●	●		
The Ambassadors of Death		●	●			●		●	TH
Inferno		●	●				●		
Inferno Special Edition		●	●				●		
Terror of the Autons		●				●	●		
The Mind of Evil		●	●			●	●	●	TH
The Claws of Axos		●					●		
The Claws of Axos Special Edition		●					●		
Colony in Space		●	●			●		●	TH
The Dæmons		●				●	●		
Day of the Daleks			●			●	●		
The Curse of Peladon		●	●				●	●	TH
The Sea Devils			●			●	●		AC
The Mutants		●	●	●	●	●		●	NP
The Time Monster		●	●				●	●	TH
The Three Doctors		●					●		
The Three Doctors Special Edition		●					●		
Carnival of Monsters		●				●	●		
Carnival of Monsters Special Edition 1		●				●	●		
2			●					●	TH
Frontier in Space		●	●				●		CH
Planet of the Daleks		●	●				●	●	
The Green Death		●	●				●		
The Green Death Special Edition 1		●	●				●		
2		●						●	TH
The Time Warrior		●	●				●		
Invasion of the Dinosaurs		●		●	●	●		●	TH
Death to the Daleks							●	●	TH
The Monster of Peladon			●				●	●	TH
Planet of the Spiders		●	●	●		●	●		
Robot	●	●	●				●		
The Ark in Space	●	●					●		
The Ark in Space Special Edition	●	●					●		
The Sontaran Experiment		●	●				●		
Genesis of the Daleks	●	●				●		●	
Revenge of the Cybermen		●			●		●	●	
Terror of the Zygons			●				●	●	MA
Planet of Evil	●	●					●	●	
Pyramids of Mars		●				●	●	●	
The Android Invasion							●	●	TH
The Brain of Morbius	●	●				●	●	●	
The Seeds of Doom	●		●		●		●	●	
The Masque of Mandragora		●					●	●	
The Hand of Fear	●	●	●				●	●	
The Deadly Assassin		●					●	●	
The Face of Evil		●					●	●	TH

	DOCTOR	COMPANION(S)	WRITER	SCRIPT EDITOR	DESIGNER	DIRECTOR	PRODUCER	OTHER(S)	MODERATOR
The Robots of Death			●				●		
The Robots of Death Special Edition 1			●				●		
2	●	●				●		●	
The Talons of Weng-Chiang		●				●	●	●	
The Talons of Weng-Chiang Special Edition		●				●	●	●	
Horror of Fang Rock		●	●					●	
The Invisible Enemy		●	●					●	
Image of the Fendahl	●	●						●	
The Sun Makers	●	●				●		●	
Underworld	●	●	●						
The Invasion of Time		●			●			●	
The Ribos Operation	●	●							
The Pirate Planet 1						●		●	
2	●	●			●				
The Stones of Blood 1		●				●			
2	●	●	●					●	
The Androids of Tara	●	●				●			
The Power of Kroll	●							●	
The Armageddon Factor 1		●				●		●	
2	●	●							
Destiny of the Daleks		●				●		●	
City of Death						●		●	
The Creature from the Pit		●				●		●	
Nightmare of Eden		●	●					●	TH
The Horns of Nimon		●	●					●	
The Leisure Hive		●			●	●			
Meglos		●	●					●	
Full Circle		●	●	●					
State of Decay		●	●			●			
Warriors' Gate		●			●	●		●	
The Keeper of Traken		●	●					●	
Logopolis	●	●	●	●					
K9 and Company		●		●				●	
Castrovalva	●	●	●			●			
Four to Doomsday	●	●				●			
Kinda	●	●						●	
The Visitation	●	●				●			
The Visitation Special Edition	●	●				●			
Black Orchid	●	●							
Earthshock	●	●							
Time-Flight	●	●			●				
Arc of Infinity	●	●						●	
Snakedance	●	●							
Mawdryn Undead	●	●			●				
Terminus	●	●	●						
Enlightenment	●	●	●			●			

iii

ERA HISTORIES
Documentaries covering notable periods of Doctor Who's production

PEOPLE

SOLO INTERVIEWS
Single subjects discussing their work, recorded for the DVDs

DOCTOR WHO STORIES

Interviews recorded for the 2003 documentary The Story of Doctor Who

PROFILES
Accounts of contributors' lives and careers

Ainley, Anthony — Planet of Fire
Camfield, Douglas — Terror of the Zygons
Courtney, Nicholas — More Than 30 Years in the TARDIS
Delgado, Roger — Frontier in Space
Dicks, Terrance — Horror of Fang Rock
Dyall, Valentine — Enlightenment
Grimwade, Peter — Kinda
Hill, Jacqueline — Meglos
Hinchcliffe, Philip — The Android Invasion
Holmes, Robert — The Two Doctors
John, Caroline — Spearhead from Space Blu-ray
Lambert, Verity [text] — The Time Meddler
Letts, Barry — The Dæmons
Luckham, Cyril — Enlightenment
Nation, Terry — Destiny of the Daleks
Newman, Peter R — The Sensorites
Pertwee, Jon — Spearhead from Space Blu-ray
Spooner, Dennis — The Romans

PRODUCTION

CREATIVE CONTRIBUTIONS
Discussions and presentations of artistic aspects

Acting — Enlightenment, Planet of Evil
Doctor's outfits — The Twin Dilemma
Incidental music — Doctor Who and the Silurians, The Visitation +SE
Mask sculpting — The Curse of Fenric
Model work — Enlightenment, The Invisible Enemy, Terminus
Monster acting — The Seeds of Death +SE
Script writing — Battlefield, The Leisure Hive, Meglos
Shawcraft Models — The Chase
Stunt work — Inferno Special Edition
Theme music (1960s) — The Edge of Destruction
Title graphics (1960s/70s) — Robot
        (1980) — The Leisure Hive
        (1982/84) — The Twin Dilemma
        (1986) — Time and the Rani
Visual effects — The Creature from the Pit, Dragonfire, Time and the Rani

ALTERNATIVE SOUNDTRACKS
See Index i for music-only and Dolby 5.1 tracks

Aztecs, The +SE (episode 4) — Arabic
Edge of Destruction, The (episode 2) — Arabic
Mark of the Rani, The (episode 1) — original music
Paradise Towers — original music
Planet of Giants — Arabic
Vengeance on Varos +SE — studio sound
Web Planet, The (episode 6) — Spanish

TITLE SEQUENCES
Original graphics and music without credits

1967 Second Doctor footage — The Tomb of the Cybermen +SE
      Second Doctor opening — The Tomb of the Cybermen +SE [eggs]
1970 Third Doctor footage — Spearhead from Space Blu-ray
      Third Doctor unused opening — Spearhead from Space +SE [eggs]
      Third Doctor opening — Carnival of Monsters +SE [eggs]
      Third Doctor opening with lava footage — Inferno +SE [eggs]
1973 Third Doctor opening and closing with 'Delaware' theme — Carnival of Monsters,
                                                    Frontier in Space [egg]
1974 Third Doctor opening and closing — Death to the Daleks [egg]
1975 Fourth Doctor unused opening — The Ark in Space +SE
      Fourth Doctor opening — The Talons of Weng-Chiang +SE [eggs]
1980 Fourth Doctor opening and closing — Meglos [egg]
1982 Fifth Doctor opening and closing — Resurrection of the Daleks +SE [eggs]
1984 Sixth Doctor opening and closing — The Two Doctors [egg]
1986 Sixth Doctor opening and closing — The Trial of a Time Lord: The Mysterious Planet
1987 Seventh Doctor opening and closing — The Curse of Fenric
Derbyshire theme arrangement remix video — An Unearthly Child
Howell theme arrangement remix video — Castrovalva, Four to Doomsday
Glynn theme arrangement remix video — The Trial of a Time Lord: The Mysterious Planet

NOW AND THEN
Revisiting the filming locations of Doctor Who

Androids of Tara, The
Awakening, The
Black Orchid
Claws of Axos, The +SE
Dalek Invasion of Earth, The
Day of the Daleks
Doctor Who and the Silurians
Invasion of the Dinosaurs
Mark of the Rani, The
Masque of Mandragora, The
Mind of Evil, The
Planet of the Spiders
Pyramids of Mars
Seeds of Doom, The
Shada
Talons of Weng-Chiang Special Edition, The
Trial of a Time Lord, The (Mindwarp)
War Games, The
War Machines, The

FICTION

COMPANIONS
Analysis of the Doctor's assistants
Role of the companions — The Tenth Planet
1960s female companions — The Romans
1970s female companions — The Three Doctors Special Edition
1980s female companions — Paradise Towers
Male companions — The Tenth Planet
Barbara and Ian — The Chase
Jo Grant — The Curse of Peladon
Romana's costumes — Warriors' Gate
K9's departure — Full Circle
Early-80s companions — Castrovalva
Kamelion — The King's Demons
Ace — Survival

THE UNIT FAMILY
Missions and development of UNIT
Part One: 1968–70 — Inferno +SE
Part Two: 1971–73 — Day of the Daleks
Part Three: 1974–89 — Terror of the Zygons

FOLKLORE FACTORS
Documentaries about recurring elements in the fiction the series
Cybermen — Attack of the Cybermen, The Tomb of the Cybermen Special Edition
Daleks — Genesis of the Daleks
  creation — The Daleks
  early years — The Chase
  voices — The Dalek Invasion of Earth
Davros — Remembrance of the Daleks Special Edition
Female villains — More Than 30 Years in the TARDIS
Gallifrey — The Invasion of Time
Guardians — Enlightenment
Ice Warriors — The Curse of Peladon
Master — Terror of the Autons
Omega — Arc of Infinity
Sontarans — The Sontaran Experiment
TARDIS — The Masque of Mandragora
Time Lords — The Armageddon Factor

CULTURAL CONNECTIONS
Documentaries on literature and film influences on Doctor Who
HG Wells — The Ark
Hammer Films — The Stones of Blood
Manchurian Candidate — The Deadly Assassin
Vampire literature — State of Decay
Victorian era — The Talons of Weng-Chiang Special Edition

FACTUAL

TELEVISION PRODUCTION
How programmes are made, often using Doctor Who *as an example*

Black-and-white era — The War Games

Colour Separation Overlay (blue screen) — Carnival of Monsters +SE

Colour production — Spearhead from Space Special Edition

Production design — The Chase

Riverside Studios — The Ark

Scene Sync — Meglos

Studio planning — The Romans

Studio recording — The Dalek Invasion of Earth, Planet of Fire

Television Centre — The Visitation Special Edition

Unions — Shada

Vision mixing — Day of the Daleks

Visual effects — Inferno +SE

RESTORATION
Explanations of film and video restoration techniques

Animation — The Ice Warriors, The Invasion

Chroma-dot Colour Recovery — Planet of the Daleks

Film rescanning — Black Orchid

Film restoration — The Aztecs +SE, Spearhead from Space Blu-ray, The Time Meddler,
                   The Tomb of the Cybermen

Recolourisation — Doctor Who and the Silurians

Recovered footage — The War Machines

Reverse Standards Conversion — The Claws of Axos +SE [egg], The Time Monster

VidFIRE — The Tomb of the Cybermen Special Edition

HISTORY AND SCIENCE
Documentaries about real-world aspects featured in Doctor Who

1960s British society — Doctor Who and the Silurians

Big Bang — Terminus

Blood — State of Decay

Cosmology — Full Circle

Entropy — Meglos

Limehouse — The Talons of Weng-Chiang Special Edition

Magna Carta — The King's Demons

Memory — Day of the Daleks

Music Hall — The Talons of Weng-Chiang Special Edition

Plastics — Terror of the Autons

Politics — The Happiness Patrol

Race and colonialism — The Mutants

Rollright Stones — The Stones of Blood

Ship disappearances — Carnival of Monsters Special Edition

Television — Vengeance on Varos Special Edition

Temporal physics — The Time Monster

Tutankhamun's tomb — The Tomb of the Cybermen Special Edition

Wars — The War Games

iii

PROGRAMMES

BLUE PETER

Extracts from the BBC1 children's magazine programme

11/10/65	Post Office Tower — The War Machines
3/2/66	Dalek cakes — The Dalek Invasion of Earth
20/6/66	War Machine — The War Machines
27/6/66	Viewers' homemade Daleks — The War Machines
27/11/67	Design-a-Monster competition — The Ice Warriors
14/12/67	Design-a-Monster winners — The Ice Warriors
21/9/70	Story of Montezuma — The Aztecs +SE
25/10/71	Daleks — Day of the Daleks
27/11/72	Monster costumes — The Mutants
4/1/73	Roman banquet — The Romans
7/6/73	Daleks stolen — Planet of the Daleks
11/6/73	Daleks recovered — Planet of the Daleks
5/11/73	Tenth anniversary — The Tenth Planet
5/11/73	Whomobile & tenth anniversary — The Three Doctors +SE
23/5/74	*Robot* sets — Robot, The Talons of Weng-Chiang +SE
20/3/75	Fan models — Genesis of the Daleks
28/4/77	Theatre make — The Talons of Weng-Chiang +SE
5/5/77	Theatre make, scenery — The Talons of Weng-Chiang +SE
19/5/77	Theatre make, sound effects — The Talons of Weng-Chiang +SE
10/10/77	Introducing K9 — The Invisible Enemy
16/2/78	Ironbridge — The Mark of the Rani
23/11/78	Fifteenth anniversary — The Stones of Blood
3/4/80	Longleat exhibition — The Leisure Hive
10/11/80	Introducing Peter Davison — Castrovalva
10/12/81	Costumes — Black Orchid
21/11/83	Peter Davison, Richard Hurndall — The Five Doctors 25th Anniversary Edition
15/3/84	Introducing Colin Baker — The Twin Dilemma
18/9/86	Robots, Colin Baker — The Trial of a Time Lord: The Mysterious Planet
2/3/87	Introducing Sylvester McCoy — Time and the Rani
Who Peter part 1 (Classic Series) — The Horns of Nimon	
Who Peter part 2 (New Series) — The Movie Special Edition	

OTHER CHILDREN'S PROGRAMMES

Extracts from other children's shows featuring Doctor Who-*related items*

18/8/71	*Behind the Scenes*: Television Centre — The Mind of Evil
6/1/74	*Billy Smart's Children's Circus*: Jon Pertwee, Whomobile — Invasion of the Dinosaurs
25/8/75	*Disney Time*: Tom Baker — Terror of the Zygons [egg]
25/10/75	*The Basil Brush Show*: Yeti — The Mind Robber
2/10/76	*Swap Shop*: Tom Baker, Elisabeth Sladen — The Hand of Fear
12/2/77	*Swap Shop*: Louise Jameson — The Face of Evil
9/5/77	*Merry-Go-Round*: Elisabeth Sladen — Terror of the Zygons
1/5/79	*Animal Magic*: Tom Baker — The Creature from the Pit
15/7/80	*Ask Aspel*: Lalla Ward — Nightmare of Eden
1/11/80	*Swap Shop*: Matthew Waterhouse — Full Circle
31/1/81	*Swap Shop*: Sarah Sutton — The Keeper of Traken
9/1/82	*Swap Shop*: Peter Davison — Castrovalva
7/10/82	*Walrus*: Dalek — Resurrection of the Daleks Special Edition

20/11/82	*Saturday Superstore*: Peter Davison — Snakedance
26/3/83	*Saturday Superstore*: Davison, Fielding, Strickson — The Five Doctors 25th Anniversary Edition
17/3/84	*Saturday Superstore*: Colin Baker, Nicola Bryant [part] — The Mark of the Rani
17/3/84	*Saturday Superstore*: Colin Baker, Nicola Bryant [full] — Vengeance on Varos Special Edition
20/9/84	*Wavelength* [radio] — The Two Doctors
2/3/85	*Jim'll Fix It*: A Fix With Sontarans — The Two Doctors
6/9/86	*The Saturday Picture Show*: Bonnie Langford — The Trial of a Time Lord: Terror of the Vervoids
13/9/86	*Roland Rat: The Series*: Colin Baker — The Trial of a Time Lord: The Mysterious Planet
29/11/86	*Saturday Superstore*: Colin Baker — The Trial of a Time Lord: The Ultimate Foe
31/8/87	*But First This*: Sylvester McCoy, Bonnie Langford — Delta and the Bannermen
14/3/88	*Science in Action*: Mat Irvine — Warriors of the Deep
19/4/89	*Take Two*: Sylvester McCoy, Sophie Aldred — The Curse of Fenric
21/11/90	*Search Out Science*: Sylvester McCoy, Sophie Aldred — Survival
25–26/10/10	*The Sarah Jane Adventures: Death of the Doctor* — The Green Death Special Edition

NEWS PROGRAMMES
Extracts from news bulletins and discussion programmes

17/1/67	*Points West*: William Hartnell in panto — The Tenth Planet
22/2/72	*Nationwide*: *Radio Times* Dalek competition winners — Day of the Daleks
22/6/73	*Nationwide*: Katy Manning leaving — The Green Death Special Edition
22/11/74	*Points West*: Tom Baker on location — The Ark in Space, Revenge of the Cybermen
17/3/75	*South Today*: Tom Baker on location — Terror of the Zygons
13/5/76	*Nationwide*: Elisabeth Sladen — The Hand of Fear [egg]
14/1/77	*Look East*: Tom Baker on location — The Talons of Weng-Chiang Special Edition
8/6/78	*Scene Around Six*: Tom Baker visits Belfast — The Ark in Space Special Edition
22/11/78	*Nationwide*: Fifteenth anniversary, Tom Baker — The Stones of Blood
9/12/78	*Scene Around Six*: Tom Baker visits Derry — The Ark in Space Special Edition
15/12/78	*Variations*: Tom Baker on location — The Power of Kroll
24/10/80	*Nationwide*: Tom Baker — Logopolis
24/10/80	*BBC1 Nine O'Clock News*: Tom Baker departure — Logopolis
5/11/80	*Nationwide*: Peter Davison — Logopolis
5/11/80	*BBC1 Nine O'Clock News*: Peter Davison casting — Logopolis
13/12/80	*BBC2 News*: Tom Baker marries Lalla Ward — Logopolis
1/3/83	*Breakfast Time*: Peter Davison, Patrick Troughton — The Five Doctors 25th Anniversary Edition
18/3/83	*Nationwide*: Verity Lambert, three Doctors — The Five Doctors 25th Anniversary Edition
28/7/83	*BBC1 One O'Clock News*: Peter Davison departure — The Caves of Androzani +SE
28/7/83	*BBC1 Nine O'Clock News*: Peter Davison departure — The Caves of Androzani +SE
29/7/83	*South East at Six*: Peter Davison, John Nathan-Turner — The Caves of Androzani +SE
19/8/83	*BBC1 Nine O'Clock News*: Colin Baker casting — Vengeance on Varos Special Edition
22/8/83	*Breakfast Time*: Colin Baker — Vengeance on Varos Special Edition
15/3/84	*Breakfast Time*: Radiophonic Workshop — Resurrection of the Daleks +SE
22/3/84	*Breakfast Time*: Colin Baker, Nicola Bryant — The Twin Dilemma
27/2/85	*BBC1 Six O'Clock News*: series hiatus — The Trial of a Time Lord: The Ultimate Foe
27/2/85	*BBC1 Nine O'Clock News*: series hiatus — The Trial of a Time Lord: The Ultimate Foe
28/2/85	*Breakfast Time*: series hiatus — The Trial of a Time Lord: The Ultimate Foe
20/10/86	*Breakfast Time*: Janet Fielding, John Nathan-Turner — Resurrection of the Daleks +SE
5/5/87	*Breakfast Time*: Location report — Time and the Rani
3/7/87	*Wales Today*: Sylvester McCoy on location — Delta and the Bannermen
8/4/94	*Wales Today*: Jon Pertwee — The Green Death Special Edition

OTHER PROGRAMMES

Extracts from other shows featuring Doctor Who-*related material*

31/12/63	*It's A Square World* — The Aztecs Special Edition
16/3/66	*A Whole Scene Going* — The Aztecs Special Edition
25/11/67	*Late Night Line-Up* — The Tomb of the Cybermen +SE
8/2/69	*Chronicle* — The Aztecs Special Edition
7/11/72	*Looking In* — Carnival of Monsters +SE
30/9–1/12/73	*Serendipity* — The Green Death Special Edition
21/12/73	*Pebble Mill at One*: Patrick Troughton, Bernard Wilkie — The Three Doctors +SE
31/3/77	*Pebble Mill at One*: Philip Hinchcliffe — The Talons of Weng-Chiang +SE
3/4/77	*Whose Doctor Who* — The Talons of Weng-Chiang +SE
14/10/78	*Larry Grayson's Generation Game*: K9 — The Invisible Enemy [egg]
22–28/12/78	*Late Night Story*: Tom Baker — The Armageddon Factor
1/1/79	*The Model World of Robert Symes*: Mat Irvine — The Stones of Blood
16/1/79	*Pebble Mill at One*: Tom Baker — The Armageddon Factor
11/4/79	*Pebble Mill at One*: Radiophonic Workshop — The Armageddon Factor
5/6/79	*The New Sound of Music* — The Armageddon Factor
17/9/80	*Where Are They Now?*: Ysanne Churchman — The Monster of Peladon
3/12/80	*Pebble Mill at One*: Peter Davison — Logopolis
26/12/80	*Saturday Night at the Mill*: Peter Davison — Four to Doomsday
23/12/81	*Pebble Mill at One*: K9 — K9 and Company
29/1/82	*Points of View* — Black Orchid
13/3/82	*Did You See..?* — Earthshock
21/12/82	*Russell Harty*: Peter Davison — Enlightenment
10/12/83	*The Noel Edmonds Late Late Breakfast Show*: Peter Davison — The Awakening
20/3/84	*Harty*: Peter Davison, Colin Baker — The Caves of Androzani Special Edition
1/3/85	*Wogan*: Cyber Controller — The Trial of a Time Lord: The Ultimate Foe
3/10/85	*The Lenny Henry Show* — The Trial of a Time Lord: Mindwarp
22/11/85	*Children In Need* — The Trial of a Time Lord: Mindwarp
25/8/86	*Wogan*: Colin Baker, Lynda Bellingham — The Trial of a Time Lord: The Mysterious Planet
17/9/86	*Points of View* — The Trial of a Time Lord: The Mysterious Planet
8/12/86	*Open Air* — The Trial of a Time Lord: The Ultimate Foe
25/1/87	*French & Saunders* [unbroadcast] — Vengeance on Varos Special Edition
18/12/87	*Victoria Wood As Seen on TV* — The Greatest Show in the Galaxy
8/10/88	*The Noel Edmonds Saturday Roadshow*: Sylvester McCoy — Delta and the Bannermen
22–23/9/90	*31 Who* (BSB) — The Three Doctors +SE
23/9/90	*31 Who* (BSB) — The Curse of Fenric
19/11/92	*Tomorrow's World* — The Dæmons
14/5/93	*The Real McCoy* — Earthshock [egg]
12/11/93	*Doctor Who and the Daleks*: Antiques — Horror of Fang Rock
17/12/93	*Doctor Who and the Daleks*: UNIT — Spearhead from Space +SE
9/7/94	*Whatever Happened to Susan?* [radio] — The Dalek Invasion of Earth
19/5/98	*One Foot in the Past*: Post Office Tower — The War Machines
13/11/99	*Doctor Who Night* sketches — An Unearthly Child

ADVERTS

Television commercials with Doctor Who *connections*

Denys Fisher toys — The Face of Evil

Prime Computer — Destiny of the Daleks

Wall's Sky Ray ice lolly — The Tomb of the Cybermen Special Edition

Weetabix — The Android Invasion

MEDIA

TOMORROW'S TIMES
Coverage of Doctor Who *in the national press*

First Doctor — The Gunfighters
Second Doctor — The Dominators
Third Doctor — The Ambassadors of Death
Fourth Doctor — The Face of Evil
Fifth Doctor — Resurrection of the Daleks Special Edition
Sixth Doctor — Vengeance on Varos Special Edition
Seventh Doctor — The Greatest Show in the Galaxy
Eighth Doctor — The Movie Special Edition

STRIPPED FOR ACTION
History of Doctor Who *comic strips*

First Doctor — The Time Meddler
Second Doctor — The War Games
Third Doctor — Frontier in Space
Fourth Doctor — The Seeds of Doom
Fifth Doctor — Black Orchid
Sixth Doctor — The Twin Dilemma
Seventh Doctor — Delta and the Bannermen
Eighth Doctor — The Movie Special Edition
Daleks — Planet of the Daleks

ON TARGET
Profiles of Target novelisation authors

Dicks, Terrance — The Monster of Peladon
Hulke, Malcolm — The War Games
Marter, Ian — Carnival of Monsters Special Edition

DR. FOREVER!
Doctor Who *media during its off-air period*

Audio adventures — The Visitation Special Edition
New Adventures books — The Ark in Space Special Edition
Revival attempts — Inferno Special Edition
Series return — The Green Death Special Edition
Toys and games — The Aztecs Special Edition

DOCTOR WHO ANNUALS
PDF files of World Distributors' annual storybooks

1966 — The Web Planet
1971 — Inferno +SE
1974 — The Time Warrior
1976 — Genesis of the Daleks
1977 — The Hand of Fear
1979 — The Armageddon Factor
1980 — City of Death

1982 — Castrovalva, Keeper of Traken, Logopolis
1983 — Arc of Infinity, Time-Flight
1983 (K9) — K9 and Company
1985 — The Mark of the Rani

OTHER PDF MATERIAL

BBC Enterprises sales document — Castrovalva
BBC Enterprises sales document — The Curse of Peladon
BBC Enterprises sales document — Frontier in Space
BBC Enterprises sales document — The Keeper of Traken
BBC Enterprises sales document — Logopolis
BBC Enterprises sales document — The Monster of Peladon
BBC Enterprises sales document — Vengeance on Varos Special Edition
BBC Enterprises sales document — The Visitation Special Edition
BBC Enterprises sales document — The War Games
BBC press release — The Trial of a Time Lord: The Ultimate Foe
Camera script — The Edge of Destruction
Design sketches — The Greatest Show in the Galaxy
New effects storyboards — Enlightenment
New effects storyboards — Mawdryn Undead
New effects storyboards — Terminus
Production handbook — Enlightenment
Promotion: Cadet sweet cigarettes — The Keys of Marinus
Promotion: Crosse & Blackwell beans — The Ark in Space Special Edition
Promotion: Kellogg's Sugar Smacks cereal — The Mind of Evil, Terror of the Autons
Promotion: Nestlé chocolate 1971 — Terror of the Autons
Promotion: Nestlé chocolate 1975 — The Ark in Space Special Edition
Promotion: Ty-Phoo tea, including *The Amazing World of Doctor Who* storybook — The Face of Evil
Promotion: Wall's Sky Ray ice lolly — The Tomb of the Cybermen Special Edition
Promotion: Weetabix cereal 1975 — The Android Invasion
Promotion: Weetabix cereal 1977 — The Android Invasion
Prop blueprints — Planet of Giants
Prop blueprints — The Rescue
Prop blueprints — The Sensorites
Prop blueprints — The War Games
Prop blueprints — The War Machines
Publication: K9 storybooks (four) — K9 and Company
Publication: *Listener*, Kit Pedler article — Attack of the Cybermen
Publication: *Making of Doctor Who* (Piccolo edition) — The Sea Devils
Publication: *Radio Times 20th Anniversary Special* — Enlightenment
Publication: *Radio Times* supplement — The Movie Special Edition
Publication: *Technical Manual* — The Ark in Space Special Edition
Publication: *Zig Zag* magazine — The Trial of a Time Lord: The Ultimate Foe
Repeat edit notes — The Seeds of Doom
Set blueprints — Frontier in Space
Set blueprints — The Horns of Nimon
Set blueprints — The Monster of Peladon
Set blueprints — Planet of the Daleks
Set blueprints — The Rescue
Studio floorplans — Mawdryn Undead
Studio floorplans — The Robots of Death +SE [not PDF, view on screen]

FANDOM

TARDIS–CAMS
Short scenes of the TARDIS made in 2001 for the BBCi Doctor Who *website*

No.1 (Cybership) — The Ark in Space +SE

No.2 (vortex) — Carnival of Monsters +SE

No.3 (desert) — The Aztecs +SE

No.4 (underwater) — Resurrection of the Daleks +SE

No.5 (snowy) — The Seeds of Death +SE

No.6 (whales) — The Talons of Weng-Chiang +SE

COMEDY EXTRAS
Recorded for the DVDs. See **Other Programmes** *for broadcast comedy sketches*

A-Z of Gadgets and Gizmos — Carnival of Monsters Special Edition

A Holiday for The Doctor — The Space Museum

Beneath the Masque — The Masque of Mandragora

Earthshock Episode 5 — Earthshock

The Elusive David Agnew — The Invasion of Time

Eye on…Blatchford — City of Death

Global Conspiracy? — The Green Death +SE

Jagaroth Battlecruiser brochure — City of Death [egg]

K-9 - A Dog's Tale — K9 and Company

Making Cocoa — The Aztecs +SE

Oh Mummy — Pyramids of Mars

Robophobia — The Robots of Death Special Edition

Scottish Falsetto Sock Puppet Theatre — The Dominators, The Horns of Nimon, The War Games [eggs]

Sid the Slyther — The Dalek Invasion of Earth [eggs]

Weird Science — The Pirate Planet

FAN OPINION
Discussion of Doctor Who *aspects from a fan's point of view*

Cliffhangers — The Trial of a Time Lord: Terror of the Vervoids

Commentaries — The Five Doctors 25th AE [egg], The Monster of Peladon, Survival, The Time Monster

Doctor's Strange Love, The — Dragonfire, The Krotons, The Movie Special Edition, Nightmare of Eden

Doppelgängers — The Androids of Tara

Misconceptions — The Three Doctors Special Edition

Nostalgia — The Tenth Planet

One-off monsters — The Ark

Regeneration — The War Games

Returning monsters — The Seeds of Death Special Edition

Scariness — The Deadly Assassin

UNIT dating — Day of the Daleks

Viewpoint — The Space Museum

FAN ACTIVITIES
How fans show their devotion to Doctor Who

Amateur drama 'Devious' — The War Games

Audio recording — The Invasion

Comedy sketches — An Unearthly Child

Convention panels — The Curse of Fenric, Ghost Light, The Three Doctors

Doctor in Distress — The Trial of a Time Lord: The Ultimate Foe

Video recording — Revenge of the Cybermen

INDEX iv **RETURNING ENEMIES**

*Stories featuring popular adversaries (and some friends) that have
appeared in the New Series, listed in broadcast order*

SILURIAN STORIES

1970	Doctor Who and the Silurians
1972	The Sea Devils
1984	Warriors of the Deep

SONTARAN STORIES

1973/74	The Time Warrior
1975	The Sontaran Experiment
1978	The Invasion of Time
1985	The Two Doctors

TIME LORD STORIES

1969	The War Games
1972/73	The Three Doctors
1976	The Deadly Assassin
1978	The Invasion of Time
1983	Arc of Infinity
1983	The Five Doctors
1986	The Trial of a Time Lord

Time Lords also appear briefly in:

1971	Terror of the Autons
1971	Colony in Space
1975	Genesis of the Daleks

Other renegade/retired Time Lords appear in:

1965	The Time Meddler
1974	Planet of the Spiders
1976	The Brain of Morbius
1979	The Armageddon Factor
1980	Shada *(unbroadcast)*
1984	The Twin Dilemma
1985	The Mark of the Rani
1987	Time and the Rani

UNIT STORIES

1968	The Invasion
1970	Spearhead from Space
1970	Doctor Who and the Silurians
1970	The Ambassadors of Death
1970	Inferno
1971	Terror of the Autons
1971	The Mind of Evil
1971	The Claws of Axos
1971	The Dæmons
1972	Day of the Daleks
1972	The Time Monster
1972/73	The Three Doctors
1973	The Green Death
1974	Invasion of the Dinosaurs
1974	Planet of the Spiders
1974/75	Robot
1989	Battlefield

UNIT personnel also appear in:

1968	The Web of Fear
1971	Colony in Space
1973/74	The Time Warrior
1975	The Android Invasion
1976	The Seeds of Doom
1983	Mawdryn Undead
1983	The Five Doctors

iv

The most credited directors and writers of Classic Doctor Who (five or more serials)

DIRECTORS

CHRISTOPHER BARRY

1963/64	The Daleks *(four episodes)*
1965	The Rescue
1965	The Romans
1966	The Savages
1966	The Power of the Daleks
1971	The Dæmons
1972	The Mutants
1974/75	Robot
1976	The Brain of Morbius
1979	The Creature from the Pit

MICHAEL E BRIANT

1971	Colony in Space
1972	The Sea Devils
1973	The Green Death
1974	Death to the Daleks
1975	Revenge of the Cybermen
1977	The Robots of Death

DOUGLAS CAMFIELD

1964	Planet of Giants *(one episode)*
1965	The Crusade
1965	The Time Meddler
1965/66	The Daleks' Master Plan
1968	The Web of Fear
1968	The Invasion
1970	Inferno *(and Barry Letts)*
1975	Terror of the Zygons
1976	The Seeds of Doom

CHRIS CLOUGH

1986	The Trial of a Time Lord: Terror of the Vervoids
1986	The Trial of a Time Lord: The Ultimate Foe
1987	Delta and the Bannermen
1987	Dragonfire
1988	The Happiness Patrol
1988	Silver Nemesis

RON JONES

1982	Black Orchid
1982	Time-Flight
1983	Arc of Infinity
1984	Frontios
1985	Vengeance on Varos
1986	The Trial of a Time Lord: Mindwarp

BARRY LETTS

1967/68	The Enemy of the World
1970	Inferno *(and Douglas Camfield)*
1971	Terror of the Autons
1973	Carnival of Monsters
1974	Planet of the Spiders
1975	The Android Invasion

Also producer 1970–75

DAVID MALONEY

1968	The Mind Robber
1969	The Krotons
1969	The War Games
1973	Planet of the Daleks
1975	Genesis of the Daleks
1975	Planet of Evil
1976	The Deadly Assassin
1977	The Talons of Weng-Chiang

RICHARD MARTIN

1963/64	The Daleks *(three episodes)*
1964	The Edge of Destruction *(one episode)*
1964	The Dalek Invasion of Earth
1965	The Web Planet
1965	The Chase

DEREK MARTINUS

1965	Galaxy 4
1965	Mission to the Unknown
1966	The Tenth Planet
1967	The Evil of the Daleks
1967	The Ice Warriors
1970	Spearhead from Space

PETER MOFFATT

1980	State of Decay
1982	The Visitation
1983	Mawdryn Undead
1983	The Five Doctors
1984	The Twin Dilemma
1985	The Two Doctors

PENNANT ROBERTS

1977	The Face of Evil
1977	The Sun Makers
1978	The Pirate Planet
1980	Shada *(unfinished)*
1984	Warriors of the Deep
1985	Timelash

WRITERS

BOB BAKER AND DAVE MARTIN

1971 The Claws of Axos
1972 The Mutants
1972/73 The Three Doctors
1975 The Sontaran Experiment
1976 The Hand of Fear
1977 The Invisible Enemy
1978 Underworld
1979 The Armageddon Factor

Bob Baker also wrote:
1979 Nightmare of Eden

TERRANCE DICKS

1969 The Seeds of Death (uncredited)
1969 The War Games (with Malcolm Hulke)
1974/75 Robot
1976 The Brain of Morbius (under pseudonym)
1977 Horror of Fang Rock
1980 State of Decay
1983 The Five Doctors

Also script editor 1968–74

BRIAN HAYLES

1966 The Celestial Toymaker (reworked by
     Donald Tosh)
1966 The Smugglers
1967 The Ice Warriors
1969 The Seeds of Death (reworked by
     Terrance Dicks)
1972 The Curse of Peladon
1974 The Monster of Peladon

ROBERT HOLMES

1969 The Krotons
1969 The Space Pirates
1970 Spearhead from Space
1971 Terror of the Autons
1973 Carnival of Monsters
1973/74 The Time Warrior
1975 The Ark in Space
1975 Pyramids of Mars (under pseudonym)
1976 The Brain of Morbius (under pseudonym)
1976 The Deadly Assassin
1977 The Talons of Weng-Chiang
1977 The Sun Makers
1978 The Ribos Operation
1978/79 The Power of Kroll
1984 The Caves of Androzani
1985 The Two Doctors
1986 The Trial of a Time Lord: Mysterious Planet
1986 The Trial of a Time Lord: The Ultimate Foe
     (one episode)

Also script editor 1974–78

MALCOLM HULKE

1967 The Faceless Ones (with David Ellis)
1969 The War Games (with Terrance Dicks)
1970 Doctor Who and the Silurians
1970 The Ambassadors of Death (uncredited)
1971 Colony in Space
1972 The Sea Devils
1973 Frontier in Space
1974 Invasion of the Dinosaurs

TERRY NATION

1963/64 The Daleks
1964 The Keys of Marinus
1964 The Dalek Invasion of Earth
1965 The Chase
1965 Mission to the Unknown
1965/66 The Daleks' Master Plan (with Dennis
     Spooner)
1973 Planet of the Daleks
1974 Death to the Daleks
1975 Genesis of the Daleks
1975 The Android Invasion
1979 Destiny of the Daleks

ERIC SAWARD

1982 The Visitation
1982 Earthshock
1984 Resurrection of the Daleks
1984 The Twin Dilemma (uncredited)
1985 Attack of the Cybermen (uncredited)
1985 Revelation of the Daleks

Also script editor 1982–86

DENNIS SPOONER

1964 The Reign of Terror
1965 The Romans
1965 The Time Meddler
1965/66 The Daleks' Master Plan (with Terry
     Nation)
1966 The Power of the Daleks (uncredited)

Also story editor 1965

DAVID WHITAKER

1964 The Edge of Destruction
1965 The Rescue
1965 The Crusade
1966 The Power of the Daleks (reworked by
     Dennis Spooner)
1967 The Evil of the Daleks
1967/68 The Enemy of the World
1968 The Wheel in Space
1970 The Ambassadors of Death (reworked by
     Malcolm Hulke)

Also story editor 1963–64

People listed in the main entries for their contributions to the extras on the DVDs. Page numbers in bold denote on-screen appearances, italics are appearances in another programme (as listed under 'Programmes' in Index iii). Names are referenced only once per title, with priority given to an on-screen appearance, but may have contributed to more than one feature on a disc. Participation in audio commentaries is listed separately, where italics indicate audio taken from an archive interview.

vi

vi

vi

vi

Coming next from Wonderful Books

A continuation of the seminal reference work,
covering every television episode, mini-episode and
prequel from the *TV Movie* to *The Time of the Doctor*

New story outlines and full cast lists, presented in
the style and format of the 1989 edition of the original
Doctor Who Programme Guide by Jean-Marc Lofficier

Available now in print from Wonderful Books

DOCTOR WHO AS YOU'VE NEVER SEEN IT BEFORE!

Now over fifty years old, *Doctor Who* is one of the longest running television programmes in the world. And probably no other is as well documented.

Ever since followers of the show started forming fan groups in the 1970s, they have sought to learn every last detail about not only the Doctor's adventures but also the making of the programme itself.

Innumerable books and websites have been written charting the production, broadcast and universe of *Doctor Who*. But these text sources only give the facts and figures, they don't present the information in a visual form that can be more easily interpreted.

This book presents a wealth of knowledge about the programme as data visualisations, using eye-catching graphics to explore the contributions of the people who have made the series, to analyse the places and people encountered by the Doctor within the show, to understand its transmission patterns and audience, and to examine how the programme has been extended beyond broadcast into print and home media.

With analysis of the data and its context, these visualisations provide a whole new way of looking at both the fact and fiction of a television series.

TIME & SPACE VISUALISER IS A FRESH PERSPECTIVE ON THE STORY AND HISTORY OF *DOCTOR WHO*